CW00797095

Rabindranath Tagore

РА́БИНДРАНАТЪ ТАГОРЪ

ЖЕРТВОПѢСНИ

(ГИТАНДЖАЛИ)

Переводъ подъ редакціей
Ю. БАЛТРУШАЙТИСА

МОСКВА.
Книгоиздательство „СОВРЕМЕННЫЯ ПРОБЛЕМЫ".
1914.

Rabindranath Tagore

One Hundred Years of Global Reception

Edited by
Martin Kämpchen
and
Imre Bangha

Editorial Adviser
Uma Das Gupta

Orient BlackSwan

RABINDRANATH TAGORE:
ONE HUNDRED YEARS OF GLOBAL RECEPTION

ORIENT BLACKSWAN PRIVATE LIMITED

Registered Office
3-6-752 Himayatnagar, Hyderabad 500 029, Telangana, India
e-mail: centraloffice@orientblackswan.com

Other Offices
Bengaluru, Bhopal, Chennai, Guwahati, Hyderabad,
Jaipur, Kolkata, Lucknow, Mumbai, New Delhi,
Noida, Patna, Vijayawada

© Orient Blackswan Private Limited 2014
First published 2014
Reprinted 2017

ISBN 978 81 250 5568 6

Typeset in
Adobe Garamond Pro 10.5/12
by Le Studio Graphique, Gurgaon 122 001

024597

14122016

Printed in India at
Glorious Printers
Delhi

Published by
Orient Blackswan Private Limited
3-6-752 Himayatnagar, Hyderabad 500 029, Telangana, India
e-mail: info@orientblackswan.com

Contents

PREFACE

I

This book was born on Rabindranath Tagore's 150th birth anniversary. On that day, in May 2011, the two editors and the editorial adviser met for a Tagore Conference at the Tagore Centre UK in London. The idea of this book emerged and we decided spontaneously to work on it together.

This book asked to be written. A little over one hundred years ago, in 1913, Rabindranath Tagore attained world fame on being awarded the Nobel Prize for Literature. This is the right time to take stock and discover what impact the poet has had globally.[1] The Nobel Prizes, including those for Literature, are being awarded only since 1901, and for its first twelve years the Literature prize had always gone to a European writer. So when Tagore, the first non-European, received the Nobel Prize, it was a signal of which the entire world took note.

This was the era when India was under colonial rule, sharing the fate of political and social subjugation with numerous other Asian and African countries. It was an era of transition and turmoil. Europe would soon erupt into a violent conflagration, termed the Great War and later known as World War I, which brought misery and poverty and upset power equations over a wide region. The Ottoman Empire which had reigned from Constantinople (Istanbul) was shattered as a result and new political regimes emerged in Turkey, in the Balkan states and West Asia. Inspired by central European social ideas, the Russian Revolution of 1917 called an end to feudalism to usher in a Communist regime with radical and bloody social transformations. Further East, China and Japan were in conflict with each other. Japan aspired to implement a Westernised social model which, however, stopped short of democratic norms of government.

Latin American countries had obtained their independence a century earlier, but struggled with political and social instability; democracy had not taken root. Around the beginning of the twentieth century, the United States of America exerted strong political influence on that part of the continent, apart from the cultural influence which Spain and Portugal wielded. This sketch indicates the overriding influence of Europe and North America in that period with all its positive and detrimental effects.

Within this context, when the Nobel Prize was conferred on an 'unknown' writer of India, the choice signalled a valorisation of Indian culture, especially of its literature, by Europe. Its cultural and political elite acknowledged with this prize that, although politically dependent and socially humiliated, the culture of a colonised country was able to bring forth a literature worthy of being compared with their own cultures and literatures. In a sense, bestowing this prize was an immensely political decision as with it Europe began to share power and prestige with the rest of the world.

After the Nobel Prize, Tagore became the *visvakabi*, the world poet, as he is known today. Within a few years his writings came to be translated into a broad range of languages and in many countries. His journeys took him to Asian countries outside India, to Western and Eastern Europe, North and South America, and to one African country, Egypt. His lectures and addresses made it clear that, while abroad, he did not speak just for himself. He assumed to have become the Voice of India, even, at times, the Voice of Asia and of the colonised world. Hence his wish to meet the personalities of consequence—statesmen, scholars, writers, artists, social leaders—in each country and exchange views with them and thus influence them. Tagore was convinced that India had something to offer to the world which no other country was able to give and which was encapsulated in his works, his lectures and in his personality. The Nobel Prize gave him the authority to speak up, and the intellectual and social elite of many countries realised the need to listen and to respond. Although a cultural or literary personality, Tagore emerged, as can be observed in this book, as an immensely *political* figure whose ideas inspired and moulded *social* movements in diverse countries in the twentieth century.

It is unique that Tagore's voice was heard not merely in one particular ideological camp or by people of one political persuasion, but he was 'used', not rarely also misused, by political, social, religious and artistic groups across the spectrum. He was made the icon of various movements which were in some sense perceived as anti-imperialist, anti-colonial, anti-nationalist and pro-freedom, pro-unity and in favour of a spiritual concept of social life. Imperialist and chauvinistic leanings were opposed by Tagore. This rejection was uncompromising. As we can see, this made his collection of speeches, *Nationalism* (1917), in some countries (e.g. Yugoslavia) and with some groups, his best-known and most relevant work.

With intrepid candour and, some contributors claim, with a measure of naiveté, Tagore enmeshed himself in the cultural politics of his time wherever he spoke. The poet's stand was, however, by no means ambiguous or fickle.

He knew how to be firm and clear in his pronouncements. Even then, this book shows that Tagore was many things to many people. He combined the strands of a spiritual visionary with the strands of a social protester. Quite pertinently one author calls him a 'romantic rebel.' These two strands combined left the field wide open for the peoples of the world to identify themselves with him. This could take various, also controversial, shapes. One example may stand for many: in Czechoslovakia, Tagore inspired the movement against German cultural hegemony, while in Germany, Tagore consoled its people ravaged by World War I. At the height of his fame, in many countries Tagore was welcomed by politicians representing the majority of a society while sometimes, religious or ideological minorities welcomed him. The attitude of certain groups to Tagore may also have changed radically over time, as was the case with Italian Fascists or Eastern and Central European Communists. Other groups, such as the Christian churches, had an ambivalent attitude towards him. Ecclesiastical sources sometimes published anti-Tagore writings, and at other times they welcomed in him a thinker who turned people back towards spiritual values.

The complex situation created by the translations of Tagore's written work is an indicator of multiple-identity politics. While most of his writings have been translated from English, they were occasionally translated from Russian, German, French, Italian, Chinese or other versions; hence, they changed language three or more times before they reached their readers. In Yugoslavia, various ethnic groups demanded their own translation although their languages may at times have been perceived as identical. In Turkey, Tagore translations were based on French and German versions, apart from the English ones. In Russia, not less than six different translations of *Gitanjali* came out between 1913 and 1915.

Tagore's grand project was to bring the 'East' and the 'West' together and make them jointly work for world peace and for a more just, more humane, more spiritual society. His lectures, conversations and letters build upon this theme with untiring constancy. At the present time, we may no longer appreciate such a neat division of 'East' and 'West', for we prefer to see the countries subsumed under these tags as a more complex reality. Asia has never been a uniform culture—with India, Japan and China, for instance, being widely different. But in Tagore's time, this broad division was a political instrument for identifying what he felt originally belonged together—the 'East'—and what needed to be brought together and complement each other—the 'East' and 'West.'

Tagore was seen as the archetypal 'wise man of the East,' as an oriental 'prophet.' The feeling of a pan-oriental solidarity evolved in many peoples from Egypt to Japan which was more spiritual and emotional than depending on social and political realities. Countries which had opted for 'Westernisation', however, opposed Tagore's Orientalism.

This volume demonstrates how many shapes this ideal of bringing together 'East' and 'West', this ideal of inclusiveness, did take. In Europe, Tagore's philosophy connected well with traditions of Romanticism and Idealism and movements leaning towards their world view. In Germany, for example, he integrated well with its tradition of Romanticism which was then a hundred years old. In the USA, he inspired nostalgic association with the spiritual back-to-nature tradition created by Thoreau, Emerson and Whitman.

Many of the political and socio-cultural movements of the early twentieth century can be seen in the light of inclusiveness, even Fascism and Bolshevism. Hence several movements could claim to be inspired by Tagore's idealism, even though some of them abused it. This influence extended into the post-colonial and post-imperialist era when Tagore's work was projected as an example of the anti-imperialist struggle and cultural wealth which had emerged from the former colonies.

Such inclusiveness was also at work in countries of the region known as the Middle East such as Turkey, Iran, and the Arab world which demonstrate the rich reception of Tagore in Islamic cultures. They present a hitherto unknown perspective, viz. that an attempt was made to 'Islamicise' Tagore's spirituality, for example in Turkey. Muslim cultures searched for the Sufi in him. A debate was initiated on the concept of 'God' in *Gitanjali* and other works. Countries with a Buddhist majority also claimed Tagore. As his interest in the Buddha is well documented, Korea, Sri Lanka and Thailand feel a special closeness to Tagore. Christian minorities within the Arab world or Japan, as well as Latin American countries with their mostly Christian populations easily found a common ground with Tagore in the Christian ideals of love and service. These examples elucidate that Tagore was able to deeply integrate into the cultural fabric of countries of different religious and cultural backgrounds, encouraging and guiding national movements towards greater inclusiveness and humanity.

However, there were dissenting voices as well. In a few countries, Tagore was deliberately censured and not published or publicised. This happened, for example, after the 1917 Revolution in Russia, during World War II in Germany and during Franco's regime in Spain. Criticism and a partial rejection of Tagore also occurred in societies which strained to rebuild themselves materially after a period of war and strife. Critics in Europe after World War I deemed Tagore's 'pacifistic' attitude and his 'Asian mildness' detrimental to the dynamic reconstruction of a country. In the USA, after World War II, the socio-political climate was unfavourable to Tagore's anti-war and anti-Nationalistic sentiments. Similarly, Tagore's stand against nationalism was rejected in Yugoslavia, Poland, Turkey and in Japan because nationalism, it was believed, was what kept these countries united in their difficult time of transition.

Journalists and writers in a few countries doubted how much Tagore understood of the implications of the socio-cultural environment to which he was subjected and forced to respond in each country. For example, in Russia, some roundly refused to listen to him as he had not lived through World War I and the sufferings of the Revolution and hence could not gauge the pain they felt. However, contrary examples have been related as well. A British soldier was known to carry *Gitanjali* with him to the battlefield; and in the Warsaw Ghetto, Jewish children enacted *The Post Office* to prepare themselves for death in the concentration camp.

Tagore became a world poet with the publication of his English rendering of *Gitanjali* in 1912. While it is unusual that a poet of such stature translates his own poetry into another language, away from his or her mother tongue, this was the one path to world recognition open to him at that time. The poet may have in his later years been ambivalent about the worth of such a step, and in letters to William Rothenstein even expressed regret.[2] However, without this fame as a vehicle, he could not have risen to become a representative of Indian and Asian culture. As *Gitanjali* was translated into English by the poet himself and was the one work which gained him the Nobel Prize, this volume became the focus of appreciation and recognition in the years immediately following 1913. In most countries it was translated soon thereafter, often several times. Interestingly, in a large number of countries Rabindranath Tagore had already been mentioned, reviewed and discussed *before* the Nobel Prize was awarded to him. This was of course mainly due to the publication of the English *Gitanjali* in London a year earlier and the publication of some of his poems in the American magazine *Poetry* and elsewhere. Some other reports valued his lectures in the United States which were later published in *Sadhana*.

As is clear from the articles, Tagore arrived in most parts of the world through the language(s) of Western colonial hegemony and this forced non-Western cultures to talk to each other through terms forced on them from outside. However, the imposed language modulated but did not obstruct cultural exchange. Many such cultures searched to accommodate Tagore in their own terms and presented him as close to the world view of Buddhism or Sufism.

It was mentioned in Yeats's 'Preface' to *Gitanjali* that Tagore was a Bengali poet primarily writing in his mother tongue who could be appreciated fully only by Bengali-knowing readers. Only few translators turned to the Bengali persona soon and made an effort to adequately translate Tagore from the Bengali. Unfortunately, in a large number of countries, for example in the Spanish- and Portuguese-speaking countries of Europe and Latin America, the 'Bengali Tagore' has not been discovered and appreciated to this day. It is one of the realisations emerging from this volume that even the 'English Tagore' had no great currency in Latin American countries since French and not English had for long been the second language of the educated class. After a 'journey' through three cultures, Tagore often arrived late in Latin American countries. One can only speculate about what would have happened if his more authentic and powerful Bengali poetry, translated congenially, had impacted those cultures at an earlier time. At present, translations from the original have been recorded from just over a dozen countries only.

Only those who have tasted the strong wine of Tagore's Bengali poems and songs can gauge what these countries are missing. We are reminded of Sri Aurobindo's words: 'One has only to compare this English prose, beautiful as it is, with the original poetry to see how much has gone out with the change; something is successfully substituted which may satisfy the English reader, but can never satisfy the ear or the mind that has once listened to the singer's own native and magical melodies.'[3]

This book demonstrates that it often depended on *one* person whether Tagore was made known and relevant in a particular country. This is vigorously demonstrated by Marino Rigon who took it upon himself to translate one volume after another from Bengali to Italian. In France, it was the writer André Gide, in Spain, another Nobel laureate, Juan Ramón Jiménez, Victoria Ocampo in Argentina, in the Netherlands Frederik van Eeden, in the Czech language Vincenz Lesný and Dušan Zbavitel, in Latvian Kārlis Egle and Rihards Rudzītis, in Arabic, the scholar Muhammad Shukri Ayyad, and in Russian the translator A. P. Gnatyuk-Danil'Chuk who pushed the Tagore legacy a giant step ahead before others took over.

In many countries it was easier to appreciate Tagore in his ideas, rather than as a poet, especially in more practical fields, for example in his *educational philosophy*. In the 1920s, Tagore collected funds for the university he founded in Santiniketan, Visva-Bharati, wherever he travelled. As a result, many of his English lectures touched upon his educational philosophy and on his experiments at Santiniketan. So this brought the educator to the fore. To understand his views on education needed no efforts of translation and with only a minimal understanding of cultural contexts it became directly relevant and inspirational. Such focus on Tagore's philosophy of education was noticeable in Brazil and other Latin American countries; popular school readers used to contain Tagore texts.

Since 1930, it was Tagore *the painter* who travelled in Europe and North America projecting in his exhibitions a face altogether different from that of the poet, educator and thinker. His pictures are fantastic in their imagination, bizarre and at times even bordering on the scurrilous giving shape to the subconscious mind. Initially, his paintings were appreciated more outside India. As a forerunner of Indian modernism in the arts, Tagore's paintings, however, are acclaimed at present mainly in his own country while Tagore the painter is overshadowed by Tagore the poet elsewhere. This is so although his paintings had given his admirers the opportunity to get close to Tagore without the distorting mirror of translations.

This volume also records the Tagore reception outside the immediate realm of literature and philosophy. Many of his poems and songs have been set to music by contemporary composers, his plays put on stage, his dance dramas converted into other cultural idioms, and his music adapted to suit other instruments, new styles and paradigms.

As translation, the projection of the Bengali Tagore on a world platform was such a problematic issue that the *personality* of Tagore played a hugely important role in disseminating his ideas. After the initial enthusiasm waned and Tagore the poet and writer was not taken with the same seriousness as around 1913, Tagore's personality, Tagore as symbolic figure, assumed greater significance in the public eye. Wherever Tagore travelled, he met people, gave lectures and addresses and as a consequence the sale and appreciation of his translated books received a boost. The preoccupation with his personality, however, tended to divert the attention away from his message and was clearly a temptation to submit to an oriental fantasy. But the reverse has also been seen, as is exemplified in Argentina, where Tagore's long visit evoked a significant and deeply-felt reaction which continues to this day.

All the contributions in this volume follow the reception of Tagore and his works up to the present. It will be noticed that hardly any country had a sustained interest in Tagore. The impact of the Bengali poet on many cultures was sometimes limited to short periods of intensity and longer periods of relative indifference. Historical changes, such as the shock of World War I, the consolidation of communism and the establishment of Indo–Soviet friendship after World War II and the creation of a new world order in the 1990s had a deep impact on the interest in the poet. However, it cannot escape the reader that in our times Tagore is only at the periphery of cultural discourse. The erstwhile 'Tagore craze' of many countries has been relegated to history. The success of modern post-colonial authors overshadows Tagore's fame. Nevertheless, his works keep being reprinted or retranslated indicating that he continues to speak to modern readers. Indeed, sometimes his voice sounds more authentic, more direct than was possible before.

II

The essays in this book are based on geographical entities, rather than on languages. This was a difficult choice to make as Tagore's impact often transcends national boundaries and moves along linguistic lines. Hence, the understanding is that the countries mentioned also include the diasporic population of the respective country in other regions and continents. This book avoids both an India-centric and a Eurocentric approach. Therefore we chose to arrange the articles in an East-to-West sequence, and within that sequence we moved from South to North. We circled the globe by beginning with Japan in the Far East and ended with Canada in the northern Far West. This does not deny the fact that the reception of Tagore originated one hundred years ago in the United Kingdom. From there most early translations, cultural influences, praises and doubts spread across the globe. So readers may be advised to begin by studying this essay on Tagore's reception in the UK.

Our desire to present a near-complete survey of Tagore's worldwide impact made us search for competent authors in all continents. Tagore's reception in India, Pakistan and Bangladesh would have required a different volume; so we excluded the Indian subcontinent here. We primarily looked for academics who were able to write on Tagore's reception in their own country or region. Many agreed to write but were later unable to comply for professional or personal reasons. As a result some geographical areas which were important to the editors could not be covered or only inadequately so. These areas lie in North Africa (only Egypt is covered), sub-Saharan Africa (only Portuguese-speaking Angola and Mozambique are represented); then Asian countries Tagore visited: Iran, Burma (now Myanmar), Singapore, Malaya (now Malaysia), Indonesia with Java and Bali; and finally, Australia. Unfortunately, we could not find contributors for the erstwhile Soviet republics, except Latvia. However, the Far East, the neighbours of the Indian subcontinent, the Middle East, East and West Europe including the Balkans, and North and South America are extensively dealt with. Due to the country- or region-wise organisation of the material, some articles have a slight overlap. We briefly cover Spanish Latin America in the article on Spain and then offer more detailed, country-wise, studies of Argentina, Costa Rica and Mexico in individual articles. Similarly, one essay covers the Arab world in its entirety while another focuses on the reception in its largest country, Egypt.

The book reflects the present state of research on Tagore's works and his impact. Some contributions go so far as presenting a detailed bibliographical account of the books by Tagore and articles and books on Tagore that were published in their respective countries. Others put more emphasis on analysing the cultural and literary influences these publications had and continue to have on the social fabric of the country. From still other contributions emerge articulate interpretations of Tagore's works and ideas in the larger context of the culture and the social movements of any given country. There, the influences Tagore exerted have become a conscious cultural input and are already fully integrated.

All essays are structured along the same guidelines, which results in a uniformity of approach and a certain completeness of dealing with the subject. The book aims to be a reference work, away from the anthology format. This also means that the analytical content always relies on presented factual data and readers do not need to be familiar with a certain culture or with every aspect of Tagore's oeuvre to fully appreciate an essay. All the essays outline the cultural relations the country in question had with India, first, and then, within that framework, delineate the immediate response to Tagore's Nobel Prize. It was important that contributors comment at some length on the translations that were published thereafter and their influence on the cultural fabric of that country. Questions on the year translations came out, which books were translated first, who were the translators and the publishers, and from which language they were translated reveal a great deal about the cultural discourses of that time. The essays also present with which movement(s) these translated volumes were being compared and associated, and, in the opinion of contemporaries, which movements supported or contradicted Tagore's poetry and ideas. It is often the reactions suggested in newspaper reviews and reports that offer some clues.

If Tagore visited a country, the essay addresses the issues that emerged on the level of both popular and elite culture. After Tagore's passing in 1941, it was especially his centenary in 1961 which was celebrated and brought forth a large volume of literature and a number of translations. Many of the essays conclude with a comment on the events related to the 150th birth anniversary of Tagore in 2011. The present research situation, apart from celebratory events, and unfinished research tasks in each country were the last points we raised. We were especially interested in finding out whether or not the Tagore specialists of the respective countries had initiated adequate translations of Tagore's Bengali writing.

The bibliographical data had to be restricted to a Works Cited section at the end of each essay. However, a website has been launched (http://tagore. orient.ox.ac.uk/) which aims at building up a comprehensive bibliography of works by Tagore and on Tagore in each country or language. Our readers are asked to refer to this website and perhaps also contribute to it.

This book is the result of a joint effort of the editors, the editorial adviser and the contributors. We thank Professor Uma Das Gupta in Kolkata who, as editorial adviser, helped to shape this volume from the beginning and actively engaged in most phases of the editorial process. Without her overview of global Tagore scholarship and wide academic contacts, this volume would have been much the poorer. We thank the contributors all of whom bore with us when we returned their manuscript with queries and requests several times. Professor Sergei Serebriany was generous with advice and editorial assistance. The Udo Keller Foundation (Hamburg) rescued Martin Kämpchen from financial worries during the three years that this volume grew. Sudeshna Banerjee in Kolkata was engaged to copyedit all the essays before they were submitted so that we could arrive at a certain uniformity of style and language.

We are grateful to Orient BlackSwan, the publishers, for accepting the challenge to bring out this complex book. As copyeditor, Suranjan Roy, with his sharp eye for detail and sense of style, helped to bring the book to its present shape. It was a joy to work with him.

SANTINIKETAN and OXFORD   MARTIN KÄMPCHEN and IMRE BANGHA

NOTES

1. There have been similar efforts on a smaller scale, starting with *Rabindranath Tagore—A Centenary Volume, 1861–1961* (New Delhi: Sahitya Akademi, 1961). One or the other aspect of Tagore's international reception has recently been addressed in a number of panels at international workshops (English Dept., Kolkata University, 2011, Budapest, 2012, etc.) but none of them had a geographically or methodologically systematic approach.
2. Tagore's letters to Rothenstein are discussed in the essay in this book by Kalyan Kundu on the poet's reception in the UK.
3. Aurobindo Ghosh, 'On Tagore,' in *Golden Book of Tagore* (Calcutta: The Golden Book of Tagore Committee 1931), 91.

Publisher's Acknowledgements

We acknowledge with thanks the permissions received from the following:

The Vice-Chancellor, Visva-Bharati University, Santiniketan and the Director, Rabindra Bhavana, Visva-Bharati, Santiniketan for reproduction of the following illustrations from their archives:

- Tagore walking past Borobodur Stupa, Indonesia (1927);
- Alex Aronson, Professor of English in Santiniketan (1937–44), photo by Sambhu Saha;
- Tagore at a Bedouin camp in Iraq (1932);
- Tagore with Indologists Moriz Winternitz and Vincenc Lesný, Prague (1930); and
- Tagore with Kurt Wolff, his German publisher (1921).

Samiran Nandy for use of his photo of open-air classes at Santiniketan (2014).

Sonia Berjman, Papers Editores, and Argentinean National Archives, Department of Photographic Documents for reproducing the picture of Tagore in the Plaza Hotel, Buenos Aires, Argentina (1924) from Berjman's *La Victoria de los jardines: el paisaje en Victoria Ocampo* published in Buenos Aires (2007) by Papers Editores.

PART ONE

East and South Asia

Open-air classes at Santiniketan. Photo by Samiran Nandy (2014).

Tagore walking past Borobodur Stupa, Jogjakarta, Java, Indonesia (1927). Courtesy: Rabindra Bhavana, Visva-Bharati.

1

JAPAN

KYOKO NIWA

INTRODUCTION

It was not long ago that Japan's whole understanding of the world revolved around three countries—India, China and Japan herself. For Japan, China had been perhaps the only civilisation she had known, and considered the country a model nation worth emulating. As for India, it was the land of Buddha beyond China. There had been almost no direct relationship between India and Japan; but the image of India for the Japanese was one of mystery and reverence.

This world view of Japan was overturned completely around the year 1868, during the time of Western influence that began with the initial steps taken by Japan towards modernisation. China and India were dislodged from their earlier position of ideal states and no longer considered to be among countries to be looked up to. Furthermore, colonised India was even seen as a 'ruined nation' with some disrespect, and people firmly determined that their own country should never make the same mistake.

In this context, we can justifiably presume that Japan would have never given the same attention to Rabindranath Tagore without the Nobel Prize, the award that came from the West. Indeed, Tagore was even called 'a poet from a ruined nation' when he first visited Japan. This distorted perception was one of the reasons why his visits to Japan failed to succeed. Not only did his lectures in Japan not receive due attention, there was confusion and controversy over Tagore and his works.

It is well known that the poet himself had once got involved in a controversy over the China–Japan War with Noguchi Yonejiro. During the war, Tagore was regarded by the authorities as a person belonging to the enemy side, so there was a proclivity to ignore him. However, after the end of the war, this attitude changed and a younger generation of scholars, translators and readers began to take a fresh look at his works.

A hundred years have now passed since the world discovered Rabindranath Tagore. And we can see for a fact that like any other country, in Japan too, the evaluation of Rabindranath has been greatly affected by the course of history. However, there also have been a number of intellectuals, translators and readers who sincerely tried to discover and introduce the true value of Rabindranath, irrespective of the prevalent social condition or context.

Here we are going to trace, chronologically, the social context of Tagore's reception in Japan together with the individual efforts made for introducing his works. Finally, we shall try to present some ideas on the future prospect of Tagore's true evaluation.

Reactions to the Nobel Prize-winning Poet and Translations from the First Period: 1913–15

Though a number of Japanese intellectuals, such as the art critic Okakura Tenshin (1862–1913) and the painter Yokoyama Taikan, (1868–1958), had visited India at the turn of the nineteenth century and got acquainted with Tagore, his literary works had not been introduced to Japan until he received due appreciation in Europe.[1]

The poet Mashino Saburo (1889–1916) was the first Japanese to translate Tagore's poems early in 1913.[2] It is worth noting that Mashino had translated those poems *before* Rabindranath Tagore was awarded the Nobel Prize when he first came across the works of Tagore published in the English magazine *The Nation*. Mashino later mentioned that the poet Miki Rofu had written to him appreciating the outstanding talent of Tagore after he published those poems in Japanese translation.[3] However, this impression of Miki Rofu was addressed to Mashino in his private letter, and we can find no other reaction.

The first report of Tagore winning the Nobel Prize headlined 'Noberu shokin-o kakutaru Indo-jin' (An Indian awarded the Nobel Prize) in the *Chugai Eiji Shinbun* (Chugai English Newspaper) on 1 January 1914 was rather insignificant. Translations of his works that appeared at this first stage did not immediately create much impression.

In early 1914, after the report of the Nobel Prize, the critic Uchigasaki Sakusaburo (1877–1947) translated a few of Tagore's poems.[4] This time again, as Uchigasaki himself said, the literary world of Japan 'remained silent and there was no reaction or comment'.[5] The writer Yoshida Genjiro (1886–1956) and the writer and translator Miura Kanzo (1883–1960) also played an active role in translating and introducing Tagore at that very early stage. Except Mashino, the other three were Christians and were closely associated with the periodical *Rikugo Zasshi*, a magazine for young Christians, which devoted a number of pages to Tagore.[6] Yoshida briefly served as editor of the magazine, Uchigasaki had always been an important member of the editorial board and Miura was a regular contributor.

Following the translations by Uchigasaki in 1914, other translators also joined the trend of introducing Rabindranath. Translations from *Gitanjali*, *The Gardener* and *The Crescent Moon* appeared in some other literary magazines. Mashino also continued translating poems from *Gitanjali*, but the first Tagore book to be published was *Sadhana: The Realisation of Life*, translated by Miura Kanzo in 1915.[7] However, this translation was much criticised, especially on the ground that Miura was not an expert in Indian philosophy as was pointed out by Kimura Taiken (1881–1930), a renowned scholar of Indian philosophy of his time.[8]

Soon after *Sadhana* was translated, Mashino published the complete translation of *Gitanjali*.[9] Miura, who had earlier translated *Sadhana*, also published his own complete *Gitanjali* under a different title.[10] Both these versions were criticised by some scholars, mainly on account of mistranslation. Besides, there was even a heated argument between these two translators. Mashino, on his part, criticised Miura saying he considered Rabindranath as a Buddhist so easily because of not knowing anything about Indian philosophy and the Brahmo Samaj, while Miura, on the other hand, attacked Mashino's translation by saying, 'I cannot bear seeing these serious mistakes' without any further specification.[11]

In 1915, the rumour of Tagore's visit to Japan triggered off an explosion in the publication of his works as well as articles focusing on these works. This phenomenon later came to be known as the 'Tagore boom.' The focus shifted beyond *Sadhana*, *Gitanjali*; with *The Crescent Moon*, *The Gardener*, *The Post Office* and *The King of the Dark Chamber* being translated into Japanese one after another in 1915; it culminated in the publication of *The Complete Works of Rabindranath* at the end of the year. This was, however, not a complete collection of Rabindranath's works. Though all these translations were done from English, they became instrumental in gradually introducing the poet to the literary world of Japan.

In Japan, no major writers or poets had taken on the task of translating Tagore's works at that early stage. Moreover, following this early introduction of Rabindranath, the 'Tagore boom' triggered off a heated controversy, not so much on his literature, but on his philosophy—more specifically on the question if his ideas were valuable to the Japanese or not.

When we survey the reviews of the translations or articles on the poet, we can easily notice by looking through the titles that quite a lot of them were written on the philosophical aspects of Tagore. Just before he was introduced to Japan, Henri Bergson and Rudolf Eucken had been welcomed as eminent philosophers by Japanese intellectuals. This was about the time when the enthusiasm for these two had cooled down so that there appeared some articles comparing Rabindranath Tagore with Bergson or Eucken. A renowned critic, Nakazawa Rinsen (1878–1920), was one of those who studied Tagore's philosophy and gave him the epithet, 'Bergson of the East.'[12] Nakazawa also described Tagore as a 'Pantheist'. However, Mashino and other translators showed much dissatisfaction with these statements. Contradicting these observations, some scholars of Indian philosophy expressed their difference of opinion by quoting from the Upanishads. Among them was Kimura Taiken, who tried to explain the background of Tagore's philosophy by referring to his association with the Brahmo Samaj together with the Upanishads and Buddhism in India.

In these circumstances, *Sadhana* was naturally the book which was the most talked about. Even when they referred to *Gitanjali*, the philosophical aspect of the poetry was the main subject and there was hardly any discussion of the poetic qualities. Furthermore, Tagore's other works were hardly discussed.

Tanaka Odo (1867–1932) and Kato Chocho (1886–1938), both literary critics, showed their distaste for this 'Tagore boom'. However, what they said was only about the mood of Japan which superficially raved over the 'Tagore boom' and did not actually enter into the realm of Rabindranath's thoughts or artistic excellence. There was a rather peculiarly mixed reaction among intellectuals as the critic and philosopher Ebu Oson, has described it:

Some people so uncritically admire Tagore as the admirers in Europe and India. Some people, however, are discriminating in their appreciation of Tagore. But some others try to reduce his importance with a reactionary indifference.[13]

It also should be mentioned here that these discussions took place mainly among scholars and translators, especially among critics and scholars of Indian philosophy and of English literature. The leading writers and poets showed little interest in them.

In these crosscurrents of popularity and adverse reaction, Mashino was one of those rare intellectuals who maintained a sincere interest in Tagore without joining any of the groups. His translations were not always highly praised and he was rather a minor poet who had hardly any influence in the literary world of Japan. But one could not but admit his sincere approach and devotion to Tagore's works. He translated *Gitanjali*, *The Crescent Moon*, and *The Gardener* one after another and humbly accepted the criticisms so that he even retranslated *Gitanjali*. According to his own testament, he came to be acquainted with Tagore and Indian thought about the time he came to know that he had been infected with tuberculosis. The more serious the disease became, the more he was engrossed in translating Tagore's poetry. He passed away just before Rabindranath visited Japan for the first time in 1916 and with the death of this devoted follower, a curtain came down on the first chapter of introducing Tagore in Japan.

FIRST VISIT TO JAPAN: 1916

Tagore visited Japan for the first time in 1916. Public figures of Japan and India met directly perhaps for the first time. However, probably unexpected by Tagore, there was already to some degree a strain in the relations between the two countries and also a kind of apprehension that the Japanese people would not listen to Tagore's message unbiasedly, as we can see from this statement of Uchigasaki:

> The visit of the greatest poet born in modern India will be a great stimulus for us to take an interest in Indian thought. There is a tendency among the Japanese in general to ignore India's philosophical ideas because of the country's political subjugation, and thus to dismiss Rabindranath as one who has come from a ruined nation. This is a great loss to us.[14]

In the context of the 'Tagore boom' of the previous year, some critics reacted unfavourably to this sudden popularity. In these circumstances, Kato Chocho used the word 'ruinous' to describe Rabindranath in his article 'Tagoru ryuko ni taisuru fuman' (My dissatisfaction with the Tagore boom) published in *Yomiuri Shinbun* for 15–18 May 1915. Uchigasaki did not mention anyone by name, but it is obvious that he was sufficiently aware of the prevailing mood among his countrymen which was to ignore Tagore as a poet from a 'ruined nation'. It is true that the ordinary Japanese had shown some excitement over his visit; but no excitement or interest can be traced among the intellectuals. Furthermore, there must have been a mood of disrespect as we can surmise from Uchigasaki's statement.

Tagore arrived in Japan on 29 May 1916 amid this ambience of conflicting attitudes. After delivering a speech titled 'India and Japan' in Osaka, he went to Tokyo and delivered his major lecture, 'The Message of India to Japan,' at the Tokyo Imperial University on 11 June. This was followed by another lecture, 'The Spirit of Japan,' delivered at Keio University in Tokyo on 3 July.

It seems the news of Tagore's visit reached the Japanese people rather late since only a few articles had appeared before his arrival. It was only after the speech at the Tokyo Imperial University that special issues of three magazines were published consisting mainly of the impressions and reflections about him or about his speeches. These three magazines which published their special editions in July 1916 were *Rikugo Zasshi*, *Shincho*, and *Shinjin*. Among these, *Rikugo Zasshi* collected articles from the widest range of people and did not limit itself to prominent writers or scholars only. In *Shincho*, there were as many as eighteen famous writers and poets of the day who presented their impressions of Tagore. In *Shinjin*, there were articles by nine scholars focusing on the lecture at the Tokyo Imperial University.

Tagore's arrival seemed to have caused a renewed 'Tagore boom' and those who were critical of it the previous year once again made unfavourable comments about its reappearance. Poet, novelist and critic Iwano Homei (1873–1920) was one of those who even had an emotional outburst, saying:

> I think it was only a year ago that you (Rabindranath) suddenly gained popularity. This was only because translators and publishing houses were trying to make money by introducing something new. We intellectuals were not really impressed by your poetry or your philosophy since your ideas were very different from those of ours.[15]

There were of course some intellectuals who were unhappy with such an attitude, and demonstrated their sympathy for Tagore though it did not lead them to take any further interest in his works or lectures.

Probably the most exhaustive work on this subject of Tagore's visit to Japan and the reaction it provoked is Stephen Hay's *Asian Ideas of East and West*. In the book, Stephen Hay summarised the 1916 visit as follows:

> The next major thrust toward Asian unity was taken by India's leading poet, Rabindranath Tagore, who visited Japan in 1916 with the express purpose of propagating the idea of a renascent Eastern civilization. He was welcomed enthusiastically by Japan's educated class not because of his friendship with their own Okakura, but because he had been awarded in 1913 one of Europe's highest accolades, the Nobel Prize for Literature. In three public lectures, 'India and Japan,' 'The Message of India to Japan' and 'The Spirit of Japan', Tagore presented his view of the Oriental civilization to which he assumed both countries belonged. Each Japanese intellectual reacted to Tagore's message in his own way but when all their comments were published it was clear that most of them disagreed with the Indian poet's concept of a spiritual East standing aloof from, and defiled by, a materialistic West.[16]

Stephen Hay put forward a persuasive analysis with his authentic research. However, there remain some misunderstandings which should not be overlooked. We have already seen the distorted circumstances of 1915 and 1916 from which it can hardly be said: 'He was welcomed enthusiastically by Japan's educated class.' It is true there was great excitement among ordinary people, but the 'educated class' remained more or less indifferent. Since they were already indifferent *before* hearing anything from Tagore, it is worth taking a closer look at their reactions to find out what they were reacting to. Let us examine one such typical statement by an intellectual who remained indifferent to Rabindranath throughout:

> This might not have been the main point of his speech, but considering his attitude as a whole, I think it was one of condemnation of science. At least his followers, I am afraid, will believe it to be so. If this notion gains in strength then I fear that it may undermine our civilization or weaken our resolve to uphold it ... What Japan is today is because we assimilated western civilization as our own. Western civilization is a creation of science. So if we reject science, we have to go backward in the course of history. It may be all right to reject science in one's personal life, but it will be quite dangerous to do so as a nation ... We are not wearing western civilization like a decoration on the surface. It has gone deep into our psyche and has become the flesh and blood of Japan.[17]

This was written by Inoue Tetsujiro, professor of Tokyo Imperial University. He often wrote articles with the purpose of enlightening his people, and we notice the same spirit here. Therefore, we may consider this not so much a response to Tagore, but an appeal to the Japanese. In the same article, he also said that Tagore was from a 'ruined nation', and was 'denouncing' civilisation. He tried to refute that denunciation by saying, 'Especially we, as the people of a rising nation, should banish such Indian notions as pessimism or the weariness of life.' Hence we cannot regard this as a direct response to Tagore's speech, but rather a warning to the ordinary people not to follow his ideas.

It is true, as Stephen Hay says, that most of the intellectuals 'disagreed with the Indian poet's concept of a spiritual East standing aloof from, and defiled by, a materialistic West.' Most Japanese intellectuals did not sympathise with Tagore's notion of East and West and this is partly because of the difference in their political situations, one colonised by the West, another established in her independence. It was in this context that critic and philosopher, Tanaka Odo, wrote:

When there was no political unity in Japan, no readiness in the Japanese army, when our ancestors were enjoying peace, then suddenly those three or four nations of the West, as if it were a bolt from the blue, visited them and threatened them ... Our ancestors were told by those nations that they must choose either death or modern civilization. And they chose modern civilization as the only way to escape death. The death which they feared was not physical death but the death of the spirit. What they feared most was yielding to violence or the loss of their independent existence ... There was only one motive in our adoption of western civilization and commencement of modernization. That motive, of course, was to maintain our independence against fears of oppression by foreign countries.[18]

Modern civilisation here meant Western civilisation and, in Tanaka's opinion, there was no choice for Japan other than to accept Western civilisation for its independent existence.

We are going to discuss one more article which expresses disagreement with Tagore's notion of 'East and West'. The excerpt below is from a piece written by Ebina Dansho (1856–1937), a Christian priest:

India is an old country and Japan is a comparatively new country ... India has many things to be proud of in her history, but Japan has hardly anything in her past and should rather have something she can be proud of in her present and future ... Considering her natural capacity for imbibing other civilizations, I would say that Japan's brothers are not China and India, but England and France. A classification of civilization cannot be easily made by its location.[19]

This statement draws our attention to how its writer looked upon his own country. This may well represent Japanese thinking more generally. What he is proud of is not ancient Japan which had closer ties with China or India, but modern Japan looking to England and France for inspiration. His image of Japan or the East clearly does not strike a chord with Tagore.

Still, Ebina did not totally disapprove of the poet's ideals, or rather he did have some appreciation for Rabindranath as is evident from the following:

However, when the poet said with indignation that the motto of 'the strong [devouring] the weak' must not be allowed in this East though it plays tyrant in the West, he struck a blow to the eagerness for territorial expansion by the Japanese. Those who are bent on such expansion, ridicule him by calling him 'a poet from a ruined nation'. But we should listen carefully to his words. If it were the time when Japan herself was apprehensive of domination by the West, she would have sympathized with the poet. However, today people are no more afraid of being colonized and moreover they themselves are rather ready to attack and invade other nations economically or politically, [so] there are many who naturally abuse the poet's words as 'ruinous.'[20]

This statement is important not only because Ebina appreciated Tagore's humanism, but also because he admitted the rise of militant nationalism in Japan. His statement deserves greater attention because he offered a possible explanation as to why Tagore's words were rejected. True, both India and Japan had faced a cultural crisis when they met the West, but Japan and India went through it in a different way and each country's notion of the 'East' was not always the same.

True, the idea of the East and the West presented by Tagore, as Stephen Hay has explained, was not acceptable to Japan. However, we have to be more careful with the investigation of Stephen Hay concerning the group of Japanese intellectuals about whom he writes:

> The greatest irony in the reaction of Tagore's idea of Asian spiritual revival by his fellow writers in Japan is that those who praised his message most warmly were men like Noguchi, who had been most deeply influenced by English and American Romantics, while those who condemned it most harshly were writers like Kawahigashi and Iwano, who were most deeply committed to the revival of Japanese traditions.[21]

There seems to be no doubt that Noguchi (Noguchi Yonejiro or Yone, 1875–1947) was a representative of the 'Westernised intellectual' and one of the foremost admirers of Rabindranath. But Noguchi was not as simple an admirer of Rabindranath as is generally believed. He came to know Rabindranath in England soon after his poetry had made a great splash in Europe. However, this does not mean that Noguchi played an important role in introducing Rabindranath to Japan. He did not translate any of his poems before 1916. Instead, he wrote four articles on Rabindranath in 1915, but these were not entirely favourable. Let us take a look at an extract from one of these articles:

> At least I cannot find anything new and surprising in Rabindranath's philosophy ... In the East, at least in Japan, the value of Rabindranath is not as much as that in the West. The Western people that [got] in touch with Eastern thought only recently must have found Rabindranath's ideas new and peculiar. However, we Japanese need to investigate our ancestors' efforts and distinguished works before we read Rabindranath's works.[22]

Here, Noguchi does not value Tagore's idea or philosophy highly and he did not change this opinion until the end as we can find almost the same view in his interview recorded in 1929.[23] This view of Noguchi is quite suggestive, in the sense that this can be one of the reasons why people did not listen to Rabindranath's 'message' seriously. Once he considered Tagore as an 'Asian' poet, he lost his earnest desire to know his philosophy or ideas relegating him as one of those wise men he knew from the past. This article was written in 1915 before Tagore's visit to Japan, but indeed this is one of the typical attitudes of Japanese intellectuals throughout the period of his visits.

We are going to look into the relationship between Noguchi and Rabindranath later again and now we should be back to the point of grouping Japanese intellectuals. In the statement quoted above, Stephen Hay only named Noguchi as an intellectual who praised Rabindranath and emphasised that he was 'deeply influenced by English and American Romantics'. But actually, it was not at all exceptional for Japanese poets and writers in those days to be influenced by Western literature or thought, and it cannot generally be said that it was the Westernised intellectuals who always praised Rabindranath.

For example, Tanaka Odo, whose statement we have quoted earlier, was a philosophy teacher at Waseda University who learned Pragmatism from John Dewey at Chicago University, and Inoue Tetsujiro, whom we have referred to, was an expert on German philosophy. Inoue spent seven years in Germany in his youth and also contributed to the highly-regarded poetry book *Shintai shishu* (poetry of new style) which was the first attempt to translate renowned Western poetry into Japanese and which became a source of modern poetry-making in Japan. These two figures, Tanaka and Inoue, were certainly influenced very much by Western ideas but had never shown any serious interest in Rabindranath and rather reacted unfavorably to the poet.

Stephen Hay mentioned two other names, Kawahigashi Hekigoto (1873–1937) and Iwano Homei (1873–1920) as those who condemned Tagore most harshly and who 'were most deeply committed to the revival of Japanese traditions'. Kawahigashi, being a Waka poet (specialising in a form of classical Japanese poetry), was sincerely committed to the revival of traditional literature. He did not approve of Tagore's speeches on civilisation describing them as 'too optimistic and unsatisfactory in the sense that they do not reflect the agony of Indian people.'[24] However, in the same article he also admitted that he was impressed by the way Tagore spoke. He was indeed a rare poet who *actually* listened to Tagore's speech. On the whole, his attitude was sympathetic rather than condemning him most harshly.

We have already seen one of Iwano's statements and there is no doubt he was harsh to Rabindranath, though what he was really irritated about was not the poet himself, but the trend of praising him uncritically. However, he cannot be classified as a traditionalist. Unlike Kawahigashi, Iwano was a modern novelist who started his career as a naturalist writer. Later, he opposed other naturalist authors and adhered to his own ideology but his main concern was not the revival of Japanese tradition.

On the whole, irrespective of the influence of Western ideas or not, most of the intellectuals were reluctant to respond to Tagore's 'message,' and even in case they did respond, most of them reacted unfavourably. However, is there anything common to those who supported him?

It has been mentioned that the Christian group of the journal *Rikugo Zasshi* played an important role in introducing Rabindranath in the first stage and indeed this group of Christians was the most attracted to him, including the Christian priest Ebina Dansho mentioned earlier. Another Christian priest Naruse Jinzo (1858–1919) was also an intellectual who supported Tagore, though he did not really join in the controversy. He studied in the United States and afterwards founded Japan Women's University. It was he who invited Tagore to the summer house of the University in Karuizawa to deliver some lectures which were memorised by the students for a long time.

People drawn to Tagore were minorities among the intellectuals, in the sense that they did not have any firm standing in the Japanese mainstream, being people such as Christians, young students or women. In Japan, 'Westernised' did not mean anything exceptional, as we can see from personalities like Tanaka or Inoue, who were 'Westernised' enough in the eyes of the ordinary Japanese, but still had their place in the mainstream. Although Christians like Ebina or Uchigasaki were highly educated, they were much less influential. On the whole, mainstream Japanese intellectuals rejected Tagore not exactly because of what he said, but rather because of the discursive frame of his reception. Even the supporters of Rabindranath, such as Ebina, could neither share his ideas on civilisation nor agree with his classification of East and West.

The Japanese in general had been accepting Western culture and science quite positively by then and there was little chance of their sharing the image of the materialistic West. Thus, Tagore's warning against militant imperialism was more or less out of tune with those people. Moreover, considering their country rather closer to the West than to the East, there was little inclination to think about Japan's role in Asia in the same way as the Bengali author had defined it.

Still, we should not underestimate the influence of Tagore among the voiceless or less influential group of minorities. They crowded the hall where he delivered his speeches, and they listened to him eagerly. The impression of the poet stayed long and deep in their minds and, because of that, Rabindranath was never completely forgotten even during the dark era of war.

Later Visits and Translations from the Second Period: 1916–29

The first visit of Tagore in 1916 was a stopover on his way to the United States and he again landed in Japan briefly in February–March 1917 on his way back home. His visits in 1924 and 1929 were of much shorter duration. The destination of his 1924 trip was China. Soon after the news of his trip to China was publicised in Japan, the idea emerged that he should be invited to Japan as well. A reporter of *Asahi Shinbun* was sent to Peking with the invitation and after showing some hesitation Tagore finally accepted the offer.[25] Tagore's last visit in 1929 took place in a situation similar to the first one in 1916. He agreed to break his journey on his way to Canada, though he declined to accept any offer to speak because of ill health. He only agreed to attend social gatherings at some places and give brief talks. However, the situation changed dramatically when he cancelled the programme in the United States because of his humiliation at the immigration office. He took a Japanese steamer to sail directly to Japan and on hearing the news, a group of people quickly organised a reception for the poet. After resting for a few days, Tagore finally delivered his five-part lecture, 'The Philosophy of Leisure' which was originally planned for the United States.

Although the enthusiasm generated during his visit in 1916 was missing in the 1920s, his lectures attracted many people. In 1924, it was reported that more than two thousand people, mainly students, came to listen to his lecture at the Tokyo Imperial University. In the same year, he also delivered a special lecture for women and, again, the hall was filled up by about two thousand women who came to listen to him.

The literary world of Japan lost its zeal to publish anything on Tagore after 1916, or even if it did publications were less frequent. However, on the occasion of his second visit in 1924, a number of new translations came out, namely, *Sacrifice*, *Gora* and *The Wreck*.[26] Among these, *Gora*, translated by Sano Jinnosuke who had been at Santiniketan for some years, was an epoch-making work in the sense that the translation was done directly from Bengali. This first translation from Bengali was done, according to the translator, with the help of the English translation, but his translation, together with its notes and explanation about the novel and its author, was fairly accurate. He had the good fortune to be able to ask the author himself about the sentences that he did not understand.[27] The novel received an appreciative though not extensively publicised review, which said in part:

> I cannot help feeling sympathy for the social uneasiness that has been described in detail by Tagore. And I also sincerely wish to examine if that uneasiness has anything in common with the reality of our country either in positive or in negative terms.[28]

Unfortunately, this article did not make the due impact because the voice was that of an unknown intellectual. It should, however, be remembered since it contained a new and insightful appreciation of Rabindranath's novels. In addition to the above-mentioned translations, new versions of works that had earlier been translated also appeared around 1924. These versions were the works of famous writers and poets. For example, the playwright Osanai Kaoru (1881–1938) translated *The Post Office*; and the poet Shiratori Shogo (1890–1973), translated *The Crescent Moon*.

Nevertheless, no special issue of any periodical was published commemorating Tagore's visit in 1924. *Rikugo Zasshi*, which had taken an active role in introducing Rabindranath in 1916, had ceased publication in 1921, and no other magazine seemed to have stepped into the breach in that respect. On the whole, the enthusiasm in introducing Tagore was on a much smaller scale in 1924 than in 1916, and the response was further reduced in 1929.

Controversy over the China–Japan War and Oblivion during World War II: 1937–45

It has been mentioned that Noguchi, who is commonly believed to be an admirer of Tagore, cannot be uncritically regarded so. He had his own independent poetic development and no definite influence of Tagore can be traced in his writings. Noguchi spent almost eleven years, from 1893 to 1904, in the West, mostly in the United States and in England, and published his English poetry books in both countries. His writings were once highly appreciated by a certain literary group in the West. His interest was not confined to the English Romantics; indeed, he had a wide circle of friends among English poets, including some of the Imagist or modernist poets. Noguchi was always active in introducing the new stream of Western literature to Japan and also played a crucial role in introducing Japanese culture and literature overseas through his great number of essays published in English magazines or lectures delivered outside Japan. He was almost the only poet who formed a personal friendship with Tagore and showed respect for the poet. However, it seems Tagore's English translations did not attract him as much as original English poetry. Being an expert in Western literature and an intellectual who actually lived in the West, he often criticised an easygoing acceptance of Western ideas in Japan. His emphasis on Japan's own cultural identity was all the more strengthened when he made various statements about Japan in the West. He tilted more and more towards Nationalistic ideas throughout the 1920s and 1930s and finally contradicted in strong words Tagore's statement on the China–Japan war.[29] Rabindranath was certainly shocked by Noguchi's refutation and there were a couple of letters exchanged between them on this subject, though neither was successful in convincing the other.

This was not their personal controversy in any way, since both of them represented their own society. As for Rabindranath, there was no contradiction being a Bengali or Indian, as well as being a poet of the world; but for Noguchi, he could not be Japanese as well as a world citizen at the same time and had to make a choice. His choice was to be Japanese:

> What I am afraid of is to be called a betrayer by my fellow countrymen. My belief, contrary to your belief, is that I want to be a true man before I am a poet. Therefore, it is important to me that I belong to a sovereign country.[30]

Noguchi's reaction shows the atmosphere in Japan at that time that did not allow him to evaluate Tagore positively.[31]

In this period of history, Tagore was considered to be an enemy, or at least of supporting the enemy, and the mood to dismiss him became the primary focus. The poet and translator Yamamuro Shizuka (1906–2000) offers an insight into the political setting of the era:

> I first published Tagore's poetry in 1943 and it was during the time Japan was at war. The inhumane war of aggression was being carried out. ... I intended to resist that, though I had little influence. That is why I translated the works reflecting such a profound love and humanity written by this great Asian poet. Tagore was almost forgotten and ignored by then, since he was considered to be belonging to the enemy side; and despite such an adverse situation, an editor of *Kawaide shobo* dared to publish the book. However, a very strict censorship was imposed during the wartime, and twelve poems were expunged from the collection at the end.[32]

It should be noted here that at the height of the war people like Yamamuro looked at the poet as a symbol of humanism and it was through his personal effort and the bold attempt taken by a publishing company that a new collection of poems came out. The spirit of Rabindranath did not totally vanish and it was silently handed down to the next generation.

REVALUATION AND TRANSLATIONS: 1946–2011

After the last visit of Tagore in 1929, the impact of the poet gradually withered. Moreover, as Japan had taken the path of militarism, as predicted earlier by Tagore, even his name disappeared from public discourse. This uneasy situation was, however, completely overturned after the end of the war, and in the late 1950s we can see the emergence of a new trend of re-discovering Tagore. Yamamuro, quoted above, published a new edition of his translated poetry and others also joined this new tide of publications.[33]

The most significant resurgence of translating and introducing Tagore after 1916 occurred around 1961, on the occasion of the Tagore centenary celebrations. In 1959, a Memorial Society of Rabindranath Tagore was established for the birth anniversary celebrations. Okura Kunihiko, who had hosted Rabindranath in 1929, was its chairman, and Yamamuro Shizuka, Shimonaka Yasaburo, a representative of a publishing company named Heibonsha, and Nakamura Hajime, a scholar of Indian philosophy, were the founder-members of the society. The society published a book of essays in connection with the celebration of the one hundredth birth anniversary, and a bibliography, of works of and on Tagore, was appended.[34] Essays by scholars like Suzuki Daisetsu, a scholar on Zen Buddhism, Tanaka Otoya, a scholar of Sanskrit literature, Ebihara Tokuo, a scholar of French literature and a specialist on Romain Rolland, and Okakura Koshiro, grandson of Okakura Kakuzo, a scholar of international politics, were included in the book.

Several new translations appeared, and a publisher named Apolonsha had planned to print an eight-volume collection of Rabindranath's works. The collection actually started appearing in 1959 and except for the second volume, which never came out, the rest were published by 1961. Among those new translations, the most important work is definitely the complete translation of *Gitanjali* by Watanabe Shoko (1907–77) in the third volume of the Apolonsha edition. Watanabe's new translation, directly from Bengali, was not only epoch-making but is recognised till today as the standard translation of Rabindranath's poetry in Japan. This translation was first published in 1961 by Apolonsha and was later reissued in an Iwanami Shoten paperback series in 1977, which is one of the oldest and most authoritative series on world and Japanese literature.

A striking feature of this book is that Watanabe translated not only all the poems of the original *Gitanjali*, but those of the English *Gitanjali* as well. He presented both translations in a single volume so that readers could compare and recognise clearly the fundamental differences between the two. This presentation opened the eyes of readers regarding the poetic genius of Rabindranath. Watanabe, the translator, himself contrasts the Bengali originals with Tagore's English versions and emphasises the importance of direct translation from the Bengali in the following words:

> If we pay attention to the style of poetry, we can easily notice that all 157 poems of the original *Gitanjali* were written in various fixed verse forms and had been meant for singing, whereas all 103 poems of the English *Gitanjali* are prose poems ... We see in this English text that many of the repetitions were omitted, peculiar words or phrases of the Indian context were replaced by English idiomatic phrases or style of saying, and sometimes even extra explanations were added ... On the whole, the English *Gitanjali* was deliberately written for English readers. And this is because even those 53 poems that are included in both the original and the English version create so different in impression ... The poems that were left out cannot be the ones the poet himself felt less confident about. We can rather recognize the peculiarity or the greatness of the poet in these poems themselves.[35]

Watanabe pointed out that the English *Gitanjali* was meant for English readers. He implied that Japanese readers can also esteem those poems which were excluded from the English version and he believed that this kind of appreciation would lead them to a real understanding of Tagore's works.

With this effort of Watanabe, the translation of Tagore's works stepped into a new stage, that is, as direct translations from Bengali. This new generation of translators, who were involved in introducing Rabindranath, all knew Bengali well and were scholars of Indian studies. Three such scholars are widely known—Azuma Kazuo, Morimoto Tatsuo and Watanabe Shoko.

Watanabe Shoko, whose complete translation of *Gitanjali* became a monumental publication, was generally known as an expert on Buddhism. He studied Indian philosophy at Tokyo University and became a professor first at Taisho University, and later at Tokyo University. He had a special talent in learning foreign languages and mastered Bengali as well as Sanskrit, German and other languages.

Azuma Kazuo (1931–2011) also studied Indian philosophy and German literature at Tokyo University and learned Bengali from Watanabe in his youth. He was appointed as professor at Waseda University and later at Tsukuba University. Meanwhile, Azuma became known as an expert on Tagore both within Japan and outside. Azuma often emphasised the importance of translating from the original and he himself made many of the translations from Bengali.

Morimoto Tatsuo (b. 1928) has a different background from the above two translators. He studied theology at Doshisha University and came to know Rabindranath during that period. He says that a missionary once recommended him *Gitanjali* and he was completely absorbed in the book right from the moment he started reading it. That was the time just after World War II and he says he had never heard the name of Tagore before. Morimoto worked on Gandhi as well as Rabindranath and has specialised in modern Indian thought. Later he learned Bengali and published his own translation. Among these, the book of Rabindranath's later poems, *Tagoru shiseino uta* (Poems of Life and Death by Tagore), was welcomed especially by senior readers.

Apart from translations, academic study on Tagore also began after the 1970s. Morimoto translated Tagore's biography by Krishna Kripalani and Azuma published a book on Tagore. And all these works of this generation were later compiled into the twelve-volume set of *Tagoru Chosakushu* (The Collected Works of Rabindranath Tagore), which started to be published in 1981.

The chief editor of this new collection was Azuma. This is an authentic introduction to Rabindranath, although there are some works that have not been translated. In the twelve-volume collection, two volumes are devoted to poems. We find names of eleven translators including some leading poets like Tamura Ryuichi (1923–98) and Ooka Makoto (b. 1931). Quite a number of the new translations were from English. Other volumes contain short stories, dramas, essays and letters. One volume is a collection of essays on different topics related to Tagore. This is undoubtedly a great achievement through which readers can approach many different aspects of his works. Several short stories, a selection of dramas, poems, a selection of essays and letters, which were translated directly from Bengali, were introduced in Japan for the first time through this collection.

There was no more nation-wide controversy over Rabindranath in this second tide of re-launching the poet. There was a genuine commitment from those who appreciated him, especially scholars specialising in Indian Studies. This time, translations directly from Bengali predominated, unaffected by evaluations from the West. Rabindranath Tagore could not be called a poet of a 'ruined nation' any more, nor could he be dismissed by the standards of Western or English literature. This approach, though new, has opened up the path to the appreciation of Tagore in the context of Indian literature.

CONCLUSION: RECENT REVIEWS ON RABINDRANATH AND THE FUTURE PROSPECT

Almost all important works by Rabindranath have already been translated into Japanese, including those that did not find place in the twelve-volume *Tagoru Chosakushu* and have been translated separately, e.g., *Ghare Baire* by Onishi Masayuki and *Shesher Kabita* by Usuda Masayuki. These translators belong to a still younger generation and their translations were done from the original Bengali.

Apart from translations, it can be said that Tagore studies have not matured yet. Except for the two books by Azuma mentioned earlier, there has been only one volume on Rabindranath published so far, written by the present author. Theses and articles published after World War II are also few in number. The above books and articles are not very much more than introductory studies on Rabindranath's life or literature; and there is much to be done, especially in the field of literary criticism.

On the occasion of Rabindranath's 150th birth anniversary, special events and programmes have been organised, though on a much smaller scale compared to the 100th birth anniversary celebrations. Still, some of the events were successful, with full audiences, which was rather unexpected. Publications were also not as profuse as at the 100th anniversary; not because there is no demand for Rabindranath's books, but because most of his works have already been published and are still in print. One of the significant publications in 2011 was the special issue of a magazine *Shi to Shiso* (Poetry and Idea). Celebrating the sesquicentennial anniversary of the poet, this magazine included nine articles on him together with a few new translations of his poetry. More than half of the articles in the magazine are by Indian writers including Sunil Gangopadhyay. This kind of publication was certainly innovative and instructive, but at the same time it shows that there are not many in Japan who are capable or competent enough to write such articles. However, when we turn our eyes to the questions and answers on the same issue, we can see that many poets *actually* read Tagore and, in most of the cases, are impressed by his poetry. From these instances, we can expect to discover many more potential readers and further serious studies in the future.

It is true that Tagore Studies in Japan have not yet matured as much as that of, say, the study of Goethe or Baudelaire, though the value of Tagore's works is no less than that of those other poets. It is a misfortune that Tagore's evaluation has been much affected by the relationship between India and Japan, and also by the rapid modernisation and Westernisation of Japan. The first contact was not at all successful and he was once almost forgotten.

However, translations continued with sincerity and we now have numerous works of Rabindranath Tagore in Japanese. As mentioned above, many of those translations were done from the original and we have at least reached the point when we can appreciate Tagore's works in the context of Indian literature. We can certainly be proud of this achievement, and should step forward to further study and evaluate Tagore as a poet of World Literature.

Notes

1. Okakura Tenshin, whose real name is Okakura Kakuzo, was the author of the influential book *The Ideal of the East* (1904). Okakura's visit and activities in India were recorded in Tagore, 'Kakuzo Okakura,' 65–72. Yokoyama Taikan was a painter who created the new style of Japanese painting.
2. Mashino, 'Indo koshi,' 43–52. There might have been a kind of confusion about the author at this point. Mashino's piece translates as 'Old poems of India,' but at the same time he clearly mentioned the name of the poet as 'Rabindranath Tagore of Bengal.'
3. Mashino, 'Shoka-no Tagoru-ron-ni tsuite,' 13.
4. Uchigasaki, 'Yoju-no kage,' 58–62.
5. In the article 'Tagoru to Indo-bunka,' 2–9, he recollected the condition of those days.
6. Kora Tomi, a Christian, who played an active part in Rabindranath's later visits to Japan, said that she too had regularly read this magazine and came to know about Rabindranath.
7. Miura, *Shinrin tetsugaku; sei-no jitsugen*.
8. Kimura, 'Tagoru shokan,' 54.
9. Mashino, *Indo shinshishu Gitanjali*.
10. Miura, *Kada-no okurimono*. ('Kada' is the Japanese form of *gatha* in Sanskrit.) It is, however, unclear on what ground Kimura Taiken criticised this title saying that it was 'not appropriate'.
11. Mashino, 'Futatabi Miura Kanzoshi-wo imashimu,' 46–54. Miura, 'Bukkyoto Tagoru-no kokoro,' 79.
12. Nakazawa, 'Beruguson to Tagoru,' 60–77. Other than that, he wrote several articles and books on almost the same topic.
13. Ebu, *Tagoru-no shiso oyobi shukyo*, 1–2.
14. Uchigasaki, 'Tagoru-shi-o mukau,' 154–5. This article was written before Rabindranath arrived, but published only after his arrival.
15. Iwano, 'Tagoru-shi-ni chokugen su,' 7. This statement criticising Rabindranath was printed with his speech at the Tokyo Imperial University. *Asahi Shinbun*, which sponsored some of Rabindranath's speeches, reported on his visit favourably throughout. But we should note here that most other newspapers showed a rather indifferent attitude and sometimes did not report at all.
16. Hay, *Asian Ideas of East and West*, 6–7.
17. Inoue, 'Tagoru-no koen-ni tsuite,' 47–8.
18. Tanaka, 'Tagoru-shi-niataeteshinonihonkan-o ronzu,' 292–3.

19. Ebina, 'Shijin tagoru-no bunmei hihyo-o yomu,' 20–1.
20. Ibid., 23–4.
21. Hay, *Asian Ideas of East and West*, 96.
22. Noguchi, 'Tagoa-wa hikkyo yomei gaku nomi,' 5.
23. An interview with Noguchi Yonejiro, *Igirisu Bungaku* [English Literature], 1, no. 7 (June 1929), 30–3.
24. Kawahigashi, 'Tagoru-no insho,' 135. Waka literally means 'Japanese poetry' and refers to poems written in the classical style consisting of 5, 7, 5, 7 and 7 syllables in each line.
25. The reporter wrote about his meeting with Rabindranath as follows: 'The poet seems very anxious [to know] if his idea of Pan-Asianism will be wholeheartedly accepted. I said "There will be no need to worry about such things. Most of the people in Japan agree with your view and they will be very happy if your visit is announced." The poet said, "I need some more invitations to impel me to go there."' *Tokyo Asahi Shinbun*, 26 April 1924, 7.
26. Those new translations are: *Gisei* (*Sacrifice*) by Oda Ritsu, *Gora* (*Gora*) by Sano Jinnosuke, and *Unmei-no fune* (*The Wreck*) by Miyahara Koichi.
27. Sano, *Gora*, 9.
28. Ono, 'Tagoru-no Gora-ni arawareta Indo-no fuan,' 106.
29. Noguchi claimed that 'it is the war of "Asia for Asia"' blaming Chiang Kai-shek as a puppet of the West. Letter from Noguchi to Rabindranath, 23 July 1938, cited in 'Poet to Poet,' *Visva-Bharati Quarterly*, 4, no. 3 (September 1938), 199. We can read the entire correspondence in the same magazine.
30. Noguchi, 'Mitabi Tagoru ni atau,' 278–9.
31. Later, Noguchi was strongly criticised for being a typical intellectual who cooperated with the war efforts and his name was almost erased from the history of modern poetry.
32. Yamamuro, *Tagoru Shishu*, 164.
33. Yamamuro published his translation of Tagore's poetry three times—in 1943, 1957 and 1966. The last one, in which the author added many new translations, has become the standard edition.
34. *Tagoru*, Tokyo, Tagorukinenkai, 1961.
35. Watanabe, *Tagoru shishu*, 3–5.

Works Cited

Studies

Azuma Kazuo. *Tagoru*. Tokyo: Kodansha, 1981.
———. *Tagoru*. Tokyo: Reitakudaigaku shuppankai, 2006.
Ebina Dansho. 'Shijin tagoru-no bunmei hihyo-o yomu' [Reading poet Tagore's criticism on civilisation]. *Shinjin*, 17, no. 7 (July 1916), 20–5.
Ebu Oson. *Tagoru-no shiso oyobi shukyo* [Tagore's Thoughts and Religion]. Tokyo: Nichigetsusha, 1915.
Hay, Stephen. *Asian Ideas of East and West*. Cambridge: Harvard University Press, 1970.

Inoue Tetsujiro. 'Tagoru-no koen-ni tsuite' [About the speech by Tagore]. *Shinjin*, 17, no. 7 (July 1916), 47–51

Iwano Homei. 'Tagoru-shi-ni chokugen su' [An appeal to Tagore]. *Yomiuri Shinbun*, 16–17 June 1916.

Kawahigashi Hekigoto. 'Tagoru-no insho [The impression of Tagore]. *Nihon oyobi nihonjin*, May 1916, 135.

Kimura Taiken. 'Tagoru shokan' [Some thoughts on Tagore]. *Chuokoron*, 30, no. 5 (1 May 1915): 53–8.

Mashino Saburo. 'Shoka-no Tagoru-ron-ni tsuite' [About the articles on Tagore]. *Seikatsu to Geijutsu*, 2, no. 10 (June 1915), 2–14.

——. 'Futatabi Miura Kanzoshi-wo imashimu' [To admonish Mr Miura Kanzo once again]. *Seikatsu to geijutsu*, 2, no. 9 (May 1915), 46–54.

Miura Kanzo. Bukkyoto Tagoru-no kokoro' [The heart of Tagore as a Buddhist]. *ARS*, 1, no. 1 (April 1915), 78–90.

Nakazawa Rinsen. 'Tagoru to seiyo-no kojinshugi' [Tagore and Western individualism]. *Chuokoron*, 30, no. 3 (March 1915), 49–54.

——. 'Beruguson to Tagoru' [Bergson and Tagore]. *Mitabungaku*, 6, no. 8 (August 1915), 60–77.

——. *Tagoru to sei-no jitsugen* [Tagore and the Realisation of Life]. Tokyo: Shinchosha, 1915.

Niwa Kyoko, *Tagoru*. Tokyo: Shimizushoin, 2011.

Noguchi Yonejiro. 'Tagoa-wa hikkyo yomei gaku nomi' [Tagore is after all a Yang-Ming follower]. *Asahi Shinbun*, 15 March 1915.

——. 'Mitabi Tagoru ni atau' [Presenting my opinion to Tagore third time]. *Bungeishunju*, 16, no. 19 (November 1938), 216–23.

Okura Kunihiko et al. *Tagoru*. Tokyo: Tagoru kinenkai, 1961.

Ono Shinichiro. 'Tagoru-no Gora-ni arawareta Indo-no fuan' [The uneasiness of India which is expressed in Tagore's *Gora*]. In *Bukkyo to gendai shiso*, 104–6. Tokyo: Daiyakaku, 1925.

Tagore, Surendranath, 'Kakuzo Okakura.' *Visva-Bharati Quarterly*, 2, no. 2 (1936–7), 65–72.

Tanaka Odo. 'Tagoru-shi-ni ataete shino nihonkan-o ronzu' [Discussion about Tagore's view on Japan]. In *Saiko geijutsuno taisei shosei*, 287–316. Tokyo: Tenyusha, 1920.

Uchigasaki Sakusaburo. 'Tagoru to Indo-bunka' [Tagore and Indian culture]. *Rikugo Zasshi*, 35, no. 5 (May 1915), 2–9.

——. 'Tagoru-shi-o mukau' [Welcoming Tagore]. *Rikugo Zasshi*, vol. 36, no. 6 (June 1916), 154–5.

Tagore's Works in Translation

Mashino Saburo, transl. 'Indo koshi' [Old poems of India]. *Zanboa*, 3, no. 2 (February 1913), 43–52.

——, transl. *Indo shinshishu Gitanjali* [New Indian poetry, *Gitanjali*]. Tokyo, Toundo shoten, 1915.

Miura Kanzo, transl. *Shinrin tetsugaku; sei-no jitsugen* [Philosophy of a forest: Realisation of Life]. Tokyo: Genosha, 1915.
——, transl. *Kada-no okurimono* [Offering of a *Gatha*]. Tokyo, Tobundo shoten, 1915.
Miyahara Koichiro. *Unmei-no fune* [*The Wreck*]. Tokyo: Daiichishuppan kyokai, 1924.
Morimoto Tatsuo, transl. *Tagoru shisei-no uta* [Poems of life and death by Tagore]. Tokyo: Ningento rekishisha, 2002.
Onishi Masayuki, transl. *Ie to sekai* [*Ghare Baire/ The Home and the World*]. Tokyo, Daisanbunmeisha, 1986.
Osanai Kaoru, transl. *Yubinkyoku* [*The Post Office*]. Tokyo: Sekai dowataikei kankosha, 1924.
Oda Ritsu, transl. *Gisei* [*Sacrifice*]. Tokyo, Nihon dokushokai kaiho, 1924.
Sano Jinnosuke, transl. *Gora*. Tokyo, Daiyukaku, 1924.
Shiratori Shogo, transl. *Shingetsu* [*The Crescent Moon*]. Tokyo: Isseido, 1924.
Uchigasaki Sakusaburo, transl. 'Yoju-no kage' [In the shade of a Banyan tree]. *Rikugo Zasshi*, 34, no. 2 (February 1914), 58–62.
Usuda Masayuki, transl. *Saigo-no shi* [*Sheser Kabita/The Last Poem*]. Tokyo, Hokuseido, 2009.
Watanabe Shoko, transl. *Tagoru shishu* [Poetry of Tagore]. Tokyo: Iwanami shoten, 1977,
Yamamuro Shizuka, transl. *Tagoru Shishu* [Poetry of Tagore]. Tokyo: Kawaide shobo, 1943 (subsequent edns.: Tokyo: Kadokawa shoten, 1957; Tokyo: Yayoi shobo, 1966).

Collections

Tagoru kessaku zenshu [Complete works of Tagore's masterpieces]. Tokyo: Bunseisha, 1915.
Tagoru chosakushu [Collection of Tagore's works]. 8 vols. Tokyo: Apolonsha, 1959–61.
Tagoru chosakushu [Collection of Tagore's works]. 12 vols. Tokyo: Daisanbunmeisha, 1981–93.

2

KOREA

Kim Woo Jo

> In the golden age of Asia
>   Korea was one of its lamp bearers
>   and that lamp is waiting
>   to be lighted once again
>   for the illumination
>   in the East.

In this poem composed on 28 March 1929 in Japan, and published a few days later in Korea, Rabindranath Tagore prophesied a bright future for the Koreans, providing a gleam of light in the darkness of Japanese colonial domination and instilling a sense of pride in Korea.[1] This may be one of the reasons why no foreign poet has ever been so deeply admired by the Korean public as Tagore. This admiration led to the installation of a bust of Tagore on Daihakro or University Street, a locality in Seoul associated with intellectuality, arts and youthfulness. The bust, engraved with the never-to-be-forgotten poem above, which also happens to be the most frequently quoted panegyric verse about Koreans, was unveiled on 7 May 2011 to commemorate the 150th anniversary of Tagore's birth.

This essay proposes to survey how Tagore was introduced to Koreans through translations and discursive writings, and then go on to discuss his influence on modern Korean literature. Unfortunately, as no information is available on new translations of Tagore's works and ways of interpreting Tagore's influence in North Korea after 1945, the study will be restricted to South Korea after that year.

PERSONAL CONTACTS

In 1916, Tagore had already dedicated a poem to Korean youth at the request of a Korean student studying in Japan. The poem 'The Song of the Defeated' is included in *Fruit-Gathering* published in 1916.[2] Its Korean translation entitled 'The Song of the Pursued' first appeared in the magazine *Cheongchoon* (The Youth) in 1917. The student who had approached Tagore with the request was Jin Hak-moon (1894–1974). He met the poet twice during his first visit to Japan and had an earnest desire to introduce him to Korea, as the first Nobel laureate from Asia. Jin Hak-moon had expressed a unique Korean view that put Tagore above other foreign authors. He said that if the poet wrote something for Koreans, it would have a far greater impact than any writing by a Western philosopher or writer.[3]

Tagore was invited to Korea twice, first in 1916 by Choi Nam-sun (1890–1957), a well-known intellectual of the time and publisher of the monthly *Cheongchoon* who assigned Jin Hak-moon to interview Tagore during his first visit to Japan in 1916, and then in March 1929 by the representative national paper *Dong-a Ilbo* (The Daily Dong-a). As a response to the first invitation he handed over 'The Song of the Defeated'. During his third visit to Japan in March 1929, he responded to the second invitation by *Dong-a Ilbo* with the manuscript of the above mentioned six-line poem, which was later entitled by Koreans as 'The Lamp of the East'. Though he planned to visit Korea on his way back to India sometime in the middle of June 1929, he was not able to make it due to his sudden illness. The following message in English expressing his regret appeared in *Dong-a Ilbo* on 13 June 1929:

> It has caused me very great regret that my ill health prevents me from fulfilling my promise to visit Korea and to offer her my greeting of sympathy. Let me assure my friends who invite me that I carry that promise with me in the hope of a more fortunate future when it may be redeemed. 8 June 1929.

INITIAL RECEPTION

Modern Korean poetry developed in the 1910s and 1920s. The Japanese adopted a repressive policy in Korea in the second decade of the twentieth century but modified it in the 1920s as a direct consequence of the 1 March Movement in 1919 (First Korean Independence Movement against Japanese Imperialism). Cultural activities were allowed, and journals, newspapers and publications in Korean flourished. Young litterateurs gathered around the magazines *Changjo* (Creation), *Pyeha* (Ruins), *Baikjo* (The White Tide), and *Geumsung* (Venus) and they felt the necessity to import literary trends from abroad in order to modernise Korean poetry. Indian literature was one of the imported foreign literatures. Apart from poems by Sarojini Naidu (1879–1949), most of the translated Indian works were those of Tagore.

One of the earliest Korean writings about Tagore, entitled *Guru Tagore, World Famous Great Poet, Philosopher and Thinker* by 'One admirer', was published in the magazine *Sinmoongye* (New Literary World) in February 1916.[4] However it was Jin Hak-moon who introduced Tagore properly in Korea. Jin Hak-moon wrote two articles about him. Although he sent the manuscripts to the *Cheongchoon* the same year (i.e., 1916), his articles appeared only in November 1917. This can be regarded as a special issue of *Cheongchoon* on Tagore. The front page carried the photo of 'The world famous Indian poet, Rabindranath Tagore' with his Bengali signature. Jin Hak-moon's essay under the same title presented Tagore's family background, the story of his winning the Nobel Prize, and translations of three poems, *Gitanjali* 93, *The Gardener* 24 and the 'Astrologer' from *The Crescent Moon*. The Korean translation of 'The Song of the Defeated', which Jin believed Tagore wrote for Koreans, was accompanied with its English source version. Jin's other essay entitled 'Tha Sunsaing Songyounggi' (An Account of our Greeting and Farewell to Guru Tagore) gave an outline of Tagore's speech 'The New Life of Modern Youth' at Waseda University in Tokyo and described the writer's second encounter with the poet. This publication had a special influence on Korean youth considering the fact that *Cheongchoon* was the only magazine at the time committed to the cultural enlightenment of Koreans at large. Jin Hak-moon's introduction opened an intensive period of Korea's intellectual engagement with Tagore, which lasted until the mid-1920s.

Han Yong-un (1879–1944), a Buddhist thinker, reformer, freedom fighter and poet, introduced Tagore to Koreans as a philosopher by publishing a translation of excerpts from *Sadhana* in his magazine, *Yoosim* (Only Mind) in 1918 (issues 1 and 2) in order to contribute to the reform of Korean Buddhism. Even though further portions of *Sadhana* could not be published owing to restrictions imposed by the Japanese authorities, the next issue of *Yoosim* published Pak Han-young's essay on 'Tago-ol-ui sigwan' (Tagore's viewpoint on poetry).

THE 1920S

The 1920s saw an increase of interest in Tagore. Several translations of his poetry were published and he was also introduced as a philosopher and educator.[5] Excerpts from *The Crescent Moon* appeared in the first issue of the periodical *Gaebyak* (Beginning of the World) in 1920 to inspire national consciousness based on the twentieth-century Korean 'Religion of the Heavenly Way' *Cheondogyo*. Excerpts from the *Gitanjali* were published in *Sinsaingwhal* (New Life) in 1922 (issue 6), a bimonthly magazine propagating nationalism with socialist values and principles, and in *Gongyoung* (Co-prosperity) in 1922 (issue 2), journal of a pro-Japanese organisation.

The most noticeable aspect was the active introduction of Tagore by authors belonging to *Changjo*, the first literary magazine in Korea. O Cheon-suk (1901–87) started translating the *Gitanjali* and published its first eighteen poems in *Changjo* in 1921 (issues 7 and 8). Although he could never complete his translation, for *Changjo* ceased publication he published a biographical sketch, *Angel of India: Tagore*, in 1921, and prepared a Korean version of *The Post Office*, which was included in the series 'Masterpieces of World Literature' (1925).[6]

Thanks to Kim Ok's (1896–?) initiative, translation of Tagore's works reached its peak in Korea. Kim Ok played an important role in introducing French symbolism through his translations. His collection of translated poems, *Onyoui Mudo* (The Dance of Agony, 1921) had a crucial impact on Korean poetry, and his *Haiphariui Norai* (Song of a Jellyfish, 1923) is considered the first modern poetry collection in Korea.

Kim Ok's translation of eleven Indian poems appeared under the title 'A Special Selection of World Masterpieces' in the special issue at the second anniversary of *Gaebyak* (July 1922). Kim Ok selected nine poems from *The Gardener* and two poems by Sarojini Naidu. Later, he translated three volumes by Tagore, *Gitanjali* (1923), *The Gardener* with the Esperanto title of *La Gardenisto* (1924), and *The Crescent Moon* (1924). Poems from *Gitanjali* and *The Crescent Moon* in his translation were also published in magazines such as *Chongnun* (The Young), the magazine of the Korean YMCA, and *Pyehoihu* (Post Ruins), a literary journal known for its slant on romantic literature. Kim Ok translated around 250 poems of Tagore: no work of any other foreign poet was introduced so comprehensively in such a short time in pre-independence Korea.[7]

Kim Ok also sought to understand the world of Tagore's poetry analytically. He wrote prefaces to the Korean versions of the three collections. He asserted that the basic sentiment of Tagore's poetry was love towards God in his article, 'Tago-a-ui si' (The Poetry of Tagore), published in the literary magazine *Josunmundan* (The Literary World of Korea, November 1924). He also discussed *Gitanjali* in his article, 'Gwangmyeong-eun donyang-eseo – deul-inun i-ui sasang' (The Light is from the East: Thought of a Devotee) in *Dong-a Ilbo* (21 July; 2 and 4 August 1925). His articles have special significance since analytical evaluation of Tagore was rare at that time. The only other substantial critical appreciation, 'Tago-a-ui wonjeong-e dehaya' (On *The Gardener* of Tagore) in *Dong-a Ilbo* (20 January 1925), came from the pen of Yi Gwang-soo (1892–1950), another pioneering figure of modern Korean literature.

The introduction of Tagore's works entered a new phase through the attempts of intellectuals who studied foreign literature at universities and were associated with the poetry magazine *Geumsung*. Among them were Baik Gi-man (1902–67) and Yang Ju-dong (1903–77) who translated some ten poems from *The Crescent Moon* and published them in the first issue of *Geumsung*. They preferred literal translation in contrast with Kim Ok, who believed in 'creative translation' or 'transcreation.' Kim Ok criticised their stance and pointed out their mistranslations. In return, Yang Ju-dong indicated errors in Kim Ok's free translations. After this famous debate on liberal or literal translation, the publication of *Geumsung* was discontinued and Kim Ok, who had been the most active translator of Tagore's works, turned to Koreanised Chinese poetry.

After the 1920s

Though by the late 1920s there was a decline in introducing new works of Tagore, his earlier translations kept being republished in newspapers and magazines.[8] Tagore's fiction was generally neglected by Koreans, but some specimens of it appeared in periodicals.[9]

The subsequent decade did not produce any remarkable new translation. Some of Tagore's essays and poems, as well as writings about him, were reissued in periodicals such as *Sinsaing* (The New Life), *Bulgyo* (Buddhism), *Sinyeasung* (New Women), *Josun Ilbo* (The Daily Josun), etc.[10]

Interest in Tagore's activities was also kept alive in the media. Since the public use of Korean language was banned in the early 1940s during Japanese rule (which ended in August 1945) and Korean newspapers were prohibited, there was no evident response to Tagore's death in 1941.[11]

After Korea attained independence in 1945, new Korean versions of Tagore's works started to appear sporadically. Most of them were new renderings of works that had appeared in the 1920s.[12] Korean scholars of English literature also presented till then untranslated works. Yoo Young (1917–2002), in particular, contributed to new publications of translations of complete books by Tagore in the 1960s and 1970s.[13]

The time of the most intensive Tagore translations, the 1920s, was also the period when modern Korean poetry was taking shape. Academic research on Tagore's influence on Korean poetry began in the 1960s and 1970s. A new wave of postmodern research came after the 1990s. Most investigation focused on Tagore's reception in modern Korean poetry in the 1920s.

Tagore's influence on Korean Literature

Tagore's influence on modern Korean poetry remains one of the most important research topics in the field of Korean literature, even as academic opinions on the extent of Tagore's influence vary. The eminent scholar Kim

Yoon-sik argued that although Tagore's impact on Korean literature has not been enormous, his direct influence on Han Yong-un is evident.[14] Kim Yong-jik, another eminent scholar, surveyed Tagore's effect on a wider range of modern Korean writers but he also asserted that it is best seen in the poetry of Han Yong-un.[15]

Young intellectuals who dominated the Korean literary world in the 1920s seemed to have been unable to appreciate Tagore's poetry which praised the oneness of the Infinite with Nature and the Finite. Kim Ok deplored in his preface to the *Gitanjali* that people tended to keep a distance from the thoughts and works of Tagore; therefore, he earnestly requested the readers not just to read these poems but to reflect earnestly on them.[16]

Although direct impact of Tagore on Korean literature was limited, his indirect influence mediated by Kim Ok's Korean versions is not negligible. As has been mentioned, Kim Ok had an ardent belief that translation is a new creation. In his prefaces, he wrote about the difficulties of creating a new style of Korean for translating Tagore and emphasised the importance of rhythm and breathing for the language. He also experimented with new rhythms in his own collections. He adopted rhythmic prose for Tagore's works, which were evidently influenced by the forms used in Han Yong-un's collection, *Nimui chimmuk* (The Silence of the Beloved).[17]

Han Yong-un

Korean literary critics admit Tagore's influence on Han Yong-un, and they normally refer to his poem 'Tagoreu-ui si "Gardenisto" reul ilgo' (After Reading Tagore's poem 'Gardenisto') in his anthology *Nimui chimmuk*.

Han Yong-un, a Buddhist thinker and freedom fighter, published his only collection of poetry, *Nimui chimmuk* in 1926 at the age of forty-seven. Although Han Yong-un was deeply involved in the 1 March movement (a public display of Korean resistance to Japanese occupation on 1 March 1919), he did not belong to any literary group. When *Nimui chimmuk* appeared, the Korean literary world was dominated by young intellectuals who had studied abroad, especially in Japan. Nobody noticed Han's collection except Ju Yo-han (1900–77), one of the pioneering figures of modern Korean literature, and the translator of the poem, 'The Lamp of the East.' He pointed out similarities in the styles of *Nimui chimmuk* and Tagore's English prose poems in his article entitled 'Han Yong-un ssi geunjak *Nimui chimmuk* dokhugam: sarang-ui gido, gido-ui sarang' (Prayer of Love, Love of Prayer: Review of Han Yong-un's recent work, *Nimui chimmuk*) in *Dong-a Ilbo* on 26 June 1926.

Academic interest in Han Yong-un emerged only in the 1960s. Song Uk, a scholar of English literature, asserted that *Nimui chimmuk* could not have come into being without Tagore's stimulus and influence and pointed out that both poets used love lyrics to talk about their religious experience.[18] Han Yong-un was not pleased with the decadent tendency in Korean Romanticism which was prevalent among young writers related to the literary magazines such as *Pyeha* and *Baikjo* in the early 1920s. In his poem 'Yesulga' (An Artist), he wrote: 'I prefer to describe my beloved's face, voice and gait as they are rather than to describe pleasure, sorrow, love and things like that.' (Han Yong-un, *Nimui chimmuk*, 22). In fact, he did not want to adopt the style of the lyrics reflecting what he thought was the decadent tendency to wallow in darkness, death, tears and groans but he wanted to develop his own style.

The central sentiment of *Gitanjali*, *The Gardener* and *The Crescent Moon* is the devotee's love for God while the focus of *Nimui chimmuk* is love for the beloved in separation. The structure of *Nimui chimmuk* is similar to that of *The Gardener*. *The Gardener* consists of a preface by the poet, a table of contents, the poems, and a separate last poem, 'O Reader' while *Nimui chimmuk* consists of 'Gun-mal' (A Murmur, i.e., preface), the table of contents, the poems and a separate last poem, 'To the Readers.' The number of poems of the two collections is almost similar, eighty-five and eighty-eight respectively. Tagore's influence is also reflected in the selection of words, imagery and concepts.[19]

Han Yong-un's artistry is reflected in his novel use of rich and delicate metaphors, philosophical depth and profound irony.[20] According to Kim Yong-jik, although the poetry of the 1920s strove for being purely lyrical, without the extensiveness of inner space it remained a superficial expression of individual emotions. *Nimui chimmuk*, however, was successful in developing a metaphysical dimension.[21] Tagore's poetry was a source of inspiration for Han Yong-un, who combined the world of beauty with the depth of thought.

The prose style of *Nimui chimmuk* based on traditional Korean rhythm was considered a key achievement by Han Yong-un. Ju Yo-han, the first person to make the observation in 1926, was moved by that poet's competence in the Korean language and expressed his opinion that the English version of Tagore's works exerted an influence on Han Yong-un, who had been thought to have invented Korean prose poetry based on his typical non-fluency in diction.[22] Since then there has been a scholarly consensus that Korean prose poetry had developed under the influence of Tagore's English poems. This is considered as Tagore's most significant contribution to modern Korean poetry. One of the most important responses to Tagore in Korea is Han Yong-un's poem 'Tagoreu-ui si "Gardenisto"reul ilgo':

O friend, my friend, like a flower blooming on the grave of my beloved you, friend, make me cry.
Like a sudden encounter with my beloved in the night of the desert without even a little bird's trace you make me glad.
You are the scent of white bones, breaking an old grave and spreading over the sky.
You are a song of hope in despair, the song you sang scattering the flowers gathered as being caught in another branch when fallen flowers were picked up to make a garland.

O friend, friend crying over broken love.
Tears cannot make a fallen flower blossom on the old branch again.
Do not sprinkle tears over fallen flower, do spread on the dust beneath the flower-tree.

O friend, my friend.
No matter how good the scent of death may be, no one can kiss the lips of white bones.
Do not enmesh his grave with golden song. Erect a bloodstained flag on the grave.
But the spring breeze says the dead earth gets motion through the song of a poet.

O friend, I am ashamed. When I listen to your song I do not know why I am so ashamed and tremble.
It is because I listen to the song alone, without my beloved.

(Translation was done by the writer of this essay, Kim Woo Jo.)

Han Yong-un portrayed Tagore as a friend with whom he could share the joys and sorrows of life. At the same time, he criticised Tagore for his attitude to life. Phrases such as 'Do not sprinkle tears over fallen flower, do spread the dust beneath the flower-tree,' 'Do not enmesh his grave with golden song, erect a bloodstained flag on the grave,' have largely been interpreted in Korea as Han Yong-un's advice or suggestion to Tagore to confront the realities of life as prevailing in Korea then.

According to Yi Ok-soon, a scholar of Indian history, Han Yong-un asked Tagore not to sing about the spiritual world of meditation highly appreciated by the West but instead focus on the dark realities in the East.[23] According to another scholarly opinion, Han Yong-un criticised Tagore for hiding his identity as a colonial intellectual in his poems.[24] Recent research supports the views of earlier Korean literary critics, such as Song Uk, who admitted that Han Yong-un criticised the lack of socio-historical consciousness in Tagore.[25]

Han Yong-un was only able to read the works of Tagore that expressed the love towards God, since most of Tagore's works had not been published in Korea at that time. As Kim Yoon-sik pointed out, Han Yong-un's critical comments on Tagore, therefore, had limited significance.[26] However, the main feature of the Korean Tagore reception was implicit in these comments. What Koreans desired to find in Tagore was not love for the Absolute but a reflection on the struggle against colonial rule and hence an echo of national consciousness.

Many Koreans became ardent admirers of Tagore because he was the first Nobel laureate from Asia. Secondly, Koreans were aware of a shared cultural background with Tagore through Buddhism, and thirdly, Indians were under colonial rule just as the Koreans were.

It can be construed that most of the Koreans inspired by national consciousness actually sought to identify Korea with India under colonial rule. Reports of the Indian freedom struggle appeared very frequently in the Korean media of those days, though it could hardly publish the news of the Korean situations due to colonial censorship. Korean media no doubt desired to instil national consciousness by publishing reports of the Indian freedom struggle.

Even though Han Yong-un expressed his dissatisfaction with Tagore's alleged lack of historical consciousness, Koreans eagerly awaited Tagore's visit, which could have meant explicit support for their urge for independence from Japan.

Tagore, an advocate of cosmopolitanism with his ideal of a 'Universal Human Being', warned against the danger of a narrow nationalism both in Japan and in Europe. National consciousness, which played an important role in Tagore's reception in Korea, was a kind of short-sighted nationalism and could not go along with Tagore's cosmopolitanism. Nevertheless, Koreans admired Tagore for his trust in the future of Korea.

THE PRESENT SITUATION

Over the past decades, infrastructure for Indian studies and for the presentation of Tagore has developed in Korea. Academic Indian studies began in the 1970s with the establishment of the Department of Indian Studies (Hindi) at Hankuk University of Foreign Studies in Seoul. Systematic research on Tagore has been undertaken by the Tagore Society of Korea, a private institution founded in 1981 by the poetess Kim Yang-sik. Samsung, a global company based in Korea, in collaboration with the Indian Sahitya Akademi instituted a 'Tagore Literature Award' in 2009. 'The Last Harvest,' an exhibition of Tagore's paintings was held at the National Museum of

Korea between 20 September and 27 November in 2011, providing Koreans a chance to recognise him as an artist.

In the past decades, Santiniketan has become a popular place to study in for Korean students. For many of them, this and other Indian universities present an alternative to the stressful Korean education system. Therefore, it is not primarily an interest in Tagore that influences their decision. Their years spent in Santiniketan, however, may invisibly influence them to bring home something from the spirit of Tagore's university.

Tagore's works have so far been translated into Korean via English. However, with the broadening of research on India, specialists with competence in Bengali can be expected to produce direct translations and a more systematic research on Tagore in the near future.

CONCLUSION

The early 1920s saw an increased Korean interest in Tagore and a number of his works were translated. While the poet's direct influence was primarily confined to Han Yong-un, indirectly it contributed to a change in Korean poetry. Although Tagore's reception in Korea responded more to Nationalistic than to literary needs, the Bengali poet has been enjoying a special status in this country for almost a century.

NOTES

1. Its Korean translation was published in *Dong-a Ilbo* [The Daily Dong-a] on 2 April and its English original in Tagore's handwriting on 3 April. It is not included in Sisir Kumar Das, ed., *The English Writings of Rabindranath Tagore*. Tagore generally expressed his positive viewpoint on the East with the imagery of light, for instance, 'the eternal light will again shine in the East. And I offer, as did ancestor rishis, my salutation to that sunrise of the East, which is destined once again to illumine the whole world' (*Nationalism*, 56). This short poem can be considered as a representative expression of Tagore's view on the East.

2. Tagore, *Fruit-Gathering*, 120–1. In the eyes of Tagore, Korea like India was a defeated country and Koreans under the repressive Japanese colonial rule deserved encouragement. 'The Song of the Defeated' is a statement of the poet's belief that it is not defeat and humiliation but subjugation with the force of arms that calls for shame. See Mohan, 'Tagore's Internationalism and his Lecture-tours,' 3.

3. Jin Hak-moon, 'Tha Sunsaing Songyounggi,' 105.

4. Quoted in Kim Yoon-sik, *Geunde hanguk munhak yeongu*, 194.

5. Tagore was introduced as an educator in Noh Ja-young's article, *The School of Nature by Tagore*, which appeared in *So-gwang* [First Light], a magazine for

current affairs (no. 7, September 1920). Since then, several articles on Tagore's School of Nature in Santiniketan have become available in Korean journals.

6. Kim Yoon-sik, *Geunde hanguk munhak yeongu*, 195.

7. See Kim Yong-jik, *Hanguk hyundesi yeongu*, 104.

8. For example, *Gitanjali* entitled *Gotongui Sokbak* [The Bondage of Agony] by Song Wan-sik appeared in 1927. This is a plagiarised version of Kim Ok's Korean *Gitanjali* of 1923 (Kim Byung-chul, *Hanguk geunde beonyeok munhaksa yeongu*, 454). The title of Song Wan-sik's translation is different but the text is the same as in Kim Ok's work.

9. The short story *Seungri* [Victory] translated by Gui-bo appeared in *Chongnun* in March 1926. An abridged version of the novel *Gora* appeared in *Dong-a Ilbo* on 26 February and 3 March.

10. The retrospective article published in *Samcheonri* [The Whole Korea] on 1 August 1934 by Jin Hak-moon can be considered as a good example of repetition or copying. The same article had already been published in *Cheongchoon* in 1917.

11. The Japanese strengthened their military rule in the 1930s, and after the outbreak of World War II, Japan sought to extract Korean resources and labour and to exterminate Korean culture to the extent that Koreans had to adopt Japanese names.

12. *The Crescent Moon* translated by Im Hak-soo (1948); 'Anthology of Tagore— Gitanjali' (1959) by Bak Hee-jin; 'Selections of Famous Tagore's Works' (1960) by Yi Soo-sik; 'Anthology of Tagore's Works' (1961) by Jang Man-young, etc.

13. Yoo Young's Tagore translations are *Collection of Tagore's Poems* (Complete Series of World Literature No. 34, 1962), *An Anthology of Tagore's Poetry: Gitanjali, The Crescent Moon, The Gardener and Fruit-Gathering* (1969), and *The Complete Works of Tagore* (1974). He also published a book of criticism, *Tagore's Literature: its Myth and Aesthetics of Mystery* (1983).

14. Kim Yoon-sik, *Geunde hanguk munhak yeongu* (Modern Korean Literature), 199.

15. According to him, Tagore's influence can be traced in Yi Gwang-soo's essay, *Self Transcendence*. Yi Gwang-soo was to become a pioneering figure in modern Korean literature, and he met Tagore in Japan in 1916. He also pointed out several poems, O Cheon-suk's 'I shall be fertiliser,' Kim So-wol's 'The Dream' and 'The Song of my Beloved' as well as Baik Gi-man's 'The Shadow of the Jinkgo Tree.' See Kim Yong-jik, *Hanguk hyundesi yeongu*, 119–37. All these three poets were also translators of Tagore. O Cheon-suk translated *Gitanjali* 1–18, Kim So-wol, who was famous for his poetry of 'Han,' the traditional Korean sentiment of sorrow expressed in folk rhythm, published a poem from *The Gardener* at the request of his teacher Kim Ok, and Baik Gi-man prepared the Korean version of some poems from *The Crescent Moon* and other collections; Kim Yong-jik, *Hanguk hyundesi yeongu*, 97.

16. Kim Ok, Preface to *Gitanjali*, translated by Kim Ok, 1.

17. Kim Yoon-sik, *Geunde hanguk munhak yeongu*, 240.

18. Song Uk, 'Yumijeok cho-wolgwa hyeokmyeongjeok agong,' 52.

19. For example, the frequent use of the words gold, lamp, scent, song in *Nimui chimmuk* came from Tagore's works.
20. Kim Jae-hong, *Han Yong-un munhak yeongu*, 231.
21. Kim Yong-jik, *Hanguk geunde sisa*, 519.
22. Ibid., *Geunde hanguk munhak yeongu*, 240.
23. Yi Ok-soon, 'Sikminji josun-ui "dongyang", tagoreu-ui "dongyang",' 71.
24. Yi Soo-jung, '*Nimui chimmuk*e natanan R. Tagoreu-ui yeonghyang gwangye yeongu,' 474.
25. Song Uk, 'Yumijeok cho-wolgwa hyeokmyeongjeok agong,' 53.
26. Kim Yoon-sik, *Geunde hanguk munhak yeongu*, 240.

Works Cited

Works by Tagore

Baik Gi-man, trans., 'Sin-wol-eseo' [From the Crescent (i.e., *The Crescent Moon*)]. *Geumsung* [La Venus], no. 2 (1924): 84–91.

Gui-bo, trans., 'Seung-ri' [Victory]. *Chongnun* [Youth], no. 29 (1926): 9–12.

Han Yong-un, trans., '"Saeng-ui silhyeon 1' [The Realisation of Life, 1]. *Yoosim*, no. 1 (1918): 47–56.

——, trans., 'Saeng-ui silhyeon 2' [The Realisation of Life, 2]. *Yoosim*, no. 2 (1918): 51–7.

Kim Ok, trans., *Kitanjari (Deul-ineun nore)* [*Gitanjali*]. Pyongyang: Imoongwan, 1923.

——, trans., *Wonjeong (Dongsanjigi)* [*The Gardener*]. Gyungsung (Seoul): Aidongseogwan, 1924.

——, trans., *Sin-wol* [*The Crescent Moon*]. Gyungsung (Seoul): Moonudang, 1924.

No-a, trans., 'Tagol-ui gitanjari' [Tagore's *Gitanjali*]. *Sinsaingwhal* [New Life], no. 6 (1922), 103–15.

O Cheon-suk, trans., 'Gitanjari takur sijip 1' [*Gitanjali*: Tagore's Collection, 1]. *Changjo* [Creation], no. 7 (1921): 60–1.

Song Wan-sik, trans., *Gotongui Sokbak* [The Bondage of Agony]. Gyungsung (Seoul): Dongyangdaehakdang, 1927.

Tae-bong, trans., 'Siseong tagol-ui danpyeon' [Some Pieces of Great Poet Tagore]. *Gongyoung* [Co-prosperity], no. 2 (1922): 97–100.

Tagore, Rabindranath. 'Dongbang-ui deungbul' [The Lamp of the East]. *Dong-a Ilbo*, 2 April 2 1929.

——. *Fruit-Gathering*. Madras: Macmillan India, 1985.

——. *Nationalism*. Madras: Macmillan India, 1985.

——. *Gora*. Dong-a Ilbo, 26 February, 3 March 1926.

Literature on Tagore

Han Yong-un. *Nimui chimmuk* [The Silence of the Beloved]. Seoul: Yeonhee, 1980 (Korean Literature, vol. 1).

Jin Hak-moon. 'Indo-ui segyejeok desi-in takur' [World famous Indian poet, Rabindranath Tagore]. *Cheongchoon* [Youth], no. 11 (1917): 95–8.

Jin Hak-moon. 'Tha Sunsaing Songyounggi' [An Account of our Greeting and Farewell to Guru Tagore]. *Cheongchoon*, no. 11 (1917): 101–7.

———. 'Myeongija geusijeol heosang (2), dongyang nebang-ui pyeonghwa-ui sangjing' [Visit to the East by the Great Poet of Peace]. *Samcheonri* [The Whole Korea], 6, no. 8 (1934): 120–7.

Ju Yo-han. 'Han Yong-un ssi geunjak *Nimui chimmuk* dokhugam: sarang-ui gido, gido-ui sarang' [Prayer of Love, Love of Prayer: Review of Han Yong-un's recent work, *Nimui chimmuk*]. *Dong-a Il-bo*, 26 June 1926.

Kim Byung-Chul. *Hanguk geunde beonyeok munhaksa yeongu* [History of Modern Korean Literature in Translation]. Seoul: Eulyoomunwhasa, 1975.

Kim Jae-hong. *Han Yong-un munhak yeongu* [Han Yong-un's Literature]. Seoul: Iljisa, 1982.

Kim Ok. 'Sidansanjaek' [Strolling the poetical circles]. *Gaebyak* [Beginning of the World], no. 46 (1924): 30–9.

———. 'Tago-a-ui si' (The Poetry of Tagore). *Josunmundan* [The Literary World of Korea), no. 2 (1924): 160–4.

———. 'Gwangmyeong-eun donyang-eseo – deul-inun i-ui sasang' [The Light is from the East—Thought of the Devotee]. *Dong-a Il-bo*, 21 July, 2 and 4 August 1925.

Kim Yoon-jik. *Geunde hanguk munhak yeongu* [Modern Korean Literature]. Seoul: Iljisa, 1973.

———. 'Hanguk sinmunhak-e iss-eoseo-ui tagoreu-ui yeonghyang-e dehaya' [Tagore's Influence on New Korean Literature]. *Jindan Hakbo*, no. 32 (1969): 199–238.

———. *Hanguk geunde sisa* [History of Modern Korean Poetry]. Seoul: Hakyunsa, 1986.

———. *Hanguk hyundesi yeongu* [Modern Korean Poetry]. Seoul: Iljisa, 1974.

———. 'Hanguk hyundesi-e michin tagol-ui yeonghyang' [Tagore's Influence on modern Korean Poetry]. *Josun Il-bo*, 6 July 1971.

Mohan, Pankaj. 'Tagore's Internationalism and his Lecture-tours in East Asia in the early 20th Century.' Paper presented as the special lecture for the Korea Foundation Cultural Centre, Seoul, 4 Feburary 2012.

Noh Ja-young, 'The School of Nature by Tagore,' *So-gwang* [First Light], no. 7, September 1920.

Pak Han-young. 'Tago-ol-ui sigwan' [Tagore's viewpoint on poetry]. *Yoosim*, no. 3: 22–30.

Song Uk. 'Yumijeok cho-wolgwa hyeokmyeongjeok agong' [Aesthetic Transcendence and Revolutionary Self-Space-'Manhe' Han Yong-un and R. Tagore]. *Sasanggye* [The World of Thought], no. 117 (1963): 38–60.

Yi Gwang-soo. 'Tago-a-ui wonjeong-e dehaya' [On the Gardener of Tagore]. *Dong-a Il-bo*, 20 January 1925.

Yi Ok-soon. 'Sikminji josun-ui 'dongyang', tagoreu-ui 'dongyang' [Colonial Korea's 'East', Tagore's 'East']. *Damron 201* [Discourse 2017, no. 2 (2005): 55–81.

Yi Soo-jung. '*Nimui chimmuk*e natanan R. Tagoreu-ui yeonghyang gwangye yeongu' [R. Tagore's Influence on *Nimui chimmuk* with special reference to *Wonjung* [*The Gardener*]. *Gwanakamunyeongu* (2003): 459–80.

3

CHINA

TAN CHUNG AND WEI LIMING

The first Asian Nobel laureate, Rabindranath Tagore, entered Chinese cultural life when the intellectuals were in the throes of a struggle between the collapse of an ancient monarchy and the uncertain destination of the new-born Republic. They were also immersed in the whirlpool of modern thinking bubbling over with individual liberation, free thinking, scientific temper, democracy, equality, and women's empowerment. When they began searching for food for thought in the jungle of foreign literature, Tagore, who synthesised quintessential Indian civilisation and modern culture within the framework of an Indian Renaissance, had much to offer. Tagore's winning the Nobel laurels and simultaneously being absorbed as a part of the English civilisation became an eye-opener to the peoples of the East whose self-confidence had been martyred to modernisation. As China lined up with other Asian colonies in search of a national salvation of sorts, Chinese intellectuals discovered the adorable Rabindranath Tagore icon from the niches of Western temples. China's reception of Tagore and her modern awakening complemented each other—greeting the Indian Nobel laureate and the New Culture Movement (that began from 1919) with equal enthusiasm.

In our study, we shall focus on the similar as well as different responses of the two ancient civilisations to the lure and challenge of Western civilisation, a process that is not concluded. We seek to especially focus on Tagore's 1924 lecture tour in China, and intend to transcend the alleged 'controversy' about this trip that makes the rounds in both knowledgeable and uninformed circles all over the world, so as to put an end to the continual hijacking of the meaningful exchanges between Tagore and China.

EARLY RESPONSE TO TAGORE

China applauded Tagore a couple of weeks *before* the Nobel Prize was announced. It was in October 1913 that Qian Zhixiu, the editor of *Dongfang zazhi* (Eastern Miscellany), one of China's earliest modern journals, who played a vital role in disseminating international knowledge and modern thinking in China, informed his readers rather cryptically: 'Tagore is an Indian poet famous for prophecy' along with displaying Tagore's photograph.[1]

In January 1915, Liang Qichao founded *Da Zhonghua* (The Great Chung Hwa Magazine), a pioneer organ blending traditional values with modern ideas. On 20 February 1916, it carried Ouyang Zhongtao's article entitled 'Jieshao Tai'a'er' (Introducing Tagore) along with a portrait of Tagore and a copy of his handwriting.[2] In the article, Tagore was introduced as a 'prophet, philosopher, preacher, educationist, Indian patriot and great man for revitalising Indian civilisation' and 'representative of Indian civilisation'. The journal also published, a few months later, a Chinese translation of Tagore's 'Autobiography.'[3]

Ouyang Zhongtao was a teacher of Tsinghua University, and his introductory article was marked 'to be continued' but was never completed. The completion was left to his colleagues and students who published a three-part biographical account of Tagore in the university journal *Qinghua zhoukan* (The Tsing Hua weekly).[4] The journal also published Song Chunfang's article on 'Guoyun yu wenxue' (The country's destiny and literature) with Tagore's writings as one of the focal points in 1918, and a translation of Tagore's short story entitled *Xiao zhuren* ('Little Master,' translating Tagore's short story 'Little Master's Return') in June 1919.[5]

Chinese readers first read Tagore's poetry through the translation of the founder of the forthcoming Communist Party of China (founded in 1921), Chen Duxiu, a Peking University professor of Chinese literature and also the founder-editor of the leftist journal, *Qingnian zazhi* (Journal of the Youth). Chen translated four poems of *Gitanjali* and published them in the journal in 1915.[6] He wrote:

> Tagore is a modern poet of India. He advocated carrying forward the Eastern spiritual culture. He was awarded *Nobel Peace* [sic] *Prize* and is famous all over Europe. Indian youths revered him as a prophet. His poetry is rich in religious and philosophical ideals.[7]

This is high approbation from the perhaps first Communist of China marred somewhat by the mistake of mentioning 'Nobel *Peace* Prize' when Literature was meant.

Chen Duxiu's journal *Xinqingnian* / *The New Youths* (the reincarnation of *Qingnian zazhi*) published two more of Tagore's poems from *The Crescent Moon* in September 1915.[8] The translator, Liu Bannong, was a young editor of the journal who later became a professor of Peking University and a famous writer. A few years later, in February 1920, Huang Zhongsu's article entitled

'Taige'erde shi shiqishou xu' (Preface to 17 Tagore Poems) appeared in the journal *Shaonian Zhongguo* (Young China).[9] This was the monthly organ of the short-lived 'Young China Association' founded by the foster mother of the Chinese Communist Movement, Li Dazhao, the Peking University librarian who was the mentor of Mao Zedong.

These two hitherto undiscovered publications are among the earliest published translations of Tagore in China. We must first credit the Chinese Communist Movement for its sensitivity in seeing merit in Tagore's poetry and their relevance to China's awakening. Second, these translations were not for idle amusement but a serious realisation of the power of the word, of progressive thinking and of the patriotic appeal in Tagore's works. Chen Duxiu's translation of 'Where the mind is without fear' from *Gitanjali* may be studied as an illustration:

Tagore's original	Chen's Chinese translation and its literal re-rendering
Where the mind is without fear and the head is held high;	远离恐怖心，矫首出尘表 Keep faraway from fear Head up above the sentient world
Where knowledge is free; Where the world has not been broken up into fragments by narrow domestic walls;	慧力无尽藏，体性遍明窈 Wisdom endless, freely available Body and nature universally enlightened and profound
Where words come out from the depth of truth; Where tireless striving stretches its arms towards perfection; Where the clear stream of reason has not lost its way into the dreary desert sand of dead habit;	语发真理源，奋臂赴完好， 清流径寒碛，而不迷中道。 行解趣永旷。 Words from fountainhead of truth Arms strive hard towards perfection Clean flow through cold desert Not astray from the middle path An eternal unbounded quest
Where the mind is led forward by thee into ever-widening thought and action— Into that heaven of freedom, my Father, let my country awake.	心径资灵诏。挈临自在天。 使我长皎皎。 Mind's path to the call of inspiration Fulfilment is disposed by Heaven I become bright and pure eternally

In 1915, Chinese literature was still in the rigid grip of classical poetry, too stiff to translate foreign poetry, especially Tagore's informal blank verse. Chen showed his mastery in adaptation by using the popular five-syllabic rhymed lines mixing colloquial expressions with classical idioms. It reads beautifully in Chinese. Our re-rendering shows that Chen did somewhat grasp Tagore's essence. This poem had inspired innumerable Indians to dedicate themselves to the struggle for freedom and independence of the motherland, just as the 'Yiyongjun jinxingqu' (Song of the Volunteers), now the national anthem of China, had done in China. Chen evidently selected it to inspire his countrymen.

Three short stories of Tagore, *Holiday*, *Kabuliwala* and *Vision*, were translated in 1917 in *Funü zazhi* (Women's journal), the first ever organ of Chinese women started in 1915 by the Commercial Press, Shanghai.[10] These translations extended Tagore's empathy for women's suffering to China and contributed to the early awakening of Chinese women who are regarded as among the most liberated and vibrant among Asian women today.

The year 1921 was a year of upsurge for Tagore translations in the Chinese press. About fifty pieces of translations were published by *Xiaoshuo yuebao* (Fiction Monthly), *Xuedeng* (Learning Lamp), *Dongfang zazhi*, *Xinren* (New People), *Funü zazhi*, and *Pingmin zazhi* (Common People's Journal), all representing the New Culture Movement. The Commercial Press brought out separate volumes of Zheng Zhenduo's translation of *Stray Birds* (in Chinese translation, *feiniaoji* ('The flying bird collection') and other works of Tagore.

Scholar-writer Wen Yiduo observed in 1923 that 'Almost every word of Tagore has moved into the Chinese language. There is very little translation of the first-rate masterpieces of Western literature.'[11] Though a gross exaggeration, it reflects the Chinese 'Tagore fever' culminating in the Jiangxueshe (Beijing Lecture Association)'s invitation to Tagore in 1923. Tagore's works were perhaps considered a part of the *Western* canon. Tagore's lecture tour took place in 1924 from 12 April to 30 May.

TAGORE IN CHINA: 1924

Amartya Sen described Tagore's 1924 China tour as a 'grand visit.'[12] The 'grand visit' has been as fondly remembered by Tagore and China as troubled by a 'controversy' theory.[13]

In a historical perspective, apart from Sri Lanka, which was then within the British Empire, China was the only foreign country that Tagore's father, Debendranath, ever visited. The visit in 1877–8 was a rich supply for entertaining and enduring gossip in the Tagore family when Rabindranath was a teenager. This must have had a bearing on Tagore's excitement on the eve of his own China visit. He even imagined half-jokingly his being held hostage in China by robbers, and his countrymen's failure of paying the ransom, compelling him to wear a pigtail and marry a Chinese girl.[14] Tagore's own China experience was much more exciting. When asked whether he had left behind anything on his departure from China, Tagore replied: 'I left behind my heart.'[15] Moreover, Tagore cherished this 'grand visit' in his last poem on his last birthday in 1941:

Once I went to the land of China,
Those whom I had not met
Put the mark of friendship on my forehead
Calling me their own.

A Chinese name I took, dressed in Chinese
  clothes.
This I knew in my mind
Wherever I find my friend there I am born
  Anew.
Life's wonder he brings.[16]

Tagore's 'A Chinese name I took' had a moving scene as described by Liang Qichao on 7 May 1924:

One day when we met, Tagore said to me: 'I don't know why, as soon as I arrived in China, I felt as though I was returning to my native place. Maybe I was an Indian monk in a previous life, who stayed on a particular mountain, in a particular cave enjoying freedom.' He then asked me to give him a Chinese name...[17]

Then, Liang Qichao gave Tagore the Chinese name of *Zhu Zhendan*/ Chu Chen-Tan ('*zhu*' for India, '*zhen*' for 'indra' and '*dan*' for 'rabi', and '*zhendan*' for China). This is not just a name, but a befitting tribute to Tagore and to the millennial affinity and friendship between India and China that Tagore symbolised.

Amartya Sen rightly points out that the Tagorean mission was unfortunately dogged by 'controversy.' With his towering vision, Tagore just could not refrain from the following observation while lecturing in China:

I have no doubt in my own mind that in the East our principal characteristic is not to set too high a price upon success through gaining advantage, but upon self-realisation through fulfilling our *dharma*, our ideals. Let the awakening of the East impel us consciously to discover the essential and the universal meaning of our own civilisation, to remove the debris from our path, to rescue it from the bondage of stagnation that produces impurities, to make it a great channel of communication between all human races.[18]

Tagore's observation was a camouflaged critical comment on the Western ethos of pursuing power at the expense of others, perhaps unaware of the

Chinese psyche when China was distressed with defeat and humiliation at the hands of world powers. The crux of the issue here is about power which China desperately wanted so that she would no longer remain a weaker and victimised member of the world where might was right. Though both have been age-old civilisations, and both have been repressed and exploited by the West, China and India have responded entirely differently to the Western challenges. The Indian response to the Western challenge as well as her success was to first awaken people's ardent affection for traditional wisdom as bestowed by their ancestors and, then, to overthrow the colonial rule by her powerful show of solidarity through the Independence movement led by Mahatma Gandhi. China took an entirely different route by first choosing the Western aggressors as her gurus, then with a Western mindset discarding the tradition of her ancestors and proceeding to overthrow the ancien régime of the old ethical teachings of China.

Tagore stood at the forefront of the Indian response to the modern Western challenges. He not only wished China to emulate the Indian example, but thought that the Chinese civilisation would be sagacious enough to uphold and carry forward her traditional values to encounter the corrosive influence of Western materialism. In his Bengali essay published in *Samajbhed* (Social Differences) in 1901, Tagore observed:

> The expansive China is restrained not by the command of the sword but disciplined by the commandments of religion. This religion comprises the relationship of fathers and sons, brothers and sisters, husbands and wives, neighbours and rural people, the king and the subjects, the preacher and the preached, all alike. Whatever upheaval hits it from outside, whoever ascends the throne, this religion controls the colossal masses of gigantic China from within. If she is hurt in her religion, China experiences death pangs and turns cruel in self-defence.[19]

We have no doubt that the word 'religion' in the quote is 'dharma' in Tagore's original which is a Bengali word inherited from Sanskrit. The word denoting 'religion' in modern Bengali is a synonym of the Chinese word 'Dao/Tao' which was the very Chinese translation of the Sanskrit word 'dharma' when Buddhism first introduced it to China two thousand odd years ago (later replaced by '*fa*'). This brings Tagore closer to his Chinese contemporary, Zheng Guanying (a leader in the 'self-strengthening movement'), who said famously in his well-known book *Shengshi weiyan* (Alarming Talks of the Booming Era) attributing Chinese civilisational strength to the synthesis of Dao/Tao (spiritual culture) and Qi (gadgets/material culture). Zheng observed that in modern times China's 'fall back into the unreal' coincided with Europe's 'advance into the real' and that 'within the unreal there is the real of Tao, within the real there is the unreal of Qi.'[20] Tagore looked more confidently at the sustainability of the Chinese Tao than Zheng Guanying who knew the Chinese weakness better than Tagore. But, both Tagore and Zheng were advocating the revitalisation of the traditional Tao–Qi dyad though Zheng's fervent advocacy for emulating the Western 'Qi' was not Tagore's cup of tea.

Zheng Guanying passed away in 1922, two years before Tagore's China visit while China continued on the road of emulating and worshipping the West. Because of the complexity of China's being ruled then by the Manchu government, this new trend gravitated towards the extreme reaction of tradition-baiting with ever increasing intensity. The patriots first turned their wrath towards the Manchu rulers, then towards the millennial Confucian tradition. Tagore had already noticed this trend before embarking on his mission in China. He said in a lecture in China:

> Some of our Eastern schoolboys may at once jump to [the] conclusion that this rebellion must take [the] form [of] imitation of the West. But they should know that while dead custom is plagiarism from our own past life, imitation would be plagiarism from other people's life. Both constitute slavery to the unreal. The former, though a chain, at least fits our figure; the latter, for all its misfit, is just as much a chain.[21]

On the surface, things were as smooth as foreign tours could go. Occasional press criticism appeared before Tagore's arrival and dogged Tagore's travel in China. But it was too feeble to mar the festivity and the 'Tagore fever'. Displeasure surfaced when Tagore was in Beijing, and, as it so happened, after Tagore had spent the happiest day of the trip on 8 May celebrating his sixty-third birthday (when he was presented with the Chinese name, and the Chinese performance of his opera *Chitra* by his Chinese hosts). The following day, 9 May, Tagore delivered his main lecture in the Zhenguang Theatre, Beijing, and some students distributed protest leaflets among the audience, the contents of which were later translated to Tagore. He was frustrated and decided to cut short his China trip, delivering his last talk in Beijing on 12 May. Tagore left Beijing on 20 May by the night train, was sent off warmly at the station by about two hundred Chinese and foreign admirers. Afterwards, he delivered only two talks, one on 25 May at Hankow (now Wuhan) and another, the 'Leave Talk' in Shanghai on 28 May.

Actually, the source of the displeasure originated from the conflict between the Tagorean mission and its opposition engineered by Tagore's earliest Chinese admirer-cum-translator, Chen Duxiu, who, as we have pointed out, had translated Tagore's 'Where the mind is without fear' for inspiring his own countrymen to wake up. Donning the hat of the Secretary of the newly founded Communist Party of China (CPC) (in 1921), Chen's mind was overcome with fear in 1924 that Tagore's spiritual power might harm the Chinese revolutionary cause which was very fragile and in its infancy. First, he published in the new leftist journal (founded in Shanghai in 1923) *Zhongguo qingnian* (Chinese Youth), Number 2 (October 1923), an article titled 'Women weishenme huanying Taigu'er?' (Why should we welcome Tagore?) capping a series of unwelcome articles which he (in his capacity as the Secretary of CPC) had urged and ordered others to write when a keenly expectant China was waiting for Tagore's arrival. Then, he published nine anti-Tagore-visit articles in *Xiangdao* (*Guide* journal, the organ of CPC) during Tagore's tour in China, in addition to several articles published in *Xiangdao* and elsewhere under the pseudonym of 'Shi'an.' Whereas these articles had little influence on the intellectual community, its weakness in argument and confusing target can be seen from the excerpt of the *Zhongguo qingnian* article below:

> I wonder why nowadays there is the vogue for the press to publish translations of Tagore. Do we welcome his art? Howsoever good, a masterpiece of literature instantly loses its value in translation. Even with mastery of translation it only shows the value of the translator which has nothing to do with the original work. Do we welcome the contents, i.e., the ideology, of his writings? But Tagore has a confused mind fundamentally opposed to material culture and science. Our own Laozi and Zhuangzi had a higher degree of confused mind that could save us the pains in translating Tagore. We had the confused minds of Laozi and Zhuangzi in addition to the confused ideology of Buddhism. I think we have had enough, we have felt the weight of the Indian gift. We don't need to add that of Tagore!

Was this the same Chen Duxiu who was the first serious Chinese admirer of Tagore, who translated 'Where the mind is without fear' of *Gitanjali* and hoped that it might help awaken the Chinese people to revitalise their nation? Yes and no. Yes, because even in the anti-Tagore-visit mood in this narrative, Chen Duxiu did not show any decrease of his high regard for Tagore. No, because his admiration for Tagore was overtaken by his allegiance to his Party's revolutionary cause. In addition to this, he had transformed himself from a scholar-writer into a politician who completely opposed the cause of translation—amounting to criticising himself, who had enthusiastically translated *Gitanjali* eight years ago.

While the 'controversy' has no substance, three bright spots of the visit are visible. The first emerges when we compare Tagore's 'grand visit' to the visits of the American statesman, John Dewey, in 1919–21 and the British philosopher, Bertrand Russell, in 1920–1 to China. Tagore's stay was shorter, but its popular reception warmer. This fact is reflected in the high number of reports and comments in the Chinese press and the surge in Tagore translations.[22] This surge is borne out by Chen Duxiu's aforesaid remark on the 'vogue in the press to publish translations of Tagore', which reiterated Wen Yiduo's statement that 'almost every word of Tagore has moved into Chinese language.' This *Tagore-fever* in the Chinese press that had begun before Tagore's arrival received a powerful boost by the visit, and continued for many years.

The second bright spot was the 'Tagore-fever' on the Tsinghua University campus which, according to the original plan, was to play host to Tagore for twenty-three days, from 28 April to 20 May. Tagore actually stayed for only six nights, from 29 April to 4 May. For those precious six nights, teachers and students of Tsinghua University had spent many months in preparation. The *Qinghua zhoukan* featured an article by Bi Shutang, an expert on foreign literature, titled 'Taige'er yanjiu zhinan' (A Guide for the study of Tagore) which is a summary of seventy-four articles on Tagore and Tagore's works published in the Chinese press from 1913 to 1923 with an appendix containing a bibliography of eighty-three English articles from the American press. When Tagore visited the Tsinghua University library, he saw a collection of twenty-four books of his own English writings. On 1 May, there were two lectures at the Tsinghua campus. At 3 p.m., Liang Qichao lectured on Sino-Indian cultural exchanges, and at 8.30 p.m., Tagore delivered one of his most serious and substantial talks in China, which became the 'To Students' section of his *Talks in China*. On 2 and 3 May, Tagore received the university students for one hour between 5 and 6 o'clock in the evening and talked on philosophy and other subjects. On 2 May, Tagore met Gu Hongming who was known as 'China's Tagore.' On the night of 3 May, the students of the university arranged for a special reception to Tagore with speeches and cultural performances.[23]

The third bright spot was the refreshing special friendship between Tagore and the Chinese poet Xu Zhimo (Hsu Tse-mou) whose name Tagore Indianised into the Mauryan 'Susima,' and whom he encouraged to address him as 'Rubidadda' (i.e., 'Rabi-dada' meaning 'elder brother, Rabi'). Tagore dedicated his *Talks in China* 'To My Friend Susima (Tsemou Hsu) to whose kind offices I owe my introduction to the great people of China'. Tagore also organised a 'tea club' at Santiniketan after he returned from China and named it the 'Susima club'. The impact of the China visit on Tagore is thus evident. The impact of Tagore's visit was even greater on Xu Zhimo who initiated and conducted Tagore's visit and wrought its success. He was Tagore's interpreter, guide, time-keeper, protector, and promoter. The Tagore–Xu, nay, 'Rubidadda–Susima', fraternity created the second Tagore visit to China in 1929—just to be the private guest of Xu in Shanghai en route to Japan and North America. We shall see the reach of Tagore's influence on the new Chinese poetry through Xu Zhimo later.[24]

TAGORE AND CHINA: ASSOCIATION OF A CENTURY

Celebrating the sixtieth anniversary of the People's Republic of China (PRC) in 2009, the *Global Times*, Beijing, featured, by popular vote, a list of '60 foreigners who helped shape China's 60 years.' The list is overwhelmingly dominated by the personalities of the West starting from scientists Newton and Einstein to the composer Beethoven, information technology pioneer Bill Gates, fashion designer Pierre Cardin, entertainer Michael Jackson and the basketball player Michael Jordan. It also included many political figures like Marx, Lenin, Stalin, Truman, Eisenhower, Kissinger, and Lee Kuan Yew. Three Indians figured in the list, viz. Tagore, Gandhi and Nehru. Tagore was in the company of only three other world-famous writers, Tolstoy, Gorky, and the Danish children's folklorist Andersen. Tagore was introduced as one who had dedicated himself to the cause of 'the meeting of the Eastern and Western civilisations' and was acclaimed as a 'sage poet.' This points to Tagore's popularity in China and obliterates any remaining trace of the so-called 'controversy' concerning him. Tagore's reputation as the most translated foreign author in China has stood the vicissitudes of times through one hundred years.

The hundred-year ties between Tagore and China have found expression in the experience of Guo Moruo who went to Japan to study in 1914, and was just in time to witness the Japanese ovation for Tagore's Nobel Prize. He read *The Crescent Moon* and other poems of Tagore with great enthusiasm and began to compose poems in the modern style emulating Tagore and others. In 1917, he translated some pieces from *The Crescent Moon*, *The Gardener*, and *Gitanjali* and sent them for publication to the leading publishers in China, the Commercial Press and the Zhonghua Bookshop, without success. Guo was an ardent revolutionary youth who was eager to return to China to join the cause while he was in love with Tagore literature. In life, he was in love with a Japanese nurse (who later lived in China with the Chinese name Guo Anna) and they also had children. But Guo was already married in China. He was tormented by this emotional entanglement which could have ruined his future career. But when Guo started reading Tagore's poems in 1916, he felt as if he had obtained '*shengmingde shengming*' (literally, 'the life of life'), and also '*shengmingde quanshui*' (literally, 'the fountain of life').[25] He drew sufficient spiritual power from Tagore's poems to overcome thoughts of suicide. He composed a poem titled 'chen'an' (Good morning) in 1920 in which he praised Tagore, and Santiniketan, which he never visited. In it Guo wrote, 'Good morning, venerable Sir Tagore of Bengal! Good morning to the academic friends of the Ashram of Nature!'[26] Unknowingly, Tagore was instrumental in the success of this Chinese intellectual who became virtually 'China's Tagore' between the 1940s and 1970s.

The overall contribution of Tagore to the development of Chinese literature is twofold: as an inspiration to the newly born Chinese 'new poetry' especially through the talented but ill-fated Xu Zhimo (Susima); and as the foster father of the first ever children's literature in China through another ardent Chinese admirer, Bing Xin.

In the annals of Chinese literature, the mid-1920s were dominated by two events: Tagore's visit and the birth of three avant-garde literary societies: Wenxue yanjiuhui (Literature Study Association) founded by Zheng Zhenduo, an ardent admirer of Tagore who topped the list of Chinese translations of Tagore in 1923 with nineteen publications, and Shen Yanbing (better known as 'Mao Dun'), the co-editors of *Xiaoshuo yuebao* (many of whose members and writers warmly welcomed Tagore's China visit); Chuangzaoshe (Creation Society) founded by Guo Moruo, ex-admirer of Tagore; and Xinyueshe (the Crescent Moon Society) founded by Xu Zhimo with many eminent intellectuals like Hu Shi (Hu Shih), Wen Yiduo, Liang Shiqiu and others as its members. It was Tagore's collection titled *The Crescent Moon* that inspired the name 'Xinyue' of the Society, and the celebration of Tagore's sixty-third birthday in Beijing was the undeclared birthday of the Society itself. Unfortunately, the Society could not survive after the untimely demise of Xu Zhimo in an air crash in 1931. Nevertheless, the pioneering role of the 'Xinyueshe' in China's 'new poetry' movement is well recognised.

Guo Moruo's spiritual connection to Tagore speaks volumes for the power of Tagorean literature and its impact on several Chinese intellectuals. Perhaps the Chinese writer most influenced by Tagore was the poetess Bing Xin who wrote in 1920 (in the same year that Guo Moruo wrote his 'Good morning' to Tagore) a poetic essay 'Yaoji Yindu zheren Taige'er' (To the Far Away Indian Philosopher Tagore). In this essay, Bing Xin, repeatedly using Tagore's word 'infinite' (in Chinese *wuxian*), wrote: 'Tagore! Majestic and solemn Tagore! When I cross the boundary of "infinite life", you would have gone beyond it to emit infinite light for mankind.' She added: 'Since we are united in "Brahma", you must have already read what I had written.'[27] Both Guo Moruo and Bing Xin read Tagore's works in English while abroad (Guo in Japan, Bing Xin in the USA) and Tagore's influence on them was therefore direct. Guo did not try to translate Tagore after his abortive trial in 1917 (as he soon joined the CPC and even the army in the anti-warlords campaign, and became very active in politics afterwards). Bing Xin became one of the eminent Tagore translators in China while retaining her own Tagorean writing style.

Bing Xin became the unchallenged apostle of children's literature in China by transplanting Tagore's affection and concern for and faith in children in her own country. She shared with Xu Zhimo not only the reputation of being the most ardent Chinese admirer of Tagore, but also of being a pioneer of China's new poetry. She built her fame on *Fan Xing* (Twinkling Stars) and *Chun Shui* (Spring River), collections of short poems emulating *Stray Birds*, published in 1922 and 1923 respectively. Bing Xin was not in China to welcome Tagore in 1924, but her *Fan Xing* and *Chun Shui* were there to impart ardour to the Tagore fever. It was in these two masterpieces that we see Chinese literature beginning its dialogue with children. For example, in *Fan Xing* (35), Bing Xin wrote (translation by Tan Chung and Zeng Qiong):

Messengers by the thousands,
Come to praise children;
Children!
Within their small bodies,
Is hidden the great soul.

And in *Chun Shui* (64), she wrote:

Baby,
In whose pulsating cry there is
Infinite mysterious language,
Brought from the primary soul
To tell the world.[28]

The emergence of an intimate dialogue with children was a revolution in Chinese literature, which had been ignored as a genre for three thousand years. Bing Xin was the unchallenged pioneer. She gained a reputation like Tagore for treating children as angels, and for being a literary companion to children. It is for this reason that Bing Xin is often compared with Tagore in Chinese literary criticism.[29] Although comparisons are made in passing between Tagore and other important Chinese writers like Lu Xun or Guo Moruo, Bing Xin always enjoys a special affinity with Tagore in spite of the fact that she never met the Nobel laureate. In 1961, the Sahitya Akademi brought out the *Centenary Volume* of Tagore, and Bing Xin was the only Chinese contributor to it. She describes in her tribute that when she read Tagore's poems, she felt 'as if I had found a hidden orchid while strolling along a mountain path.' Her conclusion is a solemn prayer: 'Let the 1,000 million people of both our countries remember forever his [Tagore's] valuable advice and continue to lay the most solid foundation-stones of friendship and unity for "struggling Asia".[30]

Tagore's zeal to develop studies on Chinese civilisation in India was appreciated during his China visit. Liang Qichao, in particular, made a promise to send a team to Santiniketan to continue the work, but that was never to be. In 1928, Tan Yun-shan joined the staff of Visva-Bharati, and dedicated himself to the task of fulfilling the wishes of Tagore. He first tried to persuade the richest Chinese person, Hu Wenhu (better known outside China as 'Aw Boon How'), to spare a hundred thousand silver dollars to build a Cheena Bhavana at Santiniketan. Mr How described the request as 'a mere pittance' in his reply, but failed to keep his promise. Tan did not give up, he established the Zhong-Yin xuehui (Sino-Indian Cultural Society) in Nanjing and obtained a 'yes' in 1933 from the supreme leader of China, Chiang Kai-shek, to make good the failed promise of Aw Boon How.[31] After the establishment of the Cheena Bhavana within Visva-Bharati, which functioned under the directorship of Tan Yun-shan and was financed by the Chinese government through the Sino-Indian Cultural Society, Tagore strengthened his fraternity with China, and firmly supported China's resistance against the Japanese aggression. There were exchanges of letters between Tagore and Chiang Kai-shek on this account.

In the wake of Tagore's demise on 7 August 1941, there were a number of condolence meetings in China's War-capital, Chongqing. On 29 September, Dai Jitao (Tai Chi-T'ao), close friend and colleague of Chiang Kai-shek (patron of the Sino-Indian Cultural Society), presided over the memorial ceremony in the presence of high-ranking government and Kuomintang officers and distinguished members of Academia Sinica (Latin for 'Chinese Academy', in Taipei) and the universities of Chongqing and other places. Zhu Jiahua (Chu Chia-Hua) (another patron of the Sino-Indian Cultural Society) delivered a passionate address. He said: 'Tagore ardently loved his country, and wanted to rescue the world from crisis and humanity from misery. His compassion for the universe and humankind and for the spirit of *Brahmatmaikya* are as great as the Buddha and the Christ.' No tribute to Tagore can surpass these words. An ambitious plan for bringing out a good memorial volume in Chinese did not materialise due to the War situation.[32]

Chinese translation of Tagore is a rich and vibrant area. During the centenary celebration of Tagore in 1961, the People's Publishing House, Beijing, brought out a ten-volume *Taige'er zuopin ji* (Works of Tagore). The source languages of this collection are English and Russian.[33] A new attempt to create a Chinese *Rabindra Racanabali* was made in 2000 when the Hebei Education Press brought out the twenty-four-volume *Taige'er quanji* (Complete Works of Tagore) edited by Liu Anwu, a Peking University stalwart, and others. The leading translators are China's Bengali experts including Bangladesh-trained Bai Kaiyuan, Shi Jingwu, and Soviet-trained Dong Youchen, Huang Zhikun, and Li Yuanshan (all of whom had studied in the erstwhile Leningrad State University). At present, a third attempt is in the offing initiated by Yu Longyu of Shenzhen University. The project will translate Tagore's works only from Bengali. When this attempt succeeds, the Chinese language will be one of the richest repositories of Tagore's golden treasury.

Tagore studies in China, being a part of South Asian (mainly Indian) Studies has its formidable base located in Peking University, Beijing, founded by Ji Xianlin, the doyen of Indian Studies in China. Its faculty, led by Zhang Guanglin, Tang Renhu and Wei Liming, has built up a wonderful department. Yu Longyu, a pupil of Ji Xianlin, is establishing a centre of Indian studies at Shenzhen University, which includes Tagore studies. There are individual Tagore experts in other universities, notably, Gong Jing and Liu Jian of the Chinese Academy of Social Sciences, Beijing, He Naiying of the Beijing Normal University, Sun Yixue of Tongji University, Shanghai, Dong Hongjun of Shanghai University, Dong Youchen of Beijing Foreign Studies University, Ai Dan of Zhejiang University of Technology, Hangzhou, Li Wenbin of the Three Gorges University, Yichang, Hou Chuanwen of Qingdao University and Yin Xi'nan of Sichuan University, Chengdu. From 1979 onwards, 2,156 articles, including PhD and MPhil dissertations, on Tagore have been published in China.

Among Tagore's admirers was the renowned Peking Opera star, Mei Lanfang, who specially performed his new drama, *Luoshen* (Goddess of Luo River) at the Kaiming Theatre, Beijing, to entertain Tagore in 1924. Tagore wore his purple gown to attend the performance, and composed a poem, writing it on a paper fan with a Chinese brush. To celebrate Tagore's sixty-third birthday, his Chinese hosts, led by Xu Zhimo, staged Tagore's *Chitra*. *Chitra* was staged once again by the students of the English Department of Lanzhou University in the Culture Centre of the Indian Embassy, Beijing, in 2007, in the presence of the Indian Ambassador, Nirupama Rao. On 24 March 2012, *Chitra* was staged in Chinese in the Lanzhou University campus in the presence of the Indian Ambassador, Dr Subrahmanian Jaishankar. The first time that Chinese musicians played the tunes of Tagore music was in a performance organised by the Central Academy of Music, Beijing, on 14 September 2007.

As a versatile writer and thinker, Tagore has been studied, appreciated, and emulated in China from various perspectives. But along with his literary accomplishment, he is most cherished for his noble spirit. In 2011, during the celebrations of the 150th birth anniversary of Tagore in China, the Chinese intellectual community enthusiastically responded to the call of the 6th Plenum of the 17th Central Committee of the CPC for ushering in a Renaissance in China. The Chinese have been drawn to Tagore with greater verve, making him all the more endearing to China.

Notes

1. Qian Zhixiu, 'The worldview of Tagore,' 1–4.
2. Ouyang Zhongtao, 'Introducing Tagore,' 1–8.
3. 'Zhuwei' (Autobiography). It is unclear what the original of this work was. *My Reminiscences* appeared in Bengali in 1912 but in English only in 1917.
4. 'Yindu shiren Taguo'er zhuan' [The Indian poet Tagore]. *Qinghua zhoukan* [The Tsing Hua Weekly] 1917, 26 April, 24 May, 106 and 31 May, 111.
5. *Xiao zhuren* [Little Master], *Qinghua zhoukan*, 1919 Summer, 1–8.
6. Chen Duxiu, 'Hymns,' 1–2.
7. Ibid., 1–2.
8. 'Tongqing' [Sympathy] and 'Haibin' [On the sea shore]. *Xinqingnian* [The New Youths] 5, no. 3 (September 1915), 229–30.
9. Huang Zhongsu. 'Preface to 17 Tagore poems.'
10. 'Chulian' [Child love = Holiday], 'Kabuer ren' [Man from Kabul = Kabuliwala], 'Mangfu' [Blind woman = Vision]. *Funü zazhi* [Women's journal], 3, no. 6, 8–13, no. 7, 1–8, no. 8, 1–8 and no. 9, 1–8.
11. See Wen Yiduo, *Collected Works*, 3, 369.
12. See Sen, 'Tagore and China,' 10.
13. A work, such as Stephen Hay's *Asian Ideas of East and West: Tagore and his Critics in Japan, China and India*, Cambridge: Harvard University Press, 1970, has led a part of Indian intellectuals down the garden path to play up the 'controversy' of Tagore's China visit. Today, some Indians still view Tagore as an 'unwelcome guest in China', ignoring the fact that thousands of Chinese intellectuals enthusiastically met Tagore, talked to him and listened to and engaged with him. A major shortcoming in Hay's work is his neglect of the wider Chinese context of the visit. Tagore spent forty-seven days between 14 April and 30 May on Chinese soil engaged in discoursing on civilisation whith Chinese intellectuals. No similar thing happened to any other eminent foreign visitor to China. Moreover, such a long stay in one country is also unique among the many foreign tours of the Nobel Laureate Tagore.
14. We owe our debt to Professor Uma Das Gupta for this information which she found in a Bengali letter Tagore addressed to his much younger friend, Ranu Adhikari, in November 1923 after he had recuperated from his illness and was about to embark on his journey to China. Tagore's letters to Ranu Adhikari were published recently in Visva-Bharati's *Chitthipatra* series (vol. 18, 2002).
15. Bing Xin wrote on 23 June 1982, in the 'Translator's preface' in her *Taige'er shixuan*, 1, about this, which she heard from a person who had looked after Tagore's stay in China.
16. Tagore, *Poems*, 203 (poem No. 123).

17. Tan Chung, 'Retracting the path to brotherhood,' 63.
18. Tagore, *Talks in China*, 99.
19. Swapan Majumdar, 'Looking East—China in Tagore's Cosmology of Thoughts,' in Tan Chung et al., *Tagore and China*, 78. We are grateful to Professor Swapan Majumdar for unearthing this valuable information and translating it from Bengali.
20. Xia Dongyuan et al., *Selected Works of Zheng Guanying*, 157–8.
21. Tagore, *Talks in China*, 99.
22. Sun Yixue *Taige'er: Zhongguozhi lü* [Tagore: China trips]. Beijing: Central Compilation and Translation Press, 2013, 202–9 provides a list of 171 reports and comments on the China visit in Chinese newspapers and magazines between 12 April and 11 June 1924.
23. Most of the information about the Tsinghua University welcome to Tagore is from Jin Fujun, 'Revisiting Tagore's stay at the Tsinghua University campus in 1924,' 60–5.
24. For details of the 'Rubidadda-Susima' fraternity see Tan Chung, 'Telepathy between Rubidadda and Susima.'
25. Guo Moruo wrote this in an article supposedly to oppose Tagore's visit to China by obliging his leftist comrade, Chen Duxiu. However, the article titled "My opinion on Tagore's China visit" turned out to be a nostalgic account of his spiritual connection with Tagore.
26. Tan Chung, 'Towards an In-Depth Understanding of Tagore, China and Asia,' in Tan Chung et al., *Tagore and China*, 180–2.
27. Zeng Qiong, 'Tagore's Influence on the Chinese Writer Bing Xin,' in Tan Chung et al., *Tagore and China*, 262, 265.
28. Ibid., 267.
29. See. Juanzi, 'The songsters of children' and Chen Wenying, 'Children in the writings of Tagore and Bing Xin.'
30. *Rabindranath Tagore (1861–1961)*, 211, 216.
31. In September 1933, Tan Yun-shan wrote from Nanjing to Tagore with these words:

    I am sorry to say Mr Aw Boon How, owing to his own unfavourable circumstances, has not yet fulfilled his promise to build in Santiniketan a Chinese Hall [Cheena-Bhavana], but now the Chinese national leader Chiang Kai-shek and Mr Tai Chi-tao, President of the Examination Yuan of the National Government of China, have in an interview with me lately promised to do what Mr Aw has failed to do. So I take the liberty of asking for your kind advice as to the necessary steps taken for its establishment, the approximate amount of finance, and the need of fund, books and other equipments.

    A copy of the letter was in the custody of Tan Chung, but now preserved in the Tan Yun-shan Sino–Indian Friendship Museum at Shenzhen University, Shenzhen, China.
32. Zhou Xiao, 'Selected data of the condolence conferences.'

33. During the 1950s and 1960s, Russian, the dominant foreign language in China, was the window to all foreign literatures. Chinese experts in the Bengali language were trained in Russia, some of whom still play important roles in Bengali–Chinese translation today.

WORKS CITED

Ai Dan. *Taige'er yu Wusishiqi sixiang wenhua lunzheng* [Polemics between Tagore and Chinese thought and culture during the May Fourth Period]. Beijing: People's Press, 2010.

Bing Xin. *Taige'er shixuan* [Selections of Tagore's poems]. Changsha: Hunan People's Press, 1982.

Chen Duxiu. 'Zan'ge' [Hymns]. *Qingnian zazhi* [Journal of the Youth] 1, no. 2 (October 1915), 1–2.

Chen Wenying. 'Taige'er yu Bing Xin bixiade ertong' [Children in the writings of Tagore and Bing Xin]. *Zhongguo xiandai wenxue yanjiu congkan* [Series of Modern Chinese Literature Studies] 1995, no. 4, 92–108.

Dong Youchen, comp. *Taige'er xiaoshuo quanyi* [Complete translation of Tagore's novels], 7 vols. Beijing: Sino-Culture Press, 2005.

Guo Moruo. 'Taige'er lai Huade wojian' [My opinion on Tagore's China visit] In *Shirende jingshen: Taige'er zai Zhongguo* [The spirit of the poet: Tagore in China], by Sun Yixue, 225–8. Nanchang: Jiangxi Higher Education Press, 2009.

Huang Zhongsu. 'Taige'erde shi shiqishou xu' [Preface to seventeen Tagore poems]. *Shaonian Zhongguo* [Young China], 2, no. 8 (15 February 1920), 48–55.

Jiang Jingkui, ed. *Zhongguo xuezhe lun Taige'er* [Chinese scholars on Tagore]. Yinchuan: Sunlight Press, 2011.

Jin Fujun. '1924 nian Taige'er zai Qinghua huodong kaozheng' [Revisiting Tagore's stay at the Tsinghua University campus in 1924]. *Nanya yanjiu jikan* [South Asian Studies Quarterly] (published by the Institute of South Asian Studies, Sichuan University, Chengdu), no. 4 (2006): 60–5.

Juanzi. 'Ertongde gezhe: Bing Xin Taige'er bijiao tan' [The songsters of children: Comparison between Bing Xin and Tagore]. *Guangxi minzu xueyuan xuebao* [Journal of the Guangxi Academy of Nationality Studies], no. 2 (1990), 92–6.

Li Wenbin. *Taige'er meixue sixiang yanjiu* [Study on Tagore's aesthetic theories]. Wuhan: Central China Normal University Press, 2010.

Liu Anwu, Ni Peigen and Bai Kaiyuan, comp. *Taige'er quanji* [Complete Works of Tagore], 24 vols. Shijiazhuang: Hebei Education Press, 2000.

Qian Zhixiu. 'Tai'e'ershi zhi renshengguan' (The world view of Tagore), *Dongfang zazhi* (Eastern Miscellany), 10, no. 4 (1913), 1–4.

Rabindranath Tagore (1861–1961): A Centenary Volume. New Delhi: Sahitya Akademi, 1961.

Ranganathan, C. V., ed. *Panchsheel and the Future: Perspectives on India–China Relations*. Delhi: Institute of Chinese Studies and Samskriti, 2005.

Sen, Amartya. 'Tagore and China.' In *Tagore and China,* edited by Tan Chung, Amiya Dev, Wang Bangwei and Wei Liming, 3–10. New Delhi: SAGE India and Central Translation & Compilation Press, 2011.

Shen Yihong, ed. *Taige'er tan Zhongguo* [Tagore on China]. Hangzhou: Zhejiang Literature Press, 2001.

Sun Yixue. *Taige'er yu Zhongguo* [Tagore and China]. Shijiazhuang: Hebei People's Press, 2001.

———. *Shirende jingshen: Taige'er zai Zhongguo* [The spirit of the poet: Tagore in China]. Nanchang: Jiangxi Higher Education Institutions Press, 2009.

———. *Taige'er: Zhongguozhi lü* [Tagore: China trips]. Beijing: Central Compilation and Translation Press, 2013.

Tagore, Rabindranath. *Poems.* Calcutta: Visva-Bharati, 1942.

———. *Talks in China.* Edited by Sisir Kumar Das. Calcutta: Rabindra-Bhavana, Visva-Bharati, 1999.

Tan Chung. 'Retracing the Path to Brotherhood: The Santiniketan Story.' In *Panchsheel and the Future: Perspectives on India–China Relations,* ed. C. V. Ranganathan, 59–75. Delhi: Institute of Chinese Studies and Samskriti publication, 2005.

———. *Tan Yun-shan yu Zhong-Yin wenhua jiaoliu* [Tan Yun-shan and SinoIndian cultural intercourse]. Hong Kong: Chinese University of Hong Kong Press, 1998.

———. 'Telepathy between Rubidadda and Susima: A Geo-civilizational Perspective.' In *Tagore and China*, ed. Tan Chung et al., 97–138 [Chapter 7]. New Delhi: SAGE India and Central Translation & Compilation Press, 2011.

Tan Chung, Amiya Dev, Wang Bangwei and Wei Liming, eds. *Tagore and China.* New Delhi: SAGE India and Central Translation & Compilation Press, 2011.

Tang Renhu, Yu Longyu, Jiang Jingkui and Wei Liming. *Taige'er wenxue zuopin yanjiu* [Studies on Tagore's literature]. Beijing: Kunlun Press, 2003.

Wang Bangwei, Tan Chung, Amiya Dev, and Wei Liming, eds. *Taige'er yu Zhongguo* [Tagore and China]. Beijing: Central Translation & Compilation Press, 2011.

Wang Zhiyan. *Zou zai Yindu yu shijiede lianjiexian shang* [Walking on the connecting line between India and the world]. Yanji: Yanbian People's Press, 2006.

Wei Fengjiang. *Wode laoshi Taige'er* [My guru Tagore]. Guiyang: Guizhou People's Press, 1986.

Wei Liming. 'Wanshide luren' Taige'er: cong Shipo, Yesu, Shashibiya dao Zhongguo [The 'eternal traveller' Tagore: from Shiva to Jesus to Shakespeare to China]. Beijing: Central Translation & Compilation Press, 2011.

Wen Yiduo. *Wen Yiduo quanji* [Collected works of Wen Yiduo]. Beijing: Sanlian Bookshop, 1982.

Xia Dongyuan et al., comps. *Zheng Guanying wenxuan* [Selected Works of Zheng Guanying]. Macau: Macau Historical Society and the Macau Association for the Concern of Historical Materials Publication, 2002.

Xiao zhuren [Little Master], *Qinghua zhoukan* [The Tsing Hua Weekly], 1919, Summer special issue, 1–8.

Yang Fei et al. *Dongfang dadide yonghengzhi sheng: Taige'er jiqi chuangzuo* [The eternal voice of Eastern land: Tagore and his creative works]. Changchun: The Time Literature & Art Press, 2001.

Yin Xi'nan. *Shijie wenming shiyezhongde Taige'er* [Tagore: From the Perspective of World Civilisation]. Chengdu: Bashu Bookshop, 2003.

Yu Longyu and Dong Youchen, eds. *Taige'er zuopin jianshang cidian* [Dictionary for appreciating Tagore's works]. Shanghai: Shanghai Dictionary Press, 2011.

Zhang Guanglin. *Yindu dashiren Taige'er* [The great Indian poet Tagore]. Beijing: Blue Sky Press, 1993.

———,. ed. *Zhongguo mingjia lun Taige'er* [Famous Chinese on Tagore]. Beijing: The Chinese Overseas Publishing House, 1994.

Zhang Yu. *Taige'er yu Zhongguo xiandai wenxue* [Tagore and modern Chinese literature]. Kunming: Yunnan People's Press, 2005.

Zhou Xiao. 'Zhongguo wenhua jiguantuanti juxing Taige'er zhuidaodahui shiliao xuan' [Selected data of the condolence conferences for Tagore by Chinese cultural organisations]. *Minguo dang'an* [Archives of the Republican Period] 2011, no. 4, 49–68.

'Zhuwei,' transl. 'Yindu dasixiangjia Tai'a'er zizhuan' [Autobiography of the Great Indian Thinker, Tagore]. *Da Zhonghua*, 2, no. 8, 1–12.

4

VIETNAM

DO THU HA AND SUPRIYA ROY

The respect with which Vietnamese intellectuals held Rabindranath Tagore for his talents, dignity, intelligence, ideals and actions might have originated from the situational identification of Vietnam and India. Both the Vietnamese and Indians experienced the evils of colonial rule, which was unable to eradicate either poverty or illiteracy, and presented hard challenges to the intellectuals. Vietnam was under French colonial rule until 1954 and in the first half of the twentieth century was administered as three different regions—North, Centre and South. Although until the end of the Vietnam War in 1975 the country was divided into North and South, the Vietnamese never accepted the separation and Communists lived and fought all around the country. Intellectuals in the early twentieth century were divided in two groups: some people advocated collaboration with the French, while others, whom we may call patriots, were against such collaboration. The patriots included both those of the 'Literati movement' who fought for the restoration of the pre-colonial order, and those with a more modern sense of nationhood.

The excitement over Tagore's Nobel Prize in 1913 was felt soon after the award, since he was the first Asian Nobel Laureate.[1] By 1924, the year of his intended stopover in the country, his works were read in Vietnam either in French or Chinese translations, as was the general practice among Vietnamese intellectuals at the time.[2] His name became increasingly well known due to his frequent international travels. He was expected to stay in Vietnam for three days in 1924 on his way back from China. However, instead of the poet, Tagore's close associate Kalidas Nag visited the country. The idea of a visit boosted Tagore's press coverage and the contemporary press presented his biography, literary career, and pictures in a number of articles.

Tagore eventually visited Saigon (now known as Ho Chi Minh City) in 1929. After that his name appeared in several articles on the nationalist movement of Vietnam written by Vietnamese and French scholars. His Vietnamese reception has been the subject of a fairly long article by Nguyen Dang Thuc, Chairman of the Vietnamese Association for Asian Cultural Relations, published in 1961.[3]

PERSONAL CONTACTS

For many people in Bengal, Vietnam is not just another country in South-East Asia. Bengalis of a particular generation, with Left leanings, who grew up in the 1960s and 1970s, would find that the name of Vietnam touched a chord in their being. Ho Chi Minh (1890–1969) was Bengal's hero, after whom an important street has been named in Kolkata as well as another road. But nearly four decades ago, it was the other way round. A poet from Bengal was lionised by the people of Vietnam. They had not yet started their struggle for independence but were in the process of searching for new ideas and ideologies that could help them find their own place in the world.

Bui Quang Chieu (1872–1945) and Duong Van Giao (1892–1945), who persuaded Rabindranath to stop over at Saigon and who organised his reception, were two prominent social reformers in the third decade of the twentieth century. Duong Van Giao, a Saigon lawyer and member of the Constitutionalist Party in French Indochina, had met Jawaharlal Nehru at Brussels in February 1927, where they attended a conference of the League against Imperialism. The annual conferences of the League enabled nationalists from different colonised countries to come together and share their experience and prepare strategies for the future. Jawaharlal Nehru invited Duong Van Giao to attend the forty-third session of the Indian National Congress as a representative of the Constitutionalist Party of Indochina. Bui Quang Chieu and Duong Van Giao travelled to Calcutta at the end of 1928 to attend this Congress session. They were both eager to understand and learn from the nationalist movement in India. They also wished to compare British and French colonial methods. This journey to India and back was fully documented by Bui Quang Chieu in a travelogue written in French, *Voyage en Inde* that was serialised in his newspaper, *Tribune Indochinoise*, between March and June 1929. Vietnamese leaders visited Santiniketan, where they found that the students were educated in their own language, literature and culture, and yet had the opportunity to study the different cultures of the world.

TAGORE'S STOPOVER AT SAIGON

In June 1929, Rabindranath represented India at the Conference of the National Council of Education in Vancouver, Canada. On his way back he spent a month in Japan. When the French Embassy came to know that Rabindranath was leaving Japanese shores, their representatives extended to the poet an invitation to visit Indo-China. Tagore sailed for India on the French mail boat, S. S. *Angers*, which called at Saigon.[4] An official reception committee, composed of French, Vietnamese and Indian members, had been formed to welcome the poet. Among the Vietnamese were Bui Quang Chieu, Duong Van Giao, Diep Van Ky, Lun Van Lang, Nguyen Van San, and Le Trung Nghia. The other members included the Foreign Secretary of the Indo-China Government, the Mayor of Saigon, and a leading Indian citizen.

On 21 June, a public holiday was declared in honour of the poet's visit. The whole city was in a festive mood and large crowds gathered near the landing stage and on the way to the State House where the poet and his companions were to stay. Festoons and decorations had been put up all along the route. Indian nationals in Saigon contributed money for an informal reception by the Mayor of Saigon and for all the expenses during Tagore's stay. A reception was held in Tagore's honour by the Mayor of Saigon, M. Béziatand, at the Hotel de Ville followed by lunch. In the evening, another reception awaited him at the Municipal Theatre. On that occasion, Bui Quang Chieu recalled the trip he and Duong had made to Santiniketan, where they saw the simple and lively spiritual communion which prevailed between the poet, the teachers and the students. Tagore then spoke of the cultural idea of a synthesis between East and West:

> ... the Poet Tagore does not cultivate a narrow nationalism... Far from being hostile to Western civilizations, the illustrious inhabitant of Santiniketan wishes with all his soul of a poet to combine the civilizations of the East and of the West in order to give to the world their full value generating beauty and goodness.[5]

Speaking after Bui Quang Chieu, Duong Van Giao praised the traditional culture of India and expressed the hope that India would revive and renew traditional ties with Vietnam. He said:

> ... in Asia, and more particularly on this Indo-Chinese peninsula, our peoples have always welcomed your formidable heritage of science, art and philosophy. We have known each other for a long time: you have given us indispensable lessons of wisdom and reason.
>
> Today, the high civilization of your country still marks ours with an indelible imprint. The wrong of fate has willed that ancient India be dismembered, looted, ravaged, conquered successively. She has served as a plaything to the most famous conquerors. All intellectual

ties seemed therefore broken between us. However, thanks to her religious faith, her centuries-old moral institutions, and her customs and manners against which time has had no influence, India still emerges amidst dispersed empires in the dust, following the course of her own destiny.

And you have come here today, Teacher, to give us proof of [India's] extraordinary vitality. Thanks to you, our traditions and our relationships are going from now on to be renewed usefully.[6]

In reply to the above greeting, Tagore said that he was deeply touched upon returning to the land where 'the heart of India had once beaten under a sunny sky', going on to state:

Please know that before human joys and human miseries, my heart always beats with the same rhythm as that of those of my predecessors who in the most distant past lived among you. My voice always expresses man's aspiration towards light, love and liberty. It is always for the triumph of the divine martyr over all that is basely cruel and selfish. I bring you the greetings of that radiant India, who lavished her light on this land as well as the message of sympathy and brotherhood of present India who lives separated from you by geographic distance and by the dead solitude of her own darkness.[7]

Apurva Chanda, the poet's sole companion on his way back, recalls this evening in his own way. As they were going to the reception, Rabindranath leaned towards him and whispered that never before had he felt so tired and empty of any ideas. But when he rose to speak, after hearing those warm felicitations, the speech that he made was the most moving one Apurva Chanda had ever heard. He sat enthralled and could not take his eyes off the poet who looked magnificent with the rays of the setting sun lighting up the Hall and his long saffron robes. Rabindranath spoke about his namesake in the sky, Rabi meaning the Sun, which was then setting and said his time of setting too was approaching. He said:

In the past, people from my country used to come to your land dreaming their dreams under your beautiful skies, singing their songs, creating beautiful things and building their temples. But in the centuries that followed, the facts of history and the barriers of geography had succeeded in interrupting that wonderful relationship. I have come to your shores today with nothing to offer you but my songs. Can I not beg of you to give me a small corner of your heart?[8]

Chanda recalls that even before Rabindranath went back to his seat, the Mayor of Saigon jumped up excitedly and translated the last part of his speech. The audience stood up and cried in one voice, 'Yes, Poet, Yes, for ever there will be an honoured place in our heart for you!'[9] Nguyen Dang Thuc writes:

> These few words, simple yet full of clear understanding uttered by the poet-prophet to the Vietnamese people, were moving indeed, at the time when all over the Indo-Chinese peninsula unarmed demonstrators fell under the colonialists' bullets and bombs, and teachers and intellectuals were sentenced by imperialist courts to death or forced labour because of their patriotism.[10]

Although these lines sound strange, since Tagore was well received by the French establishment in Saigon, it should be mentioned that Saigon, unlike the North under direct colonial rule, was administered as an autonomous region.

The 1929 March–June issue of the *Tribune Indochinoise* gave the following description of the reception at the Municipal Theatre of Saigon, which showed how enthusiastically the Vietnamese people welcomed the poet:

> As speeches followed one another in a dignified atmosphere and as the audience listened intently to the precious words, which if scattered throughout the world tomorrow will continue the poet's holy work, one felt the same admiring fervour for the illustrious old man soar up from the depth of all hearts. From all paying seats which were taken by storm the same attention was drawn to the stage.[11] Everyone, men and women, was in communion in the same atmosphere of spirituality. It was indeed all Saigon, all Cochin-China in the most diverse ethnic elements of hers celebrating the glory which, triumphantly received in the whole world in its biggest capital cities, has deigned to stoop over this little corner of Indo-China.

Incidentally, Rabindranath had a complete Vietnamese outfit made for him. According to Nguyen Dang Thuc, 'when he donned the Vietnamese costume—a black tunic over white trousers—and sat among Vietnamese for a photograph, he could pass easily for a Vietnamese Confucian scholar sitting among his children and grandchildren in a typical Vietnamese family.'[12]

On 22 June, the poet had an interview with the Governor, who came to Saigon from Hanoi, where he had been on tour, with the express purpose of meeting Rabindranath. Tagore had a long conversation with the Governor, who seemed well informed about ancient Indian history, art and sculpture and spoke about Buddhism and about Indian influence on Asian countries. He referred to the work being done by the École Française d'Extrème

Orient to preserve the monuments in Indochina.[13] Tagore then visited the Association of Indian Merchants, and in the afternoon went on a trip to Bien Hoa, about twenty miles east of Saigon, to see the École d'Art, which specialised in teaching ceramics and bronze sculpture. After this, he paid a visit to the tomb of Le Van Duyet (1763/64?–1832), a nineteenth-century Mandarin political figure who had rescued Christian missionaries and was one of the most venerated Vietnamese personalities. In the evening, he spent his time at the Eden Cinema in Saigon. He watched an early Pathé newsreel, a film on the traditional ceremonies of Tonkin. He also went sightseeing in the Halong Bay and attended a social function at the house of M. Nguyen Van Cua, the director of a publishing house in Saigon.

On 23 June, the poet went to the little town of Cholon where he bought some local souvenirs, visited a Chinese Pagoda and was received by a Chinese congregation. He also visited an Annamite Pagoda, and the Temple of the Chettys. He met local Indians at a ceremony on Ohier Street. He left Saigon the next morning and sailed back to India.

RESPONSES TO THE VISIT

While Rabindranath's visit made an enormous impact on the Vietnamese, not all reactions were positive. During his stay, he was approached by the nationalists of the Labour Party, but their efforts to draw him into discussing political issues were thwarted by the members of the reception committee. The Vietnam scholar Christopher E. Goscha observed, 'To the disappointment of the Vietnamese, Tagore was more interested in visiting Angkor Wat than discussing comparative reformist policies.'[14] It should be mentioned that Tagore had a demanding programme in Japan and his health was weak. He had been ordered complete rest by the doctors.[15] Rabindranath's interest in Southeast Asia was never at the level of daily politics but rather that of culture. He was eager to see remnants of ancient Indian civilisation in the different countries of this region. One of the reasons why he agreed to this detour in spite of his ill-health was that he was very keen on seeing Angkor Wat. He was visiting Indochina as a State guest of the French Government, and it would have been improper to discuss the faults of his hosts. However, Rabindranath was keenly sensitive to oppression of any kind. If he had a chance for discussion outside the French Protectorate, he would have responded in all seriousness. Did he not take the Korean students' complaints against Japanese oppression with indignation?[16]

Poets and writers have left ample evidence of their joy in having Rabindranath in their midst. As a poet, Rabindranath was appreciated and loved. Translation of his works started even before he landed in Saigon and continues unabated even today. His works also keep on being discussed as Rabindranath's versatility could satisfy a wide range of readership. Nguyen Dang Thuc writes that if the surface of Vietnam is clothed with a form of Chinese culture found among the ruling class, inwardly and hidden a lively stream of Indian culture flows in the hearts of the masses. So Tagore's *Sadhana* says:

> In love at one of its poles you find the personal, and at the other the impersonal. At one, you have the positive—Here I am; at the other, the equally strong denial—I am not. Without this ego, what is love? And again, with only this ego, how can love be possible?[17]

The Vietnamese poet Tan Da (1889–1939) writes about the existence of man and love:

> Who could this be, a person just like me?
> I thought somebody else, but it turned out to be you and me.
> Although two, we are really one,
> You and I. We are one but at the same time two.[18]

During Tagore's stay in Vietnam, the press was full of articles on and photos of him, as well as his speeches, treatises, and poems in Vietnamese. The most impressive articles on his visit were found in *Phu Nu Tan Van* (Women's Newspaper) and *Than Chung* (The Early Morning Bell). The impact of his visit can be measured by the words of the eminent poet Xuan Dieu, over thirty years later, on Tagore's birth centenary in 1961, uttered in a voice charged with emotion:

> I still remember that day over thirty years ago when I was ... a student at Quy Nhon School. It was in June 1929. That day, I accidentally read an article in *Phu Nu Tan Van* weekly, informing me of the great Indian poet Rabindranath Tagore's visit to Vietnam. I still remember the photo printed in that issue that pictured a man with deep eyes and a thick, long beard that touched his Asian-styled tunic. Although I was ... small then, I could feel, in his Vietnamese-translated poems, in his biography and his photo, something high and wide. This, for example, can be found in this line: 'My heart is a bird of [the] desert which has found the sky in your eyes.' I was filled with emotion after reading such lines of verse. I still feel it now. Those students who were aware of the loss of the country at that time could find in him something that caused sleepless nights, a liberal and great appeal, and a mind that is like a light in a long night... It was written in the article that he had a talk with the Study Encouragement Society. I thought that our city of Saigon then was holding the precious thing of human intelligence.[19]

One of the sentences spoken by Tagore during that trip, 'I stand outside your houses to find a place in your hearts,' was repeated many times by the great poet and artist, Doan Phu Tu (1910–89), to the young generations at the Literature Publishing House where he worked as an adviser during the 1960s. This also imparted to future enerations of Vietnam's writers a fund of affection for the great Indian poet, Rabindranath Tagore.

Tagore's brief visit to Saigon is considered a memorable landmark in the cultural relationship between the two nations. Therefore, in 2009, on the eightieth anniversary of that event, poet Nguyen Khoa Diem, who had grown up during the Vietnam War and had formerly been a leader of the Vietnam Writers' Association for many years, collected several articles published in the issue of *Than Chung* newspaper, released on 23 June 1929, that detailed Rabindranath Tagore's visit to Saigon, and had them re-published in an issue of the *Tho* (Poem) Magazine of the Vietnam Writers' Association.

INTELLECTUAL ENGAGEMENT WITH TAGORE

The first detailed introduction to and analysis of Tagore's philosophy was perhaps an article entitled 'Patriotism in Tagore.' It was published just two days before Tagore's aborted visit, on 16 June 1924 in *La Cloche Fêlée* (The Broken Bell), a newspaper established by the patriotic revolutionary Nguyen An Ninh.[20] The article was written by the editor-in-chief himself under the pen-name of Nguyen Tinh. Early translations include the treatise *The Declaration of the East*, published in issue 89 of *Nam Phong* (Southern Wind) Magazine (1924) and translated by its editor-in-chief, the scholar Pham Quynh, under the pen-name of Hoa Duong, and *The God of Love*, published by Nhat Duc Publishing House in 1929 and translated by Diep Van Ky.

The younger generations are lucky to have access to a great number of Tagore's works in Vietnamese, including dozens of poetry anthologies, short stories, novels, dramas, several treatises, and even his memoirs. Much attention has been paid particularly to the translation of his works into Vietnamese since 1961, the poet's birth centenary year, in Hanoi. Before that, only a few stray pieces and volumes were published in the Vietnamese press. In 1961 alone, two books on his life and career, accompanied by Vietnamese translations of his selected works, were simultaneously introduced to the public. One of them was *Collection of Rabindranath Tagore's Poems on the Hundredth Anniversary of his Birth*, published by the Literature Publishing House. It included studies and translations such as *Song Offerings (to Life): Gitanjali* and *The Gardener* by several leading poets of Vietnam, including Huy Can (1919–2005), Xuan Dieu (1917–85), Huyen Kieu (1915–95), Yen Lan (1916–98), Nguyen Viet Lam (b. 1919), Dao Xuan Quy (1924–

2007), Nguyen Dinh Thi (1924–2003), Hoang Trung Thong (1925–93), and Che Lan Vien (1925–89).

Another Vietnamese book, *Tagore: Poems, Short Stories, and Dramas*, was brought out by the same publishing house. The book was composed of pieces selected and translated by two leading writers and scholars, Cao Huy Dinh (1927–75) and La Con (b. 1924).

The translation of Tagore's works became part of the long-term project of the Culture Publishing House, later known as the Literature Publishing House, which at that time specialised in publishing classic and modern literary works both local and from overseas. Apart from Rabindranath Tagore's works, it published representative pieces of Indian literature including the Ramayana, the Mahabharata, the drama *Shakuntala*, Baren Basu's *The Recruit*, Bhabani Bhattacharya's *He Who Rides a Tiger* and Premchand's *Godaan: The Gift of a Cow*. Literature Publishing House employed a great number of translators, including researchers, laureates in former competitive examinations, and experienced writers and poets who were fluent in foreign languages. Unfortunately, there were no experts in modern Indian languages who could understand Tagore's original versions. Despite the harsh conditions of the Vietnam War, Indian literature in general and Tagore in particular were disseminated through translations made from intermediate languages such as English, French, and Chinese.

This achievement may be partly attributed to the support received from Indian friends who helped to train people to gather expertise on Indian culture and literature. This was followed by material support. For instance, during the 1980s when Vietnam was still suffering from the aftermath of the freshly terminated War, the Indian Government, via the Embassy of India, supplied Literature Publishing House, Hanoi, with hundreds of tons of paper to be used in the printing of valuable books such as the three-volume epic Ramayana and the *Discovery of India* by Jawaharlal Nehru.[21] Rabindranath Tagore's works, especially his poems, figured prominently in the project. Since the publication of the first two books in 1961, many poets and translators contributed to translating his works.

Tagore's Poems, a selection from Tagore's different works, collected and translated by Dao Xuan Quy, was published by Literature Publishing House, in 1979, with a print run of 10.200 copies. Dao Xuan Quy was also the translator of the *The Crescent Moon*, which included Vietnamese translations of Tagore's poems, published by the Culture-Information Publishing House in 2000. The release of *Tagore's Poems* and the over-hundred-page *Selected Works: Poems and Plays*, translated by writer and teacher Phan Khac Hoan and published by the Vietnam Writers' Association Publishing House in 1999, marks a new phase in Vietnamese translation history. It was the first time in Vietnam that translations were not forced into the traditional Vietnamese metre but reflected the modern idiom.

Vietnamese translations of Tagore's poems had also been made by scholars and released by different publishing houses in South Vietnam before 1975. They include *Song Offerings to Life* (i.e., *Gitanjali*) translated by Pham Hong Dung and Pham Bich Thuy and published by Light Source Publishing House in 1969, *Heart Offerings* (i.e., *The Gardener*) translated by Do Khanh Hoan and published by both An Tiem Publishing House and Ba Vi Publishing House in 1969, *Word Offerings* (a second translation of *Gitanjali*) also translated by Do Khanh Hoan and published by Ba Vi Publishing House in 1969 and by An Tiem Publishing House in 1972, *Song Offerings, Gitanjali* with Three Other Works: *Lover's Gift, The Crescent Moon*, and *Stray Birds* translated by Pham Hong Dung and Pham Bich Thuy and published by Light Source Publishing House, and *Tagore: The Lover of Life* including selected translations of Tagore's poems compiled by Nhat Chieu and Hoang Huu Dan and published by Vietnam Writers' Association Publishing House in 1991.

Literature Publishing House, Hanoi, also released two prose books of Tagore in succession: *The Cloud and Sun* (a collection of short stories) translated by Hoang Cuong and Nguyen Tam in 1986; and the two-volume novel *The Wreck* translated by Luu Duc Trung, Truong Thi Thu Van, and Hoang Dung in 1989. Also in 1989, Da Nang Publishing House introduced to the public the Vietnamese translation of the novel *Binodini* (*Chokher Bali*) made by Hong Tien and Manh Chuong. Several short stories have also been translated for publication by Youth Publishing House in 1973. *Kabuliwala, Broken Illusion*, and *The Judge*, translated by Pham Vien Phuong and Hoang Cuong, were included in the *Collection of Nobel Prize-Awarded Short Stories* published by the Literature Publishing House in 1997.

Nearly ten plays by Tagore, which had been translated by La Con and Luu Duc Trung over thirty years and appeared gradually, were finally assembled in the two-volume *Selected Works of Rabindranath Tagore*, published by the Labor Publishing House and the East-West Center for Cultures and Languages in 2004.

Works of Tagore have been included in textbooks for secondary and tertiary schools, as well as in anthologies, such as *Collection of Nobel Prize-Awarded Short Stories, Collection of Short Stories of World's Literature, Selected Poems of the World*, and *Nobel Prize-Awarded Works*. Many have also been quoted in academic studies on world literature, Asian literature, Indian literature, and on Tagore's life and career, which have been printed by different publishers all over Vietnam. Tagore's life and works have been also been the subject of studies by Vietnamese scholars. They include the introductory passages in the *Selected Works of Rabindranath Tagore* published by Literature Publishing House in 1989; *Tagore: Selected Works*, the chief editor of which was Luu Duc Trung, published by Labor Publishing House and the East-West Center for Cultures and Languages; and the Ph D. dissertation 'Lyricism and Philosophy in the *Gitanjali*' by Nguyen Van Hanh, a lecturer at Vinh Teachers' Training University. The 500-page monograph *Tagore: His Life and His Works* by the author of the present essay came out from the Culture and Information Publishing House in April 2005.[22] The monograph, the first of its kind in Vietnam, presents Tagore not only as a poet but also as a novelist, short-story writer and educator. It also analyses the extent to which Tagore's thinking was rooted in Indian soil. The monograph is used as a textbook for Vietnamese students at undergraduate and postgraduate levels.

CONCLUSION

Tagore was one of the most outstanding creative artists and among the greatest humanists the world has ever seen. His reputation and his large number of works imbued with lofty and humane ideas have moved Vietnamese readers. Indian literature and culture in general, and Rabindranath Tagore's literary legacy in particular, will be studied, translated, and popularised, admired and enjoyed in Vietnam well into the future.

NOTES

1. Truong Truc Dinh, 'Nhà Thơ Ấn Độ R. Tagore' [An Indian poet: R. Tagore], *Báo Nam Việt* [South Vietnam], 1 February 1914, 15–16.
2. Ibid.
3. Thuc, 'Tagore and Vietnam,' 359–64.
4. Roy, 'Stopover at Saigon.'
5. Chieu, 'Sự đáp lời của Tagore,' 8.
6. *Tribune Indochinoise*, 21 June 1929 cited in Thuc, 'Tagore and Vietnam,' 362.
7. Ibid.
8. Chanda, 'With Rabindranath to Canada,' 25.
9. Ibid.
10. Thuc, 'Tagore and Vietnam,' 362.
11. These were seats for the elite who paid for charity.
12. Thuc, 'Tagore and Vietnam,' 362.
13. The École Française d'Extrême-Orient (EFEO) is a French institute dedicated to the study of Asian societies. It was founded in 1900 with headquarters in Hanoi in what was then French Indochina. Its main fields of research are archaeology, philology and the study of modern Asian societies.
14. Chanda, 'With Rabindranath to Canada,' 19.
15. Thuc, 'Tagore and Vietnam,' 360.
16. Chanda, 'With Rabindranath to Canada,' 17.

18. *Tuyển tập Tản Đà*, 361.
19. Dieu, 'Thơ Tagore.'
20. Tinh, 'Long yeu nuoc cua Tagore' [Patriotism in Tagore], quoted on 16 June 2004 in the newspaper, *La Cloche Fêlée*, 9.
21. Ba, *Ramayana*, vols. I–III.
22. Ha, *R. Tagore, Văn và Người*.

WORKS CITED

Ba, Pham Thuy, transl. *Ramayana*, 3 vols. Hanoi: Literature Publishing House, 1983.

Chanda, Apurva. 'With Rabindranath to Canada.' In *Homage to Rabindranath Tagore*, edited by B. M. Chaudhuri, 15–30. Kharagpur: Tagore Centenary Celebration Committee, IIT, 1961.

Chieu, Quang. 'Sự đáp lời của Tagore tại một rạp chiếu phương Tây tại Sài gòn' [Tagore's Reply at a Western Cinema in Saigon]. *Phu Nu Tan Van* [Women in Modern Literature] (Saigon), 23 June 1929, 8–9.

Dieu, Xuan. 'Thơ Tagore' [Tagore and His Poems]. In *Tập thơ kỷ niệm 100 năm ngày sinh Rabindranath Tagore* [Collection of Rabindranath Tagore's Poems on the Hundredth Anniversary of His Birth] edited by Thuy Toan, 2, II–III. Hanoi: Literature Publishing House, 1961.

Dinh, Truong Truc. 'Nhà Thơ Ấn Độ R. Tagore' [An Indian poet: R. Tagore]. *Báo Nam Việt* [South Vietnam], 1 February 1914, 15–16.

Ha, Do Thu. *R. Tagore. Văn và Người* [Tagore: His Life and His Works]. Hanoi: Culture and Information Publishing House, 2005.

Roy, Supriya. 'Rabindranath Tagore: Stopover at Saigon.' Paper presented at the International Conference on Rabindranath Tagore's 150th Birthday Anniversary, Hanoi, Melia Hotel, 19 November 2012.

Thuc, Nguyen Dang. 'Tagore and Vietnam.' In *Rabindranath Tagore: A Centenary Volume, 1861–1961*, 359–64. New Delhi: Sahitya Akademi, 1961.

Tập thơ kỷ niệm 100 năm ngày sinh Rabindranath Tagore [Collection of Rabindranath Tagore's Poems on the Hundredth Anniversary of His Birth]. 3 vols. Hanoi: Literature Publishing House, 1961.

Tuyển tập Tản Đà [Collection of Tan Da]. Hanoi: Literature Publishing House, 1996.

5

TIBET

FRANÇOISE ROBIN

The history of Rabindranath Tagore's literary reception among Tibetans is a paradoxical one marked by a belated beginning. In spite of Tibet's relative geographical closeness to India, Tagore's works remained unknown until the late 1970s among the exiled Tibetan community and the early 1980s in Tibet proper, when they wound their way across the high Tibetan plateau and were met by enthusiastic young Tibetan intellectuals, ironically enough, via Chinese translations. Since then, Tagore has been regularly translated into Tibetan, and, as a token of Tagore's popularity among Tibetan literati, *Gitanjali* has been translated three times by three different translators, a rare phenomenon as far as modern Tibetan literature is concerned. More generally, it can safely be said Tagore is one of the most, if not the most, frequently translated modern poet in Tibetan since the year 2000.

INDIA AND TIBET

In the early twentieth century, Tibetans would cross over the Himalaya range and go to India, mainly for three reasons. First, for educational motives: in the 1920s, the elite of the Central Tibetan society started enrolling their children at English-speaking Christian schools in Darjeeling (St Joseph's College, North Point, was a favourite) and Kalimpong.[1] Others would go to India for business. Some wealthy Tibetan merchants had commercial trading agencies in Kalimpong, and Tibetan caravans would regularly cross over the Himalayan passes, loaded with wool, musk, yak tails, etc. Of course, the third and most important reason for Tibetans to go to India was religious. Pilgrimage to the holy Buddhist sites in Nepal and India was considered the apex of a Tibetan Buddhist's life.

On the diplomatic level, Western historians concur to say that Tibet became independent de facto, if not de jure, after the collapse of the Manchu Qing dynasty in China (1912), which in the last decades of its existence had held little, if any, control over Tibet anyway. Between 1912 and 1947, Great Britain and Tibet (more precisely, the half of Tibet that was headed by the Dalai Lama since 1642) enjoyed cordial links, eventually leading to the establishment of a British delegation in Lhasa in 1936.

In 1947, when India secured independence, things carried on almost unchanged on the Indo–Tibetan diplomatic front. An Indian Mission took over from the British Mission in Lhasa and India supplied Tibet with weapons without referring to China. But India grew increasingly uneasy about supporting an independent Tibet, especially since the new Mao-led China, a potential Socialist ally, became more and more assertive about Tibet being part of China. Moreover, Jawaharlal Nehru did not wish to threaten the solidarity of the Socialist countries in the so-called 'Third World' which emerged after World War II.[2] In March 1959, Tibet lost its de facto independence. India quickly aligned with the Chinese view that Tibet was part of China, but still offered shelter to the Dalai Lama and his tens of thousands of followers who took to life in exile.[3] The flow of people and goods between Tibet and India, which had been constant until then, became unthinkable, with the Chinese army strictly guarding the border. The Sino-Indian war in 1962 only heightened the tension between the two countries. Contacts between Tibetans and Indians became extremely scarce, hardly any Tibetans making their way to Nepal and India any longer. The Cultural Revolution (1966–76) in China perpetuated the status quo. India remained inaccessible to 'China' Tibetans until 1980, when some of them were released from prison and allowed to visit their relatives in India, or when exiled Tibetans were allowed to resume contact with their families in Tibet.

Since the early 1980s, Tibetans have resumed their visits to India, by legal and, more often, clandestine means. Sometimes they crossed the Himalayan range on foot if they did not have a passport, to obtain an audience with the Dalai Lama and to go on pilgrimage to holy Buddhist sites of India. Children continue to be sent by their parents to Tibetan schools set up in India, hoping that they will be granted a better and more culturally-suited education there than in China, where Buddhism is not included in the curriculum and where Tibetan language and history are neglected. In the meantime, with the prospect of winning their hearts, the Chinese authorities have been allowing more and more Tibetans to return from exile to their homeland for short visits and to set up business in the now flourishing Chinese economic environment. But the circulation of Tibetans across the Himalayas has come virtually to a halt since the Tibetan uprising in 2008.

The material used in this article is mostly taken from literary journals in Tibetan language appearing in Tibet, as well as, since 2006, from literary websites. This contribution will try to evaluate the importance of Tagore in today's literary scene, as well as suggest interpretations for the great reputation enjoyed by the Bengali writer today among the young Tibetan literati.

RECEPTION IN 1913–14

As far as we can tell, there was no response in Tibet to Tagore's Nobel Prize. Although the thirteenth Dalai Lama was then initiating a wave of modernisation and had started opening Tibet to non-Asian influences, it was quite unlikely that the Tibetans' knowledge of the Western world included an awareness of the Nobel Prize. Another reason why Tibetan knowledge of Western current affairs was shallow is that there was no newspaper in Tibet or in the Tibetan language at that time. But we know for sure of two instances of Tagore's name reaching the Tibetan elite some years later. First, in 1931 the thirteenth Dalai Lama himself heard of Tagore via Tan Yunshan, a Chinese follower of the poet. Tan Yunshan was sent to Tibet in 1930 as a 'special emissary' of the Guomintang government, 'for a certain official business.'[4] When Tan met the thirteenth Dalai Lama in early 1931, he 'had to answer many questions put by the late Dalai Lama, the thirteenth one, and his ministers about India. By the way, I used to tell them what Gurudeva [Tagore] and Gandhiji were doing in India and how their inspiration was going to change India's destiny.'[5] Although there was an interest on the part of the Tibetan pontiff about Gandhi, we do not know how the Dalai Lama or his entourage reacted to Tan's introductory praise of Tagore.

Later in that decade, Tagore's name appeared in a Tibetan newspaper that had been newly founded in north-east India in 1925, the *Tibet Mirror*.[6] Published in Kalimpong, it relayed important news from Tibet, India, and the world. Its founder, Reverend Babu Tharchin (1890–1976), dedicated one page to Tagore's visit to Kalimpong in April 1938. *Tibet Mirror* had readers in the Tibetan elite, so we can surmise that the name of Tagore, again, made its way to a small coterie in Lhasa via this article. But nothing is known of the reaction it evoked. Interestingly, the 1938 article included a large hand-drawn portrait of the poet and it insisted upon his links with Tibetan literary and Buddhist heritage, mentioning mainly that Tibetan was taught at Santiniketan, but did not refer much to his work as an eminent author.[7]

Tagore knew many foreigners who were engaged with Tibet—the explorers Sven Hedin, Nicholas Roerich, and Ekai Kawaguchi, as well as Reverend Dr John Anderson Graham, a missionary who lived in Kalimpong and was close to Babu Tharchin. More significantly, Tagore believed that mastery of the Tibetan language could enable one to 'restor[e] some of the forgotten Indian texts, luckily preserved in Tibetan translation.'[8] He had thus 'inspired Pandit Vidhushekhar Shastri to learn Tibetan' in this hope and, quite logically, introduced Tibetan studies in Santiniketan.[9] Tagore met the most eminent Tibetan scholar of his time, Gendun Chophel (1903–51), in the 1930s, when the latter paid a visit to Kalimpong.[10] Tagore invited him to the position of a Tibetan teacher at Santiniketan, 'well-paid and offering some security, but he [Gendun Chophel] declined the offer, as he had come to India to "wander, to see and to learn, and not to settle down in a comfortable situation".'[11] Gendun Chophel, himself a translator familiar with Indian culture, does not seem to have translated any of Tagore's works into Tibetan.

TRANSLATIONS

The first mention of a Tibetan translation of Tagore appears in 1976: a footnote in the *Tibet Journal* says that the short story *Natir Puja* was translated by Samten Norboo, a graduate student of St Joseph's College in Darjeeling. It is not possible to tell whether the translation was made from Bengali or from English.[12] The reason for translating this particular work, among the tens of short stories that Tagore wrote, may be attributed to the fact that it includes, according to one critic, 'magnificent invocations to the Buddha ... fine examples of the free handling of Buddhist themes,' undoubtedly an appealing feature for Tibetans.[13]

In Tibet proper, Tibetans were engulfed in heavy Maoist politics and then in the Cultural Revolution until the late 1970s, leaving little room for literary translations. The discovery of Tagore's texts therefore did not happen before the mid-1980s, when Chinese state-run literary magazines were launched. These served as a medium to introduce Tibetans to 'modern,' non-religious literature and included poems and prose works, some essays, and short stories. Occasionally they would publish texts from world literature, always translated from Chinese, as the new Tibetan elite had not been offered any training in English.[14] The first translation that seems to have appeared in Tibet itself was 'Mahamaya', in Tibetan, 'Bu mo Ma hā ma ya'i sgrung' [The story of the young girl, Mahamaya], published in 1985.[15] It was translated from the Chinese by Lodro Gyamtso, about whom little is known, and published in a collection of short stories from world literature that included works by Maupassant, Ibsen, Chekhov, O. Henry, Mark Twain, and Daudet.

Translation of Short Stories

Two other short stories were translated in 1992: 'Bsod nams' [Merits] and 'Gsang ba'i nor rgyun' [Secret Treasure].[16] I have not been able to identify the former, but the latter is 'Goupto Don' [Hidden Treasure]. In 2001, 'Nyin gcig' [One day], a very short story, was also translated and published, but here again I could not identify with certainty its original.[17] These short stories have probably been translated from the Chinese, but there is no information about the translators. 'The Parrot's Tale' (called 'The Parrot's Training' in English) was translated from English in 2012. While it is usually hard to figure out what the translators' motivations are for choosing a particular short story, Dawa Shonu, the translator of 'The Parrot's Tale,' has indicated that he had chosen this short story because it dealt with education. An online reader of the story commented that Tibetan educationists should carefully read it—this is especially true since 2010, when the topic of education for Tibetans has become a major social concern.[18]

Tagore's views about education do seem to be of interest to Tibetans: 'My School,' a lecture that Tagore gave in the USA and that supports full freedom in education, was translated in 2011 and published on the official website of the Central Tibetan Administration in exile.[19] The Tibetan government in exile and, more generally, exiled Tibetans' knowledge of Tagore's works can be ascribed to the fact that English-language teaching material used in Tibetan schools in India is borrowed from the Indian curriculum, thus featuring a high number of works by Tagore. The young blogger Dawa Shonu, an exiled Tibetan student in Benares, who introduces himself as a reader of Orwell and Garcia Marquez, has not only translated 'The Parrot's Tale,' but also a number of poetic works by Tagore.[20] Four of them are difficult to identify.[21] The translator indicates that he likes these poems because they remind him of some figures of speech from the classical poetics treatise Kavyadarsha, translated into Tibetan in the thirteenth and fourteenth centuries; it had been the beacon of elegant poetic writing till now.[22] In 2009, Dawa Shonu had already translated the poem which had as its first line: 'Go not to the temple to put flowers upon the feet of God,' making him one of the most regular translators of the Bengali poet into Tibetan (see also below for his complete translation of The Gardener).[23]

Translation of the Novel Gora

More remarkably, Tagore's novel Gora was translated into Tibetan, under the title 'Gho ra' (2001). Very few foreign novels share the privilege of being available in Tibetan.[24] The translation was done in India by a monk from Ngawa, in Amdo (North-Eastern Tibet), called Chodrak. It was then distributed for free by the Education Ministry of the Tibetan government in exile, thanks to the support of the then Tibetan Prime Minister in exile, Samdhong Rinpoche, an admirer of Indian culture and of the Bengali Nobel

Prize winner, whom Samdhong Rinpoche often quoted in his works and speeches. The print run was 2,000 copies, half of which were distributed among Tibetans in the diaspora and the other half sent to Tibet.

Along with this translation in two volumes came a book entitled '*Gho ra gleng ba*', 'Discussing *Gora*,' which included essays or reviews about the novel and its significance for Tibetans. This also was a novelty and, to my knowledge, has not been done for any other foreign writer. Among others, Beri Jigme, Dorje Wangchuk, Chabdak Lhamokyab, and Chung Tsering, renowned writers and commentators in the Tibetan exile society, contributed to this collection of comments. Chabdak Lhamokyab chose to express his appreciation of the novel through a poem where he praised the social and political values explicitly put forward in *Gora*.[25] Beri Jigme's essay insisted upon the high standard of the Tibetan translation, which he attributed (according to him) to the translator's mastery of the art of classical Tibetan poetics derived from Sanskrit poetry, along with his knowledge of Buddhism, Hinduism, Brahmanism, Shivaism, and the Vedas. The translator, he said, was 'as skilled as Dandin [sixth or seventh century Sanskrit author of prose romances and expounder on poetics] and Kalidasa' and managed to produce a translation with 'a sweet fragrance of genuine traditional culture.'[26]

Beri Jigme, in his lengthy praise of *Gora*'s translation, also underscored several times the similarities of the inner and ethical conflict between tradition and modernity faced by Gora, the novel's protagonist, and Tibetans today: Gora, although deeply supportive of his own language and culture, had to face the negative aspects of tradition and reassess it critically. Tibetans today are faced with the same dilemma, treading a fine line between the imperative need to protect their endangered culture and their will to embrace modernity. Beri Jigme drew a parallel between the colonial situation of India at the time when the novel takes place in the latter part of the nineteenth century and the current situation of Tibet, thus legitimising the choice of this book for a Tibetan translation.

The Nationalistic content of the novel did not fall on deaf ears in Tibet: A commentator wrote in a survey of the novel: 'Gora, the protagonist, is a very patriotic Hindu, he is a stubborn and determined young man. As soon as he graduates from university, he heads a patriotic organisation and takes upon himself to get rid of the English colonisers so as to free his people.'[27] Such an apparently innocuous comment may be interpreted in the Tibetan context as a veiled and critical reference to the current Tibetan situation. Still, the book made a more nuanced impact on the political thinking of another blogger: in a piece posted online in November 2012, for the 150th anniversary of the birth of Tagore [somewhat belatedly, as he was born in May 1861], he (or she) writes that Gora made him (or her) wonder whether 'nationalism and patriotism, which we all highly consider, unifies the peoples or destroys coexistence [among them].'[28]

Translation of Poetry

More than short stories and novels, the genre that has attracted most of the Tibetans' attention and translation skills is poetry and, particularly, *Gitanjali*. At least three extensive translations exist, with a fourth one being published at the time of writing (2013), and other extracts published here and there. This is unique in the history of contemporary Tibetan translations of a foreign text. In 1984, Ngodrub Gashawa from the Central Institute of Higher Studies in Sarnath (Varanasi) translated *Gitanjali*. Samdhong Rinpoche wrote the foreword and the afterword when this translation was republished, in 2000, by the Tibet House in Delhi.[29] It is not clear from what language (English, Hindi or Bengali) this translation was done. The translation was versified (heptasyllabic).

While the Tibetan literary magazine *Rlung rta* published a translation of an extract of *Gitanjali* in 2001, another full translation of the text appeared that year, when a Tibetan professor, Chapdrak Gonpokyap, translated the text under the aegis of an American foundation that sponsored the translation into Tibetan of some major world literature texts.[30] At this point of my research, I do not know whether Chapdrak Gonpokyap chose *Gitanjali* himself or if, as is more likely, the translation was commissioned to him by the foundation. It was a major breakthrough but, due to distribution problems, few people actually got access to the book. The translator chose to translate the text in prose, not in verse, and the translation was made from an earlier Chinese version.

In 2002, Phunor, a graduate from the Tibetan Department of the Central Institute for Nationalities in Beijing, a poet himself, who works for the Tibet Autonomous Region public radio, published his own prose translation of *Gitanjali* from the Chinese.[31] This translation sold rather well, according to Phunor himself, indicating that there was a genuine interest for Tagore among Tibetan readers.[32] After a few years when apparently no new translation was published, the forty-fifth song of *Gitanjali* went online ('Have you not heard his silent steps?'), as well as the seventy-sixth ('Face to face'), and, more recently, the sixth ('Flower') and the first half of the twenty-fourth ('If the day is gone').[33]

In 2012, three more extracts from *Gitanjali* were published online: one translated from Hindi by an unspecified translator (song 1); one by a hitherto unknown translator called Na bun [song numbers 6, 12, 17, 35, 46, 54, 57, 83, 87, and 92]; and the third by the rising young poet Sangdor, from the Chinese this time.[34] The latter only included song numbers 1 to 9, all translated in enneasyllabic (i.e., composed of lines having nine syllables) verse. Sangdor explained in his introduction that he had opted for regular verses to emulate the original Bengali *Gitanjali*, itself versified. The fact that it was published online made it possible for readers to react immediately, which they did, enabling us to fathom the reception of this translation among interested Tibetan readers. The translation generated an impressive number of comments. They mostly praise it, but a number of them are quite spiteful. At some point, Sangdor even erased all comments, as criticism was getting out of control. Those supporting Sangdor's translation pointed to his mastery and elegance in Tibetan. Sangdor being a skilful young poet, the general appreciation of his translation pertained to the fact that the Tibetan text flowed smoothly, contrary to previous translations which, according to most commentators, were quite obscure or lacked fluidity. One commentator even wrote that he could understand for the first time what *Gitanjali* was about, and comprehend at last why Tagore was so appreciated.

It is true that, among all translators, Sangdor is the one whose poetic talent is most accomplished, contrasting for instance with Chapdrak Gonpokyab, who is a biology teacher. But other commentators questioned Sangdor's capacity to translate the poems accurately, due to his deficiency in foreign languages: they argued that he did not know either Bengali or English and his knowledge of Chinese, the source for his translation, was paltry. One blogger dedicated a whole article to Sangdor's lack of mastery of Chinese and, as a consequence, of proper qualification to translate from Chinese into Tibetan.[35] Sangdor's preface to his translation had somehow anticipated this criticism: he wrote that he was aware of a number of extant Tibetan translations, but, he added, they were rather 'difficult to understand' and 'not very [pleasing] to the ear' (a comment that is often made by Tibetan readers). He went on to say that, if the famous name 'Tagore' had not been attached to those previous translations, readers would have discarded them as just 'not understandable, poorly versified, with little meaning.' He admitted that his translation was very personal and he expected that critics would discard his own translation of Tagore's *Gitanjali* due to its being nothing more than 'Sangdor's poetry.' To this he replied that 'translating is creating.'

Heated discussions raged on the Internet for two or three weeks, but they focused more on the personality of Sangdor and his opponents, or on the translation of the text, rather than on *Gitanjali* itself, or on Tagore. What is certain is that this controversy about Sangdor's translation renewed interest in Tagore. On Sangdor's own website, two weeks after he offered his own and personal translation of *Gitanjali*, a Tibetan blogger posted online the translation of Tagore's Nobel Prize acceptance speech in Stockholm,

1921 (the year he went to formally receive the Prize announced in November 1913, Tagore being awarded a medal in Santiniketan some months later), a translation that had apparently already appeared in a Tibetan magazine previously.[36] One week later, the exiled blogger and monk-poet Lunyon Heruka wrote a versified anaphoric (i.e., using a word that refers to or replaces another word used earlier in a sentence) celebration of Tagore, describing at length how, in many different situations and places in India, he hoped and prayed to meet the 'great writer' and the 'skilled poet', with his flowing beard, his sparkling eyes, his floating garment, his blazing wisdom and his ever-moving pen.[37] This was not the first poetic tribute to Tagore: in 2011, Dransong Namgyal, a Bonpo (follower of an ancient religious creed of Tibet and Nepal which predates Buddhism) scholar living in Nepal, had penned a versified tribute to the poet, entitled 'Remembering the famous poet Tagore.'[38]

Besides the *Gitanjali*, other poetic works by Tagore have been translated: in 2004, Bashung Khyungthargyal, a poet himself from Amdo, produced a translation of the first sixty poetic aphorisms of *Stray Birds*, under the Tibetan title 'Dab chags gling' (The World of Birds).[39] It was published in the main and most authoritative literary magazine of the Tibet Autonomous Region, 'Tibet Literature and Art.' The first two poems of 'Stray Birds' were translated again and published online in 2009 by a Tibetan in India.[40] The collection entitled *The Gardener* is also a favourite: in 2009, a translation in two instalments of the first thirty poems appeared on a Tibetan literary website.[41] I have also found translations of the introduction in the form of a dialogue, 'In the morning I cast my net into the sea' (*The Gardener* 3), the poems 11 to 20, 'You are the evening cloud' (*The Gardener* 30), 'My Love, Once upon a time' (*The Gardener* 38), three translations of 'Paper boats' (*The Gardener* 70), 'Infinite Wealth' (*The Gardener* 73), and 'Who are you, reader?' (*The Gardener* 85).[42] Other 'isolated' poems were also translated increasingly, possibly as knowledge and awareness of Tagore among Tibetans is getting more established as years go by: 'Vocation,' 'My Polar Star,' 'The End,' 'Authorship,' 'Sympathy,' 'The Chanpa Flower,' and 'The Little Big Man' were translated and posted online in 2013.[43] In late November 2013, the publication of the translation of *The Gardener*, under the title *A Garland of Flowers*, was announced. The translator is Dawa Shonu, who lives in exile. He has contributed a lot to the spreading of Tagore's writings among Tibetans, through his translations.[44]

It may be mentioned that Tibetans have also published some analyses and short essays about Tagore. In 1994, the state-sponsored literary magazine *Honey Rain* offered a portrayal of the Bengali author, as part of a series that included Dumas père and fils, Hugo, Maupassant, Pushkin, Cervantes,

Goethe, Lu Xun (1881–1936), Guo Moruo (1892–1978), Mao Dun (1896–1981) and Ba Jin (1904–2005).[45] In 2001–2, the same magazine introduced significant works of world literature (*The Divine Comedy, Faust, Eugénie Grandet* and *Père Goriot,* both by Balzac, the *Iliad,* the *Odyssey* and others); Tagore's *Gora* (alternately translated as *Kar la,* or *Gho ra*) featured among the surveyed works.[46]

CONCLUSION

Most introductions to Tagore praise him, not surprisingly, as the first Asian who received a Nobel Prize. This is especially meaningful to Tibetans as, in spite of their small number, they can also boast a Nobel Prize winner in none other than the Dalai Lama, who received the Nobel Peace Prize in 1989. The fact that quoting his name is forbidden in the public sphere in China may explain the Tibetans' elation at mentioning Tagore's prize, a hint at 'their' own Nobel Prize. The fact that Tagore was a strong advocate of education in the Bengali language and that he supported Indian independence is often quoted. This we can also interpret easily as a tribute to nationalism in the colonial context. He is still also appreciated as a modernist poet. Those Tibetans who value 'obscurity' in poetic expression, a trend that has been popular among young Tibetan poets since the 1990s following the 'obscure' movement in Chinese poetry in the 1980s, are strong supporters of Tagore, whom they see as a precursor.[47]

His position as a social commentator and reformer is also relevant to young Tibetan writers. Taking Tagore as a model, they mostly reflect upon the direction that Tibetan society should take in the future, choosing between tradition and modernity. The topic of religion, central to self-reflection on Tibetan identity, is to be found for instance in Tagore's poem 'Go not to the temple to put flowers upon the feet of God,' which was translated into Tibetan in 2009 by Dawa Shonu. It is most likely that this text has appealed to Tibetans for the non-dogmatic view on religion that emanates from it.

Finally, it may be recalled here that Tagore represents a literary bridge to Bengal and, more generally, India, the sacred country (Tibetan: '*phags yul*) as it is called in Tibetan. India is the source of their writing system, the source of their dominant religion, the source of their literary art—India has always featured as an ideal, godly place for Tibetans.[48] It is thus no coincidence that Phunor gave as a reason for translating *Gitanjali* the wish to 'draw India and Tibet closer,' an argument that can apply to most translations, explaining the late but persistent 'Tagore fever' in Tibet until now.

NOTES

1. Central Tibet refers to a Tibetan division of the Tibet plateau: Central Tibet actually includes Southern and Western Tibet, and is called 'Central' due to its historical and political centrality, with Lhasa at its heart.
2. For an overview on Indo–Tibetan diplomatic relations between 1947 and 1949, see Arpi, 'India–Tibet relations, 1947–49.'
3. The Tibetan population in India was estimated in 2009 by the Central Tibetan Administration in exile at 94,000, but the actual figure may be higher.
4. Pachow, 'Tan Yun-shan,' 48.
5. Tan, 'My First Visit to Gandhiji,' 193.
6. A brief mention should be made here about the rendering of Tagore's name into Tibetan: I have so far found nine different spellings for the seemingly non-problematic transcription of 'Tagore.' These are, in Wylie transliteration (in this system, capital consonants indicate a reversed stem letter, or retroflex; capital vowels indicate an elongated vowel): the kor; The kor; the gor; The gor; ThA kur; ThA kUr; krwa ghor; khre sgor. The 'Tibet Mirror,' which offers the oldest transcription that I know of, gives TA gor. The name itself has also been translated semantically into Tibetan as Nyiwang Gonpo, meaning 'Lord of the Sun.' This type of translation, called *don 'gyur* in Tibetan (meaning 'translating the meaning'), is rather common for proper names of Indian luminaries. Starting in the eighth century, Tibetan Buddhists and grammarians have translated Sanskrit religious and philosophical treatises extremely faithfully, and they included persons' and places' names in their translation endeavours, pondering over their original meaning and etymology and striving to find a strict semantic equivalent in Tibetan: to give a few examples, Kalidasa became 'Nag mo khol,' Dandin 'Dbyug pa can,' Shantideva 'Zhi ba'i lha,' Nagarjuna 'Klu grub,' Bodhgaya 'Rdo rje gdan,' and these are only a very limited numbers of examples.
7. I thank Paul Hackett (Columbia University) who made a digitalised version of this issue available to me. The 1941 issues not being available to the public, I cannot tell whether Tagore's death was commented upon, although it is likely that it was.
8. Nag, 'Tagore: Pioneer in Asian Relations,' 117.
9. Ibid. It was not the only place in India where Tibetan was taught: a Bhutanese monk, Padma Chandra, was the instructor in Tibetan language in Calcutta from 1922–3: see McKay, *Tibet and the British Raj*, 113. For a confirmation of Tagore's interest in Tibetan language, see also Bhattacharya, *Bhota-Prakāsa*, ix.
10. Stoddard, *Le Mendiant de l'Amdo*, 190.
11. '... *bien rémunéré et lui assurant une certaine sécurité, mais il déclina l'offre, car il était venu en Inde 'pour errer, pour voir et apprendre, non pour s'établir dans une situation confortable*' (Stoddard, *Mendiant*, 208). Stoddard adds that, in 1939, a Tibetan called Wangdu taught Tibetan at 'Viśwa-Bhārāti' (Stoddard, *Mendiant*, 377–87).

12. *Tibet Journal*, 1976, n. p. Another translation was announced in the early 1990s by Stoddard as being under process, but I was not able to get any confirmation. See Stoddard, 'Tibetan Publications and National Identity,' 154.

13. Bhikku Sangharakshita, in www.buddhismtoday.com/english/sociology/004-modernworld.htm. All websites were checked and accessed in June 2012, unless otherwise stated. This motivation was mentioned in passing in the footnote in the *Tibet Journal* 1976.

14. Literary magazines in the Chinese language aimed at a Tibetan readership educated in Chinese were launched in the early 1980s. They included a substantial number of works by Tagore in Chinese translation, and other Indian authors (V. S. Naipaul, R. K. Narayan, etc.). I thank L. Maconi (INALCO) for this information.

15. Tagore, 'Bu mo Ma hā ma ya'i sgrung', in *Phyi gling ba'i sgrung thung phyogs bsgrigs*, Sangs rgyas ed. (Xining: Mtsho sngon mi rigs dpe skrun khang, 1985), 147–57.

16. See Tagore, 'Bsod nams,' *Sbrang char* 4 (2002); and Tagore, 'Gsang ba'i nor rgyun,' transl. Tshe ring don grub, *Bod kyi rtsom rig sgyu rtsal* 4 (2002).

17. Tagore, 'Nyin gcig.'

18. http://www.tibettimes.net/blogs.php?id=112&post_id=3810.

19. See http://www.sherig.org/tb/?page_id=5599. Reprinted in http://dekhang. blogspot.fr/2011/05/blog-post_05.html.

20. See his own presentation in Tibetan and English on http://www.blogger.com/profile/04184556303291763526.

21. http://dawashonu.blogspot.fr/2011_06_01_archive.html and http://www.khabdha.org/?p=30577.

22. http://dawashonu.blogspot.fr/2012/01/blog-post.html.

23. http://khabdha.org/?p=3346 (accessed 22 March 2014).

24. About ten were published: *La Dame aux Camélias* by Dumas fils, *Water Margins* by Shi Nai'an, *The Sorrows of Young Werther* by Goethe, *The Old man and the Sea* by Hemingway, and two plays by Shakespeare (*Hamlet* and *Romeo and Juliet*). *Animal Farm* by Orwell as well as *The Little Prince* by A. de Saint-Exupéry and the first two volumes of *Harry Potter* have been published too.

25. See http://www.chapdaklhamokyab.fr/%EO%BD%91%EO%BD%94-%EO%BD%91-%EO%BD%96%EO%BD%A2-%EO%BD%91/%EO%BD%A2-%EO%BD%98-%EO%BD%A2-%EO%BD%82-%EO%BD%91%EO%BD%94-%EO%BD%91-%EO%BD%96%EO%BD%A2-%EO%BD%91/

26. While acknowledging the great amount of effort and care the translator put into his work, some readers I interviewed resented the fact that the translation was not smooth in Tibetan and required constant effort on the part of the reader.

27. Gru gzings, 'Dzam gling brtsams chos grags chen gyi mtshams sbyor,' *Sbrang char* 3 (2001): 152.

28. Brag gzhis bu, 'Snyan ngag gi yab chen rjes su dran pa,' www.tibetson.com/Item/Show.asp?m=1&d=2447 (accessed 22 June 2013).

29. See Tagore, *Gitanjali*, transl. Dngos grub Ga sha ba (Varanasi: Bibliotheca Indo-Tibetica, 2000). I thank T. Tsering (Amnye Machen Institute, Dharamsala) for this information (email, 26 January 2004). The name of the translator sometimes appears as K. Angrup Lahuli, a remote rendering of his original Tibetan name. It is also mentioned on a Tibetan website in 2009 http://gdqpzhx.com/bo/html/news/2009/05/09/100/. Lara Maconi, 'La longue marche translinguistique,' In *France-Asie : un siècle d'échanges littéraires*, ed. Muriel Détrie (Paris: You-feng, 2001), 212, footnote 27, mentions a translation published in Dharamsala in 1983, but I was not able to spot it. It may be the very same text as the one referred to here.

30. According to Hartley, 'Contextually Speaking,' 400. Tagore, *Snyan ngag gi mchod pa (Ke thān kyā li)*, transl. Chab brag Mgon po skyabs (Beijing: Mi rigs dpe skrun khang, 2001). The translation is followed by three appendixes: the original introduction to the text by W. B. Yeats; the speech delivered by Harald Hjärne, of the Nobel Academy, when the Nobel Prize was awarded to the Bengali poet on 10 December 1913; and, finally, some reflections about Tagore's work.

31. Tagore, *Gi tan ca li*, transl. Phun nor (Lhasa: Bod ljongs mi dmangs dpe skrun khang, 2002).

32. When I met him in July 2002, he was considering translating (from the Chinese) *War and Peace* by Tolstoi, some short stories by Gogol, and some plays by Molière.

33. Translated from the Chinese by a blogger whose pen name is Xicangren (http://blog. amdotibet.cn/xicangren/archives/41463. aspx); http://blog.amdotibet.cn/sonamdargye/archives/30270.aspx; and www.sangdhor.com/blog_c. asp?id=10407&a=2342D (accessed 2 February 2013). For reasons that are unclear, the translator translated only the first half of *Gitanjali* 24.

34. http://www.tibetcm.com/html/list_10/201202254161.html; http://blog. amdotibet.cn/Tnawin/archives/70791.aspx. The other seven translated poems could not be identified with certainty. This blogger also translates speeches by famous freedom fighters (Mandela) or Third World leaders (Nehru), indicating that he (or she) has a rather strong political leaning—some of his (her) translations have been censored—that fit with the view of Tagore as a nationalist and freedom-loving poet; and http://www.sangdhor.com/blog_c. asp?id=7134&a=sangdhor. He (or she) writes in the introduction that he (or she) based his (or her) work on the Chinese translation by the female poet Bing Xin.

35. http://www.rdrol.net/node/719.

36. See http://www.sangdhor.com/blog_c.asp?id=7346&a=sangge. The Tibetan magazine is said to be *Od dus deb* (literally 'Light Magazine'), a magazine about which I have no details; the issue is number 6 and the translator is Tenpa Tsering. The blogger begs Tenpa Tsering and the magazine editors' forgiveness for having re-posted the translation online, without their permission. The blogger who celebrated online the 150th anniversary of Tagore's birth (see Note 28) mentions this speech and insists that it made an impact on him (or

her), as he (or she) understood that mental formatting started with schooling and kept going on all life long.

37. www.sangdhor.com/blog_c.asp?id=7512&a=1000.
38. Drang srong Rnam rgyal, 'Grags can snyan ngag pa The kor rjes su dran pa' [Remembering the famous poet Tagore], in *Gangs thigs. A piece of snow*, Kathmandu, Vajra, 42–45.
39. Tagore, "Dab chags gling,' transl. 'Ba' gzhung Khyung thar rgyal, *Bod kyi rtsom rig sgyu rtsal* 3 (2004), 42–6.
40. http://sangdhor.com/blog_c.asp?id=318&a=admin.
41. http://www.gdqpzhx.com/bo/html/special/2009/12/04/483/ and http://www. gdqpzhx.com/bo/html/special/2009/12/04/484/
42. http://tibettimes.net/blogs.php?id=197&post_id=3672; http://blog.amdotibet.cn/ gomar/archives/28553.aspx; http://www.rangwang.net/index.php?essayId=1069; www.dawashonu.blogspot.fr/2011_06_01_archive.html;http://www.tibetcm.com/ html/list_10/201206074570.html; http://blog.amdotibet.cn/xicangren/archives/ 42758.aspx, dhege.com/ཧེ་གེར་གྱི་རྩོམ་ཡིག་འགའ/ and blog.amdotibet.cn/sangey/archives/ 79902.aspx (the second and the third accessed 28 August 2013); and http://www. tibetcm.com/html/list_10/201212155080.html.
43. Posted respectively on: www.sangdhor.com/blog_c. asp?id=10304&a=2342D, dhege.com/ཧེ་གེར་གྱི་རྩོམ་ཡིག་འགའ/, http://www.tibetcm.com/html/list_10/201305235450. html, blog.amdotibet.cn/sonamdargye/archives/82708.aspx, http://ti.tibet3. com/culture/2013-02/04/content_448442.htm (all websites accessed 29 August 2013). I have also found 'Impoverished mind' (2011) and 'Beloved' (2012), but I could not identify their sources with certainty.
44. http://www.lhatso.com/comment/literature/2013-11-26/725.html (accessed 14 December 2013).
45. Gru char, 'The kor,' *Sbrang char* 4 (1994): 43, 54–6.
46. Gru gzings, "Dzam gling,' 152, gives 1910 as the first year of publication, but other sources give 1907 for the Bengali version and 1924 for its English translation.
47. 'Skya-bha [a Tibetan literary critic] also quotes the French poet Mallarmé and the Indian poet Tagore regarding the value of obscure poetry' (Hartley, 'Contextually Speaking,' 387).
48. For more details on this literary fascination for India among Tibetans, see Kapstein, 'The Indian Literary Identity in Tibet.'

WORKS CITED

Arpi, Claude. 'India–Tibet relations, 1947–49: India Begins to Vacillate.' Paper presented at the International Conference on Exploring Tibet's History and Culture, Delhi, Delhi University, 19–21 December 2009, downloadable on http://www.claudearpi.net/maintenance/uploaded_pics/ Tibet_India_1947_1950.pdf

Bhattacharya, Vidhushekhava. *Bhota-Prakāsa: A Tibetan Chrestomacy*. Calcutta: University of Calcutta, 1939.

Gru char. 'The kor' [Tagore], *Sbrang char* [Honey Rain] 4, 1994, 43, 54–6.

Gru gzings. ''Dzam gling brtsams chos grags chen gyi mtshams sbyor' [Outline of famous works of world literature], *Sbrang char* [Honey Rain] 3, 2001, 146–54.

Hartley, Lauran R. 'Contextually Speaking: Tibetan Literary Discourse and Social Change in the People's Republic of China (1980–2000).' PhD diss., Indiana University, 2003.

Kapstein, Matthew. 'The Indian Literary Identity in Tibet.' In *Literary Cultures in History*, edited by Sheldon Pollock, 747–802. Los Angeles: California University Press, 2003.

Maconi, Lara. 'La longue marche translinguistique.' In *France-Asie : un siècle d'échanges littéraires*, edited by Muriel Détrie. Paris: You-feng, 2001, 205–36.

McKay, Alex. *Tibet and the British Raj.* Richmond: Curzon, 1997.

Nag, Kalidas. 'Tagore: Pioneer in Asian Relations.' In *In the Footsteps of Xuanzang: Tan Yun-shan and India*, edited by Chung Tan. New Delhi: Gyan Publishing House, 1999, 117–19.

Pachow, W. 'Tan Yun-shan and the Renewal of Sino-Indian Cultural Interaction.' In *In the Footsteps of Xuanzang: Tan Yun-shan and India*, edited by Chung Tan. New Delhi: Gyan Publishing House, 1999, 41–52.

Stoddard, Heather. *Le Mendiant de l'Amdo.* Paris: Société d'ethnographie, Recherches sur la Haute-Asie 9, 1985.

——. 'Tibetan Publications and National Identity.' In *Resistance and Reform in Tibet*, edited by R. Barnett and Shirin Akiner. Delhi: Motilal Banarsidass, 1996 [1994], 121–56.

Tagore, Rabindranath. *Bu mo Ma hā ma ya'i sgrung* [The Story of the young girl Mahāmaya], transl. Blo gros rgya mtsho, in *Phyi gling ba'i sgrung thung phyogs bsgrigs* [Anthology of foreign short stories], edited by Sangs rgyas. Xining: Mtsho sngon mi rigs dpe skrun khang, 1985, 147–57.

——. *Gitanjali.* Translated by Dngos grub Ga sha ba. Varanasi: Bibliotheca Indo-Tibetica, Series 45, 2000 [1984].

——. transl. Skal bzang rin chen. 'Nyin gcig' [One day], *Bod kyi rtsom rig sgyu rtsal* [Tibet Literature and Art] 3, 2001, 25.

——. *Snyan ngag gi mchod pa* (*Ke thān kyā li*) [An offering of poetry (Gitānjāli)]. Translated by Chab brag Mgon po skyabs. Beijing: Mi rigs dpe skrun khang, 2001.

——. *Gi tan ca li* [Gitanjali]. Translated by Phun nor. Lhasa: Bod ljongs mi dmangs dpe skrun khang, 2002.

——. 'Bsod nams' [Merits], *Sbrang char* [Honey Rain] 4, 2002.

——, transl. Tshe ring don grub. 'Gsang ba'i nor rgyun' [The Secret Treasure], *Bod kyi rtsom rig sgyu rtsal* [Tibet Literature and Art] 4, 2002.

——, transl. 'Ba' gzhung Khyung thar rgyal. ''Dab chags gling' [The World of Birds], *Bod kyi rtsom rig sgyu rtsal* [Tibet Literature and Art] 3, 2004, 42–6.

Tan, Yun-shan. 'My First Visit to Gandhiji.' In *In the Footsteps of Xuanzang: Tan Yun-shan and India*, edited by Chung Tan. New Delhi: Gyan Publishing House, 1999, 193–7.

6

Thailand

Sawitree Charoenpong

Being located, as it is, on the trade route between India and the Far East, Thailand has had cultural and economic relations with India since ancient times and inherited various aspects of Indian culture, especially religions and languages.[1] Most importantly, Thailand has been a land of deep-rooted Buddhism, which originated in India. However, Indo–Thai relationships in the past were conducted through the medium of Indian merchants and priests whose names have neither been recorded in historical documents nor become well known. By the beginning of the twentieth century, Thailand had had a good relationship with India for a long time, but no well-known Indian personality recognised by both countries had visited Thailand. Rabindranath Tagore is supposed to have been the first famous Indian to visit Thailand when, in 1927, he made his ninth tour abroad, a voyage to several countries in Southeast Asia. Hence, we will examine Tagore's reception in Thailand from two perspectives: the reception of his visit and the subsequent reception of his works.

Visit to Thailand

Tagore visited Thailand during the period 8 to 16 October 1927 at the invitation of Indian and Chinese residents.[2] Although he was not invited by the Siamese government (Siam was renamed Thailand in 1939), he was, in the end, treated as a 'distinguished guest of the government.'[3] Therefore, accommodation was arranged for him at the Phyathai Palace Hotel, which had been the palace of the late King Vajiravudh (King Rama VI, 1910–25).[4] In every official letter circulated among those who took responsibility for this reception, the clause 'a well-known poet of the world' was added after his name in order that he would be welcomed honorably.[5] During this visit, although Prince Dhani Niwat, the Minister of Education, was the most important host, Phra Rajadharm Nides, the Secretary to the Minister of Education, was assigned to act as Tagore's liaison.[6]

With regard to the purposes of the visit, apart from promoting the synthesis of different cultures and raising funds for Visva-Bharati—the common purposes of his visit to other countries—Tagore also hoped that a Chair of Buddhism could be established in Visva-Bharati with the support of the King of Thailand, King Prajadhipok (King Rama VII, 1925–34). As he said in an interview on 10 October 1927 (a Monday):

My aim is the unity of man to bring about the internationalisation of education. We have different chairs at our university but we have no chair of Buddhism and it is essential that one should be established to fit into the scheme which we have undertaken. We greatly need such a chair to give to students proper guidance.

You may ask why it is that I have sought to develop my scheme in India. The answer is that India in her long history has been a cultural centre. It may be said then without exaggeration that India has attracted all races and cultures to her bosom. India, therefore, is the centre for such an institution that aims at the unity of man, a unity of cultures, Eastern and Western, so necessary if the various civilisations are to have peace.

I, therefore, have come to Siam to seek your co-operation and your help in the desire to establish a chair in Buddhism, and also, if possible, to bring a message in a wider perspective.[7]

Unfortunately, there is no documentary evidence indicating what action, if any, the King took on this proposal.

The itinerary set for Tagore during his one week in 1927 in Thailand follows:[8]

8 October
7:30 p.m.   arrives at Bangkok Railway Station by southern line train from Penang.

9 October
10 a.m.   meets Prince Dhani Niwat, Minister of Education.
6 p.m.   meets Sankaraja, the Buddhist Supreme Patriarch.

10 October
10 a.m.   meets Prince Boripatara, Prince of Nakorn Sawan, the King's elder brother.
11 a.m.   lays wreath before the royal remains at the Dusit Maha Prasad and visits the Grand Palace and the Temple of the Emerald Buddha.

3:30 p.m.   meets Prince Traidos Prabandh, Minister of Foreign Affairs.

5 p.m.   has afternoon tea with Prince Damrong Rajanupap (Prince Damrong), the King's uncle.

6 p.m.   meets Prince Bhanurangsi, the King's uncle.

11 October

10 a.m.   visits Vajiravudh Library, the National Museum, and two important Buddhist temples: Wat Pra Jetupon (the Temple of the Reclining Buddha), and Wat Mahathat.

4 p.m.   meets Prince Kittiyakara, Prince of Chantaburi, the King's elder brother.

5 p.m.   joins the Hindu reception at the Phyathai Palace Hotel.

8 p.m.   has dinner with the Minister of Foreign Affairs.

12 October

10 a.m.   visits Vjiravudh College and Wat Benjamabopitara (the Marble Temple).

2:30 p.m.   travels along the Chaopraya River and nearby canals, including Wat Arun (the Temple of Dawn).

13 October

9 a.m.   meets Prince Narissaranuwattiwong (Prince Naris), the King's uncle, visits Wat Suthat (the Temple of the Big Buddha) and the Hindu shrine nearby, Ananta Samakhom Throne Hall, and the pavilion for white elephants.

1 p.m.   has lunch with the Minister of Education and delivers speech to an audience at Chulalongkorn University.

5 p.m.   joins the Chinese reception at Pei-ing Chinese school.

9.45 p.m.   escorted by Prince Dhani Niwat to the presence of the King at Dusit Palace.

10 p.m.   delivers speech to the King, the Queen, some members of the royal family and high-ranking officials.

14 October

9 a.m.   calls on two high dignitaries of the Buddhist Church of Siam at two important Buddhist temples: Wat Bowoniwet and Wat Tepsirin, including a Pali language school at Wat Tepsirin.

3 p.m.   visits 'Poh Chang' College of Arts and Crafts.

4:30 p.m.   delivers speech to an audience at the National Museum.

7.30 p.m.   has dinner with a German Minister.

15 October
6:28 a.m.   visits Lopburi and Ayutthaya by train.
In the evening visits the Vishnu temple at Windmill Road and delivers
         a short address in Hindustani.

16 October
In the morning leaves Bangkok for Penang by train.

Tagore's itinerary reflects that his main purpose in visiting Thailand was cultural. This itinerary can be divided into three types of activity: meeting members of the elite and scholars of Thai society, visiting historic places and places of cultural and educational importance, and attending receptions and delivering speeches.

It is noteworthy that all of Tagore's meetings with members of the elite and scholars of Thai society were with individuals well known for their outstanding cultural contributions. Prince Damrong, for example, was the 'Father of Thai History' and President of the Royal Institute. Prince Boripatara and Prince Bhanurangsi were experts in Thai classical music, although their styles were grounded in different schools. Prince Naris was versatile in every kind of Thai art, especially Thai traditional architecture, and Prince Kittiyakara was a scholar of Pali.

Yet, while those Thai intellectuals and artists had all been responsible for producing outstanding cultural work, they were also key individuals with important roles in the politics of their time because they were all members of the Supreme Council of State.[9] This means that, during his visit, Tagore actually met both outstanding cultural figures and key Thai politicians.

With respect to the speeches he delivered, he gave five lectures on different subjects at different occasions:

  (i) 'India's Roles in the World' at the Indian reception;
 (ii) 'Child Education' at Chulalongkorn University;
(iii) 'Chinese Birth' at the Chinese reception;
 (iv) 'Asia's Continental Culture' in the presence of the King and the Queen, some members of the royal family and high-ranking officials at Dusit Palace; and
  (v) 'Ideals of National Education' at the National Museum.[10]

The members of the audience at these lectures were listed in certain newspapers. Two interesting points can be made regarding the names on these lists. Firstly, some of them (who were not part of the reception committee) attended more than one reception or one lecture. Secondly, all of them were members of the elite of Thai high society, regardless of whether they were Thai, Indian, Chinese, or others such as foreign diplomats living in Bangkok. Both men and women were represented, and most of them were members of the royal family and high-ranking aristocratic families.[11] However, there is no evidence to show that Tagore's works were read in Thailand at that time.

The itinerary and activities demonstrated that, although Tagore stayed in Thailand for only one week, he met Siamese people from different backgrounds and various social strata. Moreover, both the visitors and the hosts had good opportunities to exchange knowledge of culture and history and to develop a better understanding of each other. On this occasion, Tagore wrote two poems which reflect his good impressions of Thailand. One, entitled 'To Siam,' was written two days after arriving in Bangkok and read before the King. This poem runs as follows:

When the thunder-voiced Prayer for the Three Refuges
rang from sky to sky across deserts and hills and distant shores,
the awakened countries poured their rejoicings
in great deeds, and noble temples,
in the rapture of self-dedication,
in mighty words
in the breaking of the bond of self.

At an unheeded, unconscious moment,
that prayer, wafted by some sudden wandering breeze,
touched the heart, O Siam, lived in thy life
and shaded it with a branching wealth of well-being.
A centre to thy revolving centuries,
and end to thy endeavours, which is freedom of spirit,—
it helped to bind thy people in a common bond of hope,
to strengthen them with the power of a single-pointed devotion
to one Dharma, one Sangha, and one immortal Teacher.

Let those words, potent with an inexhaustible creative urge,
ever direct thee to the adventures of new ages,
light up new truths with their own radiant meaning,
and in one single garland string all thy gems of knowledge, newly
gathered.

I come to-day to the living temple that is one with thee,—
to the altar of united hearts
in which is seated on his lotus seat Lord Buddha,
whose silence is peace, whose voice consolation.

I come from a land where the Master's words
lie dumb in desultory ruins, in the desolate dust,
where oblivious ages smudged the meaning of the letters
written on the pages of pillared stones,
the records of a triumphant devotion.
I come, a pilgrim, at thy gate, O Siam,
to offer my verse to the endless glory of India
sheltered in thy home, away from her own deserted shrine,
to bathe in the living stream that flows in thy heart,
whose water descends from the snowy height of a sacred time
on which arose, from the depth of my country's being,
the Sun of Love and Righteousness.[12]

This poem shows that Tagore appreciated the fact that Thailand had preserved certain aspects of Indian culture very well, especially Buddhism, which had not played a significant role in India at least since the beginning of the Mughal Empire, some seven centuries earlier. Thus, he compared India to a 'deserted shrine,' whereas Thailand was still a 'shelter' for 'the endless glory of India.' This poem was also later translated into Thai by Phra Rajadharm Nides.

Another poem by Tagore, 'Farewell to Siam,' offers a message of farewell, as follows:

The signet ring of a primaeval friendship
        had secretly sealed thy name, O Siam, on my mind, in its
        unconscious depth.
This is why I felt I had ever known thee,
        the moment I stood at thy presence,
and why my traveller's hasty hours
        were constantly filled with the golden memory of an ancient love,
        and centuries' silent music overflowed
            the brink of the seven short days
that surprised me with the touch
        of an immemorial Kinship
in thy words, worship and aspiration,
        in thy numberless offerings to Beauty's shrine
fashioned by thy own hands,
        in thy fragrant altars
with their candles lighted
        and incense breathing peace.

> To-day at this sad time of parting
> I stand at thy courtyard,
>   gaze at thy kind eyes,
> and leave thee crowned with a garland from me
>   whose ever fresh flowers had blossomed ages ago.[13]

Taken together, these two poems reveal that Tagore was impressed by at least two aspects of Thai culture that derived from India and had flourished in Thailand since ancient times: its religion and its language. His appreciation of Thailand is further reflected in the thanks that, before leaving Bangkok, he asked Phra Rajadharm Nides to convey to Prince Dhani Niwat and all others concerned for the kind of reception accorded to him. His message was as follows:

> The Princes I have met are the most cultured in the East. My conception of Siam is that she still has a living Kingship, Righteousness and Religion. I shall always cherish the memory of my most pleasant stay. I shall treasure the privilege of giving a lecture before the First Eastern Monarch. The programme drawn up by Prince Dhani has been marvelously accomplished to the letter, and I must say I have been greatly impressed by the warm hospitality accorded me by the Thai people as a whole.[14]

Even after returning to India, he still kept in touch with the royal court. We have evidence that he sent a postcard to the King in 1929. The contents of this card are given below:

> My salutation is to him
> Who knows me imperfect
>   and loves me.
>   Rabindranath Tagore
>
> Santiniketan
> Founders' Day
>
> 7th Paush, 22nd December 1929[15]

This card is preserved at King Prajadhipok's Museum in Bangkok. While Tagore conveyed his impressions of Thailand to the Thai people through the two aforementioned poems, there exists at least one poem from a member of the Thai elite that expresses a response to Tagore's visit. It was written under the pseudonym 'Prem Chaya', by Prince Prem Burachatra who was the Thai Ambassador to India from 1967 to 1972. The complete poem follows:

> To the learned master, whose vision gave
> Reality to this poor poet's pen,

Are dedicated these few lines of verse
Lauding the Sage of Santiniketan
Who, from the far land where the mind was free
Though the body was in chains, spoke to us
With vibrant voice of hope and dignity
Of the glories of India in our home.
Then one day he came and moved in our midst,
Giving us words of wisdom and knowledge;
Extolling the Faith born in his own land,
And transplanted here in the days of yore.
He understood the Buddha's Middle Way;
He did not want a world replete with hate.
He saw on Siam's soil the fulfillment
Of the Great Teacher's whole enlightened dream;
Where the [fog] of ignorance had lifted,
Where the barriers of hatred were down,
And where the tongue and mind were not enslaved.
Here he breathed deep the air of our common
Heritage, forming a glorious bond
'Twixt India and Siam, which shall endure
While freedom, knowledge, wisdom, faith and love,
And the Buddha's Truth, sway the hearts of men.[16]

THE RECEPTION OF RABINDRANATH TAGORE'S WORKS IN THAILAND

The two poems Tagore wrote about Thailand during his visit may be the first of his works to be known in Thailand. At a later date, Phra Rajadharm Nides translated them into Thai verse. They were published after the end of World War II in the journal *Wong Wanakadi* ('Inside Literary Circles') which was popular and circulated among those who were interested in Thai literature.[17] This means that Tagore's works, especially the works about his impression of Thailand, could be accessed by a greater number of Thai people.

Gitanjali, the work by Tagore that is best known around the world, was translated from the English version and first published in Thai in 1969. It has been reprinted in several editions since then. The translators were the married couple Karuna and Ruang-Urai Kusalasaya. In the foreword to the first edition, the Ambassador of India to Thailand, Purnendu Kumar Banerjee, praised Karuna Kusalasaya or Acharn Karuna, the main translator, as follows:[18]

Mr. Karuna Kusalasaya ... undertook a work of tremendous responsibility when he launched upon the project to produce a rendering of *Gitanjali* in the Thai language. This only shows his literary competence and courage and determination to do a piece of work for which he was by temperament and training amply suited, for who would be more competent and better trained than Mr. Karuna to render Tagore's highly philosophical and thought-stimulating poetry into Thai. Mr. Karuna has spent years in India and at Santiniketan which is a living [monument] to Gurudev's concept of education.

... I have no doubt that Mr. Karuna's work will be read widely all over Thailand and his commendable and great literary talent will receive the attention and recognition it so richly deserves.[19]

Acharn Karuna is considered the most prominent translator of Tagore's works in Thailand. He was also one of the best-known Indologists in Thailand. He entered monkhood as a novice at the young age of thirteen and, shortly thereafter, in 1933, went on a pilgrimage to India. In India, he was under the patronage of the Mahabodhi Society in Sarnath and began to study Hindi, English, and Pali. Finally, he sat for the national examination in Hindi and won top marks. This allowed him to enroll in Visva-Bharati, Tagore's university, in 1939. His studies there focused on Sanskrit and Indology, dealing mainly with Indian culture, literature, religions, and philosophy.[20] He also had a chance to meet Tagore, as he has described below:

At the time I was in Santiniketan, Poet Rabindranath Tagore was already in the ripe old age of about 80 years. He did not himself teach as before but still acted as the Grand Old Man radiating fatherly influence on every aspect of the institution. I had met and entered into conversation with him during which he spoke of his visit to Siam in B.E. 2470 (1927) during the reign of King Rama VII. He was so kind as to give me an autographed photograph of himself.[21]

Apart from university life, Acharn Karuna also experienced many aspects of Indian culture by spending his life in intimate contact with Indians. After returning to Thailand in 1946, he worked as a staff member of the Thai–Bharat Cultural Lodge and also worked at the Indian Embassy in Bangkok when the two countries established diplomatic relations following India's independence.[22]

As writers and translators, he and his wife, Acharn Ruang-Urai, contributed more scholarly books on India, both ancient and contemporary, than any other Thai of the present generation or before.[23] He was declared a National Artist (Literature) by the Office of the National Culture Commission of Thailand in 2003.[24]

Besides *Gitanjali*, Acharn Karuna and Acharn Ruang-Urai translated other works by Tagore. These were collected in a book entitled *Meuan Nueng*

Nok Thi Chak Rang 'Like a Bird Strayed from Its Nest' which contains twenty-three short stories and two plays.[25] The two plays in this book are *Heaven and Earth,* and *Chitra.*[26]

Although Acharn Karuna and Acharn Ruang-Urai are accepted as the most prominent Indologist couple in Thailand, some of Tagore's works were also passed on to Thai society by other translators. Thus, *Chitra,* one of the poet's best-known plays, has appeared in more than one Thai version. In addition to Acharn Karuna and Acharn Ruang-Urai's prose translation of this work, Indrayuth and Sang Thong presented the dialogue in the form of poetry.[27] The works translated by other scholars include *Sadhana, The Crescent Moon, Fireflies, The Gardener, The Garden, Stray Birds, Sanyasi, Malini, Sacrifice, Karna and Kunti, Binodini,* and *Lipika.* These comprise poems, plays, and short stories. Other collections of Tagore's works were also translated, such as, *Later Poems of Tagore,* and *Love Poems of Tagore.* Some of these works have been republished in many editions, and some of them were translated more than once.

Almost all translators retained the forms of the originals: poetry, drama, or short story; prose or verse. Many works were presented in Thai/English bilingual editions. As Thais generally did not know Bengali, all of these works were translated from English, not directly from Bengali.

According to their own statements, all of the translators, regardless of whether they were professionals or amateurs, were interested in certain aspects of India. For example, some had experience in India for a certain period, while others were fascinated by Indian religions and philosophy. One of them, Acharn Preecha Chopathumma, the translator of *Stray Birds, The Crescent Moon,* and *Poems of Love,* was also a product of Tagore's University. He won a scholarship from the Thai–Bharat Cultural Lodge to study Comparative Religion at Visva-Bharati in 1964 and did his BA in 1967. He went to Visva-Bharati again for further special courses on contemporary India and Tagorean literature.[28] Of these translators, three have been declared as National Artists. In addition to Acharn Karuna, who has already been mentioned, there are the two co-translators of *Fireflies,* Professor Dr Rawee Pavilai and Acharn Prakin Chumsai na Ayutthaya, who became National Artists in 2006 and 1993 respectively.[29] However, within Thai society as a whole, Tagore's works are now familiar to only a limited circle, primarily those who are interested in literature, philosophy, or Indology.

RABINDRANATH TAGORE IN THAI MEMORY

Although Tagore remained well known only among certain groups, all of his important anniversaries have been celebrated in Thailand. On the occasion of his birth centenary in 1961, Thailand joined in commemorating him. Prince Dhani Niwat, the most important host of Tagore's visit in 1927, was the chairman of the committee that took responsibility for this celebration. Books commemorating Tagore were issued, and *Chitra* was performed as a special television programme.[30]

From 16 to 17 June 2011, Chulalongkorn University in cooperation with the Embassy of India in Bangkok, the Indian Council for Cultural Relations (ICCR), and the Rockefeller Foundation organised a series of activities to commemorate his 150th birth anniversary. An international conference was held with the theme 'Tagore's Vision for Asia: Human Solidarity beyond Nationalism', and an exhibition of his life, voyage, and paintings was imported from India. Many participants, local and international experts, diplomats, mass media, and students, joined these activities.[31] On the occasion of the official opening of Chulalongkorn University's Indian Studies Centre on 16 March 2012, the dance-drama *Chitrangada* by Tagore was performed by an Indian theatre group.[32]

NOTES

1. Before 1940, Thailand was known as Siam.
2. *Lak Muang*, 17 October 1927, cited in Das Gupta, *Tagore's Asian Outlook*, 121.
3. Sonakul Dhani, 'Tagore's Visit to Siam' in *Rabindranath Tagore: A Centenary Volume 1861–1961* (New Delhi: Sahitya Akademi, 1987), 306.
4. Telegram of 2 August 1927 from the Minister of Foreign Affairs of Siam to the Siamese Consul General in Singapore, National Archive of Thailand, Document of Ministry of Foreign Affairs 33.6.7/4: Rabindranath Tagore and his party will visit Siam.
5. Ibid.
6. Sonakul Dhani, 'Tagore's Visit to Siam', 306.
7. *Siam Observer*, Monday, 10 October 1927 cited in Das Gupta, *Tagore's Asian Outlook*, 104–5.
8. Letter of 8 October 1927 from Prince Dhani Niwat, Minister of Education, to Prince Traidos Prabandh, Minister of Foreign Affairs, National Archive of Thailand, Document of Ministry of Foreign Affairs 33.6.7/4: Rabindranath Tagore and his party will visit Siam, Document of Ministry of Education 22.4/5: Dr Rabindranath Tagore and his party will visit Siam (30 September–13 October 1927), Das Gupta, *Tagore's Asian Outlook*, 91–2, 94–6, 109, 114–15.
9. Chris Baker and Pasuk Phongpaichit, *A History of Thailand* (New York: Cambridge University Press, 2005), 112.
10. Das Gupta, *Tagore's Asian Outlook*, 90.
11. Ibid., 98–9, 102.
12. *Siam Observer*, Saturday, 15 October 1927, cited in Das Gupta, *Tagore's Asian Outlook*, 128–9. See also *The English Writings of Rabindranath Tagore*, vol. 4: A Miscellany, ed. Nityapriya Ghosh. New Delhi: Sahitya Akademi, 2007,

95–6. In *The English Writings of Rabindranath Tagore*, vol. 4 (95), the first line of the poem reads, 'When the great Prayer for the Three Refuges,' which is different from the first line of the poem in this essay. The line quoted in the essay is taken from the newspaper(s) where the poem first appeared.

13. Das Gupta, *Tagore's Asian Outlook*, 129. *The English Writings of Rabindranath Tagore*, vol. 4: A Miscellany, ed. Nityapriya Ghosh. Sahitya Akademi, New Delhi 2007, 96–7. The text in this essay has four deviations from the poem 'Farewell to Siam' as given in *The English Writings*. These are printing mistakes in *The English Writings* which have been corrected by the author of this essay.

14. *Bangkok Times*, Monday, 17 October 1927, cited in Das Gupta, *Tagore's Asian Outlook*, 103.

15. King Prajadhipok's Museum, Photographs, and Documents during the reign of King Rama VII, 09: Lottery and Postcards.

16. Prem Chaya, 'Rabindranath Tagore' in Rabindranath Tagore, *Gitanjali*, trans. Karuna and Ruang-Urai Kusalasaya, 6th edition (Bangkok: Mae Kum Pang, 1991), 306.

17. *Ruam Nipon Rabindranath*, 3.

18. Usually, 'Acharn' (Acharaya in Indian languages) is a title for someone whose job is to teach in a school or college. However, it can be used for someone who is an expert in his/her profession, too.

19. Tagore, *Gitanjali*, 14–15.

20. Kusalasaya, *Life without a Choice*, 88–92.

21. Ibid., 92.

22. Sulak Sivaraksa, 'A Virtuous Life in the Service of Humanity.' *Bangkok Post*, 8 September 2009, accessed 14 October 2011, http://www.Bangkokpost.com/print/23450.

23. Sulak Sivaraksa, preface to *Life without a Choice* by Karuna Kusalasaya.

24. 'Karuna Kusalasaya,' National Artist Website, accessed 25 September 2011, http://art.culture.go.th/index.php?case=artistDetail&art_id=428pic_id=&side=book.

25 The book's title derives from the Thai name of one of the short stories in the series: 'The Home coming.' These short stories are 'Lotus Offering,' 'The Strange Beggar,' 'The Auspicious Vision,' 'Raja and Rani,' 'The Skeleton,' 'The Supreme Night,' 'The Postmaster,' 'Master Mashai,' 'The River Stairs,' 'The Home coming,' 'The Love of Rahu,' 'The Wedding,' 'Meenu,' 'The Trophy of Victory,' 'Saved,' 'Name,' 'Guru Govinda,' 'The Horse,' 'Price of A Head,' 'Elder Sister,' 'Retribution,' 'The Fairy,' and 'The Last Song.'

26. This is a lesser known play by Tagore, published in: Tagore: *The Golden Boat*, transl. Bhabani Bhattacharya. London: George Allen & Unwin, 1932, 111–21. Karuna and Ruang-Urai Kusalasaya, *Meuan Nueng Nok Thi Chak Rang*.

27. Indrayuth and Sang Thong, *Chitra*.

28. Preecha Chopathumma, *Nok Tieun*, 3–4.

29. 'Professor Dr Rawee Pavilai,' National Artist Website, accessed 18 June 2012, http://art.culture.go.th/index.php?case=artistDetail&art_id=2918pic_id=&side=book. 'Prakin Chumsai na Ayutthaya,' National Artist Website, accessed 18 June 2012,

    http://art.culture.go.th/index.php?case=artistDetail&art_id=318pic_id=&side=
    book.
30. *Ruam Nipon Rabindranath*. Ruang-Urai Kusalasaya, 'Rabindranath's Life and
    Works,' *Thai–Bharat Journal* 5.15 (1977): 70.
31. 'Tagore's Vision for Asia: Human Solidarity beyond Nationalism,' accessed 15
    June 2012, http://www.20100324.chula.ac.th/chulaglobal/index.phb/seminar/
    2010/seminar-conference.
32. Dance-drama 'Chitrangada', accessed 15 June 2012, http://www.20100324.
    chula.ac.th/chulaglobal/index.phb/home/2 latest/74-dance-drama-qchitrangadac.

WORKS CITED

Primary Sources (Unpublished)

King Prajadhipok's Museum, Photographs, and Documents during the reign of King
    Rama VII, 09: Lottery and Postcards.
National Archive of Thailand, Document of Ministry of Education 22.4/5:
    Dr Rabindranath Tagore and his party will visit Siam.
National Archive of Thailand, Document of Ministry of Foreign Affairs 33.6.7/4:
    Rabindranath Tagore and his party will visit Siam.

Books

Baker, Chris, and Pasuk Phongpaichit. *A History of Thailand*. New York: Cambridge
    University Press, 2005.
Chopathumma, Preecha. *Nok Tieun (Stray Birds)*. Bangkok: Tan Tawan, 1991.
Das Gupta, Shakti. *Tagore's Asian Outlook*. Calcutta: Nava Bharati, 1961.
Indrayuth and Sang Thong. *Chitra*. Bangkok: Sivalai, 1979.
Kusalasaya, Karuna. *Life without a Choice*. Bangkok: Sathirakoses-Nagapradipa
    Foundation, 1991.
Kusalasaya, Karuna, and Ruang-Urai Kusalasaya. *Meuan Neung Nok Thi Chak Rang*
    (Like a Bird Strayed from Its Nest). 6th edition. Bangkok: Dok Ya, 1994.
Rabindranath Tagore: A Centenary Volume 1861–1961. New Delhi: Sahitya Akademi,
    1987.
Ruam Nipon Rabindranath (Collected Works of Rabindranath). Bangkok:
    Rabindranath Tagore Centennial Anniversary Celebrations Committee, 1961.
Tagore, Rabindranath. *Gitanjali*. Translated by Karuna and Ruang-Urai Kusalasaya.
    6th edition. Bangkok: Mae Kum Pang, 1991.

Article

Kusalasaya, Ruang-Urai. 'Rabindranath's Life and Works.' *Thai–Bharat Journal*, 5,
    no. 15, 1977, 62–72.

Websites

Dance-drama 'Chitrangada.' Accessed 15 June 2012.http://www.20100324.chula. ac.th/chulaglobal/index.phb/home/2 latest/74-dance-drama-qchitrangadac.

Karuna Kusalasaya, 'National Artist Website.' Accessed 25 September 2011. http://art. culture.go.th/index.php?case=artistDetail&art_id=428pic_id=&side=book.

Prakin Chumsai na Ayutthaya, 'National Artist Website.' Accessed 18 June 2012. http://art.culture.go.th/index.php?case=artistDetail&art_id=318pic_ id=&side=book.

Professor Dr Rawee Pavilai, 'National Artist Website.' Accessed 18 June 2012. http://art.culture.go.th/index.php?case=artistDetail&art_id=2918pic_ id=&side=book.

Sulak Sivaraksa, 'A Virtuous Life in the Service of Humanity.' *Bangkok Post*, 8 September 2009. Accessed 14 October 2011. http://www.Bangkokpost.com/ print/23450.

Tagore's Vision for Asia: Human Solidarity beyond Nationalism. Accessed 15 June 2012. http://www.20100324.chula.ac.th/chulaglobal/index.phb/ seminar/2010/seminar-conference.

7

Sri Lanka

Sandagomi Coperahewa

As a poet, it is my mission to restore that ancient association of mind through my efforts that speak through a direct language of art.

Rabindranath Tagore, 1934

Introduction

In the twentieth century, among the foreign individuals who exerted an influence on Sri Lankan arts and culture, the greatest was Rabindranath Tagore.[1] It is not an exaggeration to say that the name Tagore became a household name in Sri Lanka and every educated Lankan is aware of his contribution to Sri Lankan music, art, literature and education. Focusing on Tagore's most well-known visits to Sri Lanka, 1922, 1928 and 1934 and other lesser known visits to the island, the first part of this essay discusses the socio-historical background of Tagore's relationship with Sri Lanka and his impact on Sri Lankan cultural life. After his travels to Sri Lanka (then Ceylon), a vast majority of the Sinhalese intellectuals welcomed Tagore's ideas, and later his literary works began to appear in the Sinhala language. By examining the ways in which he interacted with the cultural personalities of that era, the second part of this essay revisits Tagore's reception in Sri Lankan cultural and intellectual life. In general, this essay provides insights into the historical context in which the image of Tagore—one that persists today— was developed in Sri Lanka and his reception in a neighbouring country.

Among the many aspects of Rabindranath Tagore's diverse personality was his fascination for travel. He kept his doors open to ideas from the East and the West. As Supriya Roy writes, Tagore's journeys to the East are quite distinct from those he made to the West; 'his travels to the West had an air of adventure, his travels eastward were like pilgrimages—in the footsteps of his ancestors who travelled to the East from India carrying a message of truth and love.'[2] Tagore visited more than thirty countries including Sri Lanka.

In fact, his last overseas visit was to Sri Lanka. During his travels, Tagore explained his ideal of Visva-Bharati and raised funds for its development and made a deep impact on the cultural life of the people. He also continued with his dream of establishing contacts between different cultures and peoples.

During the early twentieth century, when Tagore visited Sri Lanka, both India and Sri Lanka were under British colonial rule. Britain's colonial relationship with South Asia led to many cross-cultural exchanges in the arts and sciences. Many South Asian intellectuals and academics established influential contacts and friendships within the region. At the same time, Bengal was the most vibrant intellectual and cultural nerve centre of South Asia. Two important institutions attracted the attention of Sri Lankan scholars: one was Calcutta University (founded in 1857) and the other was Visva-Bharati at Santiniketan founded by Tagore in 1921. It must be mentioned that in the late nineteenth century Bengal also experienced a revival in Buddhism due to the untiring efforts of Anagarika Dharmapala (1864–1933), a Sri Lankan Buddhist activist. Tagore himself had shown a great interest in the Sri Lankan people and had an emotional attachment to the island's history. Tagore's fascination with Sri Lanka seems to have been prompted by two factors: first, from the general belief that the Sinhalese, the majority of Sri Lankans, descended from immigrants from Bengal; and second, from the profound respect for Theravada Buddhism and the Buddhist heritage of the island.[3]

TAGORE AND SRI LANKA: EARLY CONTACTS

According to Kalidas Nag, the historian and a student of Tagore, Tagore's father, Debendranath Tagore, had visited Sri Lanka in the 1860s with his son Satyendranath.[4] This shows that the Tagore family had an abiding interest in the island. In the 1890s, as the editor of the literary journal *Sadhana*, Tagore invited articles on Buddhism. He was already aware of Anagarika Dharmapala's Buddhist revival work in India. The *Maha Bodhi*, a journal started by Dharmapala as the organ of the Mahabodhi Society, was patronised by Indian intellectuals such as Tagore who contributed articles and poems to it. Moreover, during 1903–5, Asit Kumar Haldar (1890–1964), an artist-colleague of Tagore, was a frequent visitor to the home of Dharmapala[5]. In the first two decades of the twentieth century, the cultural and spiritual collaboration between India and Sri Lanka was deepened through the initiatives of Dharmapala, Asutosh Mookerjee and Tagore. While in India, Sri Lankan art critic and historian Ananda Coomaraswamy (1877–1947) formed a close relationships with the Tagore family, and was involved in both Bengal's literary renaissance and the Indian *Swadeshi* movement.

On 13 November 1913, when it was announced that the Nobel Prize for Literature had been awarded to Tagore by the Swedish Academy; the Bengali poet became a world figure almost overnight. Soon after World War I ended, in May 1920, Tagore sailed for Europe, where he was received with great enthusiasm and warmth. Before 1913, the name of Rabindranath Tagore was hardly known to anybody in neighbouring Sri Lanka except for a few personal contacts. The award of the Nobel Prize to Tagore enhanced the prestige of the Asian people who were under British colonial rule, and also created an interest about his works and life in Sri Lanka. In an article titled 'Tagore and Ceylon', Martin Wickremasinghe (1890–1976), Sri Lanka's foremost Sinhala writer in the twentieth century, stated:

> Tagore would have been ignored by the majority of our English-educated intelligentsia if he was not the recipient of the Nobel Prize for literature. When I was young, I read the Rev. Edward Thompson's 'Life of Tagore' in which he ironically related the criticisms of Tagore by some Bengali Sanskrit scholars and university professors. The latter gave passages from Tagore's prose works and told matriculation students to re-write them in chaste Bengali! This attempt to humiliate the genius of Tagore, before he was offered the Nobel Prize, was the result of the influence of English culture and colonialism that prevailed in Bengal.[6]

In 1915, two years after winning the Nobel Prize, there is a noting in *Sinhala Bauddhaya* (27 May 1915), a Sinhala weekly newspaper of the Mahabodhi Society, that a visit of Tagore to Sri Lanka was postponed.

Tagore's First Visit to Sri Lanka: October 1922

The beginning of the twentieth century saw a remarkable social, political and cultural change in Sri Lankan society. The English-educated elite were politically involved in constitutional reform activities and at the same time they were interested in various cultural and reform movements.[7] It is clear that during the early 1920s Tagore had many connections with Sri Lankan Buddhist priests, politicians and intellectuals, including D. B. Jayatilaka, Dr W. A. De Silva, and Ven. Rambukawelle Siddhartha. All of them studied at Calcutta University and Tagore had a close association with the university. In 1918, Tagore laid the foundation for his ideal institution Visva-Bharati at Santiniketan and made adequate provision for the study of Buddhism and Pali there.[8] Ven. Ambalangaoda Dharmadhara (1858–1936), one of the earliest Buddhist monks to collaborate with Dharmapala in his efforts to revive Buddhism in India, was also a close associate of Tagore. Ven. Dharmadhara served as the first professor of Buddhism and

Pali (1918–22) at Visva-Bharati.[9] Moreover, the socio-cultural atmosphere that existed in Sri Lanka in the early decades of the twentieth century and Tagore's connections with Lankans paved the way for his visit to his neighbouring country.

Tagore's first visit to Sri Lanka in October 1922 was on the invitation of Dr W. Arthur De Silva (1869–1942), a scholar, politician and philanthropist, who was an alumnus of Calcutta University. Tagore was accompanied by C. F. Andrews. In this visit, Tagore first stayed at Sravasti in Colombo, the home of De Silva, and then went to Kandy, and spent a week in Nuwara Eliya. At this time, the political elite were founding the Ceylon National Congress (1919), following the example of the Indian National Congress. Tagore's friend De Silva was a Member of the Executive Committee of the Ceylon National Congress and became the President of the Congress in 1928. Tagore gave a lecture at the Ceylon University College (established in 1921). He spoke on the 'Ancient Indian Universities' and the 'tradition of close engagement between the *guru* and *shishya*.'[10] Robert Marrs, Principal of the College, presided over the event. On 10 November 1922, Tagore visited Ananda College in Colombo as the chief guest of the annual prize-giving ceremony. During his visit to Kandy, he was honoured by politician George E. De Silva and Albert Godamunne and also gave a lecture at Trinity College. During this visit he addressed gatherings in Colombo, and at the Mahinda College, Galle. At this time, Kalidas Nag served as the principal of Mahinda College. In one of his speeches, Tagore said:

> Although the political constitution of modern Ceylon separates this country from India, it is no secret that its history, religion, language, morals, culture and everything else are closely linked to India. Briefly stated, the fact that Ceylon became great because of India is no exaggeration. Although the spiritual bond between the two countries that was there in the past has collapsed, time has come to put that together again and strengthen it.[11]

TAGORE'S SECOND VISIT TO SRI LANKA: MAY 1928

In 1928, the University of Oxford invited Tagore to deliver the Hibbert Lectures. Tagore had embarked on a ship on 12 May 1928 but had to cancel his trip to the UK due to illness. Instead, he visited his Sri Lankan friend Arthur De Silva in Colombo. The visit lasted for ten days, from 29 May to 11 June 1928. Tagore again stayed at Sravasti and then went to Nuwara Eliya. C. F. Andrews accompanied him on this trip too. When Tagore visited Sri Lanka in 1928 he was much better known to the Sinhala intelligentsia as a recipient of the Nobel Prize for Literature and also as a 'Great Indian Poet'

(Bharata Maha Kavi). Sinhala and English newspapers announced the arrival of the great Indian poet. In connection with this visit, the Sinhala daily *Dinamina* published several poems in praise of 'Maha Kavi Ravindranth Tagore' including one written by the Sinhala poet, Katunayaka Lionel W. De Silva, wishing Tagore good health.[12] During the early 1930s, Arian Williams (Sri Aryanayakam), a Sri Lankan Tamilian from Jaffna, served as the poet's Secreteray and worked as a teacher at Santiniketan.[13] He also acted as a translator during Tagore's vist to Malaya in 1924. Moreover, Tagore's interaction with Sri Lankan students in Santiniketan provided scope for another visit to the island.

TAGORE'S LAST VISIT TO SRI LANKA: MAY 1934

During 1931–2, Visva-Bharati had financial difficulties and his friends and well-wishers in Sri Lanka invited him to the island and helped him raise funds for resuscitating the institution. Tagore's last visit to Sri Lanka was in May 1934. It was his most important visit, and the invitation was extended by an admirer, Wilmot A. Perera (1905–73), a business magnate who had visited Santiniketan in 1932. The friendship between Perera and Tagore had a profound influence on the cultural relationship between the two countries. When Tagore arrived in 1934, the country and the people of Sri Lanka were undergoing various socio-political and constitutional reforms. With the introduction of universal adult suffrage by the Donoughmore Constitution in 1931, this period saw various socio-political developments in the island nation, such as the broadening of political participation, and the emergence of organised political parties and associations which inspired the government to adopt the people's 'own language' (*swabhasha*) in education and administration.[14]

On 9 May 1934, Tagore and a group of twenty-three students from Santiniketan arrived in Colombo by the sea route. The poet's seventy-third birthday was celebrated on board the ship. He was accompanied by his daughter, Mira Devi, his daughter-in-law, Pratima Tagore, and the renowned artist, Nandalal Bose. Huge crowds welcomed Tagore and his group with warmth and enthusiasm. The personalities who were present to receive him included Sir D. B. Jayatilaka, the Leader of the State Council of Ceylon and an alumnus of Calcutta University, and W. L. Murphy, the Mayor of Colombo. On his arrival in Lanka, Tagore said:

> I know your island and her beauty. I have been here more than once. And this time I have a special mission. I have bought some part of our culture which *Santiniketan* represents. I hope I will be able to please you. I hope my mission will be fulfilled ... I have bought something

from India, some aspect of the culture, some delight of her arts and I hope you will realize that it is of eternal value. With politics I am not concerned. My mission is spiritual delights of art and beauty far and wide.[15]

Tagore stayed as a guest at Helena Wijewardena's Colombo residence, *Sri Ramya*. The publicity accorded by the Sinhala and the English press was quite overwhelming. Both Sinhala and English daily newspapers carried the news of Tagore's visit on the front page. The Sinhala daily, *Dinamina*, considered Tagore as the 'Sage of Santiniketan' or the Great Poet (*Maha Kavi*) of India. On 9 May 1934, an editorial appeared under the title 'Tagore and National Revival' while Martin Wickremasinghe again wrote a feature article on Tagore's life and works for *Dinamina*. During his stay in Colombo, Tagore gave interviews to English newspapers expressing his views on national culture and language problems, and he delivered several lectures. D. B. Dhanapala, a leading English journalist who interviewed Tagore in 1934, gives the following interesting account:

> I remember an interview both of us [D. B. Dhanapala and H. A. J. Hulugalle] had with Rabindranath Tagore when he was the guest of Wijewardene at Sri Ramya, now occupied by the American Embassy. Both of us listened to Tagore for two hours, only now and then putting a timid question to him. We came away without taking down a single note. He wrote down from memory half the interview and I wrote the other half in the first person singular in Tagore's own words. We sent the proof to Tagore for approval keeping our fingers crossed. It came back with only one word altered—'catastrophe' changed to 'cataclysm'—just in time to be rushed to the front page to be published as 'The Island of Lotus Eaters'.[16]

On 10 May, Tagore delivered a talk on Visva-Bharati, 'Ideals of an Indian University', which was broadcast over Radio Ceylon. He also recited his poems at the YMBA (Young Men's Buddhist Association) and YMCA (Young Men's Christian Association) and spoke in Jaffna, Kandy, Horana and Panadura. His speeches made a deep impression at that time. On 12 June 1934, speaking at the Jaffna Central College, Tagore said:

> The spirit of India once visited Lanka. The best moral ideals, the deepest spiritual philosophy which had been produced in that land, travelled across the barriers of mountains and seas, consecrating this beautiful land. But centuries passed by and she became alienated from India, and today India's gifts lie disassociated from their sacred

source. As a poet, it is my mission to restore that ancient association of mind through my efforts that speak through a direct language of art.[17]

The artistes accompanying Tagore performed the Bengali dance-drama *Shapmochan* in Colombo and Jaffna. On the evening of 12 May, the Santiniketan artistes presented their first show at the Regal Theater, Colombo. It was a memorable performance which was reviewed for the *Ceylon Daily News* by S. W. R. D. Bandaranaike, an Oxford graduate in Classics who became the Prime Minister of Sri Lanka in 1956. The following is an excerpt from his review:

> The curtain went up, and my first impression was one of aesthetic satisfaction at the setting and the grouping, which had the simplicity and the beauty which Greek drama alone has yet been able to achieve. There was Tagore seated at one end, [appropriately] garbed in a yellow robe, a typical bard and seer with his flowing grey hair and beard. The first thing that struck me was the beauty of his shapely hands and the long tapering fingers; only a great artist could have hands like that. The music started, low and soft, and the slow movement of the dance. ... Love and wrath and sorrow and joy and chivalry—all human emotions find their place in this play, and the delicate and sure touch with which they are conveyed by the music and dancing is a revelation of art at its highest.[18]

According, to Martin Wickremasinghe, 'Tagore's dance-drama which was a visual presentation of an aspect of Indian culture made an impression on the educated section who were ignorant of their own language and culture.'[19] Furthermore, the English press acclaimed this dance drama as 'A Feast of dance and song music', and the 'Greatest within living memory.'[20] This dance-drama was so popular that it was extended to three performances in Colombo and three in Jaffna. *Shapmochan* brought a new theatrical experience to the local theatre and later several plays came to be modelled on it which were staged in Colombo and other provincial towns.[21]

On 14 May 1934, an exhibition of Arts and Crafts of Santiniketan was opened at the Colombo Art Gallery by Sir Graeme Tyrell, the Chief Secretary. At the opening ceremony, Tagore spoke on 'The Ideals of Indian Art.' The exhibits included paintings by Tagore, Nandalal Bose and students of Kala Bhavana, the school of art at Santiniketan. This exhibition created an awareness and enthusiasm of the traditions of Indian art among Sri Lankans. Tagore was delighted to find that some of the pupils of his art school had already served as teachers of drawing and painting at the Ananda College, Colombo and other institutions.[22] At this time, there was also a suggestion to hand over the task of painting the murals of Kelaniya Buddhist Temple to Nandalal Bose.[23] On 16 May, Tagore was accorded a reception by the Colombo Municipal Council and the following day he delivered a lecture and recited his poems at the YMCA building in Colombo.

During this last visit, besides giving lectures and interviews, on 20 May 1934, Tagore laid the foundation for Sri Palee in Horana. Sri Palee was a dream institution of Wilmot A. Perera. He had visited Santiniketan in 1932 with his wife on a scholarly pursuit, Mrs Perera joined Kala Bhavana and learnt a number of arts and crafts, while Wilmot Perera spent the whole time to study the Santiniketan method of teaching. After his return home from Santiniketan, Wilmot A. Perera engaged himself in building a school for rural reconstruction on similar lines as Sriniketan, another of Tagore's projects near Santiniketan. To inaugurate the new institution he invited Tagore. Tagore even gave the name for this institution. He called it 'Sri Palee'—'a place where the goddess of Fine Arts lives.' At the founding ceremony of Sri Palee, Tagore said:

> My heart goes out to these simple people from the neighbouring villages and I feel unhappy that I am not able to speak to them in their own language, but I hope that they will realise that they have my heartiest blessings and I wish them well. It reminds me of my own work in Bengal, this institution which you have started, and I feel that this will be a channel of communication of hearts between your island and our institution in Bengal. It makes me feel so happy.[24]

The establishment of Sri Palee at Horana based on Tagore's concept of education and culture was a ground-breaking event for fostering local culture and fine arts. It was the direct result of a close relationship that developed between Tagore and Perera, its founder. Many former pupils of Sri Palee (which is now the government-owned Sri Palee College) have vivid memories of their school education which aimed 'to provide a humane education in harmony with [the] environment with inputs from aesthetic fields for the overall development of the students'.[25]

On 22 May, Tagore visited Galle and then Matara, the two major towns in southern Sri Lanka, where he witnessed a traditional mask-dance. On 4 June, he visited Kandy where he was fascinated by the Kandyan dance on which he wrote a beautiful poem[26]. Tagore encouraged inmates of Santiniketan to learn and imbibe these dance forms and he adapted some elements of those dances in his later choreographic productions. Moreover, his words of encouragement helped the Kandyan dance form emerge into the mainstream of Sri Lankan dance culture. During this visit, Nandalal Bose, who travelled with Tagore, did some beautiful paintings and sketches; they included the dress of a Kandyan dancer. While in Kandy, Tagore completed his novel, *Char Adhyay* (Four Chapters). After a visit to Anuradhapura and other places of historic interest, he went to Jaffna on 9 June where *Shapmochan* was performed on three successive evenings. During Tagore's stay on the island, he translated a poem from the original Bengali to commemorate the *Vesak* (Vaisākha or Buddha Purnima) and sent it to the *Ceylon Daily News*.[27] On Vesak Day (28 May), the poem was published under the title *To Buddha*.[28] During this last visit, he travelled to almost every important town, and at every place he was accorded an enthusiastic reception. He left Jaffna on 15 June and returned by way of Danuskodi–Madras to Calcutta by rail.[29]

It needs to be mentioned here that Tagore visited Sri Lanka at a time when the English-educated Sri Lankan elite treated with contempt the ancient cultures of India and Lanka. The decades of the 1920s and 30s also marked 'linguistic decolonization'—actions taken to undo the social, political and cultural effects of the dominance of the colonial language within the Sinhala and Tamil communities.[30] For example, at this time there was a general trend in Sinhalese society to adopt Arya-Sinhala or Sanskrit names. In the aftermath of Tagore's visits, many Sinhalese intellectuals who proceeded to Santiniketan abandoned their Anglo-Portuguese names and adopted Sanskrit names in order to defend their Sinhalese identity.[31] In this socio-cultural context, Tagore truly believed in the mutually interactive relationship between the two cultures and often showed his regard for the glorious history and cultural traditions of India and Sri Lanka. In one of his speeches during this visit, Tagore had said:

> I thought it was my mission to come [to] Ceylon to spread this message of our Oriental culture to those who by some unfortunate external circumstances have forgotten their own past and who are ready to disown their richest inheritance.[32]

TAGORE'S LESSER-KNOWN VISITS TO SRI LANKA

Apart from these three main visits undertaken by Tagore in 1922, 1928 and 1934, three other, lesser known, visits to Sri Lanka have been recorded. These were stopovers rather than visits.

In September 1924, on his way to Argentina he stopped at Colombo and was the guest of W. Arthur De Silva at Sravasti. He was accompanied by his son, Rathindranath, daughter-in-law, grand-daughter and Surendranath Kar.

In 1929, on his way to Canada via Japan, he left Bombay on board SS *Naldera* and stopped over at Colombo on 4 March for a brief halt. On 5

March 1930, Tagore stopped at Colombo on his way to Oxford to deliver the Hibbert Lectures.

Tagore's visits to Sri Lanka and his close contacts with Sri Lankans had a profound influence on the socio-cultural relations between India and Sri Lanka. An important cultural landmark was thus established in the relationship between the two countries.

Impact of Tagore, Translations and Commemorative Events

Tagore's three visits to Sri Lanka and three transit halts there clearly left an abiding imprint. Moreover, his extensive interaction with artists and literary personalities of Sri Lanka contributed to the country's cultural resurgence, inspiring young artistes, dancers and singers to develop their genres to attain classical forms. A reporter wrote on Tagore's visit to Lanka in 1934 thus:

> Here in Ceylon, Tagore has kindled a new enthusiasm. He has awakened a great yearning, he has held aloft a great idealism. It is not this generation that will thank him for his inspiration to Ceylon. Generations cannot measure the value of his services. It is not history that will record his achievements. Even history cannot give a niche to 'an impetus' that has opened our eyes to a vision of the joy and grandeur of our song and music, of our art and culture.[33]

Tagore's popularity in Sri Lanka reached its peak in 1934–5. Several young intellectuals and artistes proceeded to Santiniketan to study music, dance, painting and Indian philosophy.[34] Some of them had an opportunity to interact personally with Tagore. Later, they became major figures in Sinhala art and literary movements and enriched the cultural life of post-independence Sri Lanka. Among them were Ananda Samarakoon, Edwin Samardiwakara, Surya Shankar Molligoda, Ediriweera Sarachchandra, Devar Suryasena, Sunil Shantha, Lionel Edirisinghe, C. De S. Kulatilleke, Chitrasena, Premakumara Epitawela, and W. B. Makuloluwa. All these men have succeeded as artistes trying to evolve a contemporary local art with its bases in the Oriental tradition. Tagore inspired many Sri Lankans to develop and appreciate their own traditions of music and song. For Ananda Samarakoon (1911–62), the composer of Sri Lanka's national anthem, *Sri Lanka Matha,* Rabindra Sangeet (songs written and mostly set to music by Tagore) had been his main source of inspiration. Other musicians like Surya Shankar Molligoda, Sunil Shantha and W. B. Makuloluwa who were trained in Santiniketan, broke new ground in developing an indigenous music tradition which was continued by their pupils and subsequent generations.

Ediriweera Sarachchandra (1914–96), Sri Lanka's well known playwright and a former professor of Sinhala (at the University of Ceylon) was influenced by Tagore. While he was at university, Sarachchandra was lucky to see a ballet performance by Tagore's Dance Troupe at the Regal Theatre in Colombo. Having graduated from the University of Ceylon, he went to Santiniketan in 1939 to study music and philosophy. In his autobiography and series of articles titled 'Through Santiniketan Eyes', Sarachchandra talks at length on the deep and enduring impact of Santiniketan on his life and work.[35] On his return to Sri Lanka in 1940, Sarachchandra became a teacher at the S. Thomas' College, a leading English school in Colombo. In his autobiography, Sarachchandra further records that he attempted to teach Tagore's poetry to students who came from an English-speaking elite background.[36]

During the 1940s and 1950s, several poets of the 'Colombo School' of Sinhala poetry were also inspired by Tagore's poetical creations. For example, the veteran Sinhala poet P. B. Alwis Perera's *Sabadahama* (1942) displays the influence of Tagore's philosophy. Several Tagore poems were published in *Dedunna*, the poetry magazine edited by Alwis Perera. In 1963, in an article on 'Tagore and Ceylon' in *Ceylon Daily News,* Sinhala writer Martin Wickremasinghe wrote:

> Tagore encouraged these young poets to break away from the traditional Sinhalese poetry which was influenced until the 13th century by the Sanskrit poetry of Magha and others ... The enduring appeal of Tagore to the intelligentsia of Ceylon is his attitude to religion and life which he expressed artistically in his poetry and with imagination and religious perception in his lectures and essays.[37]

However, it has been pointed out recently that pioneer writers of modern Sinhala have failed to grasp the artistic depth and poetic value of Tagore's works.[38]

When Tagore died in 1941, *Dinamina*, the main Sinhala daily newspaper of the island, carried the news on the first page, followed by an editorial and feature articles describing Tagore's contribution to literature and the arts.[39] In connection with Tagore's death, M. Balasunderam, a leading Tamil educationist from Jaffna, who had invited Tagore in 1922 to address students at the University College, contributed an incisive and informative article titled 'Unchronicled Anecdotes about Tagore' to the Jaffna-based newspaper *Kesari*.[40] In 1944, a large portrait of Tagore painted by Dilip Das Gupta was presented by the Calcutta Art Society to the government of Sri Lanka. Today that portrait hangs facing the entrance to the library of the University of Peradeniya (University of Ceylon). On this occasion, Sir D. B. Jayatilaka, who had extended a cordial reception to Tagore on his arrival in 1934, said, 'When the portrait of the great poet, thinker, and social worker is hung up in the library of the University of Ceylon, it will be a continuous source of inspiration to lofty aspirations and high endeavours of the youth of Ceylon for all time.'[41] C. W. W. Kannangara, the Minister of Education at that time, mentioned in a message that Tagore himself 'treated Lanka as a daughter of Bengal and the emotions of the youth of this country were touched by the beautiful and musical prose with which he clothed lofty ideals of eternal value.'[42]

The Tagore Society in Sri Lanka was formed in 1944; under the auspices of this society several commemorative functions were organised mainly to create an awareness of the poet's works. In 1961, on the occasion of Tagore's birth centenary, the Ven. Udakendawela Sarnanakara, a Buddhist monk who spent some time in Santiniketan, compiled a special issue of his journal *Navalokaya* on Tagore. It contained several Sinhala articles on Tagore's contribution to Sri Lankan arts and culture. The Sinhala daily *Dinamina* also carried a special supplement to commemorate the birth centenary of the poet.[43]

It needs to be mentioned here that in Sri Lanka the reputation and impact of Tagore in the fields of music and the arts was high from the 1920s to the 1940s, but his fame as a literary figure came only after the publication of Tagore's works in Sinhala translation. His works had not yet appeared in local languages in the 1920s, so only a section of the English-educated intelligentsia had the opportunity to read Tagore's works in English.[44] As more and more of his works began to appear in Sinhala, Tagore became popular. Even today, Sinhala writers are keen to translate his works. In Sinhala newspapers, we can find translations of Tagore's poems and short stories. Tagore is perhaps the foreign figure most translated into Sinhala. In the decade 1961–71, the popularity of Tagore with the Sinhala reading public even increased. The early Sinhala translations of Tagore's works include *Gitanjali* (1950), *Crescent Moon* (1954), *The Gardener, Lover's Gift, Natir Puja* (1960), *Gora, Chitra* (1961), *Mashi and Other Stories* (1962), *Chandalika* (1964), *Sacrifice* and *The Post Office* (1966). During the last decade several other works by Tagore have been translated: *Fruit-Gathering, Reminiscences; The Wreck* (2000), *Broken Ties and other Stories* (2002), *Chokher Bali, The Home and the World* (2003), *My Boyhood Days* (2005), *Four Chapters* (2008) and *Stray Birds* (2009). All translations were done from English, except a Sinhala translation of *Gora* (1999) and of *Chaturanga* (2007), which were based on the original Bengali. Among these translations *Gitanjali* gained such popularity that more than one translation of the work appeared. Now there are seven Sinhala translations of *Gitanjali*, the latest from 2010.[45]

The life of Tagore also inspired deep interest in the Sinhala readership. The first Sinhala biography of Tagore appeared in 1947; at present, we have four Sinhala biographies of Tagore written by different authors.

In 2011, the 150th birth anniversary of Tagore provided an opportunity to celebrate the poet and also to review Tagore's contribution to the country. A series of lectures, seminars, exhibitions, film festivals and the re-staging of *Shapmochan* were organised to commemorate Tagore and develop an appreciation of his work and life.[46] On this occasion, the Ministry of Postal Services of Sri Lanka released a postal stamp on Tagore. A special commemorative volume *Remembering Rabindranath Tagore* was published by the University of Colombo with the support of the India–Sri Lanka Foundation containing articles in Sinhala, Tamil and English which highlight the poetic, philosophical and cultural expressions of Tagore and their relevance in the contemporary world.[47] In June 2012, a one-day seminar on 'Tagore and Sri Lanka' was held in Colombo under the auspices of the Indian Cultural Centre, Colombo, and in association with the Centre for Contemporary Indian Studies (CCIS), University of Colombo. The seminar, which was coordinated by an Indian author and literary critic, Radha Chakravarty, focused on the travels of Tagore to Sri Lanka and the cultural exchange they helped to enhance. During the academic sessions, both Indian and Sri Lankan scholars revisited Tagore's contribution and cultural exchanges and the impact of his visits to the island. On 26 June 2012, a bronze bust of Rabindranath Tagore, sculpted by Janak Jhankar Narzary, a renowned sculptor and Professor of Art History in Kala Bhavana, Visva-Bharati, was unveiled by G. L. Peiris, the Minister of External Affairs of Sri Lanka, in the presence of Ashok K. Kantha, the High Commissioner of India in Sri Lanka, at the main library of the University of Colombo; it had been gifted by the Ministry of Culture, Government of India, on the occasion of the 150th birth anniversary of Tagore. The unveiling of the bust marked the end of the year-and-half long celebrations in Sri Lanka of that event.

NOTES

1. In general, he is referred to as Tagore—the Anglicised form—but those who are conversant with the Bengali language pronounce his surname as Thakur, conforming to its Bengali spelling.
2. Roy, *Rabindranath Tagore*, 2.
3. Nag, *Rabindranath Tagore and Ceylon*, 5; cf. Dharmadasa, 'Tagore and Sri Lanka', 2.
4. Nag, *Rabindranath Tagore and Ceylon*, 4.
5. Haldar, 'Asit Kumar Haldar,' 132.

6. Wickremasinghe, *Buddhism and Culture*, 69.
7. Coperahewa, *The Politics of Language*,' especially, Chapter 2.
8. Nag, *Rabindranath Tagore and Ceylon*, 5.
9. Guruge, *From the Living Fountains*, lxii.
10. Goonetileke, 'Introduction,' 51.
11. Cited in Dharmadasa, 'Tagore and Sri Lanka', 4.
12. *Dinamina*, 31 May 1928.
13. Nag, *Rabindranath Tagore and Ceylon*, 7.
14. See Chapter 4 in Coperahewa, *The Politics of Language*.
15. Cited in Nag, *Rabindranath Tagore and Ceylon*, 2.
16. Dhanapala, *Among Those Present*, 174–5.
17. *Ceylon Daily News*, 13 June 1934; also cited in Nag, *Rabindranath Tagore and Ceylon*, 3.
18. Ibid., 21 May 1934.
19. Wickremasinghe, *Buddhism and Culture*, 69. At this time, the English-educated elite condemned the local arts and culture and in that context Nobel laureate Tagore's dance drama created an enthusiasm among the educated elite.
20. *Ceylon Daily News*, 21 May 1934
21. Ariyratne, 'An Insight into the Impact,' 158.
22. Nag, *Rabindranath Tagore and Ceylon*, 7.
23. See *Dinamina*, 31 May 1934.
24. Cited on the Sri Palee College website http://www.sripaleecollege.lk/guru.html
25. Kumara, 'Wilmot A Perera,' 356.
26. The following is the English translation of the poem by Professor Sitangshu Roy of the Sangeet Bhavana of Santiniketan.

What a tremendous Kandyan dance I did witness in Sinhale [Ceylon]
Like Sal trees uprooted and blown by a violent storm!
Negating all bondage, all bars
No looking back, no indulgence in dreamy sensuousness
The Kandyan dance is unlike the soft swinging creepers
Nor is it the slender shivering of leafy twigs
It is a blaze, a forest fire!
The ocean waves asked the dancers
Do you feel the rhythm of my veins?
The storm commanded them—
"Let your anklets jingle strongly
with the force of my dance steps"!
Their robust arms raised in the space
will save the full moon
From the greedy gape of Rahu!
Nandi is worked up at
Mahadeva's break of meditation
Shiva's wrath, charged in all his limbs,
Makes him dance like violent flames
His dance of trance will dispense sensuous infatuation

Nataraj is the original male
His tandava is his mode of worship
He releases his might to liberate himself
With the shock of force he conquers fear of all fears
He surpasses himself with his own dance
Joyful and tremendous!

27. Buddhist festival to commemorate Buddha's birth, enlightenment and passing away.
28. Nag, *Rabindranath Tagore and Ceylon*, 12.
29. Mukhopadhyaya, and Roy, eds. 'A Chronicle of Eighty Years,' 496.
30. Coperahewa, 'The Politics of Language in Colonial Sri Lanka, 1900–48'. Chapters 3 and 4.
31. See Dharmadasa, 'Tagore and Sri Lanka,' 6.
32. *Ceylon Daily News*, 21 May 1934.
33. Cited in Nag, *Rabindranath Tagore and Ceylon*, 8.
34. See Ariyaratne, *An Insight into the Impact*; and Dharmadasa, *Tagore and Sri Lanka*, 5.
35. Sarachchandra, *PinAeti Sarasvi Varamak Denne*, 85–112. Also see Sarachchandra, *Santiniketanaye Æsin*.
36. Sarachchandra, *PinAeti Sarasvi Varamak Denne*, 121.
37. Wickremasinghe, *Buddhism and Culture*. 71.
38. Wijesooriya, 'Nutana Sinhala Sahitya Kala Sambhashanaya ha Ravindranatha Thakur' in *Remembering Rabindranath Tagore* edited by Sandagomi Coperahewa, 83.
39. See *Dinamina*, 8 August 1941.
40. Goonetileke, 2001, 51.
41. Nag, *Rabindranath Tagore and Ceylon*, 14.
42. Ibid., 15.
43. *Dinamina*, 8 May 1961.
44. See Sarachchandra, *PinAeti Sarasvi Varamak Denne*, 91.
45. See Coperahewa and Ramanayaka, 'A Bibliography of Rabindranath's Works in Sinhala', 129.
46. See *Sandesh*, June/July 2012.
47. Coperahewa, ed., *Remembering Rabindranath Tagore*.

WORKS CITED

Ariyratne, Sunil. 'An Insight into the Impact of Rabindranath Tagore on Sinhala Art and Music,' *Vidyodaya Journal of Social Sciences*, 1, January 1999, 157–65.
Ceylon Daily News, 1934
Coperahewa, Sandagomi. 'The Politics of Language in Colonial Sri Lanka, 1900–48' [unpublished PhD dissertation], University of Cambridge, 2009.
——, ed. *Remembering Rabindranath Tagore* (150th Birth Anniversary Commemorative Volume), Colombo: University of Colombo, 2011.

Coperahewa, Sandagomi, and B. Ramanayaka. 'A Bibliography of Rabindranath's Works in Sinhala,' in *Remembering Rabindranath Tagore*, 128–31.

Dhanapala, D. B. *Among Those Present.* Colombo: M. D. Gunasena, 1962.

Dharmadasa, K. N. O. 'Tagore and Sri Lanka: The Highlights of an Abiding Relationship' in *Remembering Rabindranath Tagore*, 1–7.

Dinamina, 1928, 1930, 1934, 1941, 1961.

Goonetileke, H. A. I. 'Introduction', *Santiniketanaye Æsin* [Through Santiniketan Eyes]. Colombo: Godage, 2001, 47–52.

Guruge, Ananda. *From the Living Fountains of Buddhism.* Colombo: Ministry of Cultural Affairs, 1984.

Haldar, Gautam. 'Asit Kumar Haldar: Rabindranath's Poet of Colour' in *Something Old, Something New: Rabindranath Tagore 150th Birth Anniversary Volume.* Mumbai: The Marg Foundation, 2011, 130–49.

Kumara, Yasasiri Janka. 'Wilmot A. Pereira: A man among men who took the less travelled path' in *The Splendour of Sri Palee* (75th Anniversary Publication). Colombo: Sri Palee Past Pupils Association, 2010, 347–57.

Mukhopadhyaya, P., and K. Roy, eds. 'A Chronicle of Eighty Years' in *Rabindranath Tagore: A Centenary Volume.* New Delhi: Sahitya Akademi, 1961, 451–503.

Nag, Kalidas. *Rabindranath Tagore and Ceylon.* Calcutta: Prabasi Press, 1944.

Roy, Supriya. *Rabindranath Tagore: Pilgrimages to the East.* Kolkata: Rabindranath Tagore Centre, 2011.

Sandesh (June/July 2012), Bi-monthly newsletter of the High Commission of India, Colombo.

Sarachchandra, Ediriweera. *PinAeti Sarasvi Varamak Denne.* Colombo: Daywansa Jayakody, 1985.

——. *Santiniketanaye Æsin* (Through Santiniketan Eyes), Sinhala translation: Sucharitha Gamlath. Colombo: Godage, 2001.

Sinhala Bauddhya, 1915.

Sri Palee Sri Vibhutiya [The Splendor of Sri Palee] Colombo: Sri Palee Past Pupils Association, 2010.

Sri Palee College Website, http://www.sripaleecollege.lk/guru.html

Wijesooriya, Sarath. 'Nutana Sinhala Sahitya Kala Sambhashanaya ha Ravindranatha Thakur' [Modern Sinhala Literary Arts Discourse and Rabindranath Tagore] in *Remembering Rabindranath Tagore*, edited by Sandagomi Coperahewa, 81–90.

Wickremasinghe, Martin. *Buddhism and Culture.* 2nd ed. Dehiwela: Tisara Prakasakayo, 1981. First published 1964.

PART TWO

Middle East and Africa

Alex Aronson, German Jewish author (Professor of English in Santiniketan, 1937 to 1944). Photo by Sambhu Saha. Courtesy: Rabindra Bhavana, Visva-Bharati.

Tagore at a Bedouin camp near Baghdad, Iraq, with his daughter-in-law Pratima Devi (in sari) standing behind him (1932). Courtesy: Rabindra Bhavana, Visva-Bharati.

Part Two

Middle East and Africa

8

Arab Countries

Ahmad Rafiq Awad[1]

Ahmad Rafiq Awad[1]

INTRODUCTION

How did Arab writers and public figures read the great Indian poet Tagore? Did they associate him with the spirit of Sufism or with that of Romanticism? Did they consider him a revolutionary fighting the British colonial occupation or an educator with his own psychology and vision? What did they make of the religious views expressed in Tagore's works, views so significantly different from those in the Arab world? Did they scrutinise him methodically or were they enchanted by him to a degree that does not allow criticism? Is the influence of this poet perceptible in leading Arabic poets or artistic trends? Can we perceive any patterns in the Arabic reception?

In this essay, an attempt is made to answer these questions, both from a historical and a comparative perspective. This research does not claim to gather all the works produced by Arabs about Tagore but rather attempts to survey the most important reactions and to capture the images of the Indian poet formed over a century beyond the expressions of fascination or admiration.

Tagore's influence on the Arabs did not necessarily coincide with the times of writing about him. He was most influential between the two World Wars, whereas the time of extensive discourse on him came years after. The interwar period witnessed the formation of Arab literary circles aiming to change Arabic poetry both in content and in form. Such circles examined Tagore as a possible example of non-Western modernity. However, after World War II and the emergence of independent Arabic states, the literary focus shifted. Writings about Tagore and translations of his poems kept being published and reached out to a considerable readership.

Arab interest in Tagore does not take its origin in the Bengali poet's unique creative work but in the fascination with a person with whom Arab intellectuals found many similarities. Tagore was an innovative author coming from the East and provided a model of facing the Westerner and his culture without arrogance and prejudice. The Arabic reception of Tagore is free from big debates. Writers presented him in an idealised way without tying him to any ideology, without pointing out his technical faults, behavioural shortcomings or controversial Nationalistic position. He was a universal man and a poet calling for human love, a 'genius' or an international figure with 'special charm' or a 'neutral' international figure who cannot be used or employed by any party; thus he does not stir or provoke anybody at the political, sectarian or doctrinal level. Tagore's universality motivated several Arab countries to include the poet's works in school or university curricula.[2]

EARLY TRANSLATIONS

In 1941, the year in which Tagore passed away, the Egyptian poet Hussein Afif published a *diwan*[3], a poetry collection, entitled *Fragrance* and dedicated it to the memory of the Indian poet. This diwan, like Afif's other works, is permeated by Sufism and reflects the spirit of the East echoing Tagore and Omar Khayyam. It also contains emotional reflections on the essence of nature, on the charm of women as well as on the meaning of life and death in gentle 'rhyming prose' with balanced sentences, similes and metaphors.[4]

This tribute to the spirit of Tagore is indicative of the Arab, and especially the Egyptian, elite's appreciation of Tagore. Indeed, Tagore's fame in the Arab world goes back to 1913 when he received the Nobel Prize and intellectuals read his English *Gitanjali* or its French translation by André Gide published soon after.

The first Arab to translate Tagore was in all probability the Lebanese poet Wadi' al-Bustani (1886–1957), who, in 1914, travelled to India and stayed with Tagore for several days. The description of his journey appeared in 1916 and contained translations.[5] The first Tagore book appeared less than a decade later. It was *The Home and the World* translated by Tanius Abduh (Cairo: Dar al-Hilal, 1925). This was followed by Wadi' al-Bustani publishing 'al-Bustani' selections from *The Gardener* in the late 1920s. Tagore translations appeared in larger numbers from the 1940s starting with Muhammad Habib She'ran's *The Gardener* in 1940, followed by the European missionary, Father Johan Comair's (Yuhanna Qumayr) *Gitanjali* in 1948.[6]

VISITS

Egyptians were privileged to be introduced to the poet in person during his visit between 27 and 29 November in 1926, when Tagore met renowned

Egyptian poets and writers including 'the Prince of Arab Poets', Ahmad Shawqi, as well as Sa'd Zaghlul, Ahmad Lutfi al-Sayyid, Hafez Ibrahim, Muhammad Hussein Heikal and Abdul Aziz al-Bashri.[7] Celebrations for Tagore went to the extent of having the session of the Parliament postponed.[8] Newspapers wrote about him extensively emphasising his different achievements. Contributors on Tagore included famous intellectuals and reformers, such as Taha Hussein, al-Aqqad, al-Rafi'i, Hikel and al-Mazini.[9]

In 1932, Tagore visited another Arabic country, Iraq, and was received enthusiastically. He also met the country's leading poets, Jamil Sidqi al-Zahawi (1863–1936) and Maruf Rusafi (1875–1945), among others. They composed and recited poems for the Indian guest. Rusafi's poem went as follows:

To you Tagore I come   to tell the life and the story
You who said the truth   frankly and metaphorically
The rules of the past were   for the Hand of God has refined you.
  not mistaken

The following lines are by al-Zahawi:

Great poet peace upon you   from a lover of any of your poems
                                                            that follows
Peace upon you every day   and peace on you in every way
You are the essence that   as the sea in the essence of the pearls
  glues poems together
When you chant this poem   despite its proximity it is unattainable.[10]

EARLY RECEPTION IN PERSPECTIVE

It is clear that the Arab world discovered Tagore early and read his works first in English and French and then in Arabic. His fame between the two World Wars can be explained by a variety of reasons.

First, the Arab world in the interwar period witnessed rich and variegated cultural and political movements. Since most Arab lands were under British, French or Italian rule, the colonisers provided models to follow or to oppose and fight. Political and intellectual movements spearheaded Arab nationalism, Islamic unity or narrower doctrinal and sectarian thoughts. Tagore represented a different role model. He was also from the Orient under colonial rule and propagated adherence to local and national culture in the context of a global framework.

Second, English propaganda played a role in the marketing of Tagore. He was a colonial subject who achieved knighthood, the highest distinction within the empire. Since he was not an extreme nationalist, the British openly supported him during his stopovers in the Arab world, during which Tagore never spoke about actual political matters. Moreover, it was the moderate political and cultural elite who received him both in Egypt and Iraq. His literary or philosophic stand did not pose a political threat to anyone.

Third, debates on the renewal of Arabic literature were at their height during this time. While the diaspora poets (who lived mostly in Latin America) freed Arabic poetry from its formal fetters and limitations, the Diwan School wanted to renew the content while maintaining the old forms, but the Apollo group, of whom Afif was a key figure, active in the late 1920s and early 1930s, tried to renew both. At the time of these debates, numerous translations of English and French works appeared and Western literary schools, such as Symbolism and Romanticism, exercised great influence. Tagore's poetry resonated with debates on modernity among Arab litterateurs and found admirers especially among the Apollo group. Tagore's interest in the major questions of human existence, his adoration of nature and women and his appreciation of both sensual and spiritual delights coincided with the interests and sensibilities of the Apollo group.

Fourth, the period witnessed major intellectual conflicts between science and faith, between the secular and the religious state, especially in terms of secular law and Sharia. (These debates still resonate today.) Tagore's works offered a compromise. It is not a coincidence that studies on Tagore at that period portrayed him as a person of spiritual Sufi experience.[11] His religion of love is one of the prime solutions to futile and never-ending debates on nationalism, ethnicity, religion and the relations with the intruder from the West.

Fifth, Tagore himself was an 'Oriental' and his culture and poetic world were not too distant from those of the region. His love for nature, his universal religion, his reformist vision, his 'moderate' political stand and the recognition of the West, all formed a model for Arab intellectuals at that time. Since Arab intellectuals were not culturally isolated they exercised a true Gramscian 'hegemony' beyond borders. Just like Tagore, they were not marginalised but were involved in action and writing. Tagore's Nobel Prize was perceived as a victory of the East over the West. Writings on Tagore lacked critical analysis; instead, essays and translations were produced in a language of celebration and glorification.

Lastly, the colonial rule imposed the English language in education and administration. Many intellectuals and reformers interacted with English culture. Reading Tagore was one of the fruits of this process. Tagore's translations in the Arab world till this day are made from English and not from the original Bengali writings.

THE MULTIPLE READING PHASE

After the Revolution of the Free Officers in Egypt in 1952 and the success of a number of liberation movements, the Arab countries entered a new stage of political, cultural and intellectual challenges. The success of the national bourgeoisie and the military troops in expelling foreign occupants had a significant impact on the adoption of Communistic or Nationalistic ideologies in particular. Engagement with Tagore was bound to be over since his thoughts did not meet the needs of Arabs searching to reconcile the conflicting ideologies of Communism, Islam and Nationalism.

However, a different interest was kindled after the birth of the Non-Aligned Movement and the emergence of independent India on the scene of global politics. Interest of Arab intellectuals in the heritage and culture of India was the result of India's spectacular success in obtaining independence, allegedly via an almost miraculous passive resistance under the legendary figure of M. K. Gandhi. A particularly good relationship was established between the Egyptian leader Gamal Abdel-Nasser and the Indian Prime Minister Jawaharlal Nehru. Both were popular and represented a ray of hope for the 'Third World' which stood up to Western domination. It was now clear that these Oriental countries produced personalities of global significance. Many turned towards Tagore as one of the great Indians with whom they had already been to some extent familiar.

The 1950s and 1960s were fruitful periods for studying Tagore. The volume *Tagore in the Centenary of his Birth* was a collection of seven essays by leading Egyptian intellectuals and published from the Egyptian Ministry of Education. A detailed survey of that book can be found in the essay on the Egyptian reception in this volume. That compilation has been so influential that a collection of essays published from Damascus in 2010 claimed to be its new edition.[12]

In 1961, Muhammad Shukri Ayyad, an Arabic language professor at the University of Cairo, produced his study on *Tagore, the Poet of Love and Peace*.[13] It was also about this time that the Egyptian critic Abdul Aziz al-Zaki wrote extensively on Tagore as an artist with a Sufi vision.[14]

In 1966, Hosni Friz translated Krishna Kripalani's biography entitled *Tagore: A Genius that Inspired the East and the West*.[15] Friz in the introduction expressed his dissatisfaction with the Tagore material available in Arabic and gave this as a reason for translating the book:

> What I know about Tagore is unconvincing and unsatisfactory, there are only some pieces that do not represent the poet, novelist, storyteller, playwright, musician, painter and his social world.[16]

NEW TRANSLATIONS

Translations and studies in the 1950s and 1960s were characterised by more in-depth discussions and a new engagement with the poet and his achievements. Badi Haqqi (b. 1922), a Syrian diplomat, novelist and translator, who among other things rendered Gogol's short stories into Arabic, published his translations of *Fruit-Gathering* and *Gitanjali* in 1955.[17] In 1958, he added to these his Arabic versions of *The Gardener, The Crescent Moon* and *Chitra*.[18] In the same year, Father Ayyub Falluh published another translation of *Fruit-Gathering*, which, following the French version, *Corbeille de Fruits*, is titled *The Fruit Basket*.[19]

In 1967, Father Johan Comair published a book entitled *Tagore: Theatre and Poetry*, prepared to mark the twenty-fifth anniversary of the poet's death.[20] He gave his own reasons for the translation, saying:

Who is more suited for translation than Tagore, the embodiment of pleasure, charming you with his poetry and art, embodying the richness of India, tasting the poetic spirit of the West, and conscious of all circumstances of the meeting of the East and the West in a deep human embrace.[21]

In his book, Comair noted that up to 1967, fifteen books of Tagore translations and five studies had been published in Arabic.[22] Dr Yahya al-Khashab observed in 1961 that Tagore's works were represented by Tahir al-Jabalawi's *The Crescent Moon, Lover's Gift* and *Sadhana, the Realisation of Life*. To these were added translations by Muhammad Badr al-Din Khalil and Muhammad Abdul Ghafur al-Attar's *Red Lilies* (i.e., Tagore's *Red Oleanders*).[23]

VARIATIONS ON TRANSLATION

When the poem *The Mother and her Child* caught the attention of the notable Lebanese poet Halim Damus (1888–1957), he prepared a prose translation from the French and published it in the newspaper *Falasteen (Palestine)* asking Arab poets to rewrite it in a poetic manner.[24] Several translations were produced on this occasion including those of two Tagore experts, Muhammad Shukri Ayyad and Badi Haqqi. Following the English original, Ayyad entitled it *The Beginning*, while Haqqi kept the same title but drastically differed in the translation. The recourse to the original English title makes it clear that both translators consulted the English version. The concluding lines of that version are as follows:

Heaven's first darling, twin-born with the morning light, you have floated down the stream of the world's life, and at last you have stranded on my heart.

As I gaze on your face, mystery overwhelms me; you who belong to all have become mine.

For fear of losing you I hold you tight to my breast. What magic has snared the world's treasure in these slender arms of mine?

Ayyad's Arabic version is close to the original:

You are the beloved of the sky, the morning light's twin, you floated on the life of the world streams, then you landed in my heart.

When I look into your face I am overwhelmed with a mystery: you who belong to The All,

I have fear to hold you to my heart. What magic caught the treasure of the world in my slender arms?[25]

Badi Haqqi's translation uses language to a higher poetic effect:

You the first beloved of the sky, you the morning ray's twin, you were swept by the current of the universe's life until you finally landed in my heart.

While I was glancing at your face, while the ambiguity was covering me, you became, you who belongs to everyone, a king for me.

For fear of losing you, I pull and draw you to my chest. What could be the magic that donated the treasure of the world to my slender arms.[26]

Muhammad Tahir al-Jabalawi's translation of the last two lines is more pantheistic:

If I look at you I am overcome by all those hidden secrets that made you mine, you who has connecting ties with everything in life

I hold you to my chest as I so much fear for you, what could be the magic that put you in my slender arms

Life's precious treasure.[27]

Did the Arab translators, whether Muslim or Christian, avoid references to symbols of religious connotation because of reticence or because of a desire to simplify the poem?

Apart from differences in the style of the Arab translations over the decades, there are also differences in the titles of poems or books, the order of poems and their contents.[28] Translators normally start from scratch and do not make use of previous translations, and they either include or exclude their own interpretations. For example, Dr Abdul Wahid Lu'lua states in the introduction of his translation of Tagore (1995):

> There are metaphors and references to some cultural, religious or philosophical matters that we must [avoid], and many translators become traitors. However, I tried my best to evade this charge though I may have hidden a line here or there, and I crossed over a whole poem as it may [hurt] the religious feeling of the Muslim.[29]

This may be the first admission that translators overlooked or evaded whatever could embarrass or injure religious sensibilities.

This evasive style intended to cover up may also account for the tolerance and fascination with the character of the poet. It may also be linked to the desire of some to present a poet who has understood the truth of existence and the eternal one God. In their study of Tagore's religion, the critics Abdul Aziz al-Zaki and Muhammad Shukri Ayyad focus on his 'Pantheism', an idea present in Islamic philosophy.[30]

Differences in the translations of Tagore's poetry may go back to differences in the temperament of the translators, in the extent of mastering their source language as well as in their religious preferences and in those of the publishing houses. Arabic interpretation of Tagore is primarily characterised by impressionism, haste, and selectiveness. Interpretations, however, were far from static and differed according to the time of the readings.

In the 1930s, particularly in Egypt, a kind of political and social liberalism allowed one to read Tagore as a romantic rebel and an authentic reformist. This was later reflected in the poetry of the Apollo group and marked the readings of Tagore in the 1950s and 1960s as a symbol of the East that was able to invade the West through its creativity and art. Tagore at that period was perceived as a symbol of the victory of the 'Third World' over the colonisers. It admitted that Tagore was complex but, in the end, he was not a poet or reformer from the colonial Western world.

BACK TO TAGORE

Interest in Tagore subsided after the 1960s. Important publications in the 1970s were limited to the sixth enlarged edition of Badi Haqqi's translations and to a study of Ayyad published as a small booklet with a modest print-run. At the end of the decade, Abdul Aziz Alzaki published several studies of Tagore in literary journals from Kuwait.

However, at the beginning of the 1990s, attention was renewed again. It is at that time that the Egyptian Muhammad Shukri Ayyad collected his earlier essays and translations of Tagore.[31] The Saudi diplomat, writer and poet Abdul Rahman al-Ghazi al-Gosaibi also translated a selection from Tagore's poetry.[32] He searched in Tagore for thoughts similar to his own ideas and went as far as mimicking Tagore in his book *Sparks*.

In 1995, the Cultural Centre in Abu Dhabi published a translation of *My Reminiscences*.[33] The same year also saw the publication of the volume entitled *Books that Changed the Human Thought*, which included a lengthy study of Tagore's works that made a significant impact on literature in East and West.[34] The author presented Tagore's life, works, personality, relationships, travels, and his literary, artistic and political influence. This was also illustrated in Abdul Wahid Lu'lua's translations. At the end of the 1990s, the Cairo journal *Viewpoints* reviewed Amartya Sen's article 'Tagore and his India.'[35]

In 2000, the Supreme Council of Culture in Cairo published Muhammad Shukri Ayyad's selected writings on Tagore in a single volume arranged in three sections, under the title *In the World of Tagore, Tagore, the Poet of Love and Peace, The Home and the World*.[36] In the same year, in Beirut, Professor Joseph Elias (b. 1939), from the Lebanese University, prepared an annotated edition of Badi Haqqi's *The Fruit Basket (Fruit-Gathering)* accompanied with a study.[37] In Damascus, Farid al-Shahf and Thair Zain al-Din published their translation of the novel *The Last Poem*.[38] The Jordanian historian Ali al-Muhafatha in his book *Characters from History* presented Tagore as an influential historical figure.[39] The large centenary volume, *Tagore, the Inspiring Indian Poet*, was also re-edited by Muhammad Sayyid al-Tahiri from Damascus (see below).

Recent translations are characterised by special attention to accuracy in regard to the original English. Translations are also more exhaustive, as, instead of excerpts, they are now given in full. Critical studies on Tagore became scarce and authors were satisfied by presenting him in a sketchy form. However, previous essays were reprinted. The decision of the Supreme Council for Culture in Egypt to publish the complete works of the critic Muhammad Shukri Ayyad on Tagore is an indication that scholarly discourse on the poet had largely ceased.

It may be mentioned here that the concerns and issues of Arab poetry in the past forty years were far from Tagore's world and, besides, the status of poetry declined significantly.

Muhammad Shukri Ayyad, the Eminent Tagore Scholar

There is no Arabic critic dedicated to Tagore more than the Egyptian scholar Muhammad Shukri Ayyad (1921–99). His Tagore scholarship was bolstered by his thorough study of Hinduism. His critical writings are the most profound and comprehensive of all Arabic studies and his views still dominate the Arab perception of Tagore.

Ayyad had an interest in the Indian poet over an extended period. His article from 1961, *The Theory of Criticism by Tagore*, was included in the volume *The Hundredth Birth Anniversary of Tagore*. In the same year he published a book entitled *Tagore, the Poet of Love and Peace*, which later was included in his book: *Between Philosophy and Criticism* (1990).

In his article, *The Theory of Criticism by Tagore*, Ayyad stated that the difficulty in determining the theory of criticism of the poet comes from Tagore's own intellectual approach:[40]

> Tagore hates the notion of defining things. What Tagore wrote on the notion of criticism is very vast, however we do not find in it a definition of what Art is, as we also cannot conclude from his works a secure definition for the word Art, because we would have planted on his thinking a framework of our own making, and if Tagore was willing to put such a framework to define his idea he would have done that, but he avoided it deliberately.[41]

Eventually, Ayyad stated that Tagore used metaphors rather than definitions. Unlike most researchers, he did not confine himself to reasoning but relied on his artistic taste or intuition and concluded that 'Tagore's thinking in the matters that fall under the theory of criticism [shows] the thoughts of a poet.'[42] Despite its ambiguities, the critic summarised the theory of criticism of the poet:

> Tagore's theory of criticism is strongly linked to his view of existence on the one hand, and to his artistic practice, on the other. For him, the theory of criticism starts with distinguishing art from entertainment. Art is the expression of our own emotions transcending our personality (*shakhsiyat*), while expression of emotions has no artistic value when it only relates to the personal. One's personality is both the foundation of awareness and its limit. The world is a personal being and each limit in it reflects the unlimited. The sense of beauty is the sense of feeling this harmony in the created world. Art is the expression of the extension of our personality—in freedom and love—to realise the unlimited in the limited.[43]

He refers again to the ambiguity in Tagore's ideas of criticism concerning truth and beauty:

> The truth sought by science, philosophy and ethics is the law in the physical world or within ourselves; while the beauty that is expressed

in art is the harmony which is the spirit of that law. He confirms in other domains that the questions of science are different from the realities belonging to the domain of the art, because the issues of science have intermediate neutral scopes that have nothing to do with our character. The realities revealed by art are the essential truths that express the contact of our character with that of the world. In other domains, Tagore indicates that science is not materialistic as it seems because in truth it is only an expression of the freedom of humans in dealings with nature. And in other topics also, he decides that the issues of science and philosophy can be artistic when they lose their abstract character and become personal.[44]

Tagore stated about his play *The Revenge of Nature* that 'its theme ... revolves around all my writings: the pleasure of achieving the unlimited within the limited.' Relying on this, Ayyad concluded that art for Tagore was 'an expression of harmony between the unlimited and the limited.' This is the basic idea, which Ayyad repeated in everything he wrote about Tagore.

The book *Tagore, the Poet of Love and Peace* (1961) is, admittedly, a 'biography of ideas and not a biography of events.' Through understanding the environment, culture and events in which Tagore lived, it is possible to understand the poet's intellectual attitudes, themes and style. Ayyad's critical methodology is close to the social approach, in which the artistic text is part of its environment, an offspring of its culture and a natural result of the surrounding challenges. Consequently, Ayyad surveyed the history of Bengal in general and of the Tagore family in particular. He also focused on Hinduism, which he called 'Brahmanist religion', the reformist movements within it, the role of the poet's family in the reforms and the impact of the British colonisation on India. Ayyad made an in-depth study of Tagore's use of ancient religious texts. Within this framework, he examined what was innovative in Tagore. He explained that in his early phase Tagore tried to avoid the limitations of both an abstract religion and of humanitarian concerns. Consequently he imbibed influences from Vaishnava folk poetry on the one hand and from his father, who was known to him for his correctional attitude, on the other.[45]

According to Ayyad:

Tagore was a disciple of the Vaishnava poets, who considered human love a way to worship the absolute. Our poet expanded even further his faith, which at the same time became poetic sensitivity. As the absolute and the partial, the ideal and the real, the essence and the figure that is depicted by this essence are always found in Tagore's sense for life, and they blend in what resembles a harmonic music. This is one of the sources of the extraordinary simplicity that we find in his poetry. In his soul, there is no conflict that arises from the contradiction between the real and the ideal, but there is—in the pace of this conflict—a kind of nostalgia or longing linking reality and image—within the terminology of Sufism. It is a longing that never rests but never reaches the limit of torment, because the ends of the reality and the ideal meet and harmonise without one losing itself in the other. This is why the poet loves the resonance of this harmony as it is reality, and not the impact that it makes. This strange essence that tells everything, and this resonance—this strange essence—is the same *Fugitive* as he mentions it in one of his poems later; because he never sees or touches it, although we feel it everywhere and find it in everything. This idea almost becomes the key to all of Tagore's works, or at least this is what the poet is telling us himself in his reminiscences [on] his play entitled *The Revenge [of Nature]*: 'The theme around which all my writing focuses is the pleasure of reaching the unlimited in the limited.'[46]

Ayyad considered the idea of conflict in Tagore's plays a Western concept. However, Tagore also presented a conflict of another kind in a 'smooth liquid movement linking the limited to the unlimited.'[47]

Ayyad's observations also ended a controversy about Tagore. Establishing harmony between the reality and the imaginary and the replacement of the concept of conflict with that of fluidity are ideas familiar to Islamic culture, which aims at replacing the idea of violating the world with that of being a partner. This culture also replaced the idea of separating oneself from any subject crossing our paths with the possibility of a convergence through revelation and the holy scripture (the Holy Qur'an) with a total rejection of pantheism.[48]

By this Ayyad meant that even if pantheism is totally rejected and monotheism is kept, one could find a smooth harmony in the convergence of the universalism between all. This may explain the desire of some Arab intellectuals, whether Muslims or Christians, to portray Tagore as a believer in 'One God', a worshipper of a God who is no different from the God known in the Middle East.[49]

Dr Ayyad's writings discussed the poet's art, philosophy, social and political views as well as his relationship to Sufism. All subsequent scholarship drew on his statements. A good example is Abdul Aziz al-Zaki who had a sustained interest in Tagore. He summarised his earlier studies on Tagore in 1977 under the title *Tagore the Artist*. Zaki stated that 'the first task of the

artist is to find the latent truth in the existence, then display it in an artistic
way to reveal it to all people.'[50]

Regarding the doctrine of Tagore's Hindu pantheism, the critic claimed:

> Tagore doesn't only follow Sufism or respond to the calls of the scholars
> of religion but he believed in it through personal experience, which
> started as a sense of intimacy between himself, nature and the people,
> then as fascination with the beauty of nature and of the human being,
> and culminated in the realisation of the existence of an embodied
> truth in the various races linking them in one comprehensive, spiritual
> unity.[51]

This is not different from Hindu or Sufi pantheism, especially as the
critic does not explain what the 'intimacy' is that links nature and people.
(In contrast, Dr Ayyad's theory of the poet's search for the unlimited within
the limited appears to stand firmer.) Yet, the critic Abdul Aziz al-Zaki came
back to find the difference, stating, after several paragraphs that the poet 'was
not able to distinguish between the object of his worship and the subject of
his art.'[52] The critic highlighted the 'moment of revelation' that pushes the
poet into this position.[53] He also tried to pinpoint Tagore the reformist who
rebelled against ancient traditions and propagated a new religion and who was
reluctant to participate in the popular national action 'because nationalism
incites hatred and chaos and calls for more violence.'[54] According to al-Zaki
the aim of Tagore's innovative work is only

> ... to highlight his deep, pantheistic faith as the basis of Hinduism and
> the most wonderful belief cherished by Indians. We are not surprised,
> when we see Tagore dedicating his various artistic talents to burn the
> brightest incenses at the altar of his faith for the unity of God, man and
> the universe in one spiritual harmony.[55]

This concept of pantheism was rejected by Ayyad saying that the
imaginary and the real are in harmony but not in unity. The critic al-Zaki
stated this idea again and tries, based on it, to interpret all of Tagore's work,
and ends by saying:

> The poet frequently talked about the similarity between the
> philosophical concepts of the real and the imaginary revolving
> around pantheism, and he succeeded in adding to the Sufi idea an
> effluent vitality and vivid transparency, but his role stopped at this
> level. People drifted from his poetry because of the boredom arising
> from the monotony of the content. His ideas are repeated over and
> over again despite their different forms.[56]

The Essays in *Tagore, the Inspiring Indian Poet* (2010)

The book edited by the Iranian Muhammad Sayyid al-Tahiri under the title *Tagore, the Inspiring Indian Poet* was published in 2010 from Damascus.[57] It claims to be the second edition of the 1961 Cairo volume *Tagore in the Centenary of his Birth* but has been enlarged with various Arab contributions. The editor also added several photographs of the poet, his family and his theatrical plays. The volume contains eighteen essays out of which only three (those by Muhammad Lutfi Fam, Muhammad Shukri Ayyad and Muhammad Kamel al-Nahhas) were present in the 1961 volume. The others seem to have been produced over the subsequent half-century but not necessarily for the 2010 edition. For example, the volume includes an essay by Sayyid Qutb (1906–66) written much earlier.

In this book, Mir Basri, a leading Jewish intellectual from Iraq, presented a new Tagore, not the poet of love and peace and of Sufism.

> He tried with his words and actions to erase the impurities that had stuck to Brahmanism, condemned by most Indians, to raise the standard of living of the people, to safeguard them from ignorance and idleness and to remove the differences that separate the Indian classes, which have their toll and paralyse national and patriotic life.[58]

Basri's ideas of class differences, social justice and combating poverty and ignorance are part of a terminology influenced by Marxist thought especially appealing in the 1960s. The writer also tried to see in Tagore a religious reformer:

> He released his father's and ancestors' religion from the chains of dissonance and disbelief, and enriched it with a new trend that provides its followers with a space to absorb the modern world civilisation and elevate them at the same time to the highest of spiritual meditation and intellectual effort.[59]

This discourse does not really differ from the debates of the Arab intellectuals in that period, searching for an intellectual formulation of progress. Facing the dilemma of Communism and Islam, they claimed that the two do not contradict each other but coalesce into an 'Arab Communism.'

The Egyptian Sayyid Qutb, famed for his writings on the Holy Qur'an, highly appreciated Tagore's works.[60]

He wrote about Tagore in an impressionistic way:

> Within my hands is his small diwan called *The Gardener* rich with eighty-five celestial chants, simple and deep written in an English resembling that of a child yet with elevated emotions. In this diwan,

Tagore seems to be a Divine Child, lisping and transcending to the heavens.[61]

Sayyid Qutb also discussed the artistic value of Tagore's poems:

The human emotions in him are as they are, experiences, palpitations and flashes. One can imagine them as moments of life lived according to internal instincts, hidden acclaim, approbations and implicit chills, not according to artistic assortment, intellectual measure or an expressive design.[62]

We can observe here how Qutb relies on his first impressions. He insists that Tagore's poems are devoid of any 'focus or consistent mental awareness.'[63] For this reason, he believes that the poems abound in

free and transparent human emotions, which are not bound by environmental limits or the circumstances of time and place. They have not been washed by intellectual thoughts or sensory barriers but injected with a tolerant Indian Sufism in its highest and purest ideals.[64]

Qutb's essay was not published in the 1961 volume. Even if he had written it before, it is astonishing that these words emanate from an Islamic thinker regarded as an extremist towards the end of his life, which ended five years later.

Abdul Hamid Farahat, an Egyptian critic, claimed that Tagore worked all his life for universalism and compared his universalism to that proposed in Bertrand Russell's *Common Sense and Nuclear Warfare* (1959) in terms of the emergence of a world government.[65] Tagore invited people to a holistic world, which is 'soft, delicate, sensitive and commended by love, tolerance and sacrifice in the framework of full conviction.'[66] The idea of universalism proposed by Tagore, as posited by Farahat, stands on the basis of love. According to Tagore love is 'the good white horse', the initiator of self-commitment, which is the first step towards world citizenship.[67] The author continues to talk about love with the thought that human behaviour should be far from becoming a slave to different influences of civilisation.

The writer did not refrain from elevated phraseology in interpreting Tagore, stating:

The call of Tagore for the universal man was a natural reaction to the current circumstances of the world. At a time that nationalism was tearing Europe apart, there came Tagore to announce that the individual human being was above all nationalisms and was more noble than any of them. For him, a human is semi-sacred.[68]

The writer expressed his fascination for the charismatic Indian poet and concluded:

> [Tagore's] doctrine accommodates the whole world, his land is the mind, his sky is the spirit, and the human being in this philosophical context is the subject, the means and the end.[69]

The Egyptian critic and poet Abdul Rahman Shalash discussed Tagore's short stories:

> [They] derive from a material taken mostly from the reality of life in his time. He was not inclined to give a fictional image to his works, but rather his emotions were real and his visions clear.[70]

The questions of realism and commitment of the artist were some of the issues that concerned Arab intellectuals in the 1950s and 1960s due to the influence of both the Marxist and Existentialist philosophies. Accordingly, Shalash explaining Tagore's realism, pointed out that:

> The literary does not emerge from a void but is the creation of one's era. Tagore was the product of the age in which he lived and of the environment from which he derived his topics expressing its concerns and aspirations. There is nothing new without the old. In our perception, Tagore was a new extension of former poets of his land and literature. His faith in the authentic Indian heritage and in the achievements of Indian civilisation was so firm that he lent himself as the image of an ancient nation.[71]

The writer, Yahya al-Khashab, from Egypt wrote that Arab interest in Tagore was the result of the Arab nation 'looking for a new philosophy that promotes the morale from within.'[72] He believed that Tagore was one of the global thinkers, 'a modern successor of the ancient Aristotle.'[73] However, the critic does not elaborate the similarity between the two men except for their opening new schools to reform education. The critic also tried to find a connection between Tagore and Islamic culture. He wrote of the possibility of Tagore being influenced by Sufis, such as Hafez Shirazi and Jalaluddin Rumi. One can find both 'the negativity of Hafez and the positivity of Rumi in Tagore's poems.'[74] It is not surprising that the critic concludes his article in a pure Islamic manner: 'God have mercy on Tagore's soul and avail people in his realm.'

Dr Muhammad Lutfi Fam wrote about Tagore's relationship with the West. He portrayed Tagore as the man of travel, of reading and learning and an advocate of science. With a penetrating sight, Tagore discovered the misery of the West, its savagery, its contempt for mankind and its sanctification of the material. The critic quotes Tagore saying at his Visva-Bharati University that 'in order to seek perfection, we have to be primitive in our vigour, civilised in our minds and thoughts.'[75]. He tries to portray Tagore as a man of politics who understands international relations, willing to protect his country from the influence of the global forces that deprive his country from its ability to solve its problems.[76] The critic emphasised that Tagore maintained a centrist approach combining national and international interests. He tried to explain in detail his approach in many of his works, especially in the novel *The Home and the World* published in 1918 (*sic!*). Was the moderation which the critic Fam talked about another expression of Non-alignment, which as a political movement reached its peak in the 1960s?

The critic Ali Shalash from Egypt stated that Tagore was 'the most accepted Asiatic modernist for the Arab intellectuals' since his poetry resembles in its form and content those of Arab poetry characterised by elevated meanings, imagination and intellectual depth.[77] He praised Tagore's love beyond the limits of time and space and summarised his opinion as follows: '... for me Tagore is the poet of love and wisdom before being the poet of peace and ... humanity.'[78]

The Egyptian, Muhammad Shukri Ayyad, was one of the most important Arab critics interested in Tagore. His study from the 1961 volume, *The Theory of Criticism by Tagore*, was reproduced in the 2010 book and has been discussed above.

Another study from the 1961 volume is of the Egyptian Muhammad Kamel al-Nahhas's writing on Tagore the educator. Nahhas discussed the poet's ideas that he implemented within his school, which envisions an education 'deeply rooted in one's immediate surroundings but connected to the cultures of the wider world, predicated upon pleasurable learning and individualised to the personality of the child'. The writer underlined Tagore's granting freedom to students to identify and learn through personal experience, renouncing religious or national extremism, his rejection of the educational curricula taken from the West and teaching the National Language as a substitute for foreign languages. By doing this, Tagore did not promote isolation, but intended to not allow foreign education to fill entirely the national mind thus killing creative opportunities for inherent intellectual powers.[79]

The author pointed out that Tagore praised Islam as an advancing culture fully integrated in the Indian life because of 'the flow of knowledge, abundance of feelings and the great democratic spirituality.'[80]

The writer addressed the 'Communism' of Tagore which he advocated within his school, in addition to the respect of freedom and love. He also emphasised the importance of basing education on national heritage. The words of this critic suggest a genuine Oriental experience as a substitute for ideas implemented in Egypt and other Arabic countries. The writer does not hide his admiration for the Tagorean experience and insinuates the possibility of implementing it in the Arab world. It is worth mentioning that education in most Arab countries has been overhauled after they gained independence in the 1950s and 1960s.

The Lebanese Fuad Jabbur wrote that Tagore was 'an ardent patriot but his nationalism was actually his human feeling applied to India.'[81] Thus, the writer tried to balance Tagore's concern for the universal and the local. He stated that Tagore's philosophy emerges from the heart of the Indian philosophy and he considers it 'one of the ingenuities of the East.'[82]

The other Lebanese writer, Raymond Francis, is unique in his ambiguous approach to Tagore. After expressing his deep admiration for the poet, he writes that 'an abundant number of Tagore's poems revolve around the same ideas to the point of affecting the reader with some sort of boredom.'[83]

From Iraq, Harith Taha al-Rawi portrays Tagore as a revolutionary nationalist fighting British occupation, and as the first Oriental thinker to transfer to the West the virtues of the East.[84] The writer describes Tagore's visit to Iraq in 1932, where Iraqi poets and intellectuals bestowed upon him titles such as 'the great poet of the East and the great guest of Iraq', 'the messenger of culture and the poet of wisdom and beauty', 'the unrivalled philosopher and upholder of human science and of the banner of justice and a representative of the Highest Spirit' and 'the Prince of the Universal Declaration'. The writer quotes a part of a speech delivered by Tagore before a gathering of the Iraqi elite, saying:

> I hereby come to you asking God to unite us to fight the danger of mutual suspicion, to fight the hypocrisy of international politics that tears the heart of civilian lives ... the brightest eras of your glorious history have spread the sovereignty of the Arabian Peninsula over half of the world in East and West and still exercise influence on the spiritual and intellectual life of India due to the presence of a great number of people of Islamic origin among us.[85]

Leila Sabbagh, a scholar from Damascus University, reiterated some general statements about Tagore, quoting Western scholars.

The Syrian author, Dr Badi al-Qasm, wrote that although Tagore himself stated during his visit to Cairo in 1926 that he was not a philosopher, he was a philosopher par excellence. Dr Qasm claimed that Tagore was 'a poet and a philosopher and a prophet all at once', since 'a poet in Indian culture is not confined to the expression of beauty.'[86] Dr Qasm considered that Tagore's philosophy was summarised in the book *Sadhana* which represents the 'liberation of the human soul from its limitations to fly towards its perfection and reach its place in the arms of the Deity.'[87] He also explains how Tagore's philosophical ideas coincide with those of Hegel, Berkeley, Bergson and Darwin. This, however, does not mean that Tagore adopted them into his philosophy since he rather relied on personal experience. So far Dr Qasm's view is reminiscent of that of Ayyad. However, he further comments:

> It might be said that the philosophy of Tagore is in the end no more than a masterful interpretation of the ancient Indian religion, trying to bring it closer to other religions and making it accept the positive elements of Western thought.[88]

It is worth mentioning that most Arab writers did not avoid the question of the relationship between Tagore's compositions and their religious references. They discussed those references with great tolerance. Moreover, Arab Christian writers readily identified Tagore's call for forgiveness, brotherhood and love with Christian ideals. Perhaps this was the reason behind the willingness of Christian intellectuals—including priests and monks—to translate Tagore at an early stage, along with the fact that they were the first to master foreign languages because of their contacts with missionaries and missionary schools.

One of the outstanding Arab translators of Tagore, the Lebanese Dr Badi Haqqi, writes that Tagore 'goes beyond wording, melody and meaning in his poetry to bring a message similar in its nobility to the message of the great intellectual reformists.'[89]

Najat Kassab Hassan presented Tagore as a holistic artist who was musician, storyteller, satirical writer, painter and playwright at the same time, concluding that 'perhaps Tagore was the perfect model of an artist in the history of mankind, because he was a full man.'[90] Her writing is an example of complete admiration for the poet avoiding any attempt to criticise him or scrutinise his work.

The writer Ahmad Fares in his article underlined the revolutionary aspect of Tagore and his fight against British colonisation.

The desire to turn Tagore into a revolutionary was not far from the general mood in the Arab world in the 1950s and 1960s when the struggle was at its highest against British and French colonisers. Ahmad Fares wanted to see the Indian poet 'standing alongside the popular revolt for freedom and raising his voice high in condemning oppression and occupation.'[91] He tried to read all the work of Tagore from a revolutionary standpoint and he stated that 'the realistic ideas of Tagore are of relatively pure social and educational context.'[92] Fares went on to say:

Tagore's nationalistic poetry has undergone major changes due to his disappointment with the principle of non-violence. Therefore, we can note sometimes the agitated and poetic images and dreams with the romantic tendencies in order to destroy the wrong, the violent and the evil from the face of the earth, as in the poem 'Seasons of The Year'.[93]

There is no doubt that Tagore was an Indian nationalist, but not as Ahmad Fares wanted to portray him. In a different book, Krishna Kripalani was more accurate when he compared Tagore and Gandhi, stating:

[P]erhaps it is not possible for two people to be this different, again, it is from the richness of the Indian cultural geniality, this geniality implanted from the past, that it was able to raise in the same generation two artistic models, in all possible ways. Yet they represent different views of the character of India with its many aspects.[94]

Dr Amir Bikatar presented Tagore the teacher, reiterating an earlier statement saying that the basis of education for Tagore can be summarised in freedom, creative expression through art, workmanship, direct contact with nature and direct relation with human social life.[95] Dr Bikatar did not discuss these ideas in terms of applicability but in a spirit of welcoming and admiration.

Portraying Tagore and considering him a creative son of the East was the focus of Abdul Latif Sharara's article.

CONCLUSION

While Tagore exercised great influence on poetry and poets in the Arab world between the two World Wars, artists' interest in him gave way to more scholarly studies and his popularity came to a low ebb as historical events overtook his world. Despite that, his name and fame are still present in the Arab world, his works keep being published and references to his poems can be found in contemporary poetry. For example, in the mid-1990s, a leading Palestinian poet Mahmud Darwish wrote in one of his poems included in his book *Why Did You Leave the Horse Alone*:

A necklace of one of Tagore's [poor]
Is crushed by the carts of the handsome prince.

This is a reference to *The Gardener* VII:

I swept aside the veil from my face, I tore the ruby chain from my neck and flung it in his path.
Why do you look at me amazed, mother?

I know well he did not pick up my chain; I know it was crushed under his wheels leaving a red stain upon the dust, and no one knows what my gift was nor to whom.

The quantity of Arabic Tagore translations is less than enough to judge the poet properly. The various translations were normally selective, presented individual interpretations and were isolated from one another. In-depth and methodological studies were remarkably few. Secondary literature described the poet as 'a genius of the East', 'a Sufi poet' or a 'Romantic'. Sometimes even straightforwardly contradictory ideas appeared about the poet who was presented both as a mystic and a socialist, as a nationalist or a universalist. It was only after the centenary celebrations that important studies started to appear, especially those of Shukri Ayyad, that gave a balanced picture of the great Indian poet. Although his interpretations varied in different periods, Tagore has been a lasting presence in Arabic culture.

NOTES

1. This essay in Arabic was translated at the request of Professor Sari Nusseibeh by Ms Sulafa S. Musallam. Note that Arabic works will be referred to by their English titles as they appear in the *Works Cited* section.
2. In 1997, the educational curricula in Lebanon adopted *Fruit-Gathering* for the third secondary year and justified the choice saying that this collection came to 'develop the literary culture of the learner through the identification of masterpieces of world literature with humanitarian tendency'. (Tagore, *Fruit-Gathering*, tr. Badi Haqqi, 5.) The Ministry of Education in the United Arab Republic (of Egypt and Syria between 1958 and 1961) also commissioned the translation of five Tagore poems and included them in school curricula. In 1966, the Jordanian Ministry of Education commissioned Hosni Friz's translation of Krishna Kripalani's monograph under the title *Tagore, the Genius that Inspired East and West*. For more information, see Yahya al-Khashab, 'Tagore' in al-Tahiri, *Tagore, the Inspiring Indian Poet*, 40.
3. Hussein Afif (1902–79) was a member of the Apollo group since its creation in 1930. For more information, see Sakkut, *Dictionary of Modern Arab Literature*, 2, 182.
4. Ibid., 182.
5. For further details on al-Bustani's first contacts with Tagore, see the article on the Egyptian reception.
6. Harith Taha al-Rawi, 'Tagore in Bagdad,' in *Tagore, the Inspiring Indian Poet* by al-Tahiri, 200; Tagore, *Song Offerings*, tr. Father Johan Comair.
7. Ali Shalash, 'Origin and Homeland,' in al-Tahiri, *Tagore, the Inspiring Indian Poet*, 116.
8. Ibid., 117.

9. The literary figures mentioned above are the most famous Arab writers and reformers. They have created innovative, critical writing styles, followed by many later writers. For more, see Fakhuri, *History of Arab Literature*.

10. Harith Taha al-Rawi, 'Tagore in Bagdad,' in *Tagore, the Inspiring Indian Poet* by al-Tahiri, 208.

11. For example, al-Manjuri, *Tagore: Spiritual Unity* was one of the first and most important books that saw in Tagore the advocate of a religion of love who addressed all continents regardless of colour, race and culture.

12. al-Tahiri, *Tagore, the Inspiring Indian Poet*. See the last part of this essay for a discussion of that book.

13. Ayyad, *Tagore, the Poet of Love and Peace*.

14. The critic's works (all published from Cairo) include 'Tagore the Philosopher,' *Journal of the Journal*, Issue 83, Cairo, November 1963; 'Tagore the Sufi,' *Journal of the Journal*, September, 1964, no. 93; 'Sinasi and the Girls Vasanti,' *Journal of the New Message*, April 1956, no. 25; *The Story of Buddha* (Cairo: New Publications Foundation, 1959); 'Gandhi between Sufism and Islamic Jihad,' *Journal of the Journal*, December 1969, no. 156; 'The Doctrine of Pantheism and its Impact on Tagore's Thought,' *al-Risala*, 1957, no. 30. In 1977, he summed up his previous writings in his study 'Tagore the Artist' in the *Alam al-Fekr* Journal from Kuwait.

15. Kreblani (Kripalani), *Tagore: A Genius*.

16. Ibid., 5.

17. Yahya al-Khashab, 'Tagore' in *Tagore, the Inspiring Indian Poet* by al-Tahiri, 40.

18. These books were reprinted six times from 1958 onwards. Later reprints include those in Cairo in 1961, in Damascus in 1965, and finally in Beirut in 1973 by Science House for Millions.

19. Tagore, *Fruit Basket*, tr. Ayyub Falluh.

20. Ibid., *Theatre and Poetry*, tr. Johan Comair.

21. Ibid., 10.

22. Ibid., 5.

23. Yahya al-Khashab, 'Tagore' in *Tagore, the Inspiring Indian Poet* by al-Tahiri, 40.

24. al-Tahiri, *Tagore, The Inspiring Indian Poet*, 358. The poem is from *The Crescent Moon*, which the critic Muhammad Shukri Ayyad described as unique in world literature, in Ayyad, *Tagore, the Poet of Love and Peace* by 89.

25. Ayyad, *Tagore, the Poet of Love and Peace*, 87.

26. Tagore: *Poetry and Theatre*, tr. Badi Haqqi, 299.

27. Tagore, *Sadhana*, tr. al-Jabalawi, 65. The text was also present in *The Inspiring Indian Poet* edited by al-Tahiri, 426.

28. The translator Father Johan Comair gives titles to poems of *The Gardener* that have no original titles. Cf. Comair, *Tagore: Theatre and Poetry*, 192.

29. Tagore, *Chants and Poems*, tr. Abdul Wahid Lu'lua, 5.

30. Pantheism (*wahdat al-wujud*) was part of the terminology of a major Sufi school founded by Ibn al-Arabi. His school faced intense criticism over the centuries. Cf. al-Takazani, *The Greater Way*, 350 ff.

31. Ayyad, *Between Philosophy and Criticism*.

32. Included in *Cultural Invasion and Other Articles* by al-Gosaibi.

33. Tagore, *My Reminiscences* (in Arabic).

34. Shanawany, *Books that Changed the Human Thought*, 3.

35. Amartya Sen's 'Tagore and his India' was published in the *New York Review of Books*, 26 June 1997 (http://www.nybooks.com/articles/archives/1997/jun/26/tagore-and-his-india/?pagination=false). It was reviewed in *Viewpoints* (Cairo), 1999, no. 7, 50.

36. Ayyad, *In the World of Tagore*.

37. Tagore: *The Fruit Basket*, tr. Badi Haqqi. Professor Elias produced similar annotated editions of *Anna Karenina, Don Quixote* and of a work by Goethe.

38. Tagore: *The Last Poem*, tr. Farid al-Shahf and Thaer Zeinaldin.

39. al-Muhafatha, *Characters from History*.

40. al-Tahiri, ed., *Tagore, the Inspiring Indian Poet*, 148.

41. Ibid., 149.

42. Ibid., 151.

43. Ibid., 168.

44. Ibid., 168–9.

45. Ayyad, *Tagore, the Poet of Love and Peace*, 18–19.

46. Ibid., 26–7. This is a direct translation of an Arabic saying.

47. Ibid., 42.

48. Cf. Abdul Wahab al-Massiri, *Encyclopedia of Jews*. The author emphasises here that any philosophy can be absorbed, even Tagore's philosophy, without changing our own beliefs.

49. Johan Comair mentioned in the introduction to his translation of *Tagore: Theatre and Poetry* that 'Tagore's father founded the society for the worship of the one, formless God.' (13). Furthermore, Abdul Aziz al-Zaki wrote that the openness of Tagore's art is only a plea in the sanctuary of religion bringing humans closer to God, the great truth and the overall unity, in 'Tagore the Artist,' by al-Zaki, 256.

50. al-Zaki, 'Tagore the Artist,' 255.

51. Ibid., 261.

52. Ibid.

53. The revelation is both a mystical and an artistic concept with a long history among Arabs, Persians, Indians and Greeks. At the time of al-Zaki, the English writer Colin Wilson revived the idea in his book *The Outsider* (1956).

54. al-Zaki, 'Tagore the Artist,' 269.

55. Ibid., 270.

56. Ibid., 284.

57. Although it claims to be the second edition of the 1961 volume, references in this article are to the version released in 2010.

58. al-Tahiri, *Tagore, The Inspiring Indian Poet*, 11.

59. Ibid.

60. The Islamic scholar and literary critic, Sayyid Qutb, was one of the most prominent critics of the 1940s. Later, he started writing on Islamic thought to the extent that he was considered one of the best ideologists of the Muslim

Brotherhood movement. He was executed by the regime of Gamal Abdel Nasser after a military trial.

61. al-Tahiri, *Tagore, The Inspiring Indian Poet*, 20.
62. Ibid., 21.
63. Ibid.
64. Ibid.
65. Russell, *Common Sense and Nuclear Warfare*.
66. al-Tahiri, *Tagore, The Inspiring Indian Poet*, 13.
67. Ibid.
68. Ibid., 33.
69. Ibid.
70. Ibid., 37.
71. Ibid., 39.
72. Ibid., 40.
73. Ibid., 41.
74. Ibid., 44–54.
75. Ibid., 85.
76. Ibid., 87.
77. Ibid., 104.
78. Ibid., 105.
79. Ibid., 174–5.
80. Ibid., 175.
81. Ibid., 188.
82. Ibid., 190 and 192.
83. Ibid., 197.
84. Ibid., 202.
85. Ibid., 211.
86. Ibid., 237.
87. Ibid., 238.
88. Ibid., 243.
89. Ibid., 247.
90. Ibid., 256.
91. Ibid., 262.
92. Ibid., 265.
93. Ibid., 267.
94. Kripalani, *Gandhi, Tagore and Nehru*, 241.
95. al-Tahiri, *Tagore, The Inspiring Indian Poet*, 283.

Works Cited

Studies

Ayyad, Muhammad Shukri. *Taghor: Sha'ir al hubb wa al-salam* [Tagore, the Poet of Love and Peace]. Cairo: Egyptian Book Organisation, 1974. [First published as *Sha'ir al hubb wa al-salam* [Poet of Love and Peace]. Cairo: Egyptian Ministry of Culture and Guidance, 1961].

Ayyad, Muhammad Shukri. *Bayn al-falsafah wa al-naqd* [Between Philosophy and Criticism]. Cairo: Friends' Book Publications, 1990.

———. *Fi 'alam Taghor: sha'ir al-hubb wa al-salam, al-bayt wa al-'ilm* [In the world of Tagore, Tagore, the Poet of Love and Peace, The Home and Learning]. Cairo: The Supreme Council of Culture, 2000.

Fakhuri, Hanna. *Tarikh al-adab al-'arabi* [*History of Arab Literature*]. 6th ed. Beirut: Police Printing House, n.d.

al-Gosaibi, Abdul Rahman al-Ghazi. *al-Ijtiyah al-thaqafi wa manshurat ukhra* [Cultural Invasion and Other Articles]. Beirut: Arab Institution for Studies and Publishing, 1991.

Kreblani (Kripalani), Krishna. *Taghor: 'Abqariyah alhamat al-sharq wa al-gharb* [*Tagore: A Genius that Inspired the East and the West*]. Translated by Hosni Friz. Amman: Dar Alkitab Alarabi, 1966.

Kripalani, Krishna. *Gandhi, Tagore and Nehru*. 2nd ed. Bombay: Hind Kitabs, 1949.

al-Manjuri, Muhammad *Taghor: al-wahdah al-ruhiya* [Tagore: Spiritual Unity]. Cairo, 1943.

al-Massiri, Abdul Wahab. *Mawsu'at al-yuhud wa al-yuhudiya wa al-sahyuniya* [Encyclopedia of Jews, Judaism and Zionism]. Cairo: al-Shuruq House, 1998.

al-Muhafatha, Ali. *Shakhsiyat min al-tarikh* [Characters from History]. Beirut: The Arab Institution for Studies and Publishing, 2009.

Russell, Bertrand. *Common Sense and Nuclear Warfare*. London: Allen Unwin, 1959.

Sakkut, Hamdi, ed. *Qamus al-adab al-'arabi al-hadith* [*Dictionary of Modern Arab Literature*]. Cairo: Dar al-Shuruq, 2009.

Shanawani, Ahmad Muhammad. *Kitab ghayyarat al-fikr al-insani* [Books that Changed the Human Thought]. Cairo: General Egyptian Assembly of the Book, 1995.

al-Tahiri, Muhammad Sayyid, ed. *Taghor: Sha'ir al-Hind al-mulhim* [Tagore, the Inspiring Indian Poet]. Damascus: Dar Ninwah (Nineveh House for Studies, Publishing and Distribution), 2010 (first published in 1961).

al-Takazani, Abu al-Wafa al-Ghonemy. *al-Tariqa al-akbariya* [The Greater Way]. Cairo: The Supreme Council for the Care of Literary, Arts and Social Sciences, 1969.

al-Zaki, Abdul Aziz. *Taghor al fannan* [Tagore the Artist]. *Alam al-fikr* [The World of Thought], 8, no. 1 (Kuwait, June 1977), 255–86.

———. *Taghor: fi al-dhikra al-mi'awiyah li miladih* [The Hundredth Birth Anniversary of Tagore]. Cairo: Ministry of Education, 1961.

Tagore's Works in Arabic Translation

Aghanin wa ash'ar [Songs and Poems]. Translated by Dr Abdul Wahid Lu'lua. Abu Dhabi, UAE: Publications of the Cultural Centre, 1995.

al-Bustani [*The Gardener*]. Translated by Wadi'al-Bustani. Beirut: al-Ma'aref House, late 1920s.

al-Qasida al-akhira [*The Last Poem*]. Translated by Farid al-Shahf and Thaer Zeinaldin. Damascus: al-Hiwar House of Publication, 2006.

al-Shi'r wa al-masrah [Poetry and Theatre]. Translated by Badi Haqqi. Beirut: House of Science for Millions, 1972.

Dhikrayati [*My Reminiscences*]. Abu Dhabi, UAE: Publications of the Cultural Centre, 1995.

Jany al-thimar [*Fruit-Gathering*]. Translated by Badi Haqqi. Beirut: al-Malayeen Printing House, 2000 (new ed.).

Qurban al-aghani [*Song Offerings*]. Translated by Father Johan Comair. Junia: Libanese Mursaleen Press, 1948.

Sallat al-fakiha [Fruit basket, *Corbeille de Fruits/Fruit-Gathering*]. Translated by Father Ayyub Falluh. Beirut: al-Yanbou' Publications, 1958.

Sallat al-fakiha: Jany al-thimar [The Fruit Basket, *Corbeille de Fruits/Fruit-Gathering*]. Translated by Badi Haqqi. Beirut: House of Science for Millions, 2000.

Taghur: masrah wa al-shi'r [Theatre and Poetry]. Translated by Johan Comair. Beirut: al-Mashreq House, 1967.

Tahqiq al-hayah [The Realisation of Life, *Sadhana*]. Translated by Muhammad Tahir al-Jabalawi. Cairo: The Anglo-Egyptian Library, n.d.

9

EGYPT

MD. BADIUR RAHMAN

Cultural bonds between India and Egypt date back a long time and the two countries have maintained strong relations over thousands of years of their history. Records show that Emperor Ashoka had contacts with Ptolemy II of Egypt (285–246 BC) and Dionysius was Ptolemy's ambassador in the court of Ashoka. The twentieth century witnessed cordial political relations too. The parallel struggles for independence of Mahatma Gandhi and of Sa'd Zaghlul of Egypt and friendly relations between Jawaharlal Nehru and Gamal-Abdel Nasser are still remembered by the people of both countries. These two leaders signed a treaty in 1955 and the establishment of the Non-Aligned Movement played a crucial role in strengthening cultural ties between the two countries.

Cultural contacts were strengthened with the establishment of the Maulana Azad Centre for Indian Culture as a department of the Embassy of India in Cairo in 1992 and by the implementation of a Cultural Exchange Programme. The Centre, in addition to popularising Indian culture through Hindi, Urdu and yoga classes and the screening of movies, also organises cultural festivals, such as the 'Days of Indian Culture' and 'Indian Cultural Week' held in 2008 and in 2010 respectively. India was the Guest Country of Honour at the Cairo International Film Festival in 2009. The strong ties between India and Egypt are evident from the affection towards India amongst the population. Three streets in Cairo are named after Indian leaders, Mahatma Gandhi, Pandit Nehru and Dr Zakir Husain.

Egyptians found in Tagore an envoy against imperialism presenting a ray of hope for freedom. Moreover, they considered him as one of themselves who revived the glorious past of the Eastern Civilisation. He was a true ambassador of love, co-operation and trust between all countries combining teachings of spirituality, peace, love and, above all, humanism. At the same time, he was also the embodiment of patriotism whose songs became national anthems of two countries. The Bengali poet is not restricted to circles of intellectuals in Egypt but many of his poems are included in school texts for promoting ethical values.

The Egyptian reception of Tagore cannot be examined in isolation from the wider Arabic reception since authors and publications circulated within the Arabic-speaking world beyond the national boundaries. This article, therefore, examines Egyptian responses to Tagore in the wider context of Arabic reception. One can observe certain peculiarities of Egyptian reception manifest in emphasising certain aspects of Tagore and neglecting others. Such highlighted aspects include Tagore's love for nature or his visit to Egypt. His patriotism is also highly emphasised. Another issue is how to account for his Hindu background. Many writers pointed out the monotheism of the Brahmo Samaj while others, such as At-Tillisi, highlighted Tagore's universalism. There is also a parallel between Tagore's pantheistic monism and the Sufi idea of the unity of existence. Arabic writings on the poet, however, neglected important aspects of Tagore, such as his awareness of science, his note of cautiousness about its development or his concern for the uplift of women.[1]

The socio-political background of this reception also presents some peculiarities. The first Arabs to react to Tagore were secularised Syrian Christians with a wide outlook on the West. Tagore's importance in Egypt increased with the emergence of the Non-Aligned Movement, in which India and Egypt fostered a close relationship. Just as in the Communist countries, celebrating Tagore could symbolise a nation's friendship with India.

THE NOBEL PRIZE

As soon as the Nobel Prize committee announced on 13 November 1913 the news of Tagore winning the Nobel Prize for literature, Egypt expressed its enthusiasm. Dailies, such as *al-Ahram, al-Muqattam, al-Muayid,* as well as journals, such as *al-Balagh, al-Muqtataf* and *al-Hilal, al-Zahra,* published articles on Tagore with his portrait.[2]

Wadi' al-Bustani (1886–1957), the Lebanese poet and translator of the Ramayana and of Omar Khayyam's *Rubaiyat,* impressed by the reports of *al-Hilal,* thanked its editor, Jurji Zaydan (1861–1924), a notable novelist and scholar, who then asked him to contribute articles on the poet. Wadi' read the English versions of *Gitanjali, The Gardener* and *Sadhana* and began to translate them into Arabic. As a member of the British administrative service, he travelled to India in 1914 and stayed with Tagore for several days as his guest. Bustani was impressed by his host's sublime disposition and by the personal care extended to him. al-Bustani published his observations in *al-Hilal* and compared the writings of Tagore to a mirror polished with sublime and elegant words, reflecting elevated ideas suffused with humanity and divinity.[3] He wrote that he had read all that was published by Tagore in English, both prose and poetry, and remarked that 'Tagore is a holy philosopher poet and a man who loves God and nature and the whole mankind.'[4] In his article, al-Bustani described his sojourn at the poet's place, and gave his brief life sketch highlighting his dedication for the development of Santiniketan, and his efforts to bring over teachers like C. F. Andrews and W. W. Pearson from Cambridge and Oxford. Bustani supplemented his article with a verse translation of poem numbered as 41 from *The Gardener*.[5]

VISIT TO EGYPT

Tagore visited several Muslim countries. Invited by Reza Shah Pahlevi, the king of Iran, he spent a few days in Tehran and in several other places of Iran in 1932; and invited by King Faisal of Iraq, he travelled to Baghdad in the same year.[6] Tagore had paid a visit to Egypt in 1926 on his way back from Europe. By that time, some English-knowing Arabs had started translating Tagore into Arabic and the author being well known was accorded a warm reception. This visit has been documented by the eminent writer and journalist Muhibb al-Din al-Khatib (1886–1969). The Damascus-born Muhibb al-Din studied and worked in several Arab countries before settling in Egypt in 1920. He edited and contributed articles to several magazines and also wrote a large number of books. As a correspondent of *al-Zahra*, he covered Tagore's visit to Cairo, which prompted him to publish a scholarly treatise on the poet in 1928.[7]

Tagore landed in Alexandria on 27 November 1926 and on the same day was accorded a grand reception in the al-Hamra Opera, where he met literary personalities, dignitaries of Egypt and Indians who lived there. Tagore addressed the gathering and talked about the existence of God in every living being of nature.[8] The Arab audience could easily link this idea to the Sufi theory of unity of existence (*wahdatul wujud*) as propounded by Ibn al-'Arabi. Tagore advocated the liberation from the shackles of self-interest and fear in the worldly affairs. He preached emancipation from lust and avarice. Tagore opined that when the thoughts are free from these fetters, one becomes able to enjoy the truth that never accepts any kind of infringement. According to Muhibb al-Din al-Khatib, this freedom attained by the poet is the source of his poetry.[9]

On 28 November, Tagore reached Cairo by train and stayed in Hotel Shepheard, the city's leading hotel. That day, Parliament held its session one hour later in honour of the poet. In the evening, he was given a reception by Ahmad Shawqi Bek (1868–1932), the greatest poet of the Arab world at that time. On that auspicious occasion, besides many Arab litterateurs, the Head of the Egyptian Parliament and former Prime Minister, Sa'd Zaghlul (1858–1927), was also present.[10] At the reception, Muhammed Abdul Wahhab, a leading national singer, recited verses from Shawqi's drama *Masra'u Kiliobatra* (Death of Cleopatra) to express love and honour to Tagore who very attentively listened.

Taha Husain (1889–1973), the 'doyen of modern Arabic literature', mentioned this reception in his autobiography;[11] while Ahmad Shawqi's son, Husain Shawqi, in his book *Abi Shawqi* (My Father Shawqi) described the occasion in more detail; he wrote:

> My father ordered me to go to Hotel Shepheard, where Tagore stayed, to accompany him to our house. Along with the poet, there were two Indian ladies of his family, and all were in Indian national dress, while Tagore [with] his tall stature, thick and curly hair was looking like a prophet as mentioned in the *Torah*.
>
> ...
>
> During his discourse, my father said to Tagore that he was all the more impressed because his readers are quite large in numbers as India consists of 300 million inhabitants. Tagore replied, 'You are right! India is a vast country but sorry to say that its every state speaks a different language. Therefore, my readers will not be more than ten million'. Thereafter he said with a smile, 'But you should be more delighted that the whole Arabic-speaking world [are] your [readers].'[12]

On 29 November, Tagore was again given a magnificent reception in the Hadiqatul Uzbukiya Opera where leading Egyptian writers, such as Ahmad Shawqi, Taha Husain, Abbas Mahmud al-Aqqad (1889–1964) and Ahmad Lutfi al-Sayyid (1872–1963) were present. While introducing the poet, Ahmad Lutfi said that Tagore pursued the philosophy of Plato, the piety of Caliph Umar and the guidance of Tolstoy throughout his life.[13]

In his address to the enthusiastic audience, Tagore mainly talked on the difference between Western and Eastern philosophies. He said that while Westerners believed in the existence of a supernatural realm and propagated that the human soul departs the world forever, Indians believed that the human soul is imperishable; it comes back to the world repeatedly until its total purification, then it is merged with the Supreme Reality.

Fuad Sarruf, who later became a famous public figure in Lebanon, was one of the members of the reception committee. He narrated that after reciting some songs of Tagore in English, their originals were sung by Bengali boys and girls residing in Cairo. He further adds that Bengali recitations and songs cast a magical spell in the hearts of all present; which proved, as Carlyle said in his lectures on *Heroes, Hero-Worship, and the Heroic in History*, that language is never a bar to aesthetic experience.

Before leaving the reception, Tagore recited the words of an ancient Indian song, the gist of which runs as follows: 'O Lord of Lords! O God of the whole mankind! O Master of our predecessors and successors! Unite our hearts, and bestow love and affection among us, and lead us to truth, justice and guidance.'[14] Thereafter, he recited his poem 'Where the mind is without fear.'

The visit, including the lectures, was covered by the Arab media with extraordinary zeal and it also directed the attention of intellectuals to Tagore. It is in this context that the outstanding writer Abbas Mahmud al-Aqqad (1889–1964) reviewed Tagore's *Sadhana* in the weekly *al-Balagh*. He wrote:

> I don't want to abridge the *Sadhana* because the book is a 'prayer' and prayers should not be shortened nor do I want to criticise its views because these are nothing but spiritual flowers and flowers are not meant for criticism or analysis.[15]

MUHIBB AL-DIN'S BOOK ON TAGORE

In his book on Tagore, Muhibb al-Din al-Khatib describes the childhood of the poet, his family background and the cultural ambience in which he grew up. The author presents Tagore as a patriot, highlighting that the Bengali Nobel Laureate travelled all over the world in his Oriental dress. He also discusses briefly how Tagore felt aggrieved during the partition of Bengal in 1905 against which he raised his voice of protest, and returned his knighthood after the brutal British massacre in Jallianwala Bagh in 1919.[16] He further added that Tagore was a patriot, philanthropist and ambassador of love and co-operation between countries.[17] Santiniketan and Sriniketan were only mentioned in passing. Muhibb al-Din like another Arab translator, al-Tillisi of Libya, highly praised the writings of Tagore available to him in English. Both of them have especially praised the poet for his excellent command over English which he aptly utilised while transcreating from the original Bengali.

INITIAL TRANSLATIONS

Muhibb al-Din also mentions that the play *Chitra* had been translated by Mahmud al-Manjury al-Afindi and that an Arabic translation of *Sadhana* had been undertaken by Azmi al-Dwairi Afindi. *The Gardener* and a collection of poems entitled *Balaka* in Bengali have been translated by Sayyid Wadi' al-Bustani under the Arabic title *al-bustani*. *The Home and the World* was rendered into Arabic by Tanius Abduh in 1927, entitled *al-bayt wa al-ʿalam*. However, in spite of mentioning *Gitanjali* several times, Muhibb al-Din does not appear to have come across any Arabic translation of it. Naturally, he was also aware of several other works of Tagore that had not been translated into Arabic by that time.[18]

Wadiʿ al-Bustani, one of the first Arabic intellectuals to discover Tagore, rendered into Arabic the *Gitanjali* and *The Gardener*. His *Gardener*, with the punning title *al-bustani* ('The Gardener'), is a close translation of thirty-three out of the eighty-five English poems.[19] The translator presented most of the poems in prose and some in verse. In his preface, he briefly discusses the beauty of *Gitanjali* and how much fame it earned both in the East and in the West. While introducing *The Gardener*, the translator quoted several reviews in *The Observer, Daily Mail* and *Daily News* and said that some of the love poems of *The Gardener* are superior to and more elegant than many poems of *Gitanjali*.[20] According to Bustani, if the *Gitanjali* poems are sublime with spirituality, which helps one ascend to the height of heaven from earth, the poems of *The Gardener* are full of passionate love, which speaks of the pathos of this mundane world of the youths, while the poems of *The Crescent Moon* draw the picture of childhood and motherhood. In the same preface, he also mentions that he had stayed with Tagore as a guest.[21] al-Bustani also stated that Tagore was not an idolater but a believer in the oneness of God. A special feature of this Arabic translation is that the translator provides annotation on Indian mythology, rituals, flora and fauna with reference to primary sources. Moreover, Wadiʿ also quoted Arabic and Urdu parallels to Tagore.

In 1941, the year in which Tagore passed away, the Egyptian poet Husain Afif, (1902–79) published an anthology of poems, *Fragrance*, and dedicated it to the memory of the Indian poet.[22]

BADI HAQQI'S *RAWAI'U TAGHUR*

Though Wadiʿ al-Bustani translated a large number of poems from *Gitanjali*, the credit of its complete translation goes to Badi Haqqi (b. 1922), a Syrian diplomat, novelist and translator. After publishing *Jany al-thimar* (*Fruit-Gathering*) in 1955, he came out with his *Jitanjali* the same year.[23] His *Rawaiʿu Taghur fi al-shiʿr wa al-masrah* (Wonders of Tagore in Poetry and Drama), published three years later, along with *Gitanjali* and *Fruit-Gathering* contained translations from *The Gardener* (eighty-five poems), *The Crescent Moon* (sixty poems) as well as the verse drama *Chitra*. The same *Rawaiʿu Taghur* revised by Professor Mustafa Habib was published from Cairo in 1961 as part of Tagore's birth centenary celebrations. Along with translations, this edition contained a forty-one-page introduction by Badi Haqqi. In 1965, Dr Najah Attar (b. 1933) enlarged the book by including the verse drama *The Cycle of Spring* and her review.

Badi Haqqi's *Introduction* opened with a Romain Rolland quote: 'When you approach Tagore you will feel as if you are in a place of worship.'[24] Then the author presents Rabindranath's life underlining his love for nature, which redeemed him from his utter despair and loneliness,[25] and how he coped with successive deaths of his loved ones through the belief that death opens a new eternal chapter, which is more opulent, luxuriant and sweet.

Apart from highlighting the beauty of Tagore's poems, he comments that his plays 'are the true reflections of the mind and thought of that great humanist and thinker.'[26] Badi Haqqi also discusses Tagore's patriotism and mentions his passion for songs and painting. He points out that his songs suit every occasion, mood and feelings of mankind. Although information on Tagore's visit to several countries is included in *Rawai'u Taghur,* Badi Haqqi does not shed further light on Tagore's visit to Egypt or to Baghdad.

Badi Haqqi discusses Tagore's symbolism with the examples of the poems *Two Birds* ('The Tame bird was in a cage...') and *Miser,*[27] and goes on to explicate how the body of his poems transcends their function of superb poetic diction, becoming a message for mankind. He also dwells on the deep spiritual content of the poems.

Describing the poet as a saintly mystic, he goes on to say that his saintliness, however, never advocates segregation and inactiveness. Since the Egyptian edition of the *Rawai'* was a centenary volume, Badi Haqqi concluded his introduction with the citation of *Who are you, o my reader, reading me after hundred years?*[28]

The Birth-centenary Volumes (1):
Taghur: fi al-dhikra al-mi'awiyya li miladih

In 1961, Egypt celebrated Tagore's birth centenary with the publication of several books including two memorial volumes, *Taghur: fi al-dhikra al-mi'awiyya li miladih* (Hundredth Birth Anniversary of Tagore), published by the Ministry of Education, and *Dhikra Tajur* (Reminiscence of Tagore), by Muhammad Tahir al-Jabalawi (1898–1979). The former is a collection of seven essays by Egyptian scholars with an introduction by the Minister of Education, Sayyid Muhammad Yusuf. Yusuf describes Tagore as one of the geniuses of the East struggling for the freedom of his country, who revived its glory through his elegant writings, poems and songs, and his University, Visva-Bharati, as the confluence of the values of the East and the West.

In his essay, Dr Muhammad Mahdi 'Allam (1900–91), the eminent, Western-educated Arabic linguist equally conversant with both Western and Islamic philosophies and literatures argues that, alongside Muhammad Iqbal and M. K. Gandhi, Tagore is one of the three great reformers of the Indian peninsula.[29] He points out that while still a young man Tagore wrote articles on Goethe, Dante, Petrarch and Victor Hugo to acquaint the readers of Bengal with European literature. He also mentions that the poet spent the £8,000 Nobel Prize money on the development of Visva-Bharati University. Citing Tagore's letter to Lord Chelmsford, Viceroy of India at that time, lambasting the massacre in Jallianwala Bagh, Mahdi 'Allam emphasises that the poet never shut his eyes to the crimes of the West, and presents an Arabic rendering of the song Tagore composed after he relinquished his knighthood, 'Ey manihar amay nahi sajey'.[30] He also cites the gist of the article *East and West* (1934) and based on Vincenc Lesný's, *Rabindranath Tagore: His Personality and Work* (1939) concludes his essay with the translation of three poems.[31]

The essay on *Tagore's Philosophy of Religion and Mysticism* by Zaki Najib Mahmud (1905–93), explains that according to Tagore the term 'eternal man' refers to God.[32]

This 'eternal man' and the humanism it implies are permanent while human beings are not. This new religion makes no difference between members of mankind on the basis of sex, colour, race or creed.

Muhammad Kamil Nahhas presents Tagore as an educator. He writes that Tagore, just like Rousseau, desired that a child should get school education in the lap of nature. However, he differed from Rousseau in being not willing to isolate the student community from society. Tagore desired that students should grow in a conducive, congenial and free atmosphere where there is no ethnic, religious, gender, racial or even national discrimination.[33] Although studying the geography and history of one's country was given great importance, this did not mean that a syllabus-oriented course should be imposed on the students. Referring to Tagore, the essayist warns that whenever we think of a university, the picture of Cambridge and Oxford flashes in our minds and we forget that European universities are entrenched in an essentially European lifestyle and environment compatible with their nature.[34] Tagore was in favour of education through the native language but never denied the worth of foreign culture, knowledge and science.[35] That is why Tagore acknowledged that Islamic culture has enriched medieval India. Tagore also advocated that an institute should share all the problems of rural society.

The next essay, *Tagore and Indian Drama*, by the poet, translator, and writer Abdur Rahman Sidqi (1896–1973) is almost like an independent monograph. Its author was an official at the Ministry of Education and the director of the *Dar al-Opera*. As a member of the Council of Arts, he travelled extensively. His publications include two collections of poems, and books on Baudelaire and Goethe. In this Tagore volume, he translated five plays—*King and Queen, Sacrifice, Chitra, The King of the Dark Chamber,* and *The Post Office* and introduced them with a scholarly preface on the formation of Tagore's interest in theatre. In the section on 'Drama and the Religious Reform Movement', Abdur Rahman Sidqi points out that the practice of polytheism in India is against the teachings of the Upanishads, which upholds the oneness of God and the perpetuity of the soul. After dealing with Buddhism, he talks about Indian religious reforms that finally took shape in the Brahmo Samaj through Raja Rammohun Roy in 1830.[36] He propagated the worship of 'the One, who is ever living, eternal, creator of the universe and is its saviour.'[37] With regard to the play *Nature's Revenge,* Abdur Rahman mentions that traditionally after attaining the fourth stage of human life, *sannyasa,* there remains no desire either for life or death.[38] However, this play opposed that philosophy.[39] Abdur Rahman notes the eclectic nature of Tagore's plays in as much as he sometimes followed the ancient Indian style while at other times he appeared greatly influenced by Shakespeare.

In his essay on Tagore's short stories, Ismail Mazhar (1891–1962), the pioneer of the educational renaissance in Egypt, writes that Tagore is the soul of the East, where all messages of humanism—those of Moses, Jesus and Mohammad emerged.[40]

The sixth essay on Tagore's aesthetic views was written by Muhammad Shukri Ayyad (1921–99), Dean of the Faculty of Arts at Cairo University. He was also a noted translator, short story writer and novelist. A few years later, he even translated *The Home and the World* (1967). He wrote that according to Tagore, art cannot be defined.[41] His theory of criticism is based on dualism, that of the Creator and the creation, the limited and the unlimited, the necessary and the superfluous.[42] According to Tagore, personality means a man's complete awareness of his existence; and this awareness touches the spirit of the whole universe.[43] Therefore, merely on account of Man's limited view of life, Art should not be made limited.

In his article *Tagore and the West,* Lutfi Fam, an expert on Contemporary French Drama, underlined that Tagore passionately studied the works of Shakespeare, Milton, Byron and others and was deeply impressed by their emotional force.[44] He was charmed by Keats's lyricism and Shelley's glorification of mental beauty.[45] According to Tagore, the West, despite its astonishing scientific and technological development, has no peace because it did not believe in non-material values.[46] On this point, Tagore agreed with the Urdu poet Iqbal (1877–1938) who also disapproved of this aspect of Western civilisation.[47] Tagore decried Europeans for World War I and he raised his voice again in 1938, when he apprehended another global conflict. In the section *Love of the Motherland and Love of the World* the reader is reminded that Tagore supported love for the motherland but not at the cost of other nations.[48] In another section, the author presents the *Opinion of the West on Tagore* claiming that the University of Oxford bestowed an honour on him. England considered him one of the greatest poets for his original contribution to English poetry. Europe had conferred on him the Nobel Prize in 1913. His French translator was André Gide, and Henry-D. Davray praised the *Gitanjali* for its spirituality.[49] His poems have also been translated into other languages of the world since Tagore did not compose poetry with a particular readership in view. His paintings also astonished the Western world, including the poet-countess Anna de Noailles (1876–1933) who wrote on Tagore's poetry and paintings.[50] His views on music were published in various French magazines and his plays also made their place in the hearts of the Europeans including the Nobel Prize winner W. B. Yeats, who, according to Fam, wrote at length on Tagore's plays. Dr Fam argued that Santiniketan consolidated the cultural bond with Europe since this institution became a centre of cultural encounters between East and West. His source about the institution was the booklet of the Frenchman M. L. Gommès, who stayed at Santiniketan between 1940 and 1942.[51]

The Birth-centenary Volumes (2): *Dhikra Tajur*

The other Arabic book published in Egypt on the occasion of Tagore's birth centenary is *Dhikra Tajur* by Muhammad Tahir al-Jabalawi (1898–1979).[52] The author produced this volume after reviewing eight books of Tagore and appended some select portions in Arabic translation from Tagore's plays, songs, poems, etc. This 151-page book presents the origins of Bengali literature, the birth and upbringing of Tagore, his literary life and his views and beliefs. It also contains selections from *Malini, Amal* (*The Post Office*), *Fruit-Gathering, The Gardener, Lover's Gift, The Crescent Moon, Sadhana* and *Stray Birds*.

In the introduction, Jabalawi emphasised Tagore's humanism in the age of materialism and covetousness. In the first chapter, al-Jabalawi pointed out that for a long time India was secluded from the world in respect of its religion and literature. Every part of India had its own language, literature, culture and even beliefs and faiths. With regard to Bengal, he wrote about the achievements of poets like Chandidas, Bharatchandra Ray and

Ramprasad Sen and their limitations.[53] He then talked of William Carey (1761–1834) and Rammohun Roy (1772–1833) highlighting that Roy stood against polytheism, idolatry, Sati and several other evils of society—and it was he who for the first time wrote literary prose in Bengali. Tagore's father, Maharshi Debendranath Thakur (1817–1905) was also his friend and bequeathed the teachings of the oneness of God.[54] A large number of orthodox Hindus were against the Brahmos, a sect to which Tagore's family belonged. Tagore emerged as a product of the Bengali Renaissance. Talking about Tagore's early life, the writer also underlined Tagore's love for nature through which he was able to listen to the whispers of the unseen, which led him to the love of the Creator lifelong.[55] Al-Jabalawi opined that the cultures of both Gangetic rural Bengal and the city of Calcutta moulded the mind of the poet. The former helped him acquire wisdom and a fervour arousing the spirit of poetry and the imagination, while the later planted in him the feelings of nationalism. While giving an account of Tagore's literary life, al-Jabalawi quoted some Bengali critics who are dismissive of Tagore's dramas marked by a European spirit.[56] He pointed out that Tagore revived Bengali literature and, at the same time, his songs and plays are for the whole world.[57] Although Tagore was not a philosopher in the technical sense, he expressed his philosophy through his plays. Even his lectures had a magical effect upon the listeners.[58] Jabalawi showed how the grief of the successive deaths of his loved ones found its way into Tagore's sublime poems and songs.[59] He also talked about Tagore's social reforms, his engagement in raising the prestige of his country, his travels, which included a visit to Egypt in 1926, when enthusiasts could see the Indian poet at al-Uzbukiya Opera in his saintly attire, standing with folded hands in the Indian manner. al-Jabalawi wrote that from Egypt Tagore had gone to Japan.

Al-Jabalawi said that at the turn of the century when the whole world was groaning under the burden of materialism, aggression and colonisation, Tagore stood up against the Western evils. He spoke against European nationalism based upon division, selfishness and lust for accumulation of wealth.[60]

Tagore says that man should benefit from nature while the West is determined to destroy nature although man and nature are indivisible. To attain this reality man has to cultivate love and brotherhood. Al-Jabalawi also talked about Tagore's relation with Gandhi and said that when Gandhi started the freedom movement Tagore supported him in 1921. However, Tagore's view was that the East is in need of the West and vice-versa. Tagore did not believe in *swaraj* the way Gandhi did.[61] Al-Jabalawi mentioned Tagore's return of his knighthood as a response to a British massacre. He concluded that Tagore was the poet of mankind in its entirety. Along with

giving selections from Tagore, al-Jabalawi discussed *Sadhana* and the end
of his book contains a group of 'brief poems' that resemble the haikus of
Japan.[62]

SUSTAINED ENGAGEMENT WITH TAGORE

As we have seen, the interest of Arab intellectuals centred on Tagore's lyric
poetry, *Sadhana*, and his dramas. Arabic translations of poems and dramas
of Tagore continued to appear after the centenary, mainly from Cairo
and Damascus.[63] To this one can add that *My Reminiscences* (1995), and
the lectures of *Sadhana*, have also been translated into Arabic by various
hands including Azmi al-Dawairi Afindi.[64] Furthermore, al-Aqqad's essay *as-
Sadhana* is a wonderful commentary on Tagore's text.[65]

Several outstanding Egyptian critics, including al-Aqqad (1889–1964),
Ahmad Amin (1886–1954) and Sayyid Qutb (1906–66), often referred to
Tagore in their various writings.

Aqqad in his book *Sha'ir andalusi wa ja'izah 'alamiyah* (A Spanish Poet
and a World-class Prize) presented an analytical review of authors who won
the Nobel Prize from its inception until Juan Ramón Jiménez.[66] Aqqad
argued that Tagore was at a far higher level than many of the Europeans
who won the Nobel Prize and urged intellectuals to translate Tagore's works
into Arabic.[67] Aqqad himself translated several verses of Tagore in many of
his articles published in *al-Hilal, al-Balagh* and *al-Muqtataf,* etc. He also
referred to Tagore repeatedly in his other book entitled *Sa'at baynal kutub*
(Hours amidst Books), which also included the brilliant essay *as-Sadhana*
written in 1927. Aqqad said that he had first skimmed through *Sadhana*
in 1922 and came to know about Brahmo philosophy through it. When
he heard this philosophy from Tagore, whose melodious voice had ever
since been resounding in his ears, he reread the book, which now seemed
to him to echo the ancient wisdom of the Pharaohs, encompassing the age-
old Indian and Egyptian treasure-house of knowledge and wisdom.[68] Aqqad
highly appreciated Tagore for his clear distinction between Western and
Indian philosophy by saying that the former developed within four walls
whereas the latter grew in the lap of thickets and open forests.[69] He also
praised Tagore's views about the position of Indian women as contained in
Sadhana.[70]

In his book *Principles of Literary Criticism,* the Cairo Professor Ahmad
al-Sha'ib, while discussing the role of the heart in expressing true beauty,
quoted almost an entire page from *Personality.*[71] A detailed comparison of
this book with *Creative Unity, Personality* and *Sadhana* may reveal that the
impact of Tagore on Ahmad al-Sha'ib was immense.

In the same way, Ahmad Amin as well as Sayyid Qutb borrowed from Tagore many ideas in their discussion of art, truth, beauty, the relationship of man and nature, the religion of the poet and his freedom in their books *al-Naqdul adabi* (Literary Criticism) and *al-Naqdul adabi: usuluhu wa manahijuhu* (Literary Criticism: its Principles and Methods) respectively. Sayyid Qutb highly applauded Tagore's poetical qualities and discussed them elaborately with citations from Greek, Iranian and Indian epics and from Arabic books.[72] He added that the great poet bequeathed to humanity a kind of tranquillity.

A number of other Arabic books also discussed Tagore's humanism, philosophy and religion.[73] Jamil Gabr wrote on Tagore in the book series named *Iqra* (Darul Ma'arif, Cairo) in 1958. Articles on Tagore are also published online.[74] Although Tagore's dramas were discussed in detail in the book *Taghur fi al-dhikra al-mi'awiyya li miladihi*, the present writer has no knowledge whether any drama of Tagore has ever been staged in Arabic in Egypt.

A new translation of *Gitanjali* by the Libyan writer Khalifa Muhammad al-Tillisi (1930–2010) entitled *Thus Tagore Sang* appeared in 1989. In the introduction, Tillisi expressed his admiration for the beauty of Tagore's English in his exquisite transcreations from the original Bengali. He presented Tagore as a lover of nature and a great humanist who is appreciated by people of all religions. A Christian finds him close to Christianity and a Muslim close to Islam.[75]

Al-Tillisi maintained that Tagore's spirituality never meant an inactive and segregated life. He also mentioned that pessimism had no place in Tagore; rather he was the spokesman of hope and aspiration. According to Tagore, happiness lies in the selfless service of mankind after renouncing the ego.[76] Al-Tillisi also discussed Tagore's role in the freedom movement of his country and his rejection of Western imperialism. He echoed Yeats while comparing Tagore with Chaucer saying, 'he writes music for words.'

Another translator of *Gitanjali* was one of the female pioneers of prose writing from the Gulf, the Emirates-born *Zabya Khamis* (b. 1958), who was arrested in Abu Dhabi in 1987 and jailed for publishing 'transgressive poetry.' She moved to Egypt in 1989. Khatib also admired Tagore's mysticism and remarked that some of his poems shone with human love while others with divine love.[77] These poems have universal appeal and just like the Bible for the Christians, they can be read to gain consolation and strength.

TAGORE'S 150TH BIRTH ANNIVERSARY

When India declared 2011 as the 'Year of Tagore,' Egypt also celebrated the great poet. As part of the celebrations for his 150th birth anniversary, a number of programmes were organised in 2011–12 including lectures, literary seminars, exhibitions from India, performances of Rabindra Sangeet and Tagore dance dramas by top Indian performers in Cairo and a number of other places.

The Maulana Azad Centre for Indian Culture in co-operation with the Cultural Development Fund of the Egyptian Ministry of Culture celebrated Tagore's 150th birthday in the Artistic Creativity Centre, Opera House Complex on 28 May in the presence of Muhammad Abu Sa'da, Director of the Cultural Development Fund, Indian Ambassador, R. Swaminathan, Bangladesh Ambassador, Mizanur Rahman and several other dignitaries. The programme included a lecture by Professor Jalal Amin, a performance of Rabindra Sangeet by a group of Bengalis living in Cairo and the screening of Malaya Bhattacharya's *Remembering the Legend*, a film about *Gitanjali*, prepared as a Public Diplomacy Initiative of the Government of India.

The Maulana Azad Centre organised further related activities throughout 2011–12. On 5 July 2011, two exhibitions concerning Tagore were inaugurated by Dr Imad Abu Ghazi, Minister of Culture, Egypt, and the Indian Ambassador. From 5 to 17 July, under the auspices of the Indian Council for Cultural Relations and Centre of Rabindranath Tagore, Kolkata, the Maulana Azad Centre in co-operation with the External Cultural Relation Division and the Division of Variegating Art, Ministry of Culture, Egypt, also organised an exhibition displaying about twenty stamps from different countries on Tagore as well as *kantha* stitch embroidery.[78] The inaugural ceremony was attended by dignitaries, students, academics and a host of Indians and Bangladeshis living in Egypt.

The Maulana Azad Centre in co-operation with the Egyptian Ministry of Culture also organised two seminars. The first one, on the *Comparison of the Poetry of Tagore with that of Shawqi*, was held at Opera House Courtyard on 28 September 2011 with the participation of two Indian and five Egyptian speakers. On 3 October, a discussion session was held at the premises of the Centre for Indian Culture, where two Indian professors discussed various aspects of Tagore; this session was chaired by the Egyptian novelist, Jamal al-Ghitani. On this occasion, the book *al-Ruju' ilal fadfada'* (Return to Deluge) by one of the leading Egyptian female writers, Iqbal Barakah, was also released.

Five award-winning films by renowned directors, such as Satyajit Ray, Tapan Sinha, Hemen Gupta and Kumar Sahani were screened between 15 and 19 April 2012 at the Artistic Creativity Centre in Cairo. Moreover, a biographical documentary on Tagore as well as a silent film in which Tagore himself acted was shown with English and Arabic title-cards. The festival commenced with a panel chaired by the film critics Rafiq al-Sabban and

Khairiya al-Bilshawi who discussed Tagore's awareness of women issues and social problems.[79]

Tagore, the worshiper of truth and lover of nature, is still a vibrant source of inspiration and hope not only to Egyptians but to the whole world especially for his message of love, harmony, humanism, global peace and cooperation. For all this Rabindranath is regarded as an outstanding poet who transcended time.

NOTES

1. For further information, vide the special issue of *Gyan o Bigyan* (Bengali), December 2010; and *Current Science*, no. 100(b) (25 March 2012).
2. See, for example, *al-Hilal*, 22, no. 4 (1913). For further information, see al-Jabalawi, *Dhikra Tajor*, 38.
3. *al-Hilal*, May 1916. As referred to at https://sites.google.com/site/mahmoudsmasoud/visitingtagore (06/01/2013).
4. https://sites.google.com/site/mahmoudsmasoud/visitingtagore (30/12/2012).
5. He translated the poem into Arabic as:

Yahummu lisani an yutarjima 'an qalbi
Wa yathnihi ma'hudu izdiraiki bil hubb
Fa ahza'u min nafsi wa sirri udhiuhu
Nikatan wa qad takfi al-isharatu dhal lubb.

The English original runs as follows:

I long to speak the deepest words I have to say to you; but I dare not, for fear you should laugh.
That is why I laugh at myself, and shatter my secret in jest.
I make light of my pain, afraid you should do so.

6. al-Rawi and al-Khayun, 'Taghur: zaifu Baghdad al-sami,' 204.
7. al-Khatib, *Taghur*. The booklet has fifty-nine pages and contains a scholarly foreword of seven pages by Syed Mustafa Sadiq al-Rafi'i (d. 1937), an Egyptian poet and writer.
8. Ibid., 23.
9. Muhibbuddin said that he came to understand the gist of the speech from the write-up of Professor Syed Abbas at-Masafi, correspondent of *al-Ahram*, Alexandria. al-Khatib, *Taghur*, 23 (note).
10. See also Tagore's 'Parashhyey' in *Rabindra Racanabali*, XI, 636.
11. Husain, *al-Ayyam*, 142.
12. Shawqi, *Abi Shawqi*, 119–23.
13. Ahmad, 'Rihlatu Taghur ila Misr,' *Thafqafatul Hind*, 89.
14. Ibid., 90.
15. Cited in al-Jabalawi, *Dhikra Tajor*, 39.
16. al-Khatib, *Taghur*, 26.

17. Ibid., 30.
18. Ibid., 35–7.
19. No year of publication is indicated in the book; but it can be conjectured that this work was published sometime between 1916 and 1928.
20. *al-Bustani*, Preface, 6.
21. Ibid.
22. For further details, see the essay on the Arabic reception in this volume.
23. These two books have no preface or introduction but the *Jitanjali* was decorated with a colour painting of a lover with his beloved by the Indian artist Sridhar Mahapatra and the *Jany al-thimar* with an image by Rizwan al-Sahhal.
24. *Rawai'u taghur fi al-shi'r wa al-masrah*, 6.
25. Ibid., 13.
26. Ibid., 36.
27. *The Gardener* (6) and *Miser (Kripan)*, from the collection *Kheya*.
28. *The Gardener*, 85.
29. He was Head of the Arabic and English Departments at Ein Shams University; Chairman of the Board of Directors of the Egyptian Organisation for Authorship, Translation, Printing and Publishing (1961–3); *Taghur: fi al-dhikra*, 15.
30. For the full text of the letter, see http://dart.columbia.edu/library/tagore-letter/letter.html (31December 2012).
31. Zabib, *Taghur: fi al-dhikra*, p. 23. Cf. Lesny, *Rabindranath Tagore*, 77–8 and 67–8.
32. Professor of Philosophy at Cairo University, who was the author of, among others, *A History of World Literature, 1934–48*, and of a book on Islamic mysticism.
33. Zabib, *Taghur: fi al-dhikra*, 65
34. Ibid., 66.
35. Ibid., 67.
36. According to Rahman, there are seven fundamental teachings of the Brahmo Samaj: (i) not to worship idols; (ii) to continuously worship one God, the exalted, the creator of all creatures, who is their saviour and cause of their life and death; (iii) to worship God in His love; (iv) to act as He loves; (v) to ensure pious life; (vi) to implore forgiveness; and (vii) to discard vices, crimes and sinful acts. Cf. Zabib, *Taghur: fi al-dhikra*, 101.
37. Ibid.
38. Ibid.
39. Ibid., 103.
40. Ibid., 173.
41. Ibid., 188–9.
42. Ibid., 191.
43. Ibid., 194–200.
44. Ibid., 215–16.
45. Ibid.
46. Ibid., 218–20.

47. See http://allamaiqbalforus.blogspot.in/2011/10/allama-iqbal-on-western-civilisation.html (31 December 2012) and http://www.habous.net/daouat-alhaq/item/1255 (31 December 2012).
48. *Taghur: fi al-dhikra*, 224–6.
49. Henry Davray, 'Un Mistique Hindou: R. Tagore' *Mercure de France* (16 août 1913). Cf. *Taghur: fi al-dhikra*, 230.
50. *Taghur: fi al-dhikra*, 234.
51. Gommès, *Introduction à Tagore*.
52. Tagore has been spelt in Arabic in various ways: Ṭāghūr; Tāghūr even as Tājor.
53. al-Jabalawi, *Dhikra Tajur*, 10–11.
54. Ibid., 18.
55. Ibid., 22–3.
56. Ibid., 32.
57. Ibid., 33.
58. Ibid., 35.
59. Ibid., 36.
60. Ibid., 43.
61. Ibid., 52. Here al-Jabalawi gives an Arabic translation of Tagore's long letter from Chicago sent to his friend Charles Freer Andrews.
62. Ibid., 125–45; ibid., 149–50.
63. Just to name a few: Ayyad, *Sha'ir al hubb wa al-Salam*, Baghjati, *Taghur wa akharūn*, Fadil, *Aghanin wa ash'ar*, Fadil, *Min rawai' ash sha'ir al-hindi: Taghur*, Salah, *Dhikrayati*.
64. www.books4all.net/showthread.php?t=8830 (23 December 2012) and http://srv5.eulc.edu.eg/eulc_v5/libraries/start.aspx?fn=SearchResult&ScopeID=1.&Id=1.3.10.5.21.&ClassNo=294.392&PageNo=4 (23 December 2012).
65. al-Aqqad, 'Kitab sadhana li al-hakim al-hindi Tajur' in *Sa'at bainal kutub*, Matb'ah al-Muqtataf wa al-Muqattam, 1929, downloaded from http://www.al-mostafa.info/data/arabic/depot3/gap.php?file=i001269.pdf (31 December 2012). It is also included in al-Aqqad's in *al-Majmua al-Kamilah lil al-Aqqad*, vol. III, 29–36.
66. See Ahmad, 'Rihlatu taghur ila misr,' 93. Note that Ahmad misquoted the title of Aqqad's book as *Sha'ir 'alami wa jaizah 'alamiyah*.
67. Ibid.
68. al-Aqqad, 'Kitab al-Sadhana,' 30.
69. Ibid.
70. *Kitab al-Sadhana* in *al-Majmua al-Kamilah lil al-Aqqad*, vol. III, 30.
71. al-Sha'ib, Ahmad. *Usulun naqd al-adabi* [Principles of Literary Criticism], 58–9. Ahmad al-Sha'ib did not mention his Arabic source. The passage was cited in Professor Yousuf Hanna's translation as it appeared in the Egyptian weekly *al-Siyasah*, 211 and 212 (no year). The English original is *Personality*, London: Macmillan & Co., 1917, 9–12.
72. Qutb, *al-Naqdul-adabi*, 14–17.
73. For example, Ubri, *Taghur al-mu'allim al-insan*; al-Jabalawi, *Dhikra Tajore*, 6 and 145–7; Zabib, *Taghur: faylasuful hind wa hakimuha* (2001); al-Hussaini,

Taghur: al-janib al-imani (2007); al-Khuri, 'Introduction' to Tagore, *Diyanatush sha'ir.*

74. Such as www.ibtesama.com/vb/showthread-t_39438.html (accessed 28 December 2012) and http://alhayat.com/Details/425059 (accessed 28 December 2012).

75. al-Tillisi, *Hakadha ghanna Taghur*, 3.

76. Ibid.

77. al-Khatib, *Taghur*, 26–7.

78. *Kantha* is a kind of light wrap, which keeps a person warm in winter. Traditionally stitching it was a popular activity for Bengali village women, who displayed their instinctive artistic taste by portraying figures from Tagore's literature or even the poet himself with a pithy saying or verse. These days, kantha stitch in saris has become popular amongst women of high status.

79. Based on the report of PTI (Press Trust of India), dated 16 April 2012.

WORKS CITED

Primary Sources

Das, Sisir Kumar, ed. *The English Writings of Rabindranath Tagore*, 3 vols. New Delhi: Sahitya Akademi, 1996.

Tagore, Rabindranath. *Sanchayita*. Calcutta: Visva-Bharati, 2011/12 (Bengali year 1418, 11th ed).

——. *Personality*. London: Macmillan, 1921.

——. *Creative Unity*. London: Macmillan, 1922.

——. *Gitanjali*. New Delhi: UBS Publishers and Distributors, 2010 (15th reprint).

Rabindra Racanabali, vol. XI. Calcutta: Visva-Bharati, 1995 (Bengali year 1402).

Works of Tagore in Arabic Translation

al-Bustani [*The Gardener*]. Translated by Wadi' al-Bustani. Cairo: al-Maarif, n.d.

Aghanin wa ash'ar [Songs and Poems]. Translated by Abdul Wahid Lu'lua. Abu Dhabi: al-Majma' ath-Thaqafi, 1995.

Dhikrayati [*My Reminiscences*]. Translated by Salah, Salah. Abu Dhabi: al-Majma' ath-Thaqafi, 1995.

Hakadha ghanna Taghur [Thus Sang Tagore]. Translated by al-Tillisi, Khalifa Muhammad. Tunisia and Libya: al-Darul 'Arabiyya lil Kuttab, 1989.

Jany al-thimar [*Fruit-Gathering*]. Translated by Badi Haqqi. Beirut: Matabi' al-Adaab, 1955.

Jitanjali [*Gitanjali*]. Translated by Badi Haqqi. Beirut: Matabi' al-Adaab, 1955.

Min rawai' ash-sha'ir al-hindi: Taghur [From the wonders of Indian Poet: Tagore]. Translated by Fadil,Hazim Nazim. Abu Dhabi: al-Majma' al-Thaqafi, 1995.

Rawai'u taghur fi al-shi'r wa al-masrah [Wonders of Tagore in Poetry and Drama]. Translated by Badi Haqqi. Beirut: Dar al-*Malaein, 1958 (2nd edn: Damascus, 1965; new edn: Beirut: Darul 'Ilm lil Mala'in, 1984.)*

Secondary Sources

Ahmad, Muhammad, 'Rihlatu taghur ila misr' [Tagore's Trip to Egypt]. *Thaqafatul Hind* (Special issue on Tagore), 62, no. 4 (2011). New Delhi: Indian Council for Cultural Relations (ICCR), 85–100.

Amin, Ahmad. *al-Naqdul adabi* [Literary Criticism]. Beirut: Darul Kuttab, 1967.

al-Aqqad. *Sha'ir andalusi wa ja'izah 'alamiyyah* [A Spanish Poet and a World-class Prize]. Beirut: Darul Kitab al-Arabi, 1971.

——. 'Kitab al-sadhana lil hakim al-hindi Tajor' [The Book of Sadhana by The Indian Philosopher Tagore]. *al-Muqtataf.* 10 December 1927.

——. *Sa'at bainal kutub* [Hours amidst Books]. Beirut: Dar al-Raihani lit –Tab'a wan Nashr, 1974 (Contains *al-sadhana,* 29–36).

Ayyad, Muhammad. *Sha'ir al hubb wa al-salam* [Poet of Love and Peace]. Cairo: Egyptian Ministry of Culture and Guidance, 1961.

Baghjati, Adnan. *Taghur wa aakharun: shu'araul hind* [Tagore and Others: Indian Poets]. Damascus: Dar al-Ahali, 1991.

Bhattacharya, Nirmal Kanti. *Words of the Master.* Kolkata: Neogi Books, 2012.

Gommès, M. L. *Introduction à Tagore.* Paris: Éditions de la Revue des Jeunes, 1947.

Husain, Taha. *al-Ayyam,* vol. III. Cairo: Dar al-Ma'arif, 1982 (sixth ed.).

al-Husaini, Suhaila. *Taghur: al-janib al-imani* [Tagore: From the Aspect of Belief & Faith]. Cairo: al-Hay'ah al-Misriyyah al-'Ammah lil Kuttab, 2007.

al-Jabalawi, Muhammad Tahir. *Dhikra Tajur* [Tagore's anniversary]. Cairo: Maktaba al-Anjlo al-Misriyyah, 1961.

al-Khatib, Muhibb al-Din. *Taghur.* Cairo: al-Maktaba al-Salafiya, 1928.

al-Khuri, Musa and al-Khuri, Ghassan, *Diyanatush sha'ir* [The Religion of a Poet]. Damascus: Dar al-Ghirbal, 1988.

Lesný, Vincenc. *Rabindranath Tagore: His Personality and Work.* Translated by Guy McKeever Phillips. London: George Allen and Unwin, 1939.

Mukhopadhyay, Prabhat Kumar. *Rabijiboni o rabindra sahityo prabeshak,* vol. III. Calcutta: Visva-Bharati, 1961.

Qutb, Sayyid. *al-Naqdul adabi: usuluhu wa manahijuhu* [Literary Criticism: Its Principles and Methods]. Cairo: Darul Fikr al-Arabi, n.d.

al-Rawi, Harith Taha, and Rashid al-Khayun. "Taghur: zaifu Baghdad al-sami" [Tagore: the Revered Guest of Baghdad]. *Thafqafatul Hind,* 62, no. 4 (2011), 199–221.

al-Sha'ib, Ahmad. *Usulun naqd al-adabi* [Principles of Literary Criticism]. Cairo: Maktaba an-Nahda al-Misriyya, n.d.

Shawqi, Husain. *Abi Shawqi.* [My Father Shawqi]. Cairo: Maktaba al-Nahda, 1947.

Ubri, Mishal. *Taghur al-mu'allim al-insan* [Tagore: the Teacher of Man]. Beirut: Darur Raihani li al-Tiba'ah wa al-Nashr, 1974.

Zabib, Najib. *Taghur: faylasuful hind wa hakimuha* [Tagore: Philosopher of India and its Sagacious Man]. Beirut: Dar al-Hadi lit Tiba'ah wan Nashr wat Tawzi', 2001.

——. *Taghur. fi al-dhikra al-mi'awiyyah li miladih* [The Hundredth Birth Anniversary of Tagore]. Cairo: Ministry of Education, 1961.

10

TURKEY

LAURENT MIGNON

'I wonder whether my sympathy [for Tagore] is caused by my interest in India and in the Indian soul. Or is it because Tagore is an Oriental?' asked Fethi Tevetoğlu (1916–89) in his short 1938 biography of Rabindranath Tagore, the first monograph of its kind in Turkey. In his introduction, Tevetoğlu, a medical doctor and a literary dilettante with ultra-nationalist sympathies, reminiscing his teenage days when a teacher introduced him to Tagore's world, wondered about the reasons that had attracted him to the prose and poetry of the great Bengali writer. He then brushed away those questions and concluded: 'These cannot be the reasons; these are nothing compared to Tagore's songs which speak to the soul. Tagore's every page is delightful. Endless beauty and the eternal poetry that he conveys are the things that bewitch [the reader].'[1] Written at a time when Tagore became increasingly popular in the Republic of Turkey, Tevetoğlu's attempt at making sense of his passion proposes some interesting lines of inquiry to study and analyse the long love story between Tagore and his Turkish readers. Interest in India, oriental solidarity and the sheer power of Tagore's writings would become some recurring arguments in the articles and essays by Tagore's Turkish translators and critics.

DISCOVERING INDIA

Interest in India in the Turkish speaking realms of the Ottoman Empire had not started with Tagore. Travellers, writers and, later, scholars had turned their attention to the Indian subcontinent in the last quarter of the nineteenth century. Though diplomatic relations between the Ottoman Empire and the Islamic states of India went back to the fifteenth century, it was only in the nineteenth century that India and its overwhelmingly non-Islamic cultures became an object of curiosity for Ottoman Turkish intellectuals. Works such as al-Bîrûnî's eleventh-century *Indica* were not unknown to the Ottoman intelligentsia, yet Western scholarship and writings on India would have a greater impact on the perception of Indian cultures and religions at the turn of the century. Not unlike their Western European peers, Ottoman Turks writing on India were particularly keen on the exotic; they were often orientalising Indian realities, transforming, in Edward Said's terms, 'instances of a civilisation into ideal bearers of its values, ideas and positions.'[2] There were authors, however, who tried to avoid the pitfalls of exoticisation and who conceptualised, contextualised and, sometimes, even relativised Indian alterity (or, otherness). Ahmed Midhat Efendi (1844–1912), a prolific novelist and influential publisher, maintained that polyandry in India, perhaps a reference to the Mahabharata, was as estranging a practice for Ottoman Muslims as Islamic polygamy was for Western Christians.[3] Strangeness was in the eye of the beholder. In *Duhter-i Hindû* (The Indian Girl, 1875), the first of several plays which explored the impact of colonialism in India, Abdülhak Hamid [Tarhan] (1851–1937), an innovative poet and playwright, referred to the practice of *sati*. By focusing on a ruthless British officer who supported the tradition of widow-burning, the play moved beyond the basic dichotomy between a barbaric East and an enlightened West which often shaped colonial writing. Hamid, nonetheless, admitted having mostly relied on French sources when writing his first play.[4]

Rare were the books written by Ottoman Turkish intellectuals which engaged with Indian religions, such as Şemseddin Sami's (1850–1904) *Esâtir* (Mythology, 1878) which presented the belief systems of the subcontinent beside other polytheistic religions, depending, here too, on Western popular and scholarly literature. Besides Western sources, Ottoman literati could also rely on Ottoman travelogues such as Ahmed Hamdi Şirvani's (1831–1890) *Hindistan ve Svat ve Afganistan Seyahatnamesi* (A Travelogue to India, Swat and Afghanistan, 1883) and Selanikli Tevfik's (1860–1910) *Musavver Hindistan Seyahatnamesi* (Illustrated India Travelogue, 1901), a rather odd travelogue as the author admittedly never went to the subcontinent.[5] At a much later date, Halide Edib [Adıvar] (1884–1964), another ground-breaking Turkish author, would have first-hand experience of India as she lectured at the Jamia Millia Islamia University in January–February 1935 and published an English-language account of her observations. She claimed that Abdülhak Hamid's plays had introduced her to India.[6] Her book *Inside India* was published in 1937, one year after the establishment of the first Indology department in Turkey by Walter Ruben (1899–1982), at the Faculty of Languages and History of Ankara University. Halide Edib, a persona non grata in her homeland because of her outspoken criticism of Mustafa Kemal Atatürk's authoritarian ways, had published her work in

English in London with the publishers George Allen & Unwin Ltd., and
the impact of her writings in Turkey was limited accordingly. It would be
the works on Indian literature by the sociologist and thinker Cemil Meriç
(1916–87), namely *Hint Edebiyatı* (Indian Literature, 1964) and its revised
and expanded new edition *Bir Dünyanın Eşiğinde* (On the Brink of a World,
1976), as well as numerous articles on Indian literatures and spiritualities
by the poet Asaf Hâlet Çelebi (1907–58), that would familiarise a growing
number of Turkish readers with India and its literary culture. Just like their
predecessors, Meriç and Çelebi relied almost exclusively on Western sources.

TRANSLATING TAGORE

There is no doubt that the translations of Tagore's works into Turkish were
the main factor that contributed to the dissemination of Indian culture
and literature in Turkey. The award of the Nobel Prize in 1913, however,
had only attracted very limited attention, apart from references to Tagore's
being the first non-Western writer to be crowned. The prestigious literary
and cultural periodical *Servet-i Fünûn* featured a two-page illustrated article
'Şair-i Hindu Tagore (Nobel Ödülü)' (The Hindu Poet Tagore, Nobel Prize)
giving an overview of Tagore's career on 25 December 1913. Though the
Nobel Prize and Tagore's recognition in the West had been causal factors
for his discovery in Turkey, it was only in the late 1930s and 1940s that
an increase in translations and publications was witnessed. Some of his
shorter pieces had been published in periodicals, but only two of his works
circulated in book form in the Ottoman script before the alphabet change
of 1928, namely, the novel *The Home and the World* (1928), translated by
Bedri Tahir [Şaman] (d.1956) and re-edited in transliteration in 1942, and
a Turkish translation of the *Crescent Moon* (1928), published by Arâyiş H.
Sami and Kenan Halet.

In a few years' time, Tagore would become the best known and most read
non-Western contemporary author in Turkey. This was truly remarkable since
the Turkish publishing world experienced major difficulties after the alphabet
change and was badly hit by economic hardships affecting the young Turkish
republic. From the 1930s to the end of the 1940s, the surge in translations
was chaotic as different translations of the same work appeared within a few
years, such as two versions of the *Gardener* in 1938, one by Orhan Burian
(1914–53), and the other by İbrahim Hoyi (1908–84) who reissued his
translations in 1941 and 1944. A third translation was published by Mehmet
Şükrü Erden in 1939. Two translations of the *Gitanjali* were published
within one year—Bülent Ecevit's (1925–2006) in 1941 and İbrahim Hoyi's
in 1942. By the end of the 1940s, Turkish readers could read the short story

'The Conclusion' (renamed 'Mrinmaji' after the name of its major female protagonist), *The Gardener, Fruit-Gathering, The Crescent Moon, Gitanjali, The Post Office, The Fugitive, Stray Birds, The Home and the World, Chitra, Lover's Gift, The Poet's Religion* and *The Cycle of Spring* in books and thus become acquainted with a significant sample of the Tagorean canon. Tagore's works even became victims of intellectual snobbery. Asked about Tagore and universalism in literature in an interview in 1946, Çelebi reprimanded his interlocutor for mentioning an author who 'had become so very banal.'[7] The poet, who was a bit of an elitist, was referring to the popularity of Tagore's works in the early 1940s, something he quite obviously frowned upon. Renewed interest in Tagore translations would again be witnessed in the 1960s after the liberalisation in the publishing world following the 1960 military coup and the centenary of Tagore's birth in 1961 and later since the 1990s, when rising interest in alternative spiritualities and non-Abrahamic (i.e., not Jewish, Christian or Islamic) religions have also contributed to a rediscovery of Tagore.

Back in the 1930s and 1940s, at a time when the Turkish state was actively promoting Western culture, Tagore's popularity among Turkey's reading classes was truly extraordinary. Whether Tagore's status in the Turkish publishing world was really a challenge to cultural Euro-centrism in Turkey is questionable however, since interest in Tagore developed years after his recognition in the West. The translations were based exclusively on English, French and German versions. Translators of his poetry in particular, as well as critics, considered this to be problematic. They noted the difficulty of rendering accurately the rhythms and musicality of Tagore's Bengali verses, a point they probably made by establishing themselves, yet again, on Western testimonies, as Turks exposed to recitals of Tagore poetry were few. A notable exception was Halide Edib who was 'held spellbound' by the Bengali singer Nuri-Jihan's recitation of Tagore songs at a concert in Kolkata.[8]

Among Tagore's earliest translators were some outstanding figures of Turkish cultural and political life. His main translator was İbrahim Hoyi (1908–84), a literary journalist and active translator who dedicated much of his life to the promotion of Tagore's works. For Hoyi, translating Tagore was a labour of love. In a short introduction to his translation of *Fruit-Gathering*, he spoke of Tagore as 'a genius poet who had given his name to his era.'[9] His translations were generally well received. After 1947, he collaborated with the Indian authorities and published booklets on Tagore that were edited by the Indian Information Office (*Hindistan Haberler Servisi*). Rasih Güven (b.1923), a Turkish philosopher and India specialist, stated that Hoyi's translations were the most successful, among the many that were published.[10] Hoyi is the translator who has contributed the most to the dissemination of Tagore's works in Turkey by translating *The Gardener* (1938), *Fruit-Gathering* (1940), *The Crescent Moon* (1941), and *Gitanjali* (1942).

Though Hoyi's translations were re-published several times, it is the young Bülent Ecevit's Turkish renderings that would attract most attention, years after their initial publication. This had to do with the way his political career would evolve and lead him, a Kemalist social-democrat, to the office of Prime Minister in Turkey. Nonetheless, Ecevit was a poet in his own right and his translations of *Gitanjali* (1941) and *Stray Birds* (1943) had an undeniable literary value, which explains their popularity even today. During his official visit in India in 2000, Prime Minister Ecevit was awarded an honorary doctorate by Visva-Bharati University for his contribution to the promotion of Indian literature. Ecevit fondly remembered how he had been introduced to Tagore by his father. It was partly due to his desire to read Tagore in the original—even though his own translations were based on the English versions — that he went on to study Bengali and Sanskrit at the School of Oriental and African Studies in London.[11] The introduction that the future statesman wrote for *Stray Birds* revealed his familiarity with Tagore's works. He emphasised, in particular, the humanist dimension of this collection which, he argued, made it different from the mystical poetry rendered into Turkish by earlier translators.[12]

Although he translated only *The Gardener* (1938), Orhan Burian, an influential critic and professor of English literature at Ankara University, too, deserves a mention among Tagore's foremost translators, as he played an important role in the promotion and translation of English language literature in Turkey and modern Turkish literature in the English-speaking world.

Notwithstanding Tagore's Nobel Prize, had he not been promoted in Europe by the likes of William Butler Yeats and André Gide, it is highly unlikely that Tagore's voice would have been heard by the Turkish intelligentsia. Local Turkish connections also played a significant role in the continued interest in Tagore. From a political point of view, support for India's independence struggle in the newly independent Turkish republic and Tagore's apparent interest in the Kemalist experiment in Turkey facilitated his introduction into the country. Tagore's positive assessment of the changes he witnessed during a short stay in 1926 when his boat was docked for two days in Istanbul was widely reported in the press. In an article, 'Rabindranath Tagore and the Turkish Movements' (Rabindranath Tagore ve Türk Hareketleri) published in the May 1930 issue of the *Hayat* periodical, the anonymous journalist reported that Tagore addressed a letter to Mustafa Kemal Atatürk in order to obtain books in Turkish for

Visva-Bharati. His wish was granted. Tagore also wrote a letter to Celal Nuri [İleri] (1881–1938), a nationalist intellectual close to the Kemalist regime, in which he expressed his admiration for the Turkish revolution. According to the journalist, Gyula Germanus, the Hungarian Orientalist who would later teach at Visva-Bharati might have influenced Tagore.[13]

Tagore's views on nationalism, his reflections on Eastern and Western civilisations and his mysticism were the themes that particularly attracted the Turkish intelligentsia's attention as they were also hotly debated in the Republic at the time. In a country where nationalism was considered as one of the founding principles of the new state and the independence war its founding event, Tagore's scepticism about he Indian independence struggle and his opposition to Gandhi were considered disconcerting, but it was something that some intellectuals, such as Cemil Meriç, a conservative cultural critic and thinker, chose to engage with. In his monograph on Indian literature, Meriç stressed the uneasy relationship between Tagore and Indian nationalism, as the Bengali poet was 'favourable to the merging of East and West and the solidarity between nations.'[14] This conflict had already interested earlier Turkish critics.[15] Meriç maintained that Tagore's philosophy could simply not fit into the narrow nationalism of his contemporaries, but that he remained quite conscious of the dangers represented by Western encroachment in Asia.[16] Tagore's discourse on the East–West divide was of particular interest in this discussion, as Westernisation in various guises had been on the agenda of the reformist intellectuals and ruling elite in Ottoman Turkey since the early nineteenth century. Some, such as Peyami Safa (1899–1961), a not untalented novelist and right-wing pundit, with a particular fondness for name-dropping, questioned Tagore's acting as the flag-bearer for Asian spirituality as opposed to Western materialism. Quoting the Italian historian, Guglielmo Ferrero (1871–1942), he maintained that this struggle existed within the West itself.[17] Meriç, on the other hand, was inclined to forgive Tagore's 'misconceptions, considering him more of a visionary than a theoretician or historian of ideas. He defined him as a bridge between East and West and opposed 'Tagore's dream' to 'Gandhi's realism.' According to Meriç, Tagore was 'peace, bliss and poetry.'[18]

Interest in Tagore's works was not focused exclusively on his ideas. From a literary point of view, the early Tagore's exploration of the Indian countryside in his fiction was attractive for Turkish authors struggling to make Anatolia the focus of their works, as recommended by the advocates of nationalist literature. The spiritual dimension of some of his parables and of his poetry attracted a different crowd. At a time when Sufi brotherhoods and expressions of religiosity were banned from the public sphere, celebrating Tagore's spirituality promised to be a way to challenge the secularisation of the ruling class. Tagore's poetry also introduced those who were uneasy with both positivism and Islam's response to spiritual cravings to alternative forms of spirituality.

Conservative writers tended to 'Islamicise' Tagore's spirituality and glossed over elements of his mysticism that would have invalidated such a reading. Meriç put an emphasis on Tagore as a seeker of 'the unity at the source of the multiplicity' thus making him fit into a framework of Islamic mysticism. Publishing houses with a strong Islamic identity also integrated Tagore into an Islamic discourse, as witnessed in the marketing of Tagore translations by the national-conservative *Dergâh* publishing house. In a foreword to an undated revised edition of the *Gitanjali*, translated by Cengiz Durkan, the publishing house suggests that they published the work in order to counter the promotion of Westernisation in the cultural sphere that had led to 'Turkey's estrangement from its essential thought' and increased ignorance about non-Western civilisations.[19] On the back cover of this edition, Tagore is made to fit the publisher's own religious nationalist outlook by being described as a 'promoter of the nationalist movement' who in his works 'mainly explored the problem of the existence of God', a programme to which the publishers subscribed.

Tagore's spirituality and quest for unity, however, also attracted writers who chose to engage with and cherish his alterity. Rather than appropriating and Islamicising him, they put the Bengali poet's non-Abrahamic spiritual heritage to the fore. The poet Asaf Halet Çelebi is a case in point. Çelebi, himself a neo-mystical poet whose works were strongly influenced by surrealism, distinguished between Tagore's and his own understanding of nirvana: 'My conception of nirvana is different from the Buddhist and from Tagore's nirvanas: Even when reaching the peak of felicity, the nirvana, I remain restless and perturbed. The balance I reach there is an uneasy one as there is still anguish in the most secret corners of my soul.'[20] This kind of critical dialogue between a Turkish poet and Tagore was, however, exceptional.

READING TAGORE

Interestingly, very little scholarly work has been produced about Tagore in Turkish. This is most probably because his intellectual output challenges linguistic, generic and disciplinary boundaries and thus does not easily fit into the well-defined categories of Turkish academia which is rarely open to interdisciplinary and comparative research. Despite his popularity, only a few monographs were written on him. Fethi Tevetoğlu's *Tagore: Hayatı ve Eserleri* (Tagore: Life and Works, 1938), a 104-page book, was devised as an introductory text to a multi-volume edition of Tagore's works.[21] It consisted of three chapters: a biography, a section on Tagore's links to Turkey and a study of his works displaying large excerpts.[22] Tevetoğlu's analysis largely relied on the studies by Heinrich Meyer-Benfey, André Gide and Henry de Zogheb. However some of the issues that he chose to emphasise were revealing of his own concerns and of the socio-political and cultural climate he was working in.

At a time when debates were still raging on the need to develop a 'literature that spoke of the homeland' which would engage with Anatolian realities (Anatolia, formerly 'Asia Minor', covers most of Turkey, roughly corresponding to its Asian part), Tevetoğlu stressed that novels such as *The Home and the World* and *Gora* were politically engaged texts where the author took on important societal questions. The short stories were of particular interest since they were most successful in conveying the Indian reality.[23] Tagore was a possible model for young Turkish authors. Turkey's modern literature was experiencing labour pains and the author maintained that 'being acquainted with personalities such as Tagore would play an important role in its development.'[24] Tevetoğlu's views on culture and literature were essentialist. He believed that the greatness of Tagore's poetry 'could only be truly conceived by an Indian.' Nevertheless, using the vague concept of 'artless art', he stressed that the 'essence' or message of Tagore's works could reach the reader in translation, even though the form and the beauty of the language got lost.[25] Quoting long excerpts from Gide's introduction to *Gitanjali,* Tevetoğlu celebrated Tagore's poetry.

There is little doubt that Tevetoğlu believed in the need for greater interchange among Eastern literatures and authors, thus challenging the exclusivist proponents of literary Westernisation. It is ironic but also sad that, while stressing the need for a greater knowledge of Indian literature, he himself remained closely dependent on Western scholarship and translations. Though he chose not to give any details, he suggested that earlier translations of Tagore's works had been unsatisfactory and he described his own methodology and sources as a translator. His translations were based on German translations by Hans Effenberger, Annemarie von Puttkamer and Marie Luise Gothein as well as on André Gide's French translations. Knowing neither Bengali nor English, he had his own translations checked by a linguist who compared their accuracy to Tagore's own English translations.[26] Tevetoğlu was conscious that misconceptions about Indian religions and polytheism could harm the reception of Tagore's works in an Islamic country, so he put particular emphasis on the monotheism of the Brahmo Samaj to which Tagore belonged though acknowledging Christian influences, and quoted Gide's view that polytheistic motives in *Gitanjali* were rare.[27] Whenever they appeared they were 'unreal and superficial'.[28] Whether

Tevetoğlu himself was so much disturbed by polytheistic and pantheistic belief systems is open to debate, as he went to the extent of comparing Tagore to God, an abomination from an Islamic point of view: 'The greatness of Tagore lies in his ability to create beauty and perfection out of plainness and simplicity. That is similar to God's creating his great work—man—from mud, as retold in the books of the religions.'[29]

Twenty-three years later, in 1961, Ülkü Tamer (b. 1937), one of the leading poets of the modernist İkinci Yeni movement, published a small anthology of Tagore's works, preceded by a translation of William Butler Yeats's famous essay 'For Tagore' which had been quite influential in promoting the Bengali poet and thinker's works in the English-speaking world.[30] Though Tamer's own short introduction focused exclusively on biographical details, the book, published by the prominent liberal publisher Varlık arguably played a role in rekindling interest in Tagore. Love for the Tagores was there in the family. Tamer's wife, Tomris (1941–2003), a short-story writer and acclaimed translator in her own right, started her literary career with the publication of her translation of the short-story Caramel Doll, by Abanindranath Tagore, in Varlık magazine in 1962.

In 1971, Rasih Güven published Rabindranath Tagore ve Ateş Böcekleri, a work that consisted of two parts: a study of Tagore as a poet, a philosopher and an educator, followed by a translation of Fireflies.[31] Güven is the only writer who can really be considered a Tagore scholar in Turkey. He studied Indian philosophy and Sanskrit at Visva-Bharati with an Indian government scholarship in 1950. After doing his BA, he went on to obtain an MA in philosophy in December 1953. He met Tagore's relatives during his stay and kept in touch with them even later, when he left to pursue doctoral research at Banaras Hindu University.[32] In his introduction, Güven regretted the fact that Tagore was only known in Turkey as a poet and writer, and that his achievements in other fields, including drama, music and education, had been overlooked.[33] Illustrated with excerpts from Tagore's poems, Güven's book provided a general overview of his lyrical poetry, laying particular emphasis, rare among other Tagore critics, on the chief Western influences on his poetry, viz. Romanticism and Bergsonism. The latter point was made in the context of his discussion of Balaka. Though outmoded by the early 1970s, Bergson's philosophy had had an impact on the conservative Turkish intelligentsia in the earlier decades. Güven's statement that Tagore questioned Bergson's idea of a perpetual becoming without a final aim[34] was an invitation to read Tagore as a philosopher engaging with Western philosophy, who could make meaningful contributions to intellectual debates in Turkey. For Güven it was obvious that Tagore the poet should not be distinguished from Tagore the philosopher. He gave information on Tagore's philosophical essays, most of which were unknown in Turkey. Interestingly, while other authors suggested the compatibility of Tagore's spiritual leanings with Islamic mysticism, Güven emphasised Christian influences on the Bengali poet and thinker. He was conscious of the impact of Brahmo Samaj on the young Tagore, but he put particular emphasis on Tagore's conception of a personalised God being close to Christianity.[35] Noting that Tagore had discussed the similarities between Buddhism and Christianity, and certain aspects of Vaishnavism and early Christian beliefs, he argued that 'Tagore's romanticism is Christian in spirit,' an argument not unknown to Tagore scholars in the West, but which in the Turkish context, always gripped by fear of Christian missionary activities, was a daring statement which could damage the poet's reputation.[36] The scholar also maintained the idea that the unity of God, man and nature were central to Tagore's thought, discussing how Tagore constructed ontological distinctions between God and man.[37]

In the final part of his study, Güven gave an overview of the genesis of Visva-Bharati and of its history, a story that had not yet been told in Turkey.[38]

Though it did not give any references, Güven's book contributed to a more holistic image of Tagore in Turkey, going beyond the often trite debates on nationalism and religion, symbolised by the obituaries which had been written at the time of the poet's death.[39] When Güven's book was re-edited by the Ministry of Culture in 2000, it appeared in a context of renewed interest in the works of Tagore that continues till today. The Internet has undoubtedly promoted the rediscovery of the Bengali poet. Popular poetry websites as well as obscure webzines often showcase unreferenced translations of his poems and poetic prose thus reaching younger generations of readers who would otherwise have remained unaware of his works. The publishing world's interest in Tagore too has been rekindled in recent years. New editions of the now classical translations of İbrahim Hoyi and Bülent Ecevit are to be found on booksellers' shelves side by side with new translations, some of which are by major figures of contemporary Turkish literature such as Tarık Dursun K (b. 1931), a novelist and short-story writer. It should be noted, however, that publishing houses have focused exclusively on the early Tagore who had enthralled André Gide, William Butler Yeats and Romain Rolland. There has been no interest in his later works, which had little or no impact in Western Europe.

Nonetheless, the variety of publishing houses involved in new publications and republications of Tagore's works, ranging from conservative Islamic to left-wing publishers, make Tagore a rather unique case of a figure appropriated by the whole intellectual and political spectrum. Though one cannot escape the feeling that, among Islamists and socialists, he was sometimes and still is showcased as a token non-Westerner to emphasise

172   Laurent Mignon

their anti-imperialist credentials, he remains a much-read, much appreciated
author for what he truly was—in Rasih Güven's words, 'one of the greatest
poets of the twentieth century' who also has had a 'central position in the
history of modern Turkish literary translations.'⁴⁰

NOTES

1. M. Atsızayoldaş, *Tagore: Hayatı ve Eserleri*, p. 9. M[engüç] Atsızayoldaş was
   one of several pseudonyms used by Tevetoğlu.
2. Said, *Orientalism*, 252.
3. Herzog and Motika, 'Orientalism "alla turca",' 145, 150.
4. Tarhan, *Tiyatroları 3*, 159.
5. Herzog and Motika, 'Orientalism "alla turca",' 163.
6. Enginün, 'Duhter-i Hindû, Finten Hakkında,' 18.
7. Çelebi, *Bütün Yazıları*, 479.
8. Edib, *Inside India*, 137.
9. Hoyi, 'Önsöz,' 8.
10. Güven, 'Bengal Edebiyatı ve Baüller,' 144.
11. Mengü, 'Tagore ile Tanışma.'
12. Ecevit, 'Önsöz,' 5–6.
13. Atsızayoldaş, *Tagore*, 31–3. This, however, is unlikely since Tagore may only
    have briefly met Germanus on 30 October, a few weeks before his stopover in
    Istanbul, at a one-hour-long, crowded reception of the Hungarian PEN Club,
    of which Germanus was the secretary-general. See Bangha, *Hungry Tiger*, 148.
14. Meriç, *Bir Dünyanın Eşiğinde*, 276.
15. Such as Atsızayoldaş, *Tagore*, 26–7.
16. Meriç, *Bir Dünyanın Eşiğinde*, 277.
17. Safa, *Doğu Batı Sentezi*, 42.
18. Meriç, 'Tagor,' in *Bu Ülke*, 245.
19. The book had originally been published by the nationalist Islamic Hareket
    publishers in 1971; [Anonymous], 'Sunuş,' 3 4
20. Çelebi, *Bütün Yazıları*, pp. 174–5.
21. The book was re-edited in 1939.
22. This short section mainly consists of the above mentioned article entitled
    'Rabindranath Tagore and the Turkish Movements,' and published in the May
    1930 issue of the *Hayat* periodical
23. Atsızayoldaş, *Tagore*, 48–58.
24. Ibid., 12.
25. Ibid., 43–5.
26. Ibid., 10–12.
27. Ibid., 14.
28. Ibid., 84.
29. Ibid., 42.
30. Tamer, *Tagore*. It was re-edited in 2001 by Yapı Kredi Yayınları.
31. Güven, *Rabindranath Tagore*.

Turkey 173

32. Ibid., 1.
33. Ibid., 2.
34. Ibid., 5.
35. Ibid., 16.
36. Ibid.
37. Ibid., 18–19.
38. Güven, *Rabindranath Tagore*, 26.
39. *Cumhuriyet* newspaper, for instance, had put the emphasis on his poetry being 'mystical and patriotic.' Anon. 'Meşhur Hind Şairi Tagor Öldü,' *Cumhuriyet,* 8 August 1941, 3.
40. Güven, 'Bengal Edebiyatı ve Baüller,' 144.

WORKS CITED

[Adıvar], Halide Edib. *Inside India.* London and Delhi: Oxford University Press, 2003.
[anonymous]. 'Sunuş' [Presentation]. In Rabindranath Tagore, *Gitanjali,* translated by Cengiz Durkan. Istanbul: Dergâh Yayınları, n.d., 3–4.
Atsızayoldaş, M[engüç]. *Tagore: Hayatı ve Eserleri* [Tagore: His Life and Works]. Istanbul: Acun Basımevi, 1938.
Bangha, Imre. *Hungry Tiger.* New Delhi: Sahitya Akademi, 2008.
Çelebi, Asaf Halet. Edited by Hakan Sazyek. *Bütün Yazıları* [Complete Articles]. Istanbul: Yapı Kredi Yayınları, 1998.
Ecevit, Bülent. 'Önsöz' [Foreword]. In Rabindranath Tagore, *Avare Kuşlar* [*Stray Birds*], translated by Bülent Ecevit, Istanbul: Hilmi Kitabevi, n.d., 3–6.
Enginün, İnci. 'Duhter-i Hindû, Finten Hakkında' [About Duhter-i Hindû, Finten]. In Abdülhak Hamid Tarhan, *Tiyatroları 3: Duhter-i Hindû, Finten* [Plays 3: The Indian Girl, Finten], edited by İnci Enginün, Istanbul: Dergâh Yayınları, 1999, 7–33.
Güven, Rasih. 'Bengal Edebiyatı ve Baüller' [Bengali Literature and the Bauls]. *Ankara Üniversitesi Dil, Tarih ve Coğrafya Fakültesi Dergisi,* 35, no. 2, 1991, 139–54.
———. *Rabindranath Tagore ve Ateş Böcekleri* [Rabindranath Tagore and the *Fireflies*]. Ankara, 1971.
Herzog, Christoph, and Raoul Motika. 'Orientalism "alla turca": Late 19th/Early 20th Century Ottoman Voyages into the Muslim "Outback",' *Die Welt des Islams,* 40, no. 2, 2000, 139–95.
Hoyi, İbrahim. 'Önsöz' [Foreword]. In Rabindranath Tagore, *Meyva Zamanı,* translated by İbrahim Hoyi. Istanbul: Remzi Kitabevi, 1960, 7–8.
Mengü, Nazan. 'Tagore ile Tanışma,' [Meeting Tagore]. *Hürriyet.* Accessed on 24 June 2013. http://dosyalar.hurriyet.com.tr/ecevit/tagore.asp
Meriç, Cemil. *Bir Dünyanın Eşiğinde* [On the Brink of the World]. Istanbul: İletişim Yayınları, 1998.
———. *Bu Ülke* [This Country]. Istanbul: İletişim, 1998.
Said, Edward. *Orientalism.* London: Penguin Books, 1991.

174 Laurent Mignon

Safa, Peyami. *Doğu Batı Sentezi* [The East–West Synthesis]. Istanbul: Yağmur Yayınevi, 1963.

Tamer, Ülkü. *Tagore*. Istanbul: Varlık Yayınları, 1961.

Tarhan, Abdülhak Hamid. *Tiyatroları 3: Duhter-i Hindû, Finten* [Plays 3: The Indian Girl, Finten]. edited by İnci Enginün, Istanbul: DergâhYayınları, 1999.

11

Jewish Diaspora and the State of Israel (Yiddish and Hebrew Reception)

Alexander Cherniak and Sergei Serebriany

Historical Background

This is probably the first attempt to describe the reception of Tagore's works in the Hebrew and Yiddish world and in the State of Israel. Therefore we are unable to provide much more beyond preliminary bibliographical data about published translations and some information about the translators. The main sources for our information have been the National Library of Israel in Jerusalem, the Internet resource Worldcat (http://www.worldcat.org/), as well as other Internet resources. Additional information has been culled from the two largest libraries in Russia: the Russian State Library in Moscow (the former Lenin Library) and the National Library of Russia in St Petersburg.

The State of Israel has two official languages: Hebrew and Arabic. English is also widely used, because prior to the proclamation of Israel in 1948, Palestine had been administered for thirty years (1918–48) by the British. But Arabic is excluded from this review, as the reception of Tagore's works in the Arabic-speaking world is the subject of another contribution. English has also been excluded for obvious reasons (even though the reception of Tagore by English-reading Israelis may differ from the reception of his works in other English-language countries). We will consider translations and some other publications only in Hebrew and Yiddish, the two most important Jewish literary languages. Not only in the diaspora, but in Israel too, at the earlier stages of Tagore's reception, his works might have been read at least as much in Yiddish as in Hebrew.

By 1913, the year Tagore received the Nobel Prize, the majority of the world's Jews lived within the borders of the Russian Empire, which still included a large part of Poland, most of today's independent Ukraine, as well as Belarus, Lithuania and Moldova (Moldavia or Bessarabia). Many

Jews lived also across the border, in Galicia, Bukovina and other parts of the Hapsburg (Austro-Hungarian) Empire. The main spoken language of Eastern European Jews was Yiddish (with its various dialects). But for all Jews, the most important and the most revered language was Hebrew, the language of the Holy Scriptures, itself called '*lashon ha-kodesh*' ('the Holy Language').[1] From the end of the eighteenth century, modern secular literatures gradually developed in both Yiddish and Hebrew.[2]

In 1861, the year of Tagore's birth, Emperor Alexander II launched his 'Great Reforms' in the Russian Empire. In 1881 (the year Tagore wrote his first drama, *Balmiki-Pratibha*), the Emperor was assassinated by a group of comparatively young people who thought that his reforms had been inadequate and fraudulent. One of the terrorists was a Jewish woman. In 1881–2, a wave of anti-Jewish pogroms swept through the Empire. These events are considered by historians as a kind of defining point in the history of East European Jews. It is since the early 1880s that the first wave of the Jewish immigration to Palestine began (the so-called First 'Aliyah'; Aliyah is the Hebrew word for 'ascent', referring to the 'return' to the Holy Land, i.e., Palestine). It is also since the early 1880s that many Jews from the Russian Empire (as well as from the Austro-Hungarian Empire) started emigrating to South and North America, but mostly to the USA. Those migrants brought to the New World the two Jewish languages, the colloquial Yiddish in the first place, but the liturgical and literary Hebrew as well. The USA became the country with one of the largest Yiddish-speaking populations. The Yiddish press as well as book printing in Yiddish grew immensely. That is why the first book of translations of Tagore's poems in a Jewish language (Yiddish) came out in the USA, in 1915. The modern Hebrew language was also cultivated in the New World, but to a much lesser degree than Yiddish.

After the disintegration of the Russian Empire in the wake of the 1917 Revolution, and through most of the 1920s, the newly independent countries Poland and Lithuania became important centres of Jewish culture and literature in Eastern Europe. As we shall see, quite a number of translations of Tagore's works into Hebrew and Yiddish appeared in the 1920s in Poland and Lithuania. But Hitler's rise to power, World War II, the Holocaust, and the subsequent emigration of surviving East European Jews to Israel brought about the end of Jewish culture and of literatures in the Jewish languages in Eastern Europe.

THE EARLY PHASE OF TAGORE TRANSLATIONS

The first book by Tagore in a Jewish language appeared in Philadelphia, USA, in 1915. It was a translation of *The Gardener* into Yiddish, translated by Oskar Dubin.[3] In 1917, a slim book about Tagore came out in New York: *Rabindranath Tagore: A Study and an Appreciation* by Moshe-Itzhak Littauer (1888–1937).[4]

The next translations of Tagore's poetry both into Yiddish and Hebrew appeared in Russia in the fateful year 1917, the year of the Russian Revolution. In the spring of the same year, Hayim Nahman Bialik (1873–1934) and a group of his fellow Jewish litterateurs brought out an anthology of modern Hebrew writings in the city of Odessa (now in independent Ukraine). Its title was *Kneset* (here meaning 'Gathering').[5] It included a translation from English of all the 103 *Gitanjali* poems. The translator was David Frischmann (alias Frishman, 1859–1922), an outstanding figure in the history of modern Jewish literature.[6] He was born in a family of wealthy merchants in the town of Zgierz, near Łódź (in an area of Poland which was then part of the Russian Empire). In 1874, at the age of fifteen, David Frishman published his first literary works, a short story in Hebrew and a translation in Hebrew of a poem by Heinrich Heine. In 1881–3, Frishman lived in Berlin, later in Warsaw, and between 1890 and 1895 he was a student of philology, philosophy and history of art at the University of Breslau. The city of Breslau (now Wrocław, in Poland) was part of Prussia and later of Germany. It means that David Frishman got his university education in German. He was a person of pan-European culture. As for the place of David Frishman in the annals of modern Hebrew letters, a historian wrote:

> Frishman constitutes a veritable landmark in modern Hebrew literature... His literary activity was versatile and all-embracing for he distinguished himself as [a] poet, critic, cultural journalist, editor, translator, and short story writer... He enriched Hebrew literature with numerous translations from German, French, and English.[7]

Translations from various languages form a large part of David Frishman's literary legacy. By the end of the nineteenth and beginning of the twentieth century, he translated into Hebrew poems of Lord Byron, Heinrich Heine and Alexander Pushkin, Henrik Ibsen's play *A Doll's House*, tales of Hans Christian Andersen and *Thus Spake Zarathustra* by Friedrich Nietzsche. Later in his life he translated tales of the Brothers Grimm and Shakespeare's play *Coriolanus*. So the translation of Tagore's *Gitanjali* was not an isolated episode in David Frishman's literary career.

When World War I broke out, Frishman was living in Berlin. He was arrested as a subject of the Russian Empire and sent back home. In 1915, he settled in Odessa. It was there that he translated the tales of the Brothers Grimm and *Gitanjali*.[8]

In 1917, some translations of Tagore's poems into Yiddish (from English) came out in Moscow, which was then also an important centre of Jewish cultural life. The translator was Menashe Halperin (1871–1960),[9] a poet who in 1917–18 was a member of a group of avant-garde Yiddish poets in Moscow. The book in which Halperin's translations of Tagore's poems were published was a small collection of poetic translations of a number of poems from various languages into Yiddish. The book (poorly printed on paper of an inferior quality) was called *Fremds* (*The Alien* or *The Foreign*).[10] Among the translated poets are Frenchmen (e.g., Charles Baudelaire, Paul Verlaine), a German (Heinrich Heine), an American (Edgar Allen Poe), and Russians (Pushkin, Lermontov). The book is divided into parts, translator-wise. The last part (pp. 180–8), titled 'From Rabindranath Tagore and others', contains rather free poetic renderings by Menashe Halperin of three poems from *The Gardener* (nos. 28, 36 and 35), one poem of Omar Khayyam (evidently from the famous Fitzgerald version), and one poem of the Russian poet, Igor Severyanin (1887–1941). Halperin's translations seem to be the first and only translations of Tagore's poetry into Yiddish ever published in Moscow.

The following year, 1918, a rich Jewish financier and entrepreneur, Avraham Yosef Stybel (1885–1946), established a publishing house in Moscow.[11] At its early stages, one of the key figures of this publishing venture was David Frishman. When, in 1919, publishing in Hebrew was outlawed by the Bolsheviks, Stybel moved to New York, but his publishing house had branches also in Warsaw and Palestine. In the late 1920s, the publishing house was relocated to Berlin and later to Tel Aviv. The *Encyclopedia of Jews in Eastern Europe* writes:

> With an endowment from Avraham Stybel, the publishing house embarked on an ambitious publishing programme focusing on translations from classical and modern Western literature. ... It also published original Hebrew literary pieces, as well as a small body of original and translated scholarship and philosophy. Its translations were particularly popular, especially in the Hebrew-speaking *Yishuv* [the Jewish community] emerging in Palestine.[12]

One of the ambitious projects of Stybel was the literary quarterly *Ha-Tekufah* (The Epoch). The first three issues, published in 1918 in Moscow, were edited by David Frishman. In the very first issue, Frishman's translation of Tagore's *The Gardener* was published.[13]

After Frishman's translation of *The Gardener*, no translations of Tagore's works into Hebrew came out in Russia. But another translation of some poems from *The Gardener*, this time in Yiddish, appeared in 1919 in the city of Khar'kov (now in independent Ukraine), in a collection of literary pieces in Yiddish, titled *Kunstring. Kinstlerisher almanakh. Bukh 2.* The compiler of this 'artistic almanac' was Kalmen Zingman (1889–1929), a remarkable figure in the history of Jewish letters.[14] Born in Lithuania, he moved to Khar'kov during World War I and in the spring of 1917, after the wartime ban on printing in Yiddish was lifted, he issued the first 'book' of the literary almanac *Kunstring*. The book which contained the translations from *The Gardener* was the second and the last in the series. In the same year, 1919, a translation of Tagore's drama *Chitra* appeared in New York.[15] The translator was mentioned as Nathan Kaplan.[16]

It seems that no complete translation of *Gitanjali* into Yiddish has ever been published. But in an essay by the literary critic, Moissaye Joseph Olgin (1874–1939), 'Rabindranath Tagore (a great Indian poet)', included in Olgin's book *In the World of Songs* (New York, 1919), we find some poems from *Gitanjali* translated into Yiddish (obviously by the author of the essay).[17]

After 1919, no translations of Tagore's works into Yiddish appeared in print either in Russia (the Soviet Union), or in the USA. At least none has been registered in existing bibliographical sources. But during the 1920s, several books by Tagore in Yiddish as well as in Hebrew were published in Europe—in Poland, Lithuania, and Germany.

In 1921, another translation of *The Gardener* into Yiddish came out in Byalystok (Poland) from the publishing house A. Albek.[18] The translation, by Libe Burshtin, was edited by Pesah Kaplan.[19] The publishing house A. Albek must have been very short-lived. In WorldCat (a large online library catalogue), only five more books in Yiddish published by these publishers are listed.

A collection of Tagore's short stories came out in Berlin in 1922, from the publishing house Vostok.[20] The Vostok (meaning 'east' in Russian) was another short-lived Jewish publishing house, which brought out books in Yiddish from Dresden in 1921 and from Berlin in 1922–23 (about twenty titles in all). The translator of Tagore's short stories, Schemarja (Shemaryahu) Gorelik (1877–1942), was a Jewish litterateur who was born near Poltava (in today's Ukraine); he wrote in Russian, Yiddish and German, lived in various countries, and in 1933 settled in Palestine.[21] In 1921, Sh. Gorelik issued another book in Yiddish (from the publishers Vostok in Dresden) titled *Groyse neshomes* (Great souls) in which he put together his essays on Michelangelo, Blaise Pascal, Thomas Carlyle, John Ruskin, Walt Whitman, Lev Tolstoy—and Rabindranath Tagore.[22]

Moving back to Poland, Tagore's book of poems *Fruit-Gathering* came out in Warsaw in 1922, translated into Yiddish under the title *Shpetzumer* (Late Summer). It was published by the firm Kultur-lige-varlag.[23] The translator,

Hersh Dovid Nomberg (1876–1927), was a noted essayist and short story writer as well as a political activist who wrote both in Yiddish and Hebrew. Besides Tagore, he translated into Yiddish the tales of *1001 Nights* and some plays of Shakespeare.[24] As for the Kulturlige, it was an important Jewish social network, first in Ukraine (till it was ousted by the Bolsheviks) and later in Poland and other East European countries.[25]

Also in 1922, in Warsaw, five books of Tagore were published by Stybel, all translations in Hebrew by David Frishman, who had moved from Moscow to Warsaw together with Stybel and died in Berlin in the same year. The translations of *Gitanjali*, first published in the *Kneset* (Odessa, 1917), and of *The Gardener*, first published in *Ha-Tekufah* (Moscow, 1918), were published as separate books.[26]

The translation of *The Crescent Moon,* first published in Warsaw, in the fifth issue of *Ha-Tekufah,* also came out as a separate book.[27] Translations of *Fruit-Gathering* and *Chitra* appeared for the first time.[28] In 1922, all the five texts were published in one volume.[29] This book was re-issued, under another title, in 1927.[30]

We may assume that the translations of David Frishman have not lost their value even for Israelis of the present time. A collection of his translations was published in Israel in the early 1950s.[31] Translations occupy four of the eleven volumes of Frishman's *Collected Works* published in 1964.[32] The literary legacy of this remarkable person deserves more attention from scholars than has been given so far.

In 1923, three more books by Tagore in Hebrew translation came out in Warsaw: *Woman* (evidently, the last chapter of his book *Personality*), *Nationalism* and *Thought Relics.*[33] They were published by Hotza'at Traklin, one more relatively short-lived Jewish publishing house, which was active from 1922 to 1929 and published about thirty books in Hebrew. The translator's name Y. Adulomi seems to be a pseudonym. Thus ends the story of how Tagore's works were translated into Hebrew in Europe.

Yiddish Translations in Europe

The story of translations into Yiddish is a bit longer. Two books were brought out between 1926 and 1929, by the publisher B. A. Kletzkin, from Warsaw and Vilno (today's Vilnius, the capital of Lithuania): *Nationalism*, first published in Warsaw in 1926 and then republished in Vilno in 1929, and the novel *The Home and the World*, published in Vilno in 1928.[34] Boris Kletzkin (1875–1937) founded his publishing house in Vilno in 1910. Until the 1920s, it was one of the largest publishers in Yiddish. The translator of *Nationalism*, Joshua (or Yoshue) Rapoport (1895–1971), was a well-known literary critic who wrote in Yiddish and Russian; he translated works of literature into Yiddish from English, French, German, and Russian.[35] The translator of *The Home and the World*, Sarah Rayzen (alias Reisen, 1885–1974), was also a noted poet, prose writer and translator.[36]

No translations of Tagore's works into Yiddish appeared after 1929 in Europe. But in 1933, in Kaunas, then the capital of independent Lithuania, a slim book about Tagore titled *Rabindranath Tagore: Life, Work, and Social Ideology*, by L. Kopelevicius, was published.[37]

We should also mention a book by Haiman Erlikh, *In shpigl fun umru* (In the Mirror of Unrest), published in 1974 in Johannesburg by Varlag Kayor.[38] The book has two parts; the first part contains seventy-four original poems by the author, and in the second we find translations (from English) of thirty-eight poems of Tagore, mostly taken from *The Crescent Moon* and *The Gardener*. Varlag Kayor was a publishing house of South Africa which brought out books in Yiddish from the early 1950s and at least up to the early 1980s.

Translations Since the 1930s in Palestine and Israel

From 1930, all translations of Tagore's works into Hebrew appeared in Palestine (or rather in Eretz-Yisra'el, 'the land of Israel') and later in the state of Israel. In 1930, a Hebrew translation of *The Home and the World* came out in Tel Aviv.[39] According to the *Lexicon ha-sifrut ha-'ivrit he-chadashah* (Electronic encyclopaedia of modern Hebrew literature) the translator, Pesach Ginzburg, was born in today's Ukraine in 1894. He studied in Odessa and published his first poem, in Hebrew, in 1911. In 1913, he emigrated to America, but in 1922, after many vicissitudes he came to Eretz-Yisra'el and lived there until his death in 1947. He wrote several original books in Hebrew, but published many more translations of Western authors. *The Home and the World* was probably the only non-Western piece of literature translated by Ginzburg.

In 1930 or 1931, a translation of another novel by Tagore came out, *The Wreck*.[40] The translator, Uriel Halperin (1908–81), is better known by his pen name Yonatan Ratosh. He was a major Israeli poet.[41] It is indeed strange that a poet undertook a translation of another poet's novel and not of his poetry.

The first translation of Tagore's poetic work, viz. his epigrams, appeared in Eretz-Yisra'el only about ten years later. It was a translation of *Fireflies* by Reuven Grossman.[42] Reuven Grossman-Avinoam (1905–74) was born in Chicago, but in 1929 he migrated to Palestine. He was a translator and a poet. In 1953, the second edition of *Fireflies* came out.[43]

From the early 1950s till the late 1970s, nine books—translations of various works of Tagore—were brought out by Puah Shalev-Toren (born 1930 in Tel Aviv). She is a poet and a translator of poetry. She has also translated into Hebrew poems by Emily Dickinson. As for Tagore's poetic books, Puah Shalev-Toren first translated *Stray Birds* (1953), then *Lover's Gift* (1954 or 1955) and *Crossing* (1957).[44] In 1960, she published a collection of Tagore's short stories (from the books *Hungry Stones* and *Broken Ties*) under the title *Be-sod ha-nashim* (Secrets of women).[45] In the early 1960s, she translated poems of Tagore from the collection *The Fugitive* and drew the title of her translations from *The Song of Songs* of the Old Testament: *Simini kakhotam* ('Set me as a seal [upon your heart]').[46] In 1969, she published her translations of Tagore's later poems, collected in English in the book *Wings of Death*, and a new translation of the book of poetic epigrams *Fireflies*.[47] In 1973, Puah Shalev-Toren's translation of Tagore's *Herald of Spring* came out, and in 1977 her translation of the drama *Red Oleanders*.[48] It may be noted that, except *Fireflies*, earlier translated by Reuven Grossman, Puah Shalev-Toren translated only those texts which had not been translated before.

In the 1960s, two more translations of Tagore's works came out: the book of essays *Sadhana*, translated by Yechiel Karmon (1962), and the novel *Four Chapters* (*Chaturanga*), translated by Naftali Golan and with an introduction by Alex Aronson (1968).[49]

In 2002, Astrolog publishers (in Hod Hasharon) published a collection of Tagore's short stories, translated from English by Liorah Karmeli, who is a prolific translator from various languages into Hebrew.[50] In 2005, one more book of Tagore's short stories, translated from English into Hebrew by Dafnah Levi, came out.[51] Dafnah Levi translates from many languages and this is so far her only translation of Tagore's works.

FUTURE RESEARCH

This completes the list of all known translations of Tagore's works into Yiddish and Hebrew. It is these translations that may have been read and may be read now in Israel (besides, of course, translations into various other languages). All translations into both languages were done only from English. Translating directly from the original Bengali is a task for the future.

Listing translations is only the first stage of *Rezeptionsforschung* (i.e., studies on the history of literary reception). It remains to be found out how these translations were read and discussed in the press and elsewhere, and how the works of Tagore echoed in works of Israeli writers and poets. These are, again, tasks for future research.

Some observations may be made about Tagore's reception in Israel's music and performance culture. At least two Israeli composers created music based on Tagore's poems or songs. Yinam Leef composed music for two songs in Reuven Grossman-Avinoam's translation (from *Fireflies*), and Ben-Zion Bushel (alias Ben-Zion Orgad, 1926–2006) composed a cycle for mezzo-soprano and flute, also using the translations of Reuven Grossman.[52] The Israeli artist Tomar Borer has prepared a dancing-and-singing performance, using Tagore's poems from the book *Lover's Gift*.[53]

Three influential Israeli personalities were acquainted with Rabindranath Tagore: Martin Buber (1878–1965), Alex Aronson (1912–95), and Shlomith Frieda Flaum (1893–1963).

Martin Buber is one of the best-known twentieth-century philosophers. Born in Vienna, he lived and taught in Germany for many years. In 1938, he moved to Jerusalem and lived there till the end of his life. Buber met Tagore at least three times: in 1921 in Darmstadt, in 1926 in Düsseldorf, and again in 1926 in Prague.[54] In 1950, in Israel, Martin Buber described their meeting in Prague, where they had discussed Jews and Zionism.[55] The attitude of Buber towards Tagore may be described as an ironical and somewhat condescending sympathy. Here is a telling excerpt of a private letter of Buber, written in 1921:

> Tagore himself is a lovable, childlike and reverent figure with a touchingly beautiful faith which, however, is inappropriate for us. He does not understand our burden and believes he could lighten it for us by explaining to us how lightly burdened he is himself. But we, while smiling at him, with wet eyes like a child, do not forget for one moment that we must not throw off anything of the full weight of our burden, and that we must scale the heights with it or fall with it into the precipice.[56]

Alex Aronson was born in Breslau. His parents were Russian Jews who had migrated to Germany from the Russian Empire at the beginning of the twentieth century. His father was a businessman and travelled between the two countries. Alex grew up speaking Russian and German, his 'two mother tongues.' Later he studied European literature in France and Britain, and in 1937, rather than going back 'home', he applied for the post of a lecturer in English literature at Visva-Bharati, Santiniketan. He lived at Santiniketan from 1937 to 1944, that is, during the very last years of Tagore's life and about three years after his death. During his stay in Santiniketan, Alex Aronson wrote two important books: *Rabindranath Through Western Eyes* and *Europe looks at India: A Study in Cultural Relations*.[57] After teaching for two years at Dacca University (now in Bangladesh), Alex Aronson joined his parents in Eretz-Yisra'el in 1946, and from then on lived there, working as a professor of English literature at various universities. Alex Aronson's personal impressions of India, and of Rabindranath Tagore in particular, have been recorded in his autobiography as well as in the preface to *Rabindranath Tagore and Germany*.[58] While living in India, Aronson did not develop much interest in Indian culture, and he did not learn Bengali or any other Indian language. According to Martin Kämpchen:'Over the years he has become one of the best-known and most revered university teachers in Israel.'[59] But he taught English, not Indian literature or Tagore's works. So it is difficult to say to what extent Alex Aronson could contribute to the wider knowledge of and appreciation of Tagore's works in Israel.

Shlomith Frieda Flaum is the author of the only (but substantial) original book in Hebrew about Tagore.[60] There exists also a book about herself in Hebrew.[61] But nothing, it seems, has been written about this remarkable woman in any language other than Hebrew. Flaum corresponded with Tagore for a number of years, and her letters have been preserved in the Visva-Bharati archives. These letters as well as the life and personality of Shlomith Flaum deserve more attention by scholars.

In this essay, only some parts of the story of Tagore's reception in Israel and in the twentieth century Jewish world could be told. It needs further research to tell the entire story.

NOTES

1. cf. 'deva-vāṇī' ('divine language') as the name of Vedic and Sanskrit.
2. cf. e.g., Waxman, *A History of Jewish Literature*; Zinberg, *A History of Jewish Literature*; Dauber, *Antonio's Devils*.
3. Tagore, *Der gertner* (1915). The book is now available on the Internet at the site http://archive.org/details/nationalyiddishbookcenter at the address: http://www.archive.org/details/nybc207752. No further information is available about the translator.
4. Littauer. *Rabindranat Tagor*. We have not been able to look into the book, nor to learn more about the author.
5. *Gitanyali* (1917); cf. Moss, *Jewish Renaissance in the Russian Revolution*, 28. A copy of the book *Kneset* is preserved at the Russian State Library in Moscow.
6. It seems that so far no book in English about David Frishman has been written. But there are at least two books about him in Hebrew (Kremer, *Frishman ha-mevaqer: Monografiyah*; Gilbo'a, *David Frishman*) and one book in Yiddish (Frydman, *David Frischmann*); cf. also Gilbo'a, *Bein re'alizm le-romantiqah*; Parush, *Qanon sifruti we-ide'ologiyah le'umit*. There are also a number of entries in English about David Frishman in various encyclopaedias, including those on the Internet. In the Wikipedia, there are pages about him in German, Hebrew, Polish, French and Swedish.

7. Waxman, *History of Jewish Literature*, 44–6.
8. There is a portrait of David Frishman, painted in 1916 by the artist Leonid Pasternak (1862–1945), the father of the poet and novelist Boris Pasternak (1890–1960); cf. http://www.rjews.net/sifrut/ogl-fri.htm.
9. Menashe Halperin (alias Halpern) was born in what today is Ukraine, but later lived in various countries of Europe and America, as well as in Israel. Died in Saõ Paulo (Brazil); cf. *Leksikon fun der nayer yiddisher literatur*, vol. 3, 1960, 29–30.
10. A copy of this book is preserved at the Russian State Library in Moscow.
11. About him, cf. Holtzman, 'Stybel, Avraham Yosef,' in *The YIVO Encyclopedia of Jews in Eastern Europe*; and a biography in Hebrew: Amichay-Michlin, *Ahavat ish: Avraham Yosef Štibel*.
12. Moss, 'Stybel,' in *The YIVO Encyclopedia of Jews in Eastern Europe*.
13. The first and some later issues of *Ha-Tekufah* are preserved in the Russian State Library in Moscow.
14. cf. Estraikh, 'Zingman, Kalmen,' in *The YIVO Encyclopedia of Jews in Eastern Europe*.
15. Tagore, *Tshitra* (1919).
16. Nathan (alias Nehemiah) Kaplan was born in 1881 in Belostok (Białystok, today's Poland), moved to New York in 1906 and published a number of translations from English and Russian as well as original books of essays and poetry till the mid-1920s. The year and the place of his death are not known; cf. *Leksikon fun der nayer yiddisher literatur*, vol. 8, 1981, 97.
17. Olgin, *In der velt fun gesangen*, 1919, 297–311. This book is now available on the Internet at the address: http://archive.org/details/nybc205681. M. Olgin was born near Kiev, in Ukraine, and went to the USA in 1915. He was a Communist activist and an author of a number of books (in Yiddish) on Communist matters. See e.g., http://archive.jta.org/article/1939/11/24/2848694/dr-m-olgin-freiheit-editor-dead-at-61.
18. Tagore, *Der gertner* (1921). This book is now available in the Internet at the address: http://archive.org/details/nybc212392.
19. Libe Burshtin (spelt Bursztyn in Polish) was born in 1901 in Sokoly (Belostok province of the Russian Empire, now in Poland), in 1921 moved to the USA, wrote in Yiddish mostly for children; died in 1940 in New York; cf. *Leksikon fun der nayer yidisher literatur*, vol. 1. 1956, 273; Pesah Kaplan, a poet and journalist, was born in Łomża (now in Poland) in 1870. He first wrote in Hebrew, but later switched over to Yiddish; translated from Russian and English. Perished in 1943 in the Belostok ghetto. Cf. *Encyclopedia Judaica*, vol. 10, 1973, 754; *Leksikon fun der nayer yidisher literatur*, vol. 8. 1981, 98–100.
20. Tagore, *Dertseylungen* (1922).
21. cf. *Encyclopedia Judaica*, vol. 7, 1973, 807. *Leksikon fun der nayer yiddisher literatur*, vol. 2, 1958, 163–5.
22. Gorelik, *Groyse neshomes*.
23. Tagore, *Shpetzumer*. This book is now available on the Internet at the address: http://archive.org/details/nybc202633.

24. cf. Weiser, 'Nomberg, Hersh Dovid,' in *The YIVO Encyclopedia of Jews in Eastern Europe*.
25. cf. Kazovsky, 'Kultur-lige,' in *The YIVO Encyclopedia of Jews in Eastern Europe*.
26. Tagore, *Gitanyali: Qorban ha-zimrah*; Tagore, *Ha-ganan*, 1922.
27. Tagore, *Ha-yareach ha-'oleh* (1922).
28. Tagore, *Asfei peri*; Tagore, *Chitra* (1922).
29. Tagore, *Zemirot*.
30. *Kitvei Rabindranat Tagore*.
31. *Targumim*.
32. *Kol kitvei David Frishman* [1964].
33. Tagore, *Ha-ishah*; Tagore, *Ha-le'umiyut*; Tagore, *Lechishot neshamah*.
34. Tagore, *Natsyonalizm*, 1926; Tagore, *Natsionalizm*, 1929: this book is now available on the Internet at the address: http://archive.org/details/nybc207748; Tagore, *Di heym un di velt*.
35. cf. *Leksikon fun der nayer yiddisher literatur*, vol. 8, 1981, 392–5.
36. cf. http://jwa.org/encyclopedia/article/reisen-sarah.
37. Kopelevicius, *Rabindranat Tagor: lebn, shafn un gezelshaftlekhe idiologye*. The author was a journalist in Kovno, but very little else is known about him; cf. *Leksikon fun der nayer yiddisher literatur*, vol. 8, 1981, 104.
38. Erlikh, *In shpigl fun umru*, 1976. This book is now available on the Internet at the address: http://archive.org/details/nybc205408. Haiman (Haim Nisson) Erlich was born in 1888 in what is today independent Latvia, in a cobbler's family. In 1906, he emigrated to South Africa, wrote for Yiddish periodicals in Johannesburg and published four books in Yiddish. The year of his death is not known; cf. *Leksikon fun der nayer yiddisher literatur*, vol. 7, 1968, 42–3.
39. Tagore, *Ha-bait we ha-'olam*.
40. Tagore, *Ha-sefinah ha-terufah*.
41. cf. e.g., Carmi, *The Penguin Book of Hebrew Verse*, 139 and 544–6; cf. also http://en.wikipedia.org/wiki/Yonatan_Ratosh.
42. Tagore, *Gachliliyot*, (702 [1941/1942]).
43. Tagore, *Gachliliyot* (1953).
44. Tagore, *Tzipporei nod*; Tagore, *Matat ohev*; Tagore, *'Alei Orach*, 1957.
45. Tagore, *Be-sod ha-nashim*.
46. Tagore, *Simini kha-chotam*.
47. Tagore, *Le-or sheqi'ah*; Tagore, *Gachliliyot* (1969).
48. Tagore, *Besorat aviv*; Tagore, *Hardufim adumim*.
49. Tagore, *Sadhana: Chayei binah*; Tagore, *Sipur be-'arba'ah peraqim*. In 1995, another edition of *Sadhana* in Hebrew came out, by the same translator, but from another publishing house: Tagore, *Binat ha-einsof*. The relations between the two books remain to be investigated;
50. Tagore, *Ha-chayim ve ha-metim ve-sipurim acherim*. (The bibliographical data are confusing. It is not clear whether one book was published, or two, or three; cf. http://www.worldcat.org/search?q=Li'orah+Karmeli++Astrolog+Tagore&qt=results_page.)
51. Tagore, *Hi: Sodot me-achorei ha-sari*.

52. Leef, 'Fireflies': two songs after R. Tagore; Orgad, Leave out my name. Yinam Leef (born in Jerusalem in 1953) is one of the most prominent and active composers in Israel today (http://www.jamd.ac.il/en/content/prof-yinam-leef).
53. cf. http://www.tamarborer.com/pages/yamuna.php.
54. cf. Kämpchen, Rabindranath Tagore and Germany, 94–7.
55. The essay was written in German; cf. an English translation: Martin Buber, 'A Talk with Tagore.' A translation in Hebrew ('Śichah 'im Tagore') is included in the volume: Buber, 'Olelot, 1966.
56. Kämpchen, Rabindranath Tagore and Germany, 94.
57. Aronson, Rabindranath Through Western Eyes; Aronson, Europe Looks at India.
58. Aronson, Brief Chronicles of the Time; ibid., Preface to Kämpchen, Rabindranath Tagore and Germany. See also Aronson's introduction in Hebrew to the translation of Tagore's novel Chaturanga: Tagore, Sipur be-'arba'ah peraqim.
59. Kämpchen, 'Alex Aronson,' 141. This is the most detailed study of Alex Aronson's life and personality.
60. Flaum, Rabindranat Tagor. There is also in Hebrew a book about Tagore and Gandhi translated from French: Baruch, Gandhi we-Tagor: mechankhei 'amam.
61. Govrin, Nosa'at almonit.

Works Cited

(The languages of the books and other publications below are being identified as H = Hebrew; Y = Yiddish)

Tagore Translations

'Alei Orach [Crossing]. Translated by Puah Shalev-Toren. Tel Aviv: Yavneh, 1957. [H]
Asfei peri [Fruit-Gathering]. Translated by D. Frishman. Warsaw: Stybel, 1922. (First published in Ha-Tekufah, no. 7.Warsaw, 1920) [H]
Be-sod ha-nashim [Secrets of women The Hungry Stones and Broken Ties]. Translated by Puah Shalev-Toren. Tel Aviv: Yavneh, 1960 [H].
Besorat Aviv [The Herald of Spring: Poems from Mohua]. Translated by Puah Shalev-Toren. Tel Aviv: Yavneh, 1973. [H]
Binat ha-einsof [Sadhana: The Realisation of Life]. Translated by Yehiel Carmon. Hertzeliyah: Hotza'at Gal, 1995. [H]
Der gertner [The Gardener]. Translated by Oskar Dubin. Philadelphia: Ozer Bros., 1915. (http://archive.org/details/nybc207752). [Y]
Der gertner [The Gardener]. Translated by Libe Burshtin, ed. by P. Kaplan. Białystok: Albek, 1921. (http://archive.org/details/nybc212392). [Y]
Dertseylungen [Short Stories]. Translated by Sh. [= Schemarja, alias Šemarjahu] Gorelik. Berlin: Farlag 'Vostok,' 1922. [Y]
Di heym un di velt: roman [The Home and the World: a Novel]. Translated by Sarah Rayzen, introduction and biographical sketch of the author by Augusta Rosenberg. Vilnius: B. Kletzkin, 1928. [Y]

Fun 'Gertner' [From *The Gardener*]. Translated by M. Halperin. In *Fremds: Shriften.*
Moscow: No Publisher, 1917, 180–6. [Y]
Fun 'Gertner' [From *The Gardener*]. Translated by I. Bleikher. In *'Kunst-ring':*
Kinstlerisher almanakh. (Kharkov) vol. 2. (1919), 15–16. [Y]
Gachliliyot [Fireflies]. Translated by Reuven Grossman. Tel Aviv: Massadah, 702
[1941 or 1942] (New ed.: 1953). [H]
Gachliliyot [Fireflies]. Translated by Puah Shalev-Toren. Tel Aviv: Yavneh, 1969. [H]
Gitanyali [Gitanjali]. Translated by D. Frishman. In *Kneset: Divrei sifrut* by Hayim
Nahman Bialik, ed. Odessa: Ha-qeren li-temikhat sofrim (Fund for supporting
writers),1917, 45–85. [H]
Gitanyali [Gitanjali]. Qorban ha-zimrah [Gitanjali: Song Offerings]. Translated by
D. Frischmann. Warsaw: Stybel, 1922. [H]
Ha-bait we ha-'olam: roman [The Home and the World: a Novel]. Translated by Pesach
Ginzburg. Tel Aviv: Mitzpeh, 1930. [H]
Ha-ganan [The Gardener]. Translated by D. Frishman. In *Ha-Tekufah* (Moscow),
1918, no. 1, 339–418. [H]
Ibid. Translated by D. Frishman. Warsaw: Stybel, 1922. [H]
Ha-chayim we ha-metim we-sipurim acherim ['Living or Dead' and other stories].
Translated by Li'orah Karmeli. Hod ha-Sharon: Astrolog, 2002. [H]
Ha-ishah [Woman]. Translated by I. Adulami. Warsaw: Traklin, 1923. [H]
Ha-le'umiyut [Nationalism]. Translated by I. Adulami. Warsaw: Traklin, 1923. [H]
Hardufim adumim: dramah be-ma'arakhah achat [Red Oleanders: Play in one act].
Translated by Puah Shalev-Toren. Tel Aviv: Yavneh, 1977. [H]
Ha-sefinah ha-terufah [The Wreck]. Translated by Uriel Halperin. Tel Aviv: Mitzpeh,
691 [1930/31] [H]
Ha-yareach ha-'oleh [The Crescent Moon]. Translated by D. Frischmann. Warsaw:
Stybel, 1922 (First published in *Ha-Tekufah*, no. 5.). [H]
Hi: Sodot me-achorei ha-sari ['She: Secrets behind the sari'; short stories]. Translated
by Dafnah Levi. Tel Aviv: Sa'ar, 2005. [H]
In shpigl fun umru [In the Mirror of Unrest]. Written and translated by Haiman Erlikh.
Johannesburg: Farlag 'Kayor,' 1976 (http://archive.org/details/nybc205408). [Y]
Kitvei Rabindranat Tagore [Rabindranath Tagore's Writings]. Translated by
D. Frishman. Warsaw: Stybel, 1927. [H]
Kol kitvei Dawid Frishman. [Collected Works of David Frishman], vol. 8: *Targumim*
[Translations]: *Rabindranath Tagore.* Jerusalem: M. Nyuman, [1964]. [H]
Kenisah asurah we-sipurim acherim [Short stories]. Translated by Li'orah Karmeli.
n.p.: Astrolog, n.d. [H]
Lechishot neshamah [Thought Relics]. Translated by I. Adulami. Warsaw: Traklin,
1923. [H]
Le-'or sheqi'ah [Wings of Death]. Translated by Puah Shalev-Toren. Tel Aviv: Yavneh,
1969. [H]
Matat ohev [Lover's Gift]. Translated by Puah Shalev-Toren. Tel Aviv: Yavneh, 1955
[1954?] (http://www.tamarborer.com/pages/yamuna.php). [H]
Mischaq be-machlaqah achat [Play in one act = *Chitra*]. Translated by D. Frishman.
Warsaw: Stybel, 1922. [H]

Natsyonalizm [Nationalism]. Translated by Y. Rapoport. Warsaw: B. A. Kletzkin, 1926. [Y]

Natsyonalizm [Nationalism]. Translated by Y. Rapoport. Vilnius: B. Kletzkin, 1929 (http://archive.org/details/nybc207748). [Y]

Sadhana: Chayei binah [Sadhana: Life (full) of Wisdom]. Translated by Yechiel Karmon. Tel Aviv: Shim'oni, 1962. [H]

Shpetzumer [Late summer]. Translated by H.D. Nomberg. Warsaw: Kultur-lige, 1922 (http://archive.org/details/nybc202633). [Y]

Simini kha-chotam [Set me as a seal = *The Fugitive*]. Translated by Puah Shalev-Toren. Tel Aviv: Yavneh, 1962 (1963, 1965). [H]

Sipur be-'arba'ah peraqim [Story in Four Parts = *Chaturanga*]. Translated by Naftali Golan, introduction by Alex Aronson. Tel Aviv, Massadah, 1968. [H]

Targumim [Translations (by David Frishman)]. Tel Aviv: M. Nyuman: Knesset [1953 or 1954] (Translations of works by R. Tagore, Rudolf Borchardt, Friedrich Nietzsche and G. G. Byron. It contains *The Gardener, Gitanjali, Fruit-Gathering, The Crescent Moon, Chitra*). [H]

Tshitra [Chitra]. Translated by Nathan Kaplan. New York: Co-operative Literature Soc., 1919. [Y]

Tzipporei nod [Stray Birds]. Translated by Puah Shalev-Toren. Tel Aviv: Yavneh, 1953. [H]

Zemirot [Songs]. Translated by D. Frishman. Warsaw: Stybel, 1922 (The book includes: *Qorban ha-zimrah [Gitanjali]*, *Ha-ganan [The Gardener]*, *Asfei peri [Fruit-Gathering]*, *ha-Yareach ha-'oleh [The Crescent Moon]*; *Chitra [Chitra]*). [H]

Secondary Sources

Amichay-Michlin, Dania. *Ahavat ish: Avraham Yosef Shtibel* [Love for man: Avraham Yosef Stybel]. Jerusalem: Mosad Byaliq, 2000. [H]

Aronson, Alex. *Europe looks at India: A Study in Cultural Relations*. Calcutta: Riddhi, 1979 (2nd ed. First published in 1946).

———. *Brief Chronicles of the Time: Personal Recollections of My Stay in Bengal, 1937–46*. Calcutta: Writers Workshop, 1990.

———. Preface to *Rabindranath Tagore in Germany: A Documentation* by Martin Kämpchen, 1–8. Calcutta: Max Mueller Bhavan, 1991.

———. *Rabindranath Through Western Eyes*. Allahabad: Kitabistan, 1943 (2nd revised ed.: Calcutta: Riddhi, 1978).

Baruch, Avraham F. *Gandhi we-Tagor: mechankhei 'amam* [Gandhi and Tagore: Educators of their people]. Translated by Adah Tsemah. Jerusalem: ha-machlaqah le-'inyanei ha-no'ar, 724 [1964]. [H]

Buber, Martin. 'A Talk with Tagore.' In *Rabindranath Tagore in Germany: A Documentation*, by Martin Kämpchen, 95–7. Calcutta: Max Mueller Bhavan, 1991.

———. *'Olelot*. Jerusalem: Mosad Bialik, 1966.

Carmi, T., ed. *The Penguin Book of Hebrew Verse*. Harmondsworth: Penguin Books, 1981.

Dauber, Jeremy. *Antonio's Devils: Writers of the Jewish Enlightenment and the Birth of Modern Hebrew and Yiddish Literature.* Stanford: Stanford University Press, 2004.

Encyclopedia Judaica. vols. 1–16. Jerusalem: Keter Publishing House, 1972.

Estraikh, Gennady. 'Zingman, Kalmen.' In *The YIVO Encyclopedia of Jews in Eastern Europe* (http://www.yivoencyclopedia.org/article.aspx/Zingman_Kalmen).

Flaum, Shlomith Frieda. *Rabindranat Tagor: ha-meshorer, ha-filosof, ha-sofer, ha-mechanekh, ha-qompozitor, ha-tzayar, ha-martzeh we-ha-nose'a* [Rabindranath Tagore: The poet, philosopher, writer, educator, composer, painter, lecturer]. Jerusalem: Shanti, 1946. [H]

Frydman, Mosche. *David Frischmann.* Warsaw: 1927. [Y]

Gilbo'a Menuchah. *Bein re'alizm le-romantiqah: 'al darko shel Dawid Frishman be-viqoret* [Between realism and romantics: On David Frishman's way in criticism]. Tel Aviv: Universitat Tel Aviv: Ha-qibbutz ha-me'uchad, [1975]. [H]

———. *Dawid Frishman: mivchar ma'amarei biqoret 'al yetzirato* [David Frishman: Selection of criticism of his work]. Tel Aviv, 1988. [H]

Gorelik, Schemarja (Šemarjahu). *Groyse neshomes* [Great Personalities]. Dresden: Farlag 'Vostok,' 1921. [Y]

Govrin, Nurit. *Nosa'at almonit: Shelomit Flaum; chayim wi-yetzirah* [A Forgotten Traveler: Shlomith Flaum. Life and work]. Jerusalem: Karmel, 2005. [H]

Holtzman, Avner. 'Stybel, Avraham Yosef.' In *The YIVO Encyclopedia of Jews in Eastern Europe.* Translated from Hebrew by David Fachler (http://www.yivoencyclopedia.org/article.aspx/Stybel_Avraham_Yosef).

Hundert, Gershon D., ed. *The YIVO Encyclopedia of Jews in Eastern Europe.* New Haven: Yale University Press, 2008.

Kämpchen, Martin. 'Alex Aronson: Refugee from Nazi Germany in Santiniketan'. In *Jewish Exile in India, 1933–45.* Edited by Anil Bhatti and Johannes H. Voigt. New Delhi: Manohar/Max Mueller Bhavan, 1999, 127–45.

———. *Rabindranath Tagore and Germany: A Documentation.* Calcutta: Max Mueller Bhavan, 1991.

Kazovsky, Hillel. 'Kultur-lige.' Translated from Russian by I. Michael Aronson. In *The YIVO Encyclopedia of Jews in Eastern Europe* (http://www.yivoencyclopedia.org/article.aspx/Kultur-lige).

Kopelevicius, L. *Rabindranat Tagor: lebn, shafn un gezelshaftlekhe idiologye* [Rabindranath Tagore: Life, Work and Social Ideology]. Kaunas (Lithuania): [s. n., i.e., *sine nomine*, publisher not known], 1933. [Y]

Kremer, Shalom. *Frishman ha-mevaqer: Monografyah* [Frishman as a literary critic. A monograph]. Jerusalem: Mosad Bialik, 1984. [H]

Leef, Yinam (music). *'Fireflies': two songs after R. Tagore for soprano, flute and harpsichord.* Translated by Reuven Avinoam. Tel-Aviv: Israel Music Institute, 1999, ©1979 (Musical score).

Littauer, Moshe-Itzhak. *Rabindranat Tagor.* New York: Lipshits Printing Co., 1917. [Y]

Moss, Kenneth B. *Jewish Renaissance in the Russian Revolution.* Cambridge, Mass., USA: Harvard UP, 2009.

———. 'Stybel.' In *The YIVO Encyclopedia of Jews in Eastern Europe* (http://www.yivoencyclopedia.org/article.aspx/Stybel).

Niger, Samuel, Jacob Shatzky, eds. *Leksikon fun der nayer yidisher literatur.* vols. 1–8. New York: Congress for Jewish Culture, 1956–81.

Olgin, Moshe. *In der velt fun gesangen* [In the world of songs]. New York: Forverts, 1919.

Orgad, Ben-Zion. *Leave out my name: Cycle for mezzo-soprano and flute.* Translated by R. Grossman, music by Ben-Zion Bushel. New York: Mercury Music Corp. [©1953] (Musical score). [H]

Parush, Iris. *Qanon sifruti we-ide'ologyah le'umit: Biqoret ha-sifrut shel Frishman be-hashwa'ah le-viqoret ha-sifrut shel Klozner u-Brener* [Literary canon and national ideology: The literary criticism of Frishman compared to the literary criticism of Klozner and Brener]. Jerusalem: Mosad Bialik, 1992. [H]

Waxman, Meyer. *A History of Jewish Literature from the Close of the Bible to Our Own Days,* vol. 5: from 1880 to 1935. New York: Bloch Publishing Co., 1947.

Weiser, Kalman. 'Nomberg, Hersh Dovid.' in *The YIVO Encyclopedia of Jews in Eastern Europe* (http://www.yivoencyclopedia.org/article.aspx/Nomberg_Hersh_Dovid).

The YIVO Encyclopedia of Jews in Eastern Europe, ed. Gershon D. Hundert. New Haven: Yale University Press, 2008.

Zinberg, Israel. *A History of Jewish Literature in 12 vols.* Translated and edited by Bernard Martin. Cleveland and Cincinnati: Case Western Reserve Press, 1972–8.

12

GOA, ANGOLA AND MOZAMBIQUE
(PORTUGUESE-SPEAKING REGIONS I)

JOSÉ PAZ RODRIGUEZ

GOA

On 17 February 1510, Afonso de Albuquerque, commanding a Portuguese fleet composed of twenty-one ships and some one thousand and six hundred men conquered the Indian territory of Goa for the Portuguese Crown. On 18 December 1961, the Indian army invaded the territory, the few Portuguese forces being unable to defend it. For 451 years, Goa was a colony of Portugal. Today it is an Indian territory which is prosperous, well organised and structured, with enormous revenue from tourism. The older people still keep alive the Portuguese language and there are countless vestiges of Portuguese culture. As the territory of Goa is situated near Mumbai, Tagore was already well known to Goan writers and intellectuals from the beginning of the twentieth century, and even more after he was awarded the Nobel Prize for Literature in 1913.

Telo de Mascarenhas (1899–1979)

José F. Ferreira Martins's translation of *Chitra* (based on the Bengali play *Chitrangada*) was published in Nova Goa in 1914, being the first book by Tagore published in Portuguese in India. Apart from Adeodato Barreto, Propércia Correia and Froilano de Melo, Telo de Mascarenhas, born in Mormugão-Goa, was the most important Portuguese-speaking Tagore scholar. A fluent speaker of Bengali, he translated Tagore from the original: *The Home and the World* (*Ghare Baire*), *The Wreck* (*Noukadubi*), *and The Four Chapters* (*Chaturanga*). He brought out an anthology of short stories by Tagore with the general title *The key to the enigma and other tales*. In 1943, he published a study entitled *Rabindranath Tagore e a sua mensagem espiritual* (Rabindranath Tagore and his spiritual message). He was an admirer of

Indian culture, which led him to publish monographs on Hindu women, Goa and Portugal, the Ramayana as well as several anthologies of Indian tales. In 1920, he went to Portugal where, at the University of Coimbra, he graduated in Law. For some time he worked as a notary and, together with Adeodato Barreto and José Paulo Teles, he had the newspaper *Índia Nova* (New India) published by the Instituto Indiano [Indian Institute] at Coimbra University, so that they might receive support from Tagore himself. In Goan newspapers, like *O Heraldo* (The Herald) and *Ressurge Goa!* (Arise Goa!), both published by him, he wrote on various occasions about the figure of Tagore, dedicating to him one or two poems and translating others by Tagore into Portuguese. In 1984, the Indian government devoted a monograph on him as part of the series 'Builders of Modern India', written by Shashikar Kelekar.[1]

Due to his love of Goa, India and her culture, the work and thought of Tagore and the support he always had for the Indian cause, against Portuguese colonisation, Telo de Mascarenhas spent several years in jail in Lisbon. Nevertheless, he was steadfast in his enthusiasm for the Portuguese language. In the name of the Comissão Organizadora do Instituto Indiano da Universidade de Coimbra (Organizing Committee of the Indian Institute of Coimbra University), he wrote to Tagore to get books by him. The response by Tagore was published in Portuguese translation in the newspaper *Índia Nova* of 7 May 1928. Tagore expressed his happiness with the foundation of the Instituto, encouraged its patrons, and promised to gift several of his books for its library.

Adeodato Barreto (1905–37)

Júlio Francisco António Adeodato Barreto, a professor, notary, journalist and poet, was born at Margao in Goa. In 1923, he went to Coimbra, and at the university there he studied for the courses of Law, Letters and Philosophy. He also took a diploma at the Teachers Training School, and for a while practised as a teacher at several educational institutions, and he also set up the Universidade Livre (Free University) of Coimbra. His social and pedagogical work in the countryside by the river Mondego for children, common people and workers was exemplary. It followed the principles of the movement of the Escola Nova (New School movement) and the Tagorean educational ideas. Unfortunately, he died very young, without being able to further develop his wonderful work. Nevertheless, he along with others established the Instituto Indiano de Coimbra and, the newspaper *Índia Nova* in 1928, to promote Oriental philosophy and humanism. Some poems on Tagore and studies on him were published. Barretto's study on Hindu civilisation

(*Autodomínio. Tolerância. Humanismo. Síntese*) (Self-control, Tolerance, Humanism: A Synthesis), published as a book by the periodical *Seara Nova* [New Crop], Lisbon, in 1936, dedicated ample space to Tagore and Gandhi. His translation of the biography of Mahatma Gandhi by Romain Rolland remains unpublished and so does a descriptive and critical study he wrote in 1929–30 with the title 'Ideias pedagógicas de Tagore' (Tagore's Pedagogical Ideas), followed by an essay on the application of Tagorean principles to Portuguese schools.

On 27 March 1931, Barreto sent a long handwritten letter to Tagore in which, among other things, he requested permission to carry out translations of Tagore's works into Portuguese. On 18 April, Tagore's private secretary, Anil Kumar Chandra, gave a positive response.

Propércia Correia Afonso de Figueiredo (1882–1944)

Born in Benaulim-Salsete (Goa), Propércia Correia Afonso de Figueiredo was a brilliant student at the Teachers' Training School in Goa. She was a teacher at a primary school and then a professor at the Teachers' Training School until her death. At various times she functioned as the director of the School and the inspector of primary education. Eventually she became a member of the Council of Education and the Council of the Overseas Province of Goa. She was a member of the Instituto Vasco da Gama in Panjim, writing for this institution's Bulletin. In 1933, she published a study about *A mulher na Índia Portuguesa* [Women in Portuguese India]. She wrote on pedagogy and had a profound knowledge of the work done by European authorities on pedagogy and psychology. This led her to her wide-ranging work *Rabindranath Tagore. O educador* (Rabindranath Tagore. The Educator)[2]. In it, she analysed the vision Tagore had as an educator, and his educational ideas on the psychology and development of children. She also analysed the educational institutions at Visva-Bharati. She based her study on the biography of Tagore by Bento de Jesus Caraça.[3] She commented especially on several poems in the book *A lua nova* (*The Crescent Moon*) and *Oferenda lírica* (*Gitanjali*).

Froilano de Melo (1887–1955)

Indalêcio Froilano Pascoal de Melo was a doctor of international renown, an extraordinary parasitologist and epidemiologist. He was born in Benaulim-Salsete (Goa) and died in Brazil. He was a prominent professor of the Medical School in Goa (now the Goa Medical College), one of the oldest and among the most prestigious in India at the time. From 1922 onwards, he also served as a professor at the Faculty of Medicine in Oporto in Portugal.

In 1944, he wrote the monograph *O cântico da vida na poesia tagoreana* (The canticle of life in Tagore's poetry). It was based on a lecture delivered on 4 February 1946 at the premises of the Liga Portuguesa de Profilaxe Social (Portuguese League for Social Prophylaxis) in Portugal. With sensibility, revealing his appreciation of Tagore's poetry, he analysed the most important poetical books like *Gitanjali, O Jardineiro* (*The Gardener*), *Regalo de amante* (*Lover's Gift*), *A Colheita* (*Fruit-Gathering*), *A lua nova* (*The Crescent Moon*) and *Pássaros perdidos* (*Stray Birds*).

Amâncio Gracias (1872–1950)

João Baptista Amâncio Gracias was born in Loutulim, Salcete (Goa). He was an illustrious historian and polymath. He wrote articles in numerous Goan publications. At various times, he also resided in Mozambique, Angola and Cape Verde. He was secretary of the Imprensa Nacional de Goa (National Press of Goa), collaborator of the periodical *O Século* (*The Century*) of Lisbon, and correspondent of the Academia das Ciências de Lisboa (Academy of Sciences of Lisbon), the Instituto de Coimbra and the Instituto Vasco da Gama of Panjim, and for many years a member of the Comissão Permanente de Arqueologia de Goa (Permanent Commission of Archaeology of Goa). Among his many articles is 'Tagore, político e poeta' (Tagore, Politician and Poet)[4] where he analysed two prominent facets of Tagore, the socio-political and poetical. He especially commented on *Nacionalismo* (*Nationalism*), *Gitanjali, Unidade Criadora* (*Creative Unity*), *A Religião do Homem* (*The Religion of Man*), and among Tagore's books of poems the *Canções vespertinas e matutinas* (Evening and Morning Songs), besides *Kori o Komol* (Hard and Tender). He also looked at Tagore's political life and his educational efforts at Santiniketan.

Renato de Sá (1908–81)

Born in Panjim (Goa), Renato de Sá was a pharmacist, a man of letters and a journalist. He studied at the Medical School in Goa. He collaborated with numerous newspapers and journals, both Goan and Portuguese, on literary and biographical subjects. His great love for Portuguese culture and language led him, in 1964, to found the Centro de Cultura Latina (Centre for Latin Culture) in Panjim. In 1968, he founded the journal *A Harpa Goesa* (The Goan Harp), in which texts by and on Tagore were contributed, fourteen in all over the years. The last one, published in December 1981, was a monograph dedicated to the memory of Renato de Sá which included a short exchange of letters between him and Tagore between 1934 and 1939.

Mariano José de Saldanha (1878–1975)

Mariano José de Saldanha, a professor and doctor, was born at Ucassaim, Bardez (Goa). He studied at the Medical School in Goa and, later, finished his studies at the Escola Colonial (Colonial School), Lisbon and took a degree in Sanskrit at the Faculdade de Letras [Faculty of Letters], Lisbon University. He was a teacher of Marathi and Sanskrit at the Liceu (High School) de Nova Goa from 1915 to 1929, and thereafter professor of Sanskrit at the Faculdade de Letras, Lisbon until 1948. For two years he also taught Konkani, besides Sanskrit, at the Escola Superior Colonial [Higher Colonial School], Lisbon; there he was deputy director of the Instituto de Línguas Africanas e Orientais (Institute of African and Oriental Languages). Morover, he served as a member of the Instituto Vasco da Gama of Panjim. He paid a visit to Santiniketan in Tagore's lifetime. Saldanha published the study entitled *O Poeta duma Universidade e a Universidade de um Poeta ou Rabindranath Tagore e a sua obra literária e pedagógica*[5] (The Poet of a University and the University of a Poet, or Rabindranath Tagore and his literary and pedagogical work). The author analysed not only the literary work of Tagore, but also his contribution to education, commenting on the theoretical and practical principles of Tagore's educational institution. This study was first delivered as a lecture on 29 May 1943 at the Faculdade de Letras of Lisbon University. It was illustrated with slides and preceded by an invocation in Sanskrit by Sudhindra M. Tagore. A Tagore song was rendered in Portuguese translation as *A lira do universo* (The Lyre of the Universe), sung by the girls of the Sanskrit course and accompanied on the organ by an instrumentalist. This was perhaps the first time that both Sanskrit and Bengali were heard in Portugal at a public function.

Publications

Further translations and studies on Tagore published in Goa are:

José F. Ferreira Martins, the translator of *Chitra* (1914), also published, in Goa, *Poemas em prosa* [Prose Poems] (1915) by Tagore.

Padre [Father] Altino Ribeiro Santana (1915–73), who was born in Pavorim do Socorro (Goa) and died in Mozambique, published *O ideal religioso de Tagore* (Tagore's religious ideal)[6].

Three biographies of Tagore have been published in Portuguese, the authors being Sitarama Quercar (1915), Damodar B. Bounsuló (1950), and Basílio Joaquim Francisco Furtado (1965).

Eugéne d'Vaz brought out his study *R. Tagore: Gitanjali uma experiência visual* (R. Tagore: Gitanjali, a visual experience) in Chennai, 2005.

Áureo de Quadros published a new Portuguese translation of *Gitanjali* (Panjim 1996).

José da Conceição Souza wrote about the religious ideas of Tagore. Especially in Goa where Christians are a strong minority (27 per cent of the population), there has always been an interest in comparing Christian ideas with the religious ideas of Tagore.

Besides the articles and statements on Tagore published in the Goan newspapers *Heraldo* (Herald), *O Heraldo* (The Herald), *Ressurge Goa!* (Arise Goa!), *Diário da noite* (Evening newspaper) and in the Bulletins of the Instituto Vasco da Gama and the Eclesiástico of the Archdiocese of Goa, mentioned earlier, *O Académico* (The Academician) and *O Ultramar* (Overseas) issued articles after Tagore's death. *O Académico* was a bimonthly magazine, the organ and property of the União Académica (Academic Union) of Nova Goa. In 1941, it published an editorial[7] with a photo dedicated to Tagore. Later in the year, the magazine brought out a monograph of fifty pages[8] as a homage to the poet. The editorial and twenty articles analysed the personality and work of Tagore, his multiple facets as writer, educator, philosopher, thinker, poet, his land, Bengal, its life and institutions, his ideals, and his work and social thought. The contributors included Ruy Sant´Elmo, Lúcio de Miranda, Pedro Correia, Berta de Menezes, Soares de Rebelo, Joaquim da Silva, Augusto Cabral, Caxinata Damodar, Áureo de A. Quadros, António Furtado, Xencora B. Camotim, Datá Caxinata and Jorge de Ataíde Lobo. Under the caption *Tagore e os portugueses* (Tagore and the Portuguese), short statements on Tagore by prominent writers like Júlio Dantas, Agostinho de Campos, E. Tudela de Castro, Augusto de Casimiro, Ferreira de Castro and Bento de Jesus Caraça were reproduced.

O Ultramar was a weekly of the town of Margao, founded in 1859, which became bi-weekly in 1905 and ceased publication in September 1941 after 5,499 issues. Before that, on 25 August 1941, a few days after Tagore's death, it dedicated a special number to Tagore. Also, number 5.497 of *O Ultramar* details the tribute that the Municipality of Margao paid to the Bengali poet, chronicling the events and the people who took part. The district judge and president of the event, Dr Siurama Bolvonta Rau, delivered a speech about Tagore. Dr António Colaço, a doctor and journalist, contributed to the *Heraldo* and *A Vida de Margão* (Life in Margao Life). He admired Tagore and also the Tagore scholar Froilano de Melo, about whom he published a monograph in 1955. Eduardo da Silva published an article 'A sua lição' (His lesson) in the penultimate number of the magazine,[9] where again Tagore is the subject.

Reproduced in *O Heraldo de Goa* of 14 February 2011 is an article entitled 'Os dramas de Tagore' [The plays of Tagore], written in 1961, by

Paraxurama Quensori. He talks of the profundity, sentimentalism, lyricism and symbolism of Tagore's dramas, and of the difficulty in performing them. Besides pointing out the importance of theatre in Bengal, he focuses on the analysis of Tagore's play *Raktakarabi* [*Red Oleanders*] in which Tagore presents a vivid portrait of the crisis of contemporary civilisation and the terrible dilemma of modern man caught in an acquisitive and materialistic society.

Angola and Mozambique

On the reception of Tagore in those African countries where Portuguese is the official language nearly everything remains to be researched. A major part of what we know has already been told when speaking of those Goans or Portuguese people who, besides writing and publishing in their countries about Tagore, also lived, performing some political, social or labour responsibility, in the Portuguese colonies of Angola, Cape Verde (since 2013, officially Cabo Verde) and Mozambique. This was the case with Froilano de Melo, Augusto Casimiro, Amâncio Gracias and Altino Ribeiro Santana, among others.

Mozambique, having been a part of the maritime bridge linking Portugal to India on the Cape route, was almost a colony of Portuguese India. Today many Goans live in this country having taken refuge after Goa was occupied by the Indian Union in 1961. Many Goan doctors, nurses and priests have settled in Mozambique including the Goan bishop and Tagore scholar, Altino Ribeiro de Santana.

As far as Mozambique is concerned, two Tagore scholars must be mentioned. Orlando António Fernandes da Costa, better known as Orlando da Costa (1929–2006) was born in Lourenço Marques (now known as Maputo), the Mozambican capital, and died in Lisbon. With a degree in Historical-Philosophical Sciences awarded by the Faculdade de Letras of Lisbon University, he was the author of several books of poetry and drama. In 1961, he wrote an article with the title 'Tagore'[10] on the life and work of Rabindranath. Here he remembers that in August 1941, when he was a child, he heard of Tagore's death while in Goa.

> On that luminous and sad afternoon, when I made my way to the Margaon Town Hall, where a tribute was being paid to the poet who had just died, my heart was anxious and confounded. It was the first time I heard of the great Indian contemporary poet. I was without blame because the anthologies and the books of stories that at the time instructed me did not include Tagore, neither Vyasa, Valmiki

or Kalidasa. After all, twenty-eight years before, in 1913, the poet Rabindranath Tagore had been consecrated by the world with the Nobel Prize of Literature. In spite of my thirteen years not yet completed, I went to that session in the Town Hall.

Da Costa is referring to the tribute we already mentioned in the section dedicated to Goa.

The other Tagorean writer was José Craveirinha (1922–2003), born in Lourenço Marques. He is probably the greatest Mozambican writer. Entirely self-taught, he was an employee of the national press, journalist and columnist in numerous African publications. He received several literary prizes, including one from the Associação Afro-Asiática de Escritores and the Camões Award. He is one of the best-known poets of the Portuguese language and one of the major African writers. If we read his beautiful verse, where love, heaven, the stars, the mother, light and life are central themes, we will realise the profound Tagorean influence in the poetry of this great Mozambican who, like Tagore, loved his country and his people, without stopping to love and to desire peace for the whole world.

The most important Tagore scholar in Angola was Wanda Ramos (1948–98). Born in Dundo-Angola, she was a poet, novelist and translator into Portuguese. She took a degree in Germanic Philology at the Faculdade de Letras of Lisbon. Besides Tagore, she translated the works of Borges, Octavio Paz, Bruno Munari and Le Carré, among others. She contributed to numerous publications, to newspapers of Angola and Lisbon, and especially to the magazine *África.* From 1970 till her death she wrote several books of poetry, five novels, a book of short stories and works in poetic prose. In her first novel *Percursos,* she presented her personal memoirs, remembering the colonial society, and making known her vision of the colonial war from a feminine point of view. In 1986, her translation from English of Tagore's novel *The Home and the World* (*A casa e o mundo*) was published by Editora Presença of Lisbon.

Translated from the Portuguese by Galician Carlos Durão.

NOTES

1. Published by the Publications Division, Ministry of Information and Broadcasting, Government of India.
2. In *Boletim do Instituto Vasco da Gama*, no. 51 (1942).
3. Published by Seara Nova in Lisboa in 1939.
4. Published also as an offprint, in the *Boletim do Instituto Vasco da Gama*, No. 51, 1941 (Bastorá-Goa, Tipografia Rangel).

5. In the magazine of the Faculdade de Letras de Lisboa, vol. X (1943).
6. In the *Boletim Eclesiástico da Arquidiocese de Goa*, no. 2, vol. A01 (1942). Another priest called Carmo da Silva, in the same Boletim quoted, no. 09 and vol. A05, of 1947, published another beautiful statement of three pages under the title 'A mensagem de Tagore'.
7. In no. 4, May 1941 of *O Académico*.
8. No. 6, September 1941 of *O Académico*.
9. No. 5.498, of 22 September 1941 of *O Ultramar*.
10. Reproduced in the newspaper *A Vida* of Goa on 20 June 2011.

WORKS CITED

Barreto, Adeodato. 'Ideias pedagógicas de Tagore' (Tagore´s Pedagogical Ideas). Goa, 1929–30. Unpublished.

———. *Civilização hindu* (Hindu Civilization). Lisboa: Seara Nova, 1935. About R. Tagore: 240–7.

Correia Afonso de Figueiredo, Propércia. 'Rabindranath Tagore-O Educador!' (RT, The Educator!). Bastorá-Goa: *Boletim do Instituto Vasco da Gama*, no. 51, 1941, 27–52.

Furtado, Basílio J. F. *Rabindranath Tagore*. Goa: Xaverian Print Press, 1965.

Gracias, J. B. Amâncio. Tagore, político e poeta [Tagore, Politician and Poet]. Bastorá-Goa: *Boletim do Instituto Vasco da Gama* no. 51, 1941, 1–26. (Also published as offprint by the same Bulletin).

Kelekar, Shashikar. *Telo de Mascarenhas*. N. Delhi: Publications Division of India, 1984.

Mascarenhas, Telo de. *Rabindranath Tagore e a sua mensagem espiritual* (RT and his Spiritual Message). Porto: Ed. Oriente, 1943.

———. *When the Mango-Trees Blossomed. Quasi-Memoirs*. Bombay: Orient Longman, 1976.

Melo, I. Froilano P. De. *O Cântico da vida na poesia tagoreana* (The Song of Life in Tagore's Poetry). Porto: O Comércio, 1946.

PART THREE

Eastern and Central Europe

Tagore with Indologists Moriz Winternitz and Vincenc Lesný, and also Ramananda
Chatterjee, Prague (1930). Courtesy: Rabindra Bhavana, Visva-Bharati.

13

RUSSIA

SERGEI SEREBRIANY

In this essay, the reception of Tagore and his works in the Russian-speaking world will be considered, which only partially overlaps with the political entity 'Russia.' In 1913, when Tagore was awarded the Nobel Prize, 'Russia' meant the Russian Empire, which included, among other territories, a large part of today's Poland and the whole of today's Finland. From 1922 up to 1991, 'Russia' was a shorthand name for the Soviet Union (the USSR) which reunited, after the civil war of 1918–20, most of the territories and peoples of the former empire. But the restored empire disintegrated for the second time in 1991, so that now 'Russia' means the Russian Federation, still a multi-ethnic state with Russians constituting about 80 per cent of its population. The reception of the Bengali poet in Poland's and Finland's cultures, in the cultures of the successor states of the Soviet Union, as well as in the non-Russian cultures of today's Russian Federation must be treated elsewhere.[1]

In the twentieth century, especially after the Revolution of 1917, the Russian-speaking world was divided between Soviet Russia and the Russian diaspora, which spread all over the world. The number of people who chose (and in many cases were compelled) to leave Russia after 1917 is not known exactly. They were millions, and many (if not the majority) of them were from the most educated strata of Russian society. As will be shown in this essay, the reception of Tagore's works in the Russian diaspora has been an important part of his reception in the Russian-speaking world as a whole.

The theme of this study is still largely unexplored. There are several papers in Russian (published between 1961 and 1986) and even one book in English by the Soviet scholar A. P. Gnatyuk-Danil'Chuk that deal with this theme.[2] All these writings, however, are now dated. Moreover, they were written under the Soviet ideological censorship, which to a considerable degree was a kind of self-censorship by the authors themselves, a result of the notorious doublethink. Quite often, the Soviet scholars who wrote about Tagore knew the truth (even if not the whole truth), but dared not put it down on paper. Besides, much remained really unknown and will remain unknown before scholars can look into archives, personal as well as state (and, especially, secret police) archives, in Russia, India and probably elsewhere.

The story of Tagore's reception in Russia, and in the Russian-speaking world as a whole, is of course closely linked to the political and cultural history of the country in the twentieth century and at the beginning of the twenty-first century. This history itself has not been properly studied so far and remains a matter of heated controversies in today's Russia, which are certainly not purely academic, but related to current politics in the country. Any study of Tagore's reception in Russia cannot possibly avoid a number of controversial issues. For a scholar, it is rather an advantage, because this makes the study exciting, a real research work with unpredictable results. Moreover, the story of Tagore's reception in Russia, as well as the story of Tagore's perceptions of Russia, may serve as a quite revealing comment on the country's history during the last hundred years. These stories, if truthfully told, may destroy some myths about (Soviet) Russia, as well as some myths about Tagore.

HOW INDIA WAS PERCEIVED IN RUSSIA BEFORE TAGORE BECAME KNOWN

In various political discourses we may often hear that the relations (allegedly cordial) between Russia and India are 'many centuries old'. But old as those relations might be, they have been, through centuries, rather meagre. It is only since the nineteenth century that meaningful contacts between the Russian and Indian cultural worlds started growing substantially.

Indian studies slowly developed in Russia during the nineteenth century. At first they were mostly Sanskrit studies pursued by Germans (locally born or immigrant).[3] One of the most important nineteenth-century Sanskrit scholars in Russia and in Europe as a whole was Otto (in Russia: Otton Nikolayevich) Böhtlingk (1815–1904), of German origin, born in St Petersburg (his ancestors had come to Russia during the reign of Peter I). He is probably best remembered as the main compiler of the *Saint Petersburg Sanskrit–German Dictionary*. In 1923, the Russian Academy of Sciences sent to Tagore, at his request, a copy of this dictionary for the Visva-Bharati University.[4]

It is only since the second half of the nineteenth century, when the Russian Empire expanded towards Central Asia and came closer to the British dominions in India, that Indian studies in Russia came to be more in demand. Ivan Pavlovich Minayev (1840–90) is sometimes called the founder of Russian Indology. He was also the first Russian Indologist to travel to India. His scholarly interests were many, but the main one was in Buddhism, which may be explained by the tradition of Buddhist studies in Russia and by the fact that the Russian empire had some Buddhist population. Minayev studied Chinese, Sanskrit, and, especially, Pali. It seems that only towards the end of his life did he recognise the importance of modern Indian languages. Minayev visited India three times: in 1874–5, in 1879–80, and in 1885–6.[5]

While in India on his third visit, Minayev attended the founding session of the Indian National Congress in Bombay and met some of the Congress leaders. He also visited Calcutta several times and met Bankimchandra Chatterji (1838–94), a pioneering Bengali writer and novelist, who presented to the Russian scholar some of his books. While in Calcutta, Minayev could have heard about the Tagore family of Jorasanko and even about the young Rabindranath. But there are no traces of such knowledge in Minayev's papers and he evidently did not take much interest in modern Indian literatures. Nevertheless, notwithstanding his bitter remarks about 'Bengali baboos' in his diaries, he understood the importance of Calcutta for the growth of modern Indian culture. In his report about his third visit to India, Minayev wrote: 'Calcutta with its baboos is going to have the same significance for India as Paris for France.'

Two pupils of Minayev became the key figures in the Russian Indological studies of the first half of the twentieth century. They were Sergey Fyodorovich Oldenburg (1863–1934) and Fyodor Ippolitovich Shcherbatskoy (alias Stcherbatsky, 1866–1942).[6] Both belonged to the generation of Rabindranath Tagore.

Sergey (or Sergei) Oldenburg was not only a scholar, and one of the major specialists in Buddhism, but also a kind of political figure. He worked as the permanent Secretary, actually the manager-in-chief of the Russian Academy of Sciences, from 1904 to 1929. After the Bolshevik takeover, Oldenburg managed to keep the Academy of Sciences as a semi-autonomous body until 1929. Oldenburg knew many languages, though he hardly read Bengali. No doubt, he read most, if not all, works of Tagore translated into English (and probably into Russian as well). There was at least one personal link between Oldenburg and Tagore: the French Orientalist Silvain Lévi (1863–1935). Oldenburg was his close friend since the 1890s, while Tagore came in touch with Lévi in the 1920s. Oldenburg had never been to India. He might have met Tagore in Europe in the 1920s, but most probably he did not. In the 1920s, Tagore missed several opportunities to visit Russia before Stalin's 'Third revolution.' Had Tagore come before 1929, he would have met Oldenburg in Russia and enjoyed his hospitality there. When Tagore actually came to Moscow in 1930, Oldenburg failed to meet him.

Fyodor Stcherbatsky is probably the Russian Indologist best known outside Russia. He was a great scholar of Buddhist thought, and his major works were written and published in English.[7] In 1910, Stcherbatsky undertook his only trip to India. In the autumn of that year he stayed for some time in Calcutta, working with the British scholar Denison Ross (1871–1940) on the translation of Vasubandhu's *Abhidharmakosha*. He might even have met Tagore in Calcutta, but he took no interest in modern Indian languages and literatures. It was only in the 1920s, in Europe, that Stcherbatsky met Tagore. The Russian scholar even entertained the idea of going to teach at Visva-Bharati, like Silvain Lévi and Moriz Winternitz (1863–1937), but the idea was not realised.

In the nineteenth century there was one more missed opportunity to establish close relations between the Tagore family and Russia. Nishikanta Chattopadhyaya (1852–1910), a relative through marriage of Tagore (Nishikanta's daughter was married to Rabindranath's nephew), came to St Petersburg in 1878 hoping to teach at St Petersburg University.[8] He stayed in Russia for about two years, till 1880. Once he visited Moscow and was shown the Kremlin by the writer Ivan Turgenev (1818–83). But for some unknown reason Nishikanta left Russia for Switzerland. His doctoral dissertation produced in Zürich on Bengali folk dramas was the first submitted by an Indian in Europe and his book *Indische Essays* was probably the first book written by an Indian in German.[9]

India was certainly known to Russian writers and poets long before 1913. As early as 1787 a Russian translation of the *Bhagavadgita* was published, and scenes from Kalidasa's *Shakuntala* came out in Russian in 1792. But in nineteenth century classical Russian literature, roughly from the time of Alexander Pushkin (1799–1837) to that of Anton Chekhov (1860–1904), India occupied only a modest place. Educated Russians looked, in general, more to the West than to the East. Thus, Pushkin in his works, both poetry and prose, very rarely refers to India, though in his personal library there was a French translation of Kalidasa's *Shakuntala*, and he even mentioned the Ramayana once in a private letter.[10] Unlike Goethe and the German Romanticists, Pushkin and other masterminds of nineteenth-century Russian literature evidently were not greatly interested in Indian culture.

It is only by the end of the century that some Russian writers and poets became curious about India and Indian culture. The most famous example is Lev Tolstoy (1828–1910). By the end of his long life he took some interest both in the Indian cultural heritage and in contemporary India. Thus he learned about Ramakrishna and read some writings of Vivekananda.[11] It is widely known that not long before his death Tolstoy corresponded with M. K. Gandhi. It is less known that since the 1880s Tolstoy had corresponded with about twenty Indians, some of them Bengalis. The last years of Tolstoy's life are meticulously documented, but the name of Tagore is not found in these records.

We may safely assume that before 1913 the name of Rabindranath Tagore was hardly known to anybody in Russia. (Besides, hardly anybody in pre-revolutionary Russia knew Bengali.)

INITIAL TAGORE TRANSLATIONS

When the Bengali poet was awarded the Nobel Prize for Literature at the end of 1913, the situation changed radically and Tagore almost immediately became popular. Translations of his works from English appeared one after another within a very short span of time. The story of those early translations deserves to be studied and described in some detail. Here I can only highlight some episodes.

We have exhaustive and fairly reliable bibliographical lists of all publications related to Tagore which appeared in Russian (as well as in other languages of the former Soviet Union) from the very beginning (that is from 1913) up to 1975. In 1961, during the centennial celebrations, a book was published from Moscow, in Russian, titled *Rabindranath Tagore: To the Hundredth Anniversary of His Birth, 1861–1961*.[12] The last five pages of the book contain a bibliographical list compiled by L. A. Strizhevskaya under the title: *Translations of Rabindranath Tagore's Works into the Languages of the Peoples of Russia and the Soviet Union: Books*.[13] The 1961 list was later expanded in two informative books, both titled *Bibliography of India*. The first one gives very detailed information about publications on India in Russian and other languages of the former Soviet Union from the beginning of the eighteenth century up to 1967.[14] The second, a much slimmer book continues the story up to 1975.[15] These bibliographical guides contain information not only on books, but also on journal publications, articles, reviews, etc. Information about books by and about Tagore published in · Russian up to 1998 may be obtained through the electronic catalogue at the site of the Russian National Library in St Petersburg.[16] Information about more recent publications in Russian, as well as about published musical scores of the music composed by Russian composers for songs of Tagore, are available through the electronic catalogue at the site of the Russian State Library (the former Lenin Library) in Moscow.[17]

One of the first, if not the very first, to translate Tagore's works into Russian (from English) was the London correspondent of the Moscow newspaper *Russkiye vedomosti* (Russian Gazette), Isaak Shklovsky (1865–1935), a Russian-Jewish journalist and ethnographer (who used the pen-name

Dioneo).[18] In fact, according to the *Bibliography of India*, Shklovsky got a review of Tagore's *Gitanjali* published in the 6 July 1913 issue of the *Russkiye vedomostî*, that is much before the announcement of the Nobel Prize award.[19] By the end of 1913, Shklovsky published in Moscow his translations of some poems from *Gitanjali* and of the short story 'Bicharak' (The Judge).[20]

It is popularly believed that Tagore received the Nobel Prize for his English *Gitanjali*. However, in the Presentation Speech (on 10 December 1913) the Chairman of the Nobel Committee of the Swedish Academy, the Swedish historian, Harald Hjärne, mentioned five books of Tagore in English translation—three books of poems: *Gitanjali: Song Offerings* (1912), *The Gardener, Lyrics of Love and Life* (1913) and *The Crescent Moon* (1913); a book of short stories entitled *Glimpses of Bengal Life* (1913); and a book of lectures: *Sādhanā: The Realisation of Life* (1913).[21]

All five of these books were translated into Russian (some of them more than once) between 1913 and 1915. It was *Gitanjali* that attracted the biggest number of translators. In 1913–15, not less than six different Russian renderings of this book were published. In 1914–15, three translations of *The Gardener* came out.

The first translation into Russian of the complete *Gitanjali* appeared as early as October and November of 1913, in the monthly journal *Severnye zapiski* (Northern Notes), in St Petersburg.[22] The translator was Liubov' Borisovna Khavkina (1871–1949).[23] Later she became known as one of the most authoritative specialists in library science in Russia.[24] L. Khavkina was a polyglot and translated from six languages. But her fine translation of *Gitanjali* was never republished, probably because it was eclipsed by other translations, done and/or edited by outstanding men of letters.

Jurgis Baltrušaitis (1873–1944), a noted Russian–Lithuanian symbolist poet (who first made a name for himself with his poetry in Russian and later wrote also in Lithuanian), got several poems from *Gitanjali* published in his Russian translations in the 1913 November issue of the St Petersburg monthly *Zavety* (Behests).[25] In 1914, the same Russian translation of the complete *Gitanjali* was published twice by two Moscow publishers, as the first volumes of two (different) about-to-be-published Collected Works of Tagore. In both cases, the subtitle said: 'Translation from English, edited by Jurgis Baltrušaitis'.[26] This translation was later republished at least twice: in 1915 and in 1916.

Even more successful was the Russian version associated with another literary figure, Nikolay Pusheshnikov (1882–1939), an established translator of European masterpieces, and a nephew of Ivan Bunin (1870–1953), who in 1933 would become the first Russian Nobel laureate in Literature.[27] Bunin himself edited his nephew's translation of *Gitanjali*. The first edition appeared in 1914 and the fourth in 1918, all in Moscow.[28] One more edition came out in 1919, in Odessa (probably either under the French occupation of the city or under the 'White' rule).[29] And it was this translation that was again republished in Moscow in 1925 (with the name of its editor Bunin dropped)[30] and in the Soviet Collected Works of Tagore in the 1950s and (partly) in the 1960s (see below).

The Gardener, also translated by N. Pusheshnikov and edited by Ivan Bunin, came out first in 1913 (then again in 1918) and was republished in 1925[31] and in the 1950s and 1960s (see further). During 1913–17, at least three more Russian versions of *The Gardener* appeared, two of them as volumes of two different Collected Works of Tagore.[32] In 1919, the translation of Ivan Sabashnikov was published and in 1923 'selected poems' from *The Gardener* in the translation by Matilda Ber came out in Khar'kov.[33] *The Crescent Moon* also appeared in more than one Russian version before 1917.[34] The book *Glimpses of Bengal Life* was translated into Russian and published from Moscow, in 1915, as volume 7 of one of the Collected Works of Tagore.[35] The *Sādhanā*, in two different translations, was included in the two *Collected Works* (both volumes came out in 1914).[36]

As has been mentioned, two Collected Works of Tagore were published from Moscow before 1917. One of them was in eight volumes and the other in six.[37] The latter one even started a second edition in 1916, but the project was stopped, evidently, by the events of 1917. These Collected Works included some pieces of Tagore not mentioned in the Nobel Presentation Speech. Thus one of the volumes published in 1915 contained Tagore's drama *The King* translated (with a particularly insightful preface) by Zinaida Vengerova (1867–1941), an outstanding woman of letters and a member of a large and reputed literary family.[38] Two other plays, *Chitra* and *The Post Office*, were also translated for those Collected Works (each twice), as well as *One Hundred Poems of Kabir*.[39]

The writer Konstantin Paustovsky (1892–1968) wrote later, in his memoirs about those pre-Revolutionary years: 'Rabindranath Tagore dominated our minds.'[40] But this 'our' must be taken cautiously. The educated society in Russia was quite differentiated in those days. Tagore was enthusiastically welcomed by some people and completely ignored by others. Thus, I have tried to find out the reactions to Tagore's writings of the two outstanding poets: Alexander Blok (1880–1921) and Osip Mandelshtam (1891–1938). Neither of the two poets has ever mentioned Tagore in their writings (including private letters).[41] A systematic survey of responses—or their lack—from leading Russian artists and intellectuals is still a work to be done and can reveal important shades of reception.

TAGORE DURING THE FIRST DECADE OF THE SOVIET UNION

The year 1917 was a decisive and tragic watershed in the history of the Russian Empire. In February/March the monarchy collapsed under the weight of its own shortcomings and popular discontent. Hopes were high for a democratic resurgence of the former Russian Empire. But the combined strain of World War I and the Revolution proved to be destructive. In October/November 1917, the Bolsheviks, a small party of bigoted extremists, staged a coup d'état, a kind of counter-revolution, which brought the country back to its archaic authoritarian traditions. The Bolsheviks projected themselves as 'Marxists' and harbingers of progress and social equity, and probably some of them sincerely believed in their ideology. But the results of their takeover, in the long run, have been disastrous for Russia and most other parts of the former empire. The Bolsheviks undertook their 'revolution' under the premise that it would be but a spark to ignite what they called the 'world revolution,' as, according to the Marxist orthodoxy, Russia in 1917 was not at all ripe for a 'socialist revolution.' Vladimir Lenin till his death in 1924 seems to have believed that the 'world revolution' was round the corner. It was only in 1925 that the Bolsheviks officially acknowledged that it was not the case. Stalin put forward the slogan of 'Socialism in one country' which was absurd from the viewpoint of orthodox Marxists, but sounded very pragmatic. Stalin's formula, in a way, was similar to the 'National Socialism' of Hitler. By the end of the 1920s, Stalin became almost an undisputed ruler of the country and launched his so called 'Third revolution' to build the 'Socialism in one country.' This excursus in history will help us to understand the history of Tagore's reception in Russia and the Soviet Union after 1917.

During the 1920s, many cultural processes which began before 1917 continued one way or another. Thus, in the decade 1917–27 the popularity of Tagore with the Russian reading public did not diminish, but probably even increased. Up to the late 1920s, many other works of the poet, in Russian translations, appeared both in the Soviet Union and in the émigré publishing houses in Western Europe. Some works were again translated more than once. For instance, the novel *The Home and the World* came out in the early 1920s at least in three translations (all from English), one of them published from Berlin.[42] In the reviews of the translations Russian critics noted the similarity between the Indian events and personalities (of the *Swadeshi* movement) described in the novel and the events and personalities of Russian literature and Russian revolutions. In fact, now it may be argued that not long before writing the *The Home and the World* Tagore could have read the English translation of the novel by Dostoevsky *The Possessed* (or *'The Devils'*) and that novel might have been reflected in a way in Tagore's work.[43]

In the 1920s, the grip of the official ideology was not yet as tight as it became later. For some time a kind of pluralism lingered. Some critics of the Communist type denounced Tagore as 'mystic' and 'idealist', but this did not prevent publishers (some of them still private or 'cooperative' in those years) from publishing his works, just as it did not prevent many readers from enjoying his poetry and prose. Thus, my grandfather's younger brother (born in 1900) told me that while wooing his future wife (it must have been in the 1920s) he recited to her poems from *Gitanjali!*

In the 1920s, a high number of new Tagore translations (mostly from English) were published. It was often the case that no sooner did an English book by Tagore appear than it was translated into Russian. Thus, *The Home and the World* was published from London in 1919, and the three Russian translations came out in 1920 and 1923 (see above). *The Wreck* (1921) came out in a Russian translation in 1923; *Gora*, published in London in 1924, came out in two different Russian translations in that very year and one of the translations was republished in 1926.[44]

The novella *Chaturanga* was published in English translation under the title *Broken Ties* in the book *Broken Ties and Other Stories* (1925) and in 1925 it appeared in three different Russian translations.[45] In the 1920s, two more books of Tagore's dramas came out, in which *Sacrifice* (*Bisarjan*) and *Sanyasi* (*Prakritir Pratishodh*) were translated for the first time and *The King* for the third.[46] The 'epigrams' of the *Stray Birds* (1916) were translated twice; *Nationalism* (1917) also twice (first in Berlin, then in Moscow); as was *My Reminiscences* (1917) (both in Russia); *Personality* (1917) and the *Glimpses of Bengal* (1921) were translated once each.[47]

Tagore's short stories were also popular both when published separately and in collections. An excellent book of stories edited by M. I. Tubiansky (with his commentaries) and published in 1925 is especially worth mentioning.[48] This series of Tagore translations came to a halt for many years after 1929 with a Russian version of the *Kabuliwallah*.[49]

No original book on Tagore was produced at that stage, though a number of engaging papers and prefaces to translations did come out. Evidently to fill the lacuna, in 1924, a German book about Tagore was published in an 'abridged' translation.

As has already been said, before the 1920s all the translations were from English, since nobody knew Bengali and the knowledge of English among Russian intellectuals was widespread enough to avoid translating from versions in other European languages.

Mikhail Izrailevich Tubiansky (1893–1937), a student of Fyodor Shcherbatsky, was the first to translate Tagore's works directly from the Bengali. After translating a poem in prose, he published prose versions of several poems from the Bengali *Gitanjali*.[50] He was, however, much more successful as a translator of Tagore's prose works. In 1926, he came out with a translation of several short stories and in 1927 with that of *My Reminiscences*.[51] The latter translation was republished in the 1960s and has remained the standard one till today.

Besides his translations from Bengali, Tubiansky, together with the philosopher I. Kolubovsky, brilliantly rendered into Russian Tagore's *Nationalism*, which had been published in 1922 and since then never republished.[52] Tubiansky also wrote a number of prefaces to Tagore's works translated by other hands, and those texts have retained much of their value till the present day. In 1927, Tubiansky went to Mongolia to study Buddhism, came back in the mid-1930s to a different country and was executed in 1937 under Stalin's terror.

The publication of Tagore's works in Russian was at its height in 1927, but practically stopped by 1929, the year of the 'Great Breakthrough', when Stalin started in earnest his 'Third Revolution'. Till 1955 practically no more works by Tagore were published in the USSR.

From available documents it seems that there was no explicit ban on Tagore's works between 1929 and 1955. His books were not withdrawn from public libraries or annihilated one way or another (unlike books of 'enemies' like Lev Trotsky or Nikolai Bukharin). Further research might uncover more definite information on this question. It is well known that the 'Communist' bosses of Russia very often did not register important decisions on paper, probably because they themselves were aware of the dubious (if not criminal) character of those decisions.

Attitudes to Tagore during the 1920s were perhaps even more varied than in the second decade of the twentieth century. There were, as I have already said, 'Marxist' authors who castigated Tagore as 'reactionary' and 'idealist' (in the Soviet discourse the latter was a term of abuse). There was also the academic appreciation of Tagore's work, represented by Sergei Oldenburg, Mikhail Tubiansky and other scholars. There was, of course, the 'silent' appreciation of common readers who readily bought books with translations of Tagore's work. Some people, again, intellectuals too, might have ignored and neglected Tagore completely, like Osip Mandelshtam, mentioned above. Some people, taking interest in Tagore as a writer and cultural figure, assumed an ironic attitude towards him. Thus, the distinguished ethnographer (anthropologist), Vladimir Bogoraz (pen name N. A. Tan, 1865–1936), who once met Tagore in Europe in the 1920s, wrote several papers about the poet (including prefaces to and reviews of translations of his works).[53] These texts are well-informed and well-meaning, but Tan-Bogoraz seems to have treated Tagore somewhat like an object of ethnographic research. And there were other critics like this. For instance, in 1923, in the fifth issue of the journal *Russia* (it was non-conformist, and soon closed by the authorities), a review of *Creative Unity* was published, titled 'The Naive Philosophy of RT' (signed 'V. Yarlsberg', most probably a pen name). For many people in Russia, who had lived through revolutions, the World War and the civil war with all their horrors, writings of Tagore might indeed have looked naïve. And this impression might have been confirmed when Tagore came to Russia in person.

It would be unfair to pass in silence over the contacts between Tagore and the Russian emigré painter Nicholas (Nikolai) Roerich (1874–1947). They first met in 1920 in London and kept in touch in later years. From time to time Roerich wrote some high-flown words, in his usual semi-prophetical style, about Tagore. The poet's friendship (if it was really this) with the painter-cum-preacher-cum-adventurist may be taken as one more evidence of the poet's naïveté. But Roerich is such a controversial (and, in my opinion, sinister) figure, that I would abstain for the time being from any other comments on him and his contacts with Tagore.

One interesting topic is the perception of Tagore by V. I. Lenin (1870–1924). We can have some idea about this from a detailed catalogue of Lenin's personal library which he formed in his office in the Kremlin after moving there in the spring of 1918.[54] In this library there were five books by Tagore, all in Russian translations: *Personality*, two [!] different translations of *Nationalism*, *The Home and the World* (a translation published in Berlin!), and an anthology published in Russia in 1923.[55] In the catalogue of Lenin's library, all his notes on the pages of books are meticulously registered, but no notes are reported in the books by Tagore. It is not even certain that Lenin actually read those five books. If he did, we do not know what he thought. But further research may yield some information on this matter.

Visit to the Soviet Union

During the 1920s, Tagore was more than once invited to visit the Soviet Union, but for one reason or another he failed to come before 1930. Some diplomatic reasons (usually of health) were offered again and again, but the real reasons of his unwillingness or inability to accept pre-1930 invitations are still to be ascertained.[56]

It is unfortunate that Tagore did not come to Russia before the 'Great Breakthrough'. In 1926 he was very much awaited. The popular magazine *Ogonyok* published his photo with a caption that the poet was coming to Moscow. In the same issue of the magazine a short note by Sergei Oldenburg read:

Around us in the world happens something which is incomparable
in its influence on human life: the fragmented, split, disjoined world
moves by slow but sure steps towards interconnection and integration
... And one of the most remarkable representatives of this great all-
human movement is the Indian poet, the Bengali, Rabindranath
Tagore.[57]

When he finally came to Moscow in September 1930, it was too late.
The phase of his highest popularity had passed. The political atmosphere in
the country was tense. The regime was suspicious of the Indian guest, and
the reception was rather restrained. The whole story of the visit has not yet
been told and probably will be told only when the archives of the Soviet
secret police are open to historians.

We have a literary testimony which shows how some (if not many)
people in Moscow perceived Tagore's visit. In the famous novel by Ilya Ilf
and Yevgeniy Petrov, *The Little Golden Calf* (1931), Tagore is portrayed as a
funny pseudo-philosopher who was completely irrelevant to the real life in
Russia.[58] The central character of the novel, a swindler named Ostap Bender,
acquires one million roubles, but does not know what to do with this money.
At this point he learns that 'a famous Indian poet and philosopher' stays
at the same hotel.[59] So Ostap decides to go and ask the guest about 'the
meaning of life.' He has to talk to the Indian guest in the presence of an
'interpreter' who is evidently a man from the secret police. The guest (whose
appearance is described in such a way that there is no doubt that he is Tagore
himself) delivers to Ostap a long sermon about the advantages of education,
especially in the USSR (he spoke in English for the first hour, in Bengali for
the second) and even sings a 'Young Pioneer song.' When in the end Ostap
insists on his question about the meaning of life, the guest tells him through
the interpreter that 'he himself came to your great country to discover the
meaning of life.' Ostap runs away disappointed.[60] Of course, this scene,
as the novel as a whole, requires a careful hermeneutic analysis. Thus, it is
possible that 'the Indian guest' only pretended to be dull because he had
realised that he too was being watched by the secret police agent.

We have another important testimony of Tagore's visit to Moscow,
written by the poet himself, the book *Rashiyar chithi* (*Letters from Russia*).
Today, with all our knowledge, incomplete as it is, of our Soviet past, Tagore's
Letters from Russia makes difficult reading. It is somewhat awkward to realise
that Tagore knew rather little about the history of Russia and very often
misunderstood what he saw in Moscow. Nevertheless, the same book shows
that Tagore was not at all the kind of irrelevant, funny old man described in
The Little Golden Calf.

The story of Tagore's *Letters from Russia* is revealing. He got published his *Rashiyar chithi* in Bengali soon after his return to India. But an English translation came out only in 1960, before the one hundredth birth anniversary of the author.[61] Some passages of the original (all in all about four pages of the Bengali text) have been omitted in the translation, and it is not always clear whether the reasons for particular omissions were stylistic or political. The first Russian translation made from the Bengali had appeared only four years earlier, in 1956, the year of the Twentieth Congress of the Communist Party of the Soviet Union.[62] The Russian rendering was abridged on obviously ideological grounds.[63] Thus, letter No. 13 (the unlucky number!) was omitted, evidently because it contained the following passage:

> Nevertheless, I do not believe that they have been able to draw the proper line of demarcation between the individual and society. *In that respect they are not unlike the fascists.* [Emphasis made by the writer of this essay.] For this reason they are loth to admit any limit to the suppression of the individual in the name of collectivity. They forget that by enfeebling the individual, the collective being cannot be strengthened. If the individual is in shackles, society cannot be free. They have here the dictatorship of the strong man. The rule of the many by one may produce good results for a time, but not for ever. It is impossible to have a succession of competent leaders.[64]

The 'Conclusion' to the 'Letters' has never been published in Russian either. I suppose the most 'offending' passage was this:

> It is not improbable that in this age Bolshevism is the treatment, but medical treatment cannot be permanent; indeed the day on which the doctor's regime comes to an end must be hailed as the red-letter day for the patient.[65]

Needless to say, the 'Communist' rulers of the country could not possibly tolerate such suggestions, because they thought they would rule for ever.

On 25 September 1930, Tagore gave an interview to a reporter from the governmental newspaper *Izvestiya* (News). Among other things, he said:

> There must be disagreement where minds are allowed to be free. It would not only be an uninteresting but a sterile world of mechanical regularity if all of our opinions were forcibly made alike. If you have a mission which includes all humanity, you must, for the sake of that living humanity, acknowledge the existence of differences of opinion. Opinions are constantly changed and rechanged only through the free circulation of intellectual forces and moral persuasion. Violence

begets violence and blind stupidity. Freedom of mind is needed for the reception of truth; terror hopelessly kills it.[66]

By 1930, the terror now associated with the name of Stalin had not yet deployed its killing capacity at its fullest, but such words, as Tagore dared to tell to his Moscow hosts, were already considered a subversive heresy. The farewell interview was published in Russian, by the same newspaper *Izvestiya*, only in 1988, under Gorbachev, at the initiative of the author of this essay.

On 15 January 1931, *The New York Times* published a letter signed by three Russian emigrés: Ivan Ostromislensky (1880–1939), the chemist, Sergei Rachmaninoff (1873–1943), the composer, and Ilya Tolstoy (1866–1933), the writer, a son of Lev Tolstoy.[67] The letter was titled 'Tagore on Russia' and contained bitter remarks on an interview given by Tagore on his arrival in the USA:

Tagore ... is considered among the great living men of our age. His voice is heard and listened to all over the world.

By eulogizing the dubious pedagogical achievements of the Soviets, and carefully omitting every reference to the indescribable torture to which the Soviets have been subjecting the Russian people for a period of over thirteen years, he has created a false impression that no outrages actually exist under the blessings of the Soviet regime ...

At no time, and in no country, has there ever existed a government responsible for so many cruelties, wholesale murders and common law crimes in general as those perpetrated by the Bolsheviki.

Is it really possible that, with all his love for humanity, wisdom and philosophy, he could not find words of sympathy and pity for the Russian nation?

By his evasive attitude toward the Communist grave-diggers of Russia, by the quasi-cordial stand which he has taken toward them, he has lent strong and unjust support to a group of professional murderers. By concealing from the world the truth about Russia he has inflicted, perhaps unwittingly, great harm upon the whole population of Russia, and possibly the world at large.[68]

This letter never seems to have been republished in Russia, though now its utterances would be accepted as true by most Russians.[69]

AFTER 1955

After the neglect in Stalin's time, when Khrushchev 'rehabilitated' India in the mid-1950s, attention was again drawn to Tagore in Russia. From 1955 onwards, new translations started to appear. The 1961 jubilee was celebrated officially on a large scale. 'Friendship' with India (the so-called '*Hindi–Rusi-bhai-bhai*-ism') must have been taken quite seriously by Khrushchev in his efforts to overplay the USA. Two more Collected Works (eight volumes in 1955–57 and twelve volumes in 1961–65) were published, rather in a hurry, especially the first series of eight volumes: the first volume was brought out to greet Jawaharlal Nehru on his first visit to the Soviet Union.[70]

The volumes of the Collected Works contained several pre-1917 translations (e.g., the translation of *Gitanjali* by Pusheshnikov) and some translations done in the 1920s (e.g., the translation of *My Reminiscences* by Tubiansky). A number of novels, dramas, short stories, and essays were translated anew or for the first time straight from Bengali. By that time a number of people were able to translate prose from Bengali. In the 1940s and early 1950s, Bengali (along with some other modern Indian languages) was taught at several places in Moscow and St Petersburg. The objective of the establishment was to get Bengali-knowing diplomats, military interpreters and functionaries for various propaganda and intelligence agencies. But, as a by-product, the country gained some scholars and translators as well.

As for translating the poetry of Tagore, the procedure widely used for translating non-Russian Soviet poets into Russian was also applied to the Tagore translations: a person who knew Bengali would prepare a literal translation of a poem, which would be passed on to a 'professional' poet who was supposed to transform this 'raw stuff' into a finished poetical 'product'. More than twenty poets were commissioned to translate Tagore's poems this way because the work was 'planned' to be done quickly. Among these poets were some of the greatest figures of twentieth-century Russian poetry, such as Anna Akhmatova (1889–1966), Boris Pasternak (1890–1960), Maria Petrovykh (1908–79) and David Samoilov (1920–90). For many Russian poets in those times translation was the main source of income. The invitation of the best poets to the Tagore project indicates, no doubt, that the establishment attached great importance to that project.

Boris Pasternak contributed several translations to the eight-volume Collected Works (by the time the twelve-volume set was under way Pasternak died), which appeared in 1957, before the scandal around his novel *Doctor Zhivago*. Pasternak had been commissioned for this work because he was deservedly considered one of the leading Russian poets of that time. But Pasternak entrusted some of the translations to Olga Ivinskaya (1912–95), who is (rightly) considered the prototype of Lara in the novel *Doctor Zhivago*. In fact, it was Pasternak who had taught Ivinskaya the art of translating poetry, which later became one of her means of living. In Ivinskaya's memoirs there are a couple of pages on which she tells the story of her apprenticeship, which included translating Tagore's poems under the tutorship of Pasternak.[71] However, Ivinskaya's translations were left out from the twelve-volume Collected Works (1961–65) since after Pasternak's death she was again imprisoned.

Anna Akhmatova also translated more than twenty poems for the Collected Works. Translations for her were certainly a source of income, because her own poems had not been published for many years and she was permanently short of money. Now Lydia Chukovskaya's formidable three-volume book, *Zapiski ob Anne Akhmatovoy* (Notes about Anna Akhmatova), provides an interesting, if slightly ambiguous, eye-witness account about how Akhmatova and Pasternak worked at their Tagore translations.[72] The book is a kind of diary, in which Lydia Chukovskaya (1907–96), a remarkable woman of letters in her own right, recorded her meetings and talks with Akhmatova from 1938 up to 1966 (with some gaps). The notes about Akhmatova's and Pasternak's work on Tagore are found in volumes 2 and 3.[73]

In the entry of 5 August 1956, Chukovskaya wrote:

> [Akhmatova] read aloud to me a draft of her translation of a poem by Tagore, *Happiness*. — 'What do you think? Shall I go on or shall I give it up. The poems are very dull' [— said Akhmatova]. — 'Give it up!' — said I, recalling that some money were to come for [the translation of a play by Victor] Hugo [*Marion Delorme*].[74]

In the entry of 5 January 1964, we read:

> She became silent and half-lied [sic] down upon a bed... — 'Heart-aches?' — 'No, it is Tagore. He gives me head-ache. After an hour of translating my head starts to break'. — I thought how good it were, if a big sum of money were given to her, so that she would not have to do translations any longer.[75]

And here is a passage from the entry dated 20 May 1964:

> Anna Andreyevna once again complained against the editor who hurried her up with the translations of Tagore's poems. And at this moment I heard from her for the first time a favourable opinion about this poet: 'He is good. I did not like him because he was terribly disfigured in translations'.[76]

In the book of Chukovskaya we find also one note about Pasternak's attitude towards Tagore's poems. In the entry of 22 April 1958, she recorded a meeting with Pasternak at her father's house. Pasternak was talking:

> He talked about art (I came at the very end of the topic), about Rabindranath Tagore (apparently, scolding him)...[77]

In a commentary to this note, Chukovskaya writes:

> Or, on the contrary, Boris Pasternak praised Tagore—I did not understand exactly. There could be both... Pasternak's attitude towards Tagore went through changes, it was different at different times...[78]

Not too many translations of Tagore, published in the bulky volumes of the Collected Works, became really successful *Russian* poems. Russian readers still have to rely on the opinions of others who tell them that Tagore is a great poet. I suppose we may draw a moral: great poetry (including poetic translations) may hardly be created to order.

Rabindranath's presence in Russian (and Soviet) music would deserve a separate paper. The catalogue of musical scores at the Russian State Library has a surprisingly large number of musical compositions created for Tagore's poems (mostly in Russian translations) by Russian (and non-Russian Soviet) composers. These pieces must have had limited circulation and the author of these lines has never heard any of them performed.

Tagore's concluding poem in the novel *Shesher Kabita* (The Last Poem) in a Russian translation by Adelina Adalis (1900–69) was put to music by Alexei Rybnikov (b. 1945) in the film *Vam i ne snilos* (You Wouldn't Even Dream It, 1980).[79]

Tagore even became a hero of popular jokes among Russians, along with Lenin and Brezhnev. One joke played out Tagore's name through the names of three popular, cheap Soviet wines in the 1970s and early 1980s: '*Rubin. Granat. Kagor (Cahor).*'

From the 1980s to the Present

Beside the four volumes of Collected Works (1981–1982), five one-volume selections of Tagore appeared from Moscow between 1972 and 1989.[80] None of them contained new translations.

The first book in this series was part of the ambitious 200-volume *Library of World Literature* published between 1967 and 1977.[81] Tagore was allotted a whole volume along with other classic writers of 'world literature' according to the late Soviet viewpoint (from Homer to Mikhail Sholokhov, who was given, like Fyodor Dostoevsky, two volumes; 'bourgeois' authors like Marcel Proust and James Joyce were not admitted to that pantheon). The Tagore volume in the series contained a selection of poems and short stories, and the novel *Gora*.

A book published in 1989 was meant for young readers.[82]

Books *about* Tagore were also produced in Russian during the later Soviet Period. Twenty years after the 1961 publication of a jubilee collection of papers (partly by foreign authors) and a monograph by A. P. Gnatyuk-Danil'chuk,[83] the Latvian scholar Viktors Ivbulis produced a study in Russian.[84] He wisely limited his approach to purely literary matters and analysed Tagore's œuvre in terms of the Soviet '*Literaturwissenschaft*': realism, romanticism, symbolism, etc. This book belongs as much to the Russian, as to the Latvian, reception of Tagore.

In 1983, an 'abridged' translation of Krishna Kripalani's biography of Tagore was published.[85] It is remarkable that foreign biographies of Tagore were abridged both in the 1920s and in the 1980s.[86]

In 1986, towards the end of the Soviet epoch, two books (prepared to commemorate the 125th anniversary of Tagore's birth) concluded the series: a collection of papers by Soviet scholars (much smaller in size than the 1961 book), and a book in English by Gnatyuk-Danil'Chuk.[87] All these books are fairly close to us in time, but they are far away in terms of language and approach. If the publications of 1961 admitted that 'two and two are ten and probably even nine,' the books of 1986 (it was the timid beginning of Gorbachev's 'perestroika') were courageous enough to say that 'two and two may be only as much as six!' The 125th birth anniversary of Tagore was celebrated in the Soviet Union on a rather low key. People at the top were busy with other matters. Relations with India were not the first priority

In 1988, a representative selection from the *Gitabitan* saw the light of day.[88] This was a kind of swan song of Boris Karpushkin (1925–87) who had done many word-for-word translations for the Collected Works and for this *Gitabitan* volume. A large number of poetic translations were produced by outstanding poets for this edition. But after 1988 no new translations of Tagore appeared in Russian. In fact, the last quarter of a century only saw the republishing of a few earlier books.

Thus, in 1999 one more volume of Tagore's selected works came out, in the series *Nobel Laureates* sponsored by UNESCO.[89] In 2005, an anthology of Tagore's writings on education was published.[90] Also in 2005, a publishing company brought out paperback editions of *The Wreck, Binodini* (*Chokher Bali*) and of some short stories. The publishers, however, renamed the books to make them more attractive to common readers. So one book was titled *A Daughter of the Ganges* (*The Wreck*), another *In the Captivity of Passion* (*Chokher Bali*), and yet another *A Game of Passion* (*Chokher Bali* and some short stories).[91] *Chokher Bali* was published as a whole in both books.

After a long interval, in 2011 and 2012, apparently inspired by the 150th birth anniversary of Tagore, some books were published (all from Moscow).

Thus, a collection of Tagore's poems came out in 2011 compiled by the poet and translator Mikhail Sinel'nikov (b. 1946).[92] Evidently, the compiler wanted to put together the best translations: by Akhmatova, Pasternak,

Petrovykh, Samoilov and other masters of the art, to which Sinel'nikov added a poetical (if a bit misinformed) introduction in prose.

In 2011 and 2012, for the first time after 1917, the translation of *Sadhana* was republished, this time in a popular series titled *Esoteric Wisdom*.[93] In 2012, the novels *The Wreck* and *Chokher Bali* came out in one volume together with some poems from the Bengali *Gitanjali* thanks to a commercial publishing company.[94]

The only new and original post-Soviet contribution to Tagore studies is the study of the songs (both the lyrics and the music) of the Bengali *Gitanjali* by Tatyana Morozova, a scholar of Rabindra Sangeet.[95]

Symbolically, it was in 1991, only a few months before the collapse of the Soviet system, that a monument of Tagore was unveiled in Moscow. This event coincided with the visit of the former Indian Prime Minister (during 1989–90) V. P. Singh as well as with the fiftieth anniversary of the poet's death and the 130th anniversary of his birth.

As new books by and about Tagore are few and far between (and they are easily lost in the ocean of books now overflowing in Russia) and as Tagore is no longer on any political agenda, younger generations in Russia have only a vague (if any) idea about the person and the author by the name of Rabindranath Tagore. Some years ago I had a class at my university, the Russian State University for the Humanities, one of the top institutions of higher education in the humanities in this country. My class comprised third-year students who specialised in Western European languages and literatures. Just by chance I asked them what they knew about Rabindranath Tagore. To my surprise I found that none of the students had even heard the name of Tagore. So, out of print—out of mind.

Sometime in the first decade of the twenty-first century, Vladimir Putin, who was then (as again now) the President of the Russian Federation, had to pronounce on a certain ceremonial occasion the name of Tagore. His speech was broadcast over TV. Paper in hand, Putin struggled for some time with the name 'Rabindranath', but in the end failed to pronounce it articulately enough. It was especially telling, as Putin articulates even difficult Russian words usually very well (unlike most of his predecessors who were notorious for their funny pronunciations). That mishap demonstrated once again that the name of Rabindranath Tagore had practically disappeared from the mental horizon of most Russians.

In 2011, the 150th birth anniversary of Tagore was practically neglected by the establishment of post-Soviet Russia. Whatever functions took place in Moscow were organised or sponsored either by the Embassy of India or by Indians who live in Moscow.

In 1961, Yevgeni Chelyshev wrote: 'In spite of the fact that Tagore's name became known in our country almost fifty years ago and during this half a century a lot has been done to make his work popular here, Soviet readers up to now do not have such a book about Tagore in which his many-sided activity would be presented fully and deeply enough and an objective scientific appraisal of his huge contribution to the treasury of world culture would be given.'[96] Another fifty years have passed, and we can repeat this lamentation (mutatis mutandis). In the 1960s and 1970s, there were scholars in Russia who could probably undertake the work, but there was not enough freedom (including the inner freedom of the mind) to do it properly. Now we have enough freedom, but do not have enough scholars.

Be that as it may, the poet and his works have to be introduced anew to most readers in this country. But in Russia today the number of people knowing Bengali is rather limited. So probably we will have first to educate a new generation of connoisseurs and translators for Bengali and its literature. It is difficult to say which parts and aspects of Tagore's work and personality may appeal most to younger generations in Russia. The author of this essay, together with a colleague, an expert in Bengali, is going to bring out a new Russian translation of *Ghare Baire*. The problems portrayed in this novel (revolutionary violence versus non-violent action; patriotism, *desh-bhakti*, versus cosmopolitanism, *visva-bhakti* or *manava-bhakti*; the use of religion in politics; the value of love and mutual trust in marriage, etc.) are topical for today's Russia (as, for that matter, for the rest of the world). Tagore's essays on various subjects (which remain to a large extent not translated into Russian) may also find a receptive readership in Russia. But Tagore was, first and foremost, a poet. And I hope that a poet may be born in Russia who will translate Tagore's poetry into the Russian language in such a way that Russians will accept those translations as their own great poetry.

NOTES

1. The first translation of Tagore's *Gitanjali* (from English) into Finnish, by the poet Eino Leino (1878–1926), was published in Tampere, Finland, in 1917, when Finland was still part of the Russian Empire. But this translation should be considered in another part of this book.
2. Gnatyuk-Danil'Chuk, *Tagore, India and the Soviet Union*, cf. note 87.
3. For more details see my paper: 'The Generation "Waves" in Russian Sanskrit Studies.'
4. See Goldberg et al., *Rabindranat Tagor*, 335.
5. The diaries of Minayev written during the last visit have been published in Russian and the Russian edition translated into English: Minayeff, *Travels and Diaries*. However, as my colleague Alexei Vigasin has recently shown,

the published version was rather severely censored. The following paragraphs about Minayev are based on Vigasin's book in Russian: Vigasin, *Izucheniye Indii v Rossii.*

6. In Russian, this aristocratic family name sounds actually like 'Shcherbatskóy' (with the stress on the last syllable). In Tolstoy's *Anna Karenina,* we meet prince Shcherbatskoy and his family.

7. Stcherbatsky, *The Central Conception*; Stcherbatsky, *The Conception of Buddhist Nirvāna*; Stcherbatsky, *Buddhist Logic,* vols. I–II. All the three books of this *'grantha-trayam'* were more than once reprinted in America and in India.

8. I base my account of Nishikanta mainly on Vigasin's book (see above). Vigasin has relied on Mookherjee, ed., *Short Life,* a compilation of newspaper reports about Nishikanta, both in English and Bengali, accompanied by a long apologetic article.

9. (a) An English version of the dissertation was published by Trübner in London in 1882. A more recent edition is Chattopadhyaya, *The yātrās*; (b) Chattopadhyaya, *Indische Essays.*

10. Stacy, *India in Russian Literature,* 47–8.

11. Serebriany, 'Leo Tolstoy Reads Shri Ramakrishna;' Gnatyuk-Danil'Chuk, *Tolstoy and Vivekananda.*

12. Goldberg et al., ed., *Rabindranat Tagor.*

13. This bibliographical list was also published as a separate booklet: *Rabindranat Tagor: bio-bibliograficheskiy ukazatel'.*

14. *Bibliografiya Indii,* 1976.

15. Ibid., 1982.

16. http://www.nlr.ru:8101/e-case3/sc2.php/web_gak/lc/97207/1.

17. http://www.rsl.ru/ru/s97/s339/.

18. He was an uncle of a much more famous Viktor Shklovsky (1893–1984), one of the founders of the Russian 'Formalist' school. Isaak Shklovsky, after about six years of banishment to Yakutia, moved to London in 1896 and lived there till the end of his life.

19. *Bibliografiya Indii* (1976), 469.

20. *Gitanjali* and 'Bicharak,' tr. Dioneo.

21. http://nobelprize.org/nobel_prizes/literature/laureates/1913/press.html. This important speech by the Swedish historian has not even been mentioned (let alone quoted) in the standard biographies of Tagore. The speech dispels some popular myths about the motives and reasons of awarding the Nobel Prize to the poet. Now an English translation of the speech is available on the Internet as well as on paper in Frenz, *Nobel Lectures.*

22. *Gitandzhali (Pesennye zhertvoprinosheniya).* Tr. from English, with an introduction by L. B. Khavkina. The translation was obviously done (and even partly published) before the announcement of the Nobel Prize award.

23. Known also as L. B. Khavkina-Hamburger.

24. Richardson, 'The origin of Soviet education for librarianship.'

25. (i) http://en.wikipedia.org/wiki/Jurgis_Baltrušaitis. (ii) *Bibliografiya Indii* (1976), 439.

26. *Zhertvopesni (Gitandzhali),* tr. from English, ed. by Baltrušaitis (1914) and *Gitandzhali. Zhertvopesni,* tr. from English, ed. by Baltrušaitis (1914).

27. Unlike Ivan Bunin, Nikolay Pusheshnikov did not emigrate after 1917 and died in Moscow in 1939.

28. *Gitandzhali: Zhertvennye pesnopeniya,* tr. from English, with an introduction by Pusheshnikov (1914). Its second, third and fourth editions by the same publishers came out in 1914, 1916 and 1918 respectively.

29. *Gitandzhali: Zhertvennye pesnopeniya,* tr. from English, with an introduction by Pusheshnikov (1919). From mid-December 1918 up to April 1919, Odessa was under French control. Then, till the end of August, Bolsheviks were in power. From the end of August 1919 till February 1920, the Volunteer Army under the command of General Anton Denikin held the city. Ivan Bunin came to Odessa in the summer of 1918 and emigrated from there to France in February 1920. The publishing house Southern Universal Library was founded in Odessa in 1918 by the Russian Jewish writer Semyon Yushkevich (1868–1927). He emigrated in 1920 and died in Paris (http://en.wikipedia.org/wiki/Semyon_Yushkevich).

30. (i) *Tsvety moyego sada.* — *Sadovnik.* — *Gitandzhali,* tr. from English by Pusheshnikov (1925). (ii) Now this translation is available on the Internet: http://bookz.ru/authors/rabindranat-tagor/98948a4aeefb0350.html.

31. *Sadovnik,* tr. Pusheshnikov, ed. Bunin (1914) (2nd ed. 1918). *Tsvety moyego sada.* — *Sadovnik.* — *Gitandzhali,* tr. from English by Pusheshnikov (1925).

32. (i) *Sadovnik: Lirika lyubvi i zhizni,* tr. [with an introduction] by Tardov (1914). (ii) *Lirika lyubvi i zhizni (Sadovnik)* and *Chitra,* tr. [from English] with an introduction by Spasskaya (1915). (iii) *Sadovnik,* tr. by Saishnikova (1917).

33. *Sadovnik.* — *Gitandzhali,* tr. Sabashnikova (1919). *Sadovnik. Izbrannye stikhi.* Tr. from English by M[atil'da] Ber (1923).

34. (i) *Lunnyy serp,* tr. by Likiardopulo. (1914); (ii) *Vozrozhdayushchayasya luna (Lunnyy serp),* tr. from English by Vasina (1916).

35. *Iz zhizni Bengalii. Rasskazy.* Tr. [from English] by Sludsky and Sludsky (1915).

36. (i) *Tvorchestvo zhizni (Sadhana),* tr. from English by Gretman and Lempitskaya (1914). (ii) *Sadhana. Postizheniye zhizni. Vosem' lektsiy,* tr. by Pogossky (1914).

37. The Collected Works in eight volumes (actually ten volumes were planned, but only eight came out) were published in Moscow, between 1914 and 1915, from the publishing house Valentin Portugalov (Collected Works No. 1). The Collected Works in six volumes were published also in Moscow by the publishing house Sovremennye problemy (Contemporary problems) (Collected Works No. 2). Some of the volumes of this series were republished as late as 1925.

38. (i) *Tsar' tyomnogo pokoya. Misticheskaya drama.* Tr. from English by Zhurin, Lepkovsky and Rodon (1915); (ii) *Korol' tyomnogo pokoya. Pochtovaya kontora.* Tr. from English by Vengerova and Spasskaya (1915). Zinaida Vengerova (1867–1941) lived in Berlin from 1921, but in 1937 moved to the USA. She was a sister of the distinguished historian of literature, Semyon Vengerov (1855–1920, cf. http://en.wikipedia.org/wiki/Semyon_Vengerov) and of the pianist Isabelle Vengerova (1877–1956, cf. http://en.wikipedia.org/wiki/

Isabelle_Vengerova). In 1919, the translation of 'The King' by Z. Vengerova was published again in Odessa (in the same series as the 1919 Odessa edition of *Gitandzhali*): *Korol' tyomnogo pokoya. Pyesa*, tr. from English by Z. Vengerova. 'Yuzhnaya universal'naya biblioteka,' 1919.

39. (i) *Chitra: Dramaticheskaya poèma*, tr. by Podgorichani (1915) (2nd ed. 1915). (ii) *Pochta. Pyesa*, tr. from English by Rodon, preface by Yeats (1915). (iii) *Lirika lyubvi i zhizni (Sadovnik)* and *Chitra*, tr. [from English] with an introduction by Spasskaya (1915). (iv) *Korol' tyomnogo pokoya. Pochtovaya kontora*, tr. from English by Vengerova and Spasskaya (1915). *Poèmy Kabira*, tr. from English by Vasin (1916).

40. Paustovsky, 'Povest' o zhizni', 325.

41. I thank my Moscow colleagues Yevgeniya Ivanova and Yuri Freidin for the information about, respectively, Blok and Mandelshtam.

42. (i) *Dom i mir*, tr. from English by Zhuravskaya (1920). (ii) *Dom i mir*, tr. from English by Karnaukhova (1923). (iii) *Dom i mir*, tr. from English by Adrianov (1923).

43. Serebriany, 'Tagore's reception in Russia' and Saraskina, Serebryany, 'F. M. Dostoevsky i R. Tagor.'

44. (i) *Krusheniye*, tr. from English by S. A. Adrianov (1923 and 1924). (ii) *Krusheniye* , tr. from English by Adrianov, ed. with an introduction and notes by Tubyansky (1925). Sergei Alexandrovich Adrianov (1871–1942) before 1917 was a noted literary critic and historian of literature, but after 1917 he evidently preferred to keep a low profile and switched over to translations. (See http://az.lib.ru/a/adrianow_s_a/text_0010.shtml.) (i) *Gora*, tr. from English by Pimenova. (ii) *Gora*, tr. from English by Voinov (1924). (iii) *Gora*, tr. from English by Voinov, ed. with an introduction and notes by Tubyansky (1926).

45. (i) *V chetyre golosa*, tr. from English by Demi, preface by Rolland (1925). (ii) *V chetyre golosa*, tr. from English by Russat (1925). (iii) *V chetyre golosa*, tr. by Khokhlova (1925). The translators probably looked into the French translation as well, which also came out in 1925 and was titled *A quatre voix*.

46. (i) *Zhertvoprinosheniye. — Otshel'nik*, tr. from English by Adrianov (1922). (ii) *Korol' tyomnogo pokoya [i drugiye pyesy]*, tr. from English by Adrianov and Fedotov (1927).

47. (a) (i) *Fragmenty*, tr. from English by Kolubovsky and Tubyansky (1923). (ii) *Zalyotnye ptitsy*, tr. from English by Shchepkina-Kupernik (1924). (b) (i) *Natsionalizm*, tr. from English by Sklyaver [1921]; (ii) *Natsionalizm*, tr. from English by Kolubovsky and Tubyansky (1922). The latter book has a particularly insightful preface by Kolubovsky, about whom no information is available. He might have been a son of Yakov Nikolayevich Kolubovsky (1863–?), a historian of philosophy in Russia (Cf. http://www.runivers.ru/philosophy/lib/authors/author64119/). (c) (i) *Moya zhizn'*, tr. from English by Gizetti (1924). (ii) *Vospominaniya*, tr. from English by Tubyansky (1924). Alexander Alexeyevich Gizetti (1888–1938?) was a remarkable person. His ancestor, a merchant of Venetian origin, came to Russia from Germany in the early nineteenth century; the merchant's nine children and their descendants

later distinguished themselves in various spheres of activity. For instance, the late Patriarch of the Russian Orthodox Church, Alexy II (né Alexey Ridiger, 1929–2008) also belonged to this family. Alexander Gizetti was a scholar, journalist, and translator. As a member of the Socialist-revolutionary Party he was imprisoned several times both before and after 1917, the last time in 1935. The date and circumstances of his death are not known, but most probably he died in prison. About M. I. Tubiansky, see below. (d) *Lichnoye*, tr. from English by Kolubovsky (1922) and *Bengaliya*, tr. from English by Chervonsky (1927).

48. *Golodnye kamni [i drugiye rasskazy]*, tr. from English by Adrianov (1925).

49. 'Chelovek iz Kabula. Rasskaz,' tr. by Veysbrut.

50. (a) 'Malen'kaya poèma v proze,' tr. from the Bengali by Tubyansky. I have not yet been able to identify the Bengali original. (b) 'Iz "*Gitandzhali*",' tr. from the Bengali.

51. *Svet i teni. Rasskazy*, tr. by Tubyansky (from the Bengali), Fedotov and Russat (from English) (1926); *Vospominaniya*, tr. from Bengali by M. I. Tubyansky (1927).

52. *Natsionalizm*, tr. from English by Kolubovsky and Tubyansky (1922).

53. Cf. http://en.wikipedia.org/wiki/Vladimir_Bogoraz.

54. *Biblioteka V. I. Lenina v Kremle. Katalog*. M.: Izdatel'stvo Vsesoyuznoy knizhnoy palaty, 1961.

55. These are *Lichnoye*, tr. [from English] by Kolubovsky (1922) (No. 1281 in the catalogue); *Natsionalizm*, tr. from English by Kolubovsky and Tubyansky (1922) (No. 1282), and *Natsionalizm*, tr. from English by Sklyaver (1921) (No. 1283); *Dom i mir: roman*, tr. from English by Zhuravskaya (1920) (No. 6448); and *Pyesy i stikhotvoreniya v proze*, ed. by Vol'sky and Chukovsky (1923) (No. 6449).

56. In 1926, for example, it was a combination of poor health and less attractive fees for his lectures that prevented the poet from visiting Poland and then travelling on to Russia. Tagore's secretary, P. C. Mahalanobis (distinguished statistician and one of the brains behind India's Five-Year Plans for development), discussed the possible options in his letter to Rathindranath (the poet's son) sent from Berlin on 1 October. See Bangha, *Hungry Tiger*, 128–9.

57. Ol'denburg, 'Rabindranat Tagor.' .

58. A recent English translation of the novel is Ilf and Petrov, *The Little Golden Calf*. See also http://en.wikipedia.org/wiki/The_Little_Golden_Calf.

59. Ilf and Petrov, *The Little Golden Calf*, 387 (the chapter of the novel is titled 'The Indian Guest').

60. Ibid., 391.

61. Tagore, *Letters from Russia*.

62. *Pis'ma o Rossii*, tr. from the Bengali by Kafitina (1956).

63. A comparison of the cuts in the two translations, that is, a comparative study of censorship, is a task that remains to be done.

64. Tagore, *Letters from Russia*, 92.

65. Ibid., 122.

66. Ibid., 215–16.

67. Cf. http://en.wikipedia.org/wiki/Ivan_Ostromislensky.

68. http://select.nytimes.com/gst/abstract.html?res=9E05E2DA173FE637 A25756C1A9679C946094D6CF&n=Top%2fReference%2fTimes%20 Topics%2fSubjects%2fC%2fCulture Cf. also Bertenson et al., *Sergei Rachmaninoff*, 272.

69. I thank Dr Amrit Sen (Visva-Bharati) for drawing my attention to this letter in 2011.

70. (i) *Sochineniya v vos'mi tomakh*, preface by Gnatyuk-Danil'Chuk ; (ii) *Sobraniye sochineniy v dvenadtsati tomakh*, eds. Bykova et al.

71. Ivinskaya, *V plenu vremeni* (1991), 24–5. Ivinskaya's memoirs were first published in Paris (Fayard, 1978); then in Vilnius (1991), and only thereafter in Moscow (Libris, 1992). The latter edition is now available on the Internet: http://www. sakharov-center.ru/asfcd/auth/auth_booka14f.html?id=84901&aid=170. It was translated into English soon after its first appearance: Ivinskaya, *A Captive of Time*.

72. Chukovskaya, *Zapiski ob Anne Akhmatovoy.*

73. It seems that only the first of its three volumes has so far been translated into English: Chukovskaya, *The Akhmatova Journals*, vol. I.

74. Chukovskaya, *Zapiski*, II, 221.

75. Ibid., III, 135.

76. Ibid., 216.

77. Ibid., II, 307.

78. Ibid., 709.

79. http://en.wikipedia.org/wiki/Alexey_Rybnikov About the film see http:// ru.wikipedia.org/wiki/Вам_и_не_снилось_(фильм). The song is available on the Internet: http://dl.dropbox.com/u/79279702/ Общее/А.%20Рыбников%20-%20Последняя%20Поэма%20(Из%20 к_ф%20'Вам%20и%20не%20снилось').mp3.

80. *Sobraniye sochineniy v chetyryokh tomakh*, tr. from the Bengali (1981–2). The preface was written by the historian Erik Komarov (1927–2013) who studied Bengali in the late 1940s. The same author wrote prefaces for several later editions of Tagore's works, permitting himself, over time, more and more freedom of expression; and (i) *Izbrannoye. Stikhi i pyesy*, preface by Komarov (1972); (ii) *Stikhotvoreniya. Rasskazy. Gora* (1973); (iii) *Izbrannoye: Stikhi. Rasskazy. Poslednyaya poèma: roman*, tr. from the Bengali (1987); (iv) *Izbrannoye: Poèziya, proza, publitsistika*, tr. from the Bengali (1987), and (v) *Zolotaya lad'ya. Izbrannye proizvedeniya. Dlya srednego i starshego vozrasta*, tr. from the Bengali (1989).

81. http://ru.wikipedia.org/wiki/Библиотека_всемирной_литературы.

82. *Zolotaya lad'ya. Izbrannye proizvedeniya. Dlya srednego i starshego vozrasta* (see Note 80)

83. Goldberg et al., ed., *Rabindranat Tagor*; Gnatyuk-Danil'Chuk, *Rabindranat Tagor.*

84. Ivbulis. *Literaturno-khudozhestvennoye tvorchestvo Rabindranata Tagora.*

85. Kripalani. *Rabindranat Tagor* (an abridged translation, 1983) .

86. See Note 51 above (1927).

87. (a) Chelyshev and Gavryushina, eds., *Rabindranat Tagor*. This book contained ten papers by nine authors (two of them from Latvia: Viktors Ivbulis and R. Putniṇa). The book opened with the paper 'Tagore in Russia and the USSR' by A. Gnatyuk-Danil'Chuk; (b) Gnatyuk-Danil'Chuk, *Tagore, India and the Soviet Union*, 1986; cf. Note 2.
88. *Sad pesen: Gitobitan*, tr. from Bengali, compiled and with notes by Karpushkin, drawings by Poplavsky (1988).
89. *Izbrannye proizvedeniya* , tr. from the Bengali, compiled by Zhdanko (1999).
90. Vasilenko, ed. *Tagor* (2005).
91. *Doch' Ganga: roman,* tr. from the Bengali by Smirnova and Tovstykh (2005). 'A Daughter of the Ganges' ("Doch' Ganga") was also the name of a film produced in Tashkent (at the film studio Uzbek-film) in 1961, a screen version of Tagore's novel *The Wreck*. The film was rather naïve. Characters greeted each other in Hindi ('Namaste!'), and at one point one of the characters read a letter written in Hindi; *V plenu strasti [roman]*, tr. from Bengali by Smirnova and Tovstykh. (2005); and *Igra strasti [roman, rasskazy]*, tr. from Bengali by Smirnova, Tovstykh and A. Gnatyuk-Danil'Chuk. (2005).
92. *Veter li staroye imya razveyal ...* , compiled and with an introduction by Sinel'nikov (2011). The title of the book is a line from the Russian translation by Adelina Adalis of the poem from *Shesher kabita* (The Last Poem) put to music by Alexei Rybnilov. The line corresponds to the two lines of the original: *chanchal beg hāwāy urāy / āmār purāno nām*. Almost simultaneously there came out a slightly abridged version of the same collection: *Ty poglyadi bez otchayan'ya* ['Have a look without despair']. Compiled and with an introduction by M. Sinel'nikov (Moscow: Èksmo, 2011). The title of this book comes from the same translation, but it does not have a counterpart in the original.
93. *Sadhana. Tvorchestvo zhizni* (2011).
94. *Èto ne son! Romany, stikhotvoreniya* (2012). The title of the book, 'It is not a dream,' is, again, a quotation from the same poem from *Shesher kabita* : *'tobu se to svapna nay.'*
95. *Gitandzhali: muzykal'nye poèmy,* compiled by Morozova (2011). For this book, Irina Prokofyeva has done new translations of poems from the Bengali *Gitanjali*. In 1993, Tatyana Morozova published a study devoted to Rabindra Sangeet as a whole: Morozova, *Robindroshongit*.
96. Goldberg et al., ed., *Rabindranat Tagor, 9.*

Works Cited

Tagore Translations in Russian

Bengaliya. Izbrannye otryvki iz pisem. 1885–95 [Bengal. Selected excerpts from letters. 1885–95]. Translated from English by O. P. Chervonsky. Moscow–Leningrad: Gosizdat, 1927.
'Chelovek iz Kabula. Rasskaz' [A Man from Kabul. A short story]. Translated by E. Veysbrut. *Krasnaya panorama*. 1929, no. 14, 10–12.

Chitra: Dramaticheskaya poèma [*Chitra*: a Dramatic Poem]. Translated by M. Podgorichani. Moscow: Portugalov, 1915) (2nd ed., 1915) (Collected Works no. 1, vol. 4).

Doch' Ganga: roman. [Daughter of the Ganges: a novel]. Translated from Bengali by E. Smirnova and I. Tovstykh. Moscow: AST-Press Kniga, 2005.

Dom i mir: roman [*The Home and the World*: a novel]. Translated from English by Z. Zhuravskaya. Berlin: Èfron [1920].

Dom i mir: roman. Translated from English by A. M. Karnaukhova. Petrograd: Mysl', 1923 (2nd ed. Leningrad: Mysl', 1925).

Dom i mir: roman. Translated from English by S. A. Adrianov. Petrograd: Petrograd, 1923.

Èto ne son! Romany, stikhotvoreniya [It is not a dream! Novels and poems]. Moscow: Èksmo, 2012.

Fragmenty [Fragments]. Translated from English by I. Ya. Kolubovsky and M. I. Tubyansky. Petrograd: Stozhary, 1923.

[*Gitanjali* (Twenty one poems) and 'Bicharak' (a short story). Translated by Dioneo (Isaak Shklovsky)]. *Slovo*, sbornik no. 1, Moscow, 1913, 127–49.

Gitandzhali: muzykal'nye poèmy [*Gitanjali*: musical poems]. Compiled by Tatyana Morozova. Moscow: Vostochnaya literatura, 2011.

'Gitandzhali (Pesennye zhertvoprinosheniya)' [*Gitanjali*: Song offerings]. Translated from English, with an introduction by L. B. Khavkina. *Severnye zapiski*, 1913: Oct., 87–101; Nov., 100–20.

Gitandzhali: Zhertvennye pesnopeniya [*Gitanjali*: sacrificial songs]. Translated from English, with an introduction by N. A. Pusheshnikov, ed. Ivan A. Bunin. Moscow: Knigoizdatel'stvo pisateley v Moskve, 1914. (further ed. 1914, 1916, 1918).

Gitandzhali: Zhertvennye pesnopeniya [*Gitanjali*: sacrificial songs]. Translated from English, with an introduction by N. A. Pusheshnikov, ed., Ivan A. Bunin (Ed. by Semyon Yushkevich. No. 6). Odessa: Yuzhnaya universal'naya biblioteka, 1919; http://www.nlr.ru8101/e-case3/sc2.php/web_gak/1c/97207/53.

Gitandzhali. Zhertvopesni [*Gitanjali*: sacrificial songs]. Translated from English, ed. by Jurgis Baltrušaitis [Introduction by W. B. Yeats]. Moscow: V. Portugalov, 1914 (Collected Works no. 1, vol. 1).

Golodnye kamni [i drugiye rasskazy]. [Hungry stones (and other stories)]. Translated from English by S. A. Adrianov. With an introduction and notes by M. I. Tubyansky. Leningrad: Mysl', 1925.

Gora: roman [*Gora*: a novel]. Translated from English by È. K. Pimenova. Leningrad–Moscow: Kniga, 1924.

Gora: roman [*Gora*: a novel]. Translated from English by P. A. Voinov. Leningrad–Moscow: Petrograd, 1924.

Gora: roman [*Gora*: a novel]. Translated from English by P. A. Voinov. Ed. with an introduction and notes by M. I. Tubyansky. Leningrad: Mysl', 1926.

Igra strasti [roman, rasskazy]. [A Game of Passion: a novel and short stories]. Translated from the Bengali by E. Smirnova, I. Tovstykh and A. Gnatyuk-Danil'Chuk. Moscow: AST-Press Kniga, 2005.

'Iz "*Gitandzhali*"' [*From Gitanjali*]. Translated from the Bengali, with an introduction and notes by M. I. Tubyansky. *Vostok*, Kniga 5 (1925), 47–57.

Iz zhizni Bengalii. Rasskazy [*From Bengal's Life: short stories*]. Tr. [from English] by A. I. Sludsky and A. F. Sludsky. Moscow: V. Portugalov, 1915. Collected Works no. 1, vol. 7.

Izbrannoye: Poèziya, proza, publitsistika [Selected Works: poetry, prose, essays]. Translated from the Bengali. Compiled and with notes by N. M. Karpovich and I. D. Serebryakov. Preface by I. D. Serebryakov. Moscow: Prosveshcheniye, 1987.

Izbrannye proizvedeniya [Selected Works]. Translated from the Bengali. Compiled by O. Zhdanko. Moscow: Panorama, 1999 (UNESCO series, 'Nobel Laureates').

Izbrannoye. Stikhi i pyesy [Selected Works. Poems and plays]. Preface by È. Komarov. Moscow: Khudozhestvennaya literatura, 1972.

Izbrannoye: Stikhi. Rasskazy. Poslednyaya poèma, roman [Selected Works: poetry, short stories; *The Last Poem*, a novel]. Translated from the Bengali. Postface by È. Komarov. Moscow: Khudozhestvennaya literatura, 1987.

Korol' tyomnogo pokoya (i drugiye pyesy) [*The King of a Dark Chamber* (and other plays)]. Translated from English by S. A. Adrianov and G. P. Fedotov. Ed. with an introduction and notes by M. I. Tubyansky. Leningrad: Mysl', 1927.

Korol' tyomnogo pokoya. Pochtovaya kontora [*The King of a Dark Chamber; The Post Office*]. Translated from English by Z. Vengerova and V. Spasskaya. Preface by Z. Vengerova. Moscow: Sovremennye problemy, 1915 (Collected Works no. 2, vol. 4).

Korol' tyomnogo pokoya. Pyesa [*The King of a Dark Chamber*. A Play]. Translated from English by Z. Vengerova. Odessa: 'Yuzhnaya universal'naya biblioteka,' 1919 (in the pre-revolutionary orthography).

Krusheniye: roman [*The Wreck*: a novel]. Translated from English by S. A. Adrianov. Petrograd–Moscow: Petrograd, 1923 (2nd ed. Leningrad–Moscow: Petrograd, 1924).

Krusheniye: roman [*The Wreck*: a novel]. Translated from English by S. A. Adrianov. Ed. with an introduction and notes by M. I. Tubyansky. Leningrad: Mysl',' 1925.

Lichnoye [The Personal]. Tr. [from English] with an introduction by I. Ya. Kolubovsky. Moscow: Gosizdat, 1922.

Lirika lyubvi i zhizni (Sadovnik); Chitra [Lyrics of love and life (*The Gardener); Chitra*]. Tr. [from English]. with an introduction by V. Spasskaya. Moscow: Sovremennye problemy, 1915 (Collected Works no. 2, vol. 3).

Lunnyy serp. Poèmy o detstve [*Moon's Sickle*. Poems about Childhood]. Translated by M. Likiardopulo. Moscow: V. Portugalov, 1914 (Collected Works no. 1, vol. 3).

'*Malen'kaya poèma v proze*' [A short poem in prose]. Translated from the Bengali by M. Tubyansky. *Vostok*. Kniga 1 (1922), 55–56.

Moya zhizn' [My Life]. Translated from English by A. A. Gizetti. Leningrad–Moscow: Petrograd, 1924.

Natsionalizm [*Nationalism*]. Translated from English by A. Sklyaver; ed. by M. N. Shvarts. Berlin: Èfron, [1921].

Natsionalizm [*Nationalism*]. Translated from English by I. Ya. Kolubovsky and M. I. Tubyansky. Preface by I. Ya. Kolubovsky. Moscow: Academia, 1922.

Pis'ma o Rossii [Letters about Russia]. Translated from the Bengali by M. Kafitina Moscow: Goslitizdat, 1956.

Pochta. Pyesa [*The Post office,* a Play]. Translated from English by M. Rodon. Preface by W. B. Yeats. Moscow: Portugalov, 1915 (Collected Works No. 1, vol. 5).

Poèmy Kabira [*Poems of Kabir*]. Translated from English by B. Vasin. Moscow: Sovremennye problemy, 1916 (Collected Works no. 2, vol. 6).

Pyesy i stikhotvoreniya v proze [Plays and Poems in Prose]. Ed. by S. Vol'sky and K. Chukovsky. Moskva – Petrograd: Gosudarstvennoye izdatel'stvo, 1923.

Sad pesen: Gitobitan [*A Garden of Songs: Gitobitan*]. Translated from the Bengali. Compiled and with notes by B. Karpushkin. Drawings by G. Poplavsky. Moscow: Khudozhestvennaya literatura, 1988.

Sadhana. Postizheniye zhizni. Vosem' lektsiy [*Sadhana.* Realisation of Life. Eight Lectures]. Translated by V. Pogossky. Moscow: Valentin P. Portugalov, 1914.

Sadhana. Tvorchestvo zhizni [*Sadhana.* Creation of Life]. Moscow: Amrita-Rus', 2011.

Sadovnik [*The Gardener*]. Tr. N. A. Pusheshnikov. Ed. Ivan A. Bunin. Moscow: Knigoizdatel'stvo pisateley v Moskve, [1914]) (2nd ed. 1918).

Sadovnik. Lirika lyubvi i zhizni [*The Gardener:* Lyrics of Love and Life]. Translated [with an introduction] by V. G. Tardov. Moscow: V. Portugalov, 1914.

Sadovnik. [*The Gardener*]. Translated by E. I. Saishnikova. Moscow: Universal'naya biblioteka, 1917.

Sadovnik. Gitandzhali. Polnyy perevod v stihakh s prisoyedineniem izbrannykh stikhotvoreniy iz drugikh knig Tagora [*The Gardener—Gitanjali.* A complete translation in verses together with selected poems from other books of Tagore]. Tr. I. Sabashnikova. Moscow: Sabashnikovy, 1919.

Sadovnik. Izbrannye stikhi [*The Gardener.* Selected Poems]. Translated from English by M[atil'da]. Ber. Khar'kov: Gosizdat Ukrainy, 1923.

Sobraniye sochineniy [Collected Works]. 6 vols. Moscow: Sovremennye problemy, 1914–16 (new edns. 1917, 1925) (Collected Works no. 2).

Sobraniye sochineniy [Collected Works]. 8 vols. Moscow: Valentin Portugalov: 1914–15 (Collected Works no. 1).

Sobraniye sochineniy v dvenadtsati tomakh [Collected Works in twelve volumes]. Eds. Ye. Bykova, A. Gnatyuk-Danil'Chuk, V. Novikova. Moscow: Gosudarstvennoye izdatel'stvo hudozhestvennoy literatury, 1961–65.

Sobraniye sochineniy v chetyryokh tomakh [Collected Works in four volumes]. Translated from the Bengali, preface by Erik Komarov. Moscow: Gosudarstvennoe izdatel'stvo khudozhestvennoy literatury, 1981–82.

Sochineniya v vos'mi tomakh [Collected Works in eight volumes]. Preface by A. Gnatyuk-Danil'Chuk. Moscow: Gosudarstvennoye izdatel'stvo khudozhestvennoy literatury, 1955–57.

Stikhotvoreniya. Rasskazy. Gora (Biblioteka vsemirnoy literatury v 200 tomakh. Seriya 3: Literatura XX veka; t. 184). [Poems. Short Stories. *Gora.* (Library of World Literature in 200 volumes. Series 3: Literature of the 20th century; vol. 184]. Moscow: Khudozhestvennaya literatura, 1973.

Svet i teni. Rasskazy [*Light and Shadows*. Short Stories]. Translated by M. I. Tubyansky (from Bengali), G. P. Fedotov and E. R. Russat (from English). Edited with notes by M. I. Tubyansky. Leningrad: Mysl',1926.

Tsar' tyomnogo pokoya. Misticheskaya drama [*The King of a Dark Chamber*. A mystical drama]. Translated from English by A. Zhurin, B. Lepkovsky and M. Rodon. Moscow: Valentin P. Portugalov, 1915) (Collected Works no. 1, vol. 6).

Tsvety moyego sada. — Sadovnik. — Gitandzhali [Flowers from my Garden. *The Gardener. Gitanjali*]. Translated from English by N. A. Pusheshnikov. Moscow: Novaya zhizn', 1925.

Tvorchestvo zhizni (Sadhana) [Creation of Life: *Sadhana*]. Translated from English by A. F. Gretman and V. S. Lempitskaya. Prefaces by P. I. Timofeyevsky and R. Tagore. Moscow: Sovremennye problemy, 1914 (Collected Works no. 2, vol. 2).

V chetyre golosa [In Four Voices]. Translated from English by Yu. N. Demi. Preface by R. Rolland. Leningrad: Seyatel', 1925.

V chetyre golosa [In Four Voices]. Translated from English by Ye. Russat. Preface by R. Rolland. Leningrad–Moscow: Puchina, 1925.

V chetyre golosa [In Four Voices]. Translated by Ye. S. Khokhlova. Ed. by V. A. Azov. Preface by R. Rolland. Leningrad: Gosizdat, 1925.

V plenu strasti: roman [*In the Prison of Passion*: a novel]. Translated from the Bengali by E. Smirnova and I. Tovstykh. Moscow: AST-Press Kniga, 2005.

Veter li staroye imya razveyal ... [≈ 'Was it the wind that has dispelled the old name?']. Compiled and with an introduction by M. Sinel'nikov. Moscow: Èksmo, 2011.

Vospominaniya [*Reminiscences*]. Translated from English, with an introduction and notes by M. I. Tubyansky. Moscow–Leningrad: Gosizdat, 1924.

Vospominaniya [*Reminiscences*]. Translated from Bengali, with an introduction and notes by M. I. Tubyansky. Leningrad: Mysl', 1927.

Vozrozhdayushchayasya luna (Lunnyy serp) [*A Moon Reborn (A Sickle of Moon)*]. Translated from English by B. Vasina. Moscow: Sovremennye problemy, 1916 (Collected Works no. 2, vol. 5).

Zalyotnye ptitsy [*Stray Birds*]. Translated from English by T. L. Shchepkina-Kupernik. Leningrad–Moscow: Petrograd, 1924.

Zhertvopesni (Gitandzhali) [Sacrificial Songs (*Gitanjali*)]. Translated from English, ed. by Jurgis Baltrušaitis [Preface by W. B. Yeats]. Moscow: Sovremennye problemy, 1914 (Collected Works no. 2, vol. 1).

Zhertvoprinosheniye. — Otshel'nik [*Sacrifice. A Hermit*]. Translated from English by S. A. Adrianov. Ed. with an introduction by V. G. Tan-Bogoraz. Petrograd: Mysl', 1922.

Zolotaya lad'ya: Izbrannye proizvedeniya. Dlya srednego i starshego vozrasta [*A Golden Boat*: Selected Works. For teenagers]. Translated from the Bengali. Compiled and with an introduction and notes by Yu. Maslov. Moscow: Detskaya literatura, 1989.

Secondary Sources

Bangha, Imre. *Hungry Tiger: Encounters between Hungarian and Bengali Literary Cultures.* New Delhi: Sahitya Akademi, 2008.

Bertenson, Sergei, Jay Leyda, and Sophie Satina. *Sergei Rachmaninoff: A Lifetime in Music.* Bloomington, IN, USA: Indiana University Press, 2001. (First ed. New York: New York University Press, 1956). Accessed 2 July 2014. http://books.google.co.uk/books/about/Sergei_Rachmaninoff.html?id =KM-dgfOaIIkC&redir_esc=y.

Chattopadhyaya, Nishikanta. *Indische Essays.* Zürich: Rudolphi & Klemm, 1883.

———. *The yātrās: or, the popular dramas of Bengal.* Calcutta: Granthan, 1976 (1st ed. London: Trübner, 1882)

Chelyshev, Ye. P., and N. D. Gavryushina, eds. *Rabindranat Tagor: zhizn' i tvorchestvo: Sbornik statey* [Rabindranath Tagore: Life and Work: a collection of papers]. Moscow: Nauka, 1986.

Chukovskaya, Lidiya. *Zapiski ob Anne Akhmatovoy* [Notes about Anna Akhmatova]. 3 vols. Moscow: Soglasiye, 1997.

———. *The Akhmatova Journals: 1938–41,* vol.1. Evanston, IL, USA: Northwestern University Press, 2002.

Engelhardt, Emil. *Rabindranat Tagor kak chelovek, poèt i myslitel'* [Rabindranath Tagore as a Person, Poet, and Thinker]. An abridged translation from the German by A. S. Polotskaya. Edited by A. G. Gornfel'd. Leningrad: Seyatel', 1924 [The German original: Engelhardt, Emil. *Rabindranath Tagore als Mensch, Dichter und Denker: eine Lebensdarstellung mit einer Auswahl aus den Dichtungen und Bekenntnissen Tagores als Einführung in sein Werk.* Berlin: Furche-Verlag, 1922.].

Frenz, Horst, ed. *Nobel Lectures, Literature 1901–67.* Amsterdam: Elsevier Publishing Company, 1969.

Gnatyuk-Danil'Chuk, Aleksandr P. *Tagore, India and the Soviet Union: A Dream Fulfilled.* Calcutta: Firma KLM, 1986.

———. *Tolstoy and Vivekananda.* Calcutta: The Ramakrishna Mission, 1986.

———. *Rabindranat Tagor: kritiko-biograficheskiy ocherk* [Rabindranath Tagore: a critical and biographical essay]. Moscow: Goslitizdat, 1961.

Goldberg, N. M., S. K. Chatterji, and Ye. P. Chelyshev, eds. *Rabindranat Tagor: K stoletiyu so dnya rozhdeniya. 1861–1961. Sbornik statey* [Rabindranath Tagore: To the Hundredth Birth Anniversary, 1861–1961: A collection of papers]. Moscow: Izdatel'stvo vostochnoy literatury, 1961.

Ilf, Ilya, and Evgeni Petrov. *The Little Golden Calf,* trans. Anne O. Fisher. Montpelier, VT, USA: Russian Life Books, 2009.

Ivbulis, Viktors. *Literaturno-khudozhestvennoye tvorchestvo Rabindranata Tagora: Problema metoda* [The Literary Work of Rabindranath Tagore: The Problem of Method]. Riga: Zinātne, 1981.

Ivinskaya, Olga V. *V plenu vremeni. Gody s Borisom Pasternakom. Vospominaniya* [In the captivity of time: Years with Boris Pasternak: Recollections]. Vilnius: Izdatel'stvo Soyuza pisateley Litvy, 1991.

———. *A Captive of Time: My Years with Pasternak.* Translated by Max Hayward. London: Harvill Press, 1978.

Kotovsky, G. G., and N. N. Sosina, eds. *Bibliografiya Indii. Dorevolyutsionnaya i sovetskaya literatura na russkom yazyke i [drugikh]. yazykakh narodov SSSR, original'naya i perevodnaya (do 1967 g.)* [Bibliography of India: Pre-revolutionary and Soviet literature in Russian and in [other] languages of the USSR, original and translated (up to 1967)]. Moscow: Nauka, 1976.

Kotovsky, G. G., ed. *Bibliografiya Indii. 1968–75. Sovetskaya i perevodnaya literatura* [Bibliography of India, 1968–75. Soviet and translated literature]. Moscow: Nauka, 1982.

Kripalani, Krishna. *Rabindranat Tagor. Sokrashchennyy perevod s angliyskogo.* (An abridged translation of Krishna Kripalani's *Rabindranath Tagore*). Moscow: Molodaya Gvardiya, 1983.

Māmūd, Hāyāt. *Gerāsim Stepānabhic Liyebedeph.* Dhaka: Bangla Academy, 1985.

Minayeff, Ivan P. *Travels and Diaries of India and Burma.* Calcutta: Calcutta Eastern Trading Company, 1960.

Morozova, Tatyana E. *Robindroshongit: muzyka Rabindranata Tagora* [Rabindra Sangeet: The Music of Rabindranath Tagore]. Moscow: Rossiyskiy institut iskusstvoznaniya, 1993.

———, ed. *Rabindranat Tagor. Gitandzhali: muzykal'nye poèmy* [Rabindranath Tagore: *Gitanjali*—Musical Poems]. Moscow: Vostochnaya literatura, 2011.

Mookherjee, Hari Prasad. ed. *Short Life of Dr. Nishi Kanta Chattopadhyaya.* Dacca: no publisher, 1902.

Ol'denburg, S. F. 'Rabindranat Tagor.' *Ogonyok.* 1926, no. 51, [no page number].

Paustovsky, K. 'Povest' o zhizni' [The Story of (my) life]. In *Sobranie sochineniy* [Collected Works] by K. Paustovskiy, vol. 3. Moscow: Goslitizdat, 1958.

Richardson, John V. Jr., 'The origin of Soviet education for librarianship: The role of Nadezhda Konstantinovna Krupskaya, Lyubov' Borisovna Khavkina-Hamburger, and Genrietta K. Abele-Derman.' *Journal of Education for Library and Information Science*, 41/2 (2000), 106–28. (http://www.worldcat.org/title/origin-of-soviet-education-for-librarianship-the-role-of-nadezhda-konstantinovna-krupskaya-lyubov-borisovna-khavkina-hamburger-and-genrietta-k-abele-derman/oclc/223980904&referer=brief_results)

Saraskina, L. I., and S. D. Serebryanyy. 'F. M. Dostoyevskiy i R. Tagor (Istoricheskaya tipologiya, literaturnye vliyaniya).' [F. M. Dostoevsky and R. Tagore: Historical typology, literary influencies]. In *Vostok — Zapad. Issledovaniya. Perevody. Publikatsii* (East–West. Research. Translations. Publications), 129–69. Moscow: Nauka, 1985, 129–69.

Serebriany, Sergei. 'The Generation "Waves" in Russian Sanskrit Studies (in the 19th–20th centuries).' In *History of Indological Studies: Papers of the 12th World Sanskrit Conference*, vol. 11.2, ed. Klaus Karttunen. Delhi: Motilal Banarsidass (in press).

Serebriany, Sergei. 'Leo Tolstoy Reads Shri Ramakrishna.' In *Russia Looks at India. A Spectrum of Philosophical Views*, ed. Marietta Stepanyants, 325–51. New

Delhi: Indian Council of Philosophical Research and D. K. Printworld, Publishers of Indian Traditions, 2010.

———. 'Tagore's reception in Russia: What can we learn from the Rezeptionsgeschichte?' in *Rabindranath Tagore: Beyond Bengali Literature*, edited by Imre Bangha. New Delhi: ICCR (forthcoming).

Stacy, Robert H. *India in Russian Literature.* Delhi: Motilal Banarsidass, 1985.

Stcherbatsky, Th[eodor]. *Buddhist Logic*, vols. 1–2 (Bibliotheca Buddhica XXVI). Leningrad: Academy of Sciences of USSR Press, 1930–32.

Stcherbatsky, Th[eodor]. *The Central Conception of Buddhism and the Meaning of the Word 'Dharma'.* London: Royal Asiatic Society, 1923.

———. *The Conception of Buddhist Nirvāna.* Leningrad: Publication Office of the Academy of Sciences of the USSR, 1927.

Strizhevskaya, L. A., ed. *Rabindranat Tagor: bio-bibliograficheskiy ukazatel'* [Rabindranath Tagore: A bio-bibliographical guide]. Moscow: Izdatel'stvo Vsesoyuznoy knizhnoy palaty, 1961.

Tagore, Rabindranath. *Letters from Russia,* trans. Sasadhar Sinha Calcutta: Visva-Bharati, 1960.

Vasilenko, V. A., ed. *Tagor.* Moscow: Shalva Amonashvili [State Pedagogical University], 2005.

Vigasin, Aleksey. *Izuchenie Indii v Rossii: ocherki i materialy* [Alexei A. Vigasin. *Study of India in Russia: Essays and materials*]. Moscow: Stepanenko, 2008.

14

Romania

Liviu Bordaş

THE STATE OF INVESTIGATION

Research on Tagore's reception in Romania started in 1961 and subsequently about a dozen articles were published as well as two books which aimed to draw a bibliographical map of it.[1] A larger list of translations and articles is found in the *Bibliography of Romanian Literature's Relationships with Other Literatures in Periodical Publications*.[2] As the sources given in these three works are incomplete, research based exclusively on them is likely to give an incorrect image of Tagore's reception. This was usually the case with previous surveys, the best researched being those published by Amita Bhose.[3] The present writer is currently working on a book on Tagore's reception in Romanian culture. A synthesis of it is given below.

From a spatial perspective, 'Romania' in this article will refer to the culture produced by Romanians living in all the territories which belonged to Great Romania, as well as in the diaspora. From a temporal perspective, Tagore's reception is divided in five periods, following the political eras of Romanian history: 1) 1913–18: The old Romanian kingdom and the provinces of Transylvania, Banat, Bukovina (in the Austro-Hungarian Empire), and Bessarabia (in the Russian Empire); 2) 1918–40: The kingdom of Great Romania, including all these territories in a single state; 3) 1940–5: World War II, during which Great Romania lost and temporarily recovered some of these territories; and 4) 1945–89. The two Romanian socialist states: one independent (S.R. Romania) and one incorporated in the Soviet Union (S. S. R. Moldova), along with some former Romanian territories granted to Ukraine and Bulgaria.[4] While all these lands produced a considerable diaspora in the non-Communist world, Soviet Moldova also generated a significant diaspora within the Soviet Union; 5) 1990–2013. The post-Communist era, with the same borders, but with Moldova becoming an independent state.

From 1913 to 1918

The First Reactions

In the summer of 1913, *Gitanjali* was announced by a few brief notes. A longer review was published in September by the literary critic and poet, Constantin Spiru Hasnaș (1873–1958). Full of enthusiasm for Tagore's profound and moving poems that sprung all of a sudden in the West like a 'miraculous flower', he translated seven poems in prose. His review was guilty of some Orientalist clichés and misrepresentations. Hasnaș placed Tagore in the current of the spiritual and religious revival of the young twentieth century. He considered him a mystical poet, gifted with the power of religious contemplation, who, by loving and singing life, detached himself from the pessimistic tradition of *nirvana*, typical to Indian poetry. Hasnaș compared Tagore's serene pantheism with Christian mysticism. Although he asserted that Tagore's poems can only be paralleled by the purest and most spiritualised parts of the *Psalms* of David, he was careful to distinguish the Christian God from the God of the 'Orientals'.

Responses to the Nobel Prize

After the Nobel Prize, by the end of 1914 almost every important journal and newspaper from the Romanian kingdom and Transylvania published an article on Tagore, with his photograph and translations from *Gitanjali*, *The Gardener*, and *The Crescent Moon*. They gave brief biographies of him, talking about his works and about Santiniketan. He was again compared with David (i.e. the *Psalms*) and considered as having surpassed Solomon in his love songs (i.e. the *Song of Songs*).

Contrasting Tagore's work with that of Kipling and the literature of the conquered with that of the conqueror, a Transylvanian cultural journal concluded that the conquerors were defeated by the spirit of the land they conquered. In another journal from Transylvania he was seen as a poet of the people who, without entering into politics, had poured the 'national consciousness' into the souls of his compatriots.

The most important article was published on 1 December 1913, from London, by the young writer, Dimitrie N. Ciotori (1885–1965). He read *Gitanjali* in English and translated four poems from it. Their mysticism appeared to him vaguer than that of the Psalmist. As Europe had grown too sceptical and wary of prophets, he believed that the Indian poet could not become the prophet of a new poetry in the West. As for *The Gardener*, he found in it the influence of British poetry—Swinburne, Shelley, Keats— which had somehow attenuated the transcendental mysticism of Tagore.

First Translations

The early articles dedicated to Tagore were accompanied by translations of his verses. From September 1913 to June 1914, almost all of them added poems from *Gitanjali*, *The Gardener*, and *The Crescent Moon*, rendered into Romanian from French, German or English. The poets Cassian R. Munteanu (1892–1921) and Ion Sân-Giorgiu (1893–1950) tried to put Tagore's poetry into verses. Ernest Poldi presented his renderings from *Gitanjali* as part of the full translation of the book (from English), which was promised to be published soon, but something—probably what later became World War I—prevented it.

The first book of Tagore in Romanian was not *Gitanjali* but *The Gardener*. Published in June 1914, it was translated in prose, from English, by the writer Mărgărita Miller-Verghy (1865–1953). Her preface noted that, in *Gitanjali*, Tagore addresses God as he would speak to his beloved and that the presence of the divine is more real for him than that of the surrounding people. However, she found the human love expressed in *The Gardener* fresh, deep and full of tenderness. The artistic simplicity of Tagore's love poems, as also their sensitivity, seemed often to come close to those of Romanian folk poetry. The book received positive reviews from C. S. Hasnaş and the leading philologist Ovid Densusianu (1873–1938).

During the War years, the number of articles and translations—noteworthy are those of the poets Marcel Romanescu (1897–1955) and Alexandru Terziman (1894–1943)—slowly trickled to zero by 1917, before gaining a new start in the spring of 1918.

The novels, short stories, plays and educational activity of Tagore were at this time almost completely overshadowed by his image as a poet. A chapter from *My Reminiscences* was translated by the writer Camil Petrescu (1894–1957), who was also interested in his dramas. Petrescu's articles referred to the political context of Tagore's works but this was almost completely ignored by the other Romanian writers. Colonial reality was only rarely invoked, mostly in Transylvania. Instead, the question of the East–West opposition was markedly present but often reduced to the schematic binarisms of mysticism–voluntarism and contemplation–action. Tagore's reception—through the medium of French, German, and English—was very prompt both in the Romanian kingdom and in Transylvania. The journals published in Bukovina and Bessarabia seemed to have ignored him till 1918. But this is not necessarily a sign that he was unknown in these lost provinces, in which Romanian language and publications were politically discriminated against. A special research needs to assess his reception in the local official language publications (German and Russian). The Romanians who lived in

Western Europe were even more exposed to Tagore's vogue. To give only one but significant example, on the evening of 11 November 1918, the day the armistice was concluded, the poetess Anna de Noailles (1876–1933) read out poems from *Gitanjali* to the French Prime Minister Clemenceau.[5]

THE INTERWAR YEARS

In the aftermath of the War translations were still few. But the year 1921 saw a real explosion, and interest in Tagore's work grew continually till the end of the decade. The articles devoted to him touched all aspects of his creation. Newspapers and literary journals kept the public updated. Almost all leading intellectuals read one or another of his works and referred to him in their writings. The climax was reached in 1926, in connection with his visit to Bucharest. From 1930 onwards, and especially after 1933, the journals and newspapers reflect a sustained decline in interest in Tagore.

Out of the fourteen volumes of his works printed between 1921 and 1933 (with three reprints in 1926), six were of poetry, translated from German and French: *The Crescent Moon* (1921, 1926 [second edition/reprint], by I. Constantinescu-Delabaia), an anthology from *Gitanjali* and *Fruit-Gathering* (1921, by G. Ulieru), *The Gardener* (1922, by S. Lorin), *Gitanjali* (1923, by G. Ulieru), *Fruit-Gathering* (1923, by V. G. Luță), and again *The Crescent Moon* (1933, by A. Terziman). There were two novels translated from the French: *The Home and the World* (1924, by S. Lerescu) and *Chaturanga* (1927, by I. Pas), and four small volumes containing short stories from *The Hungry Stones* and *Mashi* (1922 and 1926, by N. Batzaria; 1931, by A. B. Luca; 1933, by M. Constanțiu). The most artistic translations were those of his essays, made from German: *Sadhana* (1922, by N. Crainic) and *Nationalism* (1922, 1926 [second edition/reprint], by A. Busuioceanu).

Tagore's Poetry

As the volumes of poetry did not excel in literary qualities and none of the translators was a well-known writer, they were ignored by literary critics. Only Silvian Lorin's translation of *The Gardener* triggered the critique of the symbolist poet Claudia Millian (1887–1961), who by comparing his translation with the English text, opened a discussion about Tagore's poetic style and its rendering into Romanian. The most active translator was George Ulieru (1884–1943), a publicist with socialist views, who disseminated dozens of poems in various reviews, journals and personal brochures.

Every year the periodicals carried dozens of translations of Tagore's poems. Several translators apparently competed to give better versions of, often, the same poems. In 1921, those written by the poets Alexandru

Gh. Doinaru (1882–1933), Nicolae N. Răutu (1891–1979), and Vladimir
Streinu (1902–70) could be observed. In 1922, interestingly, most of the
translators were orthodox priests and theologians, like Vasile Turtureanu
(1852–1937), Nicolae Regman (1881–1951), known as a writer under the
pen name Z. Sandu, and the poet Emil Serghie (1897–1977). New attempts
at translation in free verse were made by the seminarians Paraschiv Angelescu
(1902–7?) and Dumitru Belu (1902–80). It is not surprising therefore that
many of these translations resemble closely Christian devotional poetry.
In 1923 and 1924, a number of college and university professors joined
the club. Some of them translated in free verse with rhyme. Especially
Constantin Popescu-Gruia (1889–1952) and Constantin Asiminei (1894–
1947) used with skill the mixed rhyme (i.e. when more than one type of
rhyme is used alternately), with or without rhythm, and sometimes even
the assonance. Along with the translations from Tagore's first four volumes,
there were new ones from *Stray Birds*, *The Fugitive* and *Balaka*. The composer
Grigore Ghidionescu (1901–68) wrote music for *Two Songs on Rabindranath
Tagore's Verses* (1925) for voice and piano.

From Tagore's visit in November 1926 till the end of the 1930s, literary
reviews, general journals and newspapers kept publishing new translations
of his poems, despite the fact that most of them were already circulating
in book form. Along with the earlier translators, the literary historians Ilie
E. Torouţiu (1888–1953) and George Baiculescu (1900–72), the literary
journalist Miron Grindea (1909–95), the poets Lotis Dolenga (1905–61),
Emanoil Ungheru (1907–43), George Demetru Pan (1911–72), Geavit
Arabolu (1917–8?), and Constantin Almăjanu (1910–41) were also active.
Some of the new translations not only transposed Tagore's poems in rhymed
verse but also surpassed in quality the old ones. Seven poems from *Fireflies*—
sent by Tagore to one of his admirers—were translated in 1927, before the
printing of the book.[6]

The first translations from Bengali were done by Mircea Eliade (1907–
86) at Calcutta and Santiniketan, in 1929 and 1930. They were poems
from *Balaka* and *Mahua*. Eliade, admittedly, learned Bengali by reading,
memorising, and translating Tagore's poetry. After his return to Romania, in
December 1931, he published a free verse translation of the poem 'Nirbhay'
from *Mahua*, a book which he used to read together with Maitreyi Devi,
when he fancied becoming a *Vaishnava* and marrying her. Eliade presented
it as the first translation from *Mahua* in a European language.[7]

The vogue of Tagore exercised a certain influence on Romanian poets,
especially in the early years of his reception. Some of the poems from the
first book of Tudor Vianu (1898–1964), written between 1914 and 1917,
evoke the atmosphere of Tagore's lyricism. However, after the war he gave

up the idea of becoming a poet and the book remained unpublished in his lifetime. The influence of Tagore on Lucian Blaga (1895–1961) was widely recognised by the critics of his first volume, *Poemele luminii* (*Poems of Light*, 1919).[8] This book received mixed reviews. While some saw Tagore's influence in a positive, creative way, others considered Blaga an imitator of the modernism and mysticism then in fashion. In his subsequent articles on Tagore one can see a slow yet definite change of attitude. What impressed him particularly was the fact that the Indian poet gave more significance to feeling over thinking. He saw Tagore as the engine of a new orientation in European culture, announcing an era characterised by a deeper inner life. But his ideas about the West changed Blaga's attitude. He had been attracted not by Tagore's philosophical constructions about modern civilisation but by his *attitude* towards the world and life, especially the way he related to nature and rural life. By 1923, the year of his last article on him, Blaga freed himself poetically from Tagorean influences. Nevertheless, Blaga's early interest in Tagore drew some of his later students as well as poets influenced by him in general to the Indian writer.

By 1923, there was already an outspoken resistance to Tagore, expressed especially in the writings of traditionalist and conservative intellectuals, such as the 'national poet' Octavian Goga (1881–1938), the writer Alexandru Hodoş (1863–1929), and the literary historian Mihail Dragomirescu (1868–1942). The poetry in Romania composed under Tagore's influence was considered as 'imported literature,' 'hybrid production,' 'strange literary psychosis' or 'imitative traditionalism.' However, leaving aside the young Blaga, a real Tagorean influence can be recognised only in the works of minor spiritualist poets, such as Z. Sandu, who wrote paeans to him even in the 1930s. Elena Văcărescu (1864–1947) gave a long lecture in Paris, in 1926, expressing her admiration and sympathy for Tagore. However, with her poetic work accomplished by 1914, one cannot speak about a Tagorean influence on it.

Tagore's Prose

The other dimensions of Tagore's creative personality were overshadowed by his poetry. Only the philosophical essays and, generally, his public statements on contemporary issues could compete with his lyrics.

Nicolae Batzaria (1874–1952), a popular writer, translated from English, in 1922 and 1926, two volumes containing eleven short stories from *Hungry Stones* and *Mashi*. Two others appeared in 1931 and 1933, in a series of weekly brochures, and a few more in literary journals.

The Home and the World, translated in 1924 by the dramatist Samuel Lerescu (1876–194?), and *Chaturanga*, in 1927 by the socialist writer, Ion

Pas (1895–1974), received no significant reviews. These novels were already read in French or German as is clear from the reviews and comments on various European translations of *The Home and the World*, from 1921 onwards, both in the literary and the general press. Original comments were made by the literary critic Octav Botez (1884–1943), the poet Alexandru Iacobescu (1875–1945), the young essayist Petre Pandrea (1904–68), and the literary historian G. Baiculescu.

Surprisingly, *Gora* attracted less attention and its English and German translations received only brief comments. The English version of *The Wreck* was reviewed by G. Baiculescu and by the renowned historian and writer, Nicolae Iorga (1871–1940), who considered it to be a real fresco of 'the India of Rabindranath Tagore.' Other pieces from his prose were occasionally published by journals of literary review. A few chapters from *My Reminiscences* were translated by the novelist and playwright, Camil Petrescu, and G. Ulieru. The traditionalist writer, Cezar Petrescu (1892–1961), reviewed its French version. Others like him were attracted by Tagore's prose as a possible ally in their resistance to modernity.

Tagore's Plays

The first article on Tagore's dramatic works was published in 1918 by Camil Petrescu. It chronicled a recent staging of *The Post Office* in Vienna, considered a fiasco. In his view, the theatre of Tagore was incomprehensible to Europeans. *The Post Office* is more a dramatic poem than a play; it may delight the lovers of exotic art, but transposed into the Western theatrical language, it remains devoid of any charm. The lack of success of 'transplanting Indian philosophy' on the Western stage reflects, according to Petrescu, the gulf existing between the Indian mystic and the European man of will and action. Other stagings of his plays (*The King of the Dark Chamber, Sacrifice*, etc.) in European theatres were chronicled during the years, especially by the daily journal *Rampa*, the main publication on theatre, music, and the arts.

G. Baiculescu had more understanding for the two types of drama written by Tagore, the literary (*Chitra, Malini*) and the symbolical (*The King of the Dark Chamber, The Post Office, Muktadhara*), and wrote sensible reflections on them.

The publication of a volume of plays, translated by A. Busuioceanu and N. Crainic, announced in September 1921, did not materialise eventually. Tagore's name appeared in the proposed repertoire of a new theatre in Jassy, The Free Theatre, founded in 1922, which for unknown reasons did not start functioning. In December 1923, a translation of *The Post Office* was read out at the dramatic art society Atelier in Bucharest, but only the third scene of the first act appeared on the front page of *Rampa*.

In August 1926, an article in *Rampa*, titled 'Ungrateful People', deplored the ingratitude of Romanians towards foreigners who liked them. Tagore was reportedly an admirer of the 'mildness and distinction of the Latin spirit' of the country which he called Luminia—a name evoking a land of lights (*lumini* in Romanian). It criticised especially the lack of any performance of his dramatic works, which contained 'treasures of beauty' and 'wonders of enchantment'.

The reprehensible indifference was set right only in November 1938, when *The Post Office* was performed at the National Theatre in Cluj. It was part of a trilogy, put together by the theatre's director, the writer Victor Papilian (1888–1956), in order to illustrate the ways in which different nations—Romanian, Spanish and Indian—conceived death. The drama was translated from the French by the literary historian Olimpiu Boitoş (1903–54) and, according to its main reviews, was a success. Those reviews remarked admiringly on its philosophical poetry and symbolism.

Some of Tagore's dramas were listed in the proposed programme of the Baraşeum Theatre, in October 1940, under the direction of the writer Felix Aderca (1891–1962), but we do not know if they were ever enacted. They must have been *Sacrifice* and *Chitra*, published after the War.[9]

Tagore as Educationist

From the very beginning of his reception, Tagore's school was mentioned, described, admired. In April 1914, a full article was devoted to it in a Transylvanian review. Its author, Professor Ion Mateiu (1884–1946)—a historian and national activist, who became the head of the province's educational system after 1918—urged his fellow Romanians to follow Tagore's pedagogical example.

During the 1920s, Santiniketan and the educational projects of Tagore became almost as well known as his poetry. In 1921, Professor Ion Simionescu (1873–1944) from the University of Iaşi wrote a long article on school reforms as a commentary on Tagore's 1916 lecture 'My School.' Like Mateiu, he pleaded for the adoption of his educational principles in rural schools.

Tagore's 1921 appeal to support an international University in Santiniketan was translated and discussed by several reviews and newspapers. The chapter 'An Eastern University' from *Creative Unity* (1922) was also reviewed and commented upon positively. However, by that year there were several voices of dissent. Nichifor Crainic (1889–1972) did not believe that an international university in India could bring about the desired synthesis of East and West and the disappearance of nationalism. Further opposition came from L. Blaga, who had earlier commended Tagore's pedagogical principles. While an educational journal, *The New School*, pleaded for a 'school of the soul,' built on the foundations laid down by Tagore and Tolstoy, Blaga advocated the creation of a school of the Romanian soul.

Tagore inspired the writings of the educationists Constantin V. Buțureanu (1870–1931) and Constantin Mureșanu (1890–1941). The latter even opened his 1926 course on *Heroic Pedagogy* with a lecture on him. Notwithstanding the interest in Tagore's pedagogical ideas, his related writings—with the exception of 'My Educational Mission'—were not translated. Instead, several articles on him written by Western authors were translated or reviewed. On that basis, the mathematician Gheorghe Beiu Palade (1874–1946), the poetess C. Millian and a few publicists spread Tagore's ideas on education through the major literary or general journals of the time.

Tagore's Philosophical and Political Works

The works of Tagore most commented upon in the interwar years were his philosophical essays and lectures. He became, along with Keyserling, one of the key authors on the topics of the destiny of the West and of the East–West encounter.

The first significant reactions to his *Nationalism* appeared in 1920. A number of writers embraced its ideas for their humanitarianism and for the proposed synthesis between the positive elements of East and West. Within the literature on this book, two opposing positions can be distinguished: one of the left (mainly socialists of various nuances, several of them Jewish), and one of the right (conservatives and traditionalists, most of them with a Christian orientation). In the first group there were people like Eugen Relgis (1895–1987), Henric Sanielevici (1875–1951), and Tudor Teodorescu-Braniște (1899–1969), and in the second were L. Blaga, N. Crainic, A. Busuioceanu, Cezar Petrescu, P. Pandrea, and N. Iorga. Between them were a variety of intermediary or individual positions. The influential philosopher Nae Ionescu (1890–1940) voiced his complete imperviousness to Tagore. The refined essayist Paul Zarifopol (1874–1934) dedicated an article of exquisite irony to the dreams of 'poetic sociology' entertained by this 'dilettante of humanitarianism.'

Sadhana was commented upon mostly on its Romanian version. In 1922, a team of prominent young scholars Nichifor Crainic and Alexandru Busuioceanu (1896–1961), gave high quality translations of both *Sadhana* and *Nationalism*. Their introductory studies, written from a scholarly, critical viewpoint, were published in advance by the cultural press. The twin volumes were the best translated and printed works of Tagore in the *interbellum*, widely read and commented upon.

At first, Busuioceanu seemed attracted by the philosophy of *Sadhana* in its opposition to the individualist, rationalist, and mechanistic West. But then he drew back, apparently through identification with the trans-historic spirit of the European civilisation. He did not believe in the possibility of a synthesis of the Occident and the Orient; in his opinion, the two cultures and civilisations were irreducible. Crainic was also busy in dispelling popular misconceptions about the Bengali poet, starting with the new literary fashion, 'Tagoreism.' He insisted that the admirers and imitators of Tagore were victims of an illusion perpetrated by the English version of his poems. In the Bengali language they follow a strict prosody through their melodies of rhythms and harmonies of rhymes. 'The exotic bard is, in fact, a personified traditionalist.' Crainic also exposed the misunderstanding of Tagore as a prophet. Although the Western emotionality embraced him, the mind of Europe remained refractive to his prophesising. The fame and fashion he enjoyed, especially in the Germanic world, were not due to a metaphysical or spiritual consonance, but to petty political considerations: a shared antipathy toward the British.

The most interesting review of *Sadhana* was penned by P. Pandrea, who rejected Busuioceanu's statements. *Nationalism* was reviewed almost exclusively at the left of the political spectrum, but by people with idealistic and spiritual inclinations. The writer T. Teodorescu-Branişte, one of the most influential journalists of the left, made use of Tagore's critique of nationalism, understood as chauvinism and imperialism, in order to propose a 'true nationalism', under the guise of a humanitarian fight against exploitation, capitalism, and fascism. Several intellectuals from Transylvania, such as Horia Petra-Petrescu (1884–1962), agreed with Tagore's criticism of imperialism and colonialism, but objected to the identification of nationalism with chauvinism. Some went further and asserted that Romanian nationalism was different from the Western or Russian nationalisms, insofar as it was dictated by an instinct of self-conservation, being thus defensive and pacifist.

Tagore's ideas about East and West were also contested in the reviews of *Creative Unity*. Reactions to these ideas came from prominent philosophers, such as Constantin Rădulescu-Motru (1868–1957), Mircea Florian (1888–1960), and Mihai Ralea (1896–1964). The most important work, though critical, on Tagore's 'political philosophy' was done by Nicolae Bagdasar (1896–1961). His 1929 lecture, 'Rabindranath Tagore and Civilisation,' presented at the Romanian Society of Philosophy, received many reviews and responses even before its publication in the journal of the Society and later on in a volume.

The political positions around Tagore became more radicalised after his 1925 visit to Italy and his subsequent declarations on Fascism. When he went to Moscow, in 1930, N. Iorga wrote a bitter article decrying the visit by an acclaimed spokesman against 'foreign domination' which would endorse 'the rough Mongolic doctrine of an oligarchy of cruel murderers.' Tagore's opposition to Western 'nationalism' had led him to moral suicide, concluded Iorga. During the latter half of the 1920s, Tagore's political stand contributed considerably to the estrangement of many Romanians who believed in the West and were worried about the red imperialism of the Soviet Union, but failed to see the consequences of the rise of fascism.

Direct Contacts

Some Romanians had the opportunity to meet Tagore or at least to see him and attend his lectures. The crown prince Carol II (1893–1953) sought his company when his party reached Calcutta during the 1920 round-the-world voyage, but the poet was himself travelling in Europe. It is there that the first recorded 'experiences' of him occurred. Among those who attended his lectures in Paris, only two could make his acquaintance: the poetesses Anna de Noailles and Elena Văcărescu. Countess de Noailles met him again every time he came to France, in 1921, 1926, and 1930, and helped to launch his paintings. In contrast to these aristocratic poetesses, the novelist Panait Istrati (1884–1935), a socialist activist, declined the invitation of his friend Romain Rolland to be introduced to Tagore in 1926.[10]

Other Romanians met him in Germany and Austria, during the 1921 tour. The group of intellectuals from *Ideea europeană*, a prestigious journal edited by C. Rădulescu-Motru, wanted to invite him to extend his tour to Bucharest, but after much deliberation, they gave up the idea. The portraits of Tagore drawn by N. Crainic and A. Busuioceanu, after his lectures in Vienna, are some of the most memorable. All those who could listen to him reported with enthusiasm about the exotic, delicate beauty of his poetry in the original Bengali, and about the musicality of his native language. A dissonant note in this chorus came from Dragoş Protopopescu (1892–1948), an Anglicist, who saw Tagore in a London club where 'with the voice of an inspired ventriloquist he gathered people around English brutality in India.'

In 1920 and 1925, there were rumours that Tagore would visit Romania. The poet himself expressed this wish to a Romanian reporter who interviewed him in Italy. Ultimately, the visit happened during the tour of 1926.[11] Tagore crossed into Romania in the morning of 19 November, at Giurgiu, a border town on the Danube, and arrived in Bucharest in the afternoon by train. There was a reception in his honour and meetings with various delegations (Writers Union, Art Union, Journalists Union, etc.). On the 20th, a Saturday, he gave a lecture on 'The Poetry of India' at the National Theatre, where he was very warmly received by the young public. Thereafter he had lunch with the King at the Royal Palace. The photo of him and Rani Mahalanobis in the royal car, surrounded by the crowds, was well publicised by the international press. There were more meetings with writers and scholars; also, a few interviews and reports of his words in various newspapers. We know about at least one poem written in Bucharest, whose revised version ('Gaudi Riti') was later published in *Prahasani* (1939).[12] On the 21 November, Tagore left for Constanţa, where he boarded a ship to Istanbul.[13]

The names of notable persons who met, saw or listened to him form a long list. The writer Ion Marin Sadoveanu (1893–1964), general inspector of theatres in the Ministry of Culture, was in charge of the entire visit. The minister of culture and arts Vasile Goldiş (1862–1934) introduced Tagore's public lecture. Among the important *hommes de lettres* who left interesting impressions on the visit and a testimony of their feelings for Tagore's personality and work are: the historian N. Iorga, the philologist Ion Bianu (1856–1935), the geographer Simion Mehedinţi (1868–1962), the mathematician Gheorghe Ţiţeica (1873–1939)—all members of the Romanian Academy, the aesthetician T. Vianu, the writers Hortensia Papadat-Bengescu (1876–1955), Romulus Dianu (1905–75), Sandu Tzigara-Samurcaş (1903–87), and I. M. Sadoveanu, the literary historians G. Baiculescu and Alexandru Dima (1905–79), et al.

Most of the press reports were positive and enthusiastic, but there were also sceptical and critical voices. As in other countries, the interest in Tagore was not purely literary: he was seen more as a prophet from 'the mysterious India' than as a poet. For Camil Petrescu, his visit was a comic example of the 'intellectual epidemic' of 'imported mysticism,' which several intellectuals wanted to adapt to Romanian clothing. Mircea Eliade, who was well acquainted with Tagore's work and mentioned him occasionally, ignored his lecture and did not report on the visit. This was very probably in solidarity with his mentor, Nae Ionescu, and as a reaction to the trivialisation of his image. In an article published thereafter, he ranged the Tagore-cult among the pseudo-spiritualities and 'Eastern gnoses' [supposedly revealed knowledge of various spiritual truths], like Theosophy and neo-Buddhism.

This brief yet significant visit was not without consequences. It did not give much impetus to the publication of new books, but was instrumental in wining attention and lasting sympathy for Tagore's oeuvre from intellectuals who were not necessarily his admirers. It was essential for cementing and consolidating the earlier efforts to make his work known. Some even dared to write to Santiniketan and received polite answers.[14]

Only few had the chance to meet the poet in India. The microbiologist, Mihai Ciucă (1883–1969) did it during a medical expedition in 1929.[15] M. Eliade, who lived there between December 1928 and November 1931, had the opportunity to come closer to Tagore. Introduced to the poet by his doctoral supervisor, Surendranath Dasgupta, he spent longer periods with him in Santiniketan. Eliade read his Bengali poetry together with Dasgupta's daughter, Maitreyi Devi, one of Tagore's close devotees. In his admiration for 'the lesser known "great man" of present times,' he kept a notebook with all their conversations and everything he could learn about the poet. After his return to Bucharest, he published three articles of impressions from Santiniketan and talks with Tagore, gave a public lecture and an interview about the same. Coming from somebody well acquainted with Indian culture and who was also admitted in Tagore's intimacy, they represent the most interesting writings on the poet during the *interbellum*.

Scholarly Interest

Academic approaches to Tagore were manifested in reviews and discussions around his works. The articles of H. Sanielevici, O. Botez, A. Busuioceanu, N. Crainic, G. Baiculescu, P. Pandrea, and N. Bagdasar—most of them reprinted in books—fall into this category, as do the articles of I. Mateiu, I. Simionescu, and C. V. Buţureanu on the educational work of Tagore. His ideas could not be ignored by prominent philosophers and social scientists: Nicolae Petrescu, C. Rădulescu-Motru, M. Florian, M. Ralea, Camil Petrescu, T. Vianu, and others.

During the 1920s, various intellectuals gave public and scholarly lectures on Tagore: the historian, Emil Panaitescu (1885–1958), the writer Nicolae Bălănescu (1866–1946), I. M. Sadoveanu, C. Mureşanu, and N. Bagdasar. 'The Humanism of Tagore', read by M. Eliade on 9 January 1932, had probably the biggest impact, especially on the young generation. He interpreted Tagore's poetry as a symbolic creation, insisting that he was not only a poet and writer, but a philosopher too. According to him, Tagore's entire work was an expression of a symbolic philosophy, which could only be truly understood in India, where 'the symbol is a driving centre, which is imbibed, assimilated.'

Eliade forms a special chapter in the reception of Tagore. He was the only scholar of Indology who manifested an interest for him during the interwar years. Eliade's writings brought about a new wave of interest for his work. His enthusiasm for Tagore decreased gradually in the following years, especially after he came closer to Gandhi's nationalism and to what he thought to be a Romanian version of it. Nevertheless, the books in which his writings on Tagore were collected—*India* (1934, 1935) and *Şantier* (Indian journal, 1935)—continued to be read and kept the Indian poet in the public attention. Even his novel *Maitreyi* (*Bengal Nights*), which had six editions between 1933 and 1946, contributed significantly to the image of Tagore, a fact which can be seen in its reviews and in the contemporary testimonies.

During World War II

By 1940—a traumatic year, in which Romania lost four provinces—interest in Tagore reached its nadir. At the beginning of 1941 a new translator Ion Oană (1920–2011), a student of Blaga, rendered in free verse several poems from the French version of *Balaka*. His were to remain the last important translations of the historical era which closed after the War.

The death of the poet in 1941 reactivated interest in him only for about a year. A dozen articles paid tribute to Tagore. Along with older translators, there were several young writers. Various journals republished some of his poems and short stories, or extracts from *Sadhana* and *Nationalism*. *Viaţa*, a newspaper edited by Liviu Rebreanu, headlined his passing in large characters as 'The greatest poet of the world has died.' Recalling his vogue during the 1920s, N. Crainic deplored the little attention paid to his demise. He concluded that Tagore had constituted a literary fashion in a moment of profound crisis of the European soul, especially of the German soul which subsequently had regained its 'volcanic spirit.' While the literary journalist Leontin Iliescu (1880–195?) asserted that Tagore remained a 'column of fire on the peaks of human civilization,' Crainic believed that it had left only 'the echo of a primary melody, sung by an exotic poet in his sacred play with the ethereal divinity of Indian beliefs.'

The newer generations were less sceptical. The journalist and diplomat, Liviu Hulea (1906–8?) stated that nobody escapes the influence of a writer such as Tagore, even if he has not read a single line of his works. Like him, the poet George Drumur (1911–92) believed that with Tagore's death, a star had fallen from the sky. For Ovid Caledoniu (1914–74), another poet influenced by Blaga, Tagore was a powerful flame of national awakening, but also a man who loved the entire mankind. The poet Tiberiu Tretinescu (1921–77) insisted that the moral value of his work was as important as its poetical and philosophical worth. Yet his wise words disseminated throughout the West, although well received by those who listened to them, faded away like a tender melody.

The most interesting articles were the two penned by I. Oană. Among other things, the first of them pointed out that, despite being a Hindu, Tagore's work had nothing exotic about it; exoticism was a way of the European. The second piece, a long survey, proved him to be one of the most intimate connoisseurs of Tagore among his contemporaries. He thought that, in cases such as his, death was the assertion of a presence; although he loved life, Tagore's inner eyes were turned toward the stage 'beyond life' which made it possible. In a third article published the next year, 'Tagore and the destiny of poetry,' Oană argued that his ideas were close to Spengler's distinction between culture and civilisation, with the difference that the Indian deemed culture and religion to be almost identical, leaving no room for aesthetic autonomy. Based on the essays from *Creative Unity*, he showed how poetry was, in Tagore's understanding, a felicitous means to proclaim an explanation of existence which is otherwise realised only through deep meditation.

During the subsequent years, there were few articles on or translations from Tagore's work in journals and magazines. But he continued to be cited and referred to in articles and books, both in the political right and the left, in relation to debates around nationalism and the East–West problem.

From 1945 to 1989

In 1945, journals and newspapers in Romania started to take more interest in Tagore. Due to lack of research, we have little information about his reception in the territories seized by Soviet Union in August 1944, especially the S. S. R. Moldova. Some journals commemorated the fourth or fifth anniversaries of the death of the poet. Pro-Communist leanings were already visible in certain articles, such as those of L. Iliescu and the novelist Dan Petraşincu (1910–97).

As in most of the countries occupied or controlled by the USSR, from 1947 almost a decade-long silence fell on Tagore. Occasionally, in ideologically motivated writings, he was characterised as an idealist and reactionary author, but there were no articles, even critical, dedicated to him. On rare official occasions, the press could not avoid talking about Tagore in positive terms. One of them was the concert given by the Indian delegation at the 4th World Festival of Youth and Students, held in Bucharest, in 1953.[16]

In 1956, translations and writings on Tagore started to appear again, but in a restricted way. Initially, certain translations or original books were rejected for publication because their content was not considered compatible with the official Communist ideology or because their authors and translators did not align themselves with the new regime. This happened with *The Post Office*, *Gora* and an anthology of poems.[17]

From 1956 to 1989, books by Tagore were published occasionally: eleven in socialist Romania and two in Soviet Moldova. The years of their printing show the oscillations of official policies attesting to the vulnerability of non-canonical authors such as Tagore in a socialist culture. In 1957 and 1958, two volumes were published in Romania. Three more followed in 1961 and four others between 1965 and 1968. Interest in the subsequent two decades was more moderate with one book in 1978 and one in 1987. In the S. S. R. Moldova, a volume in 1959 was followed by one in 1979. Although this is, proportionally, less than in the interwar period, the printing was of good quality and the print runs, varying between 10,000 and 40,000, were higher. They also received numerous reviews.

Since Tagore's poetry was still considered to be mystical, initially his plays, novels, and short stories, which showed 'the life of the people,' were preferred: *Sacrifice, Citra, The Wreck, Gora*, a selection from *Hungry Stones*, and a larger collection of short stories. From the six books of poetry, two represent full volumes, *The Gardener* and *The Crescent Moon*, while the others contain large selections from *Gitanjali, The Gardener, The Crescent Moon, Fruit-Gathering, The Fugitive, Stray Birds, Gitabitan*, and *Balaka*. One volume was entirely dedicated to Tagore's brief poems from *Kanika, Lekhan, Sphulinga*, and *Stray Birds*. An anthology in 1961 included writings on education, a censured version of *Letters from Russia*, and 'Crisis in Civilisation.'

Two of the early translations—*The Wreck* and a collection of short stories—were made from the Russian. *Gora, Hungry Stones*, and some of the books of poetry were based on English editions.[18] Other poetry was translated from the French. In Soviet Moldova, all translations were done from Russian. The only volume rendered directly from Bengali was a selection of letters from *Chinnapatravali*, in 1978.

The translators of Tagore were themselves poets and writers, educated in Greater Romania or before the Communist regime was imposed. The most prominent of them was the poet and essayist Alexandru Philippide (1900–79), a member of the Romanian Academy. The most prolific was the poet George Dan (1916–72), with three volumes of poetry. The writer Feodosie Vidrașcu (1929–2010) was an important Communist leader in Soviet Moldova (head of the Radio and Television broadcast services). Other writers were: Henriette Yvonne Stahl (1900–84), Petre Solomon (1923–91), George Popa (b. 1923), Iuliu Victor Martinovici (1924–2005), and Pavel Darie (b. 1930).

Two of Tagore's plays were translated by Nela Stroescu (191?–199?), playwright and stage director, and probably Felix Aderca. The educationist Iosif Antohi (1914–97) translated Tagore's pedagogical writings. Amita Bhose (1933–92), a Bengali scholar naturalised in Romania, lecturer of Bengali and Sanskrit at the University of Bucharest, was responsible for the first ever translation from *Chinnapatravali*. Tagore's philosophical essays could not be published at this time. But in an anthology of *Bengali Proverbs and Aphorisms* (1975), Bhose included many quotations from them.

By way of compensation so to speak for the small number of volumes, every year many poems were translated in literary journals. From 1977 on, Bhose published around two dozen poems, rendered directly from the Bengali, and some more were translated by her students. The other translators were all poets educated before the war: Eugeniu Speranţia (1888–1972), Petre Pascu (1909–94), Taşcu Gheorghiu (1910–81), Dan Faur (1911–61), et al. One translation was done by the literary critic and historian Zoe Dumitrescu-Buşulenga (1920–2006), who wrote often, and perceptively, on Tagore. In contrast with the interwar years, there were more translations in free verse than in prose but fewer attempts to put the poems in rhymes.

Tagore's prose was less represented in literary journals: only some short stories, six new chapters from *My Reminiscences*, and selections from various essays. Bhose translated the social comedy *Sesh Raksha*, but only the third act was published in a literary almanac. It was performed by her students in June 1981, at the University House in Bucharest.[19]

Almost all books contained forewords and introductions, sometimes by the translators themselves, more often by other personalities: Dumitrescu-Buşulenga, the writer Radu Boureanu (1906–97), and the art and literary critics Petru Comarnescu (1905–70), Alexandru Oprea (1931–83), and Mihai Cimpoi (b. 1942).

The ideological control of culture under communism allowed no book on Tagore to be published. The one completed in the late 1950s by the Indologist Vlad Bănăţeanu (1900–63), was rejected several times. Instead, in the centenary year, 1961, the Romanian Commission for UNESCO published the booklet *Tagore in Romania*, containing the first bibliographical research on Tagore's reception, compiled by the Arabist Virgil Cândea (1927–2007). There were new volumes which included essays or studies on Tagore. Some of the interwar articles (by G. Ulieru, L. Blaga, I. M. Sadoveanu, O. Botez, Camil Petrescu, N. Bagdasar, and P. Zarifopol) were reprinted in collected works.

Generally, publishing books was more difficult than to contribute to periodicals, which came to contain numerous articles on various aspects of Tagore's work. The list of the authors is long. The most active and competent of them all was V. Bănăţeanu, founder and president of the Association of Oriental Studies. Besides writings by scholars already mentioned, mostly literary critics and historians—T. Vianu, E. Speranţia, I. M. Sadoveanu, A. Dima, I. Antohi, Z. Dumitrescu-Buşulenga, A. Oprea, A. Bhose, M. Cimpoi—there were percipient articles by Gheorghe Iancovici (1924–92), Nicolae Balotă (b. 1925), and Cornelia Comorovski (1926–2013).

Among poets and writers, Tudor Arghezi (1880–1967), A. Philippide, R. Boureanu, P. Pascu, P. Solomon, and G. Popa deserve to be mentioned. There was a unique theological exegesis by Fr. Constantin Galeriu (1918–2003), who discussed Tagore's conception of God, man and religion.

Some of these intellectuals also published abroad, especially on the occasion of Tagore's centennial celebration. Philippide contributed to the Sahitya Akademi's *Centenary Volume*, Bănăţeanu to the one issued in Moscow by the Institute of Asian Peoples, and Arghezi to the Tagore number of Sahitya Akademi's *Indian Literature*. Vianu and Bănăţeanu were featured in other Indian journals, while A. Bhose published articles on the reception of Tagore in Romanian culture in two special Tagore issues of the Bengali magazine *Desh* (1961, 1989).

Most of the writings on Tagore discussed his poetry and prose. Prior to the détente of 1965, they were generally influenced by the official thinking. Tagore was painted as a progressive author, with revolutionary accents, interested in the life of the people, a defender of the downtrodden, a fighter against colonial domination, a critic of feudalism, Fascism and the 'retrogressive' bourgeois spirit. It had to be conceded that he manifested some inevitable myopia and made 'concessions' to age-old Indian traditions and the bourgeois ideology of his era. But a general insistence on his humanitarianism made such shortcomings appear to be of little consequence. Another way to make him acceptable was to construe an evolution of his ideas, from the early mystical ones to more progressive social and political preoccupations, especially after the 1930 visit to Soviet Union. Occasionally, there were discussions of his dramas (V. Bănăţeanu), paintings (Dan Hăulică, P. Comarnescu), and educational work (I. Antohi, V. Cândea). His social and political ideas were examined, especially by V. Bănăţeanu, not without compliance with the dominant Marxist ideology. He (and later on A. Bhose) wrote on Bengali literature in general, situating Tagore in its context.

After 1965, even a look at the titles of the writings on Tagore shows a difference of perception. They refer to his 'universalistic spirit', to the 'cosmic sense' of his poetry, to Indian wisdom, or they call him an Indian Orpheus. In her doctoral thesis on Mihai Eminescu (1850–89) and India, published in 1978, A. Bhose compared the Romanian 'national poet' with Tagore, a theme which was further developed in a series of articles and lectures.

There were occasional translations of articles on Tagore written by very diverse Western, Russian and Indian authors (R. Rolland, Alfred Antkowiak, Vasily V. Brodov, Krishna Kripalani, Amalendu Bikash Guha, Balvant Gargi, Debipada Bhattacharya), and several interviews with Maitreyi Devi, during her 1973 visit.

Since almost all of the authors/translators were educated before the change of Romania's borders and political regime, it may be assumed that there is a direct link between the agents of Tagore's post-War reception and the great popularity which the poet enjoyed during the interwar years. Clearly the 'new man' was less responsive to the world of ideas and sentiments represented by him.

In the exile circles Tagore did not elicit much attention, as his stance was irrelevant to their anti-Communist cultural agenda. There were some exceptions among leftist intellectuals, like E. Relgis (Montevideo), M. Grindea (London) and Alphonse C. Vinescou (Jerusalem). In Rome, D. Petraşincu, who became a proponent of Indian and Religious studies under the name of Angelo Morretta, wrote several articles in major newspapers and literary magazines. He also participated at the Tagore Centenary celebrations organised in Bombay in January 1961.

From 1945 onwards, Eliade's novel *Maitreyi* (*Bengal Nights*) was published in many languages, but English was carefully avoided. However, Maitreyi Devi responded with the novel *Na hanyate* (1974) and translated it into English (*It Does not Die*, 1976). Tagore is a memorable presence in both of them. Eliade's book of reportage, *India*, with two chapters on Tagore, was translated into French (1978, 1990). In the last ten years of his life, he published reminiscences of Tagore in the book of conversations *Ordeal by Labyrinth*, in his *Autobiography* and post-War *Journal*, all translated into several languages.

A number of cultural programmes, TV and radio broadcasts, as well as public and scholarly lectures were dedicated to Tagore. In the centenary year 1961, the most important events were an exhibition about his life and work and a conference organised by the Association of Oriental Studies. Other functions featured state institutions and intellectuals with official patronage. An oak tree in Tagore's memory was planted in the Herăstrău Park of Bucharest. In other years, scholarly papers were read at the Association of Oriental Studies (V. Bănăţeanu, A. Bhose), Society of Classical Studies (Constantin Ciopraga) and the Romanian Academy (Maitreyi Devi). A. Bhose gave lectures on multiple occasions. In the academic year 1985–6, she delivered a series of lectures on Eminescu and Tagore at the Open University in Bucharest. In 1982, she participated in a documentary film made by Romanian Television. From 1977 to 1985, she organised an annual 'Tagore day' at the University of Bucharest, where her students read from his poetry, sung his songs and presented papers on his work.

From 1990 to 2013

While under Communism ideologically motivated censorship restricted writings on the spiritual aspects of India, during the post-Communist era publications on Indian culture flourished without hindrance. One of the first books was a reprint of Crainic's translation of *Sadhana*. Other books of the 1920s, '60s and '70s followed: *The Gardener, Fruit-Gathering, Gora,* and *Chinnapatravali*. *The Home and the World* and *The Crescent Moon* were published as audiobooks, while miscellaneous poems were included in audiobooks containing selections from world poetry.

Besides these reprints, there were sixteen new volumes. As earlier, poetry dominated with ten volumes. The most prolific translator was the poet G. Popa. After an augmented edition of his earlier anthology (1998), he published complete translations of *Gitanjali* (2000), *Balaka* (2001), *Fruit-Gathering* and *The Fugitive* (2003). I. V. Martinovici also collected his earlier translations in a new anthology (2005). Another anthology was published in 2002 by the poetess Florica Madritsch Marin (b. 1951). The poems translated from Bengali by A. Bhose were compiled posthumously into a volume (2011). A new version of *Gitanjali* (1995, 2009 [second edition/reprint]) is the work of the poet-priest George Remete (b. 1954). A bilingual edition of *The Gardener* (2006) was brought out by the aesthetician Alexandru Husar (1920–2009), and a translation of *Fireflies* (2013) by the cultural journalist Adelina Patrichi (b. 1961). While the other translators followed mostly French versions, the last two used the English editions.

Tagore's *prose* was translated from English. The first new book, in 1991, contained two novelettes, *Farewell, My Friend* and *The Garden*, together with seven short stories. This was followed by new versions of *The Home and the World* (2004) and *Chaturanga* (2008).

A. Bhose's translation of *Sesh Raksha* appeared in 2011. Two new versions of *Sadhana* were published (2009, 2013), one translated in close conformity with the Bengali edition by the Indologist Dana Sugu (b. 1966).

If in the late 1990s and early years of the new millennium the Tagore book market was dominated by G. Popa's translations of poetry, since 2008 the main initiatives belong to three publishing houses. In the 'Indian Library' series of Casa Cărţii de Ştiinţă publishing house, Mihaela Gligor (b. 1977) published Tagore's *Sadhana* and a translation of Maitreyi Devi's *With Rabindranath at Mongpu*. The Cununi de Stele publishing house, created especially for A. Bhose's works, published three volumes of translations from the Bengali. A. Patrichi, director of Taj Books, initiated a very ambitious 'Tagore Project'. *Chaturanga* and *Fireflies* are being followed by a translation of the Bengali *Gitanjali*, done by Ramona Ceciu (b. 1979). Other volumes in the publishing plan are *Noukadubi, Chokher Bali, Charulata, Yogayog, Sphulinga, Shyamali,* and two anthologies of verses and prose.

Since the print runs ceased to be mentioned in the early 1990s, it is hard to make estimations about the spread of Tagore's work. The reprint of *Sadhana* ran to 30,000 copies but in the following years the print runs gradually decreased. The book containing *Farewell, My Friend* and *The Garden* had 15,000 copies. In recent years, the volumes published by Taj Books had print runs of 1000–2000 copies. Yet there were exceptions: *Gora,* reprinted in the Nobel collection of 'Library for All' series, had 25,000 copies. However, from the fact that, not long after their publication, Tagore's books could hardly be found in the bookshops, one can infer that there is constant demand for his work among a section of the reading public.

In this period we find fewer translations in periodicals. Occasionally there were translations of other Indian authors, like Maitreyi Devi's *It Does not Die* (1992, 1999, 2010) and Amartya Sen's *The Argumentative Indian* (2010). Interviews with Satyajit Ray and Mrinal Sen about Tagore's work were published by the film critic Adina Darian (b. 1933) in her book *The Indian World and its Movies* (1990, English 2009). An interview with Ketaki Kushari Dyson and a paper written by Uma Das Gupta appeared in 2011.

Almost all translations were well reviewed in a variety of literary journals and magazines. There were also many independent articles on Tagore's work.

Eliade's books, articles and interviews referring to Tagore and Santiniketan were reprinted or translated and went through several editions. His work gained further international diffusion. The English translation of *Maitreyi (Bengal Nights)* was published in 1993 and reprinted together with *It Does not Die,* as companion volumes. *India, Şantier (Indian journal)* and a collection of Indian articles titled *Mystic Eroticism in Bengal,* including one about Santiniketan, were translated into French, Italian, and Spanish.

In the years 1990–2, Amita Bhose was active translating, writing articles, lecturing on Tagore, speaking on TV and the radio, etc. After her death in 1992, several of her unpublished writings came to light, the last one being the series of lectures *Eminescu and Tagore* (2013). Her earlier works were also reprinted.

A documentary film by A. Patrichi, *The Santiniketan Experiment,* was broadcast by Romanian Television in May 1996. Her visits to Santiniketan and Calcutta resulted in a number of articles and book chapters. A few books placed Tagore in comparative perspectives: *Three Faces of the Sublime: Shakespeare, Hölderlin, Tagore* (2004) by G. Popa; *The Poetry of the East from Khayyam to Tagore* (2005) by the literary critic Marius Chelaru (b. 1961); and *Fatalism and Mysticism in Emil Cioran, Omar Khayyam and Tagore* (2005), by the theologian Bogdan Marius Ionescu (b. 1983). He inspired an album of choral music on his verses, *My light* (1997), by the composer Grigore Cudalbu (b. 1967), and the volume *Tagore's Garden* (2007, English 2008) by the poet Petre Tǎnǎsoaicǎ (b. 1955).

The fiftieth anniversary of Tagore's death was commemorated by a number of events, especially at the Open University of Bucharest and Romanian Television. In September 1998, a statue of Tagore, sculpted by the Bengali artist Gautam Pal (b. 1949), was installed in the hall of the National Theatre. In 2007, Ranjit Kumar Saha lectured at the Romanian–Indian Cultural Association on his Hindi translation of *Gitanjali*. During recent years, the publishing houses Taj Books and Cununi de Stele organised events related to Tagore, including round table sessions on the reception of Indian literature in Romania, interpretation of his songs, and dance to music composed by the poet.

The Romanian–Indian Cultural Association coordinated various functions during the anniversary year 2011, including a dance performance at the National Theatre. Rabindranath Tagore Cultural Centre, founded the same year, is co-organising the annual *Namaste India Festival*, during which *Rabindra Sangeet* is regularly performed. The events in 2011 included a lecture by Uma Das Gupta. At the George Enescu International Music Festival, Ustad Amjad Ali Khan gave his interpretation of Rabindra Sangeet. Several Tagore songs were also sung in the drama *Maitreyi* (directed by Chris Simion), based on the twin novels, which had its premiere in December 2011 and has been performed regularly since throughout the country.

CONCLUSION

During Tagore's lifetime, despite the fact that the number of volumes and the quality of most of the translations were not particularly high, his works and ideas enjoyed widespread attention. They were discussed, accepted or opposed, by some of the most important figures of the intellectual life of Romania. A larger number of translations were published in the periodicals. The relatively low figure of books is explained by the fact that the educated and middle classes read French and German.

Translations favoured the poetic works, while discussions engaged with Tagore's philosophical and political views. His work exerted influence on several leading writers and thinkers, but it was mostly limited to the early years of their careers. The most important influence was probably that on the early poetry of Lucian Blaga. The young Nichifor Crainic and Alexandru Busuioceanu were captivated by the philosophical and political essays of Tagore, but shortly afterwards became critical of them. While in India, Mircea Eliade had a serious involvement with Tagore's work and personality, but a few years after his return to Bucharest he left it completely behind him. Theological circles did not show hostility, as they found his mystic poetry and religious ideas compatible with and useful to the spreading of their own message.

During this period there were three waves of Tagore's reception in Romanian culture: (i) in 1913, after the publication of *Gitanjali* and the award of the Nobel Prize; (ii) increased interest after the War especially after 1921; and (iii) sustained attention after Tagore's visit, in 1926. After 1933, the interest in him declined steadily. A comeback in 1941 was rapidly put down by the War.

Tagore was a banned author beyond the Iron Curtain till 1956, and his subsequent reception was controlled by the Communist Party. If in the interwar period his image was situated mostly on the religious and spiritual register—mystic poet, prophet, and sage—in Socialist Romania and Soviet Moldova he was appropriated as a progressive and anti-imperialist author. After an initial preference for his prose until the political liberalisation of 1965, his poetry—considered earlier to be mystic—started to be published extensively. His philosophical and political essays were not published and only little discussed. The translations done during this period were of higher literary quality and the print runs superior to those of the interwar years. However, most of those responsible for them, as well as for the writings on Tagore, were not representatives of the 'new man', but intellectuals educated before the Communist era. In Soviet Moldova, because of the dominant status given to Russian language and culture, the reception of Tagore in Romanian was considerably weaker, especially during the first two decades.

After the fall of Communism in Romania and Moldova in December 1989 and August 1991 respectively, and the freedom of publication, Tagore was initially absorbed into the popular interest in the spiritual East. Later he was rediscovered as a poet through a series of reprints and new translations. The past five years have seen a more complex process of reception, through new translations (along with reprints) from the Bengali, publications of the novels, plays and essays, a promising 'Tagore Project,' as well as an integration of his poetry with music and dance.

There are signs that the growing interest seen in these years is the beginning of a longer ascending curve. The availability of works not translated before is likely to encourage the scholarly study of Tagore and stimulate new articles and books about his oeuvre. After A. Bhose's death in 1992, Bengali ceased to be taught in the University and her former students could not make a career in this field. Only in the past five years, through Romanians studying in Bengal, new translations from the Bengali have been

published and more are expected to come. It is hoped that the scholars of
Bengali would also contribute with new academic writings on Tagore.

NOTES

1. Cândea, *Tagore en Roumanie*; Neacşu, *Tagore: Romania Remembers*. For
economy of space, in what follows the reader will only be directed to some of
the main secondary sources. For all the primary sources, see the forthcoming
articles by Bordaş, 'Tagore in Romanian culture. The first three decades (1913–
45),' and 'Tagore in Romanian culture: The Communist era (1945–89).' My
special thanks to Imre Bangha for his help with translation from the Bengali
and information which helped me to identify the original of some of Tagore's
works.

2. Lupu and Ştefănescu, *Bibliografia relaţiilor literaturii române*, vol. 3, 156–8;
Brezuleanu et al., *Bibliografia relaţiilor literaturii române*, vol. 9, 212–27.

3. Bhose, 'Rumaniyay Rabindranath,' 'Rabindranath Tagore şi România,'
'Romaniyay rabiraşhmi,' 'Romaniyar rajnitir pate bharatbarsha o rabindranath,'
'Rabindranath Tagore, prietenul României.'

4. It is likely that Romanians from these regions also produced responses to
Tagore, but the study of the Romanians from Ukraine, Russia, Soviet Union,
etc., is at a rudimentary stage.

5. Tagore, *On the Edges of Time*, 227. See also Kripalani, *Rabindranath Tagore*,
293, and Dutta and Robinson, *Rabindranath Tagore*, 228, 428.

6. Antohi, 'Rabindranath Tagore şi România,' 90–2; Bordaş, 'Licurici
transcendentali,' 7–26.

7. For Eliade's rapport with Tagore, see Bordaş, 'Tagore în România' and Handoca,
'De la Tagore la Eliade.'

8. For Tagore's influence on Blaga, see Vaida, *Lucian Blaga. Afinităţi şi izvoare*,
134–9.

9. Bercovici, *O sută de ani de teatru evreiesc în România*, 175. The translation of
Sacrifice and *Chitra* is jointly signed by Nella Stroescu and 'Maria Adele Felix,'
an obvious psendonym which must have belonged to Felix Aderca.

10. Bordaş, 'Istrati, Rolland e i rappresentanti del "Risorgimento indiano",' 517–
28.

11. Accounts of Tagore's visit to Romania by direct witnesses: Tagore, *On the
Edges of Time*, 145–6; Mahalanobis, *Kabir sange yurope*, 246–7; Sadoveanu,
'Omul care a trecut... (Impresii),' 272–3; Sadoveanu, 'Amintiri despre Tagore,'
1; Sadoveanu, 'Rabindranath Tagore: Amintiri,' 8; Radovici, 'Rabindranath
Tagore la Giurgiu,' 1; Dianu, 'Rabindranath Tagore la Bucureşti,' 17; Dima,
'Personalitatea marelui indian,' Vianu, 'Tagore în România,' 6.

12. A satirical poem, as an answer to the letter of a Bengali friend, written on 20
November 1926 in Rani Mahalanobis's notebook. Mahalanobis, *Kabir sange
yurope*, 246–7.

13. See also some of the historiographic accounts of the visit: Vianu, 'Tagore's
'26 visit,' Popişteanu, 'Umanistul Rabindranath Tagore,' Cleja-Gârbea,

60 Liviu Bordaş

'Rabindranath Tagore la Bucureşti,' Dinu-Ciubotariu, 'Vizita poetului indian Rabindranath Tagore.'
14. For the letters received by the headmaster and amateur painter Florica Botez (1876–1956), see the articles referred to in Note 6. The letters of the journalist Lazăr Beneş and the University of Bucharest Professor Mihail Vanghelovici are preserved in *Tagore Papers*, Rabindra Bhavana, Santiniketan.
15. Iftimovici, 'De la Iaşi în Extremul Orient,' 192.
16. Costin, 'Tineri soli ai unor tradiţii străvechi,' 2.
17. Derdena, 'Petre Hossu,' 12–13; Bănăţeanu, 'Indian Studies in Rumania,' 252–3, 258.
18. On the Romanian translations of Tagore's novels, see Bordaş, 'Căutarea identităţii,' 25–34.
19. See the chronicle of Coroiu, 'Omagiu Tagore,' 162.

Works Cited

Antohi, Iosif. 'Rabindranath Tagore şi România: La trei decenii de la moartea sa' [R. Tagore and Romania: At Three Decades after his Death], *Almanahul educaţiei* (Bucharest), 1971, 90–2.
Bănăţeanu, Vlad. 'Indian Studies in Rumania in the Past and in the Present.' *The Visva-Bharati Quarterly* (Santiniketan), 27, nos. 3–4 (1961–2), 239–59.
Bercovici, Israel. *O sută de ani de teatru evreiesc în România* [Hundred Years of Jewish Theatre in Romania]. Bucharest: Integral, 1998.
Bhose, Amita. 'Rabindranath Tagore, prietenul României' [R. Tagore, the Friend of Romania], lecture to the Open University, Bucharest: 16 May 1991, http://amitabhose.net/Books.asp?SID=4.
———. 'Rabindranath Tagore şi România' [R. Tagore and Romania]. *România literară* (Bucharest), 10, no. 20 (19 May 1977), 19.
———. 'Romaniyar rajnitir pate bharatbarsha o rabindranath' [India and Rabindranath in the political canvas of Romania]. *Korak: Sahitya patrika, Bangabda* (Bengali year)1398 *Sharadiya* (Autumnal number) (1991), 15–32.
———. 'Romaniyay rabirashmi' [The Rays of Sun/Rabindranath in Romania]. *Desh* (Calcutta), 56, no. 47 (23 September 1989), 19–43.
———. 'Rumaniyay rabindranath' [Rabindranath in Romania]. *Desh* (Calcutta), 28, no. 27 (6 May 1961), 181–7.
Bordaş, Liviu. 'Căutarea identităţii. Patriotism şi dragoste în *India capta*' [The Search for Identity. Patriotism and Love in *India Capta*], introduction to: R. Tagore, *Gora*. Translated by H. Y. Stahl, vol. 1, Bucharest: Litera, 2012, 25–34.
———. 'Istrati, Rolland e i rappresentanti del "Risorgimento indiano"' [Istrati, Rolland and the Leaders of 'Indian Renaissance']. *Annuario dell'Istituto Romeno di Cultura e Ricerca Umanistica* (Venice), vol. 10–11(2008–9), 531–42.
———. 'Licurici transcendentali. Poemele scurte ale lui Tagore şi receptarea lor în limba română' [Transcendental Fireflies. The Brief Poems of Tagore and their Reception in the Romanian Language], introduction to R. Tagore, *Licurici*. Translated by Adelina Patrichi, Bucharest: Taj Books, 2013, 7–26.

Bordaş, Liviu. 'Tagore în România' [Tagore in Romania], *Bibliotheca Indica* (Bucharest), vol. 4, 1999, 21–36.

———. 'Tagore in Romanian Culture: The Communist Era (1945–89),' *Historical Yearbook* ('Nicolae Iorga' History Institute, Bucharest), vol. 14, 2017, forthcoming.

———. 'Tagore in Romanian culture: The first three decades (1913–45).' In Imre Bangha (ed.), *Tagore: Beyond His Language*, Delhi: Primus Books, 2016, pp. 82–138.

Brezuleanu, A.-M., I. Mihăilă, V. Nişcov, M. Şchiopu, C. Ştefănescu, eds. *Bibliografia relaţiilor literaturii române cu literaturile străine în periodice (1919–44)*, vol. 9. Bucharest: Saeculum, 2008.

Cândea, Virgil. *Tagore en Roumanie. Bibliographie sélective* [Tagore in Romania: Selected Bibliography]. Bucharest: Commission Nationale de la R.P.R. pour l'UNESCO, 1961.

Cleja-Gârbea, Claudia. 'Rabindranath Tagore la Bucureşti' [R. Tagore in Bucharest]. *Bucureşti. Materiale de istorie şi muzeografie* (Bucharest), vol. 6, 1968, 333–7.

Coroiu, Irina. 'Omagiu Tagore. Actori pentru o seară' [Homage to Tagore: Actors for One Evening]. *Teatru* (Bucharest), vol. 26, nos. 7–8 (July–August 1981), 162.

Costin, D. 'Tineri soli ai unor tradiţii străvechi. Concertul de gală al grupului artistic al delegaţiei tineretului indian' [Young Messengers of Immemorial Traditions: The Gala Concert of the Artistic Group of the Indian Youth Delegation]. *Scânteia* (Bucharest), 22, no. 2739 (13 August 1953), 2.

Derdena, M. S. 'Petre Hossu,' *Cuvântul românesc* (Hamilton, Ont.), 27, nos. 7–8 (July–August 2002), 12–13.

Dianu, Romulus. 'Rabindranath Tagore la Bucureşti' [R. Tagore in Bucharest]. *Ramuri* (Craiova), 7, no. 4 (15 April 1970), 17.

Dima, Alexandru. 'Personalitatea marelui indian' [The Personality of the Great Indian]. *Gazeta literară* (Bucharest), 8, no. 32 (3 August 1961), 8; no. 33 (10 August 1961), 8.

Dinu-Ciubotariu, Ştefania. 'Vizita poetului indian Rabindranath Tagore in România (noiembrie 1926)' [The Visit of Indian Poet R. Tagore to Romania (November 1926)]. *Anuarul Muzeului Literaturii Române* (Iaşi), vol. 2, 2009, 115–21; also in *Istorie şi civilizaţie* (Bucharest), 3, no. 1 (January 2011), 58–62.

Dutta, Krishna, and Andrew Robinson. *Rabindranath Tagore: The Myriad-Minded Man*. London: Bloomsbury, 1995.

Handoca, Mircea. 'De la Tagore la Eliade' [From Tagore to Eliade], *Jurnalul literar* (Bucharest), 22, nos. 19–24 (October–December 2011), 11; 23, nos. 1–6 (January–March 2012), 9, 17.

Iftimovici, Radu. 'De la Iaşi în Extremul Orient' [From Iaşi to the Far East]. In *Fraţii Mihai şi Alexandru Ciucă* by R. Iftimovici [The Brothers Mihai and Alexandru Ciucă]. Iaşi: Junimea, 1975, 183–96.

Kripalani, Krishna. *Rabindranath Tagore: A Biography*. Calcutta: Visva-Bharati, 1980 (2nd ed.).

Lupu, I., and C. Ştefănescu, eds. *Bibliografia relaţiilor literaturii române cu literaturile străine în periodice (1859–1918)*, vol. 3. Bucharest: Ed. Academiei, 1985.

Mahalanobis, Nirmal Kumari. *Kabir sange yurope* [With the Poet in Europe]. Calcutta: Mitra-o-Ghosh, 1969.

Neacşu, Daniela, ed. *Tagore: Romania Remembers / Tagore—România—Amintiri.* Bucharest: Paideia, 1998 (2nd ed., Bucharest: Sophia, 1999).

Popişteanu, Cristian. 'Umanistul Rabindranath Tagore printre bucureşteni. Însemnare la un instantaneu fotografic' [The Humanist R. Tagore among the People of Bucharest: Gloss to a Photographic Snapshot]. *Magazin istoric* (Bucharest), 1, no. 1 (April 1967), 80–1.

Radovici, Eugen, 'Rabindranath Tagore la Giurgiu' [R. Tagore in Giurgiu]. *Torţa* (Bucharest), 1, no. 2 (14 January 1945), 1.

Sadoveanu, I. M. 'Amintiri despre Tagore' [Recollections about Tagore]. *Rampa* (Bucharest), 16, no. 4053 (27 July 1931), 1.

——. 'Omul care a trecut... (Impresii)' [The Man who Just Passed by... (Impressions)]. *Gândirea* (Bucharest), 6, nos. 9–11 (October–December 1926), 272–3.

——. 'Rabindranath Tagore: Amintiri' [R. Tagore: Memories]. *Gazeta literară* (Bucharest), vol. 8, no. 21 (18 May 1961), 8.

Tagore, Rathindranath. *On the Edges of Time.* Bombay: Orient Longmans, 1958.

Vaida, Mircea. *Lucian Blaga. Afinităţi şi izvoare* [Lucian Blaga: Affinities and Sources]. Bucharest: Minerva, 1975, 134–9.

Vianu, Tudor. 'Tagore în România' [Tagore in Romania]. *Albina* (Bucharest), 63, no. 699 (17 May 1961), 6.

——. 'Tagore's '26 visit: Message of peace.' *Amrita Bazar Patrika* (Calcutta), 40, no. 335 (6 December 1958), 6.

15

BULGARIA

NIKOLAY NIKOLAEV

BULGARIA AND INDIA

B ulgaria, being on the outskirts of Europe, has long suffered rather than benefited from its geographical position. Its peripheral situation allowed Bulgaria only a limited access to mainstream European culture. For half a millennium Bulgarians, oppressed and preoccupied with their own survival under the Ottoman Empire, did not get much exposure to the cultural and literary tendencies of the time. Divided in two, Bulgaria managed to reunite only in 1912. That year and the next were years of wars on the Balkan Peninsula that saw the young and newly liberated country getting embroiled in conflict with its neighbours.

Just a few decades after the Bulgarian liberation from Turkish oppression in 1878, two World Wars shook the world. After World War I, Bulgaria was ruled by Monarcho-Fascist governments till 1944 with tight control over culture, especially literature and the arts. With a chequered history, Bulgarians never had the chance to establish direct connections with distant lands, such as India, before the twentieth century, and the first Indian personality to enter into the wider cultural life of Bulgaria was Rabindranath Tagore.

The leading writer and literary and art critic Vicho Ivanov (1901–79) wrote in his article *Tagore in Bulgaria*:

> The subject of Rabindranath Tagore in Bulgaria leads up to that of Indo-Bulgarian relations in the past and to-day.[1]

THE INITIAL RECEPTION

The turmoil of the two Balkan Wars followed by World War I explains why there is no evidence that even the leading literary figures wrote about Rabindranath Tagore or translated anything written by him until 1918. It is unlikely that the event of awarding the Nobel Prize for Literature had not reached the Bulgarian elite and the literati, although there is no written record of any reaction to it. Interestingly, the first Tagore translation into Bulgarian was that of *The Gardener* in 1918. *Gitanjali*, the work Tagore became known to the world with, was translated into Bulgarian only in 1920. The early translations were not even made from English. *The Gardener* was translated from the Italian, and *Gitanjali* from Russian.

After that, the interest of the Bulgarian public and literary figures in Rabindranath and his works increased gradually, and reached its climax in 1926 (the year when the poet visited Bulgaria for three days in November), and in the following year. In the words of the eminent Bulgarian literary figure Vladimir Svintila (pseudonym of V. Georgiev Nikolov):

> The public sentiment in Bulgaria in the twenties was particularly receptive to Tagore's ideas. There were many reasons for it. Towards the last two decades of the nineteenth century, a number of Russian scholars had turned their eyes to the East. These moods in Russia resounded in Bulgaria as well.[2]

Visit in 1926

Rabindranath Tagore's visit to Bulgaria was a major catalyst in the development of a range of social movements, some of them positive, others not quite so. Part of the Bulgarian public viewed his thoughts and written works as a source of great inspiration and would not hesitate to use them, in their quest to defend their cause through Tagore's words of wisdom. Many, from freedom fighters to cooperative movement advocates, educationists and humanists, religious figures or monarchists, Russophiles or Russophobes, or defenders of women and their rights, seemed to have found exactly what they needed in Tagore, and they referred to his personality and used his words and ideas to promote their own cause.

In the Bulgarian sources, one can find deliberate omissions in Rabindranath's translated works and distortion of the truth about facts of his personal life and travels. Sometimes his works would be intentionally misinterpreted or presented in a way Tagore would have remained oblivious to. Journalists and public figures would occasionally offer their audience 'facts' that were fictional in nature.

Tagore initially did not intend to visit Bulgaria. In October 1926, while on his European tour, he fell ill in Vienna and following the advice of his doctor he took a route back to his motherland through countries where he would be less exposed to the severity of the approaching European winter. From Lake Balaton in Hungary, Rabindranath headed for Zagreb and Belgrade and visited Bulgaria on his way to Romania, from where he returned to India via Istanbul, Greece and Egypt. Rabindranath Tagore was accompanied by his son Rathindranath, his daughter-in-law Pratima Devi, and their adopted daughter Nandini, as well as his secretary, Prashanta Chandra Mahalanobis, and his wife Nirmal Kumari (also known as Rani) Mahalanobis.

Bulgarian literary and cultural institutions competed over whose guest Tagore would be. The House of Arts and the Press, with which unions of writers, journalists and artists were affiliated, took pride in being able to invite the poet, and several of their representatives met him at the Yugoslav–Bulgarian border. Some sources state that the Bulgarian King had sent a carriage to bring the poet to Sofia—others that the Ministry of Railways had released a special coach. Some even go further and state that Rabindranath Tagore was an official guest of the Bulgarian King Boris and the Bulgarian Government. Other sources categorically deny this, and state that Rabindranath Tagore, having been informed in advance of the situation in Bulgaria, and how the ordinary people and the intelligentsia were oppressed, had explicitly stated that he was a guest of the Bulgarian people and not of the regime, and had refused to meet any representative of the Government or the King.

The reason stated in some Bulgarian sources as to why Tagore objected to being considered an official guest of the Bulgarian Government was that the first anti-Fascist uprising in the world, which took place in September 1923 in Bulgaria, was drowned in blood. Many people were also killed in a second uprising in April 1925. Some of the victims were the most progressive intellectuals and literary figures of the time.

A short announcement in the *North China Star* (Beijing) on 22 November 1926 stated that 'According to Sofia reports Rabindranath Tagore was received by King Boris and Princess Eudoxie.' However, the sources of the 'Sofia reports' are not mentioned.

A note titled 'Poet's Home-Coming' in the Indian *Daily Telegraph* (Lucknow) on 19 December stated: 'While in the Balkan States he was the guest of governments, the kings of Romania and Bulgaria invited him to their palaces for lunch.' However, other sources state exactly the opposite. In an article in the Indian *Mainstream* magazine on 7 August 1976, the Bulgarian journalist Vladimir Svintila stated:

> In Tagore the Bulgarian public honoured the exponent of democratic ideas. On the way to the hotel he was warned that a fascist dictatorship had been established in this country whereby all rights and freedoms were suppressed. The proud Indian bard immediately took the side of the oppressed people—he refused to meet any official persons. In

his interviews with journalists, he stressed that he was a guest of the Bulgarian people, implying that he was not a guest of the Bulgarian Government.

Since the fascist coup in 1923, the authorities had not allowed entry into the country [of] any foreign representatives of progressive thought. Therefore, the visit of India's great son was hailed as a triumph of the democratic ideas. Was it not true that Tagore was the son of a country whose people, too, were oppressed in those days? His book *The Rebel Gora* was a manifesto of the freedom of the spirit.

The visit was an exhilarating occasion for the progressive Bulgarian intelligentsia. Tagore met representatives of the leftist movements, held talks with them and expressed his sympathy. Thus he helped to keep up their spirit.

From the thousands who greeted him at the station and on the streets, 'guarded and respected' by mounted and foot police, that have taken part in both his lectures, delivered on 17 and 18 November in the hall of the 'Free Theatre' in Sofia, Rabindranath Tagore realised the real situation of the people. Being an absolutely unexpected 'guest' for those who had seized the right to rule the lives of the people, Tagore had avoided all meetings and ceremonies with [monarcho-fascist] representatives of the authorities, and stayed with his close companions in hotel Imperial.

Bearing in mind the situation in the country, many eminent figures in Bulgaria, including some of Tagore's interpreters, wanted to give the impression to their readers that Tagore was an active revolutionary. The students and the ordinary people were in need of following a colossal figure, such as Tagore. They transferred all their hopes onto this great poet, writer, playwright, composer, artist, thinker, philosopher and humanist. Though initially there was just a small note published in one of the Bulgarian newspapers, *Utro*, thousands of people came to know and flocked at the Sofia Railway Station to meet Rabindranath. It is reported that all educational institutions were formally closed for the day of his arrival.

Rabindranath Tagore was perceived as a messiah or a biblical prophet. There have been speculations about Tagore's connection with Petar Dunov, the leader of the White Brotherhood movement. Some sources state they wrote to each other regularly; however no evidence of this exists and very likely they did not. Moreover, they never met each other. Tagore's visit to Bulgaria in 1926 stirred up the entire society. An article kept at the Rabindra Bhavana Library at Santiniketan from the *Zora* newspaper, most probably of 20 November 1926, entitled 'Rabindranath Tagore in Sofia:

The Singer of Bengal/. The Sage of India/The Welcome at Tzaribrod/The Solemn Reception in Sofia/What Tagore Says', does not bear any important news or information, and has many inaccuracies in it. However, the aim of the article is quite obvious and it is mentioned pointedly that 'up to now nobody from Russia [*sic*] has been invited.' The conclusion is in capital italics: '*RABINDRANATH TAGORE DOES NOT BELIEVE THAT THE AGGRESSIVE NATIONALISM, WHICH IS MUCH FELT IN SOUTH-EASTERN EUROPE, WILL IMPROVE THE SITUATION. MUCH JEALOUSY AND SUSPICION EXIST BETWEEN THE NEIGHBOURS.*'

Moreover, obvious animosity comes through against Russia and the neighbours of Bulgaria throughout the article. A similar article from the Sofia-based French-medium periodical *La Bulgarie* of 22 November 1926 entitled 'Notes of a Passer-by: Rabindranath Tagore' states that though the Bulgarians had the chance of meeting Rabindranath Tagore for only less than two days, the time had been enough to greet one of the greatest pacifists of the time, a man who had been called by Clemenceau (1841–1929) 'Homme Candide [the straightforward man].' Even Tagore himself had been surprised at the exceptionally cordial reception at Sofia station. He said it was not clear to him what kind of mysterious force had brought all these people, big and small, to come and meet him. Then follows the explanation of the author of the article—Tagore's personality emanates sincerity and truthfulness, as it is with the writer Tolstoy.

The crowd understands him and his pure soul, the article states, because the hearts of the people in this crowd are also pure and they started beating as one with the pulse of the great poet. Then follow the remarks that in no other country on the Balkan Peninsula would Tagore have a similar reception nor would he be as sincerely understood as he was in Bulgaria, though he spoke in languages many did not know:

> Rabindranath Tagore spoke in English and recited his poems in Bengali. But in whatever unknown language he would have spoken to us, we would have understood him—so much are his thoughts similar to ours. Anyway, we are much in doubt that it would be the same everywhere, and more precisely in some Balkan states. There, to be well understood, the Hindu poet could have held his lecturers on the subject of love and fraternity between people and the nations in the language of the country, and even then it is very doubtful that he would have made them understand.

The article was signed only by the initial 'P.' The verbal attacks are again clearly directed at the neighbouring countries.

In the first Bulgarian translation of Rabindranath's novel *Gora*, an important qualification was added to the original title in order to boost the morale of people involved in active struggle against their oppressors: to the Bulgarian public it became known as *The Rebel Gora*. It was translated from the German. Interestingly, in the preface of the novel, the translator Dr Vera Plocheva says: 'His [Rabindranath's] characters are creative personalities, immersed in religiousness. Their strong longing for the "eternal" makes them really close to God.' The change in the title, and this passage in the *Preface* present an interesting mixture of support for the political struggle that was then raging and of seeking support in Tagore's characters in particular and in God in general.

In 1927, the writer and literary critic Vasil Stavrev (1885–1929) published his book *Rabindranath Tagore: Life and Creativity*. The author writes that he 'had apparently been another witness and participant in the improvised Tagore *mela* in Sofia,' and draws the following portrait of Tagore with an abundance of biblical references and terms.

> In order to make the features of this extraordinary man stand out more clearly, I shall take the liberty of saying a few words also about his so interesting outer appearance.
>
> A tall, sturdy old man who, in spite of the great exhaustion of his constant travels, will never stoop and, like some Colossus, always towers above those around him. Long white hair crowns his broad and tall forehead like a halo. The features of his face are composed and absolutely regular—the features of a truly Aryan face. His dark coppery complexion, more yellowish than reddish, is characteristically offset by the surrounding whiteness of the hair and the long beard of a Biblical prophet, which completes his amazingly handsome portrait. Yet, the deep intelligent eyes piercing to the bottom of one's soul, are the most striking part of this face. How penetrative they are, those dark, large eyes! And his gentle kind smile too, as pure as that of a child! Isn't it the best expression of the childlike purity of his soul? And, lastly, his voice! If it is true that the voice can sometimes be the best interpreter of the inner spiritual manifestations, it is Tagore's voice that is the surest proof of that. The poet has such a sweet and melodious voice that even the commonest prose acquires with him the tone of a divine chant.[3]

Some famous Bulgarian artists also came to be very close to Rabindranath. Boris Georgiev painted his portrait on several occasions. Copies of Tagore's portraits are kept nowadays in both the Kala Bhavana (Department of Arts) of Visva-Bharati as well as in the Modern Art Gallery in New Delhi.

MYSTIFYING TAGORE

The author of a monograph on Boris Georgiev, Irina Mihalcheva, while connecting Tagore with Russia and Tolstoy, remarked:

> Soon after his arrival in India Boris Georgiev was invited by Rabindranath Tagore to visit his University at Santiniketan, near Calcutta, Bengal. Tagore established this school on the estate of his father like Tolstoy's Yasna[ya] Poliana... He invited and insisted that Boris Georgiev should assist in the University in the arts field. The invitation was an honour to our artist, as in India the teacher's profession is a much-respected one. Georgiev refused the offer, because he had a planned program in advance, and continued travelling around the country, collecting material for his cycle of Indian paintings. Nevertheless, his friendship with Rabindranath Tagore continued.[4]

A Bulgarian article from 1994 went even further claiming that Boris Georgiev '[taught] for some time at the University of Rabindranath Tagore because of his [Tagore's] explicit request.'[5] However, it is very unlikely that Georgiev ever visited Santiniketan.

It is not only Bulgarian sources that have written irresponsibly or stated erroneous facts about Tagore, his stay in Bulgaria and his connections with famous Bulgarians. The Indian artist Chintamany Vyas, wrote a monograph titled *Boris Georgiev*, in corresponding Hindi and English texts. The effort is an interesting one though the author has allowed many inaccuracies and mistakes to creep into his text. Vyas states:

> Living with Roerich for some time, Boris gained deep insights into the Himalayas and nature as a whole and made some paintings of the great mountain. From Nagger [perhaps Naggar in Himachal Pradesh], on being invited by Rabindranath Tagore, he went to Santiniketan where he came in contact with Acharya Nandal [*sic*] Bose, Gaganendranath Tagore, Bireshwar Sen, Sass Brunner, Upendra Maharathi, Binod Bihari Mukherji and others. During his stay in Santiniketan he exchanged views with some noted artists and as a result his approach got changed considerably. Earlier his art was inspired and influenced by the European values and standards. Leonardo da Vinci, Michelangelo and Titian and Renaissance values in general had left a mark on his paintings.[6]

While researching Rabindranath Tagore's connections with Bulgaria in Santiniketan, I found the statement quoted above, as well as numerous other 'facts' stated in Vyas's book to be fictitious and lacking in any truth or substance.

In contrast with scholarly articles, distortions in the popular press were few. There were only a few hints that there was something more than a normal working relationship between Rabindranath Tagore and the wife of his secretary, Mrs Nirmal Kumari Mahalanobis. For instance, the 20 November 1926 issue of *Vestnik na zhenata*, a Bulgarian weekly for literature, social life and housekeeping, carried on its front page a photo of the poet with Mrs Mahalanobis with the caption: 'Rabindranath Tagore (On the photo next to him is one of his millions of female admirers—Mahalanobis).'

However, some of the frivolities in publishing imaginary facts in the press at that time were surprising. A source stated that Tagore had been on an outing around Sofia, and visited some villages and a monastery. In fact, his entire company did go, but the poet stayed in his hotel room—he was too exhausted by his lectures and travels to join them.

Even in recent years similar 'facts' did appear in the press. The newspaper *Vsichko za vseki* carries an article titled 'The Bulgarian Heavenly Apples' by Misho Hristov[7] (more often signing himself as Mihail Topalov), where Rabindranath Tagore's stay in Bulgaria has been mentioned. Mihail Topalov was a person, who regularly authored 'recollections', mostly with a nostalgic monarchic slant. In his article, Mikhail Topalov stated that Tagore really loved Bulgarian apples, especially those from the Kyustendil region. When this author met him in person to inquire about the information he had about Rabindranath Tagore and his stay in Bulgaria in 1926, Topalov denied any knowledge of such facts and stated that he had just made up the story for the sake of publishing one of his 'reminiscences'!

There is a case of an almost certain 'deliberate' mistake regarding Rabindranath Tagore and his works translated into Bulgarian. Letter No. 13 from *Letters from Russia* has been consistently omitted from the Soviet editions as well as in translations into Bulgarian. The letter itself was written by Tagore to Kalimohan Ghosh (1882–1940). The reasons for its exclusion from the translations could only be that Tagore compares the Communists with the Fascists, and though the letter itself is a beautiful piece of literature, that comparison would have been enough for the letter to be considered an anathema by the regime, and be removed from publication. This is probably the most notable intentional 'error' in presenting Rabindranath Tagore to the closed world behind the former 'Iron Curtain'. Otherwise, *Letters from Russia* is an edition much appreciated in the former Soviet Union as well as in some socialist countries at that time because of its broad support of the Communist way.[8]

The Bulgarian translation of the letter by the author of the present essay, published in the literary magazine *Plamuk,* was the first direct translation from Bengali into Bulgarian.[9] Even to date, the translation of the concluding part of the original book, as well as the appendixes are missing from the Bulgarian translation of *Letters from Russia* (*Rashiar Chithi*).[10]

ENGAGEMENT WITH TAGORE'S IDEAS AFTER THE POET'S DEATH IN 1941

Obviously, Rabindranath Tagore has stirred up many a mind in Bulgaria, as he has done elsewhere too. Decades after his visit his personality and his literary works are found to be relevant to people of unconventional thinking. In the years before socialism gripped the country, the supporters of the cooperative agricultural movement interpreted Tagore and his ideas in an article in their magazine *Kooperativna prosveta* of 1 October 1941 (No. 14), with the title 'Rabindranath Tagore. The Writer and the Co-operator':

> We know him [Rabindranath Tagore] from his literary works as an ethical poet, philosopher and a person, who is seeking God. We also know that he takes a stand regarding agriculture and unequivocally and openly he supports the cooperatives.

Tagore has been quoted as assisting the *Bengal Cooperative Journal*. The magazine continues further:

> All fruitful activities develop within the framework of a common cooperative effort. All that is human creation, has been achieved through the work of a huge majority that benefits a minority, and it is a pity to many that the riches nowadays are concentrated in the hands of a small capitalist group.

The aim of the magazine is clear and the article ended up by urging the people to unite and organise their efforts and work in cooperatives.

Even the literary editions that were meant to be only informative could not stay neutral. The bias towards the socialist ideas is quite distinct in the *Short Bulgarian Encyclopaedia* (1969). It contains the following brief and sometimes convoluted account of who Rabindranath Tagore was:

> Rabindranath Tagore ... is an Indian writer, who wrote in Bengali. He is an author of lyrical poems, dramas and historical novels, directed against feudalism. His verse has a philosophical character. In 1901 he opened a school—Abode of Peace, and in 1921a national University. He created the first social novels in Indian literature—*The Wreck* (1902), *The Rebel Gora* (1910)—a broad picture of the Bengali life. He takes part in the struggle for the liberation of India. His works are filled with hatred towards imperialism and tyranny. He mixes realism, romanticism and symbolism. In 1926 he visited Bulgaria. He had

been in the USSR and had written *Letters from Russia* (1930). Nobel Prize winner (1913).[11]

Clearly biased (and unexplained) are the claims about how and when Tagore took part in the struggle for the liberation of India. Undoubtedly, these claims had in mind Tagore's taking part in the movement of 1905 against the partition of Bengal. The hatred towards imperialism leaves no doubt against whom these lines were written. Other countries, which Tagore visited—some of them many times—have been ignored in favour of the only country that mattered to the authors of the above entry—the Union of the Soviet Socialist Republics (USSR). One is directed to think that *Letters from Russia* is one of the most important works penned by Rabindranath Tagore out of the wealth of his literary heritage.

Speculations about Tagore are rife even nowadays. People try to attract attention to the great personality, and associate him with various societies and clubs, even those shrouded in mystery for the masses, such as the Masons (also known as Freemasons). An article in the Bulgarian newspaper *24 Chasa* of 12 November 1994 titled 'The Local Masons Held the Power: 26 Years the Slogan "Hear, See and Stay Silent" Leads Their Activities' mentions Rabindranath Tagore as one of the most notable Masons of all time. The Masons were also mentioned in Irina Mihalcheva's monograph on Boris Georgiev where she wrote about his portrait of Tagore's close associate C. F. Andrews:

> In the summer of 1932 Boris Georgiev is in Simla... There he makes portraits of the Commander-in-Chief of Gwalior, Raja Rajewade and his wife Rani Rajewade, of Princess Indu Raji, of Mr. Andrews from England (who invites him to become a Mason, but Boris categorically refuses).[12]

The time of Rabindranath's death coincided with big tensions in Europe and the world, when the attention of all people was turned more to survival during the World War II years than engaging in literature and culture. After the War not much of Tagore was translated and published in Bulgaria under its Socialist regime, despite good relations between India and Bulgaria. The period since 1945 has seen only seven Tagore books translated or retranslated and a three-volume edition of selected works published. The first book translated after the War, *The Wreck*, appeared as late as in 1958. My survey of Bulgarian publications of that period resulted in finding references to Tagore in a further twenty-seven books, and forty-nine articles.[13]

The complexities of social, political and literary life in this small Balkan country account for a multifaceted and unique reception of Rabindranath in Bulgaria.

TAGORE IN THE BULGARIA OF TODAY

Nowadays, regrettably, not much is being discussed about Rabindranath Tagore on the web in Bulgaria. In the Internet age Bulgarians probably remain preoccupied with more basic needs than finding Tagore again.

In the new century Bulgaria has seen only two books on Tagore so far. In 2008, Dr Stefania Dimitrova published a volume *Rabindranath Tagore: The Mythical Sentry* and has recently given interviews to journalists and Bulgarian TV regarding Tagore and her book.

Another book that was published in 2009 by Visva-Bharati in Kolkata in English was *Rabindranath Tagore and the Bulgarian Connection* by Anna Nikolaev and Nikolay Nikolaev containing their research done mainly at Santiniketan, exploring the connection of Rabindranath Tagore and Bulgaria through the Bulgarian contemporaries of Tagore whom he had been in touch with during his lifetime. *The Statesman* of 9 May 2009 wrote about the book:

> ... a series of monographs has been launched on Rabindranath's relationship with the outside world. Shailesh Parekh's *Tagore in Ahmedabad* and *Rabindranath Tagore and the Bulgarian Connection* by Anna and Nikolay Nikolaev are slim volumes with well-documented material drawn from hitherto untapped sources.

However, there is hope that interest in Rabindranath Tagore could be revived for the Bulgarian public. The first steps are evident in some on-line queries by followers of Petar Danov, the founder of The White Brotherhood movement, as to whether Tagore and Danov ever met. Though the two great sages have never seen each other nor corresponded with each other, the spiritually charged audience of Petar Danov is exploring the connection between the two great personalities beyond the simple facts of whether they met or not. They are rather intent on a comparison of their philosophy, world view and thoughts on spirituality.

NOTES

1. Quoted in Ivanov, 'Tagore in Bulgaria,' 323.
2. Svintila, 'Tagore in Sofia,' 6. The article gives an account of Bulgarians connected directly or indirectly with India and with Tagore.
3. Stavrev, *Rabindranat Tagor*, 161–2.
4. Mihalcheva, *Boris Georgiev*, 43. When I met the author Irina Mihalcheva, she stated that she did not recall where she had obtained this information, and one cannot conclude for certain whether Boris Georgiev was invited by Tagore to teach art at his university.
5. *Standart* (Sofia), 28 January 1994, 11.
6. Vyas, *Boris Georgiev*, 52.

7. *Vsichko za vseki*, 4–10 November 1997, 2.
8. The *Postscript* to the letters was also left out. It was probably because translators at that time did not always consider that part of a book as worth translating.
9. *Plamuk* 1992, no. 1–2, 122–4.
10. For further discussion of Tagore's *Letters from Russia*, see the essay on 'Russia' in this volume.
11. See the 'Tagore' entry in Georgiev, *Kratka B'lgarska Entsiklopediya*, 75.
12. Mihalcheva, 46–7.
13. For a select bibliography of the Bulgarian Tagoreana, see Nikolaeva and Nikolaev, *Rabindranath Tagore and the Bulgarian Connection*, 125–32.

Works Cited

Biswas, Amalendu, Christine Marsh, and Kalyan Kundu, ed. *Rabindranath Tagore: A Timeless Mind*. Kolkata: Shishu Sahitya Samsad, 2011.

La Bulgarie, a French-language newspaper published in Bulgaria in November 1926.

Dimitrova, Stefania. *Rabindranath Tagore: The Mythical Sentry*. Sofia: Alpha-Omega Publishing House, 2008.

Georgiev, Vladimir, ed. *Kratka B'lgarska Entsiklopediya* [Short Bulgarian Encyclopaedia], vol. 5. Sofia: Bulgarian Academy of Sciences, 1969.

Ivanov, Vicho. 'Tagore in Bulgaria,' in *Rabindranath Tagore: 1861–1961: A Centenary Volume*. New Delhi: Sahitya Akademi, 1961, 323–31.

Mainstream, weekly magazine published from New Delhi, 7 August 1976.

Mihalcheva, Irina. *Boris Georgiev: Monografiya* [Boris Georgiev: A Monograph]. Sofia: Bulgarski hudozhnik, 1987.

Nikolaeva, Anna, and Nikolay Nikolaev. *Rabindranath Tagore and the Bulgarian Connection*. Kolkata: Visva-Bharati, 2009.

Tagore, Rabindranath. *Gradinaryat'* [*The Gardener*]. Translated from Italian by D. Hr. Maksimov. Sofia: Tzviat Publishers, 1918.

———. *Gitandzhali* [*Gitanjali*]. Translated from Russian by Metodi Vecherov. Sofia: Tzviat Publishers, 1920 (De Luxe edition).

———. *Letters from Russia*. Translated by Sasadhar Sinha. Calcutta: Visva-Bharati, 1984 (1st ed., 1960).

———. *Buntovnik't' Gora* [The Rebel Gora]. Translated by Vera Plocheva. Sofia: Pravo Publishing House, 1927 ('Pearls of World Literature' series).

The Statesman, Indian newspaper, 9 May 2009. http://thestatesman.net/page.arcview.php?clid=3&id=286289&usrsess=1.

Stavrev, V. *Rabindranat Tagor—Zhivot i tvorchestvo* [Rabindranath Tagore: Life and Creativity]. Sofia: Acacia Publishers, 1927. ('Giants of Mankind' series, vol. 5).

Svintila, Vladimir. 'Tagore in Sofia.' *Mainstream*, 7 August 1976.

Vyas, Chintamany. *Boris Georgiev*. New Delhi: The All India Fine Arts & Crafts Society, 1980.

'Rabindranath Tagore' [Photograph] *Vestnik' na zhenata* 257, 20 November 1926.

16

Yugoslavia and its Successors

Ana Jelnikar

INTRODUCTION

When Rabindranath Tagore got the Nobel Prize in 1913 and his name spread rapidly across the globe, there was as yet no Yugoslavia.[1] The essay will therefore tackle not only Tagore's reception in the political entity known as Yugoslavia but also in its cultural predecessors and successors. The lands that came to comprise the South-Slavic state ('*yug*' in Yugoslavia means 'south') were in 1913 still split between the Austro-Hungarian and Ottoman Empires, the latter already on the verge of disappearing from the Balkans. But notions of South-Slavic cultural and linguistic unity go back to at least the second half of the nineteenth century. Bishop J. J. Strossmayer, a notable nineteenth-century advocate of Yugoslav unity in the nineteenth century, for example, founded the so-called Yugoslav Academy of Arts and Sciences in Zagreb as early as 1867 with the intention to promote cultural unity of the South Slavs.[2]

The so-called 'first Yugoslavia' came into being as the Kingdom of Serbs, Croats and Slovenes following the collapse of the Austro-Hungarian Empire after World War I. It re-emerged from Nazi occupation in 1944, after World War II, as the Socialist Federal Republic of Yugoslavia, or SFRY, led by the former Partisan leader Josip Broz, or Marshal Tito. This federation consisted of six republics: Bosnia and Herzegovina, Croatia, Macedonia, Montenegro, Serbia, and Slovenia. Following the Tito–Stalin split in 1948, Yugoslavia strove for a position of neutrality in the Cold War era; and in the 1960s it became one of the founding members of the Non-Aligned Movement. Against its diverse ethnic, linguistic and religious composition, consisting of Muslims, Catholic, Protestant and Orthodox Christians, and others, Tito's official line cultivated a Socialist fraternity and an ideal of unity in diversity intended to override particularistic ethnic and religious identities. A decade after Tito's death, however, in an atmosphere of compounded economic and political crisis, with separatist nationalisms growing and the inter-republic talks breaking down, the country disintegrated amidst horrific violence.

Direct politico-cultural relations between the former Yugoslavia and India date back to no more than six decades, when Yugoslavia joined the Non-Aligned Movement. But their literary and cultural associations have a much longer history, with earliest connections traced in the Indian origins of ancient Slavic myths.[3] A notion of ancient political unity of the South-Slavic peoples and India in Great Macedonia was propagated even by Croatian humanists. The sixteenth-century Croatian historian Vinko Pribojević, considered as a precursor of the Pan-Slavic ideology, for example, spoke of a great Slavic empire extending from the Adriatic Sea to the Ganges. Alexander the Great, appropriated as a Slav, became a subject of many popular Slavic romances. The fables of Barlaam and Josaphat with their reworking of the life of the Buddha entered the medieval literatures of former Yugoslavia (Serbian and Croatian) via the Byzantine cultural realm. The *Panchatantra*, transmitted into Europe through Persian, Arab and Greek translations, found its way from early Greek adaptations into the literary Old Slavonic and may have exerted an influence on old Yugoslav prose writings as early as the thirteenth century with a reworking of Kalila and Dimna in the Serbian-speaking region.[4] The notion of India as a land of plenty, a paradise on earth, was captured by many South-Slavic folksongs, tales and sayings throughout the Middle Ages and subsequent centuries and has survived to the present day in the popular phrase 'India Koromandia' ('*Koromandia*' refers to the Coromandel Coast where St Thomas preached Christianity.)[5]

As Sanskrit, alongside classical Greek and Latin, came to be an essential component of philological education in Europe in the nineteenth century, Indian literature in this part of Europe too became associated with ancient Indian texts. The first direct translations from Sanskrit were undertaken by the Croatian Petar Budmani (1835–1914) and the Slovene Karol Glaser (1845–1913), who each translated a selection of Sanskrit tales and dramas, including Kalidasa's *Shakuntala*, into Serbo-Croatian and Slovenian respectively.

The acquaintance with Indian philosophy, Vedanta and Buddhist thought first came through German scholarship, and first reached those parts of former Yugoslavia that were under the Austro-Hungarian Empire. India was seen as a land of profound wisdom, albeit still tinged with exoticism. The Ottoman Empire, on the other hand, left a legacy of another version of 'the Orient'. In 1955, Svetozar Petrović was still able to write that Yugoslav Orientalist studies were limited almost entirely to the study of Arabic, Persian and Turkish languages and literatures.[6] Indology as a scholarly discipline came late in the day, the first academic institute established in the 1960s at the University of Zagreb. To this day Zagreb is the only capital in the former Yugoslavia to systematically offer courses on Indian languages and cultures.[7]

As the first modern Indian author to be read in this part of the world, Tagore in the former Yugoslavia soon became one of the most widely translated foreign authors of the time. His reputation went through different phases and his works met with various responses in different parts of the former Yugoslavia. Overall, his fame seems to rest secured, as old and new translations are being published and reprinted to this day, and his poetry and novels are being taught at secondary school and university levels, increasingly associated with world and post-colonial literatures.

First Encounters

The initial response in the former Yugoslavia to Tagore's unexpected Nobel Prize was shaped largely by considerations other than the poet's literary merit. As elsewhere across Europe, the deeply meditative poems of *Gitanjali* were readily imbibed as the book of the soul and its author seen as a prophet and mystic from the East. The full translation of the Nobel-winning collection of poetry first came out serially in 1914 in a Zagreb daily (*Jutranji list*) and published in book form a year later.[8] Christian intellectuals of the day were keen to assimilate Tagore's perceived mysticism into their own strivings to reject the world of materialism and secularism.[9] Yeats's famous 'Introduction' to the English *Gitanjali*, which launched some of the more persistent misconceptions about the Indian poet, found its way into the earliest writings on Tagore also in the former Yugoslavia. For example, in Slovenia, one of the first articles to be written on Tagore was almost entirely based on Yeats's laudatory piece.[10]

For the Slavic peoples who were most exposed to the Germanisation pressures under the Hapsburg rule, Tagore's winning the Nobel Prize became a matter of preference over the Austrian poet Peter Rosegger (1843–1918). Certainly the Slovenes resented Rosegger for his associations with the nationalist organisation Südmark Schulverein that aided German-language schools in ethnically Slovene or mixed territories in Southern Carinthia and Southern Styria. Similarly, Croatians sympathised with Tagore rather than his unpopular rival.[11] The sentiments that Austria was an absolutist state in a constitutional form were also widely held amongst the Croatian intellectuals of the day.[12]

The old Slavic–Germanic animosity transposed itself into a literary duel that was waged in the daily press across Central and East-Central part of Europe. One of the first substantial articles to come out on Tagore in 1914 in the Slovenian press was tellingly titled 'Last year's rivals for the Nobel Prize.' Described as 'a spiritual giant of enormous horizons,' Tagore is contrasted with Peter Rosegger, a parochial writer fanning 'the flames of nationalist hatred'; thus Tagore's expansive love of humanity came to be hailed in contrast to Rosegger's narrow love of nation. His patriotic songs are described as perfect expressions of 'his universalism.'[13] The article, in its adulatory strain, goes on to describe 'a patriot' whose voice is tuned to the deepest harmonies of humanity, refusing to surrender the task of his country's liberation from under foreign rule to a nationalist agenda. Tagore's anti-nationalist message and his alternative model of anti-colonial struggle would become relevant once again in the context of the post-War border realignments, as Italy came to rule over parts of Slovene and Croat-populated territories and enforced Italianisation became the order of the day.

Publishing History, Performances and Translations

Apart from a few translations of individual poems, often appearing anonymously in the press within months of Tagore's winning the Nobel Prize, the 1914 edition of *Gitanjali* published from Zagreb, first serially and then as a book, marks the first substantial effort to present Tagore to a new Croatian readership and wider Yugoslav audiences.[14] The translator was a young student of philosophy Pavao Vuk-Pavlović (1894–1967). He also translated Tagore's poetic drama *Chitra* (most probably from German),[15] which was staged at Croatia's National Theatre in Zagreb in October 1915. This may have been the earliest staging of *Chitra* in Europe. The production also marks a joint effort of young searching minds starting out in their careers; thus, the task of directing *Chitra* was given to an as yet entirely unknown twenty-year-old Croatian by the name of Alfons Verli (best known for his staging of Krleža and Shakespeare in the 1930s), who was educated in Berlin and Leipzig. With established actors playing the parts, and the music written by another freshman in his early twenties who was to become a leading Croatian composer, Krešimir Baranović (1894–1975), *Chitra* put Tagore on the map as it was 'warmly welcomed by the critics and filling the house for three nights in ten days.'[16] In the words of one critic, 'This was theatre's victory over all those sceptics who think it impossible that true, profound poetry can find embodiment in a mimetic form.'[17]

There were indeed some sceptics who did not share the enthusiasm over the newly-discovered Indian author. Miroslav Krleža (1893–1981), considered one of the finest Croatian writers of the twentieth century, struggled to relate to Tagore. As he noted in his diary some three weeks after the premiere:

It's getting to me. Rabin-Dranath-Tagore. Alfons Verli. Directing
'Chitra'. ... For all the ecstatic appreciation of the Upanishads and
Rigveda, Tagore, while conjuring up a suggestive picture of the East,
of India, Asia, the Ganges and Buddha, in what makes for a heady,
melodious read, then crosses over into a pseudo-lyrical monotony
that becomes bothersome like tropical rain, and then starts to irk and
it irks more and more. What sort of a lesson is this? For snobs? Or is it
that I don't get it at all?[18]

Arising out of a stock set of perceptions on the one hand and a lack of
context on the other, this kind of misgivings about the intentions of Tagore
were not uncommon amongst the literati of the time. But Verli's enthusiasm
for Tagore survived the war, and just before settling down once again in
Berlin, he stopped in Prague in 1921 to hear Tagore speak.

The earliest translations of Tagore into Serbo-Croatian were generally
not done by writers or poets.[19] This was different from the start in Slovenia.
Soon after the poet Župančič brought out his short piece on Tagore largely
based on Yeats, he published a few translations of Tagore's poems in the
journal *Literarna pratika*. The short-story writer France Bevk (1890–1970)
translated a selection of Tagore's short stories from the German publication
Die Erzählungen, and poet Miran Jarc (1900–42), rendered *Chitra* into
Slovene. The play was staged in the Ljubljana City Theatre in 1953, to be
followed in 1958 by *The Post Office*, translated by another major poet Jože
Udović (1912–86). But the greatest credit for giving Tagore a permanent
place within the Slovenian world of letters goes to the noted poet Alojz
Gradnik (1882–1967). The personal enthusiasm and taste of translators
cannot be overemphasised in this respect. By his own admission, Gradnik
was so taken by what he read as he chanced upon a copy of *The Crescent
Moon* in a bookshop in Trieste during the war that he decided to introduce
as much of Tagore's poetry as was then available in English to Slovenian
readership:

How I grew to love this wonderful Indian is evident from the fact that
I transposed five of his books into Slovene. All these translations were
motivated by my wish that Slovenes too get to know this wonderful
poet, philosopher and apostle of peace and brotherhood between
nations.[20]

Tagore's first poetry collection to come out in Slovene was not the
Nobel-winning *Gitanjali*, but the volume of Gradnik's personal choice, *The
Crescent Moon* (1917),[21] to be sold out within months and republished in
1921. One after another the following collections were to appear: *Stray Birds*

(1921), *The Gardener* (1922), *Fruit-Gathering* (1922) and finally *Gitanjali: Song Offerings* (1924). If it were not for Gradnik's personal commitment, it remains doubtful whether so much of Tagore's poetry would have been translated into Slovene. *The Crescent Moon* and *Fruit-Gathering*, for example, did not make it into Serbian or Croatian until very recently.[22]

Gradnik's translations closely followed the Macmillan text of Tagore's own English reworkings.[23] They strove to be faithful renditions of Tagore's rhythmic English prose. Luckily, the adopted forms of 'thou' and 'thee,' which gave the English poems an antiquated air, alien both to the original Bengali and contemporary poetry being written in English, were lost in Slovene (and Serbo-Croatian) translation, since, as in Bengali, their grammatical equivalents do not sound archaic in these languages. Still, Gradnik's translations were full of archaisms and inversions, in line with the pervasive biblical style through which Tagore's poetry was domesticated in Europe, and which made Tagore seem less a contemporary and more of a poet from a bygone era. Gradnik may have realised this when he came to revise his own translations in the late 1950s, dispensing entirely with old-fashioned vocabulary and antiquated inversions. Similarly, in Croatia, *Gitanjali* was retranslated in a more contemporary idiom by the poet, writer and translator, as well as a great Indophile, Vesna Krmpotić in the 1980s.[24] Recently, another sensitive translation of *Gitanjali* came out in Croatia. In fact, between 2005 and 2008, Robert Mandić, who runs a small publishing house in Split, translated and brought out six of Tagore's works, some of which saw the light of day for the first time across former Yugoslavia.[25]

Interestingly, the one feature of the early translations which seems to have had a stylistic impact on the poets of the 1920s is the fact that these translations came in the guise of prose poetry. Tagore himself noted that the reason for the popularity of his English *Gitanjali* with the English poets was their prose reincarnation at a time when the prose-poem in Europe was growing in popularity. The poets in Europe, Tagore felt, were ready to accept his translations 'as part of their own literature.'[26] In Slovenia, Srečko Kosovel (1904–26)—the foremost avant-garde voice in the interwar period, who looked to the Indian poet for intellectual and aesthetic nourishment—was indeed ready to receive his prose renditions of what in the original Bengali was formally intricate verse. Part of Kosovel's poetic experimentation involved a shift to free verse, which also led him to the prose poem. Other literary antecedents notwithstanding, some of Kosovel's lyrical prose pieces carry an undeniable Tagorean imprint.[27]

In contrast, Janko Moder's Slovene translation of *Song Offerings* from 1973, in what is presumably an attempt to bring these poems closer to the Bengali original, sets out the poems in regular stanzas rather than short prose paragraphs. These translations arc being republished in recent editions in Slovenia.[28] But the penchant for the genre of an unrhymed rhythmical prose has survived and is reflected in the recent addition to Tagore's poetry opus in Slovene translation—his short sketches *Lipika*.[29]

With Tagore's works in the so-called Serbo-Croatian, we must note the following: practically there was never just one translation of Tagore's most popular works, but invariably a book would be taken up for translation separately in Serbia, Croatia, as well as in Bosnia and Herzegovina. For example, *The Gardener* came out in 1923 in two translations of what was officially one language: Iso Velikanović's translation was published in Zagreb, and David S. Pijade's in Belgrade. Similarly, Tagore's most popular novel in the Yugoslav 1920s, *The Home and the World*, saw three different translations between 1922 and 1926 (the 1923 Belgrade translation was done, unusually, from French by Petar St Bešević, while the Croatian and Bosnian variants were based on the English version). When the novel *The Wreck* became the order of the day with the Yugoslav readership, it also came out in three different translations within a span of ten years, first in Belgrade, then Zagreb and finally in Sarajevo.

Clearly there was a strongly-felt need amongst the separate peoples of former Yugoslavia, even in the early Yugoslav days, to have their own specific translations of Tagore. This is rich and as yet uncharted territory for translation studies, which could reveal a variety of translation strategies that take the differences between existing translations beyond the more obvious aspects of lexicography, syntax and idiom that differentiate Croatian, Serbian and Bosnian languages, even as these languages remain, to this day, mutually intelligible and, as some would argue, are one and the same language.

INTELLECTUAL ENGAGEMENT WITH TAGORE IN THE 1920s

The second, most significant, wave of Tagore's popularity in former Yugoslavia came after World War I, gaining momentum around 1921 and further bolstered by Tagore's visit to Zagreb and Belgrade in 1926. In this five-year period, more than ten books of Tagore's writings were translated—that is almost a third of the entire production between 1913 and 1961.[30] Poetry and drama were now supplemented by prose writings (short stories, the novels *The Home and the World*, and *The Wreck,* and his essays on *Nationalism*). The pendulum of advocacy for his work swung from Christian critics, who now dismissed him as a pseudo-mystic, to intellectuals of a more liberal persuasion. The latter primarily claimed Tagore as a spiritual leader of a new civilisation that should supplant the doomed civilisation of the West. They regarded themselves as proponents of a new humanism, and for them Tagore could offer a more holistic paradigm than the old dualistic way of thinking. Tagore's religiosity got reconfigured from supposedly close affinities with a particular faith tradition to a looser association with a more general state of being, bringing it closer to his own non-sectarian endorsement of religion as an essentially humanist enterprise.[31]

The sense of doom and spiritual bankruptcy following the events of World War I in many ways set the stage for Tagore's impact on the minds of men and women of letters in the 1920s. The West was once again in need of spiritual resuscitation from the East. Srečko Kosovel captures the moment well when in a poem he writes of 'a tired European' gazing into 'a golden evening', from where hope and regeneration were to come.[32] The colour gold is a direct allusion to Tagore, from whom he borrowed the title for his first intended collection of poetry, *The Golden Boat*.[33]

Besides World War I, the other key event that was crucial in eliciting a response from intellectuals across Yugoslavia and elsewhere in Europe was the October Revolution of 1917. As the colonial era came face to face with the age of the proletariat, the anti-imperialist struggle was increasingly seen as an extension of the anti-capitalist one. Sympathies for the worker extended to the sympathies for the colonised, both seen to be at the receiving end of rapacious capitalism. For the first time in Europe a more prominent culture of anti-hegemonism emerged and questioned, more radically, Europe's role in global politics.[34] Many leftist intellectuals responded to the civilisational crisis in anti-bourgeois and anti-capitalist terms and saw in the Bolshevik revolution a realistic hope (however short-lasting) for the ideal of a new classless society. Tagore for them was now a prominent Eastern anti-imperialist voice who also spoke up for the downtrodden worker. With this the Indian poet got delinked from some of the earlier Orientalist associations propagated by Yeats. He was no longer a voice representing ancient India, but rather a contemporary, who addressed issues of global concern, spanning nationalism, scientific and technological revolutions, environmentalism, and feminism alike.

The most sympathetic readers of Tagore from this part of Europe seemed to be those who identified with the Indian poet and his anti-imperialist struggle from their own position of being dominated by a foreign power after the War.[35] Illustrative of this type of response which stemmed from a sense of commonality and joint purpose with the Indian poet is yet again that of Srečko Kosovel, who came from a region that was allocated to Italy in the post-War era. When Kosovel turned towards the 'East' in the spirit of hope and identification, he turned as much towards the promises of socialism as he did towards the ideals of an alternative liberation struggle represented by Tagore's anti-nationalist sentiments and Gandhi's call for non-violence.[36] It is not surprising then to see that 'the most important work of Tagore for the Yugoslav twenties,' as Petrović noted, was his book of essays on *Nationalism* (1917, first published in Croatian translation in 1921), with its uncompromising attack on the creed of nationalism and patriotism the world over. Tagore's novel *The Home and the World*, which became popular at the same time, was often read as no more than a literary corollary to the ideas advanced in *Nationalism*.[37]

In poetry, *Gitanjali* was now superseded in popularity by the more secular love lyrics of *The Gardener*. In Serbia, the excellent translation of Pijade went into countless reprints after its first publication in 1923, far more than anywhere else in Yugoslavia. On occasion, the print runs reached 50,000 copies.[38] The popularity of this particular collection, the reasons for which would require a separate study, has survived down to the present: since the new millennium, it has been republished over thirty times with some twenty-three publishers across the country.[39]

It may be true that in the 1920s Tagore's political ideas took precedence over his work as a poet in former Yugoslavia, but we should perhaps not underestimate the impact of his poetry on the creative expression of the avant-garde poets and artists of the day. This is an area that needs further research, and I would not wish to suggest any straightforward link between the European or Yugoslav avant-garde and the Indian poet. Yeats and Pound, as we know, lost their interest in Tagore precisely because they did not see him to be modernist enough. Within the Yugoslav cultural milieu, the Belgrade avant-garde circle spearheaded by the controversial figure of Ljubomir Micić and founder of Zenitism strongly objected to the Indian poet's visit to Yugoslavia in November 1926 on the grounds that he was a fake portender of a new civilisation.[40]

Tagore's Visit and its Aftermath

If Tagore's reputation in the Yugoslav twenties was confined largely to the rather exclusive circle of academics, artists and intellectuals, it became more of a mass popular response once Tagore visited Zagreb and Belgrade in 1926. Recovering from severe exhaustion at the sanatorium at Lake Balaton in Hungary on what was his fifth and longest European tour, Tagore wrote in a letter to Leonard Elmhirst:

> Doctors advise me to take the shorter eastern route to India through Yugoslavia, Serbia [*sic*], Constantinople, Greece and Egypt. The prescription is very much like the French wine ordered for me in Milan; it is tempting. The people in this eastern corner of Europe are perfectly charming—their personality unshrouded by the grey

monotony of a uniform civilization that has overspread the western world. It is mixed with something primitive and therefore is fresh and vital and warmly human.[41]

His return journey to India thus took him on a whistle-stop tour of the Balkans. Between 13 and 17 November, he spent two days in Zagreb and two in Belgrade, before proceeding to Bulgaria, Romania, Greece and Egypt, and finally returning to India. The four days in Yugoslavia were jam-packed with the obligations any celebrity has to face: receptions and parties in his honour, attending meals with dignitaries, giving interviews and, lectures in auditoria filled to the last seat. The media played a key role in turning his visit into a sensation, and Tagore's every step, his appearance, meeting and spoken word were recorded minutely by the press of the day.[42]

Tagore arrived in Zagreb on the Saturday morning of 13 November by the overnight train from Budapest to be warmly welcomed on the platform by 'many ladies,' as one newspaper related the events, alongside his main host Hinko Hinković, a one-time politician turned president of the local Theosophical society, and other representatives of various associations.[43] In the evening, he lectured to a packed hall of the Zagreb Musical Conservatory. According to one report, his talk was on 'Europe, the conflicts and troubles plaguing Western nations,' with a clear message 'to seek happiness not on the path of empty intellectualism, economy, technology, politics and national hatred, but on that of contemplation, artistic imagination, wisdom, love, faith and self-sacrifice.'[44] The lecture was followed by a recital from *The Gardener* in the original Bengali. The event was a major success and Tagore was asked impromptu to speak again the next morning for a different crowd.

Tagore left Zagreb for Belgrade on the 14 November and was again met on his arrival by a welcoming crowd, greeting him with '*Živeo!*' (Long live!). His visit was well prepared for. The Zagreb interview, in which he spoke candidly on Fascism and Bolshevism, recognising the former's threat to parts of Yugoslavia, was duly reproduced in one of the major Belgrade dailies *Politika* the day before his arrival. In this interview, Tagore also condemned colonialism and spoke of the difficulty of European and Eastern civilisations coming harmoniously together unless Europe overcame her drive to conquer and dominate new markets so as to satisfy her greed for luxury.[45] Earlier in the month, a prominent literary journal published nine of Tagore's poems in a new translation.[46] Essays and lectures on the social realities of India and Tagore's work as a poet and philosopher were not long in coming.[47]

Allegedly 'the whole of Belgrade', ordinary workers as much as scholars, came to his first lecture on contemporary civilisation and the meaning of progress at the main University hall in Belgrade.[48] The following day was taken up by a round of press meetings, a visit to the museum to see the collection of national crafts (he was gifted an eighteenth-century gold-embroidered traditional costume from Kosovo),[49] a tea party at the local YMCA, ending with another lecture in the evening, this time on the meaning of art and at a reduced price.

For the most part, Tagore's visit was a success, but not everyone was impressed with the poet speaking against crude materialism and greed of Western civilisation and the stiff entry-fees charged for his lectures. The sentiments of disenchantment were forcefully expressed by a group of the Belgrade avant-garde at the first of his lectures. They denigrated the poet's presence by shouts of 'Down with Tagore! Long Live Gandhi!' and threw pamphlets in the air with an open letter addressed to Tagore in Serbian and English translation. Signed by poets Ljubomir Micić and Branko ve Poljanski, the letter protested against Tagore's perceived pro-Western and bourgeois stance in India's independence struggle, as opposed to the grass-roots Gandhian approach. The dichotomous view probably owed something to Rolland's book on Mahatma Gandhi.[50] Couched in a discourse of conceit and self-pity, the letter was vitriolic:

> Your verses are lemonade, your philosophy dung, your mysticism, like all mysticism is—mystification. ... We speak truth and only in the name of truth declare ourselves publicly against you today ... the best sons of this country of the Balkans are strangers in their own land...[51]

In the eyes of these self-proclaimed 'barbarians', whose notion of a 'Barbarogenius' (a Balkan adaptation of Nietzsche's *Übermensch*) was invented as the Balkans' antidote to a spiritually depleted (Western) Europe, Tagore was but a fake trader of 'empty phrases.' Such fundamental mistrust may have had something to do with the unfortunate circumstances of Tagore's 1926 tour. There was Tagore's contentious earlier meeting with Mussolini, which was reported again in the media on the eve of Tagore's arrival. The fact that parts of his tour were orchestrated by dictatorial regimes made his political leanings suspect, and the commerciality surrounding his visit with high entry fees jarred with the content of his addresses. One newspaper condemned the outburst as a 'scandal,' and the disruption was apparently swiftly brought under control, so that Tagore, visibly disturbed, was able to begin his lecture.[52] It is unknown how this affected Tagore.[53]

Overall, Tagore's visit in 1926 greatly increased his popularity in Yugoslavia, particularly amongst the general reading public. Articles continued being written on him weeks after his departure, and a more concerted effort was made to try and locate him within the wider Indian context and understand his multifaceted personality. Tagore was also appreciated as a defender of women's rights and one who understood women's creative needs.[54] Jelena Dimitrijević (1862–1945) a remarkable writer and traveller, considered one of the earliest Serbian feminists, felt impelled to go to India just to see Tagore in his home environment so as to appreciate his work more fully. Her *Letters from India* presents an engaging account of her arduous journey via Bombay (now Mumbai) to Calcutta (Kolkata) and finally Santiniketan, where Tagore, suffering from malaria, could only see her for a few minutes. She could not conceal her disappointment, a sense of wounded national pride even, that Tagore had nothing to say about his visit to Serbia only two years earlier.[55] Another Tagore enthusiast wrote a booklet of twenty-eight pages—in translation titled *Rabindranath Tagore as Poet and Philosopher* (1936)—relating Tagore's background and influences, and outlining his main ideas through poetry and philosophy.[56] But perhaps the most original engagement with Tagore at the time came with the essays of a major Croatian poet Tin Ujević (1891–1955). Ujević's essays on Eastern religions and cultures, published in major periodicals and running into hundreds of pages, include well-informed, independent-minded essays on Tagore, Bengali literature and Tagore's educational efforts in Santiniketan. For the most part they resist Orientalist platitudes, arguing instead for a less Eurocentric appreciation of Tagore's creative writing that needed to be seen in the context of a long history of Bengali letters.[57] Ujević also questioned the constant need to trace in Tagore's writings European influences, suggesting we might instead look for traces of ancient Indian philosophy in the 'versified pantheism of Byron and Shelley.'[58]

POST-WORLD WAR II RESPONSES: ENTERING THE SCHOOL CURRICULA AND SCHOLARLY ENGAGEMENT

Even before World War II, India's struggle for independence was one of the major news items in the former Yugoslavia, and progressive Yugoslavs had always sympathised with it.[59] In this regard, Gandhi's popularity as a key figure in India's resistance against the British cannot be overstated. By implication, Tagore could be seen as too Westernised or not anti-British enough. When India became independent, Tito was the first foreign head of state to visit the country. The Non-Aligned Movement (NAM) was the brainchild of Nehru, Tito and Egypt's Nasser, with support from Indonesia's Sukarno and Ghana's Nkrumah, and the first NAM summit was held in Belgrade in 1961. With Yugoslavia becoming part of the global South, close ties were forged with non-European cultures also through direct contact via student exchange programmes and economic and cultural collaborations.

Following a lull in the 1930s–40s, Tagore's reputation was about to enter its third important phase. His writings were introduced in primary and secondary school curricula across Yugoslavia. With his reputation, Tagore was clearly the most obvious and representative voice of modern Indian poetry,[60] making him a part of the learning experience for young people. He was, and still is, widely known amongst the general reading public.

This was also the period when his works went into new editions, now for the first time with serious, scholarly introductions.[61] His poetry was now printed also in selected volumes, and the range of his essays to appear in translation expanded, though *Sadhana* and *The Religion of Man*, for example, had to wait some decades before appearing in Serbo-Croatian and Slovene translations for the first time. *Personality* was translated into Croatian only a few years ago by Robert Mandić. To mark the centenary of his birth in 1961, a volume of Tagore's essays entitled *Towards Universal Man* was brought out in Serbia the same year as it was published by Asia Publishing House in London.[62] In Slovenia, a new translation of the *Gitanjali* together with the first translation of *Gora* came out in the prestigious Nobel Prize Winner series in 1973. Tagore's name also became a standard entry in anthologies, encyclopaedias and compendiums of world literature.[63] A genuine wish to understand more about the world brought much closer through recent political events was now being satisfied for the first time by translations of other Indian writers, notably Mulk Raj Anand, Bhabani Bhattacharya, Kamala Markandaya, R. K. Narayan, and Premchand (translated from Hindi and Russian). Nonetheless, Tagore was still at the top of the list, this time with his novel *The Wreck*. In a big public library in Zagreb in 1959 and 1960, he was one of the most frequently read modern-day writers.[64] As two of his plays were taken up by the Ljubljana City Theatre in the late fifties, Tagore's work as a playwright was discussed in depth for the first time.[65]

The year 1981 presented another anniversary occasion to celebrate the Indian poet, with writers, translators and artists responding once again to Tagore's work. The Croatian Writers Union organised a round-table discussion on Tagore at which poet Dragutin Tadijanović (1905–2007) read out a poem he wrote in remembrance of hearing Tagore speak back in 1926, and the composer Bruno Bjelinski (1909–92) played his compositions inspired by a few *Gitanjali* poems. There was a screening of Satyajit Ray's documentary on Tagore, and, probably for the first time in Yugoslavia, a small exhibition of Tagore's paintings was put on display.[66] This was also the occasion for which the Indologist Klara Gonc Moačanin wrote a perceptive appreciation of Tagore's life and work for a wider readership, after which she published two more scholarly papers, one in defence of Tagore's novels largely misunderstood in the West, and another on Tagore's poetry. These were reprinted in her book *Sahrdaya; književno putovanje sa srcem u Indiju* (Zagreb, 1996). Tagore found sympathetic and knowledgeable critics in a number of other scholars throughout the 1980s and 1990s. A substantial volume entitled *Tagore and the World* came out in 1982 in Zrenjanin (Serbia), featuring all of the established Yugoslav scholars who had written on Tagore before the eighties (Petrović, Krmpotić, Sekulić, Ujević), alongside a few first-time contributions.

It was prescient that in 1990, with Yugoslavia on the brink of collapse, *Nationalism* was republished in Serbia in 2,000 copies, and reprinted in 1992. But just as Tagore's anti-nationalist message went unheeded in his day, so it fell on deaf ears at the end of the twentieth century. The years of war that followed did not stop new publications and reprints coming out across the country.[67]

The academic and specialist interest in Tagore gathered momentum once again around the occasion of the poet's 150th birth anniversary. For the first time, a truly international angle was brought to bear on Tagore scholarship across the region. International conferences on Tagore were held in Ljubljana, Zagreb and Zrenjanin, hosting Tagore specialists and South Asian scholars from the world over. *Tagore Days in Ljubljana* combined an international conference on Tagore's legacy for today's world with the launch of the first substantial volume of Tagore's short stories in Slovene translation and an evening of poetry reading.

The 'Days of Indian Culture in Croatia' in May 2011 offered a rich programme of exhibitions (including one of Tagore's paintings), workshops, poetry readings, a few classics of the Bengali cinema and lectures by eminent Croatian and foreign scholars. William Radice spoke to the Croatian parliament in Zagreb. Besides the Croatian capital, parts of the programme were also held in Rijeka and Split.

In Serbia, the philosophy teacher Aleksandra Maksić was the primary force behind the 'Days of Indian Culture and Philosophy,' which hosted an international conference on 'Contemporizing Tagore and the World,' with Dipannita Datta giving the keynote address.

CONCLUSION AND OUTLOOK

Ideally, Tagore's creative writings should be translated from the original Bengali. This has not happened in any of the countries that made up former Yugoslavia, and the short-term prospect of direct translations from Bengali seems unrealistic, since the only modern Indian language to be taught in the region is Hindi. Robert Mandić, Tagore's Croatian translator, has noted a marked decrease even in translations from Sanskrit over recent decades.

According to him, the emergence of new sovereign states has also weakened the potential for such enterprises, and globalisation and the Internet culture are more detrimental still. Nonetheless, Mandić makes an important point that motivated his own translations of Tagore into Croatian: Tagore's authorial English translations, even if a distance from the original, are no mere translations; rather they offer 'a different perspective of a poet on his own work,' and are in that sense originals in their own right. This is 'poetry in prose of great lyrical charge and profound thought' which deserves to be brought closer to the Croatian readership in a new contemporary idiom.[68] This is no doubt a viable translation strategy, as dated translations need to be supplemented by new ones. Another possibility, especially in view of the necessity of expanding Tagore's Yugoslav opus, is to take the excellent new English translations and use these as the closest we can so far get to the original. I have adopted this strategy in translating a few of Tagore's poems from Radice's and Ketaki Kushari Dyson's translations, and in selecting the short stories for the Slovenian short prose publication. The same strategy was adopted when Tagore's play *The Post Office* was staged in Sarajevo in 2002. The organisers based their translation on William Radice's recent English translation as opposed to the old Macmillan one (i.e., Tagore's English translation).

Although known for almost a century, Tagore has been presented as a figure of world literature across Yugoslavia especially from the 1960s onwards. He is indisputably seen as one of the foremost modern lyricists. It remains questionable, however, how much of Tagore's literary imagination gets conveyed to the young Internet generations, who appear to be unmoved by Tagore's emblematic *Gitanjali*.[69] Perhaps it is time for us to jettison the paramount status of *Gitanjali* in relation to Tagore, and aim towards understanding and presenting him in a wider cross-genre perspective, for which the seeds have already been planted. This is a task for translators, scholars, and publishers alike. Only when the false aura of mysticism that still all too often clings to the Indian poet in this part of the world is discarded will Tagore shine through as our contemporary and as a major post-colonial voice, both in thought and creative imagination.

Notes

1. This essay is not a comprehensive account and analysis of the complex story of Tagore's reception in former Yugoslavia. I am limiting myself to Slovene and Serbo-Croatian sources, the dominant languages of former Yugoslavia. Therefore, when I speak of Tagore's reception in former Yugoslavia, my research is based primarily on the sources from present-day Slovenia, Croatia, Serbia, and Bosnia and Herzegovina. I regret not being able to comment on

the Macedonian reception of Tagore and for saying nothing about Tagore in Montenegro or by the Kosovo Albanians, as well as too little on Tagore in Bosnia and Herzegovina.

2. For more on *Yugoslavism* (the idea of Yugoslavia), see Rusinow, 'The Yugoslav Idea before Yugoslavia.'

3. Šmitek, *Southern Slavs and India*. Subsequent account relies on Petrović, 'Jugoslaveni i Indija' and Slamnig, 'India and the Yugoslavs.'

4. Petrović, 'Jugoslaveni i Indija,' 384.

5. Šmitek, *Southern Slavs and India*, 75–92.

6. Petrović, 'Jugoslaveni i Indija,' 398.

7. All prior academic Indological research was done elsewhere in Europe and published in German and English.

8. Serbia followed suit in 1921 and Slovenia in 1924.

9. An enthusiastic piece titled 'Mistika' ('Mysticism') came out in the newly launched Croatian Catholic monthly *Hrvatska prosvjeta* in 1914. Tagore is hailed as a 'poet of God's love' who has 'taught us Catholics a deserved lesson' in that 'mysticism belongs to us though it need not be Christian in its essence.' Cited in Petrović, 'Tagore in Yugoslavia,' 7.

10. Župančič, 'Rabindranath Tagore,' 31–2. Excerpts of it are paraphrased in another article, Lokar, 'Lanska tekmeca za Noblovo književno nagrado,' 242–7. Whole sections are cited also in the preface to the first Slovene edition of Gradnik, *Gitanjali*, Preface, iii–iv.

11. See Moačanin, 'Reception of Tagore's Work in Croatia,' 72.

12. See, for example, Ujevič, 'Revolver u parlamentu', 40–1.

13. Lokar, 'Lanska tekmeca za Noblovo književno nagr,' 246. Translation by this writer.

14. An anonymously translated poem from *Gitanjali* appeared in the journal *Slovenec* at the end of November 1913.

15. Moačanin, 'Pavao Vuk-Pavlović i Rabindranath Tagore.' Pavlović translated two other Tagore plays, *Malini* and *The King of the Dark Chamber* (*Raja*) but unlike *Chitra* they remained unpublished. See Moačanin, 'Reception of Tagore's Work in Croatia,' 72.

16. Petrović, 'Tagore in Yugoslavia,' 5.

17. The critic is Branko Gaella, cited in Batušić, 'Prve Režije Alfonsa Verlija,' 205.

18. Cited in Batušić, 'Prve režije Alfonsa Verlija,' 205. Translation by this writer .

19. The formation of Yugoslavia spelt a demand for a unified standard. Serbo-Croatian became the official language from 1918 to 1991. The separate ethnic groups would refer to it as 'Croatian', 'Bosnian', 'Serbian', or 'Montenegrin' without really implying a different language. All four standards are based on the same dialect and are mutually intelligible. After the dissolution of Yugoslavia along ethnic and linguistic lines, the use of the term 'Serbo-Croatian' has, however, become controversial.

20. Cited in Rudolf, Foreword to *Spevi* by Rabindranath Tagore, 83–4. Similarly, in the one-page preface to the first Croatian edition of *Gitanjali*, translator Vuk Pavlović writes in the first sentence: 'This translation is the outcome of immediate infatuation.'

21. The edition contains glossary of Indian terms and notes and four colour reprints of paintings by Nandalal Bose, Asit Kumar Haldar and Surendranath Ganguly.
22. In 2006, Robert Mandić, another Tagore enthusiast, took up the initiative and came out with the selected poems of Tagore entitled *Sakupljanje voća i još poneki plod* (*'Fruit-gathering and some other fruits'*; poems from *Stray Birds, The Crescent Moon*, and *Fruit-Gathering*), published by Paralele in Split (Croatia).
23. The same can be said for those done into Serbo-Croatian, or rather, Serbian and Croatian.
24. Published in 1981 by Prosvjeta, Zagreb. It is a pity that Krmpotič did not undertake the translations from the original Bengali having spent almost two years in India in 1962 as a student, studying also the Bengali language.
25. Besides *Gitanjali*, Mandić translated *Lover's Gift and Crossing, Fruit-Gathering and Other Fruits, The Religion of Man, Personality* and *Sadhana* in print runs of five hundred copies each, except for *Gitanjali*, which was printed in a thousand copies.
26. Tagore, 'The Prose Poem,' [1938], 333.
27. See Jelnikar, 'Towards Universalism,' 227.
28. Most recently in 2012 by Mladinska knjiga in Ljubljana.
29. Tagore, *Lipika*.
30. Komandić, *Tagore in Yugoslavia*, 1–16.
31. Petrović, 'Tagore in Yugoslavia,' 8–9.
32. Kosovel, 'Kons,' in *The Golden Boat*, 100.
33. The collection *Zlati čoln* never made it into print. Kosovel died before it was published, and the manuscript was lost. He must have known of Tagore's *Sonar Tari* as a collection in Bengali from the press coverage. Kosovel was an enthusiastic reader of Tagore, the most frequently mentioned foreign author in his collected works. He read him in Slovene, Croatian and German translations.
34. See Brennan, 'Postcolonial Studies between the European Wars,' 191.
35. Imre Bangha has noted something similar in relationship to Hungary; see Bangha, *Hungry Tiger*, 14. I have found it useful to call this model of reception 'situational identification' (borrowing the term from Patrick Colm Hogan), where sympathies are forged between individuals and inspirations derived from a sense of shared predicaments. I related this specifically to Kosovel's reading of Tagore, but also to some other responses from within Europe. See Jelnikar, 'Turning "East,"' 165–78.
36. See Jelnikar, 'Srečko Kosovel and Rabindranath Tagore,' 79–95.
37. Petrović, 'Tagore in Yugoslavia,' 9.
38. Tagore, *Gradinar*. The blurb relates something of an infatuation: '*The Gardener* is one of the best of Tagore's poetry books. This is a book of love—towards woman, earth, towards man and the world in general.'
39. In contrast, in Slovenia, since its first edition in 1922, the collection was republished only once, in 2009, with a small publisher and a print run of 250 copies.
40. The movement formed around the review *Zenit* (Zenith), a leading journal for the dissemination of new art and culture in the Kingdom of Serbs, Croats

and Slovenes. First launched in 1921 in Zagreb by Ljubomir Micić, then transferred to Belgrade in 1923, the journal produced forty-three issues before it was banned by the authorities in 1926 on the grounds of alleged Bolshevik propaganda. (The digital version of the review is available online through Narodna Biblioteka Srbska at http://www.digital.nbs.bg.ac.yu/novine/zenit/swf.php?lang=scr). It had a strong international orientation, publishing articles in French, German, Russian, Flemish, Hungarian, Italian, and Esperanto.

41.   Tagore, letter dated 7 November 1926, in Dutta and Robinson, *Selected Letters,* 339–40.

42.   To mention the main ones: *Obzor, Vjesnik, Jutro, Prosveta* from Croatia; and *Politika, Vreme, Pravda, Novosti* from Serbia; Slovene daily press also reported the events (*Jutro, Slovenec, Narodni dnevnik, Slovenski narod*).

43.   Borko, 'Rabindranath Tagore v Zagrebu,' 6.

44.   Ibid.

45.   Morović, 'Intervju s R. Tagorom,' 5.

46. Popović, tr. 'Rabindranath Tagore ,' 434–8.

47.   F. Mirski wrote a paper on Indian nationalism, published on 15 and 16 November in *Politika* (4 and 6 respectively), and Dr J. Stojanović was to lecture on Tagore in the Christian Society Hall at 6 p.m. on 15 November. It is not known whether Tagore was present at the lecture. Pejčić, 'Tagore u Beogradu,' 66.

48.   [Unknown author]: 'Beograđani oduševljeno pozdravili velikog indijskog pesnika: dva predavanja Rabindranatha Tagora' ('Belgraders greet great Indian poet with enthusiasm: two lectures by Rabindranath Tagore'), *Politika,* 17 November 1926, 6 (Cyrillic).

49.   [Unknown author]: 'Kosovski kostim kao dar g. Tagori' ['Kosovo costume as gift to Tagore'], *Vreme,* 17 November 1926, 4 (Cyrillic).

50.   Gandhi's attitudes to the Indian political struggle were influential amongst the opponents of monarchy in the old Yugoslavia. It is telling that the leader of the Croat Republican Peasant Party Stjepan Radić authored the introduction to the translation of Roman Rolland's book *Our Gandhi* in 1924. Slamnig, 'India and the Yugoslavs,' 6. Ironically, when Tagore was asked in an interview from the newspaper *Vreme* what lessons Serbia could take from contemporary India he said: 'India today sends forth a new light to the world, and that is Gandhi.'

51.   Micić and Ve Poljanski, 'Lettre Ouverte a Rabindranath Tagore,' 17–20.

52.   [Unknown author]: 'Škandal na predavanju Rabindranatha Tagore' [Scandal at the lecture of Rabindranath Tagore], *Vreme,* 17 November 1926, 5 (Cyrillic).

53.   The only letter in the Tagore archives sent from Belgrade makes no mention of the incident.

54.   See his interview in Belgrade on the subject of feminism, 'Mišljenje g. Tagore o feminizmu [Tagore's thinking on feminism],' *Politika,* 16 November 1926, 4 (Cyrillic).

55.   Dimitrijević, *Pisma iz Indije.*

56.   Aršič, *Tagora kao pesnik i filozof.*

57.   Ujević, *Sabrana dijela.*

58. Ibid., vol. 8, 63.
59. Radio Ljubljana, for example, broadcast a special programme devoted to covering India's struggle for independence.
60. In the National Library of Ljubljana, I had occasion to access the archives of old primary school textbooks from former Yugoslavia and was able to find examples of seventh grade and eighth grade primary school readers for literature and language for Slovenia, Croatia, Serbia and Bosnia which contained at least one poem in translation from Tagore. The same is most probably true of secondary school textbooks. For certain, he was included—and still is—in Slovenia and in Serbia (see Kos, et al., *Svetovna književnost*, 121–3; Stanisavljević *Prilozi nastavi književnosti*, 36–7.
61. See first-rate introductions by (i) Petrovič, introduction to *Dom i svijet* (*The Home and the World*), and (ii) Pacheiner-Klander, an Indologist and foremost Slovene translator from Sanskrit, to the same novel in Slovene translation.
62. Tagore, *Eseji*.
63. See Ježič and Krklec, eds., *Antologija svjetske lirike*; Žmegač et al., *Strani pisci*; Kos, Pirjevec and Mihelić, *Svetovna književnost*.
64. Petrović, 'Tagore in Yugoslavia,' footnote nos. 1, 22.
65. Kreft, 'Rabindranat Thakkur in indijsko gledališče.'
66. Moačanin, 'Reception of Tagore's Work in Croatia,' 74–5.
67. A new translation of *The Gardener* in 1994 in Croatia; first translation of *The Religion of Man* into Slovene (1994); at least three reprints of *The Gardener* and one of *Gitanjali* in Serbia.
68. Robert Mandić, email message to author, 3 July 2012.
69. I draw on Moačanin's experience of teaching *Gitanjali* at Zagreb University; 'Reception of Tagore's Work in Croatia,' 75.

Works Cited

Aršič, B. *Rabindranath Tagora kao pesnik i filozof* [Rabindranath Tagore as poet and philosopher]. Skoplje: [publisher unknown], 1936.

Bangha, Imre. *Hungry Tiger: Encounters between Hungarian and Bengali Literary Cultures.* New Delhi: Sahitya Akademi, 2008.

Batušić, Nikola. 'Prve Režije Alfonsa Verlija.' [First stagings of Alfons Verli]. *Dani Hvarskoga kazališta: Građa i rasprave o hrvatskoj književnosti i kazalištu*, 34, no. 1, 2008, 197–208.

Borko, Božidar. 'Rabindranath Tagore v Zagrebu. [Rabindranath Tagore in Zagreb]. *Jutro.* 7, no. 265, 17 November 1926.

Brennan, Timothy. 'Postcolonial Studies between the European Wars: An Intellectual History.' In *Marxism, Modernity and Postcolonial Studies*, edited by Crystal Bartolovich and Neil Lazarus. Cambridge: Cambridge University Press, 2002, 185–201.

Dimitrijević, Jelena. *Pisma iz Indije.* [Letters from India]. Belgrade: National University of Belgrade, 1928.

Dutta, Krishna, and Andrew Robinson, eds. *Selected Letters of Rabindranath Tagore*. Cambridge: Cambridge University Press, 2005.

Gradnik, Alojz. Preface to *Gitandžali (Žrtveni spevi)* by Rabindranath Tagore, translated by Alojz Gradnik, i-vi. Ljubljana, Učiteljska tiskarna: 1924.

Jelnikar, Ana. 'Towards Universalism: Rabindranath Tagore and Srečko Kosovel: A Joint Perspective in a Disjointed World.' PhD diss. School of Oriental and African Studies, University of London, 2009.

——. 'Srečko Kosovel and Rabindranath Tagore: Points of departure and identification.' *Asian and African Studies*, 14, no. 1, 2010, 79–95.

——. 'Turning "East": Orientalist Variations on Tagore from the "Eastern Corner of Europe,"' in *Rabindranath Tagore: A Timeless Mind*, edited by Amalendu Biswas et al. London: The Tagore Centre UK, 2011, 165–78

Ježič, Slavko, and Gustav Krklec, eds. *Antologija svjetske lirike*. [Anthology of world lyrics]. Zagreb: Kultura, 1956.

Komandić, S. M., ed. *Tagore in Yugoslavia: A Bibliography*. Belgrade: Union of Yugoslav Writers and Committee for Foreign Cultural Relations: 1961.

Kos, Janko, Dušan Pirjevec and Stane Mihelič. *Svetovna književnost; izbrana dela in odlomki*. [World literature; select works and excerpts]. Ljubljana: Mladinska knjiga, 1964.

Kos, Janko, Tomo Virk, and Gregor Kocijan Kos. *Svet književnosti 3*, [World of Literature 3]. Ljubljana: Založba Obzorja, 2002.

Kosovel, Srečko. *The Golden Boat*. Translated by Bert Pribac and David Brooks. Cambridge: Salt Publishers, 2008.

Kreft, Bratko. 'Rabindranat Thakkur in indijsko gledališče.' [Rabindranath Tagore and Indian theatre]. *Naši razgledi*, 30 June 1961.

Lokar, Janko. 'Lanska tekmeca za Noblovo književno nagrado' [Last Year's rivals for the Nobel Prize]. *Slovan*, vol. 12, no. 6, 1914, 242–7.

Micić, Ljubomir, and Branko Ve Poljanski. 'Lettre Ouverte a Rabindranath Tagore.' [Open Letter to Rabindranath Tagore]. *Zenit*, 6, no. 43, 1926, 17–20.

Moačanin, Gonc, Klara. 'Reception of Tagore's Work in Croatia.' *Asian and African Studies*, 14, no. 1, 2010, 71–8.

——. 'Pavao Vuk-Pavlović i Rabindranath Tagore' [Pavao Vuk-Pavlović and Rabindranath Tagore], in *Pavao Vuk-Pavlović život i djelo*, edited by Pave Barišić. Zagreb: HAZU-Institut za filozofiju, 2003, 99–105.

Morović, Olga. 'Intervju s R. Tagorom.' *Politika*, 14 November, 1926.

Pacheiner-Klander, Vlasta. Introduction to *Dom in svet [The Home and the World]*, translated by Vladimir Levstik. Ljubljana: Cankarjeva založba, 1977, 199–206.

Pejčić, Jovan. 'Rabindranath Tagore u Beogradu.' *Kulture Istoka* , 5, no. 15, 1988, 6–68.

Petrovič, Svetozar. Introduction to *Dom i svijet [The Home and the World]* by Rabindranath Tagore, translated by Mira Vodvarška. Sarajevo: Svjetlost, 1959, 5–15.

——. 'Jugoslaveni i Indija.' [Yugoslavs and India] *Republika*, 11, no. 1, 1955, 382–400.

——. 'Tagore in Yugoslavia.'*Indian Literature*, 13, no. 2, 1970, 5–29.

Popović, Branko, tr. 'Rabindranath Tagore: Devet Pesama.' [Rabindranath Tagore: Nine Poems] *Srpski književni glasnik*, 20, no. 6, 1926, 434–8.

Rudolf, Branko. Foreword to *Spevi* by Rabindranath Tagore, translated by Alojz Gradnik. Ljubljana: Mladinska knjiga, 1958, 83–92.

Rusinow, Dennison. 'The Yugoslav Idea before Yugoslavia,' in *Yugoslavism: Histories of a Failed Idea, 1918–92*, edited by Dejan Djokić. London: Hurst and Company, 2003, 11–26.

Slamnig, Ivan. 'India and the Yugoslavs: A Survey of the Cultural Links.' *The Indian Institute of World Culture*, Transaction No. 35, 1967. Accessed 7 July 2012. http://www.iiwcindia.org/transactions/transaction35.pdf.

Šmitek, Zmago, ed. *Southern Slavs and India: Relations in Oral Tradition.* Calcutta: Sampark, 2011.

Stanisavljević, Vukašin. *Prilozi nastavi književnosti.* [Select chapters in teaching literature], vol. 3. Beograd: Nauka, 1997.

Tagore, Rabindranth. *Eseji.* [Essays] Translated by Svetozar Brkić. Beograd: Nolit, 1961.

——. *Gradinar.* [The Gardener] Translated by David S. Pijade. 7th edition. Belgrade: BIGZ, 1985.

——. *Lipika.* Translated by Miriam Drev. Celje: Mohorjeva družba, 1998.

——. 'The Prose Poem,' in *Rabindranath Tagore: Selected Writings on Literature and Language,* edited by Sisir Kumar Das and Sukanta Chaudhuri. New Delhi: Oxford University Press, 2001, 331–4.

Ujević, Tin. 'Revolver u parlamentu' [Revolver in the parliament, 1912], in *Eseji, razprave, članci* Part 3, edited by Miroslav Vavpotić. Zagreb: Znanje, 1963, 37–49.

——. *Sabrana dijela.* [Collected Works] vol. 8, 60–4, and 191–7; vol. 11, 176–83. Zagreb: Znanje, 1965.

Žmegač, Viktor, Franco Čale, Aleksander Flaker, Vladimir Vratović and Mate Zorić, eds. *Strani pisci: Književni leksikon.* [Foreign writers: Lexicon of Literature] Zagreb: Školska knjiga, 1961.

Župančič, Oton. 'Rabindranath Tagore.' *Slovan*, 12, no. 6, 1914, 31–2.

17

LATVIA

VIKTORS IVBULIS

The award of the Nobel Prize for Literature to Rabindranath Tagore in 1913 was an event of far-reaching international literary and political significance. It honoured not only Tagore's poetic power and love of man but also the Indian literary tradition he represented. Indeed, he became the spiritual ambassador of India to the whole world and certainly also to Latvia. Although he did not visit Latvia in person, the motherland of this writer welcomed translations of his works with extraordinary warmth.

The Latvian reception of Tagore can be divided into several periods. There was scant interest in him before World War I because Latvia was a part of Russia with limited exposure to information. However, a few years after the War, translations from English began to appear, and Tagore became one of the most—if not *the* most—widely published and read foreign authors in Latvia. In 1940, the two territorial occupations—German and Soviet—of the country began, and only after Stalin's death in 1954 could Tagore again become a beloved author in the Soviet Union. In a little more than ten years, eight volumes of *Works* and twelve volumes of the *Collected Works,* translated from the original Bengali or English, were published in Moscow in very large print runs. This gigantic translation project resulted in many further translations of individual works from Russian in many other languages—except Latvian. The Russian publication of the poet's *Collected Works* in 1961–5 was perhaps the most important achievement in the history of Western Tagoriana after the successful introduction of Tagore by British intellectuals to Western readers. As far as national translations of Tagore's poetry, novels, stories and plays are concerned, the efforts of the well-known Latvian intellectual Kārlis Egle (1887–1974) may be second only to those of the Spanish Nobel laureate Juan Ramón Jiménez and his wife Zenobia Camprubí Aimar.[1] There is a noteworthy parallel between the two translators: Kārlis Egle, just like Jiménez, was greatly helped by his wife, Elmīra Egle; who also was more proficient in English. However, she never allowed her name to be put down in print.

LATVIAN VIEWS ON INDIA BEFORE TAGORE

From the very beginning, Latvia's intellectuals, with very few exceptions, received the Bengali poet as if he were a close ethnic relative. India had been receiving increased attention in Latvia since the middle of the nineteenth century, when German linguists proved that Lithuanian, our only sister tongue, was more closely related to Sanskrit than any other living European language. At the end of the nineteenth century, and even until 1940, Indians were called brothers by the Latvian press; in this way we, that is, Latvians, identified ourselves with their great civilisation rather than with those of the the Germans or the Russians who had ruled Latvia before (the Germans ruled from the thirteenth century and the Russians were added to them at the beginning of the seventeenth century).

In Europe, it was the Romanticists who after centuries of admiring the classical Greco-Roman culture looked beyond Greece towards the East. In Latvia, many aspects of Romanticism survived until World War II, which also contributed to the popularity of the Bengali poet.[2] In our many conversations during the last ten years of his life, this idea was always stressed by Kārlis Egle, whose efforts, as well as the work by his friend and companion Rihards Rudzītis (1898–1960), were perhaps the most decisive factors in establishing Rabindranath's long-standing fame in Latvia.

THE FIRST REACTIONS

The Indian poet entered Latvian culture via an article written by Andrejs Upīts (1877–1970), a knowledgeable, talented, influential and politically controversial prose writer and critic. He published a remarkable and long article in the journal *Domas* (Thoughts) in August 1913, that is, *before* Tagore received the Nobel Prize. Andrejs Upīts called Tagore 'a strange, attractive and splendid phenomenon.' He points out that

[Rabindranath] in his admirable simplicity and sincerity really reminds us of legendary saints... And yet someone who can sit so calmly and desribe to us the bird's morning song or man's passionate aspiration for love is not a 'saint' after all. He knows life in its loftiness and meanness. He has been as aware of human passions as few others... This Indian is a man of the people, but great and free he stands above the base and the brutal. One feels in him an heir of an old culture who tries to seek out the inner value in all phenomena of life... He believes that God and man are one, that death is not the end but only a transition, that visible things are both real and symbols of another unknown life, that an individual human soul, overcoming and discarding everything sordid, comes near the Universal Soul – all this for him goes without saying and is beyond doubt and criticism.[3]

The first article written after the poet became world famous appeared in the widely read newspaper *Dzimtenes Vēstnesis* (Motherland's Messenger) on 16 November 1913. Its unknown author reproaches *The Times* and other conservative British newspapers for ignoring the award of the Nobel Prize to Tagore because he was a hostile 'local' (i.e. 'native'). One can doubt if this reproach was deserved, yet it is clear that the Latvian newspaper expressed sincere appreciation for the honour bestowed on the Indian poet. The same article contains a brief biography of Tagore, as well as a few translations from his *Gitanjali*. The December 1913 issue of the literary monthy *Druva* contains admission charge that the Swedish Academy in the past had erred in not awarding the Nobel Prize to great European writers, such as Tolstoy, Ibsen and Anatole France. 'Yet it will be hardly possible to deny that this time the award was received by a poet who truly deserves it.' But the author of the article expressed a view that subsequently was shared by very few Latvian intellectuals: 'The content of Tagore's writings is mainly contemplatively religious; they are full of transcendental and mystical thoughts and are far from politics.'

INITIAL TRANSLATIONS: 1913–21

The Latvian treatment of the poet is interestingly characterised by the fact that the first translations by Valts Dāvids, which appeared in periodicals at the end of 1913, were from *The Crescent Moon* and not from the *Gitanjali*, so celebrated at the time of the Nobel Prize. (The same collection was also the first to be translated by Zenobia Camprubí Aimar and Juan Ramón Jiménez in 1915.) *Gitanjali* in Spanish came three years later, after other works, including *The Gardener*. Valts Dāvids soon rendered *The Crescent Moon* in full and also translated *Chitra* (*Chitrangada*).

The entire *Gitanjali* was translated by 'Austra' (the pen name of a poet who remains unknown) in 1913–14. Teodors Lejas-Krūmiņš in 1921 published a number of Tagore's short stories under the title *Indian Women*.

Kārlis Egle translated *The Post Office* in 1921, which was followed by *The Gardener* in the same year. By 1940, the collection had run into five editions. *The Gardener* is the first work in the comprehensive Latvian Tagore collection *Lirika* (Lyrics, 1961 and 1967) and in the nine-volume *Raksti* (Works) (1927–39). Looking back in 1967 on the history of his translations, Kārlis Egle mentioned the first edition of *The Gardener* as 'the small booklet in yellow covers, which made me so glad as none of the books prepared by me later. I held it in my hands already a few weeks after [submission].'[4]

The Gardener poems, which Bengali and Western critics regard as less well translated from English by Tagore than those of the *Gitanjali*, were the compositions that the highly respected and well-loved actress Elza Radziņa was fond of reciting. Clad in a red sari, she addressed thousand-strong audiences about sixty times between the 1960s and the 1980s. Studying the reception of Tagore in the West, I have never encountered such an ardent admirer of Tagore in the world of theatre. When Elza Radziņa recited Tagore in the 1970s and 1980s, I was usually priviliged to make introductory remarks on the poet and his life's work. *The Gardener* may have appealed to the actress and her audiences because the translation by Kārlis Egle conveyed a vivid picture of Bengali life in beautiful Latvian making use of a metre close to iambus, which, on the whole, is not characteristic of our poetry. (We do not feel this rythm so well in his translations of the rest of Tagore's poetry. In the nine-volume *Raksti*, Egle's companion Rihards Rudzītis also translated some of the poetry but in clear prose as Tagore did.)

THE *COLLECTED WORKS* PROJECT OF KĀRLIS EGLE AND RIHARDS RUDZĪTIS: 1927–39

Reception in the 1920s was at par with the promising beginnings before the war and the best of Tagore's writings from those then available were published as a collection in nine volumes between 1927 and 1939. A good stimulus for this ambitious undertaking was the eight-volume German edition in 1921 called *Rabindranath Tagore: Gesammelte Werke* (Collected Works; München, 1921). These volumes had neither introductions nor commmentaries. Possibly, Kārlis Egle and Rihards Rudzītis were also inspired by two unfinished collected works projects in Russian before World War I. For the nine-volume edition, Kārlis Egle translated poetry, novels (*The Wreck, Gora, The Home and the World*) and stories, and the acknowledged poet Rihards Rudzītis translated mainly Tagore's plays and essays (*Sadhana, Personality* and others).

Kārlis Egle provided each volume of *Raksti* with explanations and brief summaries of its contents, which often are particularly pertinent. For instance, the essence of *Gora* is compressed in just a few sentences:

> It reflects the time full of impetuous and ardent enthusiasm in India when the national prayer created by Bankim Chandra Chatterji, the *Bande Mataram*, began to be heard. Gora, in reality, an Irishman brought up in India (Bengal), gives himself up to the national dreams and aspirations so profoundly that he sinks into one-sidedness and intemperance, almost fully denying the new India until his foster-mother, Anandamoyi—a wonderful image personifying woman as

mother in Tagore's works—opens his eyes and enables him to discern the true shape of India, the shape that can be seen only with clear humane eyes, not fettered by dogmas and fanaticism.[5]

In the first volume, in addition to the long and laudatory introductory essays by Egle on Tagore's life and work and by Rudzītis on his philosophical, social and religious views, articles on the poet's contribution to Indian music (by Jānis Zālītis) and Indian painting (by Alberts Praude) were also included. After the ban on publishing Tagore's works in the Soviet Union was lifted, his previously published poems and novels could reappear in Latvian. The new editions could also use the Russian spelling of Bengali names, which are closer to the Bengali original than they are in the English translations. The text in the earlier editions was also slightly changed as Kārlis Egle tried to improve on his own work.

Kārlis Egle's writing on the poet is generally matter-of-fact when he discusses Tagore's closeness to nature, his treatment of woman or his pedagogical activities. However, his style changes when discussing the poet's verse, for

[in] his poetry Tagore raises the reader above everyday life, raises him to such spiritual heights where all worldly noises disappear, where the vastness of eternity and the depths of everlasting peace open up, which fascinates and stirs the reader's soul.'[6]

In such utterances, Egle approaches Rudzītis, who goes into particular detail about the poet's religion and his attitude to the ancient Indian spiritual heritage. Nevertheless, Rudzītis never forgets to mention the challenges facing India—the need to overcome caste inequality, to raise the status of women, to educate people, and to get rid of foreign rule. He does not call Tagore a prophet, but, surprisingly, he states that the poet is not interested in politics. At the same time, Rudzītis analyses the political importance of his lectures on *Nationalism* published during World War I.[7] Rihards Rudzītis stresses:

Tagore wants to present to us the initial religious surmises which essentially were the same in all ages and in all religions but which were revealed in the consciousness of only some people or race... Tagore believes in the unity of all races and peoples in their rich diversity. Humanity is above all nations. But man's mission should adapt itself to the mission of all peoples.[8]

It is to be noted that the use of the word *race* here contains nothing offensive to any person whatever their origin. In some circles it is now in vogue to affirm that even outstanding Western Indologists in the colonial epoch succumbed to a racist attitude; it is even asserted (usually without mentioning any names) that such an attitude was dominant in British Indology as a whole. I dare say that the attitude to Tagore in Latvia or Russia, and in the West as a whole, except for some authors in Germany and France in the mid-1920s, refutes such sweeping accusations. Everywhere Tagore was received as equal—if not superior—to the best national poets and his works did not lack readers. True, this attitude did not last in all countries for long. But it was hardly so because the people had realised that he was racially unacceptable. Tagore's high reputation in Germany, in the English-speaking countries and partly also in France suffered greatly for other reasons—because of his denouncement of both sides involved in the War, as we see in his *Nationalism* lectures, and the spreading influence of modernist ideology in Western Europe and the USA, the authors of which professed disbelief in all social and political 'utopias.' They expressed this disbelief also in literature. Something of that can be perceived in Tagore's late poetry. But the indomitable idealist as we see in him also in the many lectures abroad could not fit well with the after-War atmosphere. In Latvia as in most Eastern European countries, the attitude towards Tagore in the late 1920s and 1930s changed much less due to their different historical situation. During the War, people of these countries had to die under foreign flags. However, their unwillingness to fight soon turned into enthusiastic establishment of their own states. Tagore's fame also could survive in the Baltic and Eastern European countries because their sympathies for the Indian national liberation struggle were greater. Besides, Romanticism which very much can be associated with Tagore was still a living force there.

Both Latvian translators (Egle and Rudzītis) were in correspondence with Tagore from 1921. On 5 April 1936, the Bengali poet wrote to Kārlis Egle:

Dear Friends,

Your letter and a mere present of a few books in Latvian gave me the greatest pleasure, and I send you my heartfelt gratitude for them. This is not the first time I have been told of the spiritual kinship between your people and mine, and it is so refreshing to learn that there are ardent souls like you in the West who are not willing to submit themselves to the grip of machine civilisation and are seeking light from the inspiring sources of Oriental philosophy and culture. I am so happy that my poems and other writings have given some hope and some peace. With warm greetings,

Yours sincerely,
Rabindranath Tagore[9]

Intellectual Engagement with Tagore

Jānis Zanders's book *Rabindranats Tagore* published in 1934 was little noticed by reviewers. The ideas expressed by this Latvian author are a mixture of laudable and unacceptable statements. This previously unknown admirer of Tagore writes appreciatingly on his poetry and calls the Bengali poet 'the greatest lyricist of our time.' He is also deeply moved by the depiction of the child by the poet and calls the novel *Gora* 'the most beautiful song Tagore devotes to his love of the motherland.' Zanders dwells on the poet's sharp criticism of Western and Japanese nationalism, but strangely concludes that Indians, being representatives of a womanly culture, could not imagine themselves as a nation. Therefore, their country is subject to the workings of fate and the wishes of strong nations. Zanders was convinced that the self-sacrifice shown by Indian freedom fighters also reveals an aspect of their womanly nature. He writes well on the Swadeshi movement depicted in Tagore's novel *The Home and the World*, but in mentioning Bimala—the 'home'—he sees her as the personification of the womanly India, which will experience great hardships upon entering a world where masculine behaviour—hatred, noise, revolts and not domestic tranquility—dominates. The author states:

> The great message to the world by Tagore and India is this: all races should be joined on the basis of a common God or, rather, idea... And the thought to unite people on the road of deity is also the thought of many Europeans.[10]

Several outstanding Latvian poets commented on Tagore's writings. The poem published in 1926 by Jānis Sudrabkalns is especially interesting.

> Rabindranath Tagore! He is received like a king, like the loveliest prima donna, like a boxing champion;
>
> he is sprinkled with flowers, his every word is listened to; words he utters in English (nobody understands Bengali; he has to speak in the tongue of India's conquerors), with fatigued eyes, full of sadness and dreams, fondling his prophet's beard;
>
> people of Europe flock around him, abandoning their work and beloved vices, for two hours he reigns supreme: and then they return to their work and their vices, for there is nothing that can make them sound and pious for more than two hours.[11]

While Kārlis Egle expressed his appreciation for the Tagore monographs of Edward Thompson and Vincenc Lesný, no exchange of letters between them is available. Correspondence was, however, frequent between Egle and the well-trained Russian Orientalist Mihail Tubyanski, but it stopped in 1928 when Tagore became an unacceptable author in the Soviet Union. It is not known why Tubyanski was arrested or when he was executed.[12] He was the first European to translate several of Tagore's shorter works and his *Reminiscenses* from Bengali into Russian in the first half of the 1920s. Kārlis Egle died in 1974. Rihards Rudzītis, after a long imprisonment in Siberia, was freed a sick man and died in 1960.

FROM THE 1960S

Since the second half of the 1960s, I have tried to continue the work of Egle and Rudzītis. My first article on Tagore appeared in 1966, and the first poems translated from Bengali were published a few years later. Two other writers under the combined pen name of Guna Bērziņa started a similar work in the 1980s but rather soon abandoned it.

The poet's 125th birth anniversary was celebrated in 1986. At that time, together with some colleagues I organised four large-scale functions in Riga and its suburbs, readings of Tagore's poetry took place on Latvian radio and television, and articles written by me appeared in all major newspapers. Four of Tagore's plays were staged. In March, the curtain was raised for the first performance of *Chitrangada* by the Valmiera Drama Theatre (one of the best in Latvia outside Riga). The Riga Art Theatre, the most popular in Latvia, staged *Raja*. Songs and dances were introduced to make *Chitrangada* longer, but *Raja* had to be shortened. The former was translated from Bengali by Guna Bērziņa, the latter (also from Bengali) by me. Both plays were on for a long time, but they still remain unpublished. *The Post Office,* which I translated from Bengali, was broadcast on Latvian radio (and has been broadcast repeatedly), and *Sacrifice,* translated from English by Rihards Rudzītis, was staged on Latvian television. During the celebrations, the former vice-chancellor of Visva-Bharati, Nemai Sadhan Basu, visited Riga and was deeply impressed by the programmes and especially by Elza Radziņa's inspired recitation of Tagore's poems.

The restoration of Latvia's independence in 1991 was marked with the abolition of censorship and with a veritable deluge of books translated from many languages. This multitude of so far unheard voices, which were often worthy of serious attention, muted Tagore's voice. Thus since the early 1990s, Tagore has been losing his high place among readers in Eastern Europe, including Russia.

The case of this author's book *Rabindranath Tagore* illustrates this well. When it was first published in 1978 it had a print run of thirty thousand copies, but in 1999 a large volume of Tagore's works translated from Bengali with a long introduction had a much smaller print run; an abridged version was republished for the 2011 celebrations. On 15 September 2011, we managed to arrange a widely attended function and to publish some papers marking the poet's 150th birthday but all that was only a shadow of the celebration in 1986.

As a researcher of Tagore's heritage in Latvia, I have written several articles on the topic from 1971 and discussed it in my works in Russian and English. In Tagore research I was still alone. Therefore, I joined the well-trained and more experienced colleagues in Moscow and St Petersburg, who kindly received me as one of their own. I am most deeply thankful to Vera Novikova, Alexander Gnatyuk-Danil'Chuk, Yelena Brosalina and other Russian scholars and translators of Tagore's work.

When I, as a researcher—younger in years and experience—at the beginning of the seventies joined this venerable circle, whose main work was done earlier, censorship practically meant self-censorship. Yet the image of Tagore established in the previous decade was not only the result of research and translations but was also moulded by the only allowed ideology, which was not to be contradicted. This created a strange situation: on the one hand there was a genuine interest in the poet's life and heritage, supported by a many-sided choice of works for the above-mentioned editions, some of which then were not translated even into English, and on the other, there appeared introductions and afterwords to them, which more and more were written by ideologically staunch but not very knowlegeable people and in which only those sides of his personality and thought were stressed that best suited the state's aim of pleasing the Indian people and trying to make India socialist not in the Nehruvian but in the Soviet understanding of this word. This situation existed until the unexpected break-up of the empire, and Tagore continued to be the greatest cultural symbol of Soviet–Indian friendship notwithstanding the fact that his most often quoted *Letters from Russia* were censored to silence even his rather mild criticism of what he saw and experienced in Moscow. The poet most probably was never informed about it and hardly knew that when he went to Moscow his works already could not be published—a situation that lasted until 1954.

My cooperation with Moscow and St Petersburg Indologists also meant that in the 1970s and 1980s most of my scholarly writings on Tagore (altogether eleven in number) and the book *Moya zolotaya Bengaliya* (My Golden Bengal, 1988), mainly devoted to the history and contemporary life of Santiniketan, were published in Moscow. Do these works belong to Latvian Tagoriana? Perhaps my main book, the Russian *Literaturno-hudozhestvennoe tvorchestvo Tagore* (The Literary Creative Writing of Rabindranath Tagore), published in Riga in 1981, can be considered as belonging to Latvia. But it received the second prize of the USSR Ministry for Higher and Secondary Special Education (1985) and was mainly reviewed in Moscow. This book was also the basis for my doctoral dissertation in philology, which I defended at the Moscow Institute of Oriental Studies in 1983. Is my book *Tagore: East and West Cultural Unity*, published by Rabindra Bharati University in Kolkata (1999) and for which in 2002 I received the Tagore Memorial Prize, a part of Latvian Tagoreana? Let critics and readers judge.

I cannot evaluate my own works. I can only say that I have studied Tagore's life and all of his writing and have also tried to evaluate the scholarship on him in several major Western languages until 1987. Since for a quarter of century I taught various courses in literary theory at the University of Latvia, it was natural for me to see Rabindranath's creative work as being a part of the world literary process. At the same time, I sought to regard him as an embodiment and the best representative of Indian intellectual life of his time.

CONCLUSION

Very few languages surpass Latvian in the number of books by Tagore and on Tagore. We have forty-nine altogether, including the nine-volume *Raksti*, published twice, and six books on Tagore along with some smaller pieces. There have been around four hundred publications of the poet's shorter works and of various articles on him in the periodicals. As for Tagore's books, three were published by Latvians in the United States after they had to emigrate in 1945. By 1986, close to 190 books by and on the poet had appeared in Russian and around ninety were published in Spanish. After English, German and French translations, the number of those in Latvian, not spoken by more than two million people, from English and the Bengali, may come next, which is remarkable. Truly, we have loved the Bengali poet. In Switzerland, this writer met a former Latvian soldier of World War II, conscripted into the German army, who had carried a booklet of Tagore's verses through all the bloody battles in which he took part.

What about the future of Tagore Studies? It is encouraging that new translations from Bengali are appearing in various languages. However, the number of people involved in this process is not large. It is encouraging to hear authoritative reports from Britain that the works translated into English by the poet himself can themselves be regarded as originals. That may stimulate publishing them also in translation from English. However, we live in an epoch different from the one Tagore experienced, not to mention the fact that the poet's world view also kept changing over the times. What is the pristine, basic Rabindranath Tagore? The quick development of India will certainly promote the recovery of his fame worldwide, but who will continue the work already done in Latvian and Latvia?

NOTES

1. Between 1915 and 1922, they translated twenty-two volumes from English into Spanish. Until the mid-1980s these volumes were published around ninety times (mainly in Spain). Their labours have been insufficiently discussed and appreciated. As a comparison, the nine volumes of *Raksti* in Latvian contain a higher number of pages than the books by the Jiménez couple.
2. People often wonder why Ezra Pound, W. B. Yeats or André Gide became alienated from Tagore rather soon after they had done so much to establish his prestige in the West. Their parting of ways may have had personal reasons, but it was also connected to their poetic development from neo-romantic and symbolist inclinations towards modernism. In a similar way, French symbolists had strongly influenced the young Jiménez, which made him receptive to Tagore and inspired him to translate *The Post Office*, *The King of the Dark Chamber* and a large part of the *Gitanjali*.
3. [Upīts], 'Cittautu rakstniecība,' 978–9.
4. Egle, 'Tagores "Dārznieks",' 3.
5. Tagore, *Raksti*, vol. 3, 587.
6. Ibid., vol. 6, 251.
7. Ibid., vol. 1, 156–8.
8. Ibid., 207
9. Ibid., 258.
10. Zanders, *Rabindranats Tagore*, 92.
11. Sudrabkalns, *Izlase*, 130.
12. On Tubyanski, see the Russia essay in this volume.
13. Notwithstanding its title, this is a collection of various works by Tagore. In 2011, the book was republished only as the novel with a new, much shortened foreword.

WORKS CITED

Egle, Kārlis. 'Tagores "Dārznieks"' [Tagore's *The Gardener*]. *Padomju jaunatne*, June 1, 1967, 3.

Ivbulis, Viktors. *Iz istorii Tagoriany na Zapade* [From the History of Western Tagoriana]. In *Rabindranat Tagor*, edited by E. P. Tchelyshev and N. D. Gavryushina, Moskva: Nauka, 1986, 118–48.

———. *Literaturno-hudozhestvennoe tvorchestvo Rabindranata Tagora* [The Literary Creative Writing of Rabindranath Tagore]. Moskva: Nauka and Rīga: Zinātne, 1981.

———. 'Romāns Mājās un pasaulē' [The novel, *The Home and the World*]. Foreword to *Mājās un pasaulē* [*The Home and the World*] by Rabindranath Tagore. Rīga: Daugava, 1999, 7–136.[13]

Ivbulis, Viktors. *Moya zolotaya Bengaliya* [My Golden Bengal]. Moskva: Nauka, 1988.

——. 'Only Western Influence? The Birth of Literary Romanticist aesthetics in Bengal.' *Acta Orientalia Vilnensia*, 2010, 145–57.

——. *Rabindranats Tagore.* Rīga: Liesma, 1978.

——. *Tagore: East and West Cultural Unity.* Kolkata: Rabindra Bharati University, 1999.

——. Tagore's Western burdens.' In *Rabindranath Tagore: A Timeless Mind*, edited by Amalendu Biswas, Christine Marsh, and Kalyan Kundu. London: The Tagore Centre UK, 2011, 154–62.

Sudrabkalns, J. *Izlase* [Selection]. Rīga: Latvijas valsts izdevniecība, 1954.

Tagore, Rabindranats. *Raksti* [Writings]. 9 vols. Translated by Kārlis Egle and Rihards Rudzītis. Rīga: Gulbis, 1927–39.

[Upīts, Andrejs; authorship is indicated]. Cittautu raksniecība [Writing of Other Peoples]. *Domas*, August 1913, 978–9.

Zanders, Jānis. *Rabindranats Tagore.* Rīga: A. Raņķis, 1934.

18

POLAND

ELŻBIETA WALTER

This text is a short study of the Polish reception of Rabindranath Tagore focusing on books of translations published in Poland and in Polish between the years 1918 and 2011. Bibliographies of translations based on the three most relevant collections in Warsaw—those of the National Library, the Library of the University of Warsaw, and the Library of the Department of South Asian Studies at the same university—as well as on private collections, have been published elsewhere.[1]

CONTACTS WITH INDIA BEFORE TAGORE

Poland's geopolitical positioning spurred a sustained interest in the Orient, focusing mainly on Tatar and Turkish culture, which had a predominant place in the development of Oriental studies in Poland. Before the nineteenth century, Poland did not have any relationship with India; hence the interest in the country was quite low.

A more in-depth interest in Indian culture arose only during the literary phase of Romanticism. Indian influences can be found in the writing of some of the major Polish poets including Adam Mickiewicz, Juliusz Słowacki and Cyprian Norwid. *Rozprawa o języku sanskryckim* (Research on Sanskrit Language, 1816) by Walenty Skorochód Majewski, and *Dzieje starożytnych Indii* (History of Ancient India, 1820) by Joachim Lelewel were two major treatises of research on India conducted during this period.

The subsequent wave of Indian influences can be seen at the turn of the twentieth century, when theosophy and Schopenhauer's philosophy were in vogue. However, the first Indian studies specialists only emerged in the interwar period. They were Andrzej Gawroński, who specialised in Sanskrit studies, and Stanisław Schayer, a scholar of Sanskrit and Buddhist studies. Modern Indology has only been properly established in Poland after World War II. As far as Bengali studies are concerned, it is a relatively new field of research. If by Bengali studies we mean not only teaching the Bengali language but also studying the language, literature and culture of historical Bengal, then Bengali studies were only established in Poland in the 1970s as an independent branch of research.

THE NOBEL PRIZE

Rabindranath Tagore is by far the most famous Indian writer in Poland. The first review about the writer in the Polish press was published in a magazine on literature and art called *Museion* a month *before* he received the Nobel Prize. E. Leszczyński's 'Współczesny mistyk indyjski' (Contemporary Indian Mystic Writer) was based on Henry D. Davray's 'Un Mystique hindou: Rabindranath Tagore' published in August in the *Mercure de France*. After Tagore was awarded the Nobel Prize his name was regularly referred to in Polish newspapers, and Polish translations of his writings started to appear. Unfortunately, the first Polish reactions to Tagore's Nobel Prize have not yet been studied in detail.[2]

MISSED VISIT

Although Tagore travelled extensively all over Europe, and came very near the Polish border at least twice, in 1921 and 1926, he never actually visited Poland.

Apparently a visit to this country was provided for in the writer's schedule, although information about this is scanty. From Polish sources, we know that around 1920 rumours spread in the Polish press that the famous Bengali poet and thinker was going to visit Warsaw.[3] The daily *Rzeczpospolita* mentioned a Hindu poet, 'who as we know is coming to Warsaw', while another daily *Gazeta Warszawska* wrote about the literary circles getting ready to welcome the famous guest. Indeed, on this occasion Antoni Lange (1861?–1929), a major Polish poet, translator, philosopher and mystic as well as polyglot and linguist (he translated, for example, from Sanskrit), was preparing himself for the reception of the exotic guest by composing in Sanskrit an address to Rabindranath Tagore, in which he expressed in warm words his love for 'beloved India' (*dla kochanych Indyj*). Lange wrote:

> This northern land of ours is a poor and cold country, and that is why so beloved to us is *Aryavarta* (India), her sky and her sun; in our dreams we have always seen her golden spring, adorned with forests of *asoka*s, *nyagrodha*s, lotuses and palms, resounding with the songs of nightingales and cuckoos.[4]

However, the poet did not come and Antoni Lange, wishing to preserve the speech written for the occasion, published it in 1925 in his collection of poems *Trzeci dzień* (The Third Day) under the title 'Hindu kavaye kasmaicit vacanam—Przemówienie do pewnego poety indyjskiego'[5] ('An address to an Indian poet').

Indian sources, however, do not mention any plans for Tagore to visit Poland at that time; they report another year instead—1926. In the detailed 'A Chronicle of Eighty Years' in *Rabindranath Tagore: A Centenary Volume, 1861–1961,* we find the following information: Tagore 'on account of indisposition can fulfil only one lecture engagement. Plans for visiting Poland and Russia have to be abandoned as the strain of quick travel is telling on his health.'[6] At that time the subject of Tagore's visit to Poland surfaced again in the Polish press. The weekly *Wiadomości Literackie* reported on 7 November 1926 that 'the visit of Rabindranath Tagore to Warsaw was cancelled because of his illness.'[7]

Tagore's secretary, P. C. Mahalanobis, discussed the possible options in his letter to Rathindranath (the poet's son) sent from Berlin on 1 October. The agency *Buturm* offered to arrange four lectures in Poland (Lwow, since 1945 known as Lviv, in the Ukraine, Cracow, Lodz and Warsaw), then one in Budapest and one in Vienna. The agent of *Wolf und Sachs* offered to arrange two lectures in Poland and one in Budapest. However, after falling ill in Vienna and Budapest, Tagore decided to avoid the approaching winter and to take a route home via the Balkans.[8]

TRANSLATIONS FROM ENGLISH AND OTHER EUROPEAN LANGUAGES

In spite of the fact that Tagore never visited Poland, he is no doubt the only writer of an earlier generation from the Indian subcontinent whose writings have been extensively translated into Polish.

The majority of Tagore's work, fifty-eight pieces (including two anthologies), have been translated into Polish—not from the Bengali, but from English (and also German, to be discussed later). As was the case with most other European languages, when Tagore was first introduced to Polish readers there were no translators who could attempt direct translation from Bengali. This may have led to the wrong assumption that Tagore was a writer of English.

The above-mentioned fifty-eight publications go back to twenty-six actual Tagore titles, since some of the works have been rendered into Polish two or more times. Most of the translations were done between 1918 and 1923. In this period, thirty different translations of Tagore's works appeared. This makes up more than half of all the Polish translations, and almost all of the titles published in Poland (twenty-three out of twenty-six). Nine volumes, all of them in prose, were published in the series *Library of*

Nobel Prize Winners. The last translation during the interwar period was published in 1930, after which nothing appeared for thirty years. The lack of Tagore translations in the Polish market in the years between 1930 and 1939 could be explained by a drop in interest in his writings during this period. However, the apparent lack of interest in the subsequent years is more likely to be due to World War II, followed by the period of rebuilding the devastated country, and to the initial Communist suspicion towards India that did not change until 1955. (See the Russian and Hungarian essays in this volume.)

The first Tagore translation to be published after the War was a 1958 reprint of *The Home and World* translated by Wincenty Birkenmajer in 1927.

Tagore's writings in a variety of genres, as listed below, have been rendered into Polish; however, not all genres have received the same attention:

Eight books of poetry: *Gitanjali, Fruit-Gathering, The Gardener, Lover's Gift, Crossing, The Crescent Moon, Fugitive, Poems* (Calcutta, Visva-Bharati 1942);

- Five plays: *The Post Office, Chitra, Malini, The King of the Dark Chamber, Red Oleanders;*
- Three novels: *The Home and the World, The Wreck, Gora;*
- Autobiography: *My Reminiscences;*
- Letters: *Glimpses of Bengal* (fragments);
- Epigrams: *Fireflies, Stray Birds;*
- Poetic prose: *Thought Relics;*
- Essays and lectures: *Sadhana, Nationalism, Personality;*
- Short story collections: *Mashi and Other Stories, Hungry Stones, Broken Ties and Other Stories.*
- Poetry translated into English by Tagore: *One Hundred Poems of Kabir.*

It is evident that the highest number of Tagore's translations into Polish represents his poetry. This does not necessarily mean though that entire pieces of work were translated, for sometimes it was only a selection or even only as few as one or two poems from anthologies of poems.

The most popular piece was, understandably, *Gitanjali,* the collection that had introduced the poet to the European world. Most translations of the *Gitanjali,* as well as many other collections of poems by Tagore, are incomplete, and sometimes include only a few poems. The first two Polish versions of the *Gitanjali* in book form were published as late as 1918. The first was done by a noted Polish poet, Jan Kasprowicz, and published in Poznań, the second, translated by Józef Jankowski, was published in Warsaw.

Both publications also include various poems from books of poetry other than *Gitanjali*. The other translators of the *Gitanjali* are Stefan Gawłowski and Julian Przyboś (1961) as well as Robert Stiller (1977). A collective translation by Jan K. Sosnowski, Ewa B. Sosnowska and Mirosław Sosnowski appeared in 2003. The reason for the relatively late appearance of Tagore's Nobel poems as a book in Polish must be the turmoil of World War I and the absence of a sovereign Polish state before 1918, owing to which infrastructure for publishing in Polish was limited.[9]

The Polish title for *Gitanjali* in all the above five translations was given as *Pieśni ofiarne*, 'Sacrificial songs.' The Bengali original, however, is a Sanskrit compound made up of the words *git* 'a song' and *anjali* 'a present given (esp. to deities) with cupped palms.' This would more appropriately translate into Polish as *Ofiarowanie pieśni*, 'Song Offerings' or *Ofiara (z) pieśni*, 'An Offering of Songs.' However, this particular interpretation of the title has been followed by only one translator, who published fragments of *Gitanjali* in 1916 in the periodical *Pro Arte et Studio*.[10]

Some of Tagore's writings have been translated several times. Apart from the *Gitanjali* (five versions, but not all of them complete in the form of book), the novel *The Home and the World* has been rendered into Polish as many as three times, as was the case with *Sadhana* and *Thought Relics*. The latter appeared under four different titles (see below), since after World War II the original title of the first translation done by Jerzy Bandrowski, *Szept duszy*, and by Witold Hulewicz, *Poszepty duszy*, has been changed to *Ostatki myśli*—much closer to the English version of the same—*Thought Relics*. The play *Chitra* has been translated twice as was also the case with *The King of the Dark Chamber* and the collection of essays, *Nationalism*. As has been mentioned, sometimes the Polish renderings were given different titles, for example, *Lover's Gift* has been translated into Polish as *Dar oblubieńca* (Betrothed's Gift) and *Dar miłującego* (The Gift of a Loving Person), *Crossing* as *Ku drugiemu brzegowi* (Towards the other bank) and *Przeprawa* (Crossing); *The Crescent Moon* has been rendered as *Księżyc przybierający* (Waxing Moon) and as *Rosnący księżyc* ('Increasing' Moon); *Thought Relics* as *Szept duszy (Soul's Whisper)*, *Poszepty duszy* (Soul's Whisper—with a more archaic word for whisper), *Myśli* (Thoughts) and *Ostatki myśli* (Thought's remnants); the collection *Fugitive* also has two titles—*Uciekinier* (Refugee) and *Zbieg* (Fugitive).

Several translators themselves admitted that the accuracy of their Polish translations can be questioned and on the title page inside the book they often put *spolszczył*, 'rendered into Polish by', *odtworzył*, 'recreated by', or *sparafrazował*, 'paraphrased by', instead of *przełożył* 'translated by'. Some other translators, including Franciszek Mirandola and Jerzy Bandrowski, misled readers by saying 'translated from the original' even when their pieces, *Mashi and Other Stories, Reminiscences* and *Glimpses of Bengal*, were originally written in Bengali and it wasn't Rabindranath who rendered them into English.[11] However, since some of Tagore's pieces were originally written in English (*Sadhana, Nationalism, Personality*), including essays and lectures presented by him in English in the USA and Japan, their Polish translations, if done from English, are actually direct renderings from the original.

As has been mentioned, entire collections of Tagore's writings were rarely translated into Polish, and new translations may include a different selection from the original piece. Robert Stiller, the translator of the book *Rosnący księżyc i inne poezje*, '*The Crescent Moon and other Poems*' (1989), writes in his preface:

> This collection is not just a reprint of the previous two that I have published but it also includes many improved translations or new ones, which are published here for the first time, among others two thirds from the original collection *The Crescent Moon*.[12]

ENGAGEMENT WITH TAGORE'S TEXTS AND IDEAS

The collection *Nationalism* triggered off some controversy in Poland, which after many years of national duress and subjugation finally became a sovereign country again in 1918. Tagore's views expressed in the essays of *Nationalism*, which criticises armed defence of the country in the fight for independence and sovereignty, faced severe criticism from some Polish readers. Tagore was admonished for his 'war against national patriotism.' One of the journalists wrote:

> Tagore's *Nationalism* is a forceful and explicit attack against national solidarity, against patriotism, against all possible bonds between a human being and his mother country.[13]

The play *The Post Office* deserves a special place among Tagore's translations into Polish. Firstly, taking into consideration all the translations of the play, also those that have not been published, as well as those published only in periodicals, it has been translated into Polish five times—three times in the form of a book, including one translation directly from the Bengali language.[14] Secondly, because one staging of this particular play was done at a crucial and tragic moment in Polish history, on 18 July 1942 in an orphanage in the Warsaw Ghetto run by Janusz Korczak, a writer, educator, medical doctor and social activist, just before Korczak and the children were taken by the Nazis to the concentration camp in Treblinka and put to death.[15] Therefore, this play is particularly important to many Polish people and is still present in the collective memory of Poland. The performance of *The Post Office* in the Warsaw Ghetto was described by Korczak in his diary.[16]

German Influence

As has been mentioned, not all of Tagore's writings that have *not* been directly translated from the Bengali were translated into Polish from English. Firstly, knowledge of English in the inter-war period, when most of the translations were done, was limited. The second language of the Polish aristocracy since the eighteenth century had been French, and later on German also became a popular language among Poles. Secondly, comparing the dates of the German and Polish translations, one can see that the Polish versions were often published shortly after the German ones, even when English translations of the same works had been done many years before.[17] For example, the play *The King of the Dark Chamber* was published in German in 1921; the Polish translation appeared in the same year, even though the English version of the play had been published as early as 1914. Both the Polish translations of *Nationalism* were published in 1921, just like the German translation, while the English version had been published four years earlier, in 1917. This might prove to be just a coincidence, as the country was involved in World War I. Unfortunately, the custom of reporting the title of the source on the Copyright page of the translation was not yet introduced at that time. However, some of the translators of Tagore's works admitted that they had translated from the German. Jerzy Bandrowski, the translator of *Sadhana*, *Thought Relics*, and *Stray Birds,* says:

> This collection (*Thought Relics*)... was originally written in English. However, I was forced to translate it from the German translation approved by the poet himself and given by him a much more beautiful title *Flüstern der Seele*. I found the most appropriate translation of it into Polish as 'Szept duszy' (The whisper of the soul). ... *Stray Birds*—the maxims ... have also been translated by me from German.[18]

Jerzy Bandrowski commented on this issue of indirect translations when he was working on two of Tagore's pieces *Thought Relics* and *Stray Birds*:

> The German translations of Tagore's writings are very meticulous. However, the difference between the emphasis laid on spiritual and intellectual aspects by Tagore versus the one given by his translator (Helena Meyer-Franck) is so enormous that the ideas of both go sometimes completely separate ways. Even if they still retain some meaning for the German reader, they would be almost completely unintelligible in Polish.[19]

AFTER WORLD WAR II

The post-War publications of Tagore are mainly reprints of translations published between 1918 and 1923 as well as several completely new translations from the Bengali. Some new translations from English came from the collection of poems *Fugitive, Fireflies* and *Poems* (Calcutta: Visva-Bharati, 1942). Moreover, all the writings included in the anthology *A Poet of the World* were translated for the first time, with the exception of fragments from *Nationalism* and *My School*.

Although the study of the Bengali language was introduced at the Oriental Institute of the University of Warsaw as early as 1935, a proper course in Bengali began only in 1957. Moreover, under the Communist regime, access to the original pieces of Tagore's writings in Bengali was made difficult. This was due to the strictly limited contacts with India at that time, both on political and economic grounds. Another huge obstacle was (and unfortunately still is) the prevailing reluctance of Polish publishers to print translations from Oriental languages, because of their apparent exoticism and dissimilarity to European literature and, as a result, the assumed limited number of potential readers.

As far as translations directly from the Bengali are concerned, until 2010 only four short stories and three plays had been rendered into Polish. The four short stories appeared in a collection of stories translated from Hindi, Urdu and Bengali and the three plays had found their place in a book on the Bengali theatre and plays; only one of these plays, *Red Oleanders*, had not previously been translated into Polish from English. Some other direct translations, such as fragments from *My Reminiscences*, and the *The Parrot's Training* had been printed earlier in magazines.[20]

The number of Polish translations from the Bengali significantly increased from 2011 thanks to the anthology entitled *Poeta świata,* 'A Poet of the World', edited by Elżbieta Walter, which was published by Warsaw University Press. This anthology, the first in Poland, was professionally prepared, translated and annotated by scholars of the Department of South Asian Studies, University of Warsaw, and is a voluminous book of thirteen chapters. The aim of the book was to present the diverse literary genres and artistic media in which Tagore had worked and excelled. It contains translations of the following writings: memoirs *Wspomnienia z mojego życia* (*Jivansmriti*) (excerpts), *Moje chłopięce lata (Chhelebela)* (excerpts); seven poems; seven songs, drama: *Poczta* (*Dakghar*), novel *Ostatni poemat* (*Shesher kabita*) (two chapters), short stories 'Zeszyt' ('Khata'), 'Subha' ('Subha'), four philosophical tales from *Lipika* ('Vidushaka,' 'Prashna,' 'Totakahini,' 'Kartar bhut'), aphorisms from *Kanika, Lekhan* and *Sphulinga*, seven poems for children, three letters to Indira Devi Chaudhurani, two letters to Mrinalini Tagore, *Listy wygnańca do Europy,* (*Yurop pravasir patra*) (excerpts), and *Listy z Rosji* (*Rashiyar chithi*) (excerpts). Each genre represented in the anthology was provided with a short scholarly introduction by the compilers and translators of the anthology. All texts were translated into Polish from the original Bengali or English, depending on which language the great Nobel Laureate himself had used. Thanks to the inclusion of pieces mapping the range of Tagore's genres and literary forms, the Bengali writer appears to the Polish reader as a versatile artist of many talents. The footnotes to the translations in the anthology enable people to understand Indian culture which, despite contacts between Poland and India becoming easier due to globalisation, remains distant, mysterious, exotic and very often incomprehensible to the Polish reader.

Most of Tagore's Bengali writings published in the anthology *Poeta świata* appeared in the Polish language for the first time, for example fragments from his memoirs, *My Boyhood Days,* two chapters of the novel, *The Last Poem,* three philosophical tales from *Lipika,* epigrams from 'Particles,' 'Jottings,' and 'Sparks' *(Kanika, Lekhan, Sphulinga),* five letters, fragments from 'Letters from an Exile in Europe,' and *Letters from Russia,* and several poems and songs. The anthology also contains first translations into Polish of some original English writings by Tagore.

All direct translations from the Bengali were published in the last forty years and authored by academics from the Oriental Faculty (or, Faculty of Oriental Studies since 2008, earlier named the Oriental Institute) at the University of Warsaw. However, without doubt many of Tagore's writings are still waiting to be translated into Polish.

Regrettably, interest in Tagore's work is diminishing in Poland as is shown by the decreasing number of new translations of his work and lack of interest from the media regarding Tagore's 150th birth anniversary (in 2011). The only initiative to celebrate the anniversary was shown by professional institutions dealing with the promotion of Indian culture in Poland, such as the Chair of South Asian Studies at the University of Warsaw (the only place in Poland where Bengali studies are conducted) that published Tagore's *Anthology* and the Indo-Polish Cultural Committee that organised performances of Tagore's musical drama *Shyama* in Kraków, Warsaw and some other cities in Poland in 2012. There was also a short interview with Elżbieta Walter, the editor of Tagore's anthology *Poeta świata,* in the second channel of Polish Radio in August 2011.

As for the Internet, information about Tagore in Polish is scarce and rather unprofessional, very often full of mistakes. There is an article about him in Wikipedia and some websites mostly with aphorisms and epigrams from his works. More information has been appearing since 2012, the Korczak Year commemorating the seventieth anniversary of the staging of *The Post Office* by Janusz Korczak and his tragic death in 1942.

NOTES

1. Walter, 'On the Translations of Rabindranath Tagore's Writings into Polish' (2006), and Walter, 'On the Translations of Rabindranath' (2011) also contain earlier versions of this essay.
2. There are only two articles that touch on the first reactions, Kowalska, 'Z dziejów recepcji Tagore' and Kocięcka, 'Rabindranath Tagore w Polsce,' both written on the occasion of the centenary of Tagore's birth in 1961.
3. *Rzeczpospolita*, 21 January 1922; *Gazeta Warszawska* , 28 March 1922. See Kowalska, 'Z dziejów recepcji Tagore'a,' 266.
4. Machalski, *Orientalizm Antoniego Langego*, 137.
5. Probably the Sanskrit outline of the biography of the first Polish Sanskritist Walenty Skorochód-Majewski (1763–1835) was meant also for Tagore. This writing survived among Antoni Lange's unpublished papers. See Machalski, *Orientalizm Antoniego Langego*, 138.
6. Mukhopadhyay and Roy, 'Rabindranath Tagore: A Chronicle of Eighty Years,' 486.
7. Kowalska, 'Z dziejów recepcji Tagore,' 266.
8. Bangha, *Hungry Tiger*, 128–31.
9. It should be mentioned that several early translations of poems from *Gitanjali* appeared in magazines but we focus here on translations published in books.
10. Mossakowski, tr., 'Z Gitanjali,' (quoted after Kowalska, 'Z dziejów recepcji Tagore,' 276).
11. *My Reminiscences* and *Glimpses of Bengal* were translated by Surendranath Tagore (cf. Kripalani, *Rabindranath Tagore*, 402) and *Mashi and Other Stories* by various hands (cf. Dutta and Robinson, *Rabindranath Tagore*, 468).
12. Stiller, tr., *Rosnący księżyc i inne poezje*, 9.
13. J. Rembieliński, 'Walka z patriotyzmem,' *Gazeta Warszawska*, 1922, no. 86, quoted in Kocięcka, 'Rabindranath Tagore w Polsce,' 134.
14. This play was also translated under the title *Biuro Pocztowe* and staged for the first time in 1918 in the Teatr Polski in Kiev. See Osiński, *Polskie kontakty teatralne z Orientem w XX wieku*, 22; the first translations of this play were published in magazines: Laura Konopnicka-Pytlińska, tr., 'Poczta,' *Pochodnia*, 1919, no. 1, 41–55; no. 2, 90–9; Bohdan Gębarski, tr., 'Poczta,' *Dialog*, 1958, no. 3, 63–76.
15. Grabowska, et al., *Z dziejów teatru i dramatu bengalskiego*, 226–30.
16. Korczak, *The Ghetto Years*, 79–81.
17. The dates of the German translations of some of Tagore's writings: *Das Heim und die Welt*, 1921 (English version, 1919), *Chitra*, 1921 (English version, 1913), *Sadhana*, 1921 (English version, 1913), *Fruchtlese* 1918 (English version, 1916), *Die Nacht der Erfüllung*, 1921 (English version, 1918).

18. Bandrowski, 'Introduction' to *Sadhana* in Bandrowski, *Sadhana, Szept duszy, Zbłąkane ptaki*, IX–X.
19. Ibid., X.
20. *Kontynenty* (1980): 32–3; *Przegląd Orientalistyczny*, 1, no. 141 (1987), 75–81; *Przegląd Orientalistyczny* 2006, no. 1–2, 99–101.

Works Cited

Bandrowski, Jerzy, transl. *Sadhana, Szept duszy, Zbłąkane ptaki* [*Sadhana, Thought Relics, Stray Birds*]. Lwów–Poznań: Wydawnictwo Polskie, 1922.

Bangha, Imre. *Hungry Tiger: Encounter between India and Central Europe—The Case of Hungarian and Bengali Literary Cultures.* New Delhi: Sahitya Akademi, 2007.

Chaudhuri, A. 'The English Writings of Rabindranath Tagore.' In *History of Indian Literature in English.* Edited by Arvind Krishna Mehrotra, 103–15. London: Hurst, 2003.

Davray, Henry D. 'Un Mystique hindou: Rabindranath Tagore' [A Hindu Mystic: Rabindranath Tagore]. *Mercure de France*, 16 August 1913, 673–998.

Dutta, Krishna, and Andrew Robinson. *Rabindranath Tagore: The Myriad-Minded Man.* London: Bloomsbury, 1995.

Grabowska, B., B. Śliwczyńska, and E. Walter. *Z dziejów teatru i dramatu bengalskiego* [From the History of Bengali Theatre and Drama]. Warsaw: Wydawnictwo Akademickie Dialog, 1999.

Kocięcka, M. 'Rabindranath Tagore w Polsce' [Rabindranath Tagore in Poland]. *Przegląd Humanistyczny*, 4, no. 61 (1961), 125–34.

Korczak, Janusz. *The Ghetto Years: 1939–42.* Tel Aviv: Hakibbutz Hameuchand, 1980.

Kowalska, A. 'Z dziejów recepcji Tagore' [From the History of Tagore's Reception) *Przegląd Orientalistyczny.* 39, no. 3 (1961), 265–81.

Kripalani, Krishna. *Rabindranath Tagore: A Biography.* London: Oxford University Press, 1962.

Leszczyński, E. 'Współczesny mistyk indyjski' [Contemporary Indian Mystic Writer]. *Museion* (Kraków), 9, no. 10 (1913), 149–50.

Machalski, Franciszek. *Orientalizm Antoniego Langego (Z zarysem bibliografii)* [The Orientalism of AntoniLange—with an Outline of Bibliography]. Tarnopol: Prace Polskiego Towarzystwa Przyjaciół Nauk w Tarnopolu, 1937.

Mossakowski, Czesław, transl. 'Z Gitanjali: Ofiara pieśni' [From the *Gitanjali: Song Offerings*]. *Pro Arte et Studio.* 1916, no. 1, 15–17.

Mukhopadhyay, Prabhatkumar, and Kshitis Roy. 'Rabindranath Tagore: A Chronicle of Eighty Years.' In *Rabindranath Tagore: A Centenary Volume, 1861*–1941. Edited by Sarvepalli Radhakrishnan, 447–503. New Delhi: Sahitya Akademi, 1961.

Osiński, Z. *Polskie kontakty teatralne z Orientem w XX wieku* [Polish Theatre Contacts with Orient in 20th Century] vol. 1 (*Kronika).* Gdańsk: Słowo/ obraz, terytoria, 2008.

Radhakrishnan, Sarvepalli, ed. *Rabindranath Tagore: A Centenary Volume, 1861–1941*. New Delhi: Sahitya Akademi, 1961.

Stiller, Robert, transl. *Rosnący księżyc i inne poezje* [The Crescent Moon and Other Poems]. Warsaw: Nasza Księgarnia, 1989.

Tuczyński, Jan. *Motywy indyjskie w literaturze polskiej* [Indian Motifs in Polish Literature]. Warszawa: Państwowe Wydawnictwo Naukowe, 1981.

Walter, Elżbieta. 'On the Translations of Rabindranath Tagore's Writings into Polish.' In *India in Warsaw. Indie w Warszawie: A Volume to Commemorate the 50th Anniversary of the Post-War History of Indological Studies at Warsaw University*. Edited by Danuta Stasik and Anna Trynkowska, 100–11. Warsaw: Elipsa, 2006.

——. 'On the Translations of Rabindranath Tagore's Writings into Polish.' In *Rabindranath Tagore: A Timeless Mind*. Edited by Amalendu Biswas, Christine Marsh, and Kalyan Kundu, 309–22. London: Tagore Centre, 2011.

——, ed. *Poeta świata: Antologia utworów Rabindranatha Tagore'a* [A Poet of the World; Anthology of Rabindranath Tagore's Writings]. Warsaw: Wydawnictwa Uniwersytetu Warszawskiego, 2011.

Willman-Grabowska, Helena. 'Indianistyka w Polsce' [Indological Studies in Poland]. In *Szkice z dziejów polskiej orientalistyki* [Outlines of the History of Oriental Studies in Poland]. Edited by Stefan Strelcyn, 237–50. Warszawa: Państwowe Wydawnictwo Naukowe, 1957.

19

HUNGARY

IMRE BANGHA

This essay presents Tagore's reception in writings in Hungarian or by Hungarians publishing in other languages. This means that sources both within and outside the political boundaries of the country will be examined. In fact, some of the most appreciative Hungarian responses to Tagore appeared outside Hungary.

INDIA AND HUNGARY

Direct cultural contacts between India and Hungary date back to the time of the traveller-scholar Alexander Csoma de Kőrös (1784–1842), the author of the first Tibetan grammar and dictionary. Csoma worked mainly in Calcutta between 1828 and 1842, and learned Sanskrit and Bengali among other languages. In the nineteenth century—apart from the accounts of some travellers—Sanskrit literature represented the culture of the Indian subcontinent for Hungarians. The only specimen of contemporary literature before 1913 was the English adventure novel *1001 Indian Nights* by Sharat Kumar Ghosh (1883–?) translated in 1908. Tagore's Nobel Prize informed the larger public in Hungary that contemporary India possessed a dynamic literature, which was, however, mostly perceived as the continued presence of a timeless India and, in the first half of the twentieth century, was represented exclusively by Bengali authors. Emphasis shifted with the establishment of the Communist regime in Hungary after World War II, and the 1950s saw a wide range of modern translations from a variety of modern Indian languages. Third World countries struggling with extreme poverty presented the clearest examples of the cruelty of Capitalism. In the second half of the century, modern Indian literature became an accepted part of world literature. The decades that followed the collapse of Communism in 1989 saw the revival of a popular interest in the spiritual East and the emergence of post-colonial literatures.

In 1913, Rabindranath surprised Hungarian readership as an Oriental man heralding the end of Europe's cultural hegemony. The initial enthusiasm lasted only for a few months and soon gave way to perplexity, and then to oblivion. In the 1920s, Tagore became a prophet with a spiritual message showing hope to a civilisation immersed in materialism and drenched in blood. After the establishment of Indo–Soviet friendship in 1955, the Soviet Bloc saw Tagore as an anti-imperialist thinker with a progressive social message and an iconic figure of the cultural richness of the emerging colonial and post-colonial world.

THE FIRST REACTIONS

The first reports about the Indian poet misspelled his name, misread his age (actually fifty-two in 1913) and apparently confused him with the musicologist Raja Sourindra Mohan Tagore (1840–1914):

> The Nobel Prize for Literature, this year, was awarded by the committee to Rayen Dranatto Tagore. Tagore is a musical composer and a historian of music. He lives in Calcutta and he is eighty-two.[1]

Although the correct details arrived the next day, this short piece of news is indicative of European discourse about the Orient that was not inclined to acknowledge that Asia possessed a living modern culture. As has been spectacularly emphasised by Edward Said to the global public in his *Orientalism,* the 'Orientalist discourse' worked with stereotypes that cast the Orient as timeless, old, effeminate, anarchic, etc. The image of an 'eighty-two'-year-old man represented this timeless Orient. Moreover, Tagore, who was awarded the Nobel Prize at just past his middle age, accepted the role of the old prophet that Europe imposed upon him.

Following the initial reports, Hungarian intellectuals began to reflect on the change in world literature initiated by Tagore's Nobel Prize.[2] Two weeks after the announcement of the Prize, a leading Hungarian poet, Mihály Babits (1883–1941), published the prose translation of three poems from English and wrote an article about Tagore, whom—following Yeats—he compared to St Francis of Assisi. Another notable poet, Dezső Kosztolányi (1885–1936), without reading much of Tagore, meditated on the end of the hegemony of European culture. After the Nobel Prize, the strange-sounding name of Rabindranath Tagore started to feature in Hungarian life so much so that the pronunciation of the poet's name became a way of testing drunkenness: the person who was able to do it was proven not to be drunk.[3] Soon, in 1914, Ferenc Kelen (1869–?), the Hungarian translator of Schopenhauer and Oscar Wilde, produced a volume of Rabindranath's poems in Hungarian.

The dominant literary movement of the first half of the twentieth century was the one marked with the name of the magazine *Nyugat* (the Occident) that endeavoured to modernise Hungarian literature by taking inspiration from the best achievements of modern Western authors. Even if the leading exponents of this movement, Babits and Kosztolányi, were enthusiastic about Tagore in their first reactions, their generation initially did not pay much attention to Eastern literatures. The Western orientation of this powerful movement can be taken as one of the reasons for the emerging neglect of or antipathy towards Tagore.

The most interesting piece of the emerging Tagore-antipathy is a humorous sketch by Frigyes Karinthy (1887–1938), the best Hungarian literary parodist of the twentieth century, who also belonged to the circle of *Nyugat*. Karinthy produced excellent caricatures of the leading literary figures of his time and later collected them into the volumes of *Így írok ti*, 'This is how you write.' In his short piece *Pályázom a Nobel-díjra* 'I am applying for the Nobel Prize,' Karinthy produced a parody of Tagore.[4] Although the English *Gitanjali* has hardly any Indian words or cultural references, the Hungarian humorist explains the success of Tagore's poems by his use of exotic gibberish.

TRANSLATIONS

In the first half of the twentieth century, many members of the Hungarian middle class also read German and a considerable number of German translations of Tagore were available in Hungary. Nevertheless, most of his works published in English were translated into Hungarian in the early 1920s. Among his different writings, naturally, his poetry was the most popular in Hungary (*The Gardener, Gitanjali, The Crescent Moon, Fruit-Gathering, Lover's Gift, Stray Birds, Crossing*—the first three of which appeared in two or three different full or partial translations). At the same time four dramas (*Chitra, Sacrifice, The King of the Dark Chamber, The Post Office*), three novels (*The Home and the World, The Wreck, Gora*), four collections of short stories (*Mashi, Auspicious Moment, Hungry Stones, Homecoming*) with some twenty stories in total, three books of essays (*Sadhana, The Inspiration of the Soul, Nationalism*) as well as *My Reminiscences* came out in Hungarian.[5] The volumes were produced fast and they usually lacked introductions and notes. Their most prolific translator was the rather pedestrian Zoltán Bartos (1890–1981). In some books his translations were complemented by those of Márton Sármay (pseudonym of Erzsébet Bleuer). Publishing Tagore's books in the early 1920s was a good business and Bartos and Sármay faced competition from others.

The Hungarian *Sadhana* published in 1921, in contrast with the other Tagore volumes, had a foreword. Its author was Mihály Földi (1894–1943), who, experimenting with psychology in his early writings, published several short stories in *Nyugat*. Later, in the 1930s, he produced bestsellers with superficial religious messages. In his foreword, Földi emphasised that Tagore's teaching about love and the harmony of man and nature was not a new idea but rather something that is forgotten again and again and mankind needed to be reminded of it.[6] He also treated at relative length Tagore's efforts to conciliate the fundamental antagonisms of life. Although both publisher and reader expect a foreword to be appreciative, in his conclusion written in a language full of biblical expressions, Földi presents his doubts:

> Are people in India happy and composed? ... How can India as a state-creating nation be compared to the stout and pertinacious European race? ... But will love be realised on Earth?... The suggestive force of god-men so far proved to be too weak.[7]

Tagore's poetry has been widely translated into Hungarian and one can distinguish various patterns. Among the earliest translators, Mihály Babits preferred the naïve prose versions to the elaborately simple Bengali originals because the prose poems reminded him of the straightforward, terse poetry of St Francis of Assisi.

There were others who made an effort to move closer to the Bengali original by introducing strophic pattern (i.e., using the same music for successive stanzas) with metre and rhyme in Hungarian. As early as 1914, the journalist-translator Vilmos Zoltán (1869–1929) published some Hungarian versions in verse that allegedly reflected the Bengali originals. Later, having heard Rabindranath reciting his poems in Vienna, Zoltán came out with a whole volume of similar translations selected from *Gitanjali* and *The Gardener*. The forms of his translations rely on traditional Hungarian patterns close to the rhythm of folk songs.

Bringing Tagore close to folk songs is a step towards the original, although it reflects only one facet of his Bengali poetry and the elaborate or the experimental aspect of his forms is lost. There are several reasons for the emergence of these folk-song type translations. The rhythmical pattern of Hungarian folk songs is in a way similar to the Bengali *dalabritta* rhythm, where syllables are counted. The most popular Hungarian patterns consist of lines of eight or twelve syllables divided into two equal units with stressed syllables at their beginning. The folk songs suggest a naïve, unsophisticated approach to life so much longed for by urban people. Thus Tagore could be presented as someone who is not detached from nature. Hungarian conservative critics, influenced by nineteenth-century Romanticism, held poetry inspired by folk literature in high esteem and in all probability welcomed such translations. In fact, conservative circles prepared the Indian poet's visit to Hungary in 1926.

Verse translations of Tagore, however, were not the exclusive domain of conservative writers. One of the leading Hungarian poets of the *Nyugat* circle, Dezső Kosztolányi, who attended Tagore's lecture in Budapest, prepared three verse translations from English. He felt free not only to create iambic strophes, but also to deviate from the original text. He may also have felt justified in his creative approach to the text by his awareness that, in his English, Tagore had deviated from the Bengali, at least in his poetic forms. Kosztolányi made the poems sound more unambiguous in their vocabulary and emotionally more intense. For example, the Buddhist story of Upagupta in the poem *The Dancing-girl* (*Fruit-Gathering* 37) celebrates the discipline and steadfastness of the monk and shows that the problem of momentary happiness turning into suffering is solved by a renunciation of the world before suffering comes. Kosztolányi was not interested in the ideals of Buddhism and he removed the didactic layer; at the same time he made the figures less serene and more vulnerable to emotions. In the Hungarian version the dancing girl is explicit about her love for Upagupta and the sadness of the ascetic suggests that he also had a touch of it. It should also be mentioned that Kosztolányi was not alone in his free approach to the contents and form. One of the most outstanding poets of a later generation, Sándor Weöres (1913–89), took a similar attitude. He translated Tagore into iambic strophes and changed the content freely.

Kosztolányi's melodious translations are among the most popular Tagore verses in Hungarian. Moreover, they served as a basis for a later translation into the Gypsy language[8] and also inspired people to set Tagore's poetry to music. György Káldas, an enthusiast of Hungarian songs in the folk style, set to music Kosztolányi's translation of the *Blind girl*.[9] This was another attempt to present Rabindranath's poems as songs close to folk literature.

INTELLECTUAL INVOLVEMENT WITH TAGORE

The highest wave of Tagore's celebrity came shortly after World War I. Unlike the third wave in 1956–61, which disconnected itself markedly from the approach of the 1920s, this second phase did not feel any discomfort in being linked to Tagore's still-remembered reputation established in 1913–14.

Tagore's mass popularity in Hungary also raised opposition to the poet. This opposition came from all directions and there was no organised political or ideological group behind it. Representatives of the churches attacked those who wanted to show Tagore as a prophet, a bearer of a new ideology, but they still recognised him as a poet: 'Rabindranath Tagore is a true gem and we are free and right to study him as we do with the pagan poets of the Ancient Age.'[10] The extent of the Catholic Church's concern is indicated by the fact that in 1926 an apologetic book about Rabindranath was produced by the theologian István Záborszky (1893–1949).[11] He examined Tagore's ideas, interpreted them in terms of Western philosophy and rejected the tenets that contradicted the teaching of the Catholic Church, such as pantheistic monism, salvation without the help of God, etc. Nevertheless, his book appreciated the noble features of the Indian poet's approach. Although the author was aware of the variegated nature of Hinduism, he considered the Indian poet as its best representative, one who had reached the highest spiritual stages, and he valued Tagore's notion of love, optimism and spiritual depth.[12]

Rabindranath received the strongest attack from a person who was far from sharing the ideas of the Church, Georg Lukács (1885–1971), who after the fall of a short-lived Hungarian Soviet Republic in 1919, settled in Vienna. He read *The Home and the World* and, in a German article published in 1922 from Berlin in the magazine *Die rote Fahne*, he labelled the novel as 'a petit bourgeois yarn of the shoddiest kind' and explained Tagore's international fame as politically motivated; 'The British bourgeoisie ... *is repaying its intellectual agent in the struggle against the Indian freedom movement.*' Lukács's attitude shows as much of his superficial understanding of Indian culture as his vision of Tagore as a rival to the Communist movement. There were also journalists who criticised the Bengali poet.

In the 1920s, leading intellectuals were less interested in Tagore than was the general public. However, writers like Sándor Márai (1900–89), Zoltán Fábry (1897–1970) and Dezső Kosztolányi—all hailing from regions that were absorbed into other countries after the War—expressed their mixed feelings about the unprecedented literary cult of the Bengali poet but eventually recognised his human values and his poetic achievement.[13]

Two of the most outstanding authors from Transylvania, Aladár Kuncz (1885–1931) and Jenő Dsida (1907–38), celebrated Tagore unreservedly. Comparing the most influential poet of his time, Endre Ady (1877–1919), to Tagore, Kuncz wrote[14] that one of the fundamental characteristics of Ady's poetry was a constant emotional awareness of community with the world and with life, and consequently, in his poetry, concepts such as Nature and Self, Life and Death live in unity. According to Kuncz, this realisation of union was no different from the Indian idea of '*tat tvam asi*' and Ady was similar to Tagore, who lived in this unity. However, while Tagore wrote about the unity of life as the basic tenet of Indian philosophy, Ady did this on intuitive and emotional grounds. Kuncz also wrote a short story entitled 'The tree that set forth: To the melody of Tagore.'[15] Jenő Dsida's early poem 'Towards the Eastern Sunrise' is an example of Hungary's disappointment with the West and its turn towards the East.[16] Loaded with political allusions to the winning powers of the War, the poem expresses the author's disenchantment with Western civilisation, which destroyed the magic in the world, and salutes a turning towards the Orient, which he also took as the homeland of tales and the ancient homeland of the Hungarians. In this poem, the West was symbolised by Paris and the cynicism of Anatole France, while Tagore was hailed as the representative of the brightness of the East.

In the 1920s, Tagore's ideas received responses from authors who were born or lived in regions lost after the World War. As has been demonstrated recently by Ana Jelnikar, the positive reception of Tagore by those dislocated by War and experiencing oppression from the imperialism of Western powers was an example of what Patrick Colm Hogan calls situational identification, 'where we develop an immediate sense of intimacy with someone as we intuit shared feelings, ideas, references, [and] expectations.'[17]

Tagore's extraordinary popularity was followed by a period of indifference starting in the late 1920s, when even people who had earlier appreciated him became critical. An important document of this period is Rózsa Hajnóczy's (1892–1944) voluminous book, the *Fire of Bengal* (1943), about her three years in Santiniketan as the wife of a visiting professor. The book is a mixture of novel and travelogue. Despite the author's superficial acquaintance with Bengali culture, the *Fire of Bengal* became the most popular Hungarian book about India and ran into eleven editions between 1943 and 1985. With a superimposed love story, it gives an account of life in Santiniketan in the early 1930s. The author presents Tagore as a tired old man. With its sense of wonder at India, its exotic romanticism, mysticism, and critique of Tagore, the *Fire of Bengal* superseded Tagore's own works in Hungarian in readership.

Shortly before World War II, some Hungarian translations of Tagore's prose works appeared outside the borders of the country. The magazine *A Híd* from Subotica (Szabadka) in Yugoslavia published Tagore's writings to help the anti-Fascist cause. Excerpts from *Nationalism* and a letter to Yone Noguchi on the Japanese aggression of China under the title of 'Letter to a Japanese Poet' were published as well as a gloss about 'Rabindranath Tagore crying out against fascism in favour of the Spanish people.'[18]

A typical expression of the decline of Tagore's fame is found in the most influential Hungarian history of world literature, written by Antal Szerb (1901–45), and published in 1941. Even today, his work is the most popular Hungarian book on the history of world literature, and Szerb's judgement on Tagore must have influenced innumerable people. He allotted two paragraphs to Tagore—strangely in the chapter about English and American literature at the turn of the century.[19] Unlike in the case of his passages on other writers, Szerb's statements on Tagore are not based on proper study and are full of surprising mistakes. Of Tagore's literary output, Szerb concluded that 'all these have in common the usual Indian musings and a certain sanctimonious mysticism that also found its way to the heart of the undiscriminating in the world of European literature.'

TAGORE'S VISIT TO HUNGARY AND HIS PERSONAL CONTACTS WITH HUNGARIANS

On his European tour in 1926, Tagore stayed in Hungary between 26 October and 12 November. In Budapest, he gave a lecture on Indian philosophy, met Hungarian writers and scholars, and was received by the Regent Miklós Horthy. Nevertheless, the first few days of the visit were an unfortunate introduction for the aged poet. In his hotel, he was besieged by enthusiastic people carrying his books and wishing to obtain his signature or at the very least catch a glimpse of him. Even an overtaxing programme did not demonstrate to him the best elements of Hungarian literary life. Moreover, his Hungarian guide Ferenc Zajti (1886–1961), was more interested in convincing Rabindranath of his theory of the existence of a racial link between Hungarians and Indians than in paying attention to the needs of the exhausted guest.

The elderly poet was already tired. His health gave way and he fell sick. He left Budapest for a sanatorium in Balatonfüred near Lake Balaton. The ten autumn days he spent near one of the largest lakes of Europe made a deep impression on him.

After the poet's return to India, several Hungarian intellectuals visited Santiniketan. The first visitor, the Unitarian clergyman Ferenc Balázs (1901–37) from Transylvania, arrived in March 1928. He found Tagore to be the 'most beautiful man on earth' and under the influence of Sriniketan he started a rural development project in Transylvania. He was followed by Ervin Baktay (1890–1963), author of two early books on the poet. Although he found Tagore distant from life and Santiniketan disordered, he appreciated Rabindranath as a poet.[20] Visva-Bharati made a rather unfortunate decision in inviting Gyula Germanus (1884–1979) as professor of Islamic studies in Santiniketan. During his stay there between 1929 and 1932, Germanus became sceptical about the idea of the meeting of East and West. The painters Elizabeth Sass-Brunner (1889–1950) and her daughter Elizabeth Brunner (1910–2001) had a different attitude. Guided by their spiritual quest, they spent several months in Santiniketan. Finding new inspiration in India they chose the country as their home and produced pictures of Indian life, visionary images and portraits of people ranging from peasants to leading figures.

Reception under Communist Rule

During the first years of its independence, India was viewed with suspicion by Communist regimes. Publications kept repeating the same propagandistic ideas, including the denial of India's independence.[21] Nehru was denounced as 'the representative of the Indian high bourgeoisie' who 'allied up with imperialism against the Indian workers and farmers.'[22] Notwithstanding its inhuman dictatorial aspects, it was the Communist literary policy that appreciated Indian realism and began translations long before the West discovered post-colonial writings. During these years Tagore was forgotten.

In 1955, however, Soviet relationship with India underwent a change. Together with the establishment of close Indo–Soviet ties came the rediscovery of Tagore as an emblematic figure of India's anti-imperialistic struggle. Due to this development Tagore had an outstanding career in Hungary too. In February 1956, a representative exhibition of modern Indian paintings included Tagore's art; in May, an appreciative article was published about him in one of the leading dailies, and in October a bust of his was installed and an alley renamed after him in Balatonfüred. This eulogistic attitude was revived at the Tagore centenary. Writing under strict censorship, Tagore's love for freedom could also be evoked in coded messages against the hegemony of Marxist ideology:

> The unquestionably pure, upright and lofty thoughts of Tagore are permeated by the idea of peace, mutual respect and understanding. He raises his ideas against blind, vindictive and partial rationalism... we should quote the words of the heroine of his novel *Gora*, 'It must not be expected that people are forced to renounce their faith, ideas, or community just in order to be together with people who are different from them.'[23]

DIRECT TRANSLATIONS FROM BENGALI

Only a few new translations have appeared during the past fifty years. The most important development is that direct contact with the Bengali language has produced translations that are closer to the originals not only in content but also in form. The first direct Tagore translation closely reflecting the original's *dalabritta* rhythm (where syllables are counted) was the outcome of a joint effort of the outstanding Indologist József Vekerdi and of the present author in 1991. Since then we have translated some ten more songs. In a similar vein in 2011, relying on my prose translation, one of the leading Hungarian poets, János Lackfi, produced a Hungarian version of two songs that Tagore wrote in Hungary in 1926. While the translations with Professor Vekerdi reflect the original closely, those by Lackfi are close in meaning but have taken liberty with the form. I have also published several translations of prose poems from the collections *Shyamali* and *Punashcha* in literary magazines, as well as Hungarian versions of the stories 'Ghater katha' and 'Musalmanir galpa.'

CONTEMPORARY RESEARCH

In 1981, the Indologist Gyula Wojtilla published an English book titled *Rabindranath Tagore in Hungary* which has also been translated into Bengali. This is the first full-fledged treatment of the poet's contacts with the country. Professor Wojtilla was also one of the key figures behind the commemoration of the fiftieth anniversary of Tagore's death in 1991 with a research article on *Fireflies*. He also contributed to the organisation of an exhibition at the National Széchényi Library. The great interest in this exhibition marked Tagore's latent popularity. In recent years, editions of old books of Tagore's work have appeared and occasionally new translations were published. The most important Hungarian translations are also available on the Internet in the Terebess Ázsia E-Tár (or, Terebess Asia Online, TAO).[24] A few scholarly articles examined Tagore's contacts with Hungarians such as the clergyman Ferenc Balázs.[25] My English book about Hungarian and Bengali literary contacts in Hungary presents a detailed study of Tagore's reception in the country and of Tagore's ideas about Hungary.[26] The 150th anniversary of the poet's birth was celebrated with another exhibition at the National Széchenyi Library. Since the exhibition was set up in the cataloguing area, more people were exposed to visual Tagoreana in Hungarian than ever before. In March 2012, an International Conference was held at Eötvös Loránd University in Budapest with the sponsorship of the ICCR (Indian Council for Cultural Relations) and the active participation of the Indian Embassy.

PERSPECTIVES

Today, Tagore cannot be expected to command the same attention that he did in the 1920s. However, compared to other European countries, his work is not well known in Hungary. No Tagore drama has ever been performed in Hungarian. Even if Tagore is present in the book market, he is rarely translated by leading poets or quoted by intellectuals. Much needs to be done regarding direct translations, probably with the help of poets who can reflect the same power of language that Tagore captures in the originals. The presentation of Tagore's English essays still remains to be done, as does the presentation of any of his plays, probably in new translations. The study of Tagore as a figure of post-colonial literature is a further way forward. Unlike in Poland and the Czech Republic, Bengali is not taught in Hungary. The most urgent need, therefore, is to find people committed to the study of the Bengali language and culture who can become authentic interpreters of Rabindranath.

NOTES

1. 'Koszorús indiai költő' *Világ*, 14 November 1913, 12 and 'A Nobel irodalmi díj nyertese,' *Pesti Hírlap*, 14 November 1913, 16.
2. For an English translation of substantial responses from 1913 and 1914, see Bangha, 'Five responses to Rabindranath Tagore in Hungary.'
3. 'Este ötkor,' *Világ*, 5 April 1914, 12. This custom survives till the present.
4. The text can be found in Karinthy, 'Pályázom a Nobel-díjra.' I was not able to find its first publication. The reference to Tagore's 'recent' Nobel Prize indicates that it must have been written in 1913 or early 1914.
5. *The Inspiration of the Soul* is a translation of *Thoughts from Rabindranath Tagore* first published under the title *Thought Relics* in 1921. The Hungarian title, just like the Polish one, follows that of the German version, *Flüstern der Seele*. See also the essay on the Polish reception in this volume.
6. Földi, introduction, iv, vii.
7. Ibid., viii.
8. 'Lovári Műfordítások.'
9. His unpublished manuscript is preserved in the Hungary file of the Rabindra Bhavana, Santiniketan.
10. Bangha, 'Baktay Ervin.'
11. The book has 1927 as its year of publication but it was reviewed in several papers in the autumn of 1926.
12. Záborszky, *Rabindranath Tagore világnézete*, 77.
13. Sándor Márai, 'Tagore,' *Kassai Napló*, 3 July 1921; [Zoltán Fábry], 'Külföldi glosszák—Tallózás külföldi lapokból: Tagore,' *Kassai Napló*, 17 December 1922, 9, and Kosztolányi, 'Érzések és gondolatok egy estélyen.'
14. Kuncz, 'Révész Béla Adyról.'
15. Kuncz, 'Megindult fa.'
16. Dsida, 'Napkelet felé.'
17. Hogan, *Empire and Poetic Voice*, 26, quoted in Jelnikar, 'Towards universalism,' 15.
18. [Laták], 'Szemelvény'; Fekete, 'Levél egy Japán költőhöz'; and *A Híd*, May 1937, 24.
19. Szerb, *A világirodalom története*, vol. 2, 381.
20. Baktay, 'Rabindranáth Tagore,' 226–7.
21. Makai, *India*, 24. See also Blaskovics et al., *Zsoldosok*, back cover.

22. Ibid., 23–4.
23. Csertői, 'Rabindranath Tagore.'
24. 'Rabindranath Tagore (1861–1941) versei': www.terebess.hu/keletkultinfo/
    tagorevers.html.
25. Mészely, 'Balázs Ferenc indiai útja,' and Bors, 'Egy erdélyi Keleten.'
26. Bangha, *Hungry Tiger.*

WORKS CITED

Baktay, Ervin. 'Rabindranáth Tagore.' In *Nobel-díjas írók antológiája* [Anthology of Nobel Prize-winning writers]. Káldor: Budapest, 1935, 226–7

Bangha, Béla. 'Baktay Ervin: Rabindranath Tagore' *Magyar Kultúra* 1921, 186–7.

——. 'Five responses to Rabindranath Tagore in Hungary: 1913–14.' In *Rabindranath Tagore: A Timeless Mind,* edited by Amalendu Biswas, et al., 1–14. London: Tagore Centre, 2011.

——. *Hungry Tiger.* New Delhi: Sahitya Akademi, 2008.

Blaskovics, József et al. tr. *Zsoldosok* [Mercenaries]. Pozsony: Magyar Kiadó, 1953.

Bors, Mónika. 'Egy erdélyi Keleten: száz évvel Kőrösi Csoma után: Balázs Ferenc' [A Transylvanian in the Orient: hundred years after Alexander Csoma: Ferenc Balázs]. In *Kőrösi Csoma Sándor és a test és lélek a keleti kultúrákban.* Edited by József Gazda et al., 120–36. Kovászna: KCsSKE, 2006.

Csertői, Oszkár. 'Rabindranath Tagore.' *Pest Megyei Hírlap*, 7 May 1961, 5.

Dsida, Jenő. 'Napkelet felé' [Towards the Sunrise]. *Pásztortűz*, 18 October 1925, 1.

Fekete, Béla [Stern, Emil] tr. 'Levél egy Japán költőhöz' [Letter to a Japanese poet]. *A Híd*, January–February 1939, 37–40.

Földi, Mihály. Introduction to *Rabindra Nath Tagore: Az élet megismerése: Sādhanā* [Rabindranath Tagore: The Knowledge of Life: *Sādhanā*]. Budapest: Révai, 1921, i–viii.

Hajnóczy, Rózsa. *Fire of Bengal.* Translated by Éva Wimmer, edited by William Radice. Dhaka: The University Press, 1993.

Hogan, Patrick Colm. *Empire and Poetic Voice: Cognitive and Cultural Studies of Literary Tradition and Colonialism.* Albany, NY, USA: State University of New York Press, 2004.

Jelnikar, Ana. 'Towards universalism: Rabindranath Tagore and Srečko Kosovel: A joint perspective in a disjointed world.' PhD Diss., University of London, 2009.

Karinthy, Frigyes. 'Pályázom a Nobel-díjra' [I am aspiring for the Nobel Prize]. In *Ne bántsuk egymást, újabb tréfák*, by Frigyes Karinthy, 98–100. Budapest: Pallas, 1921.

Kosztolányi, Dezső: 'Érzések és gondolatok egy estélyen' [Impressions and Thoughts at a Soirée]. *Nyugat* vol. 19 (1926), 782–84.

Kuncz, Aladár. 'Révész Béla Adyról' [Béla Révész about Ady]. *Nyugat* vol. 15 (1922), 871–5.

——. 'Megindult fa: Tagore dallamára' [The Tree that Set Forth: To the Melody of Tagore]. *Aurora*, 1923, 274–7.

[Laták, István] Cs., tr. 'Szemelvény Tagore Rabindranath Nacionalizmus című művéből' [Excerpt from Rabindranath Tagore's *Nationalism*]. *A Híd*, April 1935, 3.

[no author mentioned]. 'Lovári Műfordítások' Zrínyi Miklós Nemzetvédelmi Egyetem, accessed 30 November 2012, http://konyvtarportal.zmne.hu/web/guest/124.

Lukács, Georg. 'Tagore's Gandhi Novel: Review of Rabindranath Tagore's *The Home and the World.*' In *Reviews and Articles from Die Rote Fahne*, by Georg Lukács, tr. Peter Palmer, 8–11. London: Merlin Press, 1983. Accessed 15 November 2012, http://www.marxists.org/archive/lukacs/works/1922/tagore.htm.

Makai, György. *India: útmutató városi és falusi előadók részére* [India: Guide for lecturers in towns and villages]. Budapest: Művelt Nép, 1952.

Mészely, Réka. 'Balázs Ferenc indiai útja. Találkozás Ghandival és Tagoréval' [The Indian journey of Ferenc Balázs: Meeting with Ghandi (*sic*) and Tagore]. *Művelődés* no. 11, 2001, 1–18.

Szerb, Antal. *A világirodalom története* [History of World Literature], 2 vols. Budapest: Magvető, 1989.

Tagore, Rabindranath. *Költői műveiből* [From his poetic works]. Translated from English by Ferenc Kelen. Budapest: Athaeneum, [1914].

Wojtilla, Gyula. *Rabindranath Tagore in Hungary.* New Delhi: Hungarian Information and Cultural Centre, 1983.

———. *Hāṅgerīte Rabīndranāth* [Rabindranath Tagore in Hungary]. Calcutta: Navayug Publishers, 1984.

Záborszky, István. *Rabindranath Tagore világnézete.* Budapest: Szent István Társulat, 1927.

20

Czechoslovakia and its Successors

Martin Hříbek

Czech Imagination of India before Tagore

The Czechoslovak republic, located in Central Europe, derived its continuity from the medieval Czech kingdom which was associated with the Holy Roman Empire. Czechoslovakia was formed in 1918 out of the territory of the original Czech kingdom and the Slav dominated northern part of Hungary which became Slovakia. Czechoslovakia split peacefully into the Czech Republic and Slovakia in 1993. This essay examines primarily the Czech reception of Tagore, with some remarks about the Slovak reception, and looks at personal contacts with the Germans of Prague.

The social, cultural and literary context of Tagore's reception in Czechoslovakia did not merely derive from Western/European discourses on the author but rather was located in the discourse of Czech national revival and the role that imagination of and knowledge about India had to play in it. The nineteenth century, in Bohemia as in Bengal, was a time of fervent nationalist activity. The Czech national revival within the framework of the Austrian (from 1867 Austro-Hungarian) Empire ran, in many ways, parallel to the Bengal Renaissance.

Czechs, as well as other nascent Slav nations in Central Europe, built their national consciousness in opposition to the German cultural hegemony and to the Austro-Hungarian state. As I have argued elsewhere,[1] the Czech imagination about India did not derive from British or French discourses on the Orient but from and in opposition to German constructions of India. While the British and the French largely construed the Orient they actually dominated over as other and inferior,[2] the German India scholars, writing in the context of German national resurgence, combined the notion of affinity between Germans and ancient Indians with that of cultural superiority over what was left of India's past glory, positing Germany as the inheritor of that ancient civilisation.[3]

The fact that India played an important role in Germany's claim for a national future did not go unnoticed by Czech revivalists whose effort reflected and countered that of German India scholars. Turning to philology and the newly discovered similarity of Slav languages with Sanskrit they argued that the Slavs' affinity with India is much closer than that of Germans. This argument developed into an extensive exploration and construction of links between Slav and Indian cultures in the field of language, mythology, and religion and even stimulated such curious experiments as Czech poetry in old Indian metres.[4]

However, our revivalists were not interested exclusively in India's past. From an early stage, they were aware of the Bengal Renaissance and the reformist effort of the Brahmo Samaj and related it directly to the struggle of Czechs against German cultural hegemony.[5] This situational identification based on parallel and coeval struggles of the two peoples against foreign oppression resulted in a sense of equality and common destiny.[6]

Tagore was thus perceived by Czechs not only as a purveyor of Oriental wisdom and a celebrated writer but also as a cultural ambassador of a brotherly nation. This affinity thesis, consistent with the dominant nationalist discourse about a small nation struggling for, and finally attaining statehood (1918), had remained for long the dominant framework for Tagore's reception in Czechoslovakia. There were, indeed, other interpretive frameworks with less influence, such as that of the revolutionary Left or the discourse of occultism and the Oriental Renaissance, which entered Czech public debate in the 1870s via the reading of Schopenhauer and the first Czech treatises on Indian philosophy interpreted in that framework.[7]

No less important for the reception of Tagore was the early establishment of Indological studies in Prague. Regular courses in Sanskrit started in 1850 and by the end of the century, full-fledged classical Indology departments were already firmly established at both Czech and German Universities. In the first decades of the twentieth century, the scope of research extended to modern Indian languages and literatures.

A periodisation of Tagore's reception in Czechoslovakia would best follow major ruptures of her modern history. The first period of early responses roughly corresponds with World War I, that is from the first reactions to the Nobel Prize to the creation of Czechoslovakia (1913–18). The second period spans the democratic Czechoslovakia from the birth of the country to the beginning of the Communist rule (1918–48), with an intermezzo during the Nazi occupation (1939–45) when Tagore was banned from the book market due to his anti-Fascist position. The third period covers the Communist rule (1948–89) and the fourth lasts since its breakdown in 1989 onwards.

At the time of writing, there were thirty-nine Czech and seven Slovak translations of Tagore published as books (excluding reprints and new editions), a large part of them done from Bengali originals; and many more individual poems, stories, and thoughts are scattered in various journals. In general, the translations in the first two periods of reception were characterised by an emphasis on reflexive poetry, spiritual aspects, and on humanism vis-à-vis the national sentiment. During the period of Communist rule the emphasis shifted to prose, realism, social criticism, and Tagore's progressive thought. The fourth period re-evaluated Tagore as a religious thinker.

EARLY RECEPTION (1913–18)

The news about the Nobel Prize for Literature awarded to Rabindranath Tagore was widely publicised in the Czech press, often in connection with the fact that his closest competitor was the Austrian author Peter Rosegger.[8] One of the first reports from November 1913, full of factual errors about Tagore, confidently concludes that he 'undoubtedly deserved the Nobel Prize (187,000 francs) more than Rosegger.'[9] A footnote to the first Czech translation of two *Gitanjali* poems from December 1913 states that Tagore 'as an author and a humanist surely stands much higher than the German writer Rosegger.'[10] This fact was again mentioned in the first reviews of Czech translations of *Gitanjali*: 'We still vividly remember all that helpless rage of the German press when Rabindranath Tagore drove out the German candidate Peter Rosegger. How many crude jokes they showered on the head of a poet they did not even know.'[11] The Rosegger issue was alive even after World War I, in the news about Tagore's prospective visit to Germany or his plays being staged there.

A more knowledgeable report from November 1913 (based on a biography of Tagore by A. C. Bhattacharyya published in *Berliner Tageblatt*) describes Tagore as 'Maharshi, or great saint' and as 'Indian national poet,' not 'Anglo-Indian poet' as the British press would have had him. The report mentions some of his original Bengali works and praises his educational efforts in Santiniketan. It further states that 'Tagore has never been interested in politics at all,' and that his works are 'philosophico-religious.' However, he 'substantially contributed to the boosting of the national sentiment of his compatriots.' Tagore is 'an Oriental poet with purely Oriental ideas and views, which often differ from European views, in particular regarding the relationship between an individual and the nation.'[12] In rare cases, Tagore would be labelled as theosophist or neo-Buddhist. Further articles throughout 1914 kept on bringing out news about Tagore's literary endeavours. The archives also bear evidence of amateur translations of individual poems by Tagore's Czech admirers.

The very first published Czech translation of Tagore (*Gitanjali* 61 and 62, *The Gardener* 7) came out in a local newspaper in December 1913.[13] It was followed by a full translation of *Gitanjali* from English in early 1914 by a philosopher, translator, and author of two treatises on Czech nationhood, František Balej (1873–1918). The demand was such that the book had to be reprinted five times till 1921. Balej also wrote an introduction to his translation and framed it with the theme of Euro–Asian relations emphasising, interestingly for our times, the notion of young Asia rising. Tagore was to him one of the symbols of that process: 'It is an exciting spectacle. India, exploited by Europe for centuries, pays back in evangelical coin; she sends us a poet, a preacher of love, freedom, joy of life, of unity and equality of all creation,'[14] Balej notes. Then he presents translated excerpts of *Sadhana*, on soul, death, and personality, in order to outline Tagore's world view without which, he believed, *Gitanjali* would be less accessible to Czech readers. Finally, he reflects in the form of open-ended questions on the reasons for Tagore's impact on readers in Europe: Could Tagore have drunk from a source of poetic and spiritual inspiration which is beyond culture and history? Does he remind us of what we have lost in the rush of our technical civilisation? Or is it an effect of the underlying unity of humankind?[15]

A review of this translation compared Tagore to Francis of Assisi and his poetry to that of two Czech symbolist poets, Otokar Březina and Antonín Sova.[16] Březina in particular, influenced by the 'Oriental Renaissance,' remained the single Czech author deemed the closest in spirit and form to Tagore. Importantly, the closeness of the two poets, the reviewer argued, proved that 'exotic' and 'timeless' Tagore was, in fact, very near to our (Czech) heart, that he had a special meaning for us, as if 'we' had a privileged access to his thought. This presumption is a leitmotif of Czech discourse on Tagore in the first two periods of reception.

The second book *Ukázky poesie i prosy* (Examples of Poetry and Prose) was translated directly from Bengali by Vincenc Lesný (1882–1953), an Indologist and founding figure of Bengali studies in Prague. Lesný originally studied languages of ancient India, namely Sanskrit and Pali, but later he became interested also in Hindi, Marathi and Bengali and wrote extensively about social and political affairs in India in the two decades before her Independence (achieved in 1947).[17] Lesný exchanged letters with Tagore from 1913 and has to be credited that he was the first European translator of Tagore directly from the Bengali originals. The book on 'Examples of Poetry and Prose' was published a few months after Balej's translation. This short book contains ten poems from the Bengali *Gitanjali* in verse, a short story *The In-Between Woman* from *Galpaguccha* and four excerpts from *Sadhana* translated from English.

In his introduction written in March 1914, Lesný mentions the reformist and literary activities of the Tagore family including the short story writing of Swarnakumari Debi and locates Tagore's work in the context of modern Bengali literature, summarising his efforts in various genres. Clearly, Lesný's goal was to present Tagore as a versatile author of world literature first, and a philosopher second; there was no mention of his being a seer or a prophet. Lesný's academic authority indeed contributed to Tagore being interpreted in the Czech discourse largely as a poet and a philosopher and only marginally as a prophet or a seer.[18] In fact Lesný systematically countered Orientalising interpretations of Tagore and India in general in favour of the affinity thesis.

Nevertheless, his translation came out in an Oriental Library series as number five, being preceded by Parables of Christ, Quran, Talmud, and 'Dharm' (Teachings of Buddha). Interestingly, the graphic design of the front cover has the name of the author 'Shri Rabindranath Tagore' in a Bengali font. The book was reprinted once in 1916, but it did not reach the popularity of the complete *Gitanjali*. A reviewer of Lesný's translation, who also knew that of Balej, concluded on the basis of both that Tagore's poetry is more prominent by its intensity rather than by the scope of ideas or emotions expressed. As for Tagore's short stories the reviewer considered them naïve.[19]

The third Czech translator of Tagore, albeit again from English, was Věra Stephanová, 'a girl twenty years of age' who asked Tagore to grant her permission to translate his works into 'Russian and Bohemian' (i.e., Czech) in a passionate letter dated 2 December 1913.[20] Věra Stephanová's Czech translation of *The Gardener* appeared in 1914 and five songs were immediately set to music by Josef Bohuslav Foerster (1859–1951) as *Milostné písně* (Love Songs) op. 96. Her translation of *The Crescent Moon* was published in 1915 (and again in 1920 and 1936). A review of *The Crescent Moon* compares it to *Gitanjali* with a gendered metaphor. In the former, Tagore 'addresses God like a man would speak to man, sometimes longing for him as a friend, sometimes submitting to him as a subject submits to a sovereign wise ruler,' while the latter is a 'typical work of a youthful female heart.'[21]

In 1916, translations of *Sadhana* and *The Gardener* by Balej further enlarged the access of Czech readers to Tagore. Balej was more precise and rendered *The Gardener* in what we might call a biblical style. While Stephanová is less truthful to the original, missing or twisting words at times, she definitely makes Tagore sound more passionate than Balej. Balej's translation gained immense popularity with seven reprints, the 1930 edition being a bibliophilic one with a print run of only 200 copies.

The initial reception of Tagore was thus based largely on those five collections. The emphasis on contemplative poetry clearly related to the horrors of World War I. The major Czech publisher of Tagore recollects in the late 1930s: 'I cannot miss to mention the great consolation that *Gitanjali* and *Sadhana* provided to our Czech soldiers during the World War in their most trying moments when they were leaving for the battlefield. Before the departure of every new contingent of recruits our sales soared.'[22] Unlike in the following periods the implicit notions of crisis of European modernity and the rise of Asia influenced Tagore's reception.[23] Nevertheless, this period built on the framework set in the nineteenth century, and despite possible diversions into an Orientalist discourse, the Nationalistic interpretation of Tagore prevailed and realised fully once independent Czechoslovakia was established.

TAGORE ON THE NATIONAL FRONT (1918–48)

This period is the most intense in terms of direct engagement of the Czech public with Tagore and his work. He visited Czechoslovakia twice, in 1921 and 1926, and invited numerous responses from Czech academia and the art world alike. Before his first visit, more translations and reviews brought him closer to Czech readers. A collection of short stories translated from English by Josef Trumpus appeared in 1919. *The Home and the World* was rendered from English into Czech by Antonín Klášterský (1866–1938) the following year. Klášterský was a popular poet and translator of William Shakespeare's sonnets. One review of *The Home and the World* termed the novel a 'political and national credo of Tagore,' which can also be expressed as an opposition of 'nationality versus cosmopolitanism' or 'Nietzsche versus Jesus.'[24] This observation, as I will show later, points to a crucial aspect of Czech reception of Tagore.

In 1920 appeared *The King of the Dark Chamber*, for a larger part translated from English by Balej (who had died in 1918), corrected and completed by Lesný from the Bengali original. An important theatre critic Václav Tille (1867–1937) published an analysis of the play where he compared Tagore's efforts in the field of drama to the works of another Nobel laureate, the Belgian symbolist Maurice Maeterlinck. Tille appreciated the play as 'the latest and the most truthful attempt' to personify on stage 'the Mysterious in the hands of which Man is a mere doll.' He further credits Tagore for 'a more realistic' representation of 'the Mysterious' on stage in the form of a character, an attempt going beyond Maeterlinck.[25] For Tille, it was the direct engagement with 'the Mysterious' and the realism of its representation which made Tagore a leading modern dramatist.

Another play, *The Post Office*, was translated from English in 1921 by Jarmil Krecar (1884–1959), a significant personality of the Czech literary decadence movement (an offshoot of romantic symbolism obsessed with decay and morbidity) who was active as a writer, poet, playwright and literary critic.[26] It was also the first Tagore play staged in Prague, albeit in a Russian production by the Moscow Art Theatre on 4 June 1923.[27]

Translations of *Nationalism in the West* by L. Haut as well as a complete translation of *Nationalism* in 1921 by Vasil Kaprálek Škrach invited many responses. Škrach (1891–1943) was a philosopher, sociologist, and translator, a close associate of the first Czechoslovak president Tomáš Garrigue Masaryk. Škrach himself felt compelled to comment upon Tagore's notion of nationalism in his afterword:

> Rabindranath Tagore uses the terms nation and nationalism in a different sense [from what] we usually do. Tagore understands nation to be chiefly an instrument of political, economic and technological civilisation. ... For us, on the other hand, a nation is a natural collective individuality whose members feel the bond of blood, love for the soil and understand fully their cultural community. ... As we can see, Tagore's opposition to Western nationalism is, in fact, very close to our humanistic nationalism. ... What he actually means by nationalism is Western etatism and imperialism.

The translator struggles to identify Czech nationalism with Tagore's humanism in order to establish a common front of Czechs and Indians against the various types of imperialisms of which he considers the Pan-Germanic the most heinous. Finally, Škrach believes that had Tagore been acquainted with the Czech case 'he could have raised many of his arguments with still more justification precisely against the Pan-Germanic nationalism.'[28]

This rather forced attempt at forging the affinity thesis however, was not shared, unsurprisingly, by the revolutionary Left. Thus Josef Hora (1891–1945), a notable poet and critic of the interwar period, referred to Tagore in his essay *Kulturní smysl doby* (The Cultural Meaning of our Times). Hora glorifies the successes of the revolution in Russia and calls for the destruction of bourgeois cultural values and tastes and of the bourgeois notion of nationalism. He further discusses Tagore's *Nationalism* and fervently criticises him as a representative of the retrograde religious-minded East as opposed to the progressive East of Russia: 'The misery of passivity, the misery of religion that destroys spirit survives today only in the East. Even today there exists a genius preaching to Indians joy of subjugation.' Tagore who 'condemned the hydra of nationalism' and 'aptly depicted the spiral of poverty encircling the world,' finally, writes on behalf of his compatriots suffering under the British whip ... 'We shall thank God that we were made to wait in silence through the night of despair, had to bear the insult of the proud and the strong man's burden, yet all through it, though our hearts quaked with doubt and fear, never could we blindly believe in the salvation which machinery offered to man, but we held fast to our trust in God and the truth of the human soul.'[29] ... How beautiful a human being is this Indian poet! And how bad a citizen! Was blood spilled just for us to pray and wait in mystical ecstasy for future truths? Thank god it is not so. European blood is more revolutionary than that. There is another East apart from India. There is Russia and the example she gave us.[30]

The affinity thesis, however, remained the most influential framework for the reception of Tagore.

The year 1921 marked the first visit of Tagore to Prague. The poet came at the invitation of Vincenc Lesný whom he had met in October 1920 in London and Moriz Winternitz (1863–1937) who had corresponded with Tagore prior to his visit.[31] Both Indologists were instrumental in presenting Tagore to the Czechoslovak public, Czech and German-speaking respectively, and both in turn accepted Tagore's invitation to become visiting professors in Santiniketan.[32] Another friend whom Tagore knew from London and who was going to become an art teacher in Santiniketan was the painter Jaroslav Hněvkovský (1884–1956).[33]

Tagore arrived in Prague on the morning of 18 June from Vienna by train and stayed for three days. The poet was felicitated by university dignitaries, scientists and the Lord Mayor of Prague. At 11 a.m., he listened to a welcome address by the Rector of Charles University in the convocation hall after which he gave a lecture on the religion of the Bauls of Bengal and Buddha's teachings.[34] Although general reports say his performance met with great applause, one highly satirical article by a noted literary critic, Arne Novák (1880–1939), points to the shock waves that Tagore sent through the more conservative section of the academic audience:

In fact, it was not a lecture, it was a holy ceremony. Great sacrificial and benedictory gestures, chants, none of that was missing. ... If he [Tagore] could observe his surroundings, he would have felt at home: Brahmins and Hanumans sit still on elevated benches of the professorial guild and strike strange poses. They are not amazed, they are not happy. At first, they do not know themselves why, but one thing they know for sure: that the sacred university soil has been abused. A scripture which mortifies will always hate spirit which enlivens. Alas, there is no method here, only intuition; there is no guild, no rank, not even the academic distance, just the monster of personality. The bureaucratic order was taken over, albeit for one hour, by the flash of a genius. Mr. Tagore of India is perhaps wise but for sure he is possessed: he drank the nectar of holy waters, not the content of an inkpot, that's why he ignores so arrogantly everything—a clear-cut framework, logical procedures, and, what worse, even the university officials and deans. And then the most horrific thing happens: Rabindranath starts singing in the convocation hall.[35]

Besides the lecture at the Charles University, Tagore also spoke on forest ashrams as centres of learning at the German university in Prague on the invitation of Winternitz. His most successful public appearance, however, was in the largest auditorium in Prague, the Lucerna Hall. The lectures were attended by many eminent personalities including the composer Leoš Janáček (1854–1928) who wrote a passionate article for a local newspaper which included a noted record of the speech melody of Tagore reciting his poems in Bengali. Janáček described it in the following words:

It was not a speech—it sounded like a song of a nightingale, smooth, simple, devoid of any harshness of the diphthongs. It occurred to me to fall in with a gay chord with the initial sounds of the poem he read out; I heard soft harmonious voices or sounds, but it was incoherent to me. The melody kept on falling down in a torrent of tones.[36]

Janáček wrote his famous male chorus with boy soprano, *Wandering Madman*, on the words of *The Gardener* 66 in 1922. The character of the boy who reveals to the madman that he had found and lost the touchstone struck Janáček deeply; there are even indications that this motif returns in his opera *The Cunning Little Vixen* (1924). The last lines of the poem are engraved on Janáček's tombstone. The students of Foerster and Janáček further enlarged the collection of Tagore-inspired Czech musical compositions, a collection that has been growing ever since.[37]

Other personalities who were deeply impressed by Tagore's lecture included the prominent Czech photographer, practitioner of *Vajrayana* meditation and collaborator of the Theosophical Society, František Drtikol (1883–1961,) who made studio portraits of Tagore during his second visit in 1926, the founder of modern Czech sculpture Josef Václav Myslbek (1848–1922) and painter Max Švabinský (1873–1962) who both were inspired to portray the poet.[38] And also Karel Čapek (1890–1938), the most prominent Czechoslovak author of the interwar period, who was instrumental in organising Tagore's second visit to Prague. Čapek met Tagore privately and observed him with a sympathetic, yet distanced and highly inquisitive eye, as evident from his description of the meeting:

In his grey attire of rough silk this delicate old man looks like Correggio's God the Father or Moses, or an apostle by an artist from Nazareth. ... His speech is soft and sweet, his silence still sweeter. ... His slightly grey-haired secretary, in keeping with ritual promise, stays away from meat but gulps down open sandwiches with ham. Does he believe it is fish or what? Rabindranath Tagore with hands cupped on his chest seems to pray. One expects a miracle will happen. Instead of a miracle the beautiful old man rises, floats around the room and says his Good Bye in a thin voice. Tomorrow he has a lecture or rather, he sings his poems. When he recites his drama, he utters the female part with a childish high pitch. His whole presence radiates not just an oriental culture of poetry and thought but, and perhaps still more forcefully, a strangely refined culture of aristocratic physical perfection and lived aestheticism which is self-conscious in every movement.[39]

In the years following Tagore's first visit, further translations of his works appeared: *Glimpses of Bengal* in 1922, *Lover's Gift* and *Fruit-Gathering* in 1923, *The Wreck* translated from English by Lesný's wife Milada Lesná-Krausová and *The Waterfall* translated by V. Lesný from the Bengali in 1924. *Chitra* was translated from English the same year.

In the first Czech production, Tagore's plays *The Post Office* and *Chitra* were staged jointly as *The Evening of Rabindranath Tagore (Drama)* at the two most prestigious venues in Prague, the National Theatre and the Theatre of Estates. The opening night's performance took place on 31 January 1924 in the latter; however, the production invited critical reviews.[40] Another five joint performances followed in February the same year. In 1925, *Chitra* was presented four times along with short plays other than Tagore's until the last show on 5 March 1925. The last performance of *The Post Office* was attended by Tagore himself on 12 October 1926.[41] *The Post Office* was also staged in 1935 in the Moravian town of Břeclav.

In the meantime, Lesný published *The Parrot's Tale* as a private printing with illustrations by Abanindranath Tagore in 1925 and the next year *Lipika*, both translated from the Bengali. The latter included most of the original stories except those that Lesný thought Tagore himself would have excluded if he presented *Lipika* to the Western readers.[42] The translation of *Gora* from English by Milada Lesná Krausová also appeared in 1926. It was the year of Tagore's second visit to Czechoslovakia, this time at the invitation of the Czechoslovak PEN Club and its president Karel Čapek.

Tagore came from Berlin on 9 October and stayed in Prague for a week. On the night of his arrival he attended a dinner reception hosted by the PEN Club at the Municipal House in the presence of the Lord Mayor of Prague, government officials, foreign diplomats, the literati and the art world. The next day at 10.30 a.m., Tagore delivered a public lecture in the Lucerna Hall. As a newspaper report goes, Tagore, 'dressed in a bright red robe,' was introduced by Lesný. Then he was reading out his ideas on art and punctuating this by dramatically reciting his poems in a melodious high-pitched voice in Bengali. Both were simultaneously translated into Czech by Lesný. A huge applause called for several more poems and finally Tagore was 'besieged by autograph hunting ladies.'[43]

On 11 October, Tagore lectured and recited for the German audience at the Commodity Exchange in Prague where he was introduced and simultaneously translated by Moriz Winternitz. In the evening of 12 October, Tagore appeared on the stage of the National Theatre where, after an introduction by Lesný, he again recited his poems. The second part of the evening was marked by the last show of *The Post Office* in a Czech production. The following day Tagore, accompanied by Lesný, Winternitz and Čapek, made a trip to the countryside of Central Bohemia. In the evening Tagore was felicitated in the New German Theatre by a musical programme which included the *Lyric Symphony* by Alexander Zemlinsky on the words of *The Gardener* and by a German production of *The Post Office*. In the evening of 14 October, Tagore delivered his last public speech in Prague on 'Civilization and Progress.' Before his departure to Vienna the next day, he bid farewell to the Czechoslovak public on the national radio.[44]

The two visits of Tagore to Czechoslovakia marked the peak of interest in the poet. Although news about his travels, success and health appeared regularly and some of his earlier published works were reprinted, it was not until the late 1930s that interest in Tagore emerged with a new intensity. In 1938, Lesný sent to print a collection of Tagore's short stories,[45] most of which he had translated earlier for various periodicals. More important, however are two original books on Tagore which appeared in close sequence. Winternitz published a monograph *Rabindranath Tagore: Religion und Weltanschauung des Dichters* (The Poet's Religion and World Vision)[46] in 1936 on the occasion of the poet's 75th birthday. In 1937, Lesný published a monograph *Rabíndranáth Thákur (Tagore): Osobnost a dílo*, which was translated into English under the title *Rabindranath Tagore: His Personality and Work* with an enthusiastic foreword by C. F. Andrews and published in London in 1939. Czech reviews of Lesný's monograph were positive, if not laudatory,[47] in as much as Lesný was laudatory about Tagore. The poet in turn praised Lesný in a letter written in Bengali on 5 August 1936, reprinted in the monograph, for he 'grasped the essence of Bengali language and his

Martin Hříbek

works in such a short time' and displayed 'a level of comprehension and strength of judgement' that Tagore did not see in any other foreigner.[48]

However, there are indications that when the English version was being prepared for print Tagore was not so enthusiastic. In a letter to C. F. Andrews dated 8 September 1938, he wrote: 'Lesný's book about me has not been a happy one. I wish he had not allowed it to be translated and published in England.'[49] The book did not attract much critical discussion after its publication as nearly the whole print run was burnt down during the London Blitz. Tagore for his part never levelled any criticism at Lesný directly. The events in Europe, approaching fast towards the conflagration of World War II dominated their correspondence in the late 1930s.

Before Czechoslovakia became a victim of Hitler's expansion, the Czech–German divide had widened, and with it resurfaced the idea of Czech–Indian affinity. Tagore expressed solidarity with Czechoslovakia on a number of occasions. The most memorable was his response to a peace appeal broadcast on all channels of Czechoslovak Radio on Christmas Eve of 1937. Karel Čapek read out the message in Czech and Professor Lesný in English with a few Bengali words at the end. Tagore responded by a cable expressing goodwill and through a poem.[50] In response to the Munich agreement Tagore wrote another poem, *Prayashcitta*, and expressed his condolences to Lesný as well to the President of Czechoslovakia Edvard Beneš. This exchange and Tagore's strongly anti-Fascist position were important for his reception in the following period.

In the years of World War II, Tagore's works were proscribed.[51] The only Tagore translation known to have been published then is a four-copy samizdat print of *Creative Unity*, translated from English by O. Jelínek and Luboš Perek. Perek who was then twenty-five, later became a noted astronomer and Chief of the Outer Space Affairs Division with the UN. Despite the ban, however, the news of Tagore's death appeared in the Czech press. The short period between the end of the War and the Communist takeover (1945–8) saw numerous reprints of Tagore's works. The only new translation was *Basanta* by Lesný published serially over 1945–6 and the very first translation into Slovak of *The Home and the World* from English in 1946.

TAGORE ON THE CULTURAL FRONT (1948–89)

During the third period of reception, Tagore was presented predominantly as a religious and social reformer, as progressive-minded and a fighter against superstitious practices; as anti-imperialist yet, at the same time, a critic of those who placed the national sentiment over social emancipation of the people. In post-World War II prefaces and afterwords to his translations, his anti-Fascist position was often emphasised, including his condemnation of the Nazi occupation of Czechoslovakia.

The years around the birth centenary of Rabindranath Tagore brought extensive editions of his works translated from the Bengali originals almost singlehandedly by our greatest scholar in the field of Bengali studies, Dušan Zbavitel (1925–2012).[52] The first collection, *Pouť za člověkem* (The Pilgrimage towards Man), published in 1954 contains a selection of poems, *Red Oleanders*, *Kaler Yatra*, several short stories, *Letters from Russia*, several articles and letters. Some of these translations were reprinted in the collected works of Rabindranath Tagore in three volumes published in 1958, 1959, and 1960 respectively.

The first volume *Básně a veršovaná dramata* (Poems and Dramas in Verses) presents a chronological selection of 162 Tagore poems from thirty-six original Bengali collections[53] and two dramas in verses, *Chitrangada* and *Kaler Yatra*. It aimed at demonstrating the development of Tagore's poetry with emphasis on worldly subjects including social and political issues. The translator kept the verse form of the original in contrast to earlier translations from English which were invariably in prose. The second volume includes two novels, *Gora* and *Two Sisters*. Zbavitel's Czech translation of *Gora* was also published separately in a Slovak version in 1960. The third volume under the title *Povídky, essaye a projevy* (Short stories, Essays and Discourses) consists of thirty-three short stories selected from *Galpaguccha* followed by *My Boyhood Days*, *Letters from Russia*, articles and open letters.[54]

Reviews of those volumes testify to the fact that the perception of Tagore has changed. A reviewer of the first one notes that the interwar period readers appreciated most the philosophical consequences of the idea of internal liberation, which, in the opinion of the reviewer, was an easy escape route from an engagement in a collective action. However, he was confident that 'had this been the only aspect of Tagore's work, the Soviet book market could hardly be stuffed with translations of Tagore's novels and the volume under review could not have made it to press either.'[55] A 1960 essay reacting to the publication of *Gora* interprets Tagore as a progressive writer who was nevertheless limited in his 'enlightened humanism' and could not see through the ultimate class nature of the conflict depicted in the novel.[56] A review of the last volume, albeit sympathetic both to Tagore and his translator, contends with respect to *Letters from Russia* that Tagore 'did not fully understand the complex dialectics of humanism and revolutionary violence.'[57]

In 1961, Zbavitel published a second Czech monograph on the poet entitled *Rabíndranáth Thákur: vývoj básníka* (Rabindranath Tagore:

The Evolution of a Poet). His appreciation of Tagore is more critical and distanced than was that of Lesný. Zbavitel puts the evolution of Tagore's poetry and prose systematically in the context of the social developments India was undergoing in his lifetime. Zbavitel places in the highest rung the aspect of critical realism in Tagore's work and presents the transformation of a self-centred lyricist from a privileged background into a socially conscious and politically engaged personality of world literature. He emphasises the impression that the visit to Soviet Russia left on Tagore and its possible influence on the last and most mature decade of the poet's work. The monograph formed a basis of the two chapters on Rabindranath Tagore in his comprehensive *Bengali Literature*.[58]

In 1961, Zbavitel translated Tagore's novel *The Last Poem* (which also was recorded as an audio-book in 1979), and *The Land of Cards* (a dramatic piece) in 1962. In the afterword to the latter, Zbavitel emphasises Tagore's struggle with Brahmanic orthodoxy and casteism, his evolutionary view of history, belief in social progress and the future role of the young generation. The same year a collection of stories for children, from nine years of age as the cover page states, appeared under the title *A Garland of Stories*. It was a joint translation of Zbavitel and a batch of his students of Bengali from *Galpaguccha*, *Lipika*, and *Galpasalpa*.[59]

An interesting contribution which fostered and in fact embodied the Czech link with Tagore was an ethnographic memoir *Obrázky z Bengálska* (Pictures of Bengal) published in 1963 by Milada Ganguli (1913–2000), a Czech woman who married into the Tagore family. She met Mohanlal Ganguli, a grandson of Abanindranath, during her studies in England and joined him as his wife in Jorasanko before the beginning of World War II. Her book is thus an insider's account and contains memories of Tagore's last *Basantotsab* (Spring festival) in Santiniketan.

In the following years Zbavitel provided the Czech readership with new translations of *The Gardener* (1966) and *Gitanjali* (1973). The form of the latter, the order of poems and their prosaic style follow the English version but the content is based on the Bengali original of *Gitanjali*. The new translations enjoyed immense popularity and were dramatised in numerous poetry evenings and radio programmes and inspired several composers to set the poems into music. To many readers, those two collections were antidotes to the pressures of the omnipresent materialist ideology.

The second new translation of *The Waterfall* from English was published in 1973; however, it did not leave much of an influence. In 1976, Zbavitel translated seven of Tagore's short stories and novellas and published them in a volume *Muž a Žena: Sedm novel o lásce a manželství* (Man and Woman: Seven novellas on love and marriage).[60] Referring to them, Zbavitel acknowledges that 'In Tagore's literary work, especially in prose, his social activism and social critique [come to the fore] ... the artistic elements are secondary.'[61] This collection has become probably the most widely read book of Tagore's prose in Czechoslovakia. In 1994 it was turned into an audiobook. For nearly twenty years it was the last Czech translation of Tagore. To complete the picture, Slovak translations should also be mentioned—*Hungry Stones*, 1961, *The Wreck* (under this title including *The Post Office*, *Gitanjali*, *The Gardener*, 1971), all from English, and, most notably, the only collection of short stories translated from Bengali by Anna Rácová as *Osamelý pútnik* (Lonely Wayfarer) in 1981. As Czech and Slovak are mutually intelligible, the more numerous Czech translations served the Slovak market as well.

Tagore after the Fall of Grand Narratives (Since 1989)

The period after the so-called Velvet Revolution in Czechoslovakia and the ensuing change of discourse allowed for broader contextualisation of Tagore's literary and intellectual endeavours. The readers were keen to absorb all that was prohibited and suppressed during the Communist regime and in that context a renewed interest in things religious and spiritual emerged. While the nationalist interpretation of Tagore largely fell into oblivion and his progressive interpretation lost ground with the fall of the regime that produced it, he remains a known figure of world literature and a representative of Eastern philosophical thought, somewhat as if his reception made a full circle. Interpretations of Tagore from the perspective of gender are a new element.[62]

The first new translation of this period was a collection of Tagore's non-fiction *Duch svobody: Myšlenky, úvahy, vzpomínky* (The Spirit of Freedom: Thoughts, Essays, Memories)[63] by Zbavitel in 1995. The texts are collected from both English and Bengali originals and their translation reflects the difference in style—vague and sometimes mysterious in the former and precise and rich in the latter.[64] In the introduction, Zbavitel postulates two major pillars of Tagore's world view: first, his rootedness in and creative reinterpretation of the Upanishadic philosophy, and second, his dialectic view of life and openness to the changes it brings.[65] In 1997, the first translation of *Fireflies* from English appeared, followed two years later by a second edition of *The Gardener* along with a new translation of *The Lover's Gift*. Both were recorded as audiobooks in 2002. *Gitanjali* and *The Gardener* in Zbavitel's translation were also turned into Braille books in 2003.

Zbavitel's successor in the field of Bengali studies, Hana Preinhaelterová, brought out a collection of two lectures from the original *Sadhana: The Realisation of Life*, namely *The Problem of Evil* and *Realisation in Love*. In her afterword, Preinhaelterová terms Tagore a 'practising philosopher' as opposed to a theorist of philosophy or science. She further emphasises that Tagore was shaped by his family ambience where he imbibed the tenets of Upanishads and Buddhism which he later creatively transformed into his own literary works.[66] The last translation so far published is a collection of love poems from the last period of Tagore's life entitled *Na břehu řeky Zapomnění* (The River of Oblivion) by Zbavitel which came out in 2005.

Although the structural change of the book market from state-operated to a commercial one reduced print runs of Tagore's translations and, perhaps, made him less visible among other authors, he does remain a part of grammar school curricula as a figure of world literature. Occasional recitals take place both in the Czech Republic and Slovakia and performances of his poems occur at recitation competitions. Prague has also a street and a neighbouring tram stop named after Tagore (Thákurova). As a curious consequence of the tram stop being located on a frequented route, Tagore's name got firmly engraved in the minds of countless Prague commuters who would otherwise remain ignorant of the great Bengali poet's existence.

Tagore also remains a source of inspiration for Czech music composers. Apart from serious music, two recent attempts exemplify well Tagore's reception in this period. A folk rock band Kacu! set Tagore's *Gitanjali* 69 to tune in their 2009 album *O ženských a chlapech, slimákovi a cibuli* (On men and women, a snail and an onion).[67] Other songs of the album use lyrics by Rainer Maria Rilke and Wisława Szymborska. In a more extravagant example, a Czech worldbeat band (i.e., a group blending Western pop or rock music with global traditional or folk music influences) called A.D.E. (After Death Experiences) turned one of the Haiku-like poems from the *Fireflies* collection into a nearly four-minutes-long song with a video clip which would have surely left Tagore astounded. The song *Kéž má láska* (Let my Love) was the biggest hit of their 1997 album *Babylon*:[68] 'Let my love, like sunlight, surround you and yet give you illumined freedom,' goes the poet. Yet in the hands of the rather punkish, Maori-style tattooed performers his idea of non-binding love turns into a Freudian drama, where the words 'illumined freedom' are punctuated with a scene of a little girl's doll being snatched and destroyed as in a voodoo ritual.[69]

Once again, Tagore is interpreted within the context of Eastern mysticism. Both the bands draw from Asian philosophies but this time, instead of juxtaposing East and West, they synthesise a collage where elements of jazz, reggae, Czech folk music, Tagore's and Rilke's lyrics and visuals of Maori tattoos fuse, in quite a Rabindric fashion, into a stream of worldbeat.

Conclusion

Each period of reception can be understood in terms of the dominant questions which Tagore's work was invoked to answer. In the period of early reactions, his contemplative poetry and interpretation of Indian philosophy were sources of consolation in time of war and presented an alternative to European modernity. In the second period, Tagore was entangled in the construction of imagined affinity between a particular Czech national project and his, by nature, cosmopolitan humanist project. Building on Czech perceptions of India in the nineteenth century, such a construction served to confirm that the struggle of an ethnic minority within the Austro-Hungarian Empire against German cultural domination, which resulted in independent statehood, is indeed an expression and embodiment of the greater and global humanist project. In other words, Tagore was sought to bridge our Home with the World. The third period encompassed the affinity thesis to the extent that the Communist regime, brought to power in the wake of World War II, encompassed the national agenda. However, the Marxist grand narrative of social progress replaced the nationalist narrative and Tagore was invoked as the torchbearer of that progress. In the last period, Tagore is primarily a source of a non-materialist world view. The affinity thesis melted away and Tagore has become one of many such sources beyond our cultural horizon out of which we can draw individual elements to patch the collage of our contemporary existence.

Notes

1. Hříbek. 'Czech Indology.'
2. Said. *Orientalism.*
3. Pollock, 'Deep Orientalism?' and Cowan, *The Indo–German Identification.*
4. Strnad, 'India, as Reflected in Czech Consciousness,' 279–90.
5. In 1845 appeared in the Review *Česká včela* (The Czech Bee) a fairly knowledgeable account of the 'Bengal Renaissance' which the author deemed to be 'an example of patriotism for our political situation.' His article ends with a proclamation: 'Blessed is a nation which has men like Dwarkanath!' Štorch, 'Braman Dwarkanat Tagor.'
6. For a discussion of the term see the *Yugoslavia and its Successors* essay in this volume.
7. See Fujda, *Akulturace hinduismu v českém okultismu*, 62–8.
8. See the *Yugoslavia and its Successors* essay in this volume.
9. Unknown author, 'Rabindra Nat Tagore.'
10. Tagore, 'Z poezie Hindů,' 10.
11. A. V., 'Rabindranath Tagore.'

12. Unknown author, 'Rabindranath Tagore, indický spisovatel, poctěný letošní literární cenou Nobelovou,' *Národní listy*, 53, no. 317, evening edition (18 November 1913), 2.
13. Tagore, 'Z poezie Hindů.'
14. Balej, Introduction, x.
15. Ibid., xxi–xxiii.
16. A.V., 'Rabindranath Tagore.'
17. For an overview of Professor Lesný's work, see Filipský, *Vincenc Lesný and Indian Studies*.
18. One of those marginal voices is one of the first reviews of Balej's 1914 *Gitanjali* translation. See Jarý, 'Rabindranath Tagore.'
19. Sekanina, 'Z nových knih básnických.'
20. See Rabindranath Tagore Correspondence Archive, Rabindra Bhavana, Visva-Bharati, Santiniketan, File 74, nos. 15–17.
21. Novák, 'Review of *Přibývající měsíc*.'
22. Šnajdr, Publisher's Afterword to *Přibývající měsíc*, 67–8.
23. See, for instance, the following comment: 'Europe handed Tagore a laurel right at his arrival and by doing so she made a decisive step in enlarging her notion of culture and civilization. That step is an important milestone in the history of mankind, a transition to a new era in which the feeling of great emotional unity would bond all continents. ... Through Tagore spoke up the voice of long-forgotten cradle of humankind, the voice of miraculous Orient suddenly awakening from ages of slumber, the voice springing up like a cultural water-source, long blocked yet now rapidly streaming to life.' *Lidové Noviny*, 22, no. 61 (3 March 1914).
24. Sekanina, 'Román z Indie.'
25. Tille, 'Král temné komnaty.'
26. His connection with things Indian may stem from the fact that he was also a school friend of Otakar Pertold (1884–1965) another Czech Indologist of Lesný's generation, the first professor of religious studies at Charles University and the first Czechoslovak consul in Bombay (1920–3).
27. N. M. P., 'Z pražské činohry: Rabindranath Thakur: Král temné komnaty.' *Lidové noviny*, 31, no. 278 (6 June 1923).
28. Škrach, Afterword.
29. This is a quotation from the Czech translation of Rabindranath Tagore, *Nationalism* (San Francisco: The Book Club of California, 1917), 60–1.
30. Hora, 'Kulturní smysl doby,' 4.
31. Lesný, 'Návštěvou u Rabíndrinátha Thákura;' Moriz Winternitz was a professor at the German University in Prague, at the Department of Indo-European Comparative Linguistics. The focus of his research was ancient Indian literature and ethnology. His most famous work is *Geschichte der Indischen Literatur* (The History of Indian Literature) in three volumes.
32. Winternitz lectured there in 1922–3, Lesný joined him in 1923 and returned in 1928.

33. Jaroslav Hněvkovský, celebrated as a Slav Gaugin, undertook the first journey to India in 1911 and stayed for two years, most of the time in Kerala. After World War I he had a successful exhibition of his Indian works in London. It was on this occasion when he met Tagore and accepted his invitation to Santiniketan as an art teacher. He spent there the spring of 1922. Hněvkovský left not only paintings from that journey, including those of Rabindranath himself, but also an extensive and vivid diary which he later published.

34. Unknown author, 'Rabindranath Thákur na pražské universitě.' *Nová doba*, 27, no. 166, 19 June 1921, 1.

35. Arne Novák (Skapíno), 'Rabíndranáth v Karolinu.' *Lidové noviny*, 29, no. 319, 28 June 1921.

36. Janáček, 'Rabindranath Tagore.'

37. For their partial review see Holman, 'Ohlas básnické tvorby Rabíndranátha Thákura v české hudbě', and Peduzzi, '... a svět zůstal hluchý.'

38. Myslbek, apparently in the last years of his life, depicted Tagore as a naked young man with long black hair, covered by a loose strip of red cloth around his shoulder, playing a lute and walking with a pair of tigers. Despite its Orientalising flavour the painting is modern in style. Max Švabinský portrayed Tagore much later. On his lithograph from 1961 Tagore is standing in front of his residence in the garden with a plantain and a palm tree next to him. Other Czech artists who made works inspired by Tagore's personality in the later periods include Miroslav Šnajdr (portrait of Tagore, 1959), Zdeněk Burian, and Irena Stanislavová (etching, 1989.)

39. Čapek, 'Rabíndranáth Thákur.'

40. See for example, Konrád, 'Večer v Nirwaně.'; Lesný, 'Glosy k premiéře Thákurovy Čitry a Poštovního úřadu.'

41. *Večer Rabindranatha Tagora (Činohra)* or *The Evening of Rabindranath Tagore (Drama)* directed by Vojta Novák. Schedule of performances and cast are available online at the website of the National Theatre Archives: http://archiv. narodni-divadlo.cz .

42. The stories in the Czech translation include 'Paye calar path,' 'Meghla dine,' 'Bani,' 'Meghdut,' 'Bamshi,' 'Sandhya,' 'Prabhat,' 'Purono bari,' 'Gali,' 'Ekti chaoni,' 'Ekti din,' 'Kritaghna shok,' 'Satero bachar,' 'Pratham shok,' 'Prashna,' 'Galpa,' 'Minu,' 'Ghora,' 'Kartar bhut,' 'Totakahini,' 'Aspashta,' 'Pratham chithi,' 'Pranman,' 'Agamani,' 'Svarga-martya.'

43. Unknown author, 'Přednáška Rabíndranátha Thákura.' *Národní politika*, 44, no. 279, afternoon edition, 11 October 1926, 3.

44. For a detailed overview of Tagore's second visit see Filipský, 'Notes on Tagore's visit to Czechoslovakia.'

45. This collection contains the following short stories: 'Shesher ratri,' 'Subha,' 'Srir patra,' 'Madhyabarttini,' 'Minu,' 'Bhul svarga,' 'Totakahini.'

46. Only recently translated into English with appendices and annotations by Debabrata Chakrabarti.

47. Šebor, 'Review of *Rabíndranáth Thákur*.'

48. Lesný, *Rabíndranáth Thákur* (*Tagore*, 6–9).
49. Dutta and Robinson, *Selected Letters of Rabindranath Tagore*, 500.
50. See Rabindranath Tagore Correspondence Archive, Rabindra Bhavana, Visva-Bharati University, Shantiniketan, File 74, No. 119.
51. Zbavitel, 'Vincenc Lesný – popularizátor', 58.
52. Dušan Zbavitel was the most prominent Czech Indologist of his time and a major figure in the field of Bengali literary studies. A student of Vincenc Lesný, he submitted his doctoral dissertation in Bengali literature in 1954. He worked at the Oriental Institute of the Czechoslovak Academy of Sciences until 1971 when he was forced to leave on political grounds, a result of the abrupt end to the Prague Spring of 1968. Dr Zbavitel continued to translate from Sanskrit, Pali, Bengali, English, and German. He returned to Charles University in the 1990s and lectured for about a decade on Hinduism and Sanskrit literature. He wrote two textbooks of Bengali in Czech, the latter of which was rendered into German and is still in use.
53. Collections and numbers of translated poems are as follows: 'Prabhat git' (1), 'Chabi o gan' (2), 'Kari o kamal' (4), 'Manasi' (2), 'Sonar tari' (6), 'Chitra' (3), 'Chaitali' (10), 'Kanika' (17), 'Kalpana' (5), 'Kshanika' (9), 'Naibedya' (5), 'Smaran' (2), 'Utsarga' (4), 'Shishu' (8), 'Katha o kahini' (2), 'Kheya' (3), 'Svadesh' (5), 'Gitanjali' (11), 'Balaka' (3), 'Palataka' (3), 'Shishu Bholanath' (5), 'Purabi' (3), 'Mahuya' (3), 'Parishesh' (5), 'Punashcha' (4), 'Bichitrita' (2), 'Bithika' (3), 'Patraput' (6), 'Sphulinga' (1), 'Prantik' (2), 'Senjuti' (3), 'Nabajatak' (6), 'Sandi' (4), 'Rogasajyay' (1), 'Arogya' (4), 'Janmadine' (5). Out of a total of 162 poems, nineteen had been earlier translated and published in various journals by Vincenc Lesný, one by Ivo Fišer and J. B. Čapek. The rest were new translations by Dušan Zbavitel.
54. The names of the stories were 'Dena-paona,' 'Ramkanaiyer nirbuddhita,' 'Taraprasanner kirti,' 'Kankal,' 'Tyag,' 'Jibita o mrita,' 'Kabuliwala,' 'Ekti kshudra puratan galpa,' 'Samasyapuran,' 'Megh o raudra,' 'Prayashcitta,' 'Bicharak,' 'Nishithe,' 'Didi,' 'Thakurda,' 'Atithi,' 'Durasha,' 'Putrayajna,' 'Ditektibh,' 'Rajtika,' 'Sadar o andar,' 'Durbuddhi,' 'Shubha drishti,' 'Ulukhader bipad,' 'Darpaharan,' 'Mastarmashay,' 'Panaraksha,' 'Haimanti,' 'Strir patra,' 'Tapasvini,' 'Patra o patri,' 'Namanjur galpa,' 'Samskar.' The order of translations follows that of *Galpaguccha*; *Letters from Russia* are limited to nos. 1–12. Articles include three pieces, namely 'Sadupay' from the *Samuha* collection, 'Shikshar samasya' from *Shiksha*, and separately published 'Sabhyatar sankat.' The selected open letters express anti-British and anti-Fascist sentiments. All translations are by Dušan Zbavitel except *Chhelebela* (trans. Milada Ganguli) and 'Shikshar samasya' (trans. Miloš Zapletal).
55. Heřman, 'Básník osvobozujícího se lidství.'
56. Pokorný, 'Mezi starým a novým.'
57. Pokorný, 'Myslitel a básník.'
58. Zbavitel, *Bengali Literature*, 247–77.

59. The collection includes 'Postmastar,' 'Subha' and 'Icchapuran' (*Galpaguccha*), trans. Dušan Zbavitel; 'Ekta ashare galpa' (*Galpaguccha*), 'Totakahini,' 'Natun putul,' 'Vidushak' (*Lipika*), trans. Miloš Zapletal; 'Parir parichay' (*Lipika*), 'Rajrani,' 'Aro satya' (*Galpasalpa*), trans. Hana Pletánková; 'Chhuti' (*Galpaguccha*), trans. Božena Pejpková.

60. The novellas or short stories include 'Adhyapak' (Professor, 1898), 'Drishtidan' (Vision, 1899), 'Nashta nir' (The Broken Nest, 1901) from *Galpaguccha II*, 'Rasmanir chele' (Rasmani's Son, 1911) from *Galpaguccha III*, 'Shesh katha' (The Final Word) from the collection *Tin sangi* (The Three Companions, 1940–1), and two novellas published individually in the original—*Chaturanga* (Four Scenes, 1916) and *Dui bon* (Two Sisters, 1932).

61. Zbavitel, 'Láska a manželství v pohledu Rabíndranátha Thákura', 278.

62. E.g., Knotková, 'The Role of Woman in the Poetry of Two Bengali Modernists.'

63. This collection is divided into several subsections according to the original source. The section *Reflections I* contains several chapters from *The Religion of Man*, namely 'Man's Universe,' 'The Creative Spirit,' 'The Surplus in Man,' 'The Vision,' 'Man's Nature,' and 'The Meeting.' The section *Reflections II* comprises Tagore's speeches to his students in Santiniketan. The Essays are taken from *Sahitya*: *Lectures and Addresses* (My School), and *Creative Unity* (The Spirit of Freedom). The Memories section is based on *Jibansmriti* and contains the following texts: 'Shikkharambha,' 'Ghar o bahir,' 'Pitrdeb,' 'Himalay yatra,' 'Sahityer sangi,' 'Bhanusimher kabita,' 'Svadeshikata,' 'Amedabad,' 'Gangatir,' and 'Prabhat sangit.' The order of Czech translation follows that of *Rabindra Racanabali*, vol. 10.

64. Preinhaelterová, 'Review of *Duch svobody*,' 527.

65. Zbavitel, 'Introduction to *Duch svobody*,' 10–11.

66. Preinhaelterová, 'Afterword to *Sádhaná*,' 79–86.

67. *Vlny* (Stream of Life), in KACU! *O ženských a chlapech, slimákovi a cibuli* (On men and women, a snail and an onion [CD]). Praha: Black Point, 2009.

68. A.D.E. *Babylon* [CD]. Praha: Monitor-EMI, 1997.

69. A.D.E. *Kéž má láska* (May my Love), directed by Longin Wdowiak, camera V. Vála, screenplay O. Anděra, produced by AA Centropa Film, publisher, Praha: Monitor-EMI, 1997.

WORKS CITED

A. V. 'Rabindranath Tagore.' *Národní listy,* supplement *Z kulturního života*, 54, no. 79 (22 March 1914), 17.

Balej, František. Introduction to *Gitándžali: Obět písní* [*Gitanjali*: *Song Offerings*], by Rabindranath Tagore, ix–xxii. Kladno: J. Šnajdr, 1914.

Čapek, Karel. 'Rabíndranáth Thákur.' *Lidové noviny*, 29, no. 308 (22 June1921), 4.

Cowan, Robert. *The Indo–German Identification: Reconciling South Asian Origins and European Destinies, 1765–1885*. Rochester: Camden House, 2010.

Dutta, Krishna, and Andrew Robinson. *Selected Letters of Rabindranath Tagore*. Cambridge: Cambridge University Press, 1997.

Filipský, Jan. *Vincenc Lesný and Indian Studies*. Praha: Czechoslovak Society for International Relations–Oriental Institute, 1982.

——. 'Notes on Tagore's visit to Czechoslovakia in 1926.' In *Rabindranath Tagore: The Poet's Religion and World Vision* by Moriz Winternitz. Translated by Debabrata Chakrabarti, 118–23. Kolkata: Winternitz Society for Literature and Culture, 2011.

Fujda, Milan. 'Akulturace hinduismu v českém okultismu: Sekularizace a zrod moderní spirituality' [Acculturation of Hinduism in Czech Occultism: Secularization and the Birth of Modern Spirituality]. PhD diss., Masarykova Universita v Brně, 2007.

Ganguliová, Milada. *Obrázky z Bengálska* [Pictures of Bengal]. Praha: Orbis, 1963.

Heřman, Zdeněk. 'Básník osvobozujícího se lidství.' *Literární noviny*, 7, no. 29 (19 July 1958), 4.

Holman, Petr. 'Ohlas básnické tvorby Rabíndranátha Thákura v české hudbě' [Czech Musical Responses to the Poetry of Rabindranath Tagore]. MA thesis, Charles University, 1973.

Hora, Josef. 'Kulturní smysl doby' [The Cultural Meaning of our Times]. *Akademie*, no. 24 (1 October 1919), 3–6.

Hříbek, Martin. 'Czech Indology and the Concept of Orientalism.' In *Understanding India: Indology and Beyond*. Edited by Jaroslav Vacek and Harbans Mukhia, 45–56. Praha: Karolinum, 2011.

Janáček, Leoš. 'Rabindranath Tagore.' *Lidové noviny*, 29, no. 308 (22 June 1921), 1–2.

Jarý, B. 'Rabindranath Tagore a jeho "Oběť písní".' *Našinec*, 50, no. 153 (5 July 1914), 11.

Knotková, Blanka. 'The Role of Woman in the Poetry of Two Bengali Modernists.' *Archiv orientální*, 68, no. 3 (August 2000), 433–40.

Konrád, L. B. 'Večer v Nirwaně.' *Cesta*, 6, no. 31 (1924), 453.

Lesný, Vincenc. 'Návštěvou u Rabíndranátha Thákura.' *Národní listy*, evening edition, 60, no. 296 (26 October 1920), 1.

——. 'Glosy k premiéře Thákurovy Čitry a Poštovního úřadu.' *Národní listy*, 64, no. 36 (6 February 1924), 1.

——. *Rabíndranáth Thákur (Tagore): Osobnost a dílo* [Rabindranath Tagore: Personality and Work]. Kladno: J. Šnajdr, 1937.

——. *Rabindranath Tagore: His Personality and Work*. Translated from the Czech by Guy McKeever Phillips. London: Allen & Unwin, 1939.

Novák, Arne. Review of *Přibývající měsíc* [The Crescent Moon], transl. Věra Stephanova, *Lumír*, 44, no. 4 (31 March 1916), 189–90.

Peduzzi, Lubomír. '...a svět zůstal hluchý.' *Svobodné slovo*, 37, no. 177 (1 August 1981), 5.

Pokorný, Dušan. 'Mezi starým a novým: K českému vydání Thákurova románu Gora.' *Literární noviny*, 9, no. 4 (23 January 1960), 8.

——. 'Myslitel a básník.' *Literární noviny*, 9, no. 49 (3 December 1960), 4.

Pollock, Sydney. 'Deep Orientalism? Notes on Sanskrit and Power Beyond the Raj.' In *Orientalism and the Postcolonial Predicament: Perspectives on South*

Asia. Edited by C. A. Breckenridge and P. van der Veer, 80–96. Philadelphia: University of Pennsylvania Press, 1993.

Preinhaelterová, Hana. Afterword to *Sádhaná: O zlu a lásce* [*Sadhana*: On Evil and Love], by Rabindranath Tagore, 79–86. Praha: Vyšehrad, 1999.

———. Review of *Duch svobody: Myšlenky, úvahy, vzpomínky* [The Spirit of Freedom: Thoughts, Essays, Memories], by Rabindranath Tagore, trans. Dušan Zbavitel. *Archiv orientální*, 68, no. 3, 2000, 526–7.

Said, Edward. *Orientalism: Western Conceptions of the Orient*. London: Penguin, 1978.

Šebor, Jan. Review of *Rabíndranáth Thákur: Osobnost a dílo* by Václav [*sic*] Lesný, *Pestrý týden*, 12, no. 32 (7 August 1937), 4.

Sekanina, František. 'Z nových knih básnických.' *Národní politika*, supplement, 32, no. 173 (26 June 1914), 2

———. 'Román z Indie — zrcadlo evropských zmatků.' *Národní politika*, Sunday Supplement, 38, no. 252 (12 September 1920), 3.

Škrach, Vasil Kaprálek. Afterword to *Nacionalism* [*Nationalism*], by Rabindranath Tagore. Translated by E. Škrachová and V. K. Škrach, 105–11. Kladno: J. Šnajdr, 1921.

Šnajdr, J. Publisher's afterword to *Přibývající měsíc* [*The Crescent Moon*], by Rabindranath Tagore. Translated from English by Věra Stephanová, 65–8. Kladno: J. Šnajdr, 1936.

Štorch, Karel B. 'Braman Dwarkanat Tagor.' *Česká včela*, 12, no. 82 (1845), 331–2.

Strnad, Jaroslav. 'India, as Reflected in Czech Consciousness in the Era of the National Revivalist Movement of the Nineteenth Century (*c*.1800–48).' *Archiv orientální*, 62, no. 3 (2007), 279–90.

Švabinský, Max. 'O portrétu Rabíndranátha Thákura.' In *Max Švabinský: život a dílo na přelomu epoch* by Ludvík Páleníček, 218–19. Praha: Melantrich, 1984.

Tagore, Rabindranath. 'Z poezie Hindů: Dítěti, Mladý princ' [From the Poetry of the Hindus: Child, Little Prince], translated from English by Lotty Trakalová-Kheilová, *Národní politika*, 31, no. 353 (28 December 1913), 10.

Tille, Václav. 'Král temné komnaty.' *Jeviště* , 1, no. 26 (1920), 298–300.

Vavroušková, Stanislava. 'Perception of India in the Heart of Europe: Transition through Centuries.' *Res Antiquitatis: Journal of Ancient History*, 2, no. 1 (2011), 13–29.

Winternitz, Moriz. *Rabindranath Tagore: The Poet's Religion and World Vision*. Translated by Debabrata Chakrabarti. Kolkata: Winternitz Society for Literature and Culture, 2011.

Zbavitel, Dušan. *Rabíndranáth Thákur: vývoj básníka* [Rabindranath Tagore: The Evolution of a Poet]. Praha: Orbis, 1961.

———. Afterword to *Země karet* [The Land of Cards], by Rabindranath Tagore. Translated from Bengali by Dušan Zbavitel, 73–7. Praha: NČVU, 1962.

———. 'Láska a manželství v pohledu Rabíndranátha Thákura' [Love and marriage from the perspective of Rabindranath Tagore], afterword to *Muž a Žena: Sedm novel o lásce a manželství* [Man and Woman: Seven novelettes on love and marriage], by Rabindranath Tagore. Translated by Zbavitel, 273–9. Praha: Odeon, 1976.

Zbavitel, Dušan. *Bengali Literature*. Wiesbaden: Otto Harrassowitz, 1976.

———. Vincenc Lesný — popularizátor' [Vincenc Lesný as populariser]. In *Vincenc Lesný a česká indologie* [Vincenc Lesný and Czech Indology], *Acta Universitatis Carolinae: Philosophica et Historica*, vol. 4 (1990), 57–9.

———. Introduction to *Duch svobody: Myšlenky, úvahy, vzpomínky* [The Spirit of Freedom: Thoughts, Essays, Memories], by Rabindranath Tagore. Translated by Dušan Zbavitel, 5–12. Praha: Vyšehrad, 1995.

Unknown author, 'Rabindra Nat Tagore.' *Národné noviny*, 44, no. 138 (25 November 1913), 4.

PART FOUR

Northern and Western Europe

Tagore with Kurt Wolff, his German publisher (1921). Courtesy: Rabindra Bhavana, Visva-Bharati.

21

FINLAND

HANNELE POHJANMIES

INDIA, BANGLADESH AND FINLAND

Finland was part of the Swedish Kingdom from the Middle Ages until 1809. After that it became an autonomous Grand Duchy of Russia for more than a century. Before Finland declared its independence in 1917, it was not possible to create any political relations with India. Finnish people sympathised with the Indians fighting for their independence. In 1918, Herman Stenberg published the book *Indian kirot* (*The Curses of India*) about the atrocities of the British in India. India became independent in 1947 and Finland established full diplomatic relations with that country in 1949. The first Finnish Ambassador to India was Hugo Valvanne, a theosophist who was well informed about Indian culture. India opened its Diplomatic Mission in Helsinki, the Finnish capital, in 1968.

On the website of the Indian Embassy one can find information on, for example, the many bilateral agreements between Finland and India, from the Trade Agreement of 1963 to the Agreement for Cooperation in the Fields of Science and Technology of 2008, as well as reports on the many high-level official visits between the two countries. There is no official bilateral development cooperation between India and Finland, but there are dozens of Finnish non-governmental organisations working in different development projects in India.

Finland established diplomatic relations with Bangladesh in 1972. The Finnish Embassy in India and the Indian Embassy in Sweden are taking care of the relations between Bangladesh and Finland. The development cooperation between Bangladesh and Finland started in 1975.

There has been no missionary work in India by the Finnish Missionary Society. However, the missionaries of the Salvation Army in Finland and the Evangelical Free Church of Finland have worked there in the twentieth century. There have been some occasional missionary projects in India and

Bangladesh, run by private citizens. For example, the Kylväjä Association has carried out development cooperation work in Bangladesh.

For most Finnish people, the earliest window to India might have been *The Jungle Book* (1894) by Rudyard Kipling, the first part of which was translated into Finnish as early as in 1898. The Finnish Oriental Society was founded in 1917 and The Finnish–Indian Society in 1949 (originally named The Finnish Friends of India). The Finland–Bangladesh Society was founded in 1974.

The first course in the Sanskrit language was organised at the University of Helsinki in 1835, the first lectureship in Sanskrit was founded in the 1840s and the first professorship in 1875. Nowadays studies continue in the Department of World Cultures under the name of South Asian Studies. Courses in Pali started in the second decade of the twentieth century. Teaching of other Indian languages—Urdu, Hindi and Tamil, occasionally also Bengali, Burushaski (spoken in Pakistan and Kashmir), Kashmiri, Kurukh (a tribal language of Odisha and surrounding areas), Malayalam and Telugu—started much later, in the 1970s.

For this contribution, I interviewed several specialists and made research in the archives of Finnish publishers, in the databases of the Helsinki University Library and public libraries, the archives of the Finnish National Theatre, the library of the Finnish Broadcasting Company and the database of the Finnish Composers' Copyright Association, Teosto. The archives of the *Helsingin Sanomat*, the largest newspaper in Finland and in the Nordic countries (founded in 1889), was a treasure mine. I have researched the issues of the *Helsingin Sanomat* starting from the year 1904.[1]

Tagore Receives the Nobel Prize for Literature

The first piece of news where Tagore was mentioned appeared in the *Helsingin Sanomat* in the summer of 1913, *before* he received the Nobel Prize. The story is entitled *The Concert Tour of Suomen Laulu*. Suomen laulu (Song of Finland) is a mixed chorus, which was founded in 1900. The story is a report 'from our own correspondent' in London, where the chorus had given three concerts of Finnish songs. The audience was thrilled and praised the conductor:

> Great musicians, world famous critics and other celebrities gave him credit, admiring the results that the chorus had achieved under his direction. In the last concert, one of the audience members was Tagore, the most famous Indian poet, a great connoisseur of music. It was delightful to [observe] how he and his wife became more and more thrilled in the course of the evening.[2]

The news on the Nobel Prize appeared on 14 November 1913, simply stating that that year's Nobel Prize for Literature had been awarded to Rabindranath Tagore, an Indian poet virtually unknown in Finland. The correspondent of the newspaper in Sweden had sent a telegram with some information about Tagore's life and works:

> Gitanjali or Song Offerings is a collection of religious poetry. Its ideological foundation is a splendid, warm pantheism. The poems breathe mysticism, which is enormously impressive. Their form is of noble simplicity. The poems are eulogies, hymns of praise.
>
> [Tagore] has translated the book by himself into English in prose form. It is of classical complexion. Its curiously elegant and soulful rhythm is enchanting.
>
> There is also another book that has been translated into English, The Gardener. It is a collection of love poetry.
>
> There is a collection of short stories in English as well, describing life in Bengal.
>
> In his own country, the poet enjoys a monumental reputation and he is held in high regard. His poems have melodies of their own. They are sung by the whole nation.
>
> The Grecian elevation and simplicity of his poetry impresses also Europeans like a revelation. It has been said, 'It augurs a new Renaissance, a union of the finest spirit of East and West.'[3]

For the following day's newspaper, the editors found a photo of the poet and some further information from the June edition of the German magazine Das Literarische Echo, where the German O. E. Lessing had described Tagore's visit to Urbana, Illinois, in the USA:

> I heard him recite his own poems in a simple, plain way, in a smoothly metallic voice... As he was reciting his poetry, his dark eyes were sparkling with an inner glow. The man, who was sitting there so straight up and calm, rendering his poems to us—poems about the morning song of birds or human beings' passionate pursuit of love— as naturally as if he had been telling fairy tales for children, was no 'saint'. He certainly knew the precipices of life as well as he knew its mountain peaks. He felt the gusts of passion like a real human being. But he restrained them and did not scorn them.
>
> As I later met Mr. Tagore several times, my impression of him grew deeper and deeper. This Indian is a human being like the rest of us, but he is standing tall and free above everything that is shallow and barbarous. He has the air of bearing the legacy of an old culture—a

culture which is trying to assess the wonders of life according to their inner value.[4]

The next day, on 16 November, there was more information, acquired from the Swedish press, and on 18 November there was a report on the reactions of the foreign press to the Nobel Prize. The Anglo-Saxon press received the news with enthusiasm but the German press appeared to be firmly against it—with a few exceptions.

At the end of November, the *Helsingin Sanomat* published twelve poems in Finnish, half of them from *Gitanjali* and half from *The Gardener*. Unfortunately, the translator of the poems remains unknown.

In December, a big advertisement appeared in the newspaper:

A SPECIAL NOVELTY BOOK!

The Gardener by the Indian poet Rabindranath Tagore, this year's winner of the Nobel Prize, is guaranteed to satisfy all admirers of great and brilliant poetry. The entire mysterious world of Indian fables, its glowing nature and the love life that is burning red, step in front of us in an amazingly modern lighting.[5]

A positive review by L. Onerva was published soon after.

Tagore's name started to appear in the news columns of the *Helsingin Sanomat*. He was mentioned when people gave presentations on him or when his poetry was recited at poetic soirées. There were also numerous brief mentions of Tagore's visits overseas. For example, in early 1917, he was reported to have visited the USA.

In October 1917, the poet Eino Leino's (1878–1926) Finnish translation of *Gitanjali* was published by Kustannusosakeyhtiö Kirja with the title of *Uhrilauluja* (*Sacrificial Songs*).

1920–41

In 1921, the *Helsingin Sanomat* wrote that Germany had made a donation for the library of world literature in India[6] to honour Tagore on his sixtieth birthday. Tagore had visited Stockholm and met the King of Sweden. Next year, the *Helsingin Sanomat* wrote that some European scholars had been invited to India to lecture at the university founded by Tagore. More books by Tagore were published in Finnish, and the reviews were positive.

On Tagore's sixty-fifth birthday, in May 1926, the paper carried a biographical essay and a photo. In the summer of that year, *Sadhana* was published and a long review of it appeared in the *Helsingin Sanomat*.

Later in the year the same paper published a long report from the Finnish correspondent in Rome. He translated a long article from 'a certain

Fascist newspaper' into Finnish. The article strongly disapproved of Tagore's visit to Italy in a way that the correspondent found comical—Tagore had been hosted as a guest of the government, but he had not written a word of praise for it. Yet another news item from Budapest tells us that Tagore had travelled to Balaton to take carbonic acid baths, following the advice of Professor Aleksander Koranyi, who had diagnosed the poet as suffering from severe nervous exhaustion.

In the spring of 1927, a short news item reported that the Lithuanian Government had banned the works of Shakespeare, Wells, Wilde and Tagore as they were considered immoral and antisocial. Interestingly, Tagore's name is followed by an exclamation mark in brackets: 'Tagore (!)' in the original text.

Later in the same year, the *Helsingin Sanomat* published a long article by Dhan Mukerji, with the title 'Tagore's India,' presenting a discussion on the books *Chitra, The Gardener* and *The Crescent Moon*. This was followed by more mentions of Tagore's journeys to the United States, the Soviet Union, Germany and Denmark.

When Tagore celebrated his seventieth birthday in 1931, the *Helsingin Sanomat* published his biography and a list of his works. The article mentioned his role as one of the leaders of the Indian National Movement as well as the university he had founded.

In honour of his birthday, Tagore's friends compiled *The Golden Book of Tagore*. The Finnish contribution consisted of greetings in Sanskrit by Professor J. N. Reuter, a letter by F. E. Sillanpää (who would later also receive the Nobel Prize for Literature, in 1939) and a sample of Tagore's poetry in Finnish—Eino Leino's translation of the poem no. 34 of *The Gardener* ('Do not go, my love, without taking my leave').

Finnish people got access to Tagore's plays initially through broadcasts by international radio stations. People listened to these stations because there were only a few Finnish broadcasts. Finns were able to listen to *The Post Office* in Swedish via Motala in 1929 and in German via Königsberg in 1931, and to *Chitra* in Swedish via Kalundborg the same year. In 1932, actors of the Finnish National Theatre produced Tagore's radio drama *The King and the Queen* in Finnish. *The Post Office* was performed on the radio for the first time in Finnish in December 1938 and in Swedish the following year. Many well-known poetry reciters kept Tagore's poems in their repertoire.

The *Helsingin Sanomat* published Tagore's photo and a biographical essay on his seventy-fifth birthday too. His books were mentioned in many articles—for example one with the title *The Sailing Bookcases;* the story was about collections of books that were sailing from continent to continent so that seafarers could read them. The collection included great names of world literature, the first on the list being Tagore.

In the hard years of World War II, Tagore was thinking about Finland, proof of which he gave in a poem entitled *Apaghat* (1939): two friends walk peacefully through the lush fields of their village which they have visited after many years. This idyllic situation is destroyed by the explosive last sentence:

A telegram comes:
'Finland pounded by Soviet bombs.' [7]

More articles and a biographical essay were published on Tagore's eightieth birthday. The news of Tagore's death appeared on 8 August 1941, with a short biographical sketch and a beautiful portrait.

RECEPTION AFTER HIS DEATH

The Post Office was heard again on the radio in 1952. The reviews were not entirely positive any more. The text was regarded as too slow and insubstantial. In the *Helsingin Sanomat* in July 1953, the art historian Sakari Saarikivi wrote about the paintings of Tagore, while reviewing the book *Modern Indian Painting* by Ramachandra Rao. In February 1955, the Finnish Friends of India organised a Tagore soirée where the eminent freethinker and pacifist Yrjö Kallinen talked about Rabindranath Tagore, Mahatma Gandhi and Santiniketan. The actor Unto Salminen recited poems from *Gitanjali,* and *Janaganamana* (India's national anthem, composed by Tagore) was sung. A play was performed, *Chandalika,* which had been translated for this occasion by Juha Savio; the poems in the play had been translated by Jorma Partanen.

In May 1961, *Helsingin Sanomat* printed an exhaustive article to celebrate the centenary of Tagore's birth, where Professor Eino Krohn introduced Tagore especially as a writer and artist. The Finnish Friends of India organised a party where Aurobindo Bose, a former student of Tagore at Santiniketan, gave a lecture. A film on Tagore's life was screened. The Finnish Broadcasting Company aired Tagore's play *Malini* as a radio play, in J. Hollo's translation. In October 1961, actors of the Finnish National Theatre presented 'An Hour of Poetry by Tagore' on stage, reciting poems from *The Gardener.* The Young Friends of India—a group of school-age girls and boys—had made a huge effort. Under the lead of the architect Atindranath Datta they had learnt to recite Tagore's *Balmiki Pratibha* in Bengali from memory and performed it in October 1961 four times, twice in the Finnish National Theatre. Datta was working at the office of the renowned Finnish architect Alvar Aalto in Helsinki; there were thirty-five songs in the play and Datta had explained their contents to the young actors. Two years later the play was performed on television. It gained a great deal of attention and was favourably reviewed. In autumn 1961, the art historian Sakari Saarikivi gave a lecture on the radio on Tagore's work as a painter. He also published three pictures of Tagore's paintings in the *Helsingin Sanomat*. Some prints of Tagore's paintings were exhibited in a meeting of the Finnish Friends of India in December.

A documentary film on Tagore by Satyajit Ray was screened at the Finnish Film Archive in December 1962. In the same year, a farmers' newspaper *Maaseudun tulevaisuus* (The Future of the Countryside) carried a full-page article with the heading 'Rabindranath Tagore: Story of a Noble Life,' with several photos. It was based on the jubilee publication of the Indian magazine *The March of India*, dedicated to Tagore. The article was so comprehensive that it could be used as an outline of a biography of Tagore.[8]

The Indian theatre and Tagore got much attention in the cultural event *Jyväskylä Summer* in 1966, where Dr Som Benegal gave a lecture on Tagore as a reformer of the Indian theatre.

Helsingin Sanomat carried an extensive article on the film *Ghare Baire* by Satyajit Ray in May 1984. In 1988, the Finnish Broadcasting Company presented a radio documentary entitled *Tagore*, written by Sahban Mroueh which projected Tagore as a religious mystic poet. The next year, the Australian actor Robin Ramsay visited Helsinki and performed a monologue he had written, *Borderland: A Celebration of Rabindranath Tagore*, which included Tagore's poems too.

In March 2006, Tagore was mentioned in a slightly surprising and unexpected context: at the 175th anniversary of the Society of Finnish Literature. The main address was given by the philosopher and historian Juha Sihvola, who spoke most of the time about Tagore and his ideas. He presented Tagore expressly as a world citizen.[9]

THE TRANSLATORS

All the Finnish translations are from English or occasionally from German. There are no translations from the Bengali language.

The first translator of Tagore's poems was Eino Leino (1878–1926), the most notable Finnish poet of all time. His knowledge of English was not sufficient, so he collaborated with L. Onerva, who was a writer and poet in her own right. Leino and Onerva were two of the most prominent personalities in Finnish literary circles at the time.

Eino Leino was linked to theosophical groups but only for a limited time. He was inspired by the love lyrics of Tagore. His translations were those of a poet. The language of the Finnish *Gitanjali* is generally not biblical. Its translation may have been a more difficult task for Leino; he had not had a chance to read anything that would have explained to him the religious thinking of Tagore. Thus there are some mistakes and misunderstandings in the poems of *Gitanjali*. Perhaps Leino's English skills were too limited.

The other books of the first decades of the twentieth century were translated by J. Hollo (Juho August Hollo, 1885–1967), a professor of pedagogy and a prolific and respected translator of classical literature. There is a literary award named after him which is given every year for high-quality non-fiction translation. Hollo was an educationist, a scholar and a sensitive translator. There are no signs in his fine translations of trying to give any specific tone to Tagore or to make him fit in some special category. The translator did careful research on many unknown aspects of Bengali culture and explained them in his footnotes.

Both of these translators tried to convey the right image of Tagore and did not make intentional changes in his texts.

In 1990, *The Religion of Man* was translated by Heikki Eskelinen, a noted translator of non-fiction. The aphorisms were translated by Sinologist Pertti Seppälä, a translator of many Chinese collections of poetry and words of wisdom. The collections of poems published in the first decade of the new millennium are translated by Hannele Pohjanmies, a writer and an independent scholar.

REACTIONS TO THE TRANSLATIONS

The first collection of poems, *The Gardener*, was published by Kustannuso-sakeyhtiö Kirja in 1913. Nobody knows who made the decision to translate *The Gardener* before *Gitanjali*. L. Onerva wrote a positive, long review on *The Gardener* in the *Helsingin Sanomat*:

> India, the ancient homeland of poetry, has reminded the world of its existence again by raising a modern poet up in the air. Rabindranath Tagore, who in his homeland has held the position of the emperor of poetry, recently won the Nobel Prize in Literature and has thus suddenly become a great international celebrity and, once again after a long while, has turned the attention of the surprised Europe towards those fabulous Eastern lands that are wrapped in the mystic dusk of a distant tale.
>
> *The Gardener* consists of prose poetry, love lyrics; the tone is very familiar and new and strange at the same time. There are tropical landscapes spreading in front of our eyes, mustard fields, mango blossoms, bamboo branches, mud coloured buffaloes, pearls and bangles, women 'with bubbling pots on their hips', the whole

Oriental colour glow of the *Song of Solomon* but not its blind heat. Sometimes a very modern mental landscape pops up, intellectual and revelling like a little short story by Peter Altenberg: I said...She said... Then what? Nothing. Just that inexplicable feeling. I thought... 'I don't know why.'...

The words of wisdom of Tagore never turn into sophistry, his expressions of pain never break into grimaces, his sense of beauty is thoroughly positive, his poetic images are like reflections by the distant sky and glimmering deep water, infinity above, infinity underneath, but the slightest detail imbued with the same world spirit.[10]

The Gardener was the only work of Tagore in Finnish for four years. Its poems were performed at recitals, and lectures on the writer were given on festive occasions. This continued for decades. The translation of *Gitanjali* was published in October 1917. There is no review of it to be found in the *Helsingin Sanomat*, maybe because Finland was preoccupied with the threatening political situation of that time. That year Finland became independent and drifted towards civil war. The translator Eino Leino's own life was turbulent, too.

In the following years, Otava Publishing Company published novels, essays, short stories and reminiscences by Tagore. The appreciation Tagore received shows in the many different editions of his books—paperback, hardcover, with leather backs printed in gold, and also in different series, for instance, a Nobel literature series.

The reviews were all highly positive. A reviewer writes in the *Valvoja-Aika*, a cultural magazine:

Tagore may have raised his voice from far away to be heard by the European world, but as a poet, writer, thinker and human being he has given his reader a precious gift: he has enhanced human being's delight in human being.[11]

A critic of the *Helsingin Sanomat* wrote about *The Home and the World*:

I am glad that *The Home and the World* has been published in Finnish, because it introduces us to the Tagore that really is worth knowing: a wise and a broad-minded world citizen from India. This book is typically Asian and also universally human at the same time. ... Rabindranath Tagore shows that he is a great and impartial man, understanding the human soul and assuming an objective attitude to the persons he describes and being fair to everybody, according to life's own laws and not according to the withered morals of human beings.[12]

The following piece appeared on *The Wreck*:

All in all we have to be most grateful to the publisher and the translator,
who have made it possible for us to get to know not only such a
great work of art as *The Wreck* but also one of the greatest spirits of
our time, who is not a dreamy mystic or an ascetic, revelling in his
renunciations, as we usually imagine the Eastern thinkers to be,—but
a man who knows the human being across the high dividers that race,
culture and all the external things in the world create, a man who
does not only stand in the midst of life but also loves it, and finally a
man who, in spite of all this, can draw away from life and stand at a
distance, so that he can judge it and look at it from a far wider angle
than perhaps any other of his contemporaries.[13]

These comments were on *Hungry Stones*:

Irrespective of the fact that Rabindranath Tagore knows European
civilization and has become part of it, our Western materialistic
worldview of today has not been able to desolate his imagination
or spirit, those Eastern worlds that yielded the clay out of which this
poet has ultimately created his own worlds. It is difficult to conclude
whether Europe in any respect has had a broadening influence on
such a ubiquitous spirit as Tagore, but something is certain—his
task is to broaden the hearts and spirits of us Europeans, us Western
people.[14]

This last review was written by Aarni Kouta, a writer and translator.
He also wrote the following rhymed verses, translated here in simple
stanzas. They appeared in the *Helsingin Sanomat* in 1923, decorated with a
drawing of Tagore's head. The writer has hidden some of his book-titles in
the text:

TAGORE
The current of the Holy Ganges,
The scent of the dark roses of the East
Fill your ideas and poems
And reveal a wise thinker.
A new melody is resounding in them,
The nature, the *Hungry Stones* live in them,
They speak the language of your spirit to us,
The deep mind of an Eastern sage.

You tell us how once *The Home and the World*
were at war,

But even though *The Wreck* threatens,
More than ashes will be left behind.
Your roses entered the land of snow,
We were endowed with the treasures of the dreams of the East,
You endowed us with harmony,
Which grants a spirit to our people and our land.[15]

In 1967, Otava Publishing House reprinted two books by Tagore in the same volume—*The Gardener* and *Sadhana*. They were noted in several newspapers in extensive reviews mostly favourably but not as ecstatically as in the beginning of the century. Only one of the reviewers was of the opinion that the books were outdated. Unfortunately, there was some incorrect information in the reviews.

In 1989, WSOY publishing house (Werner Söderström Corporation) reprinted *Gitanjali* with the title *Lauluja*, 'Songs'. Some critics praised it as religious poetry in reviews entitled 'Fascinating Verses' or 'Tagore and the Heart of Mankind', but others were rather hoping for a new edition of *The Gardener* or headed their review differently, for example, 'A One-sided Image of Tagore.' Jukka Heiskanen in *Kansan Uutiset* saw Tagore as a mystic, but in an interesting way:

Nowadays it is easy to laugh at the bridal mystics, but there was surprising critical strength in their doctrine in the Middle Ages. The mystic believed he was an intimate trustee of God and thus had the right to ignore the doctrine of the church and use his discretion to do whatever he wanted. Some of the mystics came up with advanced, even subversive ideas.[16]

Inspired by the book, the *Helsingin Sanomat* published a well-informed article by Elina Grundström, who had studied in Calcutta, under the title 'Tagore was a mystic prophet in the West, a renovator in the East.' It was an interview with Amita Sen (mother of Amartya Sen, the Nobel Prize-winning economist), who had grown up and lived in Santiniketan. The article gives a comprehensive image of Tagore as a path-breaker in literature and dance, as well as a social reformer.

In the beginning of the year 2002, the collection of aphorisms *Stray Birds* was published in Finnish in Pertti Seppälä's translation. The philosopher Eero Ojanen wrote a delightful review of it in the *Helsingin Sanomat*, with the title 'It is a pleasure to find Tagore again.' The book was also introduced on television.

In December 2007, Professor Juha Sihvola, the leader of the Researcher Collegium of Helsinki University, wrote a review on two poetry collections

that were translated by Hannele Pohjanmies, *Lover's Gift* and *Fruit-Gathering*
for the *Helsingin Sanomat*.

The tradition of translations, started by Eino Leino and J. Hollo, has
got a beautiful continuation. Both collections include a well-informed
foreword and explanations. ... In the poems you can hear the strong
voice of an Indian world citizen.[17]

Other reviews of the translations by Hannele Pohjanmies have been
positive too. In the magazine *Minä olen*, Erkki Lehtiranta reviews *The Poems*
and wrote that Tagore is one of the great masters of literature. In his beautiful
text, Lehtiranta mentioned that the translator has brought the poems of the
Bengali poet to life and made them sing also in Finnish:

These poems speak directly from heart to heart. Tagore's message
of love plays the chords of the soul and helps us to crystallize our
understanding of the human condition, its valleys and its mountaintops,
its pain and its pleasure.[18]

Scholarly Interest

No academic research has been done on Tagore in Finland. There are no
biographies or books on Tagore in Finnish. However, Tagore is remembered
in Finnish encyclopaedias at length. The first Finnish encyclopaedia
Tietosanakirja contained a long article on Tagore, written by Eino
Wälikangas.[19] The only foreword in the 'old' translations is in *The Home and
the World*; the writer of these two pages is unknown. The facts are however
correct.

Hannele Pohjanmies and Pertti Seppälä have written long forewords to
the collections that they have translated—because of the lack of a Finnish
biography of Tagore. The forewords to *Lover's Gift* and *Stray Birds* cover the
life and works of Tagore and the one to *Fruit-Gathering* his religious thinking.
The Poems has a foreword of thirty pages, discussing the life and poetry of
Tagore. *The Crescent Moon* has a foreword of two pages and *Crossing* a short
introduction to Tagore. The new translation of *Gitanjali* by Pohjanmies has
an introduction of thirty pages. The translations by Pohjanmies also have
explanations of the poems and a glossary of the Bengali words. Her most
important sources have been the writings of Buddhadeva Bose, Ketaki
Kushari Dyson, Krishna Kripalani, Martin Kämpchen, William Radice,
Jadu Saha and Amartya Sen.

Hannele Pohjanmies participated in an International Conference on
Rabindranath Tagore in Budapest in March 2012 as one of the speakers.
Pohjanmies has published an article in *Parabaas* with the title 'In Phalgun,

One Night.' The article is an imaginary dialogue between the writer and Buddhadeva Bose discussing Rabindranath Tagore.[20] She also published the article 'Tagore ja luonto' (Tagore and Nature) in her blog.[21] In 2012, Ulrika Juselius published all the poems of *The Gardener* in Eino Leino's translation in her blog.[22]

A SUMMING-UP

The reception of Tagore in Finland might have been a little different from that in other European countries. This is due to its remote geographical location and also its history. For centuries Finland belonged to Sweden and for more than a hundred years to Russia. The possibilities for travelling to other countries were slight, and Finland was far away from the metropolises of the world. Finland did not have any colonies. Finnish people had a humble image of themselves. As a small and poor nation, we did not feel superior to others.

This is the soil from which the reception of Tagore has grown. *The Gardener* was the first book to be translated and for four years after the Nobel Prize it was the only book of Tagore available in Finnish. *Gitanjali* became more famous elsewhere. It was not translated into Finnish until 1917. Finland became independent in that year and drifted into civil war. The novels and short stories by Tagore that were translated in the 1920s however got a good reception.

During these hundred years, the poems of *The Gardener* have been performed on the radio, festive occasions and recitals more than those of *Gitanjali*. Finnish theosophists have respected India and Tagore, but their mystical interest has been much more aimed at *The Kalevala*, the national epic of Finland.

The image of Tagore was not that of a prophet, and he was not seen as a product of Western culture. Rather, we could detect a tinge of grim pleasure in the writings, scoffing at certain aspects of Western countries. In the texts written on Tagore, there are some occasional mistakes. The most persistent one is the claim that Tagore studied law in England. But on the whole the writers were surprisingly well-informed and the texts gave a good image of this many-sided personality.

The poem *Apaghat* in which Tagore mentioned Finland was translated into Finnish by Hannele Pohjanmies, via the English translation by William Radice, and published in the collection *The Poems* in 2008. These days Tagore is not very well known among the public at large but he has some faithful friends.

372   Hannele Pohjanmies

NOTES

1. *Helsingin Sanomat,* 1904–2012 (Helsinki: Sanoma Osakeyhtiö, since 2008, Sanoma News Oy).
2. Ibid., 28 June 1913 (Helsinki: Sanoma Osakeyhtiö). Note: There is a slight error here: the journalist is mistaking Tagore's daughter-in-law for his wife.
3. Ibid., 14 November 1913.
4. Ibid., 15 November 1913.
5. Ibid., 14 December 1913.
6. Actually, the donation of books was made in favour of Tagore's institution, Visva-Bharati.
7. 'Bombshell,' in Rabindranath Tagore, *Selected Poems.* Translated by William Radice (London: Penguin Books, 1985), 119.
8. *Maaseudun tulevaisuus,* 8 March 1962 (Helsinki: Maataloustuottajain Keskusliitto).
9. *SKS, Suomalaisen Kirjallisuuden Seura, toiminta vuonna 2006* (Helsinki: SKS 2006).
10. *Helsingin Sanomat,* 21 December 1913 (Helsinki: Sanoma Osakeyhtiö).
11. Ibid., 9 October 1923.
12. Ibid.,15 October 1922.
13. Ibid.,19 December 1922.
14. Ibid.,7 October 1923.
15. Ibid.,14 October 1923.
16. *Kansan uutiset* 6.9.1989.
17. *Helsingin Sanomat* 30.12.2007 [Helsinki: Sanoma Osakeyhtiö].
18. *Minä olen* 5/2008 [Helsinki: Minä olen-kustannus Oy, 2008].
19. *Tietosanakirja* [Helsinki: Tietosanakirja Oy, 1909–22].
20. Hannele Pohjanmies, *In Phalgun, One Night.* An imaginary dialogue with Buddhadeva Bose on Rabindranath Tagore. Published in May 2008. www.parabaas.com/rabindranath/articles/pHannele.html
21. Ibid., *Tagore ja luonto* [Tagore and Nature]. http://hpohjanmies.blogspot.com/2009/03/tagore-ja-luonto.html
22. Web pages of Ulrika Juselius *Kotikirjaston uumenista,* published in 2012. http://www.phpoint.fi/ulrikaj/bookshelf/puutarhuri.html

WORKS CITED

Works by Tagore

Poems

Gitanjali [*Gitanjali,* 1912]. New translation by Hannele Pohjanmies. Helsinki: Basam Books, 2013.
Hedelmätarha [*Fruit-Gathering,* 1916]. Translated by Hannele Pohjanmies. Helsinki: Memfis Books, 2007.
Kuukeinu [*The Crescent Moon,* 1913]. Translated by Hannele Pohjanmies. Helsinki: Therapeia-säätiö, 2010.

Puutarhuri [*The Gardener*, 1913]. Translated by Eino Leino. Helsinki: Kustannus-osakeyhtiö Kirja, 1913; Otava, 1924, 1967.

Rakkauden lahja [*Lover's Gift*, 1918]. Translated by Hannele Pohjanmies. Helsinki: Memfis Books, 2006.

Tähtitaivaan runot [*Poems*, 1942]. Translated by Hannele Pohjanmies. Helsinki: Memfis Books, 2008.

Uhrilauluja [*Gitanjali*, 1912]. Translated by Eino Leino. Helsinki: Kustannusosakeyhtiö Kirja, 1917 (reprint entitled *Lauluja*, Helsinki: Werner Söderström Osakeyhtiö, 1989).

Villilintuja [*Stray Birds*, 1916]. Translated by Pertti Seppälä. Helsinki: Memfis Books, 2002.

Other Works

Ahnaat paadet ja muita kertomuksia [*Hungry Stones and Other Stories*, 1916]. Translated by J. Hollo. Helsinki: Otava, 1923.

Haaksirikko [*The Wreck*, 1921]. Translated by J. Hollo. Helsinki: Otava, 1922.

Ihmiskunnan uskonto [*The Religion of Man*, 1931]. Translated by Heikki Eskelinen. Helsinki: Biokustannus Oy, 1990.

Koti ja maailma [*The Home and the World*, 1919]. Translated by J. Hollo. Helsinki: Otava, 1922, 1937.

Sadhana [*Sadhana*, 1914]. Translated by J. Hollo. Helsinki: Otava, 1926, 1967.

Musical Compositions

In 1914–18, Erkki Melartin composed songs on four poems of Tagore: *Sinä päivänä, Skyar, Sagan om vårt hjärta, Smärtan.*

Eeli Kivinen has composed *Sotilaan rapsodia* (1977) and Hannu Virtanen *Tämä yö* (1993).

Merja Ikkelä has composed nine songs (2006): *The wind is up, Oh the waves, Listen, my heart, I would ask for still more, I filled my tray, This autumn morning, In the night when noise is tired, I have come to thee* and *My life when young*, all taken from *The Song of Love*, a selection translated by Hannele Pohjanmies.

Minna Leinonen has composed the song cycle *Shom* for female voice and the accordion (2009). It consists of parts *The day with the noise, Man goes into noisy crowd, The world, When the sun goes down, Put out the lamp, Man goes into noisy crowd II* and *The day with the noise II.*

Arto Koskinen has composed the series *Laulu suuresta kaipuusta* [*Song of a Great Yearning*] in 2010 to the poems of Rabindranath Tagore (among others); the poems of Tagore are *Thou art the sky, Thou hast made me endless, Stranger,* and *Art thou abroad on this stormy night?*

22

Scandinavia
(Denmark, Sweden and Norway)

Mirja Juntunen

India and the Scandinavians

The small Buddha statuette found at Helgö, an ancient Viking settlement in the vicinity of Stockholm, is held to substantiate early contacts between Indians and Scandinavians. The statuette is from north India and dates from the sixth century. In any event, the Vikings did travel far in the East in their looting expeditions and certainly they were in contact with people who belonged to the area under the cultural influence of India.

Apart from travel accounts by Scandinavians who had visited India, most of the knowledge of India in Scandinavia was mediated by scholars of Oriental languages and littérateurs who had spent some time in European universities in the late eighteenth and the nineteenth centuries. The Scandinavian scholars were as thrilled as their European contemporaries at their first contacts with Sanskrit dramas, the Upanishads and the Sanskrit language. After returning home from the European seats of learning— mostly in France and Germany—these scholars got chairs of Indology and Oriental languages established in the leading universities of Scandinavia. Ancient Indian literature was translated into the Scandinavian languages, most often direct from Sanskrit or Pali. The Eighth International Congress of Orientalists was held in Stockholm in 1889. Scandinavian scholars seemed to have similar interest in Oriental issues as the rest of Europe.

The political and economic contacts with India were mostly dominated by affairs related to Danish missions. The Danish East India Company started a trade mission in Tranquebar (now called Tharangambadi, in Tamil Nadu) in 1620 and expanded it to Serampore in Bengal and to the Nicobar Islands in 1750s. The Danish colonies were sold to the British administration in 1850s, but nevertheless, the Scandinavian interest in India had been aroused and acquisition of first-hand knowledge of India initiated.

Scandinavian missionary activities were lively and intensive in India and constituted an important part of the social interaction between Indians and Scandinavians. The missionaries were deeply involved in health care, education and social work. They turned their missionary stations into meeting places for people of various cultural and religious backgrounds. One of the most eminent missionaries was the Norwegian linguist and folklorist Paul Olaf Bodding (1865–1938) who created the first alphabet and wrote the first grammar for the Santali-speaking tribe.

This essay examines the reception of Tagore in Scandinavia—the historical cultural-linguistic region that includes the three countries Sweden, Norway and Denmark. It aims at collating the prevailing attitudes and the receptiveness of intellectuals to Tagore's works and message.

Tagore's writings were received in Scandinavia with childlike enchantment. Divinity and a purifying influence were the attributes ascribed to him in most Scandinavian accounts that appeared in 1913 and later during his visits to Scandinavia in 1921, 1926 and 1930. The excitement and the interest in Tagore, however, were short-lived, even though a number of Scandinavian twentieth century-writers and intellectuals based their works on the spiritual and existential legacy of Tagore.

THE CHOICE OF THE NOBEL LAUREATE AND THE IMMEDIATE SCANDINAVIAN RESPONSES

On the eve of the announcement of the Nobel Prize for Literature in 1913, Werner von Heidenstam (1859–1940), a Swedish poet of the romantic–idealistic school (who was to receive the Nobel Prize in 1916), visited the explorer Sven Hedin (1865–1952) at his residence in Stockholm, and exultantly exclaimed his delight at the choice of the next Nobel laureate in literature. As the Member of the Swedish Academy he could of course not reveal the name but he called out: 'You can't imagine who it will be! The foremost *scald* of our times, who has written the best in the idealistic line.'[1] Heidenstam had been introduced to Tagore's poetry collection *Gitanjali* in the spring of 1913 by the Swedish writer Andrea Butenschön (later also the translator of *Gitanjali*). Many years later she recalls this spring in her essay on Heidenstam and writes how she, after having received the poetry collection from the Indian Society in London, had visited Heidenstam and provided him with a copy of the book in English.[2]

Heidenstam seems to be the one who inspired and influenced the Swedish Academy to award the Nobel Prize to Tagore. Normally, the Nobel Committee presents the name(s) to the Academy, which usually confirms the choice of the Nobel Committee. In 1913, an exception was made to this

rule and the Academy did not accept the Nobel Committee's choice, which
was the French author and literary critic Émile Faguet (1847–1916), instead
preferring Rabindranath Tagore. Heidenstam was a member of the Swedish
Academy but not a member of the Nobel Committee of the Academy. The
recently elected secretary of the Academy, the writer and critic Per Hallstrøm
(1866–1960), had written expert appraisals on the candidates of the year.
There are two such appraisals on Tagore in the archives of the Swedish
Academy written by him. In the first and short one of April 1913 he admits
that his knowledge of Indian literature was limited and he compares *Gitanjali*
with catholic mysticism and the Song of Solomon in the Bible, in line with
Yeats's assessment of Tagore. He was also doubtful whether the prize should
be given for purely religious poetry. The second expert opinion also delves
into the religious atmosphere of Tagore's poetry, but it draws attention to the
universal tone of absorption of unity and harmony in the poetry. By now the
Nobel Committee had also access to *The Gardener* and *Sadhana* in English
translation. Hallstrøm's relatively sceptical initial attitude towards Tagore
may also be explained by the fact that he himself had nominated the Danish
fellow writer and ideological brother Jacob Knudsen (1858–1917) for the
Nobel Prize and he may have been interested in getting him elected. On the
other hand, many of the Academy members and contemporary intellectuals
in Scandinavia nominated each other during this period.[3]

Heidenstam kept on raving about Tagore's poetry in the letter that he
sent on 18 October 1913 to Erik Axel Karlfeldt (1864–1961), a member of
the Nobel Committee and a symbolist Swedish poet. He compared Tagore
to Goethe and continued, '... by reading these poems we have become
acquainted with one of the greatest poets of our time. ... I have not met
anything comparable in lyrical literature for decades.' He was deeply moved
by the poems in *Gitanjali*. According to him, reading the poems gave him
'hours of intense enjoyment, it was like drinking the water of a fresh, clear
spring.'[4]

The wording of 'fresh spring' was taken up by the chairman of the Swedish
Academy, the historian Harald Hjärne (1848–1922), in his presentation
speech on the Nobel ceremony on 10 December 1913.[5] He accounted for
the reasons for the selection of the literature laureate and gave a presentation
on Tagore as well as of Tagore's works. He characterised the poems and ideas
of Tagore as 'fresh and bubbling springs of living water.' The selection of
the laureate was based mainly on his English translation of *Gitanjali*, but
The Gardener as well as the story collection *Glimpses of Bengal Life* was also
available to the selection committee. The Nobel Library had received three
works of Tagore in Bengali in July 1913 even though it is dubious whether
the Orientalist scholar and writer Esaias Tegner Jr. (1843–1921), who was

one of the five committee members and knowledgeable in Bengali, had been consulted in the matter.

First of all, Harald Hjärne pointed out in his presentation speech that the prize of the year was being awarded to a poet who had written the finest poems of an idealistic tendency in conformity with the last will of Alfred Nobel (1833–96). Secondly, he pointed out that the poetry of Tagore by no means should be regarded as exotic but truly universally human. Then he proceeded to elaborate on the criteria that may have played the major role in the selection: '… the features of this poetry that won immediate and enthusiastic admiration are the perfection with which the poet's own ideas and those he has borrowed have been harmonized into a complete whole; his rhythmically balanced style, his austere taste in the choice of wording.' Hjärne seems here to hint here at Tagore's inclusive attitude towards Christianity. He even states that the 'Christian mission has exercised its influence as a rejuvenating force in India.'

The persons who promoted Tagore in the Academy constituted the conservative intellectual élite in Sweden, and the selection of Tagore seems to have served several purposes. It gave sustenance to the romantic ideas still prevailing among the intellectuals, it fuelled exoticism and escapism and it also highlighted the cultural connection with an ancient civilisation that was needed in the process of building up the sense of Swedish national identity with roots in a larger context. A poet like Tagore was needed at this point of time to dispel the worries of the approaching war and enliven the stagnant literary stage. Tagore was also needed to keep up the balance against the realistic trend in literature—in Sweden represented by August Strindberg, who had passed away in 1912.

The immediate Swedish reactions to Tagore were published in the newspapers on 14 November 1913, the day after the announcement of the Nobel laureate. Almost all the daily papers in Stockholm reported in similar wording. His poetry was described as 'fresh', 'pure' and 'spiritually religious,' even 'naively fresh.'[6] Not only were Tagore's literary qualifications mentioned, but his poetry was also characterised as a representative of ancient Indian wisdom and civilisation, and Tagore himself was seen as an incarnation of that ancient wisdom and religion.[7] The picture that was given in the reviews and articles on his poetry was romantic and idealistic. The poetry and the poet were said to represent the best of mankind in their most simple and honest way. The common Indo–European connection between Scandinavia and India was incidentally touched upon in some of the newspaper accounts in 1913. The organ of the Swedish Social Democratic Party, *Social-Demokraten,* wrote that the Nobel Prize for Literature was 'a tribute to the cultural world of India, racially similar to ours.'[8] (The references to the racial connection were more pronounced in news media during Tagore's first visit to Sweden and Denmark in May 1921, when he came to Scandinavia to deliver his Nobel Prize speech in Stockholm.)

Tagore's literary production that was available by 1914 was sensitively analysed by Per Hallstrøm in his lengthy essay on Tagore. Not only the poetry of Tagore but also the plays and short stories were reviewed by him. Hallstrøm especially mentioned *Glimpses of Bengal Life* paying attention to the plot construction in the stories, which according to him turned them to small pieces of drama rather than stories.[9]

The Norwegian papers were equally appreciative but the image of Tagore that they presented was less eulogising than the image that the Swedish papers and contemporaries had presented. In an article in a Norwegian regional paper a certain Matias Jørum analysed the authorship of Rabindranath Tagore after the announcement of the Nobel Prize winner.[10] He characterised the poetry of Tagore as sweet and moving, and harmonious in tone. By giving extracts from Tagore's rhythmical prose in Norwegian translation, he pointed out that the religious content that was obvious in *Gitanjali* was not present in *The Gardener*. Jørum connected the message in the poems with the Bengali philosophy of life, but he also pointed out that Tagore in many respects resembled Leo Tolstoy (1828–1910) when it came to the deeper religious issues and the focus on peasant life. By mentioning this he might have wanted to remind his readers that Tolstoy was never awarded the Nobel Prize even though he had been nominated several times. He had developed a world view similar to Tagore's and he profoundly excelled in literary production. He noted that Tagore was the second author after Kipling (in 1907) from British India who had been awarded the Nobel Prize for Literature.

The Norwegian Indologist Sten Konow (1867–1948), professor of Indic philology at the Christiania University (Oslo), had a long review of Andrea Butenschön's Swedish translation of *Gitanjali* on the front page of the leading daily *Aftenposten* soon after the announcement of the prize.[11] He started with hinting at a secret plot in the choice of the Nobel laureate of the year; he was doubtful about the criteria for the selection. He interpreted Tagore as the representative of the values that Europe was craving for at the moment and he even hinted that this was known and discussed prior to the selection. However, Konow did not disparage Tagore's poetic originality. He was appreciative of his poetical expressions and the way in which Tagore portrayed affection and love and created an intense religious atmosphere in *Gitanjali*.

The Danish audience got acquainted with Tagore's authorship soon after the name of the laureate was announced through newspaper notices.

For the first time after two years a longer article written by the writer and editor Louis v. Kohl (1882–1962), who also translated *Gitanjali* and *The Gardener* into Danish, was published in a leading daily.[12] Kohl had studied German philology and Oriental literature and languages. He was known for his friendly attitude to Germany and was considered a controversial figure in Danish political and cultural life.

The Danish actor and theatre director Johannes Poulsen (1888–1938) had visited Tagore and his family during his travels in India and he reported about the visit in an article and later on in his travelogue.[13]

TRANSLATIONS

Almost all the Swedish as well as Danish and Norwegian translations of Tagore's writings were made from English. The Swedish translation by Andrea Butenschön of *Gitanjali* with Yeats's introduction was published as early as 1913. Butenschön, a Sanskrit scholar and writer, had studied Indology in London and it was through her connection with The Indian Society in London that she had obtained a copy of Tagore's English poems. By 1920 the book had been reprinted eight times. The publishing house Norstedts engaged six translators immediately after the announcement of the Nobel Prize. Many of the translators were reputed Swedish cultural personalities of that time—for example, the versatile translator Hugo Hultenberg (1870–1947) and Harald Heyman (1889–1962), a noted critic of literature. Prince Wilhelm of Sweden and Norway (1884–1965)—of the latter only until 1905 when the union was dissolved—who had visited Calcutta in 1912 and interacted with the Tagore family even though he did not meet Rabindranath Tagore, translated *Fireflies* into Swedish in 1927.

Not surprisingly Tagore's poetry seems to have attracted the interest of the Swedes: *The Crescent Moon*, *The Gardener*, *Fruit-Gathering*, *Stray Birds*, *Lover's Gift* and *Crossing* (combined in one volume) were all available in translation by the beginning of the 1920s. His plays were also translated during this early period: *The Post Office* in 1916, *The King of the Dark Chamber* in 1917, *Sacrifice* in 1919 and *Chitra* in 1921. There are several story collections in Swedish rendering from the same period (*Mashi and Other Stories*, *Auspicious Moment*, *Hungry Stones* and *Homecoming*) as well as the essays *Sadhana: The Realization of Life*, *Nationalism*, *Personality* and *The Religion of Man*.

In the late 1950s and early 1960s, three more books were translated into Swedish (*My Boyhood Days*, *A Collection of Stories* and *Quartet*, the last two from French). In 1961, the year of the Tagore Centenary Celebrations, Stockholms Stadsteater (Stockholm City Theatre) staged *The Post Office*.

A few other Tagore plays were performed in Sweden later on the stages of independent theatre companies, among them *Chitra* in the late 1990s. During the recent decades the independent scholar Per Olov Henricson seems to be one of the few who has kept up an interest in Tagore's writings in Sweden. He has published a number of translations of Tagore's poems in Swedish literary and cultural magazines, inspired by the new English translations by William Radice. Also the small Bangladeshi diaspora in Scandinavia has valiantly published articles on Tagore and translated his poems and stories into the Scandinavian languages in their cultural magazines. But unfortunately these magazines are rarely acknowledged by the wider audience of the Nordic cultural establishment.

By the middle of the 1920s, a number of works of Tagore were available in Danish translation. *Gitanjali* and *The Gardener* (translated by the above-mentioned Louis v. Kohl) were the first ones, followed by *Stray Birds, The Crescent Moon, Hungry Stones, The Home and the World, Lover's Gift, Crossing, My Reminiscences, Fruit-Gathering* and *Fireflies*. The drama *The Post Office* was translated into Danish in 1921 by the leading Danish dramatist and actor Johannes Anker Larsen (1874–1957), who was known for his interest in Eastern religions. The play was staged at Dagmarteatret in Copenhagen in 1922 and adapted as a radio drama and broadcast in 1932. During Tagore's visit to Copenhagen in 1930 on the occasion of the inauguration of the exhibition of his paintings, he recited his own poetry on Danish Radio. *Chitra* was translated and broadcast on Danish radio twice during the 1930s and 1940s. *The King of the Dark Chamber* is also available in Danish. In 1957, *The Crescent Moon* was reprinted, and in 1964 *The Gardener* and *Gitanjali* (the latter again in 1981) as well. *Stray Birds* was being republished again in 2013 in Danish.

One who translated several books of Tagore (*Stray Birds, The Crescent Moon* and *Fireflies*) into Danish was the poet, critic, journalist and above all translator Kai Friis Møller (1888–1960). He was celebrated for his delicate translations of French literature and he had also translated Kipling into Danish. Strangely enough, he did not include any of Tagore's poems in the poetry anthologies that he compiled in the 1940s and 1950s.[14]

The first book of Tagore that was translated into Norwegian *bokmål* (one of the two standard literary languages) was *The Gardener* in 1915. The translator was Villa Thrap (pen name for Johanne Wilhelmine Segelcke Wahl, 1888–1968), herself an author of several books. There were regular announcements in the daily papers about the translation,[15] and within two weeks after the first edition, the second edition was announced with a note that Rabindranath Tagore and his love lyrics had been received with great interest by the Norwegians.[16] In 1917, Lars Eskeland (1867–1942), author and educator, translated *The Gardener* into *nynorsk*, the other standard literary language of the Norwegians. A reviewer described *The Gardener* as 'not an exciting story, not a novel about bizarre mating or weird people, but elated beautiful poetry, pure and soulful.'[17] Maybe here the reviewer contrasted Tagore to Henrik Ibsen! Eskeland also translated *Gitanjali* in 1918. It was well received and reviewed in many Norwegian regional and national dailies. The other works of Tagore that were translated into Norwegian during this period were *The Crescent Moon* (1919) and *Fireflies* (1926). Some of Tagore's stories and poems were published in poetry anthologies and in *For Bygd og By*, a family journal run by Severin Eskeland (1880–1964), the brother of Lars Eskeland. The translation of *The Post Office* into Swedish in 1916 was noticed in Norwegian papers but the play seems not to have been published in Norwegian although it was presented to the Norwegian public in 1921 by the actor-couple Sigurd and Abigail Magnussen, with Abigail, an internationally reputed actress, playing Amal.[18] The Norwegian translations of Tagore are less in number than the Danish and Swedish ones, but a perusal of the library catalogues and news items shows that the major part of Tagore's production is available in Norway in one of the Scandinavian languages.

If we talk about Scandinavia in a broader sense, two more languages should be mentioned, namely Icelandic and Faroese. Magnús Árnason rendered *Gitanjali* into Icelandic in 1919 and *Stray Birds* in 1922. In 2011, *The Post Office* came out in Faroese, the language spoken in the Faroe Islands (Danish territory situated between Norway and Iceland) and mutually intelligible with Icelandic in writing though not in speech.

TAGORE'S IMPACT ON SCANDINAVIAN INTELLECTUALS

By and large the Scandinavian contemporary intellectual elite were appreciative about Tagore. He was met with admiration, and obviously his wide interests and his versatile and practical approach towards religion, literature and politics had something to offer to everyone. Scandinavian authors, especially those with a conservative outlook, saw a kindred spirit in Tagore. Tagore's English critics were regarded as a reference point and intellectuals with a pro-German attitude regarded Tagore as their ally. Sven Hedin was one of Tagore's admirers. He met Tagore in Stockholm in 1921 and 1926, and several times afterwards elsewhere in the world, both in Asia and Europe. In his appreciative essay on Tagore, Hedin expressed his fascination with Tagore's sublime and simple language as well as the content of universally applicable verities—and, Tagore's Germanic, tall physique impressed him.[19]

Many Scandinavian authors were influenced by the intellectual movements of Romanticism and Orientalism and they loved the dream of India, if not its reality. Tagore tried to introduce the reality of India, but his writings were mostly taken as romantic descriptions of universal love and pastoral values. There were many authors and intellectuals as well as theologians in Scandinavia who shared Tagore's political conservatism. The Archbishop of Uppsala and outspoken pacifist, Nathan Söderblom (1866–1931), evidently found Tagore's pantheistic world view attractive and appreciated his work for India's independence and self-government.[20] He invited Tagore to Uppsala in 1921 and organised a meeting in Uppsala Cathedral where Tagore was commended for the excellent work he had carried out for humanity. Nathan Söderblom and Tagore had broadly similar views on religion. During the same occasion in Uppsala, Tagore visited the parental home of Dag Hammarskjöld (1905–1961) whose father Hjalmar had been Prime Minister of Sweden, during 1914–17; Dag was then a schoolboy—and apparently the meeting impressed Hammarskjöld since he quoted Tagore many times in his speeches while serving as Secretary General (1953–61) of the United Nations.

One who was inspired by the theosophical movement was the Swedish working-class author Dan Andersson (1888–1920). His poetry was rooted in the charcoal burner's experiences, but it also had a touch of a search for God and elements of mysticism. Dan Andersson got introduced to Tagore's works while attending courses at a Folk High School (an institution for adult education). One of his teachers had been present in Uppsala Cathedral during Tagore's visit there and had been inspired by Tagore's ideas of unity and spiritual vision.[21] In his autobiographical works Dan Andersson mentioned two works of Tagore that had specially attracted his attention, namely the plays *King of the Dark Chamber* and *The Post Office;* he regarded the first play as extraordinary from the message point of view and the second one unusual for the Western audience from the thematic point of view, i.e., its approach to life and death.

The romantic language of Tagore and his approach to existential issues inspired other Scandinavian authors directly or indirectly. The Swedish author Pär Lagerkvist's (1891–1974) existentialist play *Himlens hemlighet* (The Secret of Heaven) from 1919 is regarded to echo Tagore. Two other Swedish authors whose works show the influence of Tagore are the modernists Gunnar Björling (1887–1960) and Karin Boye (1900–41). The Norwegian poet and novelist Tarjei Vesaas (1897–1970) was directly influenced by Tagore's romantic-sentimental language. In the early 1920s, he wrote poetry in prose, which he said he did 'as Tagore in India had done.' He called his *Til mi Solmøy* ('To My Solmøy') 'a high-flown prose poem on the lines of Tagore.' He had come in contact with Tagore's works while attending a Folk High School in 1917–18 where Lars Eskeland, the educator and translator of *The Gardener* into *nynorsk*, used to read out Tagore's poetry at social gatherings. Vesaas recollects those days later on and tells us that most of the students found Tagore's unrhymed poetry extraordinary.[22]

Tagore has inspired Scandinavian composers to set his poetry to music. The Danish composer Rued Langgaard's (1893–1952) allegorical religious mystery opera *Antikrist* (Antichrist) is partly based on Tagore's poetry collection *Gitanjali*. It was composed in the early 1920s, reworked in 1930, but premiered as late as in 1999 at the Tiroler Landestheater Innsbruck (Austria) and only in 2002 in Copenhagen. *Chitra* was set to music by the Swedish composer Wilhelm Stenhammar (1871–1927) in 1921 ('Chitra', incidental music, op. 43). Other Scandinavian composers like the Swedes Edvin Kallstenius (1881–1967) and Maurice Karkoff (1927–2013), and the Danes Otto Sandberg Nielsen (1900–41) and Finn Høffding (1899–1997), to name a few, have employed Tagore's poetry in their musical compositions. Tagore's poem 'Stilla min själ' (Silence My Soul) has found its way into the Swedish Hymn Book (No. 910 in the supplement from 2000).

TAGORE'S VISITS TO DENMARK, SWEDEN AND NORWAY

Rabindranath Tagore came to Stockholm to deliver his Nobel Prize lecture in May 1921 while touring Europe, eight years after he had been awarded the Prize. He arrived at Copenhagen on 21 May and travelled to Stockholm two days later. After having spent five days in Sweden, he proceeded to Berlin. He did not visit Norway although it seemed to have been on his agenda and the Norwegians were waiting for him.[23]

Judging from the media coverage, the cultural élite in Sweden and Denmark (and a part of the common people as well according to the reporting) was almost overwhelmed with enthusiasm. Now, the newspaper articles were less focused on his literary production even though a considerable number of translations had come out in Scandinavian languages after 1913. The focus of the media reporting was on Tagore's personality and appearance. He was described as a prophet-like saint from the world of ancient wisdom and a grand civilisation. The headlines—often on the front pages—talked about the 'fever' or 'intoxication' that Tagore had stirred up as soon as he set foot on Scandinavian soil. He was received like royalty or even as a god. Danish papers described the reception at the railway station as an event of uncontrolled excitement. People rushed towards him gazing intently at his imposing appearance.[24] The Swedish dailies were not slow in comparing the arrival of Tagore at Stockholm with that at Copenhagen and pointed out that the Swedish reception was indeed controlled and respectful but by no means less enthusiastic than the Danish one. Tagore was revered more as a religious icon than a literary one. His movements were minutely reported. Thus we learn that during his few days in Copenhagen he interacted with the philosopher and theologian Harald Høffding (1843–1931), the Danish historian Kristian Erslev (1852–1930) and the historian of religions Vilhelm Grønbech (1873–1948) who had been interested in Indian religions at the beginning of his career. Women's rights activist Henni Forchhammer (1863–1955) met Tagore as did the writer Sophus Michaëlis (1865–1932). There were many more people he met; this sample shows the range of his connections. Georg Brandes (1842–1927), who was among the most influential and productive Scandinavian cultural personalities of this time, invited Tagore to his home. Tagore's visit to Copenhagen that summer was a climactic experience for many. Apart from all the meetings with cultural personalities Tagore delivered public lectures and gave interviews. The headlines reported about his wrath directed at the British colonial power in India and his criticism of Western culture. A Christian newspaper saw him as an associate in the joint struggle against the iniquity in the world.[25]

In 1926, Tagore visited the three Scandinavian countries. He was still an object of curiosity even if the media interest was not as extensive as it had been five years earlier when he visited Sweden and Denmark. On 21 August he sailed to Oslo from England. This was his first visit to Norway, and while in Oslo he interacted with distinguished Norwegian academics and cultural personalities. He addressed the Norwegian Oriental Society where King Haakon VII was also present among the audience. Tagore delivered a public lecture in the University Hall and visited the studio of sculptor Gustav Vigeland (1869–1943), who had also designed the Nobel Prize Medal. While in Oslo, Rabindranath Tagore met the explorer Fridtjof Nansen (1861–1930) who, besides Sven Hedin, was one of the most famous Scandinavian adventurers. The Norwegian papers reported extensively about Tagore's movements in Oslo and quoted his speeches, also those which criticised the Western mode of life.[26] After Oslo, Tagore proceeded to Sweden where he was received as an honorary guest, but not as enthusiastically as five years earlier. He targeted Western materialism in newspaper interviews, but he also showed generosity towards the Christian heritage in the Western world. Since Tagore had expressed his eagerness to meet Sven Hedin in Stockholm, Hedin organised a lunch for him and for a few of the Swedish Academy members including Per Hallstrøm and Anders Österling.

Tagore visited Scandinavia once again. It was in August in 1930 when he inaugurated the exhibition of his paintings at Charlottenborg in Copenhagen.[27]

Scholarly Interest in Tagore in Scandinavia

The interest in Tagore faded rapidly after his 1926 visit to the Scandinavian countries. Swedish newspapers mentioned Tagore now and then, the Danish ones were almost silent after his exhibition in Copenhagen in 1930, while the Norwegian ones kept on reporting at regular intervals.

Scholarly interest in Tagore in the three Scandinavian countries has not been very extensive, but as discussed above, traces of his legacy of unity and tolerance can be discerned in many writings of Scandinavian intellectuals. In the early period his works were analysed and discussed by writers and scholars, and there were some critical voices as well who saw the superficial sides of the Tagore cult in Scandinavia.[28]

Göran O. Eriksson (1929–93), the Swedish author, actor and translator, summarised the Swedish attitudes to Tagore since the heyday of 1920s in his preface to the Swedish translation of some of Tagore's stories that were published in 1961: 'It is a long time ago since we really *read* Tagore in this country with a response to his writings and letting his writings influence our literature and our approach to literature.' The lyrical writings of Tagore no longer attracted the literary circles of Scandinavia. Instead, the stories about Bengal peasant life seemed to find an interested readership. '[The stories] have a genuineness and there is nothing romantic about them', Eriksson concluded and thus clearly rejected the previous apprehension about Tagore's stories.[29]

However, Tagore's writings have drawn little scholarly or critical attention in Scandinavia during the last few decades. Recent scholarly interest in Tagore has been focused on examining the impact of Tagore's religious ideas on Swedish fiction or on the image of Tagore in Sweden during his two visits[30]. In Norway, the influence of Tagore on Vesaas has been critically analysed.[31]

The Future of Tagore in Scandinavia

To the best of my knowledge, there are no direct translations of Tagore's works from Bengali to any of the Scandinavian languages. Bengali is no longer being taught at Scandinavian universities. The recent celebrations of Tagore's 150th birthday have, however, brought him back to the intellectual arena of Scandinavia. The universities in Uppsala, Stockholm, Lund, Oslo and Copenhagen organised cultural and academic programmes in honour of the Nobel laureate of 1913. The University of Copenhagen also exhibited Tagore's paintings. If the poetry of Tagore—for that matter any poetry— does not find appreciative readers any more in our part of the world, at least Tagore's complex novels about the contradictions in society and in individual

Mirja Juntunen

lives should attract a wider audience in Scandinavia. They should be made available in our Scandinavian languages, preferably in direct renderings from the original Bengali.

NOTES

1. Hedin, *Stormän och kungar*, 353–4. A *scald* is a Norwegian or Icelandic folk singer.
2. Butenschön, *Heidenstam som jag kände honom*.
3. See Svensén, ed., *Nobelpriset i litteratur*.
4. The letter is in Svensén, ed., *Nobelpriset i litteratur*, vol. 1, 305ff.
5. 'Nobelprize.org. http://nobelprize.org/nobel-prizes/literature/laureates/1913/press.html. Also in Frenz, ed., *Nobel Lectures*.
6. See e.g., 'Det litterära Nobelpriset till en bengalisk skald [Nobel Prize in Literature to a Bengali Poet],' *Aftonbladet*, 14 November 1913; 'Nobelpristagaren i litteratur i år: Indiska skalden Rabindranath Tagore [Nobel Laureate of This Year: The Indian Poet Rabindranath Tagore],' *Dagens Nyheter*, 14 November 1913.
7. 'En hindu får årets litterära Nobelpris [A Hindu Gets the Nobel Prize of this Year],' *Svenska Dagbladet*, 14 November 1913.
8. 'Årets Nobelpristagare [The Nobel Laureate of the Year],' *Social-Demokraten*, 14 November 1913.
9. The essay on Tagore is found in Per Hallström, *Levande dikt: Essayer* [Living Poem: Essays]. Stockholm: Bonnier, 1914, 277–372.
10. 'Den nye vinnaren av Nobelprisen for dikting [The New Winner of the Nobel Prize in Literature],' *Intrøndelagen*, 24 November 1913.
11. Rabindranath Tagore, *Gitanjali* (Sångoffer), *Aftenposten*, 23 November 1913.
12. Ibid., *Politiken*, 20 November 1915.
13. Johannes Poulsen, 'Et besøg hos Indiens berømte digter'[A Visit to the Famous Poet of India], *Politiken,* 3 December 1915; Ibid., *Gennem de fagre riger.*
14. See Stinus, 'Indisk litteratur i Denmark,' 17.
15. E.g., *Aftenposten*, 10 December 1915, in both morning and evening editions, *Aftenposten*, 12 December 1915, *Aftenposten*, 15 December 1915.
16. *Aftenposten*, 23 December 1915.
17. Tagore: 'Hagemannen [*The Gardener*],' *Nordenfjeldsk Tidende*, 7 December 1917.
18. See Gandhi's foreword to Hemmilä, *Tagore in Sweden*, v.
19. Hedin, *Stormän och kungar*, 348–62.
20. Söderblom, *Sundar Singhs budskap*. Sundar Singh (1889–1929?) was a Sikh who had converted to Christianity and considered himself a Christian *sadhu*.
21. The teacher was Niklas Bergius (1871–1947) and his booklet *Tagore: Föredrag vid Brunnsviks folkhögskolans midsommarfest, 1921* [Tagore: Lecture Delivered on the Occasion of the Midsummer Celebration at Brunnsvik's Folk High School 1921], Stockholm: Tiden, 1921, was read and reviewed.

22. See the autobiographical text 'Om skrivaren' [About the author] in *Ei bok om Tarjei Vesaas* [A Book about Tarjei Vesaas], edited by Leif Mæhle, Oslo, 1964. Also Sehmsdorf, 'Tagore og Vesaas' [Tagore and Vesaas] in *Norsk litterær årbok*, Oslo: Det Norske Samlaget, 1982, 35–46.

23. For example, *Firda Folkeblad* on 31 May 1921reported that Tagore was in Copenhagen and Stockholm and he might pay a visit to Oslo as well.

24. *Politiken*, 22 May 1921.

25. See 'Indisk forfatter tog danskerne med storm [An Indian Writer Took the Danes by Storm].' *Kristeligt Dagblad*, 14 November 2011, for reporting of Tagore's visit in the same paper in May 1921.

26. E.g., 'Tagore gaar tilfelts mot Europas mekanisering [Tagore Attacks European Mechanisation],' *Nordre Bergenhus Amtstidende*, 27 August 1926.

27. *Berglinske Tidende* on 10 August 1930, on the front page, reported about the exhibition with a picture of Tagore flanked by Danish celebrities.

28. For example, the Swedish Historian of Religions Tor Andræ (1885–1947) brought up some aspects of uncritical reception of Tagore's aesthetic and religious ideas. See Tor Andræ, *Modern mystik: En blick på teosofien och den ockulta vetenskapen* [Modern Mysticism: A Look at Theosophy and Occult Science], Stockholm: Bonnier, 1930.

29. See Tagore, *Den landsflyktiga*, 7.

30. Hemmilä, *En yogi kommer till stan*; on the occasion of the replacement of Tagore's Nobel Medal to Rabindra Bhavana in Santiniketan on 7 May 2005, a booklet about Tagore's two visits to Sweden was launched: Hemmilä, *Tagore in Sweden*. The original medal was stolen in 2004 and the Swedish Nobel Foundation presented two replicas of the medal to the Indian Government. Also, Kongstad, *Tagorefeber i Stockholm*, unpublished thesis.

31. Sehmsdorf, 'Tagore og Vesaas', 35–46.

Works Cited

(The languages of the books below which are not in English are identified as D = Danish; S = Swedish; N = Norwegian)

Bergius, Niklas. *Tagore: Föredrag vid Brunnsviks folkhögskolans midsommarfest 1921* [Tagore: Lecture Delivered on the Occasion of the Midsummer Celebration at Brunnsvik's Folk High School 1921]. Stockholm: Tiden, 1921. [S]

Butenschön, Andrea. *Heidenstam som jag kände honom* [Heidenstam as I Knew Him]. Uppsala: Lindblad, 1941. [S]

Frenz, Horst, ed. *Nobel Lectures: Literature, 1901–67*. Amsterdam: Elsevier Publishing Company, 1969.

Gandhi, Gopalkrishna. Foreword to Olavi Hemmilä, *Tagore in Sweden, 1921 & 1926*. New Delhi: Embassy of Sweden, 2005.

Hedin, Sven. *Stormän och kungar: Senare delen* [Dignitaries and Kings, Part 2].Helsingborg: Fahlcrantz & Gumælius, 1950. [S]

388 Mirja Juntunen

Hemmilä, Olavi. *En yogi kommer till stan: Indisk religiösitet i svensk skönlitteratur med särskild tonvikt på Dan Anderssons författarskap* [A Yogi Comes to Town: Indian Religious Thinking as Reflected in Swedish Fiction with Special Focus on the Works of Dan Andersson]. (Stockholm Studies in History of Literature 46). Stockholm: Almqvist & Wiksell, 2002. [S]

———. *Tagore in Sweden, 1921 &1926.* New Delhi: Embassy of Sweden, 2005.

Kongstad, Hannes. 'Tagorefeber i Stockholm: En studie av synen på den indiske författaren Rabindranath Tagore i svensk tidningspress 1913 och 1921' [Tagore Fever in Stockholm: A Study of the Image of the Indian Writer Rabindranath Tagore in Swedish Newspapers in 1913 and 1921]. Lunds Universitet: Historiska institutionen, 2013. Unpublished thesis. [S]

Poulsen, Johannes. *Gennem de fagre riger* [Through the Fair Realms]. København: V. Pios, 1916. [D]

Sehmsdorf, Henning G. *Tagore og Vesaas: Påvirkning eller slektskap?* [Tagore and Vesaas: Influence or Congeniality?] in *Norsk litterær årbok.* Oslo: Det Norske Samlaget: Oslo, 1982. [N]

Söderblom, Nathan. *Sundar Singhs budskap* [The Message of Sundar Singh]. Stockholm: Geber, 1923. [S]

Stinus, Erik. 'Indisk litteratur i Denmark' [Indian Literature in Denmark] in *Indien–Denmark: Forbindelser og Samarbejde* [India–Denmark: Contacts and Cooperation] edited by Kika Mølgaard. København: Den indiske ambassade i Danmark, 1983. [D]

Svensén, Bo, ed., *Nobelpriset i litteratur: Nomineringar och utlåtanden, 1901–50* [The Nobel Prize in Literature: Nominations and the Nobel Committee's Reports, 1901–50], vol. 1: 1901–20, vol. 2: 1921–50. Stockholm: Svenska Akademin [Swedish Academy], 2001. [S]

Tagore, Rabindranath. *Den landsflyktiga.* [Stories] Göteborg: Gösta Skoogs bokförlag, 1961. [S]

Vesaas, Tarjei. *Om skrivaren* [About the author] in *Ei bok om Tarjei Vesaas* [A Book about Tarjei Vesaas] edited by Leif Mæhle. Oslo, 1964. [N]

23

GERMANY, AUSTRIA AND SWITZERLAND

MARTIN KÄMPCHEN

INTRODUCTION

The German language-area includes what is now Germany and Austria and the northern part of Switzerland. A hundred years ago, Germany had already been formed approximately within its present borders. However, Austria was still the central part of the Hapsburg Monarchy which had disintegrated by the end of World War I in 1918, leaving Austria with Vienna as the capital of a truncated country. The catastrophe of World War I (1914–18) which originated from Germany delayed the proper reception of Rabindranath Tagore by the German-speaking countries by a number of years, at least until after the War. Later, the consequences of the War dominated this reception.

The German-language culture first came into contact with India at the beginning of the nineteenth century when the Romantics discovered India as their ideal. Disillusioned with European civilisation, and with the utilitarianism of the Enlightenment, they saw in India an alternative culture with childlike, innocent people who lived in harmony with nature. This romanticising of India has remained a *leitmotif* of the German reception of Indian culture as a whole until today. At the scholarly level this led to an earnest study of India's languages, philosophy and mythology. In 1818, the first University Chair for Sanskrit was founded in Bonn marking the inception of Indology at the German universities, with August Wilhelm Schlegel the first to hold the chair. This affinity to Indian studies also strongly influenced the way Germans saw Rabindranath Tagore. Many felt that he was the fulfilment of Germany's romantic yearning for the ideal man and an ideal culture. This is what the philosopher Hermann Keyserling exclaimed: 'Rabindranath Tagore is the greatest man I have had the privilege to know ... There has been no one like him anywhere on our globe for many and many centuries.'[1]

Tagore on the other hand was deeply aware of the Germans' idealising love for India and did not get tired of emphasising his appreciation. Helmuth von Glasenapp, a noted Indologist, said: 'Germany means to [Tagore] not only the country of poets and thinkers (*Dichter und Denker*), the country of Goethe and Kant, but first of all the country which has shown an unselfish interest in the study of Indian languages and religions.'[2]

In the nineteenth century, contact with India was restricted to the early translations of Hindu and Buddhist sacred texts and to some travelogues. Germany and the Hapsburg Monarchy had no colonial stake in the Indian subcontinent. Hence, German-speaking explorers, administrators, businessmen and scholars had no special interest in visiting India. However, at the turn of the century and in the early twentieth century, first diplomats, often from the German aristocracy, wealthy explorers and travellers, and finally intellectuals and writers began to flock to India. Their writing contributed to a direct knowledge of the country which was more varied and diverse than the naïve fantasies which earlier generations of Germans had to contend with.

Noteworthy among the writers visiting India are, in chronological order of their visits, Waldemar Bonsels (who visited India in 1904), Max Dautendey (1905–6 and again later), Rudolf Kassner (1908), Stefan Zweig (1908–9), Hanns Heinz Ewers (1910), Hermann Hesse (1911), Hermann Keyserling (1911–12), Melchior Lechter (1910–11), Karl Wolfskehl (1910), and René Schickele (1913). Keyserling's *Travel Diary of a Philosopher* (1918) was widely read, and Hesse's visit to neighbouring Ceylon (now, Sri Lanka) (he did not enter India proper) had far-reaching effects on Hesse's thinking, his later literary works and on the India-fascination of a post-War hippie generation which took Hesse's 'Indian novel' *Siddhartha* (1922) as its guiding star.

Germany suffered defeat in World War I and was subjected to severe economic restrictions under the Versailles Treaty (1919) imposed by the victor nations. This not only led to an economic crisis but amounted also to a humiliation that was keenly felt by the German people, giving rise to an emotional and cultural crisis. Tagore reiterated in his speeches that he felt a deep sympathy for the suffering German people and that he visited Germany to offer spiritual consolation.

The cultural void experienced in post-War Germany created a wave of messianic movements. Spiritual masters, real and assumed, and various esoteric paths, for example Theosophy and Anthroposophy, also including life with nature, nudism and 'spiritism,' gained currency. A flight from reality into interiority or into an imagined East was a popular option. Not only did the writers and scholars who visited India in the early twentieth century nourish a genuine interest in an Indian world view, but a wide spectrum of the German-speaking intelligentsia also felt similarly inclined. Tagore's philosophy, personality and appearance had great acceptance within this scenario.[3]

RESPONSES TO TAGORE BEFORE AND AFTER THE NOBEL PRIZE

Rabindranath Tagore was almost 'unknown' before the award of the Nobel Prize was declared on 14 November 1913. However, one O. E. Lessing wrote a brief essay on Tagore whom he had met at Urbana, Illinois (USA) where Tagore spent the winter of 1912–13; this was published on 1 June 1913.[4] Lessing described the Indian poet in terms which was to become characteristic soon: as 'a beautiful, tall man with grey hair and beard and a strange gown.' Lessing heard Tagore's lectures in Urbana, describing his 'serenity', his 'dark eyes' and 'inner fervour'; he saw in him 'a legend' even before the Nobel Prize set off a multitude of romanticised stories about Tagore's life. The wise-man image was already evident.

Two renowned personalities from the German–Austrian intellectual circle, however, knew of and appreciated Tagore before he shot to fame. This was the German cultural philosopher Hermann Keyserling (1880–1946) and the poet Rainer Maria Rilke (1875–1926, born in the Hapsburg Monarchy). In 1911–12, Keyserling, hailing from an aristocratic family in the Baltic region, went on a trip around the world which resulted in his philosophical travelogue *Travel Diary of a Philosopher*. In Kolkata, Keyserling attended a musical soirée of Indian classical music at Jorasanko, the home of the Tagore family. Singling out Rabindranath from among his many relatives, he wrote: 'Rabindranath, the poet, impressed me like a guest from a higher, more spiritual world. Never perhaps have I seen so much spiritualized substance of soul condensed into one man.'[5] After returning to Germany, Keyserling corresponded with Tagore regularly, suggesting which personalities to meet in Germany when Tagore contemplated a visit in the summer of 1913, and in Japan when Tagore wanted to visit that country. His letters testify to the genuine admiration of the German count for the Indian poet.

Rainer Maria Rilke received information about Tagore as early as in September 1913 from an essay probably by Frederik van Eeden (1860–1932); this he mentioned in a letter to Lou Andreas-Salomé.[6] In December 1913, Rilke (in a letter to Kurt Wolff) praised André Gide's translation of *Gitanjali* into French[7] and Kurt Wolff immediately offered to publish a German translation of *Gitanjali* but, after some consideration, Rilke declined to translate and explained his reason in a letter to Wolff:

There is a reason for refusing which in fact renders all other reasons superfluous: namely that I do not find within myself that irrefutable call for the proposed assignment, from which alone could emerge a definitive and responsible work. Although much in these stanzas has a familiar ring, it seems, so to speak, to be borne towards me on a tide of unfamiliarity whose movement I would hardly know how to reproduce without somehow doing violence to myself. This may be partly due to my meagre acquaintance with the English language.[8]

One legend which keeps cropping up in various contexts is that Kurt Wolff, who was to become Tagore's German publisher, initially refused to publish *Gitanjali*. He had either received the manuscript from the English publisher, Macmillan, or the German translation from Marie-Luise Gothein. Wolff claimed in two letters and in a radio talk that he accepted the text for publication *before* the declaration of the Nobel Prize. Various newspaper reports, however, maintained that Wolff accepted it only after it became known that its author was to receive the Nobel Prize.[9] After the Nobel Prize was declared Kurt Wolff was triumphant that he could present a Nobel laureate to the German reading public, greatly helping his nascent publishing firm.

The reaction of the public came in two phases: first, immediately after the declaration of the Prize; and then in 1921, when Tagore visited Germany for the first time. The newspapers in Germany and Austria had several common themes. First, the disappointment that Peter Rosegger (1843–1918), an Austrian writer who had been touted to be the likely awardee, did not receive the Nobel Prize. Second, as the Nobel Prize Committee had issued sparse biographical data, the newspaper reports built up an imaginary Tagore using clichés that would stamp him until the present day. He was seen as a 'saint', a 'recluse' who lived in 'quiet seclusion and lonely meditation', as a mystic with a Christ-like appearance.[10] Alternatively, he was pictured as an aristocrat of fabulous wealth and fame. Some reports quoted Tagore's British friend William Rothenstein and particularly Frederik van Eeden, the Dutch poet and Tagore's translator, who lectured on Tagore in German[11] and claimed that it was he who brought Tagore to the notice of the Nobel Prize committee.[12] Van Eeden glorified the 'religious wisdom, contemplation, coexistence with the Divine which has become so uncommon with us.'[13]

More articles in the same vein appeared after the first German translation of *Gitanjali* was published in January 1914. In the same year the first German biography of Tagore, written by Paul Cremer, appeared.[14] It is said to be the first biography of Tagore in any European language, arriving one year before

Ernest Rhys's English biography; its forty-eight brief pages are, however, ill-informed and sketchy.

Kurt Wolff, a publisher of distinction, well remembered even today, got down to publishing every book by Tagore as soon as it appeared in English. In the short span of eleven years (1914 to 1925), Wolff's firm, Kurt Wolff Verlag, printed twenty-four books by Tagore as well as an eight-volume Collected Works (*Gesammelte Werke*) in 1921. Wolff claimed a monopoly on publishing Tagore. However, newspapers and journals of the time printed versions by other translators, some, in contrast to the English originals, in verse and rhyme, even by well-known authors of the time.

In his monograph on Kurt Wolff Verlag, Wolfram Göbel wrote that by the end of 1923 'more than one million copies' of Tagore books had flooded the German-language market making it an early bestseller in German publishing history.[15] In 1923 though, a decline set in due to post-War inflation, bringing the publication of Tagore's books to a closure in 1925, with *Gora*.

TRANSLATIONS FROM ENGLISH AND BENGALI

Wolff employed various translators. *Gitanjali*, Tagore's first volume in English, was translated by Marie-Luise Gothein who with her son Percy figured in the *George-Kreis*, the circle of followers around the poet Stefan George (1868–1933). Kurt Wolff's wife, Elisabeth Merck (1890–1970, a descendant of the Merck family which is an important name in German cultural life and runs a pharmaceutical company), translated the play *Chitra*. Elisabeth Merck's sister, Annemarie von Puttkamer (1899–1921), translated several early prose volumes. Other translators were Hans Effenberger, Hedwig Lachmann, Gustav Landauer, and Emil Engelhardt.

Most notable among Tagore's translators was Helene Meyer-Franck (1873–1946), a school-teacher from Hamburg who began translating in 1918, and from 1919 onwards became the sole translator, publishing in all fourteen volumes.[16] With her husband, Heinrich Meyer-Benfey, she also brought out the eight-volume Collected Works. Moreover, deeply dedicated as Helene Meyer-Franck was to Tagore and his ideas, she corresponded with him from 1920 to 1938[17] and was the first person to translate him into German from the original Bengali. After she was no longer in demand for translations from English, Meyer-Franck learnt Bengali with the help of Bengali students and books and, over the years, translated three stories and a selection of poems.[18] Unfortunately, they evoked no debate and exerted no influence in post-World War II Germany and have not been reprinted.

These early translations adopted the sentimental lyrical language imitating a romantic folk style which looks antiquated today. Moreover, after 1945, the German public was not inclined to appreciate emotional literature. It had revelled in an excess of emotionalism during the Nazi era and was suspicious of any emotional or romantic language. This is a feature which persists until today. That is why, when the successor of Kurt Wolff Verlag, the Hyperion Verlag, began to republish the old translations, some were retranslated in a more modern idiom. The new translators are F. Fiedler, Winfried Zillig, Gabriele Maria Muncker, Adam Haas, Karlernst Ziem, Gisela Petersen, Hella Rymarowicz, Joachim Marten, and Dieter Dunkel.[19] On the whole, Tagore did not regain the popularity which his books enjoyed between the two World Wars. Hermann Hesse, asked for a reaction to Tagore's descent into oblivion, commented wisely:

> Tagore's partial eclipse in the West at the present time is a phenomenon based on a universal historical truth. Today's man of fame falls into oblivion after his death, and only after a lapse of time—sometimes prolonged—does the world take the trouble to re-examine and reappraise both his former fame and his present neglect. Indeed, the greater the fame the more obdurate the oblivion that follows. This is the state of Tagore's reputation in the West today. In Europe, in the years following the First World War, Tagore was not only famous, he was also very much in fashion. But such is the world that it likes to make its former favourites pay the price for gifts once bestowed.... however, I see no cause for bitterness or complaint. He owes part of his reputation to the rich heritage of ancient Indian philosophy, for which he reclaimed a place of honour in the West, at least for a time. In some minds and hearts the effects have lived on and borne fruit, and this continuing influence—impersonal, silent and in no way dependent on fame or fashion—may in the final analysis be more appropriate to an Indian sage than fame or personality cults.[20]

Translations from Bengali resumed during Tagore's birth-centenary year, 1961. The erstwhile German Democratic Republic [Communist East Germany] officially celebrated the poet as an internationalist and propagator of the brotherhood of man. In East Berlin a street was named after Tagore. An anthology containing stories, aphorisms and poems, partly translated from English and partly from Bengali,[21] marked this beginning. In the course of time, Verlag Volk und Welt, the government's publisher for non-European literature, brought out four volumes of a Tagore Selected Works series (*Rabindranath Tagore Ausgewählte Werke*) in which translations from English and Bengali were mixed. It presented only prose works,[22] while the scheduled volume of poetry could not appear as a result of the reunification of Germany (in 1989). Noteworthy among them is Gisela Leiste's mature translation of the novel *Gora* (*Gora*, 1982) and of the story 'Nashta Nid' (*Das zerstörte Nest*, 1985), both from Bengali which were re-published in West Germany.[23] Gisela Leiste participated also in the direct translations in other volumes, along with Christiane Agricola and Gisela Petersen.

Heinz Mode (1913–92), a professor of archeology in Halle (East Germany) met Tagore at Santiniketan in 1934 and studied Bengali and Pali at Visva-Bharati and became the university's first teacher of German. From 1956, Mode revisited India almost annually. Tagore Studies owes him two books. The first one is *Rabindranath Tagore: Auf den Spuren des Dichters und Denkers in Indien und Bangladesh* (Rabindranath Tagore: In the Foot-Steps of the Poet and Thinker in India and Bangladesh; 1976), the poet's first full-fledged German biography; unfortunately, it is heavily laced with Communist ideology which gives Tagore's life an unjustifiable slant. The second book is *Rabindranath Tagore: Aquarelle, Gouachen, Zeichnungen* (1985) which is so far the only German book introducing Tagore as a painter; it includes reproductions of Tagore's paintings and drawings as well as interpretative essays.

A curiosity is the translation of *Letters from Russia* from a Russian translation into German[24] and a translation of Tagore's sermons *krishtu* from the Italian.[25] The Swiss translation of poems from Bengali to German, prepared by Aurobindo Bose and Ilse Krämer, needs a mention.[26] The German text is, however, more in the nature of a paraphrase lacking the accuracy of a philological translation.

The next step was the translation of *poems* from the original Bengali by Lothar Lutze and Alokeranjan Dasgupta with brief notes, aiming at a philologically correct and poetically adequate rendering of the original.[27] The title *Der andere Tagore* (The Other Tagore) points to the translator's determination to move away from the 'mystical,' 'sentimental' poet and explore his realistic, existential, sometimes desperate poetry of his later years. Thereafter, Martin Kämpchen began translating Tagore's poetry from Bengali on a wide scale covering the different phases from his early poetry up to his last poems written on his deathbed and incorporating Tagore's various moods and styles. Kämpchen's initial four volumes of poetry translation have been collected in *Das goldene Boot* (The Golden Boat) which also contains the translations of two plays, a novel, two stories, essays and letters, and Tagore's conversations with Albert Einstein, some of which were prepared by several other translators.[28] Tagore's 150th birth anniversary in 2011 was the occasion for a final collection of translated poems.[29] Kämpchen's stated aim was to present Tagore as a poet of world literature. For the first time his poetry came out in direct translation with renowned German publishers of world literature (Insel Verlag and Verlag Artemis & Winkler). This report does not include the numerous gift books which came out in the last fifty years with quotations from Tagore and photographs on diverse themes. Two audio-CDs with recitations of Tagore poetry (in Kämpchen's translation) have also been published.

When Tagore's popularity was at its peak, four of Tagore's plays had been performed to wide acclaim. *Chitra* began to be staged from 1916, *The King of the Dark Chamber* from 1920, and *Sacrifice* from 1921. During the 1920s the combined number of performances of these three plays was sixty-two. The fourth, *The Post Office*, became by far the most popular play. Between 1918 and 1929, it was performed 314 times at 105 theatres; in 1921, Tagore attended a performance in Berlin. The graph shows that with the decline in Tagore's popularity the number of productions and performances also dropped.[30] After World War II, *The Post Office* was adapted as a radio-play, and it was performed by amateur groups during the centenary year of 1961. In the last twenty years, a direct translation of *The Post Office* was performed professionally in Chur (Switzerland) and as a puppet-play in Magdeburg.[31] No other play was performed after the War. Even the 150th birth anniversary in 2011 could not resurrect Tagore as a playwright. However, Tagore's ballad *Snatched by the Gods* (*Debatar Gras*) was transformed into a modern opera (libretto by William Radice, the translator of the ballad; music by Param Vir) and produced at the Third Munich Biennale International Festival for New Music Theatre in 1992.

Tagore's poems and songs were set to music by numerous German-speaking composers soon after his books appeared. A few of these pieces are still being performed regularly. Notable among the composers are Karol Szymanowski who, though of Polish nationality, set to music the German translation of four songs. Alexander von Zemlinsky, a leading Austrian composer and conductor of his time, wrote the Lyrische Symphonie opus 18 in 1922–3 which sets to music seven songs.[32] To celebrate Tagore's 150th birth anniversary, the German composer Bernd Franke wrote a choral work basing the words on the German translation of a Tagore song.[33]

TAGORE'S VISITS TO GERMANY, AUSTRIA AND SWITZERLAND

Tagore visited Germany, Austria and Switzerland each three times:

Germany: May–June 1921, September–October 1926, and July–August 1930;
Austria: June 1921, July, and October 1926;
Switzerland: April–May 1921, June–July 1926, and August–September 1930.

These dates indicate that Tagore combined the visits of these countries, possibly seeing them as a single cultural entity. Tagore had contemplated visiting Germany even before 1913 and again during his first trip to Europe in 1920 after World War I had ended. The difficulty of getting a visa at short notice prevented him from entering Germany.

In 1921, the poet entered Switzerland from France and first stayed at Geneva where his birthday was celebrated (6 May) by a gathering at Geneva University. He travelled to Lucerne, Basle and Zürich, lecturing at each place. Tagore's meeting with Romain Rolland and his friends at Villeneuve near Geneva was the most noteworthy part of the trip. (See Tagore Reception in the France chapter) The second visit to Switzerland started off at Villeneuve to meet Rolland again and continued to Zürich and Lucerne. On the third visit in 1930, Tagore visited Geneva yet again with the intention to address the League of Nations. From there he travelled straight to Russia.[34]

In May 1921, Germany had been suitably prepared for Tagore's visit by the wide dissemination of his books. Accordingly, the response to Tagore's visit was highly successful. He lectured to overflowing halls, and received attention from politicians, public figures, scholars and writers. Hermann Keyserling who lived in Darmstadt (near Frankfurt) suggested to Tagore that, rather than him travelling around Germany, he could ask Germany's intellectuals to gather in Darmstadt to listen to him; Tagore rejected this attempt at monopolising him in no uncertain terms. Arriving from Switzerland, Tagore's first brief stop was, however, in Darmstadt. From there he went to Hamburg and spent some days in the company of Helene Meyer-Franck and her husband. This visit is amply documented in their correspondence.[35] Tagore briefly visited Denmark and Sweden to formally receive the Nobel Prize. He then returned to Germany, visiting Berlin, Munich and Darmstadt. In Berlin, he lectured at the Humboldt University and had to repeat his lecture on popular demand. The police had to pacify the crowds which could not enter the packed hall. Keyserling had been successful in persuading the poet to spend a week at Darmstadt. From 9 to 14 June, Tagore delivered daily several lectures in the palace of Archduke Ernst Ludwig which were translated by Keyserling. He addressed a gathering of enthusiastic people from a hilltop making them sing German folksongs, and he received groups of children with flower bouquets. These carefully orchestrated events mythified Tagore into the Wise Man and great educator of the people as which he is remembered in Germany.[36]

A large number of well-known scholars and writers attended the 'Tagore Week' at Darmstadt. Keyserling requested Thomas Mann to attend and write a promotional article; Mann however refused. His reply to Keyserling is characteristic of a dissenting German voice. Thomas Mann, the 'ironic German,' as he was labelled, wrote:

> Dear and Respected Count Keyserling,
>
> I cordially thank you for your letter. It exudes so much enthusiasm that I almost packed my bags and went to Darmstadt. However this would have been easier than writing an article, particularly one canvassing for this famous Indian of whom I have, whether you believe it or not, no understanding, or almost none, up till now. I am familiar with isolated, intensely soulful poems of his which, however, reading them in German, made no immediate impression on me, as indeed is the case with all translated poetry. The image I have always had of him is picturesque but pallid. Surely I do him an injustice in assuming that the subjective pallor of this image reflects reality; in presuming him to be a typical Indian pacifist, animated by a somewhat anaemic humanitarian spirit and a mildness which I deemed almost hostile in the years I spent engrossed in violent emotional conflict. Surely the man is totally different. Since I understand from your letter that he has made a deep impression on you, he must be great. But as it is you who are under his personal spell, how can you think that someone else, for example myself, could be the right person to write an essay publicizing the Tagore Week in Darmstadt? This you have to do yourself! You have to do it with the immediate and appealing enthusiasm of your letter. This will give an altogether different impression than if I were to squeeze out of myself some mediocre little piece, devoid of inner compulsion and only because I find it difficult to refuse you.[37]

Thomas Mann came face to face with the poet, rather unwillingly, when the latter visited Munich. Mann and his wife accepted the invitation to a lecture and a reception where they were introduced to each other. However, Mann shied away from speaking to him, and Tagore did not recognise that it was Thomas Mann who pushed his wife in front to let her do the talking. The incident is both comical and pathetic.[38]

Among the others who congregated at Darmstadt for the 'Tagore Week' were the philosopher Paul Natorp, the Jewish religious philosopher Martin Buber, the Protestant theologian Rudolf Otto, the cultural philosopher Leopold Ziegler, the writer Helene von Nostitz, Tagore's publisher Kurt Wolff, the Indologist Heinrich Jacobi and the Sinologist Richard Wilhelm. None of them, except the latter two, had any personal or academic relationship with India or Indian thought, yet each of them expressed a profound and sophisticated interest in Tagore. While his personality in its dignity and genuineness was highly appreciated, some critics commented that the exotic and romantic image Tagore created in spite of himself was exploited and even sensationalised. The lecture Tagore gave in most places bore the title 'The Message of the Forest.' It detailed his ideal of education which he was about to implement at Santiniketan by founding Visva-Bharati. Wherever he went he asked for donation of books for Visva-Bharati's future library. From Darmstadt, Tagore visited Frankfurt for a day and then moved on to Vienna.

In 1926, the fervent interest in Tagore had died down to a great extent. Germany had plunged into an economic crisis and was then on the road to recovery. No new books could be published after 1925. He also had to realise that, sadly, the royalty from the sale of his books had been whittled down by inflation. Although the public response was more modest, Tagore visited more cities than on his first visit and delivered a larger number of lectures. He revisited Hamburg and Berlin and toured Munich, Nürnberg, Stuttgart, Cologne, Düsseldorf and Dresden before returning to Berlin. From there he left for Prague.

The visit of 1930 was unique as Tagore arrived especially to promote his own paintings. Returning from England, he once again stopped first at Berlin where he mounted his first exhibition at the Galerie Ferdinand Möller from 16 July; next, he exhibited his paintings in Dresden at the Kunstmuseum and finally at Munich at the Galerie Caspari. The responses he received demonstrate the struggle of German viewers to connect with Tagore's uncommon style. The noted art historian Heinrich Lützeler commented:

> ... what surprised me in Tagore's paintings was the close connection with Europe, contrary to his literary work which has its roots entirely in Indian tradition. The form, especially colours and lines, but also the themes of Tagore's paintings are strongly influenced by symbolism and the 'Jugendstil.'[39]

Tagore himself denied any direct European influence in his paintings, but this did not stop the public from making speculative comparisons. Those most frequently made in newspaper reports were with the works of Edvard Munch, Emil Nolde and Paul Klee.[40]

During the same visit, Tagore took a special interest in the German Youth Movement, visiting at least two castles associated with it, the Hohnstein castle near Dresden and the Waldeck castle of the Nerother Wandervögel, a popular Youth Movement group, in the Rhine Valley near Koblenz. Some members of that group had visited Santiniketan in January 1928. Moved by the play they had performed, Tagore had promised them a visit when he next toured Germany, a promise he faithfully kept. A high point of that stay in Germany with considerable consequences was Tagore's visit of the Odenwaldschule (Odenwald School) near Heidelberg and meeting their founders, the noted educationist Paul Geheeb (1870–1961) and his wife Edith. Requested by one of his earlier students at Santiniketan, Aurobindo Mohan Bose (1892–1977), who was associated with the school, Tagore came on a visit and discovered a great deal of similarities in the educational concept Paul Geheeb practised, and his own. The aim both pursued was that their school children had the freedom to choose their subjects according to their interests. Apart from conventional subjects, they both integrated practical activities and spontaneous learning processes into their syllabus. Tagore and Geheeb kept up a decade-long relationship. The school which had to be moved to Switzerland in 1934 for fear of Nazi repression, and was renamed Ecole d'Humanité, continues to foster its Santiniketan ties. Bose lived in this school till his last days, and became Tagore's translator (into English and German) and in some ways his 'ambassador' in Europe, delivering lectures and publishing articles on Tagore.

Tagore visited Germany for the last time in 1930. Apart from the cities mentioned, Tagore lectured in Frankfurt and Marburg and attended the famous Passion Play in Oberammergau which moved him deeply. This experience was the basis of Tagore's well-known English poem *The Child*.

Tagore's three visits to Austria were confined to Vienna, where he lectured at the University and among others met Sigmund Freud. On his way to Vienna in 1921, he changed trains in Salzburg and talked with the writer Stefan Zweig, an urbane, widely educated personality in public life who was in touch with other pan-European figures, particularly with Romain Rolland and Hermann Hesse. Zweig was enthusiastic about his meeting with Tagore, describing it to Kurt Wolff: 'I have encountered this great personality, of whom I formed a strong and profound impression.'[41]

POPULAR AND SCHOLARLY INTEREST SINCE 1921

The tenor of the popular reaction to Tagore's visits to Germany, Austria and Switzerland was enthusiasm bordering on adulation. The newspapers were overflowing with reports of his every move. There was plentiful publication of interviews, summaries of his various lectures and addresses, along with reminiscences of visitors to Tagore's receptions and their personal conversations. Photographs of his venerable figure abounded in the press. Naturally, some sections of the public voiced their dissent. Zweig mentioned the 'hollow jokes' and condescension that Tagore encountered.[42] The sudden reverence also provoked some cultural envy. The following newspaper report, for example, makes this clear:

Without wanting to alter and belittle what is without doubt the great importance of the works of this Indian poet and novelist, it should not be forgotten that within the borders of Germany, writers and personalities are at work who deserve to be celebrated and made famous in foreign countries.[43]

Another aspect of this undercurrent of resentment was the fear in certain Christian quarters that Tagore wanted to draw his audience towards Hinduism. Therefore, in an attempt to integrate what was strange and threatening and thus render it harmless, some newspapers reacted by claiming that Tagore's philosophy was 'nothing but the elementary, simple and basic ideas of the Christian world-view.'[44] While most reports naïvely admired Tagore's flowing hair, long robes and dignified demeanour, others considered it a 'pose.' They poured their sarcasm over the 'itinerant human circus of morality.'[45] The terms 'Tagore-Kult' (cult of Tagore) and 'Tagore-Rummel' (Tagore-mania) were bandied about in the press.

Tagore's cherished wish to bring 'East' and 'West' together, which preoccupied his mind especially when he toured Europe in the 1920s, was accepted by all those who found solace in his poetry, philosophy and his appearance, radiating peace and harmony. This section was certainly in a majority; yet, the reconciliatory approach created resentment. It was felt that he should not preach love to a subjugated people like the Germans, but rather address himself to the subjugators, i.e. the victorious nations of World War I. They did not want to listen about the heroism of suffering from somebody who was not a victim himself.

Some argued that Tagore advocated 'East-West unification without any real familiarity with the West in its fateful realities. Therefore he cannot be our savior, but merely a "curious stranger" to the masses.'[46] These writers saw East and West as irreconcilable opposites. Eastern mildness and passivity could not help Germans and Austrians to rebuild their nations after the War. Rather, they had, it was asserted, to activate the European ideal of dynamism.

The productive interest of writers and scholars in Tagore arose soon after translations became available. But the principal drawback was that none of them had access to the Bengali original, and most could not even imagine the serious difference between the English translations and the Bengali works. Thus, true scholarship could not develop. Mention has been made of the first biography in German by Paul Cremer. A more informed biography came out by Heinrich Meyer-Benfey, professor of literature at Hamburg University, who received information through Tagore's associates.[47] A long and rambling interpretation of Tagore's works with numerous quotations, a short biography and a lengthy chapter on Tagore's religion and world view was written by Emil Engelhardt,[48] one of the poet's translators. A greater intellectual format was revealed in Paul Natorp's short book *Stunden mit Rabindranath Thakkur* (Hours with Rabindranath Thakkur).[49] He described his encounter with the poet in Darmstadt during the 'Tagore Week.' Natorp, like many other commentators, admired Tagore's personality, placing it above the impression which his books created. In his evaluation, Natorp praised Tagore, saying that he 'does not want to convert the West to the religion and culture of the East or vice versa. He wants that East and West should cooperate in order to save the afflicted humanity.'[50]

Noteworthy academic works by distinguished scholars include a lucid essay by the German-speaking Indologist Moriz Winternitz (1863–1937) of Prague on Tagore's religion and world view;[51] and a critical examination, *Rabindranath Through Western Eyes*[52] by the German Jewish scholar Alex Aronson (1912–1995) from Breslau; the latter is the first evaluation of the foreign, especially German, response to Tagore.[53] Winternitz spent about a year in Santinketan teaching at the newly founded Visva-Bharati (1922–3) and maintained a life-long friendship with the poet. Aronson found shelter at Santiniketan (1937–44) from Nazi persecution. He taught English, started the archive on Tagore at Santiniketan, and wrote extensively on Tagore in English-language journals. Aronson spent the final two years of his stay in the Indian subcontinent in Dacca (Dhaka), teaching at the University, before he migrated to Israel. As a University teacher in Tel Aviv and Haifa, he maintained links with Santiniketan until his death. His three-volume biography testifies to his enduring love for Tagore and Santiniketan.[54]

The Austro–Slovakian art historian Stella Kramrisch (1896–1993) arrived at Santiniketan towards the end of 1921 and stayed for about two years teaching art history. Thereafter, she joined Calcutta University as professor of Indian Art and stayed until 1950. She wrote on the artists in the Tagore family and often referred to Rabindranath Tagore with whom she maintained a close relationship. She was one of the early art historians appreciating Tagore as an artist.

The eminent theologian, philosopher, musicologist and physician Albert Schweitzer (1875–1965) dedicated the final chapter of his book *Die Weltanschauung der indischen Denker. Mystik und Ethik (Indian Thought and its Development)*[55] to Tagore's world- and life-affirming philosophy. Schweitzer contrasted it with the long Indian tradition of world- and life-negation. The foremost Austrian Indologist Heinrich Zimmer wrote a tract comparing the story of Tagore's play *The King of the Dark Chamber* with early Hindu myths.[56] As Zimmer continues to be well appreciated among students of Indian culture, this essay too is still being read.

Hermann Keyserling referred to Tagore in a number of his books and essays. However, he has not authored a comprehensive study of Tagore's philosophy, chiefly because he was more deeply affected by Tagore's personality than by his books. Besides, Keyserling's treatment of Tagore is more in the nature of eulogies than of analytical essays. He has penned the largest correspondence with Tagore, after the one by Helene Meyer-Franck. Unfortunately, all letters by Tagore to Keyserling, except one, have been destroyed by the ravages of World War II.

Among the prominent German-speaking men of literature only Stefan Zweig and Thomas Mann met Tagore personally. Stefan Zweig, as mentioned, was enthusiastic about Tagore when he met him in Salzburg. He consequently wrote a long essay about Tagore's world view. It is an imaginary dialogue between an 'Older Writer' and a 'Younger Writer.' The Older Writer argues in favour of Tagore's values and gradually convinces his younger colleague.[57]

The teenaged Bertolt Brecht wrote a rave review on *The Gardener*. Among the writers of that time, Hermann Hesse was closest to Tagore's world view. He however lived in seclusion in the Ticino mountains (Switzerland) and for that reason never met the Indian poet. He did write three book-reviews (on *Gitanjali*, *The Gardener* and *The Home and the World*) expressing critical appreciation.

Apart from Winternitz and Aronson, one more German-speaking scholar of note shared his life with Tagore at Santiniketan for some time. He is the Mahayana Buddhist monk Brahmachari Govinda (1898–1985) who stayed at Santiniketan teaching Buddhist Psychology, European Philosophy, Architecture and French. He met Tagore in Darjeeling, probably in 1931, and followed the poet to Santiniketan where he stayed on until 1935/36. It was there that he met his future wife, the Parsi artist Rati Petit, who became a Buddhist nun and changed her name to Li Gotami. Govinda accompanied Tagore to Ceylon (Sri Lanka) in 1934. Under the name Lama Anagarika Govinda, he later founded a modern Buddhist order and became the author of numerous well-known books on Buddhism.

A special and significant place on this list is occupied by Albert Einstein (1879–1955), the physicist. He and Tagore met in Berlin in 1926 and 1930 and again in New York at the end of 1930. That year, two conversations between Tagore and Einstein were recorded, which freely covered philosophy, religion and music.[58] They clarified the opposite metaphysical positions of these two thinkers. These meetings attained an iconic status not because of the significance of these conversations, but rather because here an eminent representative of 'the East' and an eminent representative of 'the West' exchanged views. It was sheer coincidence that the East was symbolised by a poet and man of religion, and the West by a physicist, a man of science, yet it was regarded as archetypal and these meetings achieved prominence for that reason. The photographs of Tagore next to Einstein taken in Berlin are some of the most publicised among Tagore's iconic pictures. To my mind, the true significance lies in the fact that these conversations demonstrate how the two men share a common vision and have an excellent chemistry with each other. Such unison Tagore enjoyed with very few persons from the West—probably with William Rothenstein, but certainly not with any other German-speaking personality.

RECENT RESEARCH

The 150th birth anniversary of Rabindranath Tagore (2011–12) generated considerable new interest in the poet in Germany. Several new translations or reprints of old translations have come out; the only German biography of Tagore in print entered its fourth updated edition. A fresh evaluation of Tagore's significance for Germany by Bernd-Peter Lange and several anthologies of essays on Tagore were published. A fresh evaluation of Tagore's significance for Germany by Bernd-Peter Lange and two anthologies of essays on Tagore were published. Lydia Icke-Schwalbe and Walter Schmitz edited an anthology on Tagore's visits to Saxony (East Germany) and the cultural debate this started. Golam Abu Zakaria edited another with essays on various aspects of Tagore's work. (see 'Works Cited' below). Seminars, poetry-readings and lectures took place in numerous German cities. Austria and Switzerland, however, did not seem to participate in these efforts. These events originated from the Indian and Bangladeshi diaspora community, the Deutsch–Indische Gesellschaft (Indo–German Association) with its many branches in all large German cities, the Indien-Institut (Munich), several Universities, as well as from the Draupadi Verlag (Heidelberg) and the India-specific journal *Meine Welt*. Germany's leading daily newspaper, the *Frankfurter Allgemeine Zeitung*, carried two articles to commemorate Tagore's 150th birth anniversary.[59]

The Deutsche Literaturarchiv (at Marbach near Stuttgart), one of the premier literary libraries and archives in Germany, organised a two-day seminar in March 2011. Four Tagore translators spoke, a book on *Rabindranath Tagore und Deutschland* (Rabindranath Tagore and Germany) was launched and a remarkable concert held presenting songs by German composers of the early twentieth century which were based on Tagore poems.[60] The Deutsche Literaturarchiv keeps dozens of original letters by Tagore in its archive. They are the letters by Tagore to Helene Meyer-Franck and letters bequeathed by Aurobindo Bose's inheritors. Martin

Kämpchen has donated his entire 'Tagore and Germany' research material to the Deutsche Literaturarchiv and his Tagore library to the Udo Keller Foundation (at Neversdorf near Hamburg).

The Merck company (Darmstadt) instituted a new prize in Tagore's name, the Merck Tagore Award. After the Tagore Culture Prize of the Deutsch-Indische Gesellschaft which exists since 1986, this is the second German prize in the name of Tagore.

The high point of Tagore's 150th birth anniversary celebrations in Germany certainly was the exhibition of paintings by Tagore in Berlin (*The Last Harvest*), organised by the Indian government together with the Asian Art Museum, Berlin.

On 14 November 2013, the Udo Keller Foundation, in cooperation with the Indian Consulate General in Hamburg, organised an event at Neversdorf to honour Tagore on the day on which he received the Nobel Prize one hundred years earlier. A Tagore bust was unveiled and Martin Kämpchen delivered a lecture.

Unfortunately, no plays or music- or dance-dramas have been staged in translation. The wide networks of theatres and music halls in Germany, Austria and Switzerland have taken no notice of Tagore's genius. Adaptations of this genre could bring out Tagore's 'message' and poetic insights in a contemporary context. Despite various efforts no new documentary film on Tagore could be produced.

Repercussions of the many Tagore-events within the wider public will take some time to be felt. The challenge before the small group of German-speaking Tagore scholars will be to attract the interest of a new young generation of educated readers of world literature. The older generation still remembers Tagore from the stories of their parents and grandparents and fondly preserves the old translations of Kurt Wolff Verlag. That generation clings to the image of Tagore as a mystic and wise man. The younger generations need to find entry into the universe of Tagore with the help of an ever-growing body of new, adequate translations from Bengali. This would assure that Tagore is read not by India-lovers alone, but by lovers of excellent literature, wherever it may originate.

Historical research on Tagore's visits in Germany, Austria and Switzerland, his interaction with men of letters and public figures need no longer be the prime target; much research has been executed in this area. Instead, Tagore's works, his ideas and philosophy need to be linked to the present prevailing discourses, especially in the fields of ecology, theology and education, apart from literature and aesthetics. Such interpretative efforts are still in a nascent state. They would ensure that Tagore's universe is not the domain of a small enthusiastic group, but enters mainstream, yet progressive and alternative, debates.

Modern German theatre, dance and opera have, as mentioned, not yet really taken note of Tagore. His music has, on occasion, been used in pop music, jazz and experimental music. These areas of public life should be made to profit from Tagore's creativity more and more.

NOTES

1. *The Golden Book of Tagore.* Calcutta: The Golden Book of Tagore Committee 1931, 127.
2. In *Deutsche Allgemeine Zeitung*, 30 May 1921; reproduced in English translation in: *Rabindranath Tagore and Germany* (Chapter: 'Rabindranath Tagore in Germany: A Cross-Section of Contemporary Reports.' Edited and translated by Dietmar Rothermund). Published by the Federation of Indo–German Societies in India, New Delhi [2011], 41.
3. See Panesar, *Der Hunger nach dem Heiland.*
4. O. E. Lessing, 'Rabindra Nath Tagore.' In *Literarisches Echo*, 15, no. 17 (1 June 1913), column 1184.
5. Hermann Keyserling, *The Travel Diary of a Philosopher.* Translated by J. Holroyd Reece. London: Jonathan Cape, 1925, 1st vol., 335.
6. See Rainer Maria Rilke/Lou Andreas-Salomé, *Briefwechsel*, ed. by Ernst Pfeiffer. Frankfurt: Insel Verlag 1975, 300 (Letter dated 30 September 1913).
7. Rilke/Helene von Nostitz, *Briefwechsel*, ed. by Ernst Zinn. Zürich: Niehans & Rokitansky Verlag/Insel Verlag, 1951, 1st vol., 336 and other sources.
8. See Kurt Wolff, *Briefwechsel eines Verlegers, 1911–63*, ed. by Bernhard Zeller and Ellen Otten. Frankfurt: Verlag Heinrich Scheffler 1966, 138–9.
9. For a detailed documentation see Kämpchen, 'The Legend: Kurt Wolff's Version'/'The Other Versions', in *Rabindranath Tagore in Germany,* 67–74.
10. *Der Tag* (Berlin), 14 November 1913; *Neue Freie Presse* (Vienna), 15 November 1913; and *Tagblatt* (Prague), 16 November 1913.
11. See Frederik van Eeden, 'Rabindra Nath Tagore: Der indische Nobelpreisträger,' in *Die neue Literatur* 1 (June) 1916, 1.
12. Neue Freie Presse (Vienna), 30 January 1914.
13. Ibid.
14. Cremer, *Rabindranath Tagore.*
15. Göbel, *Der Kurt Wolff Verlag,* column 640.
16. See Kämpchen, *Rabindranath Tagore and Germany: A Bibliography.*
17. See *My dear Master.*
18. Tagore, *Aus indischer Seele*; Ibid., *Mit meinen Liedern hab ich dich gesucht.*
19. See Kämpchen, *Rabindranath Tagore and Germany: A Bibliography.*
20. Preface to Tagore, *Later Poems,* transl. by Aurobindo Bose. New Delhi: Orient Paperbacks, 1974, 7.
21. Tagore, *Kabuliwallah, O Kabuliwallah.*

22. See Kämpchen, *Rabindranath Tagore and Germany: A Bibliography*, nos. 186, 189, 193, 206.
23. *Gora* in 1988 by C. H. Beck Verlag in Munich; *Das zerstörte Nest* by Manesse Verlag, Zürich 1989.
24. See Tagore, *Briefe über Russland*.
25. Ibid., *Jesus, die Große Seele*.
26. Ibid., *Schwingen des Todes*.
27. Ibid., *Der andere Tagore*. These translations have been included in *Das goldene Boot*.
28. Ibid., *Das goldene Boot*.
29. Ibid., *Gedichte und Lieder*.
30. These data have been taken from Sanatani, *Rabindranath Tagore und das deutsche Theater der zwanziger Jahre*, 66–80.
31. By Martin Kämpchen, published in *Das goldene Boot*, 251–82.
32. See Suddhaseel Sen, 'The Art Song and Tagore: Settings by Western Composers,' in *Rabindranath Tagore: Reclaiming a Cultural Icon*, d. by Kathleen M. O'Connell and Joseph T. O'Connell. Kolkata: Visva-Bharati, 2009, 148–73.
33. The choral work by Bernd Franke has the title 'Pran' and is based on the German translation of Tagore's song 'Prakriti 205' (in *Das golden Boot*, 129).
34. See P. V. Roy Chaudhury, 'Tagore in Switzerland,' in *Modern Review*, May 1971, 366–70.
35. See *My dear Master*.
36. For a detailed account of the 'Tagore Week,' see Kämpchen, *Rabindranath Tagore in Germany*, 46–57.
37. Thomas Mann, *Briefe, 1889–1936*, ed. by Erika Mann. Frankfurt: S. Fischer Verlag 1961, 188–9.
38. For details, see Kämpchen, *Rabindranath Tagore and Germany: A Documentation*, 32–6.
39. Heinrich Luetzeler, 'Tagore's Paintings,' *World Window*, 2 no. 1 (May) 1962, 10; Jugendstil is a form of art nouveau.
40. See Martin Kämpchen, 'Rabindranath Tagore's Paintings in Germany,' in *The Last Harvest: Paintings of Rabindranath Tagore*, ed. by R. Siva Kumar. Ahmedabad: Mapin Publishing, 2011, 30–3.
41. Wolff, *Briefwechsel eines Verlegers, 1911–13*, 413.
42. Ibid.
43. Johannes Schrapel, 'Nachrichten' [title and date of publication illegible] (Rabindra Bhavana archive).
44. E. Weber, 'Rabindranath Tagore,' in *Neues Volksblatt* (Vienna),19 June 1921 (Rabindra Bhavana archive).
45. Anton Kuh, 'Rabindranath usw. Bekenntnisse eines Nicht-Lesers,' in *Der Morgen am Montag* (Vienna) 20 June 1921 (Rabindra Bhavana archive).
46. E. K. Fischer, 'Tagore und wir. Ein Schlußwort zur Tagore "mache,"' in *Allgemeine Zeitung* (Chemnitz) 3 July 1921.
47. See Meyer-Benfey, *Rabindranath Tagore*.
48. See Engelhardt, *Rabindranath Tagore als Mensch, Dichter und Denker*.

49. Natorp, *Stunden mit Rabindranath Thakkur.*
50. Ibid., 39.
51. See Winternitz, *Rabindranath Tagore.*
52. See Aronson, *Rabindranath Through Western Eyes.*
53. Ibid., 25–40 and 59–71.
54. Ibid., *Brief Chronicles of the Time,* Calcutta: Writers Workshop 1990; Ibid., *The Seeds of Time,* Calcutta: Writers Workshop 1994; Ibid., *For the Time Being,* Calcutta: Writers Workshop 1995.
55. Albert Schweitzer, *Die Weltanschauung der indischen Denker. Mystik und Ethik,* Munich: C. H. Beck 1965 (first published in 1935); section on Tagore: 190–9. English translation: Albert Schweitzer, *Indian Thought and its Development.* Transl. by Charles E. B. Russell. London: Hodder & Stoughton 1936; section on Tagore, 238–49.
56. Heinrich Zimmer, 'Der König der dunklen Kammer. In drei Verwandlungen vom Rgveda bis Tagore,' in *Zeitschrift der Deutschen Morgenländischen Gesellschaft.* N.F. 8 (1929) 3–4, 188–212.
57. Stefan Zweig, 'Rabindranath Tagore's *Sadhana,* in *Das literarische Echo,* 1 October 1921.
58. These conversations have been reproduced in full by *The Kenyon Review & Stand Magazine,* 13 (2001) 2, 1–33.
59. Martin Kämpchen, 'Tagore Superstar. Übervater der Nation: Indien feiert seinen Dichter,' in *Frankfurter Allgemeine Zeitung* 15 June 2011; Thomas Meissner, 'Selig sei er gepriesen, aber besser noch gelesen,' *Frankfurter Allgemeine Zeitung,* 6 May 2011
60. Kämpchen, *Rabindranath Tagore und Deutschland.*

Works Cited

Studies on Tagore

Aronson, Alex. *Rabindranath Through Western Eyes.* Allahabad: Kitabistan, 1943.
Cremer, Paul. *Rabindranath Tagore.* Berlin: Wilhelm Borngräber Verlag Neues Leben, 1914.
Engelhardt, Emil. *Rabindranath Tagore als Mensch, Dichter und Denker. Eine Lebensdarstellung mit einer Auswahl aus den Dichtungen und Bekenntnissen als Einführung in sein Werk.* Berlin: Furche Verlag, 1921.
Göbel, Wolfram., *Der Kurt Wolff Verlag, 1913–30: Expressionismus als verlegerische Aufgabe.* Frankfurt: Buchhändler-Vereinigung, 1977.
Icke-Schwalbe, Lydia/Walter Schmitz, eds. *Bengalen und Sachsen. Tagore in Dresden* [Bengal and Saxony. Tagore in Dresden]. W.E.B. Universitätsverlag, 2012.
Kämpchen, Martin, ed. *Rabindranath Tagore and Germany: A Documentation.* Calcutta: Max Mueller Bhavan/Goethe-Institut, 1991.
———. *Rabindranath Tagore and Germany: A Bibliography.* Santiniketan: Rabindra Bhavana/Visva-Bharati, 1997.
———. *Rabindranath Tagore in Germany: Four Responses to a Cultural Icon.* Shimla: Indian Institute of Advanced Study, 1999.

Kämpchen, *Rabindranath Tagore und Deutschland*. Marbach: Schiller Gesellschaft/
   Deutsches Literaturarchiv, 2011.
———. *Rabindranath Tagore*. Rowohlt Verlag, Reinbek (4th ed.), 2011 [biography
   with comprehensive bibliography]
Lange, Bernd-Peter. *A Classic Eclipsed: Tagore in the West*. Südasienwissenschaftliche
   Arbeitsblätter Band 11. Ed. by Rahul Peter Das. Halle: Martin-Luther-
   Universität, Halle, 2011.
Meyer-Benfey,   Heinrich.   *Rabindranath   Tagore*.   Berlin: Brandus'sche
   Verlagsbuchhandlung, 1921.
Mode, Heinz. *Rabindranath Tagore: Auf den Spuren des Dichters und Denkers in
   Indien und Bangladesh*. Berlin, 1976.
———, ed. *Rabindranath Tagore: Aquarelle, Gouachen, Zeichnungen* [Water colours,
   gouaches, drawings]. Leipzig: Insel Verlag, 1985.
Natorp, Paul. *Stunden mit Rabindranath Thakkur*. Jena: Eugen Diederichs, 1921.
   English translation: 'Hours with Rabindranath Tagore,' in *Rabindranath
   Tagore and Germany* (Chapter: 'Rabindranath Tagore in Germany: A Cross-
   Section of Contemporary Reports,' ed. and tr. by Dietmar Rothermund),
   New Delhi: Federation of Indo-German Societies in India, [2011], 22–40.
Panesar, Rita. 'Der Hunger nach dem Heiland.' Das Bild des indischen Dichters und
   Philosophen Rabindranath Tagore in Deutschland während der Weimarer
   Zeit' [Hunger for the Saviour: The image of the Indian poet and philospher
   Rabindranath Tagore in Germany during the Weimar Republic]. Universität
   Hamburg, Hamburg, 1997 [M.A. thesis in typescript].
Sanatani, Reeta. *Rabindranath Tagore und das deutsche Theater der zwanziger Jahre:
   Eine Studie zur Übersetzungs- und Wirkungsgeschichte seiner Dramen in
   Deutschland* [Rabindranath Tagore and the German theatre of the 1920s: A
   study on the history of the translation and reception of his plays in Germany].
   Frankfurt/Bern: Peter Lang, 1983.
Winternitz, Moriz. *Rabindranath Tagore. Religion und Weltanschauung des Dichters*.
   Prague: Verlag der Deutschen Gesellschaft für sittliche Erziehung, 1936.
   English translation: Moriz Winternitz, *Rabindranath Tagore: The Poet's Religion
   and World Vision,* ed. by Debabrata Chakrabarti. Kolkata: Winternitz Society
   for Literature and Culture, 2011.
Zakaria, Golam Abu, ed. *Rabindranath Tagore: Wanderer zwischen Welten.*
   [Rabindranath Tagore: Wanderer between Two Worlds]. Bangladesch
   Studien- und Entwicklungszentrum e.V., Ulm and Münster: Verlag Klemm
   + Oelschläger, 2011.

Translations from Bengali

Dasgupta, Alokeranjan. *Mein Tagore* [My Tagore]. Heidelberg: Draupadi Verlag,
   2011 [selection of prose and poetry translations]
Tagore (Thakur), Rabindranath. *Aus indischer Seele* [The stories 'Samapti,' 'Atithi'
   and 'Durasha']. Transl. by Helene Meyer-Franck, Afterword by Heinrich
   Meyer-Benfey. Leipzig: Reclam, [1930?]

Tagore (Thakur), *Mit meinen Liedern hab ich dich gesucht* [Poems from *Gitanjali* and several other collections.]. Gedichte. Tr. Helene Meyer-Franck. Hamburg: Deutscher Literatur-Verlag Otto Melchert, 1946.

———. *Kabuliwallah, O Kabuliwallah.* Ed. by Karlernst Ziem. Berlin: Alfred Holz Verlag, 1961. Translations from Bengali by Sushanta Kumar Sinha in collaboration with Karlernst Ziem.

———. *Schwingen des Todes* [poems written between 1937 and 1941]. Tr. Aurobindo Bose and Ilse Krämer. Bern: Benteli 1961.

———. *Der andere Tagore. Eine Werkauswahl* [The other Tagore: A Selection]. Tr. Lothar Lutze and Alokeranjan Dasgupta. Freiburg: Wolf Mersch, 1987.

———. *Das goldene Boot. Lyrik, Prosa, Dramen* [The golden boat. Poetry, prose and plays]. Ed. by Martin Kämpchen. Tr. from Bengali by Rahul Peter Das, Alokeranjan Dasgupta, Hans Harder, Martin Kämpchen and Lothar Lutze; tr. from the original English by Andor Orand Carius and Axel Monte. Düsseldorf and Zürich: Verlag Artemis & Winkler, 2005.

———. *Gedichte und Lieder* [poems and songs]. Transl. from Bengali byMartin Kämpchen. Berlin: Insel Verlag, 2011.

Translations from Other Languages

[This does *not* include the translations from English published by Kurt Wolff Verlag, Leizig/München, from 1914 to 1925. For this see Martin Kämpchen, *Rabindranath Tagore and Germany: A Bibliography.* Santiniketan: Rabindra Bhavana/Visva-Bharati, 1997.]

Tagore, Rabindranath. *Briefe über Russland.* Tr. Arnold Boettcher. Leipzig: Philipp Reclam Jun. [1961] [from Russian]

———. *Jesus, die Große Seele.* Ed. by Victor Mendes. Munich, Zürich, Vienna: Verlag Neue Stadt 1995.[from Italian]

Correspondence

My dear Master. Correspondence of Helene Meyer-Franck and Heinrich Meyer-Benfey with Rabindranath Tagore. Ed. by Martin Kämpchen and Prasanta Kumar Paul. Kolkata: Visva-Bharati (2nd edition), 2010.

24

THE NETHERLANDS AND BELGIUM

VICTOR A. VAN BIJLERT

THE DUTCH IN THE NINETEENTH CENTURY

The Netherlands was, like several other countries, caught in the vortex of a storm that Tagore generated in 1913. In the context of Western colonialism in Asia, it was considered almost a miracle that the prestigious Nobel Prize went to an Indian, a citizen of a subject nation. To the Dutch reading public, an Indian poet was probably more exotic than for the British. The Dutch had given up the last vestiges of their trade settlements in India at the beginning of the nineteenth century, when they concentrated all their energies on colonising the Indonesian Archipelago into the Dutch Indies. With the rise of Theosophy in the late nineteenth century, some Dutch religious seekers were aware of India as a wonderland inhabited by mystics and mahatmas. There was also an academic interest in India's rich cultural heritage, for in 1865 the noted Dutch Orientalist Hendrik Kern (1833–1917) was appointed the first professor of Sanskrit in the Netherlands, holding the chair created at Leiden University. This appointment aroused comments in the press to the effect that money should not be wasted on such useless eccentricities as Indian languages.

Since the 1880s, Dutch literature, especially poetry, had experienced a revolution. Gone was the sanctimonious Calvinist utilitarianism in literature. 'The most individualist expression of the most private emotion' became the new literary creed of the loosely-knit group of young poets and writers. The sonnets of Jacques Perk (1859–1881, the 'Keats' of this group) and Willem Kloos (1859–1938); the lyrical epic *Mei* (May, 1889) by Herman Gorter (1864–1927, the 'Shelley' of the group); and the lyrical *Bildungsroman* (1885) *De Kleine Johannes* (Little Johannes) by Frederik van Eeden (1860–1932) set new standards for Dutch literature. These young Dutch authors did not conceal their admiration for Shelley, Keats, Heine and Wagner. The Dutch movement of the 1880s was a late offspring of English and German Romanticism.

Frederik van Eeden, an Early Translator

The influence of this late-Romantic movement of the 1880s on Dutch literary taste lingered on well into the third decade of the twentieth century. Frederik van Eeden has been one of its most important protagonists. It fell on Van Eeden to be the first Dutchman to get acquainted with and inspired by the English poetry of Tagore. This happened in early 1913, before the Nobel Prize was declared, in London when the Italian actress Eleonora Duse (1858–1924) suggested to van Eeden to read *Gitanjali: Song Offerings*. Van Eeden began reading these poems and was deeply moved by them. In his diary, Van Eeden noted on 11 May 1913: 'Yesterday I've read the songs of Tagore, the Bengali poet. This is beautiful. It moved me like no other contemporary has moved me so far. Could I ever meet this man? This is better than Omar Khayam.'[1] For Van Eeden, Tagore represented the ideal he thought he himself could not fully realise: 'I know very well what I lack. Tagore has it. He feels the proximity, he feels Him, he is sure of it and he is full of it. I have to make do with mere fancy, and mediation and momentary annunciation ... to me Tagore seems to be the profoundest to which we can aspire in our days.'[2]

Van Eeden's Dutch translation of the English *Gitanjali* came out in November 1913, under the title *Wij-zangen* (Song of devotion), and ran into eight reprints in 1914 alone. Until 1933, *Wij-zangen* was reprinted seventeen times, testifying to the immense popularity of the volume with the Dutch public. The fact that the widely respected author and poet Van Eeden made the translation may have contributed to the popularity of the book. Van Eeden saw himself as Tagore's herald in the Netherlands. The editions of *Wij-zangen* as well as all subsequent Tagore translations by Van Eeden were acquired by the Amsterdam publishing house Versluys, which also published writings by other 1880s poets such as Gorter and Kloos. The covers of all these Tagore translations (ten cm x fifteen cm) were printed in green, orange and white and showed floral motifs typical of the early twentieth century. Stylistically Van Eeden tried to remain faithful to the English original of *Gitanjali*, using a slightly affected, sentimental prose style. As the English originals were in prose, Van Eeden never attempted to turn his translation into rhymed verse. Perhaps it never occurred to Van Eeden that the English itself was a prose recreation of rhymed Bengali verses. The Dutch text of Van Eeden captures the atmosphere and the diction of the English quite well, including the somewhat archaic expressions (which Tagore's English seems to have borrowed to some extent from Keats). Van Eeden applied this style of translating also to *De Hoovenier*, (*The Gardener*, 1916); *Kabir* (One Hundred Poems of Kabir, 1916) and *De Wassende Maan* (*The Crescent Moon*, 1917).

Other translations like *Sadhana* (1918), *Chitra* (1918), *Hongerige Steenen*, (*Hungry Stones*, 1920), *Huis en de Waereld*, (*The Home and the World*, 1921), 'De Vluchtelinge (*The Fugitive*, 1923) were all done with assistants whose names do not appear on the title page.[3] If the printing history of all these translations gives an indication of the public reception of these writings, it is clear that only *Wij-zangen* survived in Dutch public esteem. The latest reprint of *Wij-zangen* dates from 1994 and *De Hoovenier* has been reprinted several times in the 1970s.

WIJ-ZANGEN

After *Wij-zangen* appeared in November 1913, the Sunday, 7 December, edition of the newspaper *Algemeen Handelsblad* carried a lengthy review. The reviewer enjoyed the beauty of many of the verses but could not help detect some 'hollow rhetoric' in poems 43, 69 and 76. The reviewer regarded the poems as intending to announce the coming of a future religion: 'It is a volume to leaf through, late in the evening, when one is sitting alone under a lamp. Then a "Song of devotion" could turn into one's private prayer ... and yet it does not give any solid hold, which is what these times demand.' The first impressions of this reviewer were repeated time and again for almost a century. For Dutch readers Tagore was primarily a wise man from the East, a mystical poet and a kind of religious prophet and preacher. It is perhaps telling that all the post-War reprints of *Wij-zangen* were brought out not by literary publishing houses but publishers of esoteric books and those on New Age cults. This mystical impression of Tagore's work can be traced to Van Eeden himself who in his diary painted Tagore in mystical colours. Ultimately the responsibility for creating the image of a mystical thinker from the East lies squarely with Tagore himself. It is difficult to picture the author of *Song Offerings* as anything else but an Eastern seer and mystic. In his travels to Europe Tagore cultivated this public persona of an Oriental prophet, and it was no different when he visited the Netherlands.

It must have been an act of foresight on the part of Van Eeden to feel attracted to *Song Offerings* and begin translating the poems into Dutch in the summer of 1913. When *Wij-zangen* reached the bookshops in November 1913 this happily coincided with the announcement that Tagore was awarded the Nobel Prize on the basis of the same volume. For Dutch readers, *Wij-zangen* was the product of two cult figures who shared similar world views: Tagore, the internationally acclaimed Asian, and Van Eeden, the Dutch poet.

TAGORE'S VISIT IN 1920

In fact, Van Eeden himself thought Tagore shared his own idealistic, socialistic and utopian outlook. Van Eeden wrote to Tagore in the summer of 1913 (well before the Nobel Prize award), expressing his desire to meet him. This became a possibility during Tagore's Netherlands visit from 19 September to 1 October 1920. But contrary to Van Eeden's expectations to quietly meet Tagore and discuss issues of culture, international politics and religion with him, Tagore hardly spent time with Van Eeden. Instead, Tagore met Theosophists and Rotterdam bankers. After all, he was looking for sponsors for his school and university at Santiniketan. Within the short span of his visit, Tagore gave lectures almost every day, usually one in the afternoon and another one in the evening, and always at different locations in the Netherlands. He was given an official reception at Leiden University on 25 September, at Amsterdam University on 27 September and at Utrecht University on 28 September. Tagore spoke mostly on his educational ideals, the meeting of East and West, and on 'Bengal village mystics.'[4] Van Eeden wrote a report on Tagore's visit, which appeared in the *Groene Amsterdammer* periodical of 22 September 1920, commenting that even Tagore—'a high-minded and free spirit'—had succumbed to economics.[5]

OTHER TRANSLATORS

Van Eeden was not the only translator of Tagore in the early period. *The Post Office* was translated by the leading novelist and journalist, Henri Borel (1869–1933). He gave his translation the title *De Brief van den Koning* ('The letter of the King', 1916). A year later this was staged in Amsterdam with the most eminent Dutch actors of the time. Borel translated *The King of the Dark Chamber* in 1919. The Javanese prince Raden Mas Noto Soeroto (1888–1951), a journalist and writer like Borel, translated some lectures by Tagore and a short story from English in a single volume, *De Leerschool van de Papegaai* (*The Parrot's Training*, 1922). In 1916, Soeroto had published a 'Biographical Sketch' on the life and writings of Tagore with Versluys in Amsterdam.

TAGORE SET TO MUSIC

It is noteworthy that in the period 1914–26 Dutch composers set texts of *Wij-zangen* to music. In most cases these compositions contain only two to four texts from *Wij-zangen*, and usually set for a single voice with piano accompaniment. Although at least a dozen composers set pieces from *Wij-zangen* to music, the more well-known are Hendrik Andriessen (1892–1981),

Jan van Gilse (1881–1944), Karel Mengelberg (1902–84), and Bernard Zweers (1854–1924). Bernhard van den Sigtenhorst Meyer (1888–1953) composed a prelude and an interlude for orchestra which were meant for the Dutch stage production of *The Post Office*, and Jan van Gilse's composition, based on German translations of the English *Gitanjali* poems, is set to a score for a full orchestra.[6]

FROM THE 1930S TO THE 1960S

Interest in Tagore's writings began to wane rapidly during the 1930s. Interesting exceptions from a musical point of view were Arnold Bake and Peter van Hoboken. Arnold Bake (1899–1963), a Dutch Indologist and musicologist, was invited by Tagore and stayed at Santiniketan from 1925 to 1932. He was initially drawn to Tagore when he heard the latter speak at Leiden University in 1920.[7] Bake published the first staff notation of twenty-six Bengali songs of the original *Gitanjali* together with a transliteration of the Bengali texts.[8] Peter van Hoboken (1901–94), a Dutch journalist and musicologist for *Radio Nederland Wereldomroep* (Radio Netherlands Worldwide), and an enthusiastic promoter of Indian music in the Netherlands, stayed in India from 1935 to 1939 and spent some months at Santiniketan.

Among notable translations of Tagore's English works, Johan de Molenaar's Dutch translation of *Stray Birds* under the title *Zwervende Vogels* (1941) must be mentioned. This translation has remained a favourite and was reprinted until 2001. The years after World War II witnessed a clean break with the political, cultural, and religious traditions of the pre-War period. Dutch society was severely traumatised by the Nazi occupation; for the first time since Napoleon the country had been overrun by a foreign power. After 1945, 'beauty had lost its visage' as the Dutch experimental poet Lucebert (1924–94) wrote. Though interest in Tagore had declined considerably, it had not entirely disappeared.

As Tagore's birth centenary was approaching, a committee was formed, the Nederlands Tagore Comité 1961, to prepare the celebrations. Members of this committee belonged to the academic, political and cultural elite of the Netherlands. The ambassador of India, R. K. Tandon, was also involved in the committee's work. The committee had a prominent patroness in the Queen of the Netherlands, Juliana. Queen Juliana had always shown a keen interest in things Indian, like her mother, Queen Wilhelmina. The programme included Jan van Gilse's orchestral composition, *Gitanjali*, exhibitions and performance of plays.

The early 1960s witnessed a minor controversy regarding Van Eeden's Tagore translations. In 1961, a number of articles appeared in the press about Van Eeden. Relatives of some of his assistants or co-translators claimed that Van Eeden had not acknowledged their work. Van Tricht produced a book documenting this controversy, providing an analysis of the facts known about Van Eeden's collaborators.[9] On the basis of original letters by Van Eeden, Van Tricht provided a list of Van Eeden's attested own translations and the ones done by his assistants.[10]

FROM THE 1960S TO THE 1990S

The late 1960s, heralded by the craze for the Beatles and the Rolling Stones, was a 'roaring' period in the Netherlands. A Dutch version of the hippie, the '*provo*', demanded that 'the imagination should rule.' The Provo Movement was inspired among others by the Russian anarchist Peter Kropotkin (1842–1921). The centre of this cultural revolution was Amsterdam, the city in which the provos even held a seat in the municipal council. Young people questioned what they regarded as the old-fashioned and authoritarian politics and culture of the 'bourgeois' 1950s (which was the post-War period of rebuilding the country). Artists, poets, pop musicians demanded the free availability of soft drugs like marijuana, and advocated liberal sexual relationships. Western culture itself was questioned and criticised for being materialistic and one-sidedly rationalistic. Many young people turned East (especially to India) to find new spiritual awakening.

A decade earlier, Dutch experimental poets had already shaken off the shackles of the literary past. The ensuing literary movement of the generation of the 1950s paralleled the movement of the 1880s. In both cases young poets and writers wished to break away from worn-out literary traditions and venture into unknown territory. Where the poets of the 1880s were inspired by English and German Romanticism, the 1950s' movement harked back to Arthur Rimbaud (1854–1891), and European Dadaism and Surrealism, and looked up to the American Beat Poets. In the 1960s, these poets from the 1950s were regarded as the vanguard of a large cultural, political and social upheaval, also known in European history as the Revolution of 1968.

One of the most colourful protagonists of the 1950s movement was the poet, journalist and novelist Simon Vinkenoog (1928–2009). He evolved into a Dutch hippie guru in the 1960s and 1970s, emulating to some extent America's best-known Beat Poet, Allen Ginsberg (1926–97). Vinkenoog (who knew Ginsberg personally) shared with Ginsberg the interest in Indian mysticism. For Vinkenoog breaking away from the past entailed the expansion of consciousness. For this reason he advocated the use of marijuana but also espoused Indian forms of meditation. Within this search for Indian wisdom, Tagore's work presented itself once more. Vinkenoog, familiar with Indian mysticism and devotional poets like Mira Bai, regarded Tagore as a kind of ally and translated into Dutch Tagore's *The Religion of Man*. This translation was published in 1977 and reprinted once in 1989.

The 1980s saw the publication of some Dutch translations of a few English books of Tagore. Wilfried Gepts translated the English *Gitanjali* into Dutch once again. He wished to create a more contemporary version than Van Eeden's translation, whose style had come to be regarded as outdated. Gepts called his translation: *Een fluitje in het riet: De Psalmen van Tagore* (A little flute among the reeds: The Psalms of Tagore, 1984). Aleid Swierenga and Mark de Sorgher translated into Dutch the English compilation, *A Tagore Testament* by Indu Dutt in 1969. The Dutch translation was published in 1989 and reprinted in 1993 and 2006. In 1991, Swierenga published a Dutch translation of Martin Kämpchen's poetic German renderings, directly from Bengali, of *Sphulinga, Lekhan,* and *Kanika*. Swierenga's translation was reprinted in 1998.[11] In both editions the title page and the introduction omit to mention Martin Kämpchen as the author of the German texts which formed the basis of Swierenga's translation. Furthermore, the 1991 edition looks identical—including all the photographs—with the German original.

TRANSLATING FROM BENGALI INTO DUTCH: 1990S ONWARDS

It is no exaggeration to maintain that William Radice's *Rabindranath Tagore: Selected Poems,* first published with Penguin Books in 1985, sparked off a totally new approach to Tagore's work. Hitherto all translations into Western languages, including Dutch, had always been made from Tagore's English writings. Radice was among the first serious translators to go back to Tagore's Bengali texts. There are some translations directly from the Bengali into English before Radice published his epochal work. But it was Radice who had set pertinent criteria for translating Tagore from Bengali: faithfulness to the Bengali original, philological exactitude, and no poetic liberties on the part of the translator. And equally important: the results in the target language should read like original poetry or prose in that language. To explicitly set such high standards seems almost superfluous. No one expects English translations from Rimbaud or Kavafis (Cavafy) to be below the mark, so why should Tagore translations from the Bengali be any different? Radice's work has shown—as well as the excellent translation work by Ketaki Kushari Dyson from 1993—how Tagore translations ought to be done in English. Could the same be done in Dutch as well? To Victor van Bijlert, Radice's work was an eye-opener and a major source of inspiration. Radice became Van Bijlert's role model for translating Tagore from the Bengali into Dutch.

Until Van Bijlert's translation of the complete Bengali *Gitali* (1914), a book of poems similar in mood and tone to *Gitanjali*, into Dutch in 1996, no work of Tagore was translated into Dutch directly from Bengali. This is due to the sparseness of Dutch translators of Bengali. Although Van Bijlert was trained as an Indologist (like William Radice) and studied Hindi and Sanskrit, he learned Bengali from his wife, Bhaswati Bhattacharya. Van Bijlert's first preference for translating Tagore, as apparently is the case with many non-Bengalis, was for the Bengali *Gitanjali*. The reason for this is that the Bengali *Gitanjali*, like its English counterpart, reads like a unity and not an anthology with different poems and a title-poem stuck somewhere in the middle, as is the case with other collections of Tagore's poetry, for example *Manasi*, *Sonar Tari*, and *Chitra*. Yet he chose *Gitali* because (a) it is a unitary book of poetry, and (b) it is less obviously devotional than *Gitanjali*.[12]

However, the Bengali *Gitanjali* saw a complete Dutch translation as well. It was prepared by the Belgian writer Jan Gysen and published in Belgium.[13] It cannot be said that Gysen's translation is very faithful and accurate. Many essential details are left out, while new ones are added. Gysen seems to have emulated what he thought was Tagore's own 'technique' of translating his own Bengali texts into English. But in Tagore's case it could be argued that the English texts are not translations at all, but they are English transcreations. Some of Gysen's *Gitanjali* translations were done before 1999 because they had been selected for the Dutch anthology of Tagore poems: *De mooiste van Tagore* (The best of Tagore) edited by Koen Stassijns and Ivo Strijtem published in 1997 and reprinted in 2007. The two editors, themselves Dutch language poets, brought together the work of various Dutch translators of Tagore's poetry, mostly done from English but in the case of Gysen done from the Bengali. This anthology also contains two of Van Bijlert's *Gitali* translations.

Promoting General Interest in Tagore

In 2007, Liesbeth Meyer published a book on Tagore's reception in the Netherlands around the time of the Nobel Prize award in 1913.[14] In her documentary study, Liesbeth Meyer also reprinted a number of characteristic reviews and articles on Tagore in the newspapers in the 1920s.

Tagore is a lasting icon of Indian wisdom not merely to a small group of indigenous Dutch admirers. Since 1975 a large group of immigrants from Surinam (a former Dutch colony in South America) has settled in the Netherlands. A large section of these migrants are of Indian origin (at present probably numbering over 100,000). These Surinamese Hindustanis (as they prefer to call themselves) evince a growing interest in Tagore, not so much because of Indian spirituality but because Tagore was a famous Indian and a Nobel Laureate. The Surinamese Hindustani poetess and writer of short stories Chitra Gajadin adapted the story of *The Post Office* in Dutch to the format of a children's story book with original illustrations by noted artist Helen Ong.[15] Surinamese Hindustani musicians and actors or playwrights have tried to establish a Tagore festival on 7 May, the poet's birthday, as a yearly cultural event. One such festival was organised in The Hague in 2001. Some short stories of Tagore were adapted for the theatre. The initiative did not see much follow-up. The Surinamese Hindu broadcasting corporation OHM, with airing time on the Dutch national TV and Radio networks, produced a one-hour documentary film on Tagore. Film crews had even visited Calcutta and Santiniketan to interview Tagore experts. This outstanding production was aired in 1995. Another documentary was made by OHM in 2007 focusing on the way Tagore inspired Indians, Surinamese and the Dutch people living in the Netherlands. The name Tagore is used by at least one Surinamese Hindustani cultural organisation in the Netherlands: *Stichting Tagore Sociëteit* (Tagore Society Foundation), founded in 1997 to promote Surinamese music.

The year 2011 was, like the Tagore centenary year in 1961, an important time for cultural and scholarly activities relating to Tagore. The Indian embassy was engaged in co-organising the 150th birth anniversary of Tagore. The resulting programme included the unveiling of two bronze Tagore busts— one in the public library at The Hague and the other at Leiden University. The municipalities of The Hague and Amsterdam hosted cultural events in May 2011, including performances of Tagore's dance dramas and plays.

In September 2011, the Society of Friends of the Kern Institute organised a two-day scholarly and cultural event on Tagore at Leiden. Bhaswati Bhattacharya acted as academic convenor and designed the cultural programme. The academic seminar comprised public lectures by international Tagore scholars. The cultural programme consisted of dance performances based on Tagore songs. The songs were rendered by professional Bengali musicians. In 2013, a Surinamese Hindustani theatre group in Amsterdam was to stage *Chandalika* (in Van Bijlert's Dutch translation from the Bengali).

THE FUTURE

It is difficult to predict how Tagore will be perceived and studied in the Netherlands in the coming years. If the past gives any indication, it is likely that Tagore will continue to be regarded as an Indian teacher of wisdom. The Dutch-speaking part of Belgium seems more interested in Tagore as an Indian artist and poet. After all, Gepts, Stassijns, Strijtem and Gysen are themselves Belgian poets. Interest in Tagore's music, however limited, is shared by both Dutch and Belgians. The musicologist Rokus de Groot who spoke at the Tagore celebrations in 2011, is after all, a Dutchman. Surinamese Hindustanis look up to Tagore as an eminent Indian, and thus by proxy he is considered to be one of them. The Dutch filmmaker Tomas Stolk who produced the OHM documentary of 2007 was attracted to Tagore's religious thought. This variety of interests and attractions reflects Tagore's multi-dimensional genius.

Notes

1. Bijlert, 'Frederik van Eeden en Tagore,' 9.
2. Ibid., 9.
3. Tricht, *Over de Tagore-vertalingen van Frederik van Eeden*, 10–16
4. Hoboken, 'Tagore in Nederland,'30–1.
5. Bijlert, *Frederik van Eeden-Genootschap*, 17–18.
6. For details, cf. Hoboken, *Tagore, 1861–1961*, 50–1
7. Ibid., 24a.
8. Bake et Stern, *Chasns de Rabindranath Tagore.*
9. Tricht, *Over de Tagore-vertalingen van Frederik van Eeden.*
10. Ibid., 16.
11. Swierenga, *Rabindranath Tagore.*
12. Van Bijlert's translation was published by the Society of Friends of the Kern Institute, a society promoting Indology in the Netherlands, and linked to Leiden University. William Radice was invited to speak at the official book launch on 2 December 1996 at Leiden University. Radice had taken the trouble to learn enough Dutch to comment on the Dutch translations which he thought 'were able to capture the strong emotions of the Bengali original.' The book launch and Radice's lecture are still fondly remembered as an important cultural event of the Kern Institute.
13. Gysen, *Gitanjali.*
14. Meyer, *Rabindranath Tagore.*
15. Gajadin, *Amal en de brief van de koning.*

Works Cited

Bake, Arnold A., et Philippe Stern. *Chansons de Rabindranath Tagore: vingt-six chants transcrits par Arnold A. Bake.* [Songs by Rabindranath Tagore: twenty-six songs transcribed by Arnold Bake]. Paris: Geuthner, 1935.

Bijlert, van V. A. tr. *Toen Jij de Snaren spande: De Gitali van Rabindranath Tagore, uit het Bengaals vertaald en ingeleid door Victor A. van Bijlert.* [When you tuned the strings: The *Gitali* of Rabindranath Tagore translated with introduction by Victor A. van Bijlert] Kern Institute miscellanea. 9. Leiden: Kern Institute, 1996.

Bijlert, 'Frederik van Eeden en Tagore: Onvolkomen Ontmoeting' [Frederik van Eeden and Tagore: Imperfect Encounter], in *Frederik van Eeden-Genootschap*, Mededelingen 36, 1999, 9–19.

Gajadin, Chitra. *Amal en de brief van de koning: naar het toneelstuk The Post Office van Rabindranath Tagore* [Amal and the letter of the king, after the play *The Post Office* by Rabindranath Tagore]. Rotterdam: Lemniscaat, 1992.

Gepts, Wilfried, tr. *Een fluitje in het riet: De Psalmen van Tagore* [A little flute among the reeds]. Sint-Baafs-Vijve: Oranje/De Eenhoorn, 1984.

Gysen, Jan. *Gitanjali: Naar een nieuwe dageraad.* [*Gitanjali*: Towards a new dawn] Tielt: Lannoo, 1999.

Hoboken, van P. C. 'Tagore in Nederland' [Tagore in the Netherlands] in *Tagore, 1861–1961.* The Hague: Information Service of India, Embassy of India, 1961, 30–8.

Meyer, Liesbeth. *Rabindranath Tagore: Een berichtgeving* [Rabindranath Tagore: An account]. Leesmijnboek. nl, 2007.

Stassijns, Koen, and Ivo Strijtem, eds. *De mooiste van Tagore* [Tagore's most beautiful poems] Tielt: Lannoo, Amsterdam: Atlas, 1997.

Swierenga, Aleid, tr. *Rabindranath Tagore: Op de stralen van het licht, Levenswijsheden* [On the rays of light, wise sayings for living]. Heemstede: Altamira, 1991.

Swierenga, Aleid, and Mark De Sorgher, tr. *Tagore: Een Testament* [Tagore: A Testament]. Uitgeverij: Altamira,1989.

Tricht, van H. Wed. *Over de Tagore-vertalingen van Frederik van Eeden.* [About the Tagore-translations] Den Haag: Nederlands Letterkundig Museum en Documentatiecentrum, 1963.

Vinkenoog, Simon, tr. *Rabindranath Tagore: De religie van de mens* [*The Religion of Man*]. Amsterdam: Wereldbibliotheek, 1977.

25

ITALY

MARIO PRAYER

India had never been at the centre of public debates or in the foreground of cultural life in Italy until 1913, and interest in that country and its 'ancient civilisation' had been confined to elitist academic circles. Indo–Italian cultural and political relations actually started in the interwar period, and have been explored by quite a few studies over the last thirty years.[1] Rabindranath Tagore's personal engagement in them has also received a fair amount of scholarly attention. The present essay takes on a broader perspective by providing the cultural context of Italy's response to Tagore as a poet and a thinker after 1913, as illustrated in articles, essays and comments accessible to the general public.

Like other countries, in Italy, too, the conferment of the 1913 Nobel Prize for Literature to Tagore created waves of enthusiasm among the people. The simple language and delicate imagery of his poems and plays, his love of children, his profound sense of humanity, divinity and life, and his clarity of vision seemed to herald a new light of hope. As the Italian people acknowledged the exceptional character of his poetry, translations of his works began to appear in bookshops. At the same time, important literary critics, scholars and general commentators were soon involved in what was their first encounter with a real, living representative of Indian civilisation.

The lively response was largely a result of certain characteristic features of Italian social and cultural ambience in the early twentieth century, which are briefly sketched in the first section of the present study. In the two following sections, the cultural interpretation of Tagore's works by different authors and the discussion of certain problems associated with translation will help to figure out how Tagore gradually became a tangible, multifaceted entity in Italy's cultural debates. The twenty-six years between 1913 and the outbreak of World War II were the most significant period in Italy's response to Tagore. During the 1950s and 1960s, with the industrial boom, development of a new urban, capitalist society, and the rise of neorealism and the so-called

Avanguardie, Tagore was pushed to the margins of public discourse. However, his works continued to be published. As discussed in the fourth section, even after World War II and despite momentous changes in the social and cultural atmosphere of the country, some of the pre-War stereotypes on India and Tagore were still firmly entrenched. This is illustrated in the views of some noted Indologists, as well as in the appreciation of Tagore by thinkers and scholars engaged in the formulation of an alternative, global culture of peace and education.

ITALY IN THE SECOND DECADE OF THE TWENTIETH CENTURY

In the early decades of the twentieth century, the strong Catholic foundation of Italian culture was recovering from the blows that Positivism and Socialism had dealt to it since the late nineteenth century. While the infatuation with positive science as the only source of real knowledge soon made room for a sense of dissatisfaction towards extreme materialism, Christian faith with all its devalued dogmas had not been entirely able to regain its undisputed centrality. The religious spirit of the Italian people had originally been attracted to Idealism, as propounded by Friedrich Hegel, Benedetto Croce and Giovanni Gentile, as well as to other, previously unknown religious traditions. This was a period when the history of religion was transcending the boundaries of university scholarship and reaching out to the people at large. Theosophy and other forms of spiritualism and occultism were on the rise in the quest for a more encompassing approach to life. Within the Church, Christian Modernism was proposing a religion more attuned to the realities of the contemporary world than to the ways and needs of the institutional church, threatening to deprive Christianity of its established philosophical and spiritual roots.

Undermining the centrality of Christianity entailed a growing perception of other cultural traditions, which would, sooner or later, result in questioning the assumed superiority of Christian and European civilisation over non-Christian and non-European ones. Nationalism was also a rising phenomenon in this phase with its projected idealisation of a flourishing collectivity placed under the safe mantle of a strong government, enlivened by shared values and interests. This could, to a fair extent, counteract the centrifugal and radical trends in Italy's cultural consciousness of the time.

All this resulted in a lively public debate carried out in the pages of a great number of journals and magazines reflecting various orientations and catering to a wide variety of readership.[2] Questions related to religion mingled with reverberations of national and European politics within a larger field of debate. Literature also played a major role in the vision for a

new national ethos, and while Croce's aesthetics were still holding sway over
Italian literary criticism, poets like Giosuè Carducci (1835–1907), Giovanni
Pascoli (1855–1912) and Gabriele D'Annunzio (1863–1938) were in turn
being held up as model examples of modern national writers.

TAGORE: INDIAN POET, ENGLISH ROMANTICIST, UNIVERSAL INDIAN

The 1913 Nobel Prize came at a favourable point in time, when Italy's public
culture was perhaps in its most responsive phase. Tagore's works immediately
became the object of intense debates in the columns of literary and other
journals, monographs and prefaces to translations. Despite differences of
opinion, these analyses shared two aspects—a sincere appreciation of the
exquisite literary quality of Tagore's poetry and, perhaps not unrelatedly,
what might be defined as a basic Orientalist approach. This Orientalism
descended from a deep-rooted Christian-centric/Euro-centric view of the
world which mingled with a sense of pride for the classical roots of Italy's
national civilisation. It was then assumed that Italy, seen as the cradle of
European civilisation, owed her supremacy in the world largely to the
historical role played by imperial and Christian Rome.

In this context, it was only natural for Italian intellectuals of the early
twentieth century to relate to India according to the established pattern
which the British had successfully exported to Europe. To them, India
belonged to an enchanted realm of spirituality, exotic refinement and
erudite scholarship, secure in the hands of British rulers, crystallised in its
civilisation beyond history. This assumption, once it was applied to Tagore,
produced paradoxical results at times. To some Italian writers, the fact that
Tagore often explicitly referred to ancient India as the original source of
contemporary Indian civilisation only seemed to confirm the soundness of
the Orientalist cliché—the spirit of India had really never changed over the
millennia, and Tagore was seen as a true Indian. The specific late-nineteenth
century origins of Tagore's defence of tradition, as well as his anti-colonial
purpose were thus entirely missed. To others, instead, Tagore could symbolise
India's emancipation because he had completely abandoned Indian tradition
in order to become a true Westerner in feeling and outlook.

Let us now consider a few examples. In offering one of the earliest
comments to Tagore's being awarded the Nobel Prize, Paolo Emilio Pavolini
(1864–1942), an eminent Sanskrit scholar teaching at the Florence Institute
of Higher Studies, presented the 'Bengali poet' to the Italian public as 'the new
interpreter of the human soul's nostalgia, of the longing for a reunion with
the divinity, of man's eternal aspiration towards God.'[3] A true representative
of India's ancient civilisation, according to Pavolini, Tagore was presenting

in a new, universally accessible poetic garb the spiritual truths of Vedanta philosophy and Indian classical literature.

Among the upholders of Tagore's Indianness were a few 'India experts,'[4] notable among whom was Ferdinando Belloni-Filippi (1877–1960), professor of Sanskrit at the university of Pisa. He wrote a learned and detailed essay to show that Tagore's poetry had purely Indian origins, both in content and form.[5] The content, Belloni-Filippi held, could be related directly to the pantheistic mysticism of the *Chandogya* Upanishad, while the form was indebted to the prosody of Bengali traditional poetry. According to Belloni-Filippi, it was in the latter aspect that Tagore's original contribution to the history of Indian literature had to be located, namely, the adoption of popular language within established poetic forms.[6] Belloni-Filippi wrote:

> Those who have seen Tagore as a Westerner, nay an Anglo-Saxon engaged in glorifying the beauty of action and life in the land of inaction and renunciation, have shown a poor knowledge of the poet and his country. ... Tagore no doubt extols the joy of living and doing, and to avoid any misunderstanding he calls this joy real and not illusory. But the action he values is not aimed at the gratification of passions ...; he glorifies the activity which is derived from the divine energy itself, and compels man to share in the work of goodness that is manifested in the universe.[7]

The polemical reference here was to Luigi Luzzatti, formerly Italy's Prime Minister (1910–11), senator, prominent jurist, economist and a man of letters. In a previous essay, Luzzatti had openly rejected the idea that Tagore represented the real (i.e., ancient) Indian civilisation, thereby giving rise to a controversy which involved scholars and other commentators for almost ten years. In Luzzatti's opinion, Tagore's works were the result of the de-Indianising influence of Western culture in India, so much so that in conferring the Nobel Prize to Tagore, Europe

> was actually praising itself, its religion, its customs, its aspirations. Tagore is Eastern by birth, but Western by everything else. He allowed the gods and sagas of his country to fade away, along with the thousand-year-old doctrines of renunciation, and has become the most remarkable example of the modern Indian man, enticed by the glow of Western civilisation.[8]

According to Luzzatti, Tagore had very little to share with India's literary history, as was evident in his treatment of nature. Whereas a genuine Indian poet (the likes of Kalidasa and Shudraka) would describe India's wildlife 'in its lively and intense colours, in its splendour, in its opulence and wildness,'

Tagore was simple, moderate, and his approach to nature was more akin to
that of 'a poet on the banks of the river Thames.'[9] In conclusion, Luzzatti
found Tagore's case interesting because,

> it proves that the lesson Europe—strong, vital and 'brutal' as it
> sometimes is—had to teach India has already borne fruit. India
> awakens, regains vigour, strengthens up her nerves, turns her gaze
> away from the past into the future, [so that today] her beloved poet
> talks to her in virile tones of grandeur and freedom: 'Where the mind
> is without fear and the head is held high.'[10]

Luzzatti's views found an echo in two eminent literary critics, Federico
Olivero and Giuseppe Antonio Borgese. Olivero (1878–1955), a well-
known Anglicist and literary contributor, grouped Tagore together with
three English writers, viz. Richard Crashaw (1613–49), Coventry Patmore
(1823–96) and Christina Rossetti (1830–94), in the chapter 'Mystical Poets'
of his book *New Essays on English Literature*.[11] Here Olivero presented Tagore
as an accessible and appealing poet and playwright, whose works had made
some original contributions to English literature, and whose Indianness was
limited to a few exotic metaphors. Giuseppe Antonio Borgese (1882–1952)
was a professor of German literature and Aesthetics in Turin, Rome and
Milan, a noted writer, a co-founder of prominent literary journals of the early
twentieth century (*Leonardo*, *La Voce*, *Hermes*), and later became an anti-
Fascist exiled in the USA. In one of his most celebrated works, a collection of
literary essays entitled *Ottocento europeo* (The European nineteenth-century),
Borgese harshly criticised Tagore as a trite and insincere 'poet-prophet,'
attractive in his appearance but devoid of substance:

> At first one is impressed by his tall stature, his thriving beard, his solemn
> attire. He looks like Leonardo Da Vinci in a wizard's dress. After
> observing him more closely, one notices a kind of negro feebleness
> across his features; as handsome as Jupiter, yes, but a mulatto Jupiter.

The comment is repeated at the literary level:

> Of [Tagore's] art a composite and mediated impression is often
> formed, and therefore, rather than Indian, it should be defined as an
> episode of European literature *made in India*.[12]

In conclusion, Borgese chastised Tagore's numerous admirers in Europe.
Their aesthetic taste, he argued, was decadent and weak. What need was there,
he asked, to go all the way to Calcutta to hear 'tired and mawkish' metaphors
such as 'the evening air is filled with the sad music of the waters?'[13] Europe
had had enough of 'this half pre-Raphaelite, half floral style,' particularly in
nineteenth-century England.[14] Therefore, he wrote:

Hindus have a right to sit in judgement of their poets and philosophers who are opening up the road to a new freedom. We Europeans, in turn, have a duty to remain loyal to our own tragic, virile style, and not to hazard, apart from empires, our primogeniture by getting lost in the imitation of obsolete languor.[15]

An attempt to find a sort of compromise between the conflicting views on Tagore's Indianness came from another scholar of ancient India, Elena Beccarini-Crescenzi, formerly a student of Pavolini's. In her essay 'The Child in Indian Literature,' she objected to Luzzatti's one-sided interpretation and pointed out that although Tagore's work did have certain European traits, its deeper nature was predominantly Indian. One should not forget, she argued, the simple fact that 'much water has been flowing down the Ganges' since the times of Valmiki and Kalidasa.[16] Having thus done a concession to historical change, Beccarini-Crescenzi moved on to reclaim Tagore to the only conceivable India, i.e. classical-exotic India, for reasons which were particularly evident in *The Crescent Moon*. In her words, this collection showed

> the 'Indianness' of the Bengali poet's thought and art, despite some coating of Western images and colours here and there. The landscape is Indian, with its luxuriant Indian trees and flowers—bamboo, *madara, bamani, bakula, kadamba, champa, tulsi, shiuli*. Lines of cranes fly over it, flocks of crows alight on it. Ganesha looks on with his huge elephant head; and *nupura*s jingle at the women's ankles.[17]

In tune with a widely accepted stereotypical view of India as the birthplace of religions, Tagore was often described by Italian authors as religious, spiritual, mystical, prophetic. The increasing popularity of not only his poems, but plays, novels and essays became alarming for Catholic writers who had already been on the defensive for a few decades. Among the new spiritualist circles, some responded to Tagore with full admiration. *Ultra*, the mouthpiece of the Theosophical League of Rome, carried a few articles in praise of Tagore, and one of the prominent representatives of Italian spiritualism, the psychiatrist Roberto Assagioli (1888–1974), penned a few articles extolling Tagore's spiritual universalism.[18]

TAGORE'S VISITS TO ITALY

Tagore's first visit to Italy was a fleeting passage through Brindisi on his way to England in 1878.[19] His second visit was in 1925 while returning to India from his South American tour. The Italian political scene at that time was still shaken by the violent events which marked Mussolini's rise to power and

428   Mario Prayer

the early years of the Fascist regime. Tagore was then a well-known figure in Italy. After landing at Genoa on 20 January, he took a train to Milan in the company of the Italian Sanskrit scholar Carlo Formichi (1871–1943); from there he would proceed to Venice to board the steamer to India. In Milan, Tagore was received by Duke Tommaso Gallarati Scotti, an intellectual with anti-Fascist leanings, and on his invitation delivered a lecture on 'The Voice of Humanity' at the Circolo Filologico on 22 January. The address contained a denunciation of violence and the politics of aggression, and was warmly received by the audience, while some official observers considered it inappropriate and tendentiously anti-Fascist. In the evening he was invited to the famous opera house La Scala for Puccini's opera *La Traviata*, directed by Arturo Toscanini; as he entered the theatre, he was noticed and greeted with a round of applause. On the following day, a programme was organised in his honour at the Teatro del Popolo, where *The Post Office* was staged.

A few days earlier, the idea had been tabled in official circles of bringing the great poet to Rome as a 'state guest'; but given his 'anti-Fascist' views, the plan was shelved. Tagore was taken ill and could not accept any further public engagements. During the days of illness he composed a hymn to Italy, which appeared in Italian in *Corriere della Sera* on 29 January.[20] On the same day Tagore took the train for Venice. Here he met a delegation from the Pro Coltura Femminile, a Turin-based cultural association for women, and a group of professors of Venice University. He left for India on 2 February.

While in Milan, Formichi had pressed Tagore for an invitation to Visva-Bharati as a visiting professor. When Tagore kept his promise by sending a telegram of invitation on 10 August, Formichi sought Mussolini's help in financing his trip to India. He tried to convince Mussolini that in Milan the Indian poet had not expressed any criticism of Fascist Italy, on the contrary he was a great admirer of Italy, and that the establishment of cultural ties with the world-renowned poet's university in India would greatly improve Italy's international reputation. Mussolini, who was himself attracted to Tagore as a spiritual figure, agreed to send Formichi to Santiniketan in the winter of 1925. Along with him went a rich donation of books on Italian history, literature and art. Moreover, the young Indologist Giuseppe Tucci was deputed to Visva-Bharati to take classes in Italian culture. During his stay in Santiniketan, Formichi and Kalidas Nag, whom he had met in Rome in 1921, worked at plans for developing academic cooperation between India and Italy. Formichi then persuaded Tagore to visit Italy again in 1926 in order to facilitate these plans. This time Tagore would go as an official guest of the Italian government.

Formichi returned to Italy early in 1926. When Tagore arrived at Naples on 30 May, Formichi took charge as Tagore's untiring tour guide and strict 'guardian,' and kept the poet under his constant watch during the two weeks that he spent in Rome. Tagore's days in the Italian capital were by all means a grand event, with a constant flow of admirers and well-wishers—artists, aristocrats, writers, students, philosophers, theosophists and common people—going to meet the poet at his residence at the Grand Hotel, in the heart of the city. The poet was taken around the city and shown both the ancient relics and the achievements of the present government. The newspapers gave extensive coverage of Tagore's tour, of his meeting King Victor Emmanuel III and Mussolini (on 1 and 13 June) and of the many celebrations organised in his honour: at the Town Hall on the Capitol Hill; at Teatro Quirino where he spoke on 'The Meaning of Art' in Mussolini's presence; at the school 'Orti di Pace,' at Rome University, at the centre for physiotherapy 'Natura Sana,' at Teatro Argentina where his play *Chitra* was staged, at the Colosseum and on the Via Appia. On 2 June, *La Tribuna* published the following message to the Italian people in Tagore's own handwriting: 'Let me dream that from the fire bath the immortal soul of Italy will come out clothed in quenchless [sic] light.'[21]

Not surprisingly, no mention was made by the Italian press of Tagore's meeting with Benedetto Croce on 14 June. The poet had explicitly requested Mussolini to help him see the Italian thinker whose theories on literature and aesthetics were well known among Bengali intellectuals. Croce, who had read all of Tagore's works then available in Italian translation, came to see him by the night train from Naples. During the conversation, Croce did most of the talking, touching on philosophy, history and other topics, while Tagore listened and agreed to what he was saying. Croce, however, abstained from making any comment on Mussolini and Fascism.

While the Italian press was trying to make political capital out of Tagore's expressions of sympathy for Italy, Tagore had adopted what he considered an apolitical stance and preferred to suspend any judgement on the contemporary political scenario. He preferred to look at Italy in the light of the historical role the country had played in the past. Heir to a centuries-old cultural heritage encompassing the Roman Empire, Christianity, Renaissance and Risorgimento, the Italian people had in recent years been able to rise again from political coercion to a new national life, thanks to their spirit of self-assertiveness and discipline, thereby setting an example for the Indian people. It is in this context that Tagore felt an admiration for Mussolini as the embodiment of man as a dynamic force in history. Endowed with a dominant character and greatness of vision, Mussolini had been able to infuse in his people a new sense of identity, leading them into a new phase of national life.[22]

After leaving Rome on 15 June, Tagore spent a few days in Florence and Turin, where more admirers were eagerly waiting to meet him. On 22 June, he finally left Italy for Villeneuve in Switzerland, where the French writer Romain Rolland was his host until 5 July. Rolland and another French writer, Georges Duhamel, made Tagore aware of the way the Italian Fascist press had all along been showing him as a friend of Fascism. This had horrified pacifists and anti-Fascists all over Europe, and a disclaimer was urgently necessary. Tagore firmly denied having ever meant to lend political support to the then Italian regime and reiterated that he had no competence to evaluate the political realities of contemporary Europe. He may also have feared that by entering into a controversy with the Italians, he would have jeopardised the promising prospects of cultural cooperation between Italian universities and Visva-Bharati. At the insistence of Rolland and Duhamel, and Giacinta Salvadori, wife of a notable anti-Fascist professor in exile, Guglielmo Salvadori, who had told him of several instances of Fascist violence to which she and her family had been subject, Tagore finally agreed to write a disclaimer, which was later sent to the *Manchester Guardian* and published on 5 August 1926. As expected, Formichi and the Italian establishment were deeply embittered by Tagore's supposed volte-face and all proposed plans of cooperation with Visva-Bharati were stopped. Harsh tirades appeared in the Fascist press. Here is one instance from *Popolo d'Italia*, a mouthpiece of the Fascist government:

> After his first experiment [in 1925], Tagore came again to Italy, appreciated the homage paid to him by the Government and its Head, strutted about in Italy's major cities, but once again the 'old man' did not arouse our liking. As far as we are concerned, when a poet does not feel the tragedy of his own people, he is a fake, not a poet. This sly hermit, whom the stupidity of others has made into a great man, has taken advantage of all that Italy, ever generous and kind towards her guests, was offering to him as a token of her respect for the Indian people, their magnificence in history and truth, their awesome mystery. Then, after crossing the border, Tagore came under the bastard pressure of his superiors, the Jewish Masonry, and obeyed their orders by speaking with great venom against Italy.[23]

This foreshadowed the ostracism which soon after erased Tagore from all forms of public and literary debates in Italy.

Tagore in Translation

The volatile and creative cultural milieu of the early twentieth century, which had managed to survive the shocks and deprivations of the years of World

War I, gave way in the 1920s to a more regimented notion of national identity with the rise and consolidation of the Fascist regime. By the early 1930s, the range and variety of Italy's periodicals were stifled and they were reduced to being mouthpieces of official culture. The frank observation on the cultural scenario of other countries was substituted by the uncompromising self-aggrandisement of autarchy. As for Tagore, despite the official veto his works continued to appear in Italian translation and receive the quiet approbation of the Italian readership.

The story of the Italian versions of Tagore's works begins with individual efforts by enthusiastic contributors to journals and magazines, who wanted to give the Italian readers a sample of the extraordinary literary phenomenon that the 1913 Nobel Prize winner represented. These include Paolo Emilio Pavolini, already mentioned above, Eduardo Taglialatela in his book on Tagore's poetry (1914), Nemi in *Il Marzocco* (1913) and Enrico Castelnuovo in *Nuova Antologia* (1914).[24] Very soon a publishing house of Lanciano, Carabba, acquired exclusive rights of translation for Italy from Macmillan; the first volume appeared in 1914. This was the *Gitanjali* with W. B. Yeats's Introduction, translated from the English version by the Italo–Irish writer and scholar Arundel Del Re (1892–1974).[25] Despite Italy's entering World War I in 1915, two more Macmillan volumes were translated and published by Carabba that year, *Il giardiniere* (*The Gardener*) and *Sadhana: Reale concezione della vita* (*Sadhana: The Realisation of Life*), while *La luna crescente* (*The Crescent Moon*) was brought out by the Florence publishing house Bemporad. The translations were entrusted to three writers, M. Sesti-Strampfer, Augusto Carelli and Clary Zannoni Chauvet respectively.[26] Two titles appeared in 1916 and two more in 1917, all from Carabba, viz. *Chitra*, *Il re della camera oscura* (*The King of the Dark Chamber*), *Ricolta votiva* (*Fruit-Gathering*) and *L'ufficio postale* (*The Post Office*). The first two were translated by the noted journalist, writer and teacher Federico Verdinois (1844–1927), and the other two by Eduardo Taglialatela and M. Sesti-Strampfer respectively.

During the 1920s and '30s, Carabba continued with the publication of Tagore's collected works covering novels, plays, poetry and essays.[27] In an attempt to improve the literary quality of the translations, the publisher tried to involve professional translators, poets and playwrights in their own capacity, and in one instance, a Bengali translator. This great effort succeeded in establishing Tagore's popularity in Italy once and for all. Even in later years, Carabba's books continued to represent the immediate point of reference for Italian publishers, and were reprinted several times. With the outbreak of World War II, however, Carabba's project was suspended and only briefly revived in 1948 with *Personalità* (*Personality: Lectures Delivered in America*) in A. Silvestri Giorgi's translation. After this, an entire decade passed without any translation being published. The first round of Tagore in Italian had thus come to an end.

As already pointed out, Tagore made his first appearance before the Italian readership in the form of English poetry in prose, and this induced some early observers to define him as an English writer altogether.[28] Very soon, however, thanks to Yeats's Introduction to *Gitanjali*, the awareness spread that this was not the original language of Tagore's poems, and that in the poet's own English translation the meaning was retained but the music and rhythm of the Bengali verses had been lost. For Italian translators, the idea of going back to the Bengali original was simply not feasible because none of them knew the language. Even scholars like F. Belloni-Filippi, who had some knowledge of Bengali, refrained from producing full-text translations, although he was perfectly aware that, in his words, Tagore's own translation of *Gitanjali* was 'a remake' rather than 'a version,' and moved away from the Bengali original 'not only in form and style, but also in the choice of words— more ornate in the English *Gitanjali* and often considerably different from the corresponding Bengali text.'[29]

In the given circumstances, professional translators had no option but to render Tagore's poems in Italian 'poetic prose.' This solution was far from satisfactory for Italian readers, who were connoisseurs of poetry. E. Beccarini-Crescenzi, in her essay of 1916 mentioned above, argued that an Italian rendition in verse was not an impossibility, and tried her hand with seven poems from *The Crescent Moon*. Her aim, she pointed out, was to rescue the 'popular character' of the stanzas by 'adjusting them to those systems of metric and verse alternation of our [Italian] language which may sound the least far removed from the matchless harmony and beauty of the Bengali text.'[30] As a result, she mostly used the versatile hendecasyllabic (eleven-syllabled) verse and actually managed to produce a musical effect, whereas her language fluctuated between erudite and trite expressions, thereby defeating her own intentions.[31]

Italian translations partly continued to be derived from Tagore's English prose translations almost till the end of the twentieth century, which shows the kind of literary prestige that surrounded the poet's interpretation of himself. Other English versions began to be used in 1961 with Augusto Guidi's and Elsa Soletta's *Le ali della morte: Le ultime liriche* translated from Aurobindo Bose's *Wings of Death: The Last Poems of Rabindranath Tagore*.[32] The question of how to propose to Italian readers a 'better' Tagore, the 'real' Tagore, however, was still unsolved. In two cases, translators adopted the Beccarini-Crescenzi's method of going beyond Tagore's English version in order to conform with the canons of Italian prosody. Girolamo Mancuso, a professional translator with a penchant for Asian literature, in his 'Note on Translation' to the Newton Compton *Gitanjali* (see below), argued that

> In his English translations ... Tagore acted as a broker between the original texts and Western sensibility; and it is, above all, this character that makes them into 'originals,' having their own function and value—which justifies their translation into Italian.

Nevertheless, Mancuso went on, he had opted for a verse translation because

> [Tagore's prose] has a unique character. Through its veil becomes discernible, at times like a remote echo, other times with great immediacy, the working of a mind used to give language a poetic form, to express thoughts in verses and songs. This 'prose', even in a literal translation, is naturally, almost 'spontaneously' organised in verses. I have done nothing but capture this working, ... letting rhythm emerge from the 'material' itself.[33]

Similarly, Elvira Marinelli, while introducing her verse translation of *Gitanjali*, pointed out that in Tagore's prose translations,

> the marked articulation of syntax and the significance of lexical choices suggest ..., even in the English version, a natural verse rendering: words arrange themselves in tune with the rhythm of thought, and thus single out concepts, images, actions within the sentence. For the present translation, therefore, the verse form has been adopted.[34]

Both Mancuso and Marinelli appreciated the poetic nature of Tagore's imagery, which 'naturally' induced the translator to swim upstream, so to say, to reach the imagined source of the lost verse. The difficulty in this kind of approach seems to lie in the distance between Tagore's Bengali verse, with its unique rhythm, musicality and word play, and the contemporary Italian blank verse where the prosodic music and rhythm of a hundred years ago are replaced by an inner meditative dimension.

In 1964, seven years before Mancuso's translation, the St Xavier's missionary Father Marino Rigon wrote the first ever Italian translation of the Bengali *Gitanjali* under the title: *Ghitangioli*.[35] Born in 1925 in a rural town of north-eastern Italy, Rigon first visited East Pakistan (now Bangladesh) in 1953 and since 1954 he had been living at Shelabunia and other villages in the southern and central districts. Rigon's translations are distinctive because of the unique transliteration system he adopted for Bengali words, where the pronunciation is brought out in Italian spelling. This had a specific purpose. Rigon, who had learnt Bengali 'in the field,' had discovered that the character

484   Mario Prayer

of Tagore's writings in Bengali was quite different from what he had earlier found in the Italian translations. The latter suffered from a dependence on both English and Sanskrit which, in his opinion, needed to be done away with, starting right from titles of works and the rendering of Bengali words. He thus embarked on the task of making the 'real' Tagore accessible to the Italian public.[36] Between 1971 and 2009 he published more than twenty books of translation.[37] In recognition of his achievements during many years of service he received several awards and prizes from prominent cultural institutions like the Accademia Ambrosiana (2012).[38]

An overview of Italian translations between 1962 and 2012 shows that about 150 individual texts, not including reprints, were published. Of these, more than half were issued in the 1990s alone by various publishers, often small-sized and interested in bringing out a limited number of translations, or purchasers of copyrights hoping to derive some income from the sale of *Gitanjali* or other equally popular books. Apart from Marino Rigon, translators generally used Tagore's or Aurobindo Bose's English versions, and produced poetic prose rather than actual verses. A consistent interest in Tagore was shown mainly by two publishers, both well known but quite different from each other in cultural profile and editorial policies, namely Guanda and Newton Compton. Gradually Tagore's work came to be identified with their editions. Guanda, first established in 1932 by a group of noted intellectuals of Florence, Parma and Milan, placed Tagore in its elegant and prestigious series of poetry *La Fenice* along with authors of some other classics of world literature: Guillaume Apollinaire, Sergei Esenin, García Lorca, Katherine Mansfield, Pablo Neruda, Jacques Prévert and Arthur Rimbaud. After the initial collaboration with Marino Rigon, Guanda entrusted the translation of Tagore's work to Brunilde Neroni, a writer and essayist with some knowledge of Indian languages.[39]

The first book thus produced was *Il giardiniere* (*The Gardener*, 1986), followed by *Fogli strappati: immagini dal Bengala* (Torn Pages: Images from Bengal, i.e. *Glimpses of Bengal: A Selection of Letters*, 1988), *La vera essenza della vita: Sadhana* (The Real Essence of Life: Sadhana, i.e. *Sadhana. The Realisation of Life*, 1988), *Il canto della vita* (The Song of Life, an anthology, 1989), *Le pietre maledette* (The Cursed Stones, i.e., *Hungry Stones and Other Stories*, 1989), *Massime per una vita armoniosa* (Precepts for a Harmonious Life, i.e. *Stray Birds*, 1992), *Il mondo della personalità* (The World of Personality, i.e., *Personality: Lectures Delivered in America*, 1993), *Petali sulle ceneri* (Petals on Ashes, poems translated from *Pushpanjali*, 1994), *Poesie d'amore* (Love Poems, an anthology, 1996), *Il Dio vicino* (The Intimate God, an anthology of poetry and prose, 1998), *La poesia della natura* (The Poetry of Nature, an anthology, 2005), and *Il vagabondo* (The Wanderer, i.e. *The Runaway and Other Stories*, 2010).

Established in 1969 at Rome, Newton Compton, on the other hand, was a popular publisher, offering famous titles of world literature at a low price and in simple design editions. It had the merit of bringing to the ordinary reader such writers who were previously the preserve of a cultural elite. To its discredit goes the often careless quality of the translations. While Guanda kept diversifying and enlarging its Tagore catalogue, Newton Compton restricted its offer to only two items, both translated from English by Girolamo Mancuso: *Poesie: Gitanjali e Il giardiniere* (combining *Gitanjali* and *The Gardener*), first published in 1971 and reprinted more than twenty times over forty years, and *Poesie d'amore* (Love poems, i.e., *Fruit-Gathering*), first published in 1976, with only five reprints. In addition to these titles that went into large print runs, editorial initiatives by daily and weekly papers like *Corriere della Sera* (2004) and *L'Espresso* (2006) further contributed towards bringing Tagore's books to the shelves of a large number of Italian households. Similarly, important world literature listings included Tagore in their catalogues of 'selected works': for instance, *Poesia. Teatro. Prosa* (Turin: Utet, 1966). Conspicuous for its absence in this context is the prestigious Mondadori book series *I Meridiani* from which one could have expected a Tagore volume.

Beyond Euro-centrism?

During the early decades after World War II, even as Italy was gradually returning to its normal pace of activities in various fields, Tagore was a marginal figure in the country's cultural scene. On the occasion of his hundredth birth anniversary in 1961, however, he became the object of a renewed interest.

The official celebrations culminated in a function at Rome's Town Hall, where representatives of Indian and Italian institutions and universities presented their speeches, and in readings of Tagore's poems and musical evenings at Ismeo (Italian Institute for Middle and Far East, a wing of the Ministry of Foreign Affairs), for which the educationist and scholar Sushil Kumar Dey and the Rabindra Sangeet exponent Rajeshwari Dutta were specially invited with the assistance of the Indian government. The proceedings of these celebrations were published in Ismeo's journal *East and West*.[40] Here we find an essay by the noted Indologist Giuseppe Tucci (1894–1984), then President of Ismeo, where most of the issues which had been raised during the previous decades are once again picked up and discussed. Going back to the years he had spent in India between 1925 and

1931, Tucci recalled the deep inspiration he had derived from Tagore and Mahatma Gandhi, embodiments of 'certain ideals of wisdom and spiritual rapture, which I had read about in books, and now saw with my own eyes.' They were, he continued, 'two clear and unmistakable voices of the spiritual renewal which was then taking place in India':

> With Gandhi and Tagore India has renewed its own religion, has communicated the exaltation of a vigorous and hopeful youth to certain visions and attitudes which stagnated in the inertia of exhausted custom. Hinduism, the world's oldest religion, reawakened at that voice and vibrated with a human ardour which had not moved it since the time of Buddha. ... Indian humanism was reborn with Tagore and Gandhi.[41]

And like the Buddha, according to Tucci, Gandhi and Tagore had 'injected new ardour into a tired religion, ... made it compassionate and universal, bringing it back from the abstract to the concrete.' Tagore, in particular, had given India and the world his message of 'solidarity with everything living.' He was, Tucci argued, neither a 'mediaeval poet or mystic' nor a 'prophet.' On the one hand, he expressed in his works an intimate relationship with nature which was unknown in India's religious and literary tradition; on the other, true to the Upanishadic principle *tat tvam asi* he was not 'immersed in history' and, as a poet, stood 'outside of history.' His concept of action was not restricted to the divisive plane of politics, but rather to a uniting dimension of universal understanding, for which he spent his best energies after the foundation of the university, Visva-Bharati. Therefore, Tucci argued, 'if perennial tradition is reborn in India from [the] ashes, this was largely the work of Visvabharati [sic].' This renewed culture was 'not that of Asia or Europe, but culture generically understood as an awareness which confers a gentle sensibility on life, devoted not merely to understanding facts, but to putting us in harmony with objects and Nature.'[42]

As to the source of Tagore's poetry, Tucci pointed out that it was neither Sanskrit nor European literature, but rather Indian popular poetry, 'the mystical lyricism of the Bahul [sic, Baul] and the Sadhu of Mediaeval India, from Dadu to Kabir.' Tagore knew European literature, but, as he himself had admitted, had no understanding of Dante or Goethe, which was, in Tucci's opinion, as natural as 'the fact that many Occidentals do not appreciate or do not feel Indian poetry, or that of Tagore himself. Everyone carries with him the weight of his own land.' Tagore's European-ness was, thus, a false problem, which was due to the fact that 'the West is reluctant to admit that something great may take place without its inspiration.'[43]

Finally, Tucci commented on the problem of translating Tagore into Western languages and opined that, since Tagore's works were like refractions of 'the musical unity of the world which he ... hears in his heart,' they were 'untranslatable.' In his words,

> the heaviness of our languages, in which the need for logical and conceptual immediacy has weakened the primitive musicality, cannot express anything but the shadow of Tagorean poetry, its scheme of images and thoughts, not the necessary and inseparable melody, like the movement of waves which dissolve on the smoothness of a shore. Translations of Tagore's lyrics are the cold echoes of vital vibrations.[44]

Tucci was less inclined to Eurocentrism than his predecessors. He was deeply involved with the object of his studies, particularly with Buddhism, and perhaps tended to view the problems of the contemporary world in a Buddhistic framework. This framework, though, might still retain some elements of Orientalism. It is significant, for instance, that Tucci viewed the ongoing renewal of Indian civilisation in terms of injecting a new spirit of 'action' and 'compassion' to Hinduism, which was otherwise stagnating 'in the inertia of exhausted custom.' This reminds one of the discourse that European liberals and Christian missionaries had been elaborating on Hindu society and religion from the beginning of the nineteenth century. His remarks on the untranslatable character of Tagore's lyrics also seem to point to a belief in the fundamental separation of cultures: on one side we have the musical, ethereal, comprehensive East, on the other the logical, heavily material, fragmented West. The separation of cultures was according to Tucci an inescapable fact for the ordinary people; only the privileged few could overcome it through study and personal exposure. All this again sounds like only a small step away from the 'rule of colonial difference.'[45]

Tucci's views are also illustrative of a general shortcoming of Indian studies in Italy, that is, the very late development of historical studies on modern India. Until the third quarter of the twentieth century, 'experts' participating in public debates on India were invariably scholars of Sanskrit, ancient philosophy and ancient religion. They naturally tended to approach contemporary India in the light of their academic knowledge. This levelled out their awareness of historical change.

Let us take two more examples. Introducing Marino Rigon's translation of *Ghitangioli* in 1964, noted Sanskritist Carlo Della Casa (1925–2014) pointed out that Tagore's belief in the search for unity in diversity as the 'deepest creed of India' was identical to a hymn of *Rigveda* (I, 164, 46). Similarly, his moving 'from the contemplation of nature on to the assertion of monism' only repeated 'the Vedic *gayatri*.'[46]

Thirty-five years later in 1999, a collection of Tagore's writings on Santiniketan was published with an introduction by noted Indologist Stefano Piano (b. 1941). Piano wrote:

> The spiritual light which illuminates Tagore's verses, as well as those of all the 'religious' poets who came before and after him, is, after all, one and the same; that light is derived from one particular vision (*darsana*) of Reality, whose origins can be traced long back in time, in the words of the ancient 'seers' (*rishis*) of the Upanisads.[47]

This combination of cultural separation and inherent Indianness was not, however, the preserve of Indologists alone. The same kind of Orientalist substratum emerges at times in the work of pedagogues and, in general, of scholars and writers searching for cultural alternatives in a world threatened by atomic annihilation and a growing culture of violence and individualism. This search brought some of these authors to study the traditions of the Orient through their most significant contemporary representatives. India played a major role in this context, and thus Tagore, among others, came to be analysed and interpreted.[48]

In principle, therefore, these studies are contributions towards the elaboration of a new education leading to a multi-polar world of universal peace, social integration and inter-cultural dialogue. In practice, however, they are often based on an equation between the ideas of Tagore, in our case, and the cultural heritage derived from India's ancient philosophy, religion and social customs—an equation which is implicitly assumed as a matter of fact.

A case in point is provided by a book written in 1990 by a professor of Pedagogy, Sandra Chistolini, where Tagore's ideas on education are studied together with those of two modern Indian 'teachers,' Sri Aurobindo and Jiddu Krishnamurti, all upholders of a 'universal conception of man as derived from the cultural and religious tradition of India.'[49] Chistolini was interested not only in Tagore's ideas on education, but more generally in the view of life, which informed his novels and short stories. What is relevant here is that Tagore's teachings are described as 'rooted in the world-view of Oriental philosophy, whose foundation, i.e. spirituality, reveals the depth of thought which thinks itself.'[50] Implicitly assuming the Upanishadic philosophy as the key to Tagore's vision, Chistolini argued that for him, as well as for Aurobindo and Krishnamurti, 'it is not the search for knowledge, but rather knowledge itself that constitutes an act [*sic*] leading to self-perfection.'[51] Moreover, according to Chistolini, in Tagore the *aim* of education was 'the realisation of our most profound relationship with Supreme Truth. Science, philosophy, art, literature can be fully developed only after attaining the sense of detachment which belongs to the spiritual.'[52]

The distinctive element in Tagore's concept of education was, according to Chistolini, the aspiration to a world free from the barriers of ignorance and prejudice, and to achieve that aim the new generations had to be imbued with belief in a 'new faith' and in some 'grand ideal.' Here lay, according to Chistolini, the limitations of Tagore's education, for an education entirely devoted to the 'realisation of an ideal,' with no adjustment to the 'historical dimension,' would be impracticable and useless. Santiniketan was, in a sense, a symbol of this excessive idealisation: 'the ashram' was, in Chistolini's words,

> such an ideal state that it is difficult to reproduce its environment in our schools, including open-air schools. ... To build up a school as a happy island, far away from influences from the society, especially the supposedly negative ones, does not seem to be an easy or useful undertaking in view of the integration of the young in the society.[53]

Similarly, 'to think in terms of belonging to the cosmic context,' as Tagore used to do, would entail 'the risk of losing the sense of history and daily life.' This ultimately amounts to accepting the Orientalistic stereotype about the absence of history in spiritual India. Between East and West, Chistolini concluded, there could not be any 'unity in diversity.' In education, as perhaps in other fields of human activity, the East could at best provide 'materials, methods, instruments' for the West to receive, screen and adjust to its own needs.[54]

CONCLUSION

Tagore's Nobel Prize was the first European literary event which compelled Italian intellectuals to come to terms with an extraordinary poetic talent belonging to a non-European culture. What emerged from this confrontation was a fundamental Orientalist approach, which fed on the Euro-centrism and Christian-centrism of Italian culture of the time, rather than on any political motivation.

Among the Italian public, Tagore acquired and retained for long a great popularity as he appeared to offer different meanings and interpretations to different kinds of readers. To admirers of ancient India he could offer the Vedas and Upanishads, to philo-Buddhists he represented a revived compassionate Hinduism, to devotees of motherhood and family he could bring affectionate images of children, to lovers of action he could show the way to build up a new humanity through education. Various elements of his thought undoubtedly appealed to the 'Italian mind.' However, what seems to really have won the love of many Italians is, after all, his poetry—despite all the hurdles posed by translations and questions of form and style.

The intuitive, non-logical nature of the Italians' infatuation with Tagore at a deeper level than ideas and theories is reflected in the relevance attached in almost all the sources mentioned in this essay to the musical nature of Tagore's verses. This 'perfect musicality' was due, according to Ferdinando Belloni-Filippi, 'not only to the [Bengali] language which is the most harmonious of Indian languages, but to the innate connection [of the Tagorean poetry] with singing.'[55] This may explain, among other things, why a considerable number of Italian musicians set Tagore's poems to music.[56] As Belloni-Filippi had pointed out in 1918, the music that accompanied Tagore's songs has little in common with European music, and yet he hoped that those melodies would some day be transposed to the Western system of harmony.[57] Giuseppe Tucci's observation, on the other hand, that Tagore's lyrics were untranslatable seemed to apply to his music as well.

While Italian official and academic initiative was, if not absent, at least marginal on the occasion of the 150th anniversary of Tagore's birth, in May 2012 an exhibition of Tagore's paintings was organised at the Galleria Nazionale d'Arte Moderna in association with the Government of India. For the first time the poet was thus presented to the Italian public in his capacity as an artist. In this respect, it may be pointed out that despite the efforts of individual scholar-singers like Reba Som and Francesca Cassio since the 1990s, Rabindra Sangeet still awaits a proper introduction to Italian music-lovers. To this end, an important contribution may come from the popularisation of the Bengali language among translators. For poetry and music, a direct access to the original version seems to be particularly necessary for those writers and performers who will want to reproduce in Italian the rhythm and depth of Tagore's Bengali poems and songs.

NOTES

1. All translations from Italian to English are this writer's. Giuseppe Tucci, 'Recollections of Tagore,' was originally written in English.
2. On the role of literary journals in Italy's cultural life during the twentieth century, see Renato Bertacchini, *Le riviste del Novecento. Introduzione e guida allo studio dei periodici italiani: Storia, ideologia e cultura* (Firenze: Le Monnier, 1984); Giorgio Luti, *Introduzione alla letteratura italiana del Novecento: la poesia, la narrativa, la critica, le riviste e i movimenti letterari* (Roma: NIS, 1985); Augusto Simonini, *Cent'anni di riviste: la vittoria della critica sulla letteratura* (Bologna: Calderini, 1993).
3. Pavolini, 'Il Premio Nobel a un poeta indiano.' I am indebted to Dr Imre Bangha for references to this journal as well as for a copy of the text quoted in note 10.
4. One exception was Giuseppe De Lorenzo, a geographer by profession but an Indologist by passion. In his article 'India e Inghilterra,' he argued that

Tagore, who had deeply absorbed British culture, had estranged himself from 'the tropical forest of Indian poetry' and therefore used to 'feel and sing like an Englishman' (363).

5. Belloni-Filippi, *Tagore*.
6. Ibid., 17–19. Similar arguments were presented by Belloni-Filippi in 'Rabindranath Tagore musicista,' 391–3; and 'Tagoriana,' 175–81.
7. Belloni-Filippi, *Tagore*, 10.
8. Luzzatti, 'Rabindranath Tagore,' 481. Luzzatti's essay also appeared as the Preface to the Italian translation of *The Crescent Moon* (*La luna crescente*, see section 4 below).
9. Ibid., 488–9.
10. Ibid., 490.
11. Olivero, 'Rabindranath Tagore,' 296–310.
12. Borgese, 'Tagore e tagorismo,' 208–9.
13. Ibid., 214.
14. Ibid.
15. Ibid.
16. Beccarini-Crescenzi, 'Il bambino nella letteratura indiana,' 372–88.
17. Ibid., 373.
18. See for instance, two quotations from Tagore's poems in *Ultra* 9, 1–2 (1915): 25; 'Di Rabindranath Tagore,' *Ultra* 11, 1 (1917): 64; 'Un poeta indiano,' *Ultra* 11, 2 (1915): 47–8; 'Un attentato a R. Tagore,' *Ultra* 12, 4 (1918): 200; 'Tagore,' *Ultra* 18, 5–6 (1924): 78; Rabindranath Tagore, 'Il messaggio,' *Ultra* 20, 3 (1926): 1; Rabindranath Tagore, 'La filosofia del nostro popolo,' *Ultra* 20, 3 (1926): 2–17; various other news and comments on Tagore's visit to Italy appeared in 1926. By Roberto Assagioli, see 'Impressioni sulla visita di Tagore in Italia,' *Ultra* 20, 4 (1926): 42–7; 'Rabindranath Tagore poeta, mistico, educatore,' *Rassegna italiana. Politica, Letteraria & Artistica* 17, 91 (1926): 684–94; *Psicanalisi e psicosintesi* (Roma: Istituto di Cultura e di Terapia Psichica: 1931).
19. This account of Tagore's visits to Italy has drawn on information from the following works: (i) Gaetano Salvemini, 'Tagore e Mussolini,' in *Esperienze e studi socialisti scritti in onore di Ugo Guido Mondolfo*, 191–206; (ii) Prabhat Kumar Mukhopadhyay, *Rabindrajibani o Rabindrasahitya*, vol. 3, 209–12, 246–54; (iii) Mario Prayer, *In Search of an Entente: India and Italy from the XIX to XX Century: A Survey*; (iv) Vito Salierno, 'Tagore e il fascismo. Mussolini e la politica italiana verso l'India,' *Nuova storia contemporanea*, 2, 63–80; (v) Giuseppe Flora, 'Tagore and Italy: Facing History and Politics,' 1025–57; (vi) Kalyan Kundu, *Itali Safare Rabindranath O Musolini Prasanga*; and (vii) Prayer, 'Tagore's Meeting with Benedetto Croce,' 265–75.
20. The poem was first published in *The Visva-Bharati Quarterly* 3, 1 (1925): 11. For an Italian edition, see *All'Italia* (note 27).
21. 'L'Italia ammantata di luce inestinguibile. Nostra intervista con Rabindranath Tagore,' *La Tribuna*, 2 June 1926, 3.

442 Mario Prayer

22. Tagore expressed these views in his talks with Romain Rolland, Georges Duhamel and others. See Romain Rolland, *Inde: Journal, 1915–43* (Paris: Gallimard, 1960), 108–65.
23. *Popolo d'Italia*, 25 August 1926; quoted in Salierno, 'Tagore e il fascismo,' 77.
24. Taglialatela, *La poesia di Rabindranath Tagore*, 69; Nemi, 'Un poeta del Bengala,' *Il Marzocco*; Castelnuovo, 'Un poeta indiano,' 594–612.
25. Del Re had worked for *Poetry Review* in London between 1911 and 1917, when he came in personal touch with Yeats.
26. Little is known about them, except that their names have ever since been associated with Tagore. Carelli also wrote a book on love and death in India, and another on Indian medicine: *Kama-yama*. *L'amore, la morte e il dolore nella sapienza dell'India* (Albano Laziale: Strini, 1928); *Contributi alla storia della medicina Indiana* (Milan: Arte e storia, 1942).
27. The Carabba series includes: *Uccelli migranti* [*Stray Birds*] in 1918 (E. Taglialatela); *Il dono dell'amante e Passando all'altra riva* [*Lover's Gift and Crossing*] in 1920 (E. Taglialatela); *Il malefizio delle pietre e altre novelle* [*Hungry Stones and Other Stories*] in 1920 (Agnese Silvestri Giorgi, a novelist and professional translator); *Mashi e altri racconti* [*Mashi and Other Stories*] in 1922 (A. Silvestri Giorgi); *Nazionalismo* [*Nationalism*] in 1923 (Ida Vassalini, a poet and Sanskrit scholar); *La casa e il mondo* [*The Home and the World*] in 1924 (M. Valli); *Oleandri rossi* [*Red Oleanders*] in 1926 (Clary Zannoni Chauvet); *Lettere di viaggio* [*Letters from Abroad*], *Sacrifizio e Il re e la regina* and *Sannyasi, o L'asceta e Malini* [both from *Sacrifice and Other Plays*] in 1927 (Giannina Spellanzon, a poet and playwright); *Ricordi* [*My Reminiscences*] in two volumes, 1928 (Antonio Fuortes); *Unità creativa* [*Creative Unity*] in 1929 (A. Silvestri Giorgi); *La macchina. Dramma in un atto* [*The Waterfall*] in 1932 (P. Ariani); *Vincoli infranti e altre novelle* [*Broken Ties and Other Stories*] in 1932 (C. Zannoni Chauvet); *Lipika* in 1934 (Promotho Nath Roy, an Indian student then residing in Italy); *Gora* in three volumes, 1935 (G. Spellanzon); *Visioni bengalesi: Dalle lettere di R. Tagore* [*Glimpses of Bengal: Selected from the Letters of Sir R. Tagore, 1885–95*] in 1938 (A. Silvestri Giorgi). Apart from these, a small number of translations appeared on special occasions in journals or in book form: 'Cielo e terra,' *Bilychnis* 2 (1921): 89–90; *All'Italia* (Roma: Tipografia Coop. Sociale, 1925); 'In Venezia: discorso pronunciato dal poeta durante il suo soggiorno a Venezia,' *Ateneo Veneto* 48 (1925), 85–96; 'La grande idea. Lirica inedita di R. Tagore,' *Nuova Antologia* 61, 1302 (1926), 361–4.
28. See for instance, A. Agresti, 'Cronaca di letteratura inglese,' *Rassegna contemporanea* 6, 661–2.
29. Belloni-Filippi, 'Tagoriana,' 179–81.
30. Beccarini-Crescenzi, 'Il bambino,' 374.
31. For instance, she translated 'You were enshrined with our household deity, in his worship I worshipped you' (from *The Beginning*) as 'Con il dio della casa protettore/intabernacolato, se adoravo/lui, te pure adoravo, dolce amore,' which sounded somewhat outdated even in those times ('intabernacolato'), and with an unnecessary touch of extra-sweetness ('dolce amore'). Beccarini-Crescenzi, 'Il bambino,' 375.

32. Tagore, *Le ali della morte.*
33. Mancuso, 'Nota alla traduzione,' 36. With more than twenty editions over thirty-five years, this was perhaps the most often reprinted Italian translation.
34. Marinelli, 'Così ricca e semplice è questa poesia,' 10.
35. Tagore, *Ghitangioli*, translated by Rigon.
36. At times Marino Rigon's transliteration system seems to reflect the regional pronunciation to which he was exposed, as in *sissu*, *somaz*, etc. Apart from translations, Marino Rigon has also been engaged in public lectures in Italy in order to spread knowledge of Bengal, its literature and art, its population, its history. In Bangladesh he has been doing the reverse by translating into Bengali and popularising Italian literature, for instance Collodi's *Pinocchio*. In his endeavours, he has been supported by Centro Studi Tagore, established at his birthplace Villaverla in 1990, and presided over by one of his brothers, Francesco Rigon. The centre's activities include collecting Tagore literature, convening seminars, setting up exhibitions of Bengali arts and crafts in Italy, supporting children of other countries in their studies, and organising long-distance adoption. Father Rigon's work also reflects a renewed interest of Italian Catholicism in Tagore, and in general in India and other non-European civilisations, which came to replace the early twentieth-century doubt and mistrust after World War II. This aspect would however require a separate study.
37. These include: *Sfulingo* (Parma: Guanda, 1971); *Noibeddo. Offerta* (Vicenza: Esca, 1974); *Poesie* (Parma-Milano: Guanda, 1975); *Balaka* (Parma: Guanda, 1976); *Lekhan* (Imola: Grafiche Galeati, 1978); *Citra. Variopinta. La scoperta del Dio della vita* (Imola: Grafiche Galeati, 1979); *Sissu* (Milano: Guanda, 1979); *Shesh lekha. Ultimi scritti* (Vicenza: Esca, 1980); *La barca d'oro* (*Sonar tari*; Imola: Grafiche Galeati, 1982); *Cioitali* (Vicenza: Esca, 1991); *Kori o Komol. Duro e tenero* (Castel Maggiore: Book, 1991); *Shemoli. Morettina* (Castel Maggiore: Book, 1992); *Il Cristo. Antologia di scritti* (Milano: Paoline, 1993); *Rogsoggiae. Sul letto della malattia* (Castel Maggiore: Book, 1993); *Kolpona. Fantasia* (Castel Maggiore: Book, 1995); *Santiniketon* (Milano: Paoline, 1995); *Kotha o kahini* (Castel Maggiore: Book, 1997); *58 poesie* (Milano: Mondadori, 1998); *Il nido d'amore. Riflessioni per una vita serena* (Milano: Paoline, 1998); *Neonato* (Castel Maggiore: Book, 2001); *Farò fiorire canti nuovi* (Milano: Paoline, 2003); *Citrangoda* (Rimini: Guaraldi, 2004); *Il tremendo gioco della gioia* (Bologna: Editrice Missionaria Italiana, 2009).
38. Among the prizes received by Father Rigon are the Kobi Jasim Uddin literary prize which was conferred on him by the President of Bangladesh Abdul Sattar in 1982; the Rocca d'oro (Golden Rock) prize for his missionary activities in 1994; the "Man of the Year' award from the US-based World Vision Association in 1995; the Honorary Citizenship of Vicenza in 1997; the Accademia Olimpica prize in 1999; and the Rotary Club Prize in 2000.
39. Before embarking on this long collaboration with Guanda, Brunilde Neroni had translated *Lipika* for the Milan-based publisher SE in 1985. While many of Neroni's works are explicitly presented as translations from the Bengali, they at times reveal a scant familiarity with Bengali culture. The transliteration

of Bengali terms and names is often inconsistent and seems to be derived
from an English original. To mention only a few examples, in *Oltre il ricordo*
(Palermo: Sellerio, 1987), professedly 'translated from Bengali' (*Jivansmrti*),
we find errors and words in English rendering or plural form, such as *Sandya-*
sangit [*sic*] (16), *bustee*s (32), Babu Aghore (48), *Yaksas* (53), Birbhoom (59),
kathakas (73), Akshay Mazudonar [*sic*] (103), *mujlis* (105), *sola-topee* (121),
instead of *Sandhya sangit, basti,* Babu Aghor, *Yaksha,* Birbhum, *kathak,* Akshay
Mazumdar, *majlis, sola topi* respectively.

40. *East and West* 12, 2–3 (1961). See also *Centenario di Tagore, 1861–1961*
(Roma: Ismeo, 1962).
41. Tucci, 'Recollections of Tagore.' Original in English.
42. Ibid., 113–17.
43. Ibid., 113; Dadu or Dadu Dayal (c16th century) was a *sant* (holy man) of the
nirgun bhakti tradition.
44. Ibid., 117.
45. See Partha Chatterjee, *The Nation and Its Fragments: Colonial and Postcolonial*
Histories (Princeton: Princeton University Press, 1993).
46. Della Casa, 'Introduction,' vii–viii.
47. Piano, 'Introduction,' xiv–xv. The volume is a translation of the French *La*
Demeure de la Paix (Paris: Stock, 1998).
48. For early attempts of this kind see Delfino, *L'ideale educativo di Rabindranath*
Tagore; Ottonello, *Rabindranath Tagore*; Stilo, *L'umanesimo integrale di Tagore*.
For the Christian side of the pedagogic interest in Tagore see Poli, *Tagore e*
Santiniketan; Benvegnù, *Il giardino di Tagore.*
49. Chistolini, *Tagore, Aurobindo, Krishnamurti,* 141.
50. Ibid., 11.
51. Ibid.
52. Ibid., 69.
53. Ibid., 64–5.
54. Ibid., 142–46.
55. Belloni-Filippi, 'Rabindranath Tagore musicista,' 392.
56. To name only a few: Franco Alfano, Alfredo Casella, Armando Gentilucci,
Giorgio Federico Ghedini, Ottorino Respighi, Vittorio Gnecchi Ruscone,
Virgilio Mortari, Nino Rota.
57. In 2004, the Italy-based Harsharan Foundation published Alain Daniélou's
re-arrangements of some of Tagore's songs in *Lied* form (1932) under the title
Songs of Love and Destiny. For further details see the website http://soundcloud.
com/tagore-danielou-project.

Works Cited

Agresti, A. 'Cronaca di letteratura inglese.' *Rassegna contemporanea* 6, 22 (1913):
661–2.
Assagioli, Roberto. 'Impressioni sulla visita di Tagore in Italia.' *Ultra* 20, 4 (1926): 42–7.
———. 'Rabindranath Tagore poeta, mistico, educatore.' *Rassegna italiana. Politica,*
Letteraria & Artistica 17, 91 (1926): 684–94.

Beccarini-Crescenzi, Elena. 'Divagazioni panteistiche: La poesia di Tagore.' *Vita e pensiero* 22 n.s., 11 (1931): 676–84.

———. 'Il bambino nella letteratura indiana.' *Rivista d'Italia* 19, 9 (1916): 372–88.

Belloni-Filippi, Ferdinando. 'Rabindranath Tagore musicista.' *Nuova Antologia* 53, 1106 (1918): 391–3.

———. 'Tagoriana.' *Nuova antologia* 57, 1204 (1922): 175–81.

———. *Tagore.* Rome: Formiggini, 1920.

Benvegnù, Antonella. *Il giardino di Tagore: percorsi di educazione interculturale.* Bologna: Editrice Missionaria Italiana, 2005.

Bertacchini, Renato. *Le riviste del Novecento. Introduzione e guida allo studio dei periodici italiani: Storia, ideologia e cultura.* Firenze: Le Monnier, 1984.

Borgese, Giuseppe Antonio. 'Tagore e tagorismo.' In *Ottocento europeo.* Milan: Treves, 1927, 208–14.

Casolari, Marzia. 'Nazionalismo hindu e fascismo. L'incontro con Mussolini dai diari inediti di B.S. Moonje.' *Nuova storia contemporanea* 3, 5 (1999): 47–78.

Castelnuovo, Enrico. 'Un poeta indiano: Rabindranath Tagore.' *Nuova Antologia* 49, 1024 (1914): 594–612.

[Various Authors], *Centenario di Tagore, 1861–1961.* Roma: Ismeo, 1962.

Chistolini, Sandra. *Tagore, Aurobindo, Krishnamurti: unità dell'uomo e universalità dell'educazione.* Roma: Euroma-Goliardica, 1990.

De Lorenzo, Giuseppe. 'India e Inghilterra.' *Gerarchia* 10, 4 (1930): 360–77.

Delfino, Giuseppe. *L'ideale educativo di Rabindranath Tagore.* Genova: Edizioni Pedagogiche, 1972.

Della Casa, Carlo. 'Introduction.' In *Ghitangioli,* by Rabindranath Tagore, vii–xx. Parma: Guanda, 1964.

Flora, Giuseppe. *Benoy Kumar Sarkar and Italy.* New Delhi: Italian Embassy Cultural Centre, 1994.

———. 'Tagore and Italy: Facing History and Politics.' *University of Toronto Quarterly* 77, 4 (Fall 2008): 1025–57.

Kundu, Kalyan. *Itali safare Rabindranath o Mussolini prasanga.* Kolkata: Punashcha, 2009.

Luti, Giorgio. *Introduzione alla letteratura italiana del Novecento: la poesia, la narrativa, la critica, le riviste e i movimenti letterari.* Roma: NIS, 1985.

Luzzatti, Luigi. 'Rabindranath Tagore.' *Nuova Antologia* 50, 178 (1915): 481–90.

Mancuso, Girolamo. 'Nota alla traduzione.' In *Poesie. Gitanjali* by Rabindranath Tagore. *Il Giardiniere,* 35–6. Roma: Grandi Tascabili Economici Newton, 1971.

Marinelli, Elvira. 'Così ricca e semplice è questa poesia.' In *Gitanjali—Universo d'amore* by Rabindranath Tagore, 9–12. Firenze-Milano: Demetra-Giunti, 2002 (first ed. 1995).

Mukhopadhyay, Prabhat Kumar. *Rabindrajibani o Rabindrasahitya*, vol. III, 209–12, 246–54. Calcutta: Prabeshak, 1961.

Nemi. 'Un poeta del Bengala.' *Il Marzocco,* 4 May 1913.

Olivero, Federico. 'Rabindranath Tagore.' In *Nuovi saggi di letteratura inglese,* 296–310. Turin: Libreria Editrice Internazionale, 1918.

446   Mario Prayer

Ottonello, Giacomo. *Rabindranath Tagore: principi educativi e scuole nuove in Oriente.* Roma: Armando, 1977.

Pavolini, Paolo Emilio. 'Il Premio Nobel a un poeta indiano.' *Il Marzocco,* 23 November 1913.

Piano, Stefano. 'Introduction.' In *La casa della pace* by Rabindranath Tagore, vii–xxv. Turin: Bollati Boringhieri, 1999.

Poli, Flavio. *Tagore e Santiniketan: l'attuazione d'un ideale pedagogico.* Bologna: Editrice Missionaria Italiana, 1982.

Prayer, Mario. 'Italian Fascist Regime and Nationalist India, 1921–45.' *International Studies* 28, 3 (1991): 249–71.

———. 'L'intervista Gandhi–Mussolini: pagine italiane dal diario di Mahadev Desai.' *Storia Contemporanea* 23, 1 (1992): 73–89.

———. *In Search of an Entente: India and Italy from the XIX to XX Century: A Survey.* New Delhi: Italian Embassy Cultural Centre, 1994.

———. *Internazionalismo e nazionalismo culturale. Gli intellettuali bengalesi e l'Italia negli anni Venti e Trenta*, Supplement no. 1, *Rivista degli Studi Orientali*, 69, Roma: Bardi, 1996. [This journal comes out with a main volume of articles, book reviews etc., and one or two stand-alone 'Supplementi,' i.e., monographs, proceedings, etc.]

———. 'Nationalist India and World War II as Seen by the Italian Fascist Press, 1938–44.' *Indian Historical Review* 33, 2 (2006): 89–111.

———. 'The Vatican Church and Mahatma Gandhi's India, 1920–48.' *Social Scientist* 37, 1–2, 428–9 (2009): 39–62.

———. 'Creative India and the World: Bengali Internationalism and Italy in the Interwar Period.' In *Cosmopolitan Thought Zones. South Asia and the Global Circulation of Ideas*, edited by Sugata Bose and Kris Manjapra, 236–59. London: Palgrave Macmillan, 2010.

———. 'Tagore's Meeting with Benedetto Croce.' In *Rabindranath Tagore: A Timeless Mind—Commemorating the 150th Birth Anniversary of Rabindranath Tagore* edited by Amalendu Biswas, Christine Marsh and Kalyan Kundu, 265–75. London: Tagore Centre UK, 2011.

Salierno, Vito. 'Tagore e il fascismo. Mussolini e la politica italiana verso l'India.' *Nuova storia contemporanea* 2, 5 (1998): 63–80.

Salvemini, Gaetano. 'Tagore e Mussolini.' In *Esperienze e studi socialisti scritti in onore di Ugo Guido Mondolfo*, edited by Critica Sociale, 191–206. Firenze: La Nuova Italia, 1957.

Sareen, Tilak Raj. *Indian National Army: A Documentary Study.* New Delhi: Gyan House, 2004.

Simonini, Augusto. *Cent'anni di riviste: la vittoria della critica sulla letteratura.* Bologna: Calderini, 1993.

Stilo, Salvatore. *L'umanesimo integrale di Tagore.* Reggio Calabria: Parallelo 38, 1982.

Taglialatela, Eduardo. *La poesia di Rabindranath Tagore.* Roma: Tipografia del Senato, 1914.

Tucci, Giuseppe. 'Recollections of Tagore.' *East and West* 12, 2–3 (1961): 111–17.

[Various Authors], *Centenario di Tagore, 1861–1961.* Roma: Ismeo, 1962.

Works by Tagore

All'Italia [*To Italy*]. Roma: Tipografia Coop. Sociale, 1925.

'Cielo e terra' [*Sky and Earth*]. *Bilychnis* 2 (1921): 89–90.

Ghitangioli [*Gitanjali*]. Translated by M. Rigon. Parma: Guanda, 1964.

Gora. Translated by G. Spellanzon. Lanciano: Carabba, 1935.

Il dono dell'amante e Passando all'altra riva [*Lover's Gift* and *Crossing*]. Translated by E. Taglialatela. Lanciano: Carabba, 1920.

Il malefizio delle pietre e altre novelle [*The Hungry Stones and Other Stories*]. Translated by A. Silvestri Giorgi. Lanciano: Carabba, 1920.

'Il messaggio' [*The Message*]. *Ultra* 20, 3 (1926), 1.

'In Venezia: discorso pronunciato dal poeta durante il suo soggiorno a Venezia' [In Venice: Speech Delivered by the Poet During his Stay at Venice]. *Ateneo Veneto* 48 (1925), 85–96.

La casa e il mondo [*The Home and the World*]. Translated by M. Valli. Lanciano: Carabba, 1924.

'La filosofia del nostro popolo'[*The Philosophy of Our People*]. *Ultra* 20, 3 (1926), 2–17.

'La grande idea. Lirica inedita di R. Tagore' [*The Great Idea: An Unpublished Poem by R. Tagore*]. Translated by Carlo Formichi. *Nuova Antologia* 61, 1302 (1926), 361–4.

La macchina. Dramma in un atto [*The machine. A One-Act Play* (*The Waterfall*)]. Translated by P. Ariani. Lanciano: Carabba, 1932.

Le ali della morte: Le ultime liriche [*Wings of Death*: *The Last Poems of Rabindranath Tagore*]. Translated by A. Guidi and E. Soletta. Parma: Guanda, 1961.

Lettere di viaggio [*Letters from Abroad*]. Translated by G. Spellanzon. Lanciano: Carabba, 1927.

Lipika. Translated by P. N. Roy. Lanciano: Carabba, 1934.

Mashi e altri racconti [*Mashi and Other Stories*]. Translated by A. Silvestri Giorgi. Lanciano: Carabba, 1922.

Nazionalismo [*Nationalism*]. Translated by I. Vassalini. Lanciano: Carabba, 1923.

Oleandri rossi [*Red Oleanders*]. Translated by C. Zannoni Chauvet. Lanciano: Carabba, 1926.

Ricordi [*My Reminiscences*]. Translated by A. Fuortes. Lanciano: Carabba, 1928.

Sacrifizio e Il re e la regina [*Sacrifice,* and *The King and the Queen* (from *Sacrifice and Other Plays*)]. Translated by G. Spellanzon. Lanciano: Carabba, 1927.

Sannyasi, o L'asceta e Malini [*Sannyasi or the Ascetic,* and *Malini* (from *Sacrifice and Other Plays*)]. Translated by G. Spellanzon. Lanciano: Carabba, 1927.

Uccelli migranti [*Stray Birds*]. Translated by E. Taglialatela. Lanciano: Carabba, 1918.

Unità creativa [*Creative Unity*]. Translated by A. Silvestri Giorgi. Lanciano: Carabba, 1929.

Vincoli infranti e altre novelle [*Broken Ties and Other Stories*]. Translated by C. Zannoni Chauvet. Lanciano: Carabba, 1932.

Visioni bengalesi: Dalle lettere di R. Tagore [*Glimpses of Bengal: Selected from the Letters of Sir R. Tagore, 1885–95*]. Translated by A. Silvestri Giorgi. Lanciano: Carabba, 1938.

26

France

France Bhattacharya

India and France before Tagore

The history of the relationship between France and India dates back to the seventeenth century at least. Then, several French travellers visited India and sought hospitality at the court of the Great Moghuls. They wrote interesting travelogues about their experiences in India on their return. The philosopher–physician François Bernier (1620–88) was a most cultured man, and the narration of his stay in India between 1659 and 1669 is a remarkable book lauded by historians. His *Voyage dans les États du Grand Mogol* (Journey in the countries of the Great Mogul) was published from 1670 in several parts; its first English translation appeared remarkably early in 1671–2 in London and went into several prints and the last French edition came out in 1981. The second important traveller was Jean-Baptiste Tavernier (1606–89), a trader in precious stones, whose travelogue *Les six voyages de Jean-Baptiste Tavernier* (The six journeys of Jean-Baptiste Tavernier) was published in 1677. The next batch of travellers to India who wrote accounts of their sojourn were Catholic missionaries, mostly in South India. *Les Lettres édifiantes* (The edifying letters), written in the eighteenth century by a number of Jesuits, added to the knowledge of India. In 1816 appeared in London an important volume, *Description of the Character, Manners and Customs of the People of India, and of their Institutions, religious and civil*, under the name of Abbé Dubois (1765–1848); the French edition came out in 1825. Between the two sets of travellers, France had lost her possessions in India, except the five Establishments (in French, *Comptoirs*), including Pondicherry and also Chandernagore in Bengal.

Anquetil-Duperron (1731–1805) translated from the Persian edition made for Dara Shekoh fifty *Upanishads* under the title *Oupnekhat* in 1801–2. The teaching of Sanskrit started in Paris in 1803, thanks to the presence of A. Hamilton, back from India, and of Antoine-Léonard de Chézy

(1774–1832). Friedrich Schlegel began learning the language in Paris. In 1815, a Chair of Sanskrit was created in Paris at the Collège de France, the first in Europe and Antoine-Léonard de Chézy was the first to occupy it. The Asiatic Society was established in Paris in 1821, the first after that of Calcutta. Eugène Burnouf, who succeeded Chézy in 1833 at Collège de France, published the first *Dictionnaire classique sanscrit-français* in 1866, after his *Grammaire sanskrite* in 1859. A second Chair of Sanskrit was introduced in 1868 and Abel Bergaigne became its first holder.

Rammohun Roy (1772–1833) whose works and writings were known to the French through several articles in *Revue encyclopédique*, as well as in *Journal asiatique*, was made Associate Member of the French Société Asiatique in 1824. In Calcutta, he met a gifted young traveller Victor Jacquemont who wrote movingly about the great Bengali in the account of his travels in India. When he came to Paris in 1832, Rammohun Roy met Garcin de Tassy who was then teaching Hindustani at the Ecole des Langues Orientales, and also Chézy, translator of *Sacountala*. Rammohun Roy was introduced to King Louis-Philippe with great honour. Garcin de Tassy wrote his notable *Histoire de la littérature hindouie et hindustanie* in 1839. In 1833, the year Rammohun died, Loiseleur-Deslongchamps published his translation of *Manusmriti*. The translation of the *Bhagavata-purana* by Eugène Burnouf appeared in several volumes from 1840 to 1884. In 1844, Burnouf published his seminal *Introduction à l'histoire du Bouddhisme*.

During the last years of the eighteenth century and the first half of the nineteenth, there was a great interest in the Orient in general, and India in particular, in literary circles. Victor Hugo published *Les Orientales*, while Bernardin de Saint-Pierre wrote *La chaumière indienne* (The Indian straw-hut) and *Paul et Virginie*. Balzac published his esoteric novel *Louis Lambert*, Théophile Gautier wrote *L'avatar*. Gérard de Nerval made a French adaptation of *Mricchakatika* that was staged in 1850. Chateaubriand and the major romantic poets such as Vigny and Lamartine, and later Baudelaire and Mallarmé, had all read about India, and added this dimension to their works, most of the time with wonder.

RABINDRANATH TAGORE AND FRANCE BEFORE THE NOBEL PRIZE

Tagore's first acquaintance with French literature was possibly through his elder brother Jyotirindranath, the translator of Molière into Bengali. At the age of seventeen, in 1878, when Rabindranath was going to England to study in the British capital, he disembarked at Brindisi and, from there, went to Paris by train. His first reaction was positive and he wrote: 'What a wonderful city!' He could only stay for one day. Yet he had a memorable

Turkish bath and got a glimpse of the International Exhibition that was taking place that year. His *Yurop-prabasir Patra* (Letters from Europe) bears witness to his discovery of the West. In 1890, he went again to London by the same route. At the time of his second visit, he was already a mature poet. Besides, he was married and the father of two children; his family however did not accompany him. He wrote this time his *Yurop-yatrir Dayary* (Diary of a traveller to Europe) from the day he left Bombay. On the way to England from Italy, he appreciated the French countryside. From the window of his train, the sight of a mountain stream evoked in him an interesting judgement on the French mentality, about which he knew very little, if at all, at that time. He wrote: 'The mountain stream is like the French: quick, restless, enthusiastic, fond of fun and sweet-tongued. But it is much purer and child natured than them.'[1] He had something to say about the relationship of the French with their countryside, particularly in the mountains. He wrote: 'Each patch is a witness to the efforts of man. There is nothing surprising in the love that these people have for their country. By their care they have made their country theirs. Here, since a long time, men have an understanding with nature, there is constantly an exchange between them, and they are bound in an intimate relationship.'[2] He stopped one day in Paris and went to see the newly built Eiffel Tower. Taking the lift he went up to the top floor. The view of the city from above impressed him and he wrote to his wife about his visit.

These two very short stays in Paris gave him an idea of the place and of some of its inhabitants, but it was much later, in 1920, that he really discovered the city and made friends there.

THE NOBEL PRIZE AND AFTER

In April 1913, a journalist, J. H. de Rosen, was the first to write an article on the Bengali poet in the literary review called *La Revue*. He added his own translation into French of fifteen poems taken from the English *Gitanjali*.[3] Rosen showered praises on Tagore who, according to him, was the hero of a new era in literature. 'Rabindranath', he wrote, 'is candid like a child, profound like a sage and humble as a saint.' In December 1913, the same *La Revue* announced the award of the Nobel Prize to the poet and, happy to have been the first in France to praise the author of *Gitanjali*, wrote: 'The Hindu poet, Rabindranath Tagore is a mystic of an unparalleled elevation of thought and a wonderful wealth of images.'[4] The first literary critics, totally ignorant of Bengali, and, more generally, of Indian literary traditions, found it easier to call him a second Francis of Assisi than to speak of him and his work in literary terms as a poet.

One year before the award of the Nobel, Saint-John Perse (1887–1975) who was to become a major poet and a senior diplomat, happened to be in London when Tagore showed his own translation of *Gitanjali* to a small number of British intellectuals and artists. In a newspaper the Frenchman read two poems by Rabindranath that W. B. Yeats had quoted in an article. Later, he read a few more 'on proofs', so he said, as he was slightly acquainted with Mr. Fox-Strangways, a musicologist whom Tagore trusted and who was instrumental in getting *Gitanjali* published by the India Society of which he was the Secretary. Saint-John Perse became eager to meet the Bengali poet and wrote to him a letter in his rather poor English asking if he could go to see him and 'bow to him.' The letter is preserved in Rabindra Bhavana at Santiniketan. Fox-Strangways had given him a letter of introduction for the Indian poet. Rabindranath welcomed Saint-John Perse 'in a charming way.' The conversation between the twenty-five-year-old Frenchman and the mature poet must have been pleasant and might have touched the subject of the *Gitanjali*'s translation into French. After the meeting, Saint-John Perse wrote to André Gide (1859–1951), already an established prose writer, on 23 October 1912: 'The *Nouvelle Revue Française*, instead of serving Arnold Bennett, would do better to be the first in Europe to serve the work of Rabindranath Tagore. An English translation, prepared by himself, which will appear in a fortnight is the only poetical work written in English for a long time.'[5] In another letter to Gide, in December 1912, he wrote again: 'As for Rabindranath Tagore, whom a very great glory awaits in England, I shall bring him to you, this summer, or I shall take the liberty of sending you this living person (*ce vivant*): a great old man on a pilgrimage, of a delicate charm and of a very solid distinction.'[6] In January 1913, he wrote again: 'Tagore's work is beautiful... You are probably the only person in France to know, at this moment, this little book, and I will write for you to Tagore: when we parted in London he had not given his rights to anyone.'[7] Probably in July 1913, Perse wrote to Tagore another letter, from Paris this time and in French, to ask if the rights for translating *Gitanjali* into French could be given to André Gide who 'on his own, gave expression to his strong desire to do the translation.' Perse had given to Gide his personal copy of the India Society edition and he informed Tagore that the great novelist had already started to translate it. The Frenchman took great pains to impress upon Tagore the importance of Gide as a writer and editor of the *Nouvelle Revue Française*. He wrote: 'His intention would be to publish it at first in a literary review to reach a greater number of readers, then, immediately afterwards, in a book, at the most advantageous conditions for you, as André Gide has no financial interest at stake.' The letter is preserved at Rabindra Bhavana in Santiniketan. The French, as well as Tagore himself, can thank Saint-John

Perse for his convincing plea. The Bengali poet had no idea of the French literary scene and was ready to give the rights of translation to unknown and much inferior candidates. In his letter Perse underlined the importance of a good translator for the success of a literary work, and put forward the example of Baudelaire translating Poe.

At that time, in Paris, there was a stiff competition for publishing 'good literature' between two literary reviews: the *Nouvelle Revue Française* (NRF) and the *Mercure de France*. Gide and Saint-John Perse were on the side of the first. During the years 1912–13, the *Mercure de France* was better placed as far as English literature was concerned because of the presence of Henry D. Davray, who was H. G. Wells's translator. He was a regular contributor of a *chronique* (or chronocle) in this periodical. In fact, in August 1913, Davray published in *Mercure de France*, under the title 'A Hindu Mystic Rabindranath Tagore', a long article accompanied by fifty-four poems or excerpts of poems, from the English *Gitanjali*, translated by one Miss Weithermer. Davray who quoted a long passage from W. B. Yeats's Introduction to the Macmillan edition, presented Tagore as a mystic and ended by saying: 'Whatever may be the literary quality of these poems, their value is mainly due to the reach and the depth of their thought, to the strange purity of their meaning, to the infinite power of their lyricism.'[8]

André Gide was displeased because of the copyright issue. On the whole, attribution of translation rights to Gide for *Gitanjali* was not as simple as Saint-John Perse had thought. After Gide finally obtained exclusive rigths for the French translation of *Gitanjali*, he worked on the text with greater eagerness. In November 1913, he wrote in his *Journal* (Diary) that a secretary came to him every morning to take down in shorthand what he dictated, and then, in the afternoon, typed what she had taken down.

On 4 December 1913, Gide gave a lecture on Tagore and *Gitanjali* at the Théâtre du Vieux Colombier, in Paris. He used the text of his speech as the introduction to *L'Offrande lyrique*, as he called the French *Gitanjali*. In 1914, Gide obtained the rights for translating *The Post Office*, and he did the translation during the month of July of the same year. Gide was eager to obtain from Macmillan the rights to translate all the future books by Tagore, particularly *The Gardener* and *The Crescent Moon*. Mary Sturge Moore—the wife of Thomas Sturge Moore, the poet who was also Tagore's friend—was already translating *The Crescent Moon* but she had not found a publisher. After World War I, Gallimard wanted to publish Mrs Sturge Moore's translation that Gide found mediocre; she accepted a few corrections as suggested by Gide and the book came out only in 1924.

In his introduction to *L'Offrande lyrique*, Gide, after a few critical comments, presented the subject of the book as a mystic journey. He wrote:

'What I admire here, what fills me with tears and laughter, is the passionate animation of this poetry, which makes of the brahmanical teaching—that one could have thought so intellectual, so abstract—something so quivering, so rustling, like a sentence of Pascal's *Mystery of Jesus* but here trembling with joy.'[9] He appreciated the pantheistic feeling of universal life: 'The joy that Tagore teaches, it is precisely beyond *Maya* that he finds it.'[10] He gave much importance to the philosopher in the poet. He quoted several passages from *Sadhana* to elucidate the meaning of particular poems. He ended with his greatest compliment: 'All the last poems of *Gitanjali* are in praise of death. I do not think that I know, in any literature, a more solemn and more beautiful accent.' Yet, though a few articles mentioning the publication appeared in 1914 in *La Critique indépendante*, *La Phalange* and *L'Art moderne*, nothing more came out later.

On 9 January 1914, Gide informed Macmillan that he was beginning to translate Tagore's lectures delivered in 1912 at Harvard, that appeared in English as *Sadhana*. At first, he wrote that he would like to publish only some portions of it in a literary review but added: 'I feel that I may be drawn to translate the whole volume, because I am greatly interested by this work.' Surprisingly, he did not do any of it. Three months later he wrote to Macmillan to inform them that he was too preoccupied with other tasks and so was giving up his rights on the other French translations of Tagore's works, with the sole exception of *The Post Office* that he finished translating in 1916. When he received *Nationalism* he wrote to Macmillan that he had partly read it and found it 'very interesting,' but that he did not wish to translate it nor did he want the *Nouvelle Revue française* to publish it. In his *Journal* Gide rarely mentioned the poet; when he did, it was only to mention that he was working on translating either *Gitanjali* or *The Post Office*, but nothing more than that. After World War I, it seems that Gide lost interest in Tagore's writings. One entry dating from 1918 reads: 'Read the *Reminiscences* by Tagore. But this Indian Orient (*Orient des Indes*) is not made to suit me.'[11] He met Tagore in 1921 and after the visit he told a lady friend of his: 'He is exquisite!'

In 1920, when Tagore went to Paris, he stayed at *Autour du monde* as the guest of the banker Albert Kahn. There he met Comtesse de Noailles, a society lady and a poetess of some distinction. She told Rabindranath that on the day the War was declared in 1914, she was with the then French Prime Minister Georges Clémenceau (1841–1929). Both, very much affected by the news they had just heard, read aloud a poem from the French translation of *Gitanjali* done by André Gide.

After the Nobel Prize, a number of French translations were published. The poet himself translated quite a few of his poems into English. It is on the basis of these and other translations that the French volumes appeared, as below:

L'Offrande lyrique (*Gitanjali*), NRF 1913; Poésie Gallimard, 1979 with La corbeille de fruits.
Le jardinier d'amour—La jeune Lune (*The Gardener—The Crescent Moon*), NRF, 1920; Poésie Gallimard, 1980.
Amal et la lettre du roi (*The Post Office*) NRF, 1922; Gallimard, 1962.
La maison et le monde (*The Home and the World*), 1921, Payot poche, 1986.
La fugitive–Poèmes de Kabir (*The Fugitive—One Hundred Poems of Kabir*), NRF, 1922; Gallimard, 1986.
Souvenirs,(*Reminiscenses*) NRF, 1924; Gallimard 1986, 1991.
Cygne (*Balaka* [Flight of Swans]), 1923, Stock.
Nationalisme (*Nationalism*), Editions Delpeuch, 1924.
La religion du poète (*The Religion of a Poet*), Payot, 1924.

Ten years after the Nobel Prize, of all these publications, including collections of poems, plays, novels and essays, only one, *Cygne*, was translated from the Bengali by Kalidas Nag and the poet Pierre-Jean Jouve: the poems are rendered into prose. In the following years, from 1925 to 1930, the pattern is about the same. The translations include a volume of short stories, two novels, two plays and a collection of poems. All, except *La machine*, are translated from English. The translation of *A quatre voix* (*Chaturanga*) is the work of Madeleine Rolland, Romain Rolland's sister, and the volume contains an introduction by Romain Rolland himself.

Mashi (*Mashi and Other Stories*) NRF, 1925.
A quatre voix (*Chaturanga* [Four Parts]), (Editions du Sagittaire), 1925.
Le cycle du printemps (*Cycle of Spring*), Stock, 1926.
Le naufrage (*The Wreck*), NRF, 1929.
La machine (*Muktadhara* [Free Fall]), Rieder, 1929.
Lucioles (*Fireflies*), Feuilles de l'Inde, Ophrys, 1930.

From 1931 onwards, the number of new publications fell somewhat. One notices also the absence of collections of poems. The translations are all from English:

Lettres à un ami (*Letters to a Friend*), Rieder, 1931.
La religion de l'homme (*The Religion of Man*), Rieder, 1933.
Kacha et Devayani, Ophrys, 1950.[12]
Sadhana, Maisonneuve, 1940; Albin Michel, 1956.
Chitra, Ophrys, 1945.

En ce temps-là (*Jivansmriti* [Reminiscences]),Ophrys, 1950.
Souvenirs d'enfance et de jeunesse (*Chhelebela* [*My Boyhood Days*]), Ophrys, 1950.

In 1961, the centenary of Tagore's birth was celebrated throughout the world. The Indian and the French governments were keen to rekindle public enthusiasm for Tagore's works. New translations were published:

Gora, Robert Laffont, 1961.
Œuvres poétiques (Poetic works), Club du meilleur livre, 1961.
Vers l'homme universel (*Towards Universal Man*), Gallimard, 1964, 1986.
Le vagabond et autres histoires (The vagabond and other stories), Gallimard, 1962, 1983, 2002.
Souvenirs d'enfance et de jeunesse (*Chhelebela* [*My Boyhood Days*]), NRF, 1964, 1985.

Gora was translated from English but, later, revised by Father Pierre Fallon, a Jesuit who knew Bengali. The last two books in the above list were translated from the Bengali by two persons, one Bengali and one French. *Le vagabond et autres histoires* was translated by Christine Bossenec and Kamaleswar Bhattacharya, and *Souvenirs d'enfance et de jeunesse* by Bossenec and Rajeshwari Datta.

Most of the earlier publications were not allowed to disappear from the bookshops, and new reprints, if not new editions, were brought out. Later, and to date, new French translations came out: one from English:

La demeure de la paix (*Santiniketan*), Stock, 1998.

and others from the original Bengali:

Epousailles et autres histoires (collection of short stories), Editions Le Félin, 1989.
L'esquif d'or (*Selected Poems*), Connaissance de l'Orient, Gallimard, 1997.
La petite mariée (suivi de *Nuage et soleil*), (*Selected Stories*), Gallimard, 2004.
Quatre chapitres (Four Chapters), Zulma, 2005.
Histoires de fantômes indiens (Selected Stories), Cartouche, 2006; Arléa, 2008.
L'écrin vert (*Selected Poems*), Gallimard, 2008.
Charulata ('Nashta nirh' [Broken Nest]), Zulma, 2009.
Kumudini (*Yogayog* [Relationships]), Zulma, 2013.

The collection of Tagore's writings in French is impressive but some of his major works were published long ago from English, and it is difficult to get them translated anew from the original Bengali. The publishers would not be interested to cast aside their previous publications for new ones.

THE CENTENARY CELEBRATIONS

In 1961, several cultural programmes were organised by the French National Committee for the Celebrations of the Centenary of the Birth of the Poet, under the patronage of the Minister of Cultural Affairs, the noted writer André Malraux, the Ministry of External Affairs and the Ministry of Education, and with the cooperation of the Indian government, its Embassy in Paris and UNESCO. A volume was published, *Hommage de la France à Rabindranath Tagore*, with contributions among others of Saint-John Perse who himself had received the Nobel Prize for Literature in 1960, Buddhadeva Bose, Louis Renou and Jean Filliozat, both leading Indologists, Alain Daniélou and Philippe Stern, Director of Musée Guimet. Many cultural programmes were organised in Paris and in the other major French cities.

TAGORE SONGS (*RABINDRA SANGEET*) IN FRANCE

Rabindranath's songs got noticed with the publication of a transcription in European notation system of twenty-six songs by Arnold A. Bake, along with their literal translation. The volume, entitled *Chansons de Rabindranath Tagore* (Songs of Rabindranath Tagore), was published in Paris by P. Geuthner in 1935. Alain Daniélou transcribed and adapted several melodies by the poet for voice and piano. Another volume, called *Poèmes chantés* (Sung poems), with notation, translation and adaptation for voice and piano, by M. de Maule, came out in Paris in 2005. Three melodies by Tagore with texts in French and English, with notations by Alain Daniélou, were published in 1961 by Ricordi. In 2005, a number of poems by Rabindranath with notation, translation and adaptation for voice and piano by Alain Daniélou were also published in Paris by M. de Maule.

MUSICAL PIECES COMPOSED ON RABINDRANATH TAGORE'S POEMS

A number of musical pieces were composed on Rabindranath's poems. The Department of Music in the French *Bibliothèque nationale* gives a list of fourteen. In 1916, Darius Milhaud, a prominent musician, composed the music on four poems.

THEATRE

In 1919, *Sacrifice*, in a French version by Henri Odier, was performed in Geneva under the direction of Georges Pitoëff who played the role of Raghupati. In 1936, Pitoëff also directed *Amal et la lettre du roi* (*Post Office*; translation by André Gide, music by Darius Milhaud) at the théâtre des Mathurins in Paris.

It should be added that, according to a letter written on 22 June 1940, by Christine Bossenec, then Superintendant of the Girls' Hostel at Santiniketan, to the Calcutta English daily *Amrita Bazar Patrika*, Tagore and herself, then staying at Kalimpong, had heard *The Post Office* on the French radio as it was broadcast from Paris on 14 June, the night before the city fell to the German army. The mention of this broadcast could not be found in the Radio Archives, but is noted in *Selected Letters of Rabindranath Tagore*[13].

In 1961 and 1962, *The Post Office* was performed at the Théâtre de l'Oeuvre and Théâtre Hébertot. The play *Chitra et Arjuna* (*Chitrangada*) was put up at Centre Mandapa in Paris in 1987, under the direction of Gérard Rougier.

DANCE

At the twentieth *Festival d'Avignon* in 1966, *Cygne* (*Balaka*) was produced by the reputed *Ballet du XXe siècle* with choreography by Maurice Béjart.

EXHIBITIONS OF TAGORE'S PAINTINGS

The first ever exhibition of Tagore's paintings outside India took place in Paris at the Galerie Pigalle in May 1931. On this occasion a catalogue was printed with a foreword by Comtesse de Noailles. A few very positive reviews appeared in the press. In 2012, an exhibition of Tagore's paintings took place at the Petit Palais, in Paris, on the occasion of the 150th birth-anniversary of the poet.

In 1961 on the occasion of the poet's centenary, an exhibition of photographs took place at the *Bibliothèque nationale* in Paris and a catalogue was printed with an introduction by Jean Filliozat, followed by *Hommage de la France à Rabindranath Tagore pour le centenaire de sa naissance, 1961*.

STUDIES ON RABINDRANATH TAGORE

Two studies devoted to Tagore were aimed at introducing the man and his works to school children. Both were entitled: *Introduction à Tagore*. They were written by Marie-Louise Gommès and were published respectively in 1942 and 1947. With the same objective, François Chan presented *Rabindranath*

Tagore, 1861–1941: Textes et documents pour les enseignements du second degré, Paris, 1965.

In 1921, Léandre Vaillat wrote *Le poète hindou Rabindranath Tagore* and published it in Paris. P. Chaize-Borel wrote an article entitled: 'Sur le mysticisme oriental de Rabindranath Tagore.' Interestingly, it was published in Paris by *La Famille Theosophiste* in 1923.

In 1961 appeared in the excellent collection *Poètes d'aujourd'hui* (Poets of today) by Pierre Seghers a volume entitled *Rabindranath Tagore*, which contained a presentation on the poet, selected texts and a bibliography, the author being Odette Aslan. Later, in 1987, Sylvie Liné wrote *Tagore, pèlerin de la lumière* (Tagore, pilgrim towards the light). It was published by Le Rocher, both in Monaco and Paris.

Several PhD theses were written about Tagore and his works in several French universities, at first mostly by students of Indian origin. Manjulal Jamnadas Dave submitted his thesis entitled *La poésie de Rabindranath Tagore* (The poetry of Rabindranath Tagore), at Montpellier University in 1927. Sushil Chandra Mitter, in 1930, wrote on *La pensée de Rabindranath Tagore* (The thought of Rabindranath Tagore); his thesis was submitted in Paris. Gita Banerjee-Delgalian wrote in 1987 a study on *Raktakarabi* (*Red Oleanders*) for a PhD at Lille university.

In 2002, a DEA (MPhil.) memoir on *La Voix dans Balaka et Gitanjali: Présence, Passages et Seuils* (The voice in *Balaka* and *Gitanjali*: Passages and Thresholds) was presented by Laetitia Zecchini at the English Department of Paris Sorbonne. In 2004, Fabien Chartier obtained a PhD of the university of Rennes 2, at the English Department, on *Réception britannique et française du poète indo-anglais Rabindranath Tagore (1912–30): utilisation d'un symbole et genèse d'un mythe* (British and French Reception of the Indo–British poet Rabindranath Tagore).

Tagore Sangam

An association called Tagore Sangam was founded by Azarie Aroulandom in 2002. Its aim is to popularise Tagore's thought and works in French-speaking countries, mainly through organising exhibitions of photographs on Tagore's life. The photographs have been collected and mounted by the founder. The bilingual exhibition comprises more than 250 photos and illustrations as well as reproductions of some of the paintings by the poet. It also includes a number of copies of Tagore's books in various languages. The exhibition was presented in March 2002 at UNESCO, Paris, under the patronage of M. Jacques Chirac, President of the French Republic. The inauguration was followed by a seminar and a cultural programme.

In 2004, the exhibition was taken to the French Caribbean island of Guadeloupe as part of the celebrations of the 150th anniversary of the arrival of Indians in the island. It was held under the patronage of Mr Abdou Diouf, ex-President of the Republic of Senegal and Acting Secretary General of the Organisation générale de la Francophonie. The association continues to organise exhibitions of photographs, participates in national poetry and literary festivals about the Bengali poet, and sponsors programmes of dances and songs composed by Tagore.

FRENCH FRIENDS OF RABINDRANATH TAGORE

Sylvain Lévi

When Rabindranath arrived from London in 1920, he was welcomed by the banker Albert Kahn in his cultural centre Autour du monde, Tagore was accompanied by his son and daughter-in-law. During his stay he was helped by the presence in Paris of Sudhirkumar Rudra, whose father was a friend of C. F. Andrews.[14] Shortly after his arrival, Kahn took the poet in his car to see the battlefields of World War I near Reims;. the poet was deeply moved.

It is during this visit to France that he met Sylvain Lévi (1863–1935), a Sanskrit scholar and a specialist on the history of Buddhism, who was born in Paris. After his brilliant studies at the higher secondary level, he was persuaded by Ernest Renan to start learning Sanskrit under Abel Bergaigne at the Ecole des Hautes Etudes. In 1886, after Bergaigne's death, the young Lévi was appointed to teach Sanskrit at his alma mater. He wrote his dissertation on the Indian classical theatre and obtained a DLitt. In 1894, he was elected professor of Sanskrit language and literature at the prestigious College de France and went to India and the Far East for the first time in 1897. Of Jewish origin, he became President of the Alliance Israélite Universelle in 1920.

The same year (1920) he met Rabindranath in Paris who spoke to him about the university that he was setting up at Santiniketan where he wanted to welcome scholars from abroad. Lévi was impressed by the poet's enthusiasm and volunteered to go to Santiniketan. He became the first European professor to do so. After their first meeting in Paris, they met again at Strasbourg where Lévi, already professor at the Collège de France, was also teaching at the university. The poet gave a lecture entitled 'The message of the forest.' At the end, Professor Lévi praised him and his work in deeply moving terms. The Strasbourg University formed a Tagore Committee to appeal for funds in order to present a collection of French classics to the new library of Visva-Bharati.

Professor Lévi arrived in Santiniketan in November 1921, as a visiting professor, accompanied by his wife. Both were present at the formal inauguration of Visva-Bharati. There Lévi taught Sanskrit, ancient Indian history in relation to Asia, and Chinese as well as Tibetan. In August 1922, the couple left Santiniketan to accompany the poet on his travels to other parts of India, after a brief sojourn in Nepal. On their return to Paris, Madame Lévy wrote a book of souvenirs entitled *En Inde (de Ceylan au Népal)*. The sixth edition appeared in 1926, and the last one in 2008. In it she gives a lively and charming account of life in Santiniketan.

Tagore and Lévi had occasion to meet once again in 1926 when the poet came to Paris from Italy after spending ten days at Villeneuve with Romain Rolland. But an incident occurred when Tagore was in Java in 1927 that resulted in a misunderstanding between the two friends. The poet was shown a press cutting from a Dutch newspaper reporting Lévi's unfavourable comments on Visva-Bharati as an academic institution. Tagore was deeply hurt and expressed his sorrow in a letter to Lévi; this letter has been preserved in the Rabindra Bhavana archives, but the date is erroneous. The professor protested and affirmed his total innocence in a letter dated 16 December 1927 in which he underlined his deep love and admiration for the poet and his work. In August 1928, on their way back from Japan, the Lévis stopped in Calcutta to meet Rabindranath and reassure him of their innocence and express their regret over the matter. But the poet was sick at that time, and it is not clear whether Lévi was able to totally convince him of his unqualified love for Visva-Bharati. Lévi was a rigorously trained academic and he may not have felt fully at home in the somewhat free atmosphere of the new university founded by a poet who, moreover, was very often absent. Yet he had a sincere love for Tagore and trained several students of Visva-Bharati in Paris, like Prabodh Kumar Bagchi. Lévi was sent to Tokyo in 1927 to become the founder and the director of the Institut franco-japonais.

In 1930, during another of his sojourns in Paris, Tagore expressed his desire to meet the Lévis again at their home. 'It will be far more tempting for me if you occasionally drop in to our place for lunch with *Didima* (Mrs Lévi) as our guardian angel, and in return ask us to tea all by ourselves.' The following year, Lévi contributed an essay to *The Golden Book of Tagore* entitled: 'An ancestor of Tagore in Javanese Literature'[15]. In Java he had come to know of a Javanese version of Bhatta Narayan's *Veni Samhara*, and remembered that the poet had mentioned that his family descended from one Bhatta Narayan who had come to Bengal from Kanyakubja! He wrote: 'Called by his (Tagore's) choice to inaugurate the teaching of orientalism in the western way in the Visva-Bharati that he was founding at that time, I have learnt much more than I have taught. Thanks to Gurudev, as we call him there, thanks to the elite of scholars and disciples who gather around him and who live [on] his inspiration, I came to know in its living reality the soul of India that the study of texts had taught me to admire. It is only at Santiniketan, in the contact of the Master and of his entourage, that I could appreciate in their incomparable charm the dignity of deportment, the nobility of feelings, the measured exaltation of thought that effortlessly combine with a witty gaiety, a spiritual fantasy, an exquisite sweetness and the perpetual communion with nature which give to the daily life the charming coloration of a Virgilian eclogue.'

After the sudden demise of the scholar in 1935, at a meeting of the Alliance Israelite Universelle, his widow published her husband's translation from the Bengali of five poems by Tagore in a literary periodical with the introduction that he had written.[16] The poems appeared in *Yggdrasill, Bulletin de la poésie en France et à l'étranger* on 25 May 1938. Tagore offered his contribution to the fund the Paris University initiated to create a Foundation in memory of Professor Sylvain Lévi. The correspondance between Rabindranath and Sylvain Lévi is housed at Rabindra Bhavana, Santiniketan. Lévi's most significant contribution to Indian studies include his volumes on Indian classical theatre and *La Doctrine du sacrifice dans les Brahmanas* (The doctrine of sacrifice in the Brahmanas). Lévi wrote also an important study on Nepal and several scholarly articles on Buddhism.

Romain Rolland

In 1916, Rabindranath Tagore had gone to Japan where he was received warmly until he lectured on the evils of Nationalism that he felt Japan had imbibed from the West. Tagore saw the Japanese people as eminently artistic and linked with India through the Buddhist faith. But he discovered that they were keener to imitate Europe, even in her follies, than befriend a poor and subjected India. He clearly condemned the materialism of the new Japan. Romain Rolland, a French writer who had just received the Nobel Prize, read the lectures that Tagore gave in Japan. They were published under the title *Nationalism*, at a time when the whole of Europe was involved in a terrible armed conflict. Romain Rolland was the citizen of a country that was fighting against its neighbour Germany for the recovery of two of its provinces lost in a previous war. The French nation was behind its army in a 'sacred union,' and patriotism was at a pitch. Yet Rolland was a declared pacifist, and remained 'above the battle' at enormous cost to his reputation in his country. He wrote: 'Any man who is a real man must learn to stand alone in the midst of others, to think alone for all—and if need be, against all', and also: 'The task of the intellectual is to search for Truth in the midst of error.'

He had written a *Declaration for the Independence of the Spirit* that, after reading *Nationalism*, he requested Tagore to sign along with other European intellectuals. Rolland felt that writers had a duty to express feelings of human brotherhood even in the most terrible conflict. The Bengali poet had no hesitation and signed the document, with a beautiful letter dated 24 June 1919: 'When my mind was [stupefied] in the gloom of the thought that the lesson of the late war has been lost and that the people were trying to perpetuate their hatred, anger and greed into the same organized menace for the world which threatened themselves with disaster, your letter came and cheered me with its message of hope.' In August, Rolland wrote a letter thanking him for the two books, *Nationalism* and *The Home and the World*, that he had received, and added: 'I have a deep pain (and I would say, a remorse, if I was not feeling more Man than European) of the monstrous abuse Europe has made of her power, of the ravage of the universe, of the destruction and debasement by her of so many material and moral riches, of the greatest strenghts of the world that even in her own interest she should have defended and increased, by uniting them with her own... It is not only a question of justice, it is a question of salvation for humanity.' Then he expressed his great desire to see a union of Eastern and Western minds in defence of humanism and wrote: 'Europe alone cannot save herself. Her thought is in need of the thought of Asia, just as the latter has benefitted from contact with the thought of Europe. These are the two hemispheres of the brain of mankind.'[17] Tagore was exactly of the same opinion.

Rolland, one of the best European friends of Tagore, was born in 1866 in a provincial middle-class family which lived in central France. His mother taught him music, and he became an excellent pianist. A brilliant student, he obtained the 'agregation' diploma in history and spent two years in Rome as member of the Ecole française de Rome. Back in Paris, he obtained a *doctorat es lettres* (DLitt.) on the origins of lyrical theatre in Europe. He started to teach musicology at the Sorbonne. At the same time, he was pursuing a literary career and, as soon as he had some success, resigned from the university. He was fluent in German and Italian but knew no English. In 1916, three years after Tagore, he was awarded the Nobel Prize for Literature. When he met the Bengali poet in 1921, he had already published more than thirty books: plays, biographies, novels and essays. His monumental novel *Jean-Christophe* had come out between 1903 and 1912 and was an enormous success. His friends were Paul Claudel, Hermann Hesse, Stefan Zweig, and among the younger writers Jean Guehenno and Georges Duhamel.

In his letter of 26 August 1919, Rolland had expressed his wish to start a periodical that would present the 'moral wealth,' both of the West and of Asia. It would be published in French and in English, and would be the meeting ground of intellectuals and writers from many countries. He asked Tagore whether such a publication would interest Asian thinkers. The poet replied assuring Rolland of his own interest in the proposal but, at the same time, his doubt about its immediate realisation because of the political situation in India. He wrote: 'The great event that was the meeting of Orient and Occident has been vitiated by the contempt of one and, in reply, the hatred of the other.'[18] This was the beginning of Rolland's persistent efforts to include the poet into his group of pacifist and idealistic European writers, who, in newspapers, literary magazines and books, were actively promoting their generous ideas.

After a somewhat unsuccessful tour in America to collect funds for his new university, Tagore returned to Europe and after spending a few weeks in London, where he spoke of the difficult political situation in India and the resulting antagonism between his country and England, he flew to France in April 1921. At that time, Rolland was living in Paris and Tagore went to meet him. They discussed several issues with the help of Rolland's sister Madeleine who acted as the interpreter. Rolland could not but appreciate the name given to the university, Visva-Bharati, or India open onto the world, and he promised to help Tagore's fledgling university at Santiniketan by informing the European intellectual élite about its aims and by trying to send French scholars to teach there. He himself would go if his health would permit, he said. Unfortunately, Rolland never went to Tagore's Bengal for various reasons, but keenly followed the events at Santiniketan.

Kalidas Nag, a young and cultured Bengali with a good command of French, was studying for a doctorate in Paris University, the Sorbonne. Tagore knew him well. Nag was introduced to Rolland, who became quite fond of him. Nag served as a bridge between Tagore and Rolland. For the first time, in May 1922, the name of Kalidas Nag is mentioned by Rolland in his diary. A month later, Rolland wrote to Nag about Tagore in these words: 'Of no poet nor thinker of contemporary Europe I feel nearer than to him, by the mind and the heart. This is a proof of the vanity of these artificial divisions established between the thought of India and that of the west.'[19] He described himself as a pure product of provincial France, without any contact with Asia until very recently. In the same letter, the French writer announced his shift of residence from Paris to Villeneuve, a small town on the shore of the Lac Leman (also known as Lake Geneva) in Switzerland.

Tagore and Rolland were both misunderstood in their respective countries. Tagore was advocating a cultural rapprochement between India and Europe at a time when India was passing through a great political upheaval and when chauvinistic tendencies were understandably very strong.

On his side, Rolland was saddened by the humiliating way Germany was treated after the victory of the Allies in 1919. Both felt isolated. At the same time, Rolland was keen to include the Bengali poet in all his efforts to promote a universal literature. Tagore gave him the right to publish in French a translation of his letters from Europe that had appeared in *The Modern Review*. With the same generosity he gave to Rolland's sister, Madeleine, the permission to translate from English into French his great novel *Gora* that Pearson was to render into English. Madeleine did not translate *Gora* but her translation of *Chaturanga* entitled *A quatre voix* appeared in 1924.

We also know that Madeleine was busy learning Bengali, from a letter Rolland wrote in March 1923.[20]

So far all the translations of Tagore's works had been made from English, with the exception of *Balaka* (*Cygne*), translated in 1923 from Bengali by Kalidas Nag and the French poet Pierre-Jean Jouve, a friend of Rolland. The publisher was Stock, whose proprietor was also a friend of Rolland. The same year, Rolland informed Tagore that he had completed a long essay on Gandhi based on the articles that had appeared in *Young India*. He would publish it in the periodical *Europe* which reflected his views. Though he wrote that he considered some of Gandhi's ideas 'a little too medieval,' he felt a great respect for the Mahatma. Later, the political and moral leadership that Gandhi embodied attracted more and more a person like Rolland who was both an idealist and an activist. Tagore, primarily a poet and an artist, was trying at that time to keep Santiniketan away from the turmoil of politics. In another letter to Kalidas Nag, dated 15 September 1923, Rolland expressed a great interest in the nascent university at Santiniketan: 'Please, my dear friend, tell our common great friend, Rabindranath Tagore, the deep affection that I have for him, my firm intention to go to Santiniketan as soon as the circumstances will permit and my desire to help him in his international task ... After a conversation with Pearson, it seems to me that the international university needs, before all, a strong organisation that will keep it, in the beginning, concentrated on a few essential courses—that will set a course programme for several years—and that will try in a friendly way to tie down students and teachers to it. A course on the general history of civilizations would seem to me fundamental. It is the axis upon which the whole construction can rise... Similarly, it would be good to proceed little by little to teach comparative literature and art.'[21] He was not discouraged by Pearson's not too favourable comments on the new university. Tagore's devoted English friend had described it as 'more ficticious than real' and complained to Rolland of its lack of an organised curriculum of studies and of a fixed timetable. The same drawbacks had probably attracted the attention of Sylvain Lévi and also of Giuseppe Tucci.

During these months, Romain Rolland met several friends and young admirers of Rabindranath. His interest in India was becoming paramount in his intellectual life. He came to know C. F. Andrews and talked to him about the poet and Gandhi. He expressed a great desire to go to India and see Tagore in his own surroundings, but he regretted that the presence of his old father and his own weak health would probably not allow him to realise his dream. With some grandiloquence, rare in a French intellectual, he added: 'The union of Europe and Asia must be, in the coming centuries, the highest task of humanity.'[22] During this period, the friendship between Tagore and Rolland was at its zenith, and they wrote long letters to each other. Rolland was greatly concerned over Tagore's tiring tours in search of funds for Santiniketan. He pleaded with him in his letters not to sacrifice poetry to the extension of his university. He also took a great interest in the *Visva-Bharati Quarterly* that his sister was translating for him. He wanted to share with the poet his 'small volume' on Gandhi and also his novel *L'Âme enchantée* (The enchanted soul). Tagore, on his side, opened his heart to Rolland. He wrote that 'there is in my nature a kind of civil war between the personality of the creative artist—to whom solitude is necessary—and that of the idealist who must find his accomplishment through works of a complex nature, requiring a vast collaboration with a great number of men.'[23]

With the passing of time their friendship had to face obstacles of several kinds. Tagore was always moving from one continent to another. Soon after he returned from China in 1924, he left for South America, and occasions for a meeting of the two friends became rare. Twice the poet had to cancel a visit to Villeneuve where Rolland, who hardly ever travelled, was waiting for him. In March 1925, the French author wrote a moving reply to the Bengali poet who had written about his sadness and solitude, even in Bengal. Rolland wrote that men like Tagore and himself remain in a state of isolation, wherever they live: 'Our country is the future,' he added. Thinking that Tagore could come to rest for sometime in Switzerland, he described the landscapes of several places in that country, mentioning a physician who could help him recover his health in a pleasant nursing home, gave the name of a hotel near his own house and even train routes to come to Villeneuve. But, by another letter, we learn that Tagore could not go to Villeneuve where all arrangements had been made. The following year in May 1926 Rabindranath announced his arrival. Delighted, Rolland wrote back mentioning the new arrangements that he was making. Once again, Tagore had to postpone his visit.

After Visva-Bharati had been set up, Tagore, eager to get funds for his university, accepted invitations from wherever they came. On the contrary, Rolland, more and more politically conscious, wanted to prevent the poet from mixing with the wrong type of politicians. In 1924, Tagore embarked from a French port to go to Peru on being invited by a dictatorial government that had promised financial help for Visva-Bharati. Rolland was irritated by Tagore's lack of discrimination and tried his utmost, over three months, by letters and messengers, to make him aware of the wrong signal that his visit to Lima would send to the democrats. When the poet left without meeting him, he wrote to Kalidas Nag: 'I am very saddened and angry.' However, the poet did not finally go to Peru and had to break journey in Argentina because of ill health. He spent two months there as the guest of the charming Victoria Ocampo. On his way back from South America, because of his poor health, Tagore failed to meet Rolland who was disappointed again. Yet, in January 1925, an enthusiastic Rolland informed Kalidas Nag of his idea of opening a Maison de l'Amitié (a Friendship House) in Switzerland, which would serve as a kind of European branch of Santiniketan. It would bring together all the living intellectual energies of Asia and Europe. Initially, a Swiss publishing house would take up this project and would also undertake to publish Asian authors, and Tagore in the first place.

The French writer was a second time, and far more deeply, perturbed and disappointed when the poet accepted an invitation from Mussolini. On a first visit to Italy, on his way back from Argentina, Tagore had spent some time in Italy on his own. There he had met Professor Carlo Formichi (1871–1943), professor of Sanskrit and Buddhist Studies at Rome University and invited Formichi to teach at Visva-Bharati. The Italian professor went there in November 1925 along with Giuseppe Tucci (1894–1984), his former student and colleague. Actually, Mussolini sent the two scholars at the expense of the Italian Government along with an important gift of Italian classics for the library. The Italian dictator who had ruthlessly started to eliminate his opponents thought that the visit of so famous an Indian poet as Tagore would add to his prestige. He wanted to make full use of the poet's reputation in support of his political activities. Formichi, an enthusiastic supporter of Fascism, was the willing instrument through which this project could be successfully accomplished. When Formichi left Santiniketan, the poet, in his farewell address, expressed his feeling of debt in regard to Italy and her Government.[24] Not much later, when the official invitation came from the Italian Government, Tagore did not think it necessary to find out more about Mussolini's Fascist regime before accepting. He was received there as an official guest of the government. Rolland, who wanted to warn the poet about the obnoxious Fascist regime, did not get a chance to see him on his way to Italy. Pained, he wrote to Kalidas Nag that he had abandoned the project of going to India the following autumn: 'I feel that my presence in Santiniketan would not be useful.'[25] He added that he was worried that the poet was losing the right, as a moral figure, to speak the language of truth in Asia and in Europe. When the poet finally went to Villeneuve in June–July 1926 for two weeks, he learnt from Rolland the exact nature of the Italian State. Through him, he met Italian refugees who told him of the horrors they had gone through. The poet was ashamed to have been caught unawares and he wrote an article in the form of a letter to C. F. Andrews which appeared in the press, both in England in the *Manchester Guardian*, and in India, in a longer version, in the *Visva-Bharati Quarterly*. Many democrats in the West, friends of Rolland, thought that the poet's condemnation of Fascism was not strong enough. A single paragraph in a long text repudiated Mussolini's regime directly[26]. Rolland got excerpts from Tagore's letter translated by his sister and published in the periodical *Europe,* though he found it very mild and unsatisfactory[27]. Rolland had to defend Tagore's reputation against quite a few European intellectuals who lost no time in blaming the poet. The French writer had attributed to himself the task to warn Tagore against the dangerous political ideologies that were coming up in Europe. In 1933, as he did not write directly to Tagore for warning him about the dangers of Nazism, he asked Kalidas Nag to do it for him.

The judgement of Romain Rolland was somewhat harsh at the time of the Italian visit. It was difficult, if not impossible, for Tagore to keep abreast of European politics and, perhaps, even in Europe at that time, the nature of Mussolini's regime was not clearly understood by many. Tagore was spending much time and effort, at a relatively advanced age, to look for funds for his university and was also distressed by the situation in India and his disagreements with Gandhi. In November 1926, Rolland writes in his diary: 'One of the reasons that, now, push me back from the projected trip to India, is that I would be torn between the two rival groups.'[28]

But, in spite of a momentary disappointment, Rolland, though more and more enmeshed in idealistic politics, never forgot that Tagore was primarily a poet and an artist. In July 1926 after Tagore's visit to Italy, Rolland wrote to Kalidas Nag about the poet: 'I understand him perfectly; and, as he is, I love him.'[29] He went on to say: 'Poet—the more one knows Tagore, the more one recognises to what extent this word essentially designates him. In his rich and enlightened personality, it is the Poet who dominates... One of the highest poets that the world has ever known.'[30] And again: 'I love him tenderly. His nature is full of charm and kindness. He has his weaknesses. But there is in him nothing that is false, not even superficial. He is true in all that he feels. He is a poet, deeply.'[31] Rolland once remarked to Prasanta Mahalanobis who was passing through Villeneuve: 'In Europe, Tagore's popularity is less due to his poetical works, that are little or not at all known, than to certain elevated and free statements pronounced during the war, to his prophetic condemnation of imperialism, of machine-worship, of the blind force of the West, and to the almost sacred role that is attributed to him.'[32] This remarkably pertinent observation may partly explain the relative lack of literary interest for Tagore's writings in France after the 1930s.

After the poet's departure on 4 July 1926, Rolland gave expression to his sadness and fear of not seeing him again. He wrote in his diary a frank assessment of the great man: 'His nature is eternally divided between his poetic aspirations, which are the deepest, and the prophetic social role that the circumstances forced him to adopt. This role is glorious; and Tagore, in moments of passionate inspiration, has been equal to it. But he does not remain at that height. The poet takes again the upper hand and also the aristocrat...'[33] Rolland wrote: 'In his avid and childish desire to travel everywhere in Europe, Tagore, who is not wealthy any more, has surrendered himself to an agent organising paying lectures for him. And only the rich and snobbish public had access to them. So everywhere, he has left behind him a bitter disappointment. And he, the most generous person, has given the impression to present himself everywhere out of vanity and for the sake of money. It is heartrending.'[34] Most of the time, Rolland chose to blame the poet's age and poor health for this. But, after the Italian visit, he wrote: 'Should I add this ? The pose that is natural to him, this patriarchal solemnity, which is an ancient Asiatic attitude, imposes itself on all that surrounds him—at first it fascinates, but later, contributes to separate him from his European friends. I love him tenderly, I worship him; and yet, (should I say it?) there was not a single meeting when I did not feel the diabolical desire to get up abruptly and to leave—to break the constraint of this solemn courtesy and of this etiquette. He does not notice it; nor do his people. It is the way of their social life... But fatally happens the shock between the old Orient and the hurried West which levels and cuts.'[35]

Both were probably expecting too much from one another, and they could never be fully satisfied. Rolland regretted that he had to depend on his sister for their mutual exchanges. Tagore would have liked to receive Rolland at Santiniketan and was disappointed that it never happened. In the spring of 1930, the poet went back to France and stayed in Albert Kahn's villa in the south. He invited Rolland to join him there but, for some reason, the French writer did not go. Rolland was more and more involved in his work on Ramakrishna and Vivekananda. In just a couple of years, his two volumes were researched, written and published. At the same period of time, his interest in Gandhi was getting stronger. Taking into account his *Brahmo* background, Tagore must have found it hard to understand the fascination of Rolland for the great mystic and his disciple. As for him, he expressed his views on spirituality in his remarkable lectures given at Oxford in 1930 and published later as *The Religion of Man*. In August 1930, Tagore was at Geneva for a few days and Rolland went to meet him. Significantly, the poet spoke of Rammohun Roy and of his father.

The rhythm of their correspondance slackened between 1930 and 1940: there were only four letters from Tagore and five from Rolland. Yet, in 1931, when Rabindranath was seventy years old, Rolland was one of those who took the initiative to edit a volume of homage to the poet published as *The Golden Book of Tagore*. The other sponsors were Albert Einstein, Costis Palamas, a well-known Greek poet, Rolland's friend, Mohandas Karamchand Gandhi and Jagadish Chandra Bose. Rolland wrote a poetic text in praise of the poet whom he described as 'for us the living symbol of the spirit of light and harmony, soaring, as a great and free bird, in the midst of storms.'[36] In *The Golden Book of Tagore*, interestingly, his contribution consists of 'three fragments of an early drama written by the author about his twentieth year, in Rome, during his sojourn at the French School of the Farnese Palace.' These lines appear at the beginning of the English translation at the end of the volume[37]. The French original, placed first in the book, is entitled *Niobé*. As a dedication, Rolland wrote: 'To the magic bird from India I offer this young song of a small blackbird from France who was making an early attempt, just out from the nest. To Rabindranath Tagore with my affection and my respect.'

Tagore had discovered in himself a passion and a talent for painting. He gave much of his time to his art but was diffident at first to show his works. He spoke of his paintings as 'products of untutored fingers and untrained mind.' But, coming once more to Europe, he was keen to have the opinion of the 'connoisseurs.' The first exhibition of his works took place in Paris. It was inaugurated at Galerie Pigalle on 2 May 1930 and was organised in a very short time, thanks to the contacts and energy of Victoria Ocampo. It took place under the patronage of the Association des Amis de l'Orient. The exhibition was a social affair, and it is known that Romain Rolland, more and more involved in his writings on Ramakrishna and Vivekananda, published in the same year (1930), and also with Gandhi, thought that Rabindranath's health had suffered and that he spent too much time with society people unworthy of him. To Kalidas Nag who came to see him the same year in June, Rolland spoke about Tagore with affection but also regret:. 'Perpetual travelling', Rolland wrote in his diary, 'has become for Tagore a sickly need, a worry that torments him. It has too many causes as we shall see.' Rolland mentioned several deaths in the poet's family, his loneliness in India and the insufficient communication with his European friends, and Rolland himself, due to the absence of a common language. He continued: 'He started painting as a diversion. And it is also because of a need for diversion, oblivion even, that he goes in search of or accepts in Paris mundane societies so little worthy of him and, for that, he is the object of the virtuous condemnations of our French friends. They have no idea of the tragedy hidden under this apparent frivolity.'[38] Victoria Ocampo came to know of Rolland's criticism, and she replied that among these 'society people' were André Gide, Paul Valéry, one of the most renowned poets on the French literary scene, Georges-Henri Rivière, the founder of Musée national des arts et traditions populaires and the inventor of a new museography, Jean Cassou, art critic, poet and translator from Spanish, Abbé Brémond, historian and member of the French Academy, and Abbé Mugnier, the spiritual director of many intellectuals and a friend of the novelist Marcel Proust. Ocampo agreed with Rolland that Tagore was passing through a crisis during which the artist had the upper hand over the guru.[39]

Paul Valéry, who had met the poet at the exhibition of his paintings, wrote in *The Golden Book of Tagore*: 'I address to the illustrious poet the homage and the very fervent wishes that my western soul inspires me for his person and his great work. I retain of him the most venerable memory.'[40] At that time, Valéry was an elected member of the Académie Française (French Academy).

Rolland wrote about the meeting between Tagore and Gandhi that took place in Calcutta that his sister had read for him from *Harijan* (20 November 1937). He also noted down what he had read about Tagore's illness and quoted a poem from *Gitanjali*. He was deeply moved and announced that the next day he would write to Rabindranath[41]. It is the last mention of the poet in Rolland's diary about India, though it ended in 1943. In his *Journal de Vézelay* (Vézelay Diary), very recently published, that contains his writings from 1938 till his death in 1944, one reads, in 1941, two short sentences about Rabindranath's death: 'Death of Tagore after an operation. Sadness because of this great [departure] in this dark hour, without any flash of lightning.'[42]

Andrée Karpelès

Andrée Karpelès (1885–1956) was one of Rabindranath's young female friends. She was born in Paris in a well-to-do family. Her father, born in Eastern Europe, came to France as a poor man but soon earned a comfortable living by importing indigo from India. The Karpelès family was regularly going to India for business and vacation. The father died, and the family was impoverished with the discovery of a chemical substitute for indigo. Andrée learnt painting in Paris. After World War I, she returned to India and stayed at Santiniketan where she taught painting and engraving.

She also took a lot of interest in folk art. She was close to the poet with whom she exchanged an affectionate correspondence once she returned to France. In 1923, she married Carl Adalrik Högman, a Swede. Andrée had a real devotion for the poet that her husband came to share. Together, they founded a publishing house, Ophrys, in the south of France where they settled and started a collection of books called *Chitra*. Andrée went to meet Tagore in 1926 when he visited Italy. In May 1930, the couple took an active interest in the exhibition of the poet's paintings in Paris. Andrée wrote a long article of appreciation of the 125 works that were exhibited. Their publishing house had a special collection on India, called *Feuilles de l'Inde* in which appeared several books by Rabindranath and by his nephew, the painter Abanindranath, all of them beautifully illustrated. Andrée predeceased her husband by two years.

Alain Daniélou

Born in an upper middle-class family from Brittanny, Alain Daniélou (1907–94) learnt music, ballet dancing and singing in his youth. In the company of Raymond Burnier, a wealthy Swiss photographer, he travelled all over Asia and visited the poet several times at Santiniketan between 1932 and 1937. A musicologist, he took a great deal of interest in Tagore's songs that he transcribed in European notation, translated and adapted to be played on the piano. Raymond Burnier took a number of photographs of Rabindranath and of the ashram, as well as of temples, especially those of Khajuraho and Konarak. Back in Europe, they set up in Paris the Association des Amis de Tagore to help in collecting funds for Visva-Bharati. In 1939, the two friends settled in Benares where Daniélou learnt Sanskrit, Hindi and classical music. In 1953, he left Benares for Madras where he became the keeper of the manuscripts in the library of the Theosophical Society at Adyar. Later, he joined the Institut Français d'Indologie at Pondicherry where he prepared editions of Sanskrit texts. In 1963, he became the director of the International Institute of Comparative Studies in Music in Berlin. He wrote more than ten books about Indian music, religion and philosophy. He also made numerous recordings for UNESCO. He spent the rest of his life in Italy where he died.

Christine Bossenec

A neighbour of the Daniélou family in Brittanny, she was sent to Santiniketan by Alain in 1935 at the request of the poet. She was put in charge of the Girls' Hostel. She remained there until Tagore's death. Then she became director of the Alliance Française, the French Cultural Centre, in Calcutta. She remained a close friend of the Tagore family. Back in France, she translated from the Bengali, with the help of Kamaleswar Bhattacharya, a volume of Rabindranath's short stories *Le Vagabond et autres histoires*, published in 1962. With Rajeshwari Datta, she translated *Souvenirs d'enfance et de jeunesse*, published in Paris in 1964.

CONCLUSION

It is often said that, in France, if not in Europe as a whole, the poet and the thinker went out of fashion after the 1930s. Tagore's criticism of Western civilisation did not go well with many intellectuals after World War I. His insistence on the spiritual nature of Eastern culture in comparison with European materialism, displeased those who were active in defence of the Christian ideals. After the award of the Nobel Prize, Rabindranath was, once for all, put into the category of a *guru*, placed on a pedestal for veneration, and kept beyond critical evaluation. His physical appearance, so dignified, and the constant presence of devoted disciples, who always surrounded him, contributed to spread the image of an Eastern seer who could only be approached with folded hands. He was no longer seen as a writer, ever exploring new literary forms, but as a prophet whose message was ever the same. The books that were translated in the 1920s, with few exceptions, presented the same inspiration as *Gitanjali*, and the French critics found them repetitive. The English renderings, made by Tagore himself or under his direction, do not read very well. At places, the poet amended his Bengali texts, probably to make them more readily acceptable to a Western public. As for the French translations, apart from those by André Gide and Pierre-Jean Jouve, no other French poet of any repute attempted to translate Tagore's poetry. So there is little of the original beauty in most of the translations.

Another reason for the lack of interest of the French élite for Tagore as a writer can probably be attributed to the great change that took place in literary taste, ten years after Tagore's Nobel Prize, due to the advent of Surrealism. The French literary scene was greatly transformed when André Breton published his first *Manifeste du Surrealisme* in 1924, and the second in 1930. It was not only a change for many writers, it was a revolution. Then, there was World War II, and new trends came out in philosophy and literature. Albert Camus, as an intellectual preoccupied with ethical issues, could have been interested by Tagore's universalistic and humanistic thought, but we do not know whether he ever read him. In Europe in general, and in France in particular, political issues were largely dominant in the years around World War II. Ideological contests between the nationalists influenced by Fascism and the socialists impressed by the Soviet Union did not allow much space for 'Indian spirituality' in intellectual discussions.

One hundred and fifty years after his birth, there is still so much to learn from Tagore and so much to enjoy in reading him. Tagore is indeed a mystic poet, but he is not merely a mystic poet. The range of his talent is astounding. As a novelist and a short story writer, he takes a stand on the burning issues of post-colonial ideology and feminist preoccupations. It is a pity that after a period of great enthusiasm he remained somewhat fossilised in the eyes of the French literary public. Yet, since the last decades of the twentieth century, there has been a return to an appreciation of Indian spirituality among a section of the public. The exhibition of his paintings, *The Last Harvest*, held in Paris in February–March 2012, received the admiring attention of several art critics. The Alliance Française at Chittagong, Bangladesh, and later in several places in India, as also in Paris, exhibited rare photographs of Rabindranath and Santiniketan taken in the 1930s by Alain Daniélou's friend Raymond Burnier. A radio programme on *France Culture* on 11 February 2012 recalled the many sides of Tagore's genius with interviews of several specialists, ex-students of Visva-Bharati, Tagore's university at Santiniketan, and a well-known Rabindra Sangeet singer. The Indian Embassy in Paris organised a *Tagore Evening* with two specialists and the founder-president of the Tagore Sangam, an association that aims at spreading the poet's message through exhibitions of photographs and lectures.

There is still much to discover in the multi-talented man that was Rabindranath Tagore. He was not only a writer of genius who gave his people a literary language of extraordinary brilliance and flexibility, he was also a pedagogue whose original ideas on education may inspire us to this day. He gave his songs and dances to his countrymen, and his paintings to the world, he once said. In his essays, he has for us important messages about issues like tolerance, universalism, respect for nature and faith in reason that liberates one from prejudices and superstitions. Tagore expects us to go beyond the narrow limits of our own self and open up to the multicultural world.

NOTES

My gratitude is due to Professor Udaya Narayana Singh, then Pro-Vice-Chancellor, Visva-Bharati, and to Sri Banerjee, then Project Officer, Rabindra Bhavana, as also to Sri Utpal Mitra, Senior Assistant (Archives), for their kindness and efficiency. I also express my thanks to Elisabeth Vernier, at the BNF, who helped me immensely with her knowledge of the Tagore fund at our *Bibliothèque nationale*.

1. *Rabindra Racanabali*, vol. 10, 392–3.
2. Ibid., 393.

474 France Bhattacharya

474

3. Jean de Rosen, 'Rabindranath Tagore,' *La Revue*, 15 April 1913, 496–503.
4. Ibid.
5. Saint-John Perse, *Œuvres complètes*, 581.
6. Ibid.
7. Ibid., 782.
8. Henry D. Davray, 'Un mystique hindou Rabindranath Tagore,' *Le Mercure de France*, 16 August 1913, 673–98.
9. Gide, *L'Offrande lyrique* suivi de *La corbeille de fruits*, 17–18.
10. Ibid., 19.
11. Gide, *Journal*, vol. 1, 644.
12. 'Kacha et Devayani' is the translation of the poem entitled 'Bidāy Abhishāp.' An English version by Tagore was published in *The Fugitive* (Macmillan, London 1921, 23–36. The title was 'Farewell Curse.' In 1924, it was translated by Edward Thompson and published as 'The Curse of the farewell.'
13. Dutta and Robinson, *Selected Letters of Rabindranath Tagore*. 521–2.
14. Mukherji, *Rabindrajibani*, vol. 3, 60.
15. Lévi, in *The Golden Book of Tagore*, 292–7.
16. 'Cinq poèmes inédits de Tagore, traduits du bengali,' *Yggdrasill Bulletin de la poésie en France et à l'étranger*. Cote BNF microfilm 4622.
17. *Rabindranath Tagore and Romain Rolland Lettres et autres écrits*, 27–8.
18. Ibid., 29.
19. Ibid., 95.
20. Ibid., 101.
21. Ibid., 102–3.
22. Ibid., 50.
23. Ibid., 54.
24. Dutta and Robinson, *The English Writings of Rabindranath Tagore*, vol. 3, 769–71.
25. *Rabindranath Tagore and Romain Rolland Lettres et autres écrits*, 128.
26. Das, ed., *The English Writings of Rabindranath Tagore*, vol. 3, 773.
27. Dutta and Robinson, *Rabindranath Tagore*, 266–76; Das, ed., *The English Writings of Rabindranath Tagore*, vol. 3, 769–76; 991–6.
28. Rolland, *Inde Journal*, 180.
29. Tagore et Rolland, *Lettres et autres écrits*, 152.
30. Ibid., 154.
31. Ibid., 156.
32. Rolland, *Inde Journal*, 153.
33. Ibid., 155–6.
34. Ibid., 184.
35. Ibid., 157.
36. Ibid., 213.
37. *The Golden Book of Tagore*, 293.
38. Rolland, *Inde Journal*, 278.
39. Kripalani, *Rabindranath Tagore*, 365.
40. *The Golden Book of Tagore*, 262.

41. Rolland, *Inde Journal*, 499.
42. Rolland, *Journal de Vézelay*, 643.

WORKS CITED

Rabindra Racanabali [Tagore's Complete Works], 15 vols., Kalikata, Paschim Banga
   Sarkar, 1368 (B.S.).(*Bangla Shon*, i.e., Bengali year, about 594 years behind
   the English calendar)
Anglès, Auguste. *André Gide et le premier groupe de La Nouvelle Revue Française*,
   vol. 3. *Une inquiétante maturité, 1913–14*, Paris: Gallimard, Bibliothèque des
   idées, 1986.
Aronson, Alex. *Rabindranath Through Western Eyes*. Calcutta: Riddhi-India, 1978
   (1st ed. 1943).
Chatterjee, Ramananda, ed. *The Golden Book of Tagore*. Calcutta: Golden Book
   Committee, 1931.
Dutta, Krishna, and Andrew Robinson. *Rabindranath Tagore: The Myriad-Minded
   Man*. London: Bloomsbury, 1995.
——, eds. *Selected Letters of Rabindranath Tagore*. Cambridge: Cambridge University
   Press, 1997.
Gide, André. *L'Offrande lyrique* suivi de *La corbeille de fruits*. Paris: Poésie/Gallimard,
   1963.
——. *Journal*, 2 vols. vol. 1: 1887–1925, vol. 2: 1926–49. Paris: Gallimard, La
   Pléiade 1996. (The quotation is from vol. 1.)
Hay, Stephen N. 'The Development of Tagore's views on the melting of 'East' and
   'West.' *Acts of the 1960 International Seminar* at Moscow.
Hommage de la France à Rabindranath Tagore, Institut de civilisation indienne. Paris:
   de Boccard, 1962.
Kripalani, Krishna. *Rabindranath Tagore: A Biography*. Calcutta: Visva-Bharati, 1980.
Lévi, Sylvain, transl. 'Cinq poèmes inédits de Tagore, traduits du bengali: Le batelier,
   Terre et ciel, Concert mystique, Le Voyageur, Saison des pluies.' *Yggdrasill,
   Bulletin de la poésie en France et à l'étranger*, 25 May 1938. Cote BNF micofilm
   4622.
Moulènes, Anne-Marie. 'Gide et Tagore.' *Etudes*, Paris: June 1969, 851–63.
Mukhopadhyay, Prabhat Kumar. *Rabindrajibani*, 4 vols. Kalikata: Visva-Bharati
   Granthabibhag, 3rd ed. 1401 (B.S.).
Rabindranath Tagore et Romain Rolland Lettres et autres écrits. Cahiers Romain
   Rolland 12, Paris, Albin Michel, 1961.
Rolland, Romain. *Inde Journal, 1915–43*, nouvelle éd. Augmentée. Paris: Albin
   Michel, 1960.
——. *Journal de Vézelay, 1938–44*. Paris: Bertillat, 2012.
Sylvain-Lévi, Mrs D. *Dans l'Inde De Ceylan au Népal*. Paris: Rieder, 6th ed. 1926.
   Reprinted by Editions Kailash, 2008.
Tagore, Rabindranath. *The English Writings of Rabindranath Tagore*. Edited by Sisir
   Kumar Das. 3 vols. New Delhi, Sahitya Akademi, 1996.
Tilby, Michael. 'Gide et l'Angleterre,' Actes du colloque de Londres *Gide et la
   littérature anglaise*, Patrick Pollard (ed.), 22–4 novembre 1985, 67–77.

27

SPAIN AND LATIN AMERICA

SHYAMA PRASAD GANGULY

PREAMBLE AND METHODOLOGY

While discussing the theme of Tagore's reception in the West, our overwhelming occupation for a long time with the English-speaking domain and to a lesser extent with some other European locations had almost completely neglected the Spanish reception. Ironically however, the Indian poet's survival, both qualitatively and quantitatively, has been much more enduring in Spanish-speaking countries as compared to the rest. After the Nobel Prize stimulus the overwhelming Spanish reaction resulted in the publication of more than two dozen Tagore translations from one source alone; more came from other sources, mainly from the English renderings published by Macmillan. However, the present essay concentrates on that expansive narrative of the principle source of the whole reception process which is associated with the work of the great Spanish poet Juan Ramón Jiménez and his wife Zenobia Camprubí. That is to say, this essay chooses to concentrate mainly on one Spanish (Castillian) language author-translator as there is too little space to refer to other translators from the same language or from other regional languages of Spain like Catalan, Galician or the Basque. Although the general framework of Spanish reception will become evident, I am conceptualising the same in terms of a conflictual dynamics that resulted from the very first moment of Tagore's appearance in Spain. Through such a study we can arrive at a plausible hypothesis which is comparative in nature and which demonstrates the mediating operations of authors who are universal in character and whose work has the capacity to negotiate discourses across cultures.[1] Many of the aspects of this reception have still not been adequately dealt with by literary critics especially in relation to its impact on the Spanish poet himself.

TRANSLATORS, WORKS AND PROPAGATORS

Although we are mainly dealing with the reception in Spain, we all know that the Spanish-speaking world covers two separate spatial entities, Spain and Latin America. But that doesn't deny it a unifying focus because of their historically determined interaction. Both these spaces have received Tagore for similar yet different reasons all of which flourished on the foundation of translations. While we have already mentioned the Spanish figure of Juan Ramón Jiménez who is inseparably linked to his wife Zenobia Camprubi's name, another name must be mentioned which is connected with the Latin American reception—Victoria Ocampo from Argentina. The engagements of both from the two sides of the Atlantic were basically responsible for Tagore's initial popularity in the Spanish-speaking world. It would be fair to underline that they were not the first ones to show interest in Tagore nor was the famed *Gitanjali* the first work to be translated in the Spanish-Portuguese domain. Besides, leading literary figures like Gabriela Mistral, Pablo Neruda (Chile), Dulce María Loynaz (Cuba), José Vasconcelos (Mexico), Cecilia Meireles (Brazil) and a series of educationists and reformers from different countries of Latin America showed deep interest in Tagore's creations.[2]

It is significant that Tagore's first book that may have been taken up for translation in the Hispanic world was *One Hundred Poems of Kabir* by the well-known Argentine educationist Joaquín V. González in 1914, an engagement that must have started immediately after the English version of 1914. In Spain even though the first work to be translated by the Jiménez couple was *The Crescent Moon* in 1915, it was the Galician intellectual Vicente Risco who made the first reference to Tagore after reading *The Mystic Way* by Evelyn Underhill in 1912. (see the essay on the Portuguese reaction.) In fact, Risco's first reaction to *The Crescent Moon, The Gardener* and *Sadhana,* published by Macmillan in 1913, was so engaging that he was even nicknamed 'the Spanish Tagore'! He also delivered a lecture on Tagore in late 1913, after the Nobel Prize announcement, at the famed institution called the Ateneo de Madrid. With time, however, Risco got disillusioned with Tagore and critical of his philosophy due to his own progressive inclination towards extreme Nationalism and Fascism.

Almost at the same time as Risco, in August 1913, the well-known author Pérez de Ayala wrote in the magazine *La Tribuna* about the great interest of the English world in *Gitanjali.* But even before the Spanish translations started appearing another prestigious writer, Ramiro de Maeztu, offered a strong criticism of what he understood as the Tagorean philosophy. To him it was something inert and 'sleep-inducing' from his reading of 'The Realization of Life' (*Sadhana*), published in the newspaper *Nuevo Mundo* on 5 March 1914. These views of Risco and Maeztu, may be considered the signal of the dynamics of reception that we are trying to elaborate.[3] Although criticism came from other writers of repute in Spain,[4] as we shall refer to a little further on, it was the outstanding works of the Jiménez couple, combined with the popular perception, that eventually led to the enduring reception.

THE JIMÉNEZ COUPLE AS THE CENTRAL SOURCE: A CASE STUDY OF *GITANJALI*

The Jiménez couple's relationship with Tagore started after Zenobia (who was then unmarried and residing in the USA)) read some of the first English poems of Tagore appearing in *Poetry*, a US periodical. She sent it to Juan Ramón, her poet friend in Spain who was already the leading literary figure there. Apart from its impact on the intimate personal lives of the Spanish couple, this is the beginning of a poetic relationship which resulted in the production of more than twenty works of Tagore in Spanish. Surprisingly, the Spanish couple's first translations were those of *The Crescent Moon* and four other collections, but not of *Gitanjali*. It was only in 1918 that they translated the latter with the title *Ofrenda Lírica* (literally *Lyrical Offering*).

Around the same time as Zenobia's encounter, another important woman of letters from Latin America, the Argentine Victoria Ocampo, also had the occasion to read some of the poems of *Gitanjali* in English translation. Her first reaction is well recorded in many books and articles published in India.[5] The Argentine reaction is included in this volume (see the essay on Argentina in Part 5). The Argentine reaction as a whole, along with the impact of the Jiménez couple's translations, evoked a profound response from many Hispanic poets and writers. Some of the best examples can be found in Jiménez's own poetic reaction to and handling of *Gitanjali* and other collections in the Spanish peninsula, as well as in the philosophical reflections on *Gitanjali*, registered in the work of the notable Argentine poet Eduardo González Lanuza in Latin America.[6] Let us briefly reflect on the phenomenon.[7]

As expected, all the 103 poems in Spanish translated by the Jiménez couple were taken from the English version, dedicated to William Rothenstein, which was a collection of poems translated from the Bengali books *Naivedya*, *Kheya*, *Gitanjali* and several others. In spite of Jiménez's efforts to find a Bengali-knowing person in Spain, all translations had to be inevitably done from the English versions. However, Jiménez did consult André Gide's French translation and it is evident from a comparison of the two that he decided to exercise more liberty than Gide. We may keep in mind the two domains of the Jiménez reception: one, the very corpus of his translation of the *Gitanjali* poems; and two, the interiorisation and enrichment of his own poetic and philosophical ideas as a result of this contact.[8] We shall avoid going into the latter aspect and only touch upon the former.

Let us point to a few details of the first aspect.[9] It may be well to remember that Jiménez himself felt that the English translations suffered from certain weaknesses. Probably this realisation prompted him to exercise some liberty, although on the whole the translations were quite faithful to the English original. Certain slight variances were also due to the differences in the structure of the languages. The high quality attained by Jiménez was of course due to his complete mastery of the genre of prose poems. Let us now cite a couple of representative examples of the operational process and impact of the translations.

A) Original in English:
My song has put off her adornments. She has no pride of dress and decoration. Ornaments would mar our union; they would come between thee and me; their jingling would drown thy whispers.[10]

Translation in Spanish:
Mi canción, sin el orgullo de su traje,
Se ha quitado sus galas para tí
Porque ellas estorbarían nuestra unión,
Y su campanilleo ahogaría nuestros suspiros

A literal translation of the above in English:
My song, without the pride of her dress,
Has put off her adornments for you,
Because they will spoil our union,

And their jingling will drown our sighs (whispers).

Spanish-knowing readers can immediately note some of the changes made by Juan Ramón Jiménez. Two phrases in English have been turned into one in Spanish; the expression 'Para tí' (for you) has been added in Spanish. Even the separating entities like 'thee' and 'me' in English have been combined into one, which is 'nuestra' (our), in Spanish. We can see a similar process in another extract, for example:

B) Original in English:
My poet's vanity dies in shame before thy sight. O master poet, I have sat down at [thy] feet. Only let me make my life simple and straight, like a flute of reed for thee to fill with music.[11]

Translation in Spanish:
   Mi vanidad de poeta muere de vergüenza ante ti, Señor, poeta
   mío. Aquí me tienes sentado a tus pies.
   Déjame solo hacer recta mi vida, y sencilla,
   Como una flauta de caña, para que tu la llenes de música.

The literal translation of the above in English:
   My vanity of poet dies in shame before you,
   Lord, my poet. Here you have made me seated at your feet.
   Let me only make my life straight and simple like
   A flute of cane, so that you may fill it with music.

Here again we can see how Jiménez coins the expression 'Señor, Poeta mío' (Lord, my poet) instead of the original 'O Master poet'. This may not suggest any major liberty, but if we compare his version with that of André Gide the differences become a little more pronounced.

Most importantly, Juan Ramón has tried to maintain his own style and structure without attempting to translate quite literally from the English version. The second paragraph of poem no. 24 of *Gitanjali* starts as 'From the traveller, whose sack of provisions is empty before the voyage is ended ..., remove shame and poverty...' Here Jiménez has moved the last part to the beginning. He has also reduced a few *alankara*s (literally, ornaments, also, figures of speech) and made them as simple as possible. At some places he has introduced some of his favourite expressions like 'no sé qué' (I don't know what). For example, in the poem no. 2 of *Gitanjali*, Tagore's 'one sweet harmony' becomes 'no sé qué dulce melodía.' The indeterminate nature of this Spanish expression introduces an additional dimension into the meaning. It is evident that Jiménez's main objective in taking this liberty was to present Tagore to the Spanish reader in the most acceptable form as a powerful poet. In this process he was able to remove the weariness and lack of variety in the English version. It is not out of place to mention that the reaction of many informed readers of poetry to the Jiménez rendering of Tagore has been as lively as the reaction of many Bengali readers to the original Bengali. In some of the Spanish lines we find the structure closer to Bengali, a feat that must have been achieved intuitively through a process of re-creation as of the English version.

As indicated earlier, the two most prominent examples of the impact were Victoria Ocampo and the Jiménez couple. Ocampo's personal relationship with Tagore grew more intense after she hosted him in Buenos Aires in 1924. She conceived this in terms of the imagery of her being like a seeking tree and Tagore the sky who provided light and nourishment to her.[12] She has also left ample written admission of the impact the *Gitanjali* verses had on her. Similarly, Zenobia mentioned in one of her letters how near to their souls Tagore has been during all these years. The impact of Tagore on Jiménez's poetic work from a certain period is also part of this nearness. His lyrical prologue to the translation of *Gitanjali* is an unparalleled testimony of the process which leads to this impact. This is what the Spanish poet has to say on the subject, in my translation:

> To Rabindranath Tagore
>
> We have tried to give a new body to your great soul, to this book where you wanted to put your full and true soul. Will it move your soul with its blood and its rhythm? Will it beat free, in our body? Tell me how does your soul find itself in this body of ours?
>
> Does our word cast its shadow a bit in your immense joy, in that sandy expanse of joy, kin only of the sea of paradise? Does it shine as the great star and come down from your night of adventures? Can you lift your fire with it to the zenith; can you make your pensive love quieter with it, like the subterranean water?
>
> You are going to be heard in our words—fortune of others—by your God! Will they be enough for your God to come to listen to your soul under our skies? Can you talk to him freely, with our Spanish voice, to a God who is yours, closer, visible, human who listens to beautiful words?[13]

Jiménez saw *Gitanjali* as a dialogue between the poet and his God. This is not a God who is just full of beauty, nor does He only appear to the poet in a human form, but He is one who also loves to listen to beautiful words.

It is this concept of beauty that explains the approach of Jiménez to Tagore. More than anything else he is keen that Tagore's God should descend under the Spanish sky with the same kind of beautiful words as were used in the Bengali poet's own language. This made the dialogue and relationship between the two so endearing, marked by nearness and visibility. Therefore Jiménez is most concerned to create such a body for Tagore's soul in the Spanish domain whose primary element ought to be the beauty of words. Here, as in other translations by him, he is keen to create a dialectic structure between the body and the soul and the new body that he creates in his poetic endeavour must let the Tagorean soul feel free and spontaneous. Through this process Jiménez tries to create for himself the proposed big challenge of a free, interactive and spontaneous flow between Tagore, his God, Jiménez himself and the Spanish readers. In the process we become aware also of the fact that Jiménez enters into the world of Tagore and turns it into a part of his own poetic world. He wouldn't have continued translating and recreating more than 1,200 pages from Tagore's œuvre had there not been an internal compulsion, an illuminating discovery while dealing with 'a truly extraordinary poetry,' as he himself admitted.

THE SPANISH LITERARY AND HISTORICAL AMBIENCE OF THE PERIOD

Around 1915, we know from Jiménez's own words how he felt the need for inspiration from a foreign poetic tradition. Since he was himself the symbol of a literary epoch, this inspiration would naturally spread to the cultural and literary ambience of the period. Francisco Garfias, the biographer of Jiménez, intimately connected to his evolution, said of Tagore:

> The moment of Tagore's appearance in Spain was crucial to Spanish poetry. The great Rubén (Darío) was dead and the neck of the modernist swan had been twisted, although it continued producing agonising songs from second-ranking poets, stiff as they were with their accent on the ante-penultimate syllables and weary of pagan deities. Spain was looking for a more intimate and natural poetry, dismounted from a cold parget or artificial marble pedestal. Unamuno, Machado and Jiménez followed different (expressive) paths and were saying things in different ways. Unamuno with his strong personality was making restive blank verses, full of humanism and tremor. Machado put an unusual truth in his moving poems, but in 1913 when Tagore gets the Nobel Prize and becomes famous worldwide, in Spain there was still no outstanding book of poetry, a book that could open new lyrical paths for future generations. In 1916, in his collection *Diary of a recently married poet* Juan Ramón Jiménez invents a new form which is so different from everything written before. From the *Diary* whose free verse came from the sea, as the poet himself was to say, arose all the later poetry: Leon Felipe, Guillen, Salinas.
>
> But before this poetic event indicated above, Rabindranath, supported by the Nobel Prize and his profusion of books of poetry, essays, dramas, aphorisms, novels and short stories, with his subtle articulations, had already captured the attention of the Spanish reader. After the slanderous spirits, the princesses and Bacchantes (of the Spanish Modernists' poetry) Tagore erupted (in the minds of the Spanish readers) with his sun, his cloud, his half-open flower, his sleeping child and his crescent moon... The poetic material used by Tagore carried the promise of communicating to the ears a poetry full of fragrance of the sunny fields, of sudden springs, of peace, of solitude and a dialogue with God, a poetry that was called upon to shake and freshen up a little the plaster-ridden dry Spanish poetry of

that period. From the Bengali poet, through Juan Ramón, many of the poets of succeeding generations drank an exquisite juice, and from the author of *The Gardener* the Chilean Pablo Neruda learnt ... his first blind and suggestive enumeration of plants and animals which were later to impress his readers so much.[14]

This reception was produced in the midst of the new realities of a post-imperial Spain that was going through major changes and adjustments in the first decades of the twentieth century. Many leading figures of artistic and intellectual life opened up to new mental horizons and experiences of knowledge. Here one notes the presence of the opportunity which historians have called the 'historical inversion' of Spain. Ortega y Gasset joined this wave in favour of the new thought and he saw in Tagore the reaffirmation of the very new humanism and the vision of reality based on what he championed as his philosophy of vital reason. He was perhaps the first Hispanic figure who unfolded a philosophical exegesis of the writings of Tagore. His famous and fascinating epistolary explanation of some of these texts, particularly of *The Crescent Moon* and *The Post Office*, offers an alternative vision of human reality.[15] He convincingly voiced the philosophical significance of the unprecedented vision represented by a child in both works. The celebration of childhood for him constituted an eternal human dimension with Tagore appearing as the unsurpassed representative of a universal spirit that can relate the child's aspirations and dreams with every individual's identity. Ortega's illuminating analysis of the child protagonist Amal in *The Post Office*—'a child that all of us carry within us'—aimed at highlighting the importance of the Tagorean discourse across cultures. He raised him to Biblical proportions and qualified him to be an 'Oriental David' who need not be defined but read, to experience how he breaks open the closed door of all sensibilities. This is akin to the creative dialogue sustained by Jiménez at the literary level in his 'colofones líricos', which was composed in response to the different works by Tagore which he translated with Zenobia.

We have referred to the fertile ground that this period of Spanish history presented during the initial decades of the twentieth century as far as the reception of external currents was concerned. This historical reality in Spain certainly contributed to the positive reception of Tagore. Known as the 'silver period,' the years between 1900 and 1936 represent a new impulse for literary, artistic and scientific movements. The national culture also acquired an intense stimulus of self-criticism and evaluation. While regional cultures got a push, there was a reformist and liberal orientation through an institutionalised attention by the central government.

One of the major influences on the first nucleus of writers of the twentieth century was the German philosopher Karl Christian Friedrich

Krause (1781–1832) whose ideas promoted the identification of a national mentality. Krause's rationalism and new humanism, as well as the *Free Institution of Learning* created earlier for promoting the reformist spirit in all spheres, opened the doors for the reception of philosophies, movements and cultural tendencies from other spaces. The fact that the 'veneration of the child, which in other words meant respect for the future', was to become an accepted objective explains why the Tagorean evocation of the child had so much of attraction for the Spaniards.[16]

The institutionalist spirit, aided by the leading intellectuals of the time, promoted the creation of various institutions that propagated the expression and free exchange of ideas. Education and national questions became the starting point for many insightful essays by thinkers and artistes. For example, the Residencia de Estudiantes and the Residencia de Señoritas were two typical centres highlighting this concern. In the open atmosphere of these institutes where intellectuals, students, writers met, the first translations of Tagore were presented and discussed by Zenobia and Juan Ramón Jiménez, who was the principal figure in the Residencia de Estudiantes. The two other outstanding figures who participated during such presentations were Ortega y Gasset and Gregorio Marañon.

CRITICAL DIMENSIONS AND RESPONSES

The most critical reactions came from equally well-established figures who found the message and content of the first translations from the Jiménez couple unacceptable mainly due to ideological implications of the Tagorean discourse. According to them Tagore should not gain preference over the dominant poetic or realist-naturalist narrative tradition of Spain. Against the furore raised by these voices, indirectly aimed at Jiménez, the latter and many others stood firm. Jiménez's own search for new canons at a particular moment of his poetic career, his creativity supported by the gradual expansion of reader response to their translations, drowned those criticisms after some time. He himself was known to have reservations about certain 'defects' of the mystics of the Orient. No less significant was the position taken by those intellectuals and pedagogues of the Spanish Catholic Church who were deeply impressed by Tagore's ideas, experiences and writings on education.

Well-known writers like Emilia Pardo Bazán and Eugenio d'Ors and some critics and journalists led this critique. In one of her last pieces Emilia Pardo Bazán, an exponent of the naturalist movement, echoed the pre-existing Western valorisation of the so-called passive philosophy of life of the East projected in Tagore's work. According to her, Tagore belonged to a race frequently given to 'dreaming with eyes open,' a race which promoted the idea of 'beatified nirvana.' By that she probably meant a passive surrender to the idea of deliverance from suffering made possible by a belief in *moksha*. That is why India, according to her, could not occupy the place it deserved with its philological aristocracy, its ethnographic purity, nobility and territorial expansion that its splendorous nature had given her.[17] This longish piece was written for a popular newspaper, probably to stem the popularity of the translations whose sales had multiplied exponentially. This popularity is also reflected in the correspondence between the Jimenez couple on the subject. Such a reaction was also due to the gradual disappearance of the prevailing movements of naturalism-realism and Spanish 'modernismo' which failed to set guidelines for the future. Bazán insisted that there was nothing new worth emulating in the mystic content of Tagore's religious philosophy. They were 'subjective emotions converted into divinity.' In that respect Bazán takes recourse to what the French philosopher and social theorist Michel Foucault conceptually calls 'comparison of measures.' According to this all analysis is done to establish relations of equality or superiority in place of doing comparison of orders. The latter would exclude any judgemental pre-eminence of one over the other between the objects compared. In Foucault's terms she was establishing hierarchical canons of primary and secondary authors, strong and weak cultures. While Jiménez and others like Ortega y Gasset saw a clear need for dialogue across cultures and a multicultural understanding of differences, Emilia Pardo Bazán stridently compared the mysticism of Tagore with that of Spanish mystics who according to her were never resigned to passive meditation because they were people of an ardent and active spirit and very sure and concrete in their thinking. She rejected the universality of the poetics of Tagore, saying that it was pure emotion and did not need any mystic adornments. One notes in Tagore's works, according to her, a type of dialogue with someone invisible and idealised. His poetry 'escapes from the soul in the same way as water from the basket.'[18]

This accusation of dilution and vagueness can be contrasted with Juan Ramón's exuberance about the lyrical precision of Tagore to whom, many years later, he devoted some very telling verses. Jiménez who has a famous poem where he asks a Supreme Intelligence to bestow on him 'the exact name of things', remembered Tagore with the following verses:

Where is the word heart
the word that softens the hard world with love
the word that gives forever—at this moment
the strength of a child
the resistance of a rose.[19]

Similarly, these other verses, perhaps the first draft of a dedicatory poem, which recall for Jiménez the close relation between life and verse, connected with his vital experience during his Tagore phase:

Luz de la atención
(Rabindranath Tagore)

Verses, pure chalices
It is there where I pour my blood
Without a single drop being wasted,
It is there where my life becomes new
Not spilled in vain for things;
Verses, loving hands   (arms)

Will keep forever, in fullness
the soul of my hands   (arms)

—lovers

of my arms
my legs and my wings.

This Spanish poet saw in Tagore the example to follow in his own search for the exact expression or name of things through words.

Emilia Pardo Bazán's criticism is perfectly explicable. The subversive potential of the vision of reality derived from another epistemological construction posed a threat to Western codes, especially in the epoch of transition. The acceptance of Tagore by a large number of Spanish readers obliged Pardo Bazán to warn them to give creditability only to those aspects of Tagore's work that were based on some measure of reality close to its Western notion. And in this sense Maeterlinck was found to be closer to a poet from the Orient. The West did not need to imitate the excessive sentimentalism and the timid orientation which was represented by the 'pillow of feathers' on which Jiménez was accused by a writer like Eugenio d'Ors to have gone to sleep; in d'Ors's view, the pillow needed to be shaken up.

We must underline the fact that the example of Tagore's reception and controversies do reflect to a large extent the conflict of ideas in Spain during the first quarter of the twentieth century. Amid alarm caused by warmongering that loomed large ever since World War I, Tagore appeared to be a messiah to many. He was seen as the harbinger of an epochal message for all humanity, but most relevant for Europe. This dimension is evident in the assessment of another great Spanish poet of the time, Antonio Machado. In one of his poems dedicated to the Indian poet, cited here only in part, he tellingly puts it thus:

Rabindranath, your heart has been heard
in this peninsula of the West.
On this autumn eve when rain clinks
on the bamboos and showers spread over
your Bengali sky, war thunders
and the river of life is becoming stormy
in the dark Europe.
Your book comes to this bleeding Europe
Clamouring with war and trouping soldiers—
Like the story of Gautama that arrived one day.
In this Europe, on the white bull,
Shiva mounts, military crests
are nothing but rude wild promises,
the war would spread through the seven seas.[20]

Machado, one of the finest poets of the famed Spanish Generation of '27, of no less literary merit than Juan Ramón Jiménez, was not only overwhelmed by the creative output of Tagore, but also enthusiastically welcomed Tagore's message after reading the first translations between 1915 and 1918. This is represented by the expression 'your book' referring to *The Crescent Moon*, *The Gardener* and *Gitanjali*.

PLAYS, PEDAGOGY, PRESS: A BRIEF CONSIDERATION

Tagore symbolised the pull of contrary forces. On the one hand, his works gave rise to raging controversies among writers; on the other, oblivious of these controversies, popular reception gave him instant approval. This is surprising, considering the limited nature of knowledge of his oeuvre. The total number of works translated by the Jiménez couple was around twenty, all done in the first few years, between 1914 and 1922; of these, eight were plays. *The Post Office* and *The King and the Queen* were staged in the famed theatre La Princesa of Madrid in 1920 and at Hotel Ritz in 1921 respectively to full houses, to wide acclaim. But the shows were never repeated. They were praised for their universal symbolism and idealism.[21]

It is difficult to avoid lamenting the cancelled visit of Tagore to Spain,[22] for, among other things, it stalled the staging of his play *Sacrifice* which was being rehearsed in honour of his visit. Incidentally, Federico García Lorca would have acted as Jaisingha. This opportunity in the history of Indo–Spanish literary relations would have not only encouraged the immediate unfolding of Tagore's other dimensions but it also would have made him conscious of the great Spanish literary tradition.

It was only in later decades that the initial impulse created the ground for further exploration in the area of his philosophy, short stories and education. Some of the unpublished translations by the Jiménez couple also came out later.[23] In 1961, Jiménez Martos wrote on Tagore as a sociologist, political thinker and essayist.[24] One of the best pieces on Tagore's creative pedagogy was written by Ramón Castelltort in 1964.[25] In fact, Spanish newspapers too, whether after Tagore's death or to commemorate his birth or death anniversaries, kept publishing eulogies, as well as analytical articles on the poet, his life, work and relevance.[26]

SOME REFLECTIONS FROM LATIN AMERICA

Looking across the Atlantic, the Chilean poets Gabriela Mistral and Pablo Neruda received Tagore in a very positive light. However, César Vallejo (Peru) and Jorge Luis Borges (Argentina) were known for their adverse opinions.[27]

Mistral, after a careful study of the Indian poet came to the conclusion that Tagore belonged to a culture which 'had the ability to completely transform knowledge into a spiritual experience.' She was deeply influenced by the fact that Tagore happened to be that 'rare poet who wields the knowledge of all sciences and yet, as Maragall would say, sings like a shepherd.'[28]—'[He] is a poet of spontaneous inspiration that transcends all demands of artificiality of reason and technique.' In her view,

> In the West, the notion of culture operated in a crude manner where the instrument is too heavily felt. The *fabrication*, as seen by Abbé Bremond, is so visible that the reader of, for example, a poem, even though not an expert, clearly sees the manipulation and tastes it and even feels the weight of a dictionary. The poet appears to be a lamppost fitted with cables and lights. In the eyes of the reader he is like a chemist with his small potions of salts and alcohol. But the chemists of literature smile at being told about this deceit. Because they are firm in their belief that everything is chemistry. Nature as well as the fruit derived without strong blows for sagacious pruning is just another word for *chemistry*. Certainly so. Perhaps Tagore also works laboriously to create lines like Valéry does, but one is immediately transported to the feel of an elevating faculty...

This faculty Mistral calls *gracia*. It 'gives the illusion of not being conditioned by reasoned will but by a happy consent.' In other words, Tagore is an inspired poet which is the test for all great poets in Mistral's view. When she had a personal encounter with Tagore during his visit to the USA. she saw the 'burning fire' of inspiration in his eyes and a creative irony in his looks, not captured by any of the images portraying him as mystic in his misleading robes.

This *grace* in poetry that Mistral talked about was responsible for Neruda's fascination too, a perspective which has still not been analysed. He appropriated Tagore in his first great adventure in verse on the theme of love[29]. Whatever the critics may hold against him regarding plagiarism, Neruda's paraphrasing of a significant Tagore poem using deep symbolism and felicity of expression is the true voice of Neruda's soul on the theme of love. The particularities are reconciled into a universal, identifying both the poets as belonging to the same domain of thought. This is so although Neruda may have erred in understanding or imitating some words while translating Tagore's English version. For example, what is 'haunt' in Tagore becomes 'hunt' in Neruda! One has often missed the point that Neruda had a fascination for Tagore's ethos from his school teacher who happened to be Gabriela Mistral. Many critics have dismissed this coincidence of poems as a simple inclination to imitate a foreign poet. But the vehemence of the criticism against Neruda as a plagiarist was only an expression of the unwillingness of poets like Huidobro and his friends to accept Tagore's influence on the kind of avant-garde modernity they were trying to introduce in Chilean and Latin-American poetry.[30]

Well-known authors like Cesar Vallejo and Jorge Luis Borges were inclined to take a stand against Tagore. Vallejo thought he was a courtesan poet serving the British masters and Borges opined that he was too metaphoric, indirect and mellifluous. But when Tagore's socio-political ideas on Nationalism were revealed, Borges did not mince words to analyse the importance of Tagore's thoughts while assessing how individual human freedom and liberty was put at stake by the repressive nation state whose basic idea evolved from Europe.

The type of Nationalism that evolved in Europe in the first quarter of the twentieth century, inevitably leading to Fascism, which Borges attacked, considered the ideas of pacifism and universal love championed by Tagore with great scepticism. Its nationalists who believed it natural that history is created through bullets, could not understand how human realities may be contemplated in the light of intuitive happiness leading to peace, liberty and love for the other.

AFTER 1941 AND THE LASTING IMPACT OF *GITANJALI*

This negative view of Tagore remained for a long time in Spain, so much so that after Tagore's death a noted Spanish journalist, Juan Aparicio, contrasted his long life with a flower of which 'not a petal remains.' A soldier, however, lives for an instant like an arrow in the middle of great action.[31] Tagore's pacifist ideas were considered as carriers of a salient virus of an antipatriotic universalism.

These apprehensions during the consolidation of Fascism in Spain do not surprise us, but what does surprise is the survival of Tagore in the face of such hard-hitting criticism. The Spanish public which received and spread Tagore's works seemed to have judged him with other, positive, criteria. Contributing factors were literary merit, spiritual vigour rooted in worldly human realities and the cultural significance presented through the Spanish versions by the Jiménez couple and thereafter by many other translators. These more recent versions are the responses of a whole group of humanist writers, poets and thinkers who were keen to delve into the true nature of human identity across cultures.

There are studies that show how many of the symbols used by Juan Ramón Jiménez are close to Indian religious thought. In this context, the Spanish scholar Seferino Santos Escudero has shown how Juan Ramón vacillated for a long time on whether to make the idea of a metaphysical presence, the divine, the principal theme of his work.[32] But it was Tagore who gradually changed Jiménez's mind and helped him to imbibe the essence of a religion that is also human. No other work better than *Gitanjali* would have helped him in this process of transformation.

One point has been repeatedly mentioned in the introductory studies of many other translations of *Gitanjali*. In his remarks for a newly translated version, Guzman Coto Mir pointed out how Tagore conceived his work as 'an intimate expansion of his soul' with poems which not even the master poet thought would be of any major interest to other readers beyond himself. Mir went on to say that certainly in Spain, but also in the rest of the West everyone 'read with wonder and increasing admiration these simple transparent verses full of transcendental lyricism that express the Indian genius's ecstasy in the face of nature' and how 'he transcends the same to achieve a supreme spiritual exaltation.'[33]

In a prologue written for another collection of Tagore translations by Jorge Rotner, eminent historian F. L. Cardona emphasised how *Gitanjali* is an 'eternal dialogue between Thee and I, God and the human soul. But its pages don't lead one to the feeling of any static piety nor an invitation to Nirvana. Such a creation cannot come only on account of the infinite love for nature but also for all creatures of the creation, expressed with the authentic soul of a child not contaminated by life.' We can see how in the Hispano–American ambit authors have tried to project the human quality of Tagore's spirituality. Cardona reiterates the same when he says, '[In] *Gitanjali* we discover a mystic pantheism where God, in spite of being one with the world, possesses also personal attributes felt by those who believe in him throughout the concrete act of adoration.'.[34] Tagore's expansive reach in capturing the nuances of human experiences and yearnings vis-à-vis life, death and beyond has been as much a source of wonder for a great number of Hispanic readers as for many of us.

It is not uncommon to find younger poets of successive generations showing familiarity with some or the other works of Tagore. One poet, writing in 1985, has even dreamed of 'walking in the footsteps' of the poetic word and language inherited from Tagore, considered as the origin of the eternal.[35] But it was his principal translator Jiménez, who considered Tagore as the 'eternal honeycomb' who remains the singular example of a deep reception process. This process is perhaps best captured in Jiménez's own poem 'Rosa del mar' from the collection *Diario de un poeta recién casado*. It is a process which enables him to enter Tagore's world only to come out enriched. Two of the lines of the poem say:

The white moon takes the sea
from the sea and gives it back to the sea.[36]

The visionary similarities of both poets expressed in the search for truth and beauty may have produced this unique response. It is this perception and deep understanding of creativity on the part of the Jiménez couple which evoked such a response. It goes beyond the mystic, religious or ideological labels defining the identities of the two different cultures.

CONCLUSION

All this may be valuable data to assess the history of Tagore's reception in Spain and Latin America. But what about our own times? Even though Tagore editions may have proliferated commercially after the copyright restrictions were withdrawn in 2001, are new generations reading or rediscovering Tagore? In a recent Tagore Festival held in Spain at different universities one co-chairperson of a session asked this question. I found out that the youth was not reading literature anyway, not even by their own master poets or prose writers. In this situation the plausible way to make Tagore relevant is to recreate him and his unknown dimensions in new forms. The outstanding British Tagore scholar, William Radice, suggested in a recent article, where he admirably compares Jiménez's and Yeats's approaches to Tagore translation, that the Indian poet has to be rediscovered by the Spanish (and Western) public by bringing him out of the crystal box created by Jiménez and adapting his creations to modern artistic expressions.[37] Is William Radice aiming at an 'Indian Tagore' rather than an 'international' one? For the more intellectually and culturally inclined it may be more rewarding to build on the affinity in the trans-cultural variables of the Indian and Hispanic traditions. One could, for example, inquire into the optimism implicit in the so-called mystic and the religious lyrics offered by Tagore. They contain a vision and images of a lively and creative future which is yet full of the experience of profound suffering. Why does that have a special appeal to people from the Hispanic mystic tradition? This vision was not available in the religious poetry of Europe signalled by the 'Wasteland' of T. S. Eliot. It is no mere coincidence that the dialectic impulse which provided the necessary dynamism for Tagore's survival in Spain equally characterises Tagore's life which went through the very deep experiences of joy and suffering.

UNESCO in its biennial project (2010–12) looked for highlighting the concept of the 'reconciled universal' by choosing to examine the affinity in the thoughts of Tagore, Neruda and Aimé Cesaire (the francophone poet from Martinique in the Caribbean). This is a stupendous project for reiterating the international relevance of Tagore today. But for all future engagements with Tagore's creative oeuvre it may be necessary for interested Hispanic scholars, even with collaborative efforts, to enter the world of Tagore through Bengali, the language of his original expression.

NOTES

1. This essay is based on some of my previous writings and talks on the subject of Tagore and the Hispanic world. The three books with me as co-author or co-editor mentioned under 'Works Cited' are specially relevant. One may also refer to my presentations in triennial Congresses of the International Association of Hispanists (cf. website of AIH): 'Los colofones líricos de Juan Ramón Jiménez a las obras de Tagore: una aproximación a la recepción y repercusión transcultural' (Barcelona 1989), 'Dinámica conflictual en la recepción de Tagore en España' (Birmingham, 1995); also (yet to be published), 'Beyond the Transatlantic Matrix: Tagore and Latin America' (in Conference Latin America–India: Literature and Culture, Lateinamerica Institut, Freie University, Berlin, 2011).
2. Essays in this volume which deal with Mexico, Costa Rica, Argentina and Brazil provide more information.
3. For a fairly detailed perspective on the entire gamut of reactions to Tagore and his works in the Spanish Press, see 'La recepción de Tagore en la prensa española' by Emilia Cortés Ibáñez in *Redescubriendo a Tagore*, ed. Ganguly & Chakravarty, 264–87
4. Ganguly, 'Tagore Criticism in Spain', in *The Kindred Voice*, ed. Ganguly, 58–63.
5. For example: (*i*) Sankha Ghosh, *Ocampor Rabindranath* (in Bengali), fourth revised edition, Calcutta: Dey's Publishing, 1989; (*ii*) Ketaki Kushari Dyson, *In Your Blossoming Flower Garden*, New Delhi: Sahitya Akademi,

1988; (*iii*) Embassy of Argentina in India and Susnigdha Dey, ed., *Victoria Ocampo, An Exercise in Indo–Argentine Relationship*, Delhi: B. R. Publishing Corporation, 1992.

6. Lanuza, 'La poesía de Rabindranath Tagore,' in *Sur* (Revista Bimestral: Rabindranath Tagore, 1861–1961, (Centenario), Buenos Aires, mayo-junio 1961.

7. It is certainly true that the maximum number of translations done in Spanish have been of *Gitanjali*. Besides Juan Ramón Jiménez and his wife Zenobia Camprubí's version we have seen, for example, translations by Abel Alarcón (Madrid, 1917) Pedro Requeña Lagarreta (Mexico, 1918), Ventura Gascól (Barcelona, 1936; Buenos Aires 1944); Enrique López Castellón, Madrid, 1981, 1984). Similar is the case with *The Post Office, The Gardner, The Crescent Moon, The Fruit-Gathering* and *Gora*.

8. For a fairly detailed discussion on this aspect, see Sisir Kumar Das, 'Jiménez and Tagore' in *The Kindred Voice*, ed. Ganguly, 41–57.

9. I cite this example from Kim Hyun Chang, 'Tagore in Spanish' in *The Kindred Voice*, ed. Ganguly, 18–40.

10. *Gitanjali* (part of Poem no. 7) as reproduced in *The English Writings of Tagore*, ed. Sisir Kumar Das, vol. 1, 44, New Delhi: Sahitya Akademi, 1994.

11. As cited in Note no. 9

12. This is evident in a handwritten text on the theme drafted by Ocampo, available with the writer of this essay.

13. Translated by me in collaboration with Sisir Kumar Das from the original in Spanish appearing in Zenobia Camprubí and Juan Ramón Jiménez, *Rabindranaz Tagore: Obra Escojida* (traducción de Zenobia Camprubí de Jiménez), Aguilar, Madrid, 1955 (11th edition, 4th reprint, 1981), 99.

14. 'Rabindranath Tagore en español', *Recuerdos*, 1961, Plaza y Janés, Barcelona, 9–10. Translations of this and subsequent quotations, originally in Spanish, are mine.

15. See 'Estafeta Romántica, un poeta indo', published in three numbers in *El Sol*, from Jan. to Mar. 1918, also reproduced in *Rabindranaz Tagore, Obra escogida*, Madrid, Aguilar, 1981 with the title 'Epistolario liminar.'

16. This assertion supposedly of the Spanish philosopher Miguel de Unamuno had a wide impact, including among the Church.

17. 'Un poco de crítica: la obra de Tagore', *ABC* 4 de mayo de 1921, 3.

18. E. Pardo Bazán, ibid. (Note no. 17)

19. *Luz de la Atención,* El observatorio, Madrid, 1986.

20. My translation of a fragment of the poem 'A Rabindranath Tagore' cited from *Tutte le Poessie e Prose Scelte* ed. with an introduction by Giovanni Caravaggi, Arnoldo Mondadori Editore S. A., Milano, 2010. Caravaggi also explains the constituents of the expression 'your book' amongst other references.

21. See 'La recepción de Tagore en la prensa española' by Emilia Cortés Ibañez in *Redescubriendo a Tagore*, ed. Ganguly and Chakravarty, 264–87.

22. The story of this cancelled visit is by now available in details in various writings like Das and Ganguly, ed., *Saswata Mouchak*; Kim Hyun Chang, 'Tagore in

Spanish' in Ganguly, ed., *The Kindred Voice*; José Paz Rodriguez, 'Tagore and his Relationship with the Latin World' in *The Visva-Bharati Quarterly*, 10, No. 1, April–June 2001, Santiniketan, India.

23. For example, Jiménez and Camprubí, *Entrevisiones de Bengala*.
24. 'Rabindranath, meditaciones,' *La Estafeta Literaria*, 15 November 1961.
25. *Educadores, Revista de la Federación Española de Religiosos de Enseñanza*, No. 28, Mayo–Junio 1964, 481–510.
26. We can mention some important ones here: 'Report on Rabindranath Tagore' in *ABC*, Madrid, 8 August 1941;'Cuando la voz ha sido escuchada', Francisco Montero Galvache, *ABC*, 7 August, 1943; 'Vida, Obra y Pensamiento de Rabindranath Tagore', Juan Roger Riviere, *Estafeta Literaria*, Madrid, 15 May 1961, 12–15; 'Recordando a Tagore', S. P. Ganguly, *Culturas/Diario 16*, núm, 311, Galicia/Madrid, 14 July 1991, 4–5.
27. Latin American countries which have separate essays in this volume, viz. Argentina, Brazil, Costa Rica and Merxico, are excluded from our purview.
28. This and the subsequent citations from Gabriela Mistral have been taken from Gabriela Mistral's essay 'La Gracia en la Poesía' included in the section 'Chile y Países del Plata' in *Vanguardia Latinoamericana: Historia, Crítica y Documentos* (Tomo 5), ed. Mendoza Teles, Gilberto and Muller-Bergh, Klaus, Edición Iberoamericana, Madrid, 2009.
29. The most popular of Neruda's works, his second collection, *Veinte poemas de amor y una canción desesperada*, published in 1924.
30. I cannot avoid the temptation of referring to how a modern Bengali poet, Shakti Chattopadhyay, attempted a reverse translation into Bengali from the Nerudian Spanish version. One critic has done a comparative study of the three versions to show how Shakti's expression captures elements of modernity as compared to the romantic notions of Tagore and Neruda. See Samir Sengupta, 'Kabi Shakti', *Patralekha*, Kolkata, September 2010.
31. Aparicio, 'La saeta y la flor', *Pueblo*, 1908–41.
32. Seferino Santos Escudero, *Símbolo y Dios en el último Juan Ramón Jiménez*, Gredos, Madrid, 1975.
33. *Rabindranath Tagore: Gitanjali, La Luna Nueva, El Jardinero*, translation and inroductory notes by Guzman Cota Mir, Zeus, Barcelona, 1959.
34. *Rabinranath Tagore: Obras escogidas*, translation by Jorge Rotner, Edicomunicaciones, S. A. Barcelona, 1999.
35. This is the subject matter of the very first poem of José López Martínez in his collection *En el mar riguroso de la muerte,* Award winning book published by the Rabindranath Tagore Cultural Association and Embassy of India, Madrid, 1985. This award which was discontinued in the late eighties has been renewed by the Spanish Instituto de Indológico in 2012.
36. Cited by Sisir Kumar Das, Note no. 7, 51.
37. William Radice, 'The Wakening of Shiva: How Rabindranath Tagore Became Global (and Spanish) and How He Could Become Global (and Spanish) Again,' in *The Kindred Voice*, ed. Ganguly, 107–21.

Works Cited

Works on Tagore

Camprubí, Zenobia, and Juan Ramón Jimenez. *Rabindranaz Tagore*: Obra Escojida (compilation of all their translations of Tagore's works into Spanish). Madrid: Aguilar, 1981 (11ᵗʰ edn., 4ᵗʰ reprint).

Castelltort, Ramón. *Rabindranath Tagore*. Madrid: EPESA, 1964.

Das, Sisir Kumar, and Shyama Prasad Ganguly. *Saswata Mouchak: Tagore o Spain*. Calcutta: Papyrus, 1987; reprinted, Kolkata: Dey's Publishing, 2011.

Ganguly, Shyama Prasad, ed. *The Kindred Voice: Reflections of Tagore in Spain and Latin-America*. CSPILAS, JNU, New Delhi, 2011.

Ganguly, Shyama Prasad, and Indranil Chakravarty, eds. *Redescubriendo a Tagore*. Mumbai: Amaranta, 2011.

Gascó Contell, Emilio. *Rabindranath Tagore*. Madrid: EPESA, 1970.

Santos Escudero, Seferino. *Símbolo y Dios en el último Juan Ramón Jiménez*. Madrid: Gredos, 1975.

Works by Tagore (Chronologically)

(This bibliography is based on the lists provided by the author and José Paz Rodríguez in the books: Ganguly and Chakravarty, eds., *Redescubriendo a Tagore*, 368–70, and Ganguly, ed., *The Kindred Voice,* 87–71; 211–14. It summarises the translations of Tagore which appeared in different Spanish-speaking countries. Hence it is relevant for the contributions on Latin American countries, except Brazil, in this volume.)

1914: *Anochecer de Julio* (July Evening), Zenobia Camprubí and Juan Ramón Jiménez, henceforth ZC & JRJ (Spain) in *La Lectura*, Revista de ciencias y artes, num. 159, marzo, 272–6.

1915: *Cien poemas de Kabir* (*One Hundred Poems of Kabir*), Joaquín V. González (Argentina), first published by the journal Atenea, La Plata. Argentina, 1914; ZC & JRJ (Spain), 1965.

–do–: *La luna nueva* (Poemas de niños) (*The Crescent Moon*). Madrid: Imprª. Clásica Española, trad. Zenobia Camprubí Aymar; A Valls I Valls (Spain) 1937; María de Quadras (Spain) 1980; Montserrat Tobella (Spain) 1984; Mauro Armiño (Spain) 1985

1917: *El cartero del Rey* (*The Post Office*), ZC & JRJ (Spain); Andres Bais (Chile) 1981; Fernando de Mier West (Spain) 1981.

–do–: *El Jardinero* (*The Gardener*), Madrid: Imprª. de Fortanet, trad. ZC & JRJ (Spain); María de Quadras (Spain) 1937: Ministerio de. Educación Nacional (Colombia) 1973; Enrique Lopéz Castellón (Spain) 1982, Mauro Armiño (Spain) 1985.

–do–: *Gitanjali*, Abel Alarcón (Spain); ZC & JRJ (Spain) 1918; Pedro Requena Legarreta (Mexico) 1918; Ventura Gasól (Spain) 1936, (Argentina) 1944; (along with La luna nueva and El Jardinero); Palma de Mallorca: Olañeta, trad. Agustin López y María Tabuyo.

–do–: *Oraciones líricas* (*Gitanjali*). Madrid: Impr^a. de M. García y G. Saez, trad. Abel Alarcón.

–do–: *Pajajaros perdidos* (*Stray Birds*), ZC & JRJ (Spain); as *Aves errantes*, H. L. Charles (Argentina) 1953.

–do–: *La Cosecha* (*Fruit-Gathering*), ZC & JRJ (Spain) Madrid; Tip^a de Fortanet; *La Cosecha de la fruta*, Muzzio Saenz-Peña (Argentina) 1917; Enrique López Castellón (Spain) 1984; Mauro Armiño (Spain) 1985. Fernando de Mier West (Spain) 1982

1918: *Ciclo de la primavera* (*Cycle of Spring*). Madrid: Tipografía de Fortanet, trad. Zenobia Camprubí Aymar; Enrique López Castellón (Spain) 1982.

–do–: *El asceta* (*Sanyasi*). Madrid: Tip. Lit. de Angel Alcoy, trad. Zenobia Camprubí Aymar.

–do–: *El rey y la reina* (*Raja o Rani*). Madrid: Tip. Lit. de Angel Alcoy, trad. Zenobia Camprubí Aymar.

–do–: *Malini*. Madrid: Tip. Lit. de A. Alcoy, trad. Zenobia Camprubí Aymar; Enrique López Castellón (Spain) 1982.

–do–: *Rabindranath Tagore, poeta Bengaíi*, (Tagore, the Bengali Poet), Joseph Maria Batista y Roca (Spain).

1919: *Chitra* (*Chitrangada*), ZC & JRJ (Spain). Madrid: Impr^a. de Fortanet, trad. Zenobia Camprubí Aymar; Heramba Lal Gupta (México) 1919; Fernando de Mier West (Spain) 1981; Enrique López Castellón (Spain) 1984.

–do–: *El rey del salón oscuro* (*The King of the Dark Chamber*). Madrid: Impr^a. de Fortanet, trad. Zenobia Camprubí Aymar; Enrique López Castellón (Spain) 1984.

–do–: *Meditaciones* (Meditations), Madrid: Escelicer, trad. Emilio Gascó Contel (Spain).

–do–: *Morada de paz* (*Santiniketan*), ZC & JRJ (Spain).

–do–: *Regalo de amante* (*Lover's Gift*), ZC & JRJ (Spain); as *Present de enaimorat* (Spain) 1985; with *Tránsito, La fugitiva* and *Cosecha*, ZC & JRJ (Spain), 1948.

–do–: *Sacrificio* (*Bisarjan*). Madrid: Tip. Lit. de A. Alcoy, trad. Zenobia Camprubí Aymar; Enrique López Castellón (Spain) 1984.

–do–: *Santiniketan-Morada de Paz*. Madrid: Impr^a. de Fortanet, trad. Zenobia Camprubí Aymar.

1920: *Mashi y otros cuentos* (*Mashi and Other Stories*), Madrid: Impr^a. de Fortanet, trad. ZC & JRJ (Spain).

–do–: *Tránsito* (*Crossing*). Madrid: Tip. de Fortanet, trad. Zenobia Camprubí Aymar; María de Quadras (Spain), 1962, Enrique López Castellón (Spain) 1984.

1921: *La hermana mayor y otros cuentos*. (Didi and other stories). Madrid: Impr^a. Maroto, trad. Zenobia Camprubí Aymar.

1922: *La fujitiva*. (*The Fugitive*). Madrid: Talleres Poligráficos, trad. Zenobia Camprubí Aymar.

–do–: *Las piedras hambrientas y otros cuentos* (*Hungry Stones and Other Stories*). México: ed. Cultura, in Spain 1st ed.: 1955. Madrid: Afrodisio Aguado, trad. Zenobia Camprubí Aymar.

1928: *La escuela del papagayo y alocuciones de Shantiniketan.* (*Tota Kahini* and *Santiniketan Speeches*). Barcelona: Cernates, trad. Guillermo Gossé.

1931: *Cartas a un amigo* (*Letters to a Friend*). Barcelona: Atenas A. G., Nicolás M Martínez Amador.

–do–: *La religión de hombre* (*Religion of Man*). Madrid: M. Aguilar, trad. R. Cansinos-Asséns, 1960.

–do–: *Jardinillos de Navidad y Año Nuevo* (Christmas Gardens and New Year). Madrid: A. Jiménez, trad. Zenobia Camprubí Aymar.

1936: *Verso y prosa para niños* (Verse and Prose for Children), (Cuba); ZC & JRJ (Spain) 1937.

1942: *Las quintaesencias* (Quintescences). Madrid: Ediciones La Gacela, trad. Pedro López Ferret.

–do–: *Sadhana, el sentido de la vida* (*Sadhana*, the Meaning of Life), Sady Concha y Aliro Carrasco (Argentina); along with *Poemas de Kabir* (*One Hundred Poems of Kabir*), Emilio Gascó Contell (Spain) 1957.

1945: *Amor, versiones, paráfrasis y recreaciones* (Love, versions, paraphrase and recreations), Eduardo Carranza (Colombia).

1952: *El naufragio* (*The Wreck*), Alicia Molina y Vedia (Argentina); Barcelona: Plaza y Janés, trad. ZC &JRJ (Spain) 1964.

–do–: *La casa y el mundo* (*The Home and the World*). trad. Alicia Molina y Vedia (Argentina); 1971. Madrid: Libra, trad. Emilio Gascó Contell; Manuel A. Penella (Spain) 1983.

–do–: *Recuerdos* (*Reminiscences*), Alicia Molina y Vedia (Argentina); ZC & JRJ (Spain) 1961.

1954: *Poesías* (Poems), Ramón Sangenís (Spain).

1955: *Obra escojida.* Madrid: Ed. Aguilar (Biblioteca Premios Nobel), trad. Zenobia Camprubí Aymar.

1956: *Sadhana o la via spiritual y Poemas de Kabir.* (*Sadhana* and *One Hundred Poems of Kabir*) Madrid: Afrodisio Aguado Escelicer, trad. Emilio Gascó Contell.

1957: *Pensamientos de Rabindranath Tagore* (Tagore's thoughts). Barcelona: Sintes, trad. Antonio C. Gavaldá.

1959: *Gitanjali, La luna nueva, El jardinero* (*Gitanjali, The Crescent Moon, The Gardener*). Barcelona: Zeus, trad. Guzman Cota Mir.

1961: *Canto del sol poniente* (*Purabi*), 2ª edición, 1981, Edición Nivicke, 1986 (Argentina), trad. Alberto Girri.

–do–: *Cuatro ensayos sobre Tagore* (Four Essays on Tagore), Ministerio de Educación, (Cuba).

–do–: *Poesias, cuentos* (Poems, Stories), contains '*The Post Office*,' 'Khokababur Protyabartan', '*Chitraganda*' and other Poem Selections (Cuba).

1962: *Gora* (*Gora*). Barcelona: Plazay Janés, trad. Ana Mariá de la Fuente; as *Una Juventud en la India* (Argentina) 1945; (Spain) 1945, Anatole y Nina Sanderman.

1964: *A cuatro voces* (*Chaturanga*). Barcelona: Plazay Janés, trad. M Agustina Pacovi.

1961–4: *Conferencias y ensayos* (Lectures and Essays). Madrid: Escelicer, trad. Emilio Gascó Contell (Spain).

1965: *Entrevisions de Bengala* (*Glimpses of Bengal*). Barcelona: Ed. Plaza y Janés, trad. Zenobia Camprubí Aymar.

–do–: *Filigranas de luz* (Fire-files), Franco (Argentina).

–do–: *Poemas de Kabir* (*One Hundred Poems of Kabir*). Barcelona: Ed. Plaza y Janés, trad. Zenobia Camprubí Aymar.

1967: *Hacia el hombre universal* (*Towards the Universal Man*). Barcelona: Sagitario, trad. Irene Soriano.

1968: *El sentido de la vida* (*Sadhana*). Madrid. Ed. Aguilar, trad. Zenobia Camprubí Aymar; Enrique López Castellón (Spain) 1982; Ed. Alianza (Spain) 1983; Mauro Armiño (Spain) 1985.

–do–: *Nacionalismo* (*Nationalism*). Madrid: Ed. Aguilar, trad. Zenobia Camprubí Aymar.

–do–: *Oriente y Occidente*, Epistolario (East and West, Epistolary). Barcelona: Juventud, trad. Nicolás María Martínez Amador.

–do–: *Sentido de la vida y el nacionalismo* (*Sadhana* and *Nationalism*), ZC & JRJ (Spain).

1978–9: *Los derechos del niño* (Compiled from *The Crescent Moon*), (Spain).

1979: *Lírica breve* (Anthology). Madrid: Susaeta., trad. unknown

–do–: *Obra selecta de Tagore* (Selected Works of Tagore), María de Quadras (Spain).

1981: *Lipika* (*Lipika*). Barcelona: Pomaire, trad. Marta I. Guastavino.

–do–: *Últimos poemas* (Last Poems), Madrid: Visor, Mariano Antolín Rato (Spain).

1983: *Una juventud en la India* (*Gora*). Madrid: Akal, trad. Anatole y Nina Sanderman.

1984: *Correspondencia entre dos guerras* (1877–1962) (Hesse, Rolland, Tagore). Barcelona: Nuevo Arte Thor, trad. Joaquín Bochaca.

–do–: *Palabra reflejada* (Anthology), José Luis Crespo Villalón (Spain).

1985: *El Alpona*, Argimon Victoria (Spain).

1994: *Cuentos* (Stories). Madrid: PPC, trad. Angel García Galiano.

–do–: *Historias cortas seleccionadas de Rabindranath Tagore* (Short Stories). Barcelona: Apostrofe Pokhara, trad. M Alejandra Medrano Pizarro.

1995: *Pequeña antología*. Madrid: Iberonet, trad. unknown.

1997: *Cristo* (Christ). Madrid: PPC, trad. Rafael Claudin López y Felicita di Fidio.

1999: *La Morada de la Paz* (*Santiniketan*). Barcelona: Oniro, trad. Rosa Alapont.

2000: *Del alba al crepusculo.* (From dawn to dusk). Palma de Mallorca: Olañeta, trad. Esteve Serra.

2008: *Mis recuerdos* (*Jibansmriti/Reminiscences*). Coruña: Ediciones del Viento, trad. Isabel García López.

2009: *El Cuentos para mi nieta* (*She*). Barcelona: La Otra Orilla, trad. Ana Herrera.

2010: *Palabra por palabra*. Barcelona: *La Otra Orilla*, trad. Ana Herrera (Translation of *Rabindranath Tagore: My Life in my Words,* ed. Uma Das Gupta).

(NB: In the above list, 'Impr^a' is a shorter form of the Spanish word '*Imprenta*' which means Press (or printed at); 'trad' signifies translator or translated by; and 'Tip^a' or 'Tip' is a short form (originally used) of *Tipografía* meaning typography, type-setting or printing.)

28

PORTUGAL AND GALICIA
(PORTUGUESE-SPEAKING REGIONS II)

JOSÉ PAZ RODRIGUEZ

GALICIA

Although Galicia is an autonomous region it is a part of Spain. It has two official languages, Castilian (it is official in the whole of Spain) and Galician Portuguese which is the mother tongue of most of its inhabitants.

Vicente Risco (1884–1963)

Vicente Risco and Carme Brei Moure, the Galician curator of Victoria Ocampo's villa in San Isidro-Buenos Aires, in which Tagore lived for more than two months in 1924, were two of the few Galicians who saw Tagore. Risco heard his lecture at the University of Berlin in 1930 and read the first editions of *Song Offerings (Gitanjali)*, *The Crescent Moon*, *The Gardener* and *Sadhana*. In 1913, Tagore received the Nobel Prize for Literature and the Ateneo of Madrid (a cultural institution founded in 1835) invited Risco to give a lecture on the writer from Bengal. On Saturday, 7 March 1914, he talked about the Bengali poet under the topic 'Rabindranath Tagore, Nobel Prize for Literature,' to a large interested audience.[1] This comprehensive lecture which bears almost no factual errors, was the first serious study made on Tagore in Galicia. Risco discovered Tagore for the people of the Iberian Peninsula.

Risco was a prolific writer on Tagore. This continued even after 1930, when he met Tagore in person and felt distressed by the hierachical attitude of Tagore with the result that some of his admiration vanished. In his Orientalist phase, represented by his avant-garde magazine *La Centuria* [The Century] (no. 5), published in Ourense (Galicia) in the years 1917 and 1918, he spoke well of Tagore's school at Santiniketan. He also remarked how Tagore's poems, when translated into English, lose the musicality present in the Bengali originals. In the same number, three poems of Tagore were published, translated by Risco. Later, several poems and stories of Tagore were published in periodicals like *A Nosa Terra* [Our Land] and *Nós* [Us] by Risco, in Galician, not Portuguese. Until his death, Risco published articles in the Ourense daily *La Región* [The Region] on special commemorations, such as on Tagore's death anniversary and his centenary. In the Vigo daily *Galicia* (11 January 1925), Risco published an article in Galician under the title *Cultura e Natura* [Culture and Nature] on Tagore, in which he analyses how Tagore interpreted these two principles, culture and nature.

Other Galician Admirers

Besides Risco, there were other Galicians who admired Tagore, and some even received literary stimulation from his works. The first in this group was João Vicente Biqueira (1886–1924).He taught at the Instituto (secondary school) of Corunna, where he travelled from Betanços for his lectures. Biqueira, who was a member of the Institución Libre de Enseñanza [Free Institution of Teaching] of Giner and Cossío, compared Tagore to the Galician autor, Castelão. In *A Nosa Terra* (10 April 1920), he wrote: 'Tagore, the most universal poet of our days, admired throughout the world, great amongst the great, who is he? A Bengali who writes in Bengali, a noble language of India which almost nobody understands in Europe.' This was originally part of a lecture delivered by Biqueira in 1920 at Corunna, at the opening of an exhibition of Castelão's work. Then in 1974, the year when the *Dia das Letras Galegas* (The Day of Galician Literature) was devoted to him, this text was published in his book *Ensaios e Poesias* [Essays and Poems].

On 19 December 1913, the thinker, journalist and writer, Antão Vilar Ponte, published an interesting article in Spanish on Tagore on the first page of a Corunna daily. The Countess of Pardo Bazán, Dona Emilia, wrote two articles in Spanish about Tagore in *La Nación* [The Nation] of Buenos Aires and the *ABC* daily of Madrid in 1921. The Countess liked the plays by Tagore, especially *Sacrifice*. In February 1954, António Avilês de Taramancos (1935–92) delivered a lecture on Tagore's poetry at Corunna. Later he wrote an essay in Galician under the title 'R. Tagore, poeta sem tempo, nem distância' (R. Tagore, a poet without time and distance).[2]

The year 1961, the centenary of Tagore's birth, was important, as his works were republished and many remembered him and wrote books, articles and statements. In several journals, Galician authors wrote about Tagore: Francisco Fernández del Riego (under the pseudonym Salvador de Lorenzana), Alberto Vilanova, Manuel Fabeiro Gómez, Dionísio Gamallo Fierros, Borobó (pseudonym of Raimundo Garcia Domínguez), José Garcia

Nieto, Cristina Picos de Amenedo, Maria do Pilar G. de Fresco and José Luis Varela. Among the Ourense writers, of particular interest are the reminiscences of Pura Vázquez, who for a number of years contributed articles on Tagore. So did her sister Dora, the pedagogue, Conceição Ramom, and the Inspector of Education, Joaquina Gallego Jorreto, with their own collaborations in *El Pueblo Gallego* [The Galician People] and the periodical *Educadores* [Educators].

José Paz Rodrigues founded in 1966 a large library devoted to Tagore literature in all major languages of the world which he subsequently donated to the Casa de la India of Valladolid. He has also published a large number of articles on Tagore in Galician and Portuguese dailies, and in periodicals like *Padres y Maestros* [Parents and Teachers], *BILE, Agália, Auria, Leer* [To Read], *A Peneira* [The Sieve], *Comunidad Educativa* [Educational Community], *Semanário Minho* [Minho Weekly], *Boletim da AGLP* [Bulletin of the AGLP] (Galician Academy of the Portuguese Language), *ABC* daily and *La Región* [The Region], as well as in Indian journals like *The Visva-Bharati Quarterly* and the Bengali *Jignasa*. The number of articles and essays published in *La Región* of Ourense outnumber those published in other periodicals and journals. This is due to the single-minded devotion of Risco who constantly wrote on the poet from the 1930s to the 1960s.

Portugal

Some translators of Tagore into Portuguese lived in what Oliveira Salazar's government euphemistically called 'overseas provinces', that is, in Goa, Macau, Angola, Cape Verde and Mozambique (see Chapter 12). The cases of Mascarenhas, Barreto, Amâncio Gracias and Froilano de Melo who were born in Goa are paradigmatic. Mascarenhas and Barreto worked in Portugal, particularly in Coimbra and Lisbon, where they published articles on and translations of Tagore. De Melo's case is exceptional. He travelled worldwide. An excellent doctor, he shared his time between Goa, Mozambique, Angola, Cape Verde, and Portugal and Brazil, where he died. We have discussed his literary influence in the section on Goa (Chapter 12 of this volume), as it was his birthplace. The same is true for Amâncio Gracias, who at various times lived in Angola, Mozambique and Cape Verde.

In the year 1910, with the fall of the Portuguese monarchy, a Republic was proclaimed. This fact stimulated the birth of important democratic and cultural groups interested in social change and in the improvement of education and culture. This continued until Oliveira Salazar's dictatorship (1932–68). As pointed out by Sovon Sanyal, the Tagore reception went through different stages running more or less parallel to the political vicissitudes of Portugal.[3] The reception was naturally stronger when cultural groups were able to voice their opinions, as opposed to the times when they were being silenced or oppressed. Among these groups were the Renascença Portuguesa (Renaissance Portuguese), based in Oporto. This was a cultural movement born in 1912, with its organ *A Águia* and the fortnightly *Vida Portuguesa*. The other group gathered around the periodical *Seara Nova*, founded in Lisbon in 1921 through Raul Proença's initiative. Both groups, with some common members, were admirers of Tagore's work. Their publications included translations of Tagore's poems and essays on his personality.

Bento de Jesus Caraça (1901–48)

Bento de Jesus Caraça was born in a family of rural workers in Alentejo's Vila Viçosa. In 1923, he obtained his degree in Economic and Financial Sciences and became a teacher of mathematics. In 1927, he became a professor, becoming one of the important specialists in his subject in Portugal. He was a member of the Portuguese League against war and Fascism, and consequently he struggled in the underground, in a legal or semi-legal way, against Salazar's dictatorship, and went on to establish with some of his colleagues, the Movimento de Unidade Democrática (MUD). He was imprisoned on several occasions and expelled from his university chair in 1946, two years before his early death.

In a letter that Caraça sent on 23 January 1933 from Lisbon to Armando M. Guedes, he explained how he wanted to organise a series of talks on the general subject of *Grandes figuras morais contemporâneas* (Great contemporary moral figures) in the UPP (Universidade Popular Portuguesa). Eminent authors and personalities who featured on this list of Caraça as subjects of the talks were Leo Tolstoy, Maxim Gorki, Zola, Anatole France, the Catalan educator Ferrer, the Belgian pedagogue Decroly, the creator of the Spanish Institución Libre de Enseñanza, Giner de los Ríos, Mahatma Gandhi, Romain Rolland, who was the subject of the inaugural lecture, and Rabindranath Tagore. Important personalities of Portuguese culture also figured in the list. The talk on Tagore was delivered by Caraça on 22 January 1939; followed by a concert, organised by Emma Romero Santos Fonseca da Câmara Reys, of five Tagorean songs, interpreted for the first time in Portugal.[4] Caraça started with these appropriate words: 'The extension of [Tagore's] work in different fields, instead of confounding us by its variety, guides us by the continuity of the general traits it presents. There is a profound unity in all his productions and it is enchanting in the extreme, for those who dive in this vast ocean, to discover ... the lines of its internal structure.' Caraça was commenting, among other books, on Tagore's works that he had read in French: *The Religion of a Poet, Letters to a Friend, The Post Office, The Crescent Moon, The Religion of Man, Song Offerings: Gitanjali,* and a collection of songs of Tagore *Chansons de R. Tagore* by Arnold Bake, *Songs of Kabir.* At the end there was the reproduction of a letter that Tagore had sent to the Japanese poet, Yone Noguchi, from Santiniketan on 1 September 1938.

Bento de Jesus Caraça was elected a director of the Centro de Estudos de Matemáticas Aplicadas à Economia (created in 1938 and defunct in 1946). In 1940, he was one of the founders of the Sociedade Portuguesa de Matemáticas (SPM), and its president, participating in numerous congresses. In Portugal, this figure is still greatly respected today, and monographs and studies on him continue to be published.

Augusto Casimiro dos Santos (1889–1967)

Born in Amarante where he did his primary and secondary schooling, Augusto Casimiro dos Santos studied at the university in Coimbra, and graduated in 1909 to follow a military career. Three years earlier he had already begun publishing as a reporter and a poet. In 1910, with the proclamation of the Republic in Portugal, he adopted immediately the republican ideas immediately. He opposed the dictatorship in 1932 and was expelled from the army (1933 to 1936) and exiled to Cape Verde. He always maintained his opposition to the Estado Novo (or 'New State', the authoritarian regime installed in Portugal in 1933) of Salazar and thus entered the MUD, to which Caraça too had belonged. He published his pieces in many newspapers, especially in the periodicals *A Águia* and *Seara Nova*. His work is vast, comprising poetry, prose, fiction, historical essays, memoirs and studies, as also socio-political articles. As an admirer of Tagore, especially of his poetry, he translated several of Tagore's poems into Portuguese.[5] These were published in 1939 with a preface by Augusto Casimiro under the title *Poesias: o músico e o poeta* by Seara Nova of Lisbon, in a volume of the series 'Cadernos da Seara Nova-Estudos Literários.' It is an anthology with poems from *The Crescent Moon, Gitanjali* and *The Gardener*. In 1943, the *Editorial Confluência* of Lisbon published a poetical anthology by Tagore, with an introduction, selection and translation by Casimiro under the title *Poesia*.[6] This anthology brought together poems from *The Gardener, Song Offerings: Gitanjali, The Crescent Moon* and *The Fugitive*, several Tagore songs from the book *Chansons de R. Tagore,* and some fragments from the book *Letters to a Friend* (letters by Tagore to C. F. Andrews).

To mark the centenary of Tagore's birth, in 1961, Casimiro published an article with the title 'Tagore e os poetas da Renascença Portuguesa.'[7] He expressed his appreciation for the poets and writers of the Renascença Portuguesa. These poets felt attracted by Tagore's pacifism, his internationalism and his idea of self-government. In its most dynamic stage, this group carried out a project of promotion of the national culture with various publications, the foundation of people's universities, the implementation of courses and colloquia and the establishment of libraries to promote reading. The magazine *A Águia* (1910–1932) functioned as the organ for their works and ideology.

Tagore in the Portuguese Press, and More Translators

Under the heading 'O Prémio Nobel de Literatura de 1913 foi concedido ao poeta anglo-indiano Rabindranath Tagore' (The Nobel Prize of Literature of 1913 awarded to the Anglo-Indian poet Rabindranath Tagore), the *Diário de Notícias* of Lisbon (13 November 1913) made it known that the Swedish Academy had conferred the Nobel Prize for Literature to Tagore. The same newspaper, dated 8 August 1941, announced Tagore's death: 'The glorious Indian poet Tagore died yesterday in Calcutta.'

For appreciation of Tagore in Portugal, it was important to have the link with Goa. The Goan writer Telo de Mascarenhas described his experiences with this link and the times he lived in Portugal in an essay titled 'O nosso passado politico' (Our political past), enjoying the beaches and landscapes in Goa, but equally his visits and stay at the Biblioteca Nacional of Lisbon. There it was possible to get to know and read important books by European authors writing on India, and even the writings by Gandhi in a French translation by Romain Rolland. Leading a group of Goan enthusiasts, Mascarenhas established a Centro Nacionalista Hindu in Lisbon in 1926. The Instituto Indiano in Coimbra and the newspaper *Índia Nova* (organ of the Goan students in the universities of Portugal), may be mentioned here.

Goan intellectuals translated works from Marathi, Hindi, Bengali and even from Sanskrit into Portuguese and published them first in Goan newspapers. The same intellectuals helped spread Tagore's work in the rest of the Portuguese-speaking world. The Portuguese editions done by Ferreira Martins in Goa, in 1914 and 1916, of Tagore's works *Chitra* and *Poemas em prosa* [Poems in Prose] were dedicated respectively to the Portuguese writers Fernando Leal and Júlio Dantas. The Goan Lúcio de Miranda who lived in the Azores discovered his love for India and delivered talks and wrote articles and a book *Índia e indianos* (1936). Two chapters were dedicated to Tagore under the headings *Tagore, o poeta* and *Santiniketan*. He mentioned

Tagore's 'modern and progressive education' which was founded on a solid scientific basis, as Tagore knew the psychology of children. Lúcio de Miranda collaborated with the Instituto Indiano of Coimbra. The 1920s were important for the spread of Tagore's ideas in Portugal. Visva-Bharati was established in 1921, and Tagore propagated its ideals by undertaking extensive lecture tours in Europe for fund raising. The appreciation of Tagore was also spreading due to the efforts of Romain Rolland, who had much influence on Portuguese intellectuals of the time. In 1922, António Figueirinhas (1885–1945), an educator, founder of several schools and of an important publishing firm for school books, translated and published a book of love poems by Tagore in Oporto. Its title was *O jardineiro d'amor* [Gardener of Love]. The translation was done by Figueirinhas from the French edition of *The Gardener*. This book was a great success, and its second edition could be published in 1925 by Casa Editora de A. Figueirinhas in Oporto. Also in 1922, Luís de Castro Norton de Matos published an article with the title 'Misticismo na Filosofia Oriental de Rabindranath Tagore' [The mysticism in the Oriental philosophy of Rabindranath Tagore].[8] De Matos commented on Tagore's spiritual ideas and his relationship with the Upanishads.

On 11 May 1923, E. Tudela de Castro delivered a lecture dedicated to Santiniketan and Visva-Bharati at the Sociedade Teosófica de Portugal describing in detail the characteristics of its pedagogical model and the importance of Tagore's teaching in unity and harmony with nature.[9] On 7 May 1928, Tagore's birth anniversary, Telo de Mascarenhas published an article on Tagore on the first page of the newspaper *Índia Nova* of Coimbra, illustrated with a photograph of Tagore.

The book most often published in different translations done by different people in this region was the novel *Ghare Baire* [*The Home and the World*]. The first edition was published in Lisbon in 1941, in a translation from the Bengali by Telo de Mascarenhas that went into two consecutive reprints in 1945 and 1955. Fernanda Pinto Rodrigues translated the same novel from English in 1973, which was republished in 1992 and 1998. In 1986, the Angolan writer Wanda Ramos published yet another translation.

Telo de Mascarenhas published translations from Bengali of the novels *Naukadubi* [*The Wreck*], *Chaturanga* [*Four Chapters*] and of a selection of stories under the title *A chave do enigma e outros contos* (Key to the Enigma and Other stories), published by Inquérito Publishers of Lisbon in 1942 and 1943. Alexandre Fonseca translated the novel *Gora* in 1947, choosing *Inquietação* [Disqietude] as its title. An anthology of poems entitled O *Coração da Primavera* (The Heart of Spring, 1958) was even brought out in a Braille edition. The translation was by Manuel Simões (1924–95), who did the selection and arranged the fifty-eight poems taken from the books *Gitanjali*, *The Gardener*, *The Crescent Moon* and *The Last Poem* [*Shesher Kabita*] including also several aphorisms from *Stray Birds*. The third edition was printed in 1990.

The Centro Cultural da Embaixada da Índia (Cultural Centre of the Indian Embassy) in Lisbon brought out Tagore's story 'Kabuliwallah.' Especially noteworthy is the anthology of poems *Poesia*, in a translation from English by José Agostinho Baptista.[10] The first edition of this collection of verses, published in 2004, had an enormous success in Portugal, so that it could be republished in 2011. The anthology contains fifteen Tagore poems from 1882–1913, fourteen from 1914–36 and eight from 1937–41, another eighteen poems taken from different periods, and twenty-one from Tagore's last poems. Content-wise we have poems of hope and defiance, some songs and fourteen texts entitled by the translator as 'poemas maravilhosos' (poems of wonder).

Tagore never visited Portugal. However, his ship stopped at the port of Lisbon on various trips. The newspapers of the capital flashed the news of the presence of Tagore. Finally, a few admirers of Tagore from among the Portuguese writers of Tagore's time deserve to be mentioned. They are Júlio Dantas (1876–1962), Agostinho de Campos, an admirer of *The Crescent Moon*, and Ferreira de Castro who called Tagore the Tolstoy of India, because the Russian is 'the poet of the snow, and Tagore of the sun.' Finally the Portuguese philosopher, educator, poet and essayist, Agostinho da Silva (1906–94) must be mentioned who especially appreciated Tagore's social and educational thought.

Translated from the Portuguese by Galician Mr Carlos Durão

NOTES

1. The lecture was reproduced in issue nos. 17 and 18 of the magazine *La Palabra*, the year is stated as 1913, but it was published later.
2. In *Luzes da Galiza*, no. 21 (February) 1993.
3. 'Tagore's reception in Portugal,' *Hispanic Horizon*, no. 29 (2010).
4. Caraça, *Rabindranath Tagore*, published in three parts in *Seara Nova*, nos. 607, 608 and 609, of 1, 8 and 15 April 1939, respectively.
5. A poem by Tagore with the title 'Um soneto de Tagore' was published in the magazine *Seara Nova*, no. 124, 1929. The same magazine published in 1939 the poems entitled: 'Farei tudo,' 'Há muito que dura a viagem,' 'Nauchini' and 'Se fores o silêncio.' All were translated by Casimiro.
6. It is no. 2 of the collection *Antologia de Autores Portugueses e Estrangeiros*.

7. *Colóquio-Revista de Artes e Letras,* no. 15, October 1961, 57–9, published in Lisbon by the Calouste Gulbenkian Foundation.
8. *Contemporânea-Grande Revista Mensal* no. 3 (Lisbon) 1, July 1922. It was republished as a book with the title *O espiritualismo oriental de Rabindranath Tagore* in 1924, the second edition being published in 1927.
9. In 1925, published as a book in Lisbon as *Shantiniketan: o asilo da paz,* printed at the Tipográfica Simões M. Santos.
10. No. 90 of the collection *Documenta poética,* Editora Assírio & Alvim, Lisbon.

Works Cited

Galicia [In the following, RT stands for Rabindranath Tagore]

Avilês de Taramancos, A. *R. Tagore, poeta sem tempo, nem distância* [R. Tagore, poet without time or distance]. Compostela: Luzes de Galiza No. 21, February 1993.

Biqueira, João V. 'Obra selecta (Poesia e Ensaio)' [Selected Works (Poetry and Essays)]. Ponte Vedra/Braga: *Cadernos do Povo-Revista Internacional da Lusofonia* No. 43–6, 1998, 92–4(Text published under the title 'Divagaciós engebristas' in *A Nosa Terra,* No. 117, 10 April 1920, 1, and in *Ensaios e Poesias* [Essays and poems]. Vigo: Ed. Galaxia, 1974, 112–27).

Casares, Carlos. *Vicente Risco.* Vigo: Ed. Galaxia, 1981, 42–4.

Gallego, Joaquina. 'Rabindranath Tagore, educador' [RT, educator]. Madrid: *Revista Calasancia,* No. 26, April–June 1961, 233–39.

Paz, José. 'Vicente Risco, descobridor de Tagore' [Vicente Risco discoverer of Tagore]. Ourense: *La Región,* 7 May 2008, 22.

———. 'Rabindranath Tagore e Galiza' [RT and Galicia]. Ourense: *La Región,* 7 August 2008, 34.

Risco, Vicente. 'Rabindranath Tagore (Premio Nobel de Literatura)' [RT, Nobel Prize in Literature]. *La Palabra* No. 17–18. Ateneo of Madrid, September 1913, 25–39. The publication of this number was delayed and came out in early 1914.

———. 'Rabindranath Tagore.' Ourense: La Centuria (*Revista Teosófica*) No. 5, October 1917, 2–3.

———. 'Rabindranath Tagore.' Ourense: Nós (*Boletín mensual da cultura galega*) No. 104, 15 August 1932.

Vilar Ponte, A. 'O poeta índio' [The Indian poet]. Corunha: *La Voz de Galicia,* 19 December 1913, 1.

Note: For several years poems, texts and stories by Tagore were published and translated into Galician-Portuguese by Vicente Risco, in the magazine *Nós* [Us], No. 104 of 15 August 1932 and the newspaper *A Nosa Terra,* No. 54 (10 May 1918), No. 56 (30 May 1918), No. 100 (15 September 1919), No. 101 (25 September 1919), No. 142 (15 June 1921), No. 160 (1-04-1922) and No. 184 (1 May 1923).

Portugal

Alves de Azevedo. 'A mensagem do génio hindu através da obra de Tagore' [A message of Hindu Genius through the Work of Tagore]. Lisboa: *Colóquio-Revista de Artes e Letras*, No. 15, outubro- (October) 1961, 59–61 (Fundação Calouste Gulbenkian).

Casimiro dos Santos, Augusto. 'Tagore e os poetas da Renascença Portuguesa' [Tagore and the poets of the Portuguese Renaissance]. Lisboa: *Colóquio-Revista de Artes e Letras*, No. 15, October 1961, 57–9 (Fundação Calouste Gulbenkian).

Castro, E. Tudela de. *Shantiniketan: o asilo da paz* [Santiniketan: the Haven of Peace]. Lisboa: Tip. Simões M. Santos, 1925.

Caraça, Bento de Jesus, *Rabindranath Tagore*. Lisboa: Seara Nova, 1939.

——. *Conferências e outros escritos* [Lectures and other writings]. Lisboa: Ed. Minerva, 1970.

Miranda, Lúcio de. *Índia e indianos* [India and Indians]. São Miguel/Ponta Delgada (Açores): Papelaria Ambar, 1936 (two chapters on Tagore: 'Tagore, o poeta' (Tagore, the Poet) and 'Santiniketan').

Norton de Mattos, Luís de Castro. 'O espiritualismo oriental de Rabindranath Tagore' [The eastern spiritualism of RT]. Lisboa: *Revista Contemporánea*, 1924 [published in 1922 as an article in the same magazine].

Saldanha, Mariano. 'O Poeta duma Universidade e a Universidade de um Poeta ou Rabindranath Tagore e a sua obra literária e pedagógica' [The Poet of a University and the University of a Poet or RT and his literary and pedagogical work]. Lisboa: *Revista da Faculdade de Letras*, 1943.

Sanyal, Sovon, 'Universalism of Tagore: Specificities of the Portuguese Reception'. *Hispanic Horizon* ((Jawaharlal Nehru University, N. Delhi) No. 29, 2010, 346–66.

29

UNITED KINGDOM

KALYAN KUNDU

In all that he did in his songs and his poetry, in his work of education and his rural renewal, Tagore urged us to accept that we must bring to our work not just science and rational thought but also the life of the spirit, that without this we are incomplete and vulnerable to a dangerous hubris ... Perhaps more than anything else it is this message of Tagore we need to hear, attend to and with great urgency act upon.

HRH The Prince of Wales
7 July 2011[1]

The Bengal Renaissance was an extraordinary phenomenon in the history of nineteenth-century India. Pioneered by Raja Rammohun Roy (1772–1833), Bengal was revitalised and uplifted from its medieval decadence. Roy's in-depth scholarship in Islamic and Hindu philosophy, and his acceptance of European liberalism, democratic ideas, education and science placed him in the role of a great benefactor and the first modern man of India. The new awakening of mind in the second decade of the nineteenth century brought about a significant change in the literary, cultural, social, economic and religious aspirations of Bengalis and spread like ripples in the latter half of the century. Roy also brought a new kind of religious movement. He discarded all ritualistic practices from the orthodox Hindu religion and founded the Brahmo Samaj, a monotheistic group accepting the Upanishadic Supreme God (Brahma).

Another remarkable Bengali, Roy's contemporary and a substantial contributor to the Bengal Renaissance, was Dwarkanath Tagore (1794–1846), an industrialist, entrepreneur and grandfather of Rabindranath Tagore. Dwarkanath set up a string of commercial ventures through his business enterprise Carr, Tagore and Company and made a fortune by diversifying into banking, indigo factories, sugar plantations, shipping companies, insurance and exports in partnership with British traders. According to

Blair Kling, 'Dwarkanath envisioned an India that was westernized and industrialized and whose inhabitants enjoyed without discrimination the rights and liberties of Englishmen.'[2]

The cultural, intellectual and commercial rekindling of India in the late nineteenth century passed unnoticed by the educated masses of Britain. The end of the nineteenth century and the beginning of the twentieth century marked the high noon of Imperial trade and commerce. This astounding economic growth, due to rapid industrialisation, generated enough wealth for the prosperity and comfort of the Crown's subjects in Britain. There was a steady flow of basic raw materials at a low price from the colony; the privileged members of mainland Britain had little concern for such exploitation, which was deemed to be a necessary part of the colonial commitment. A binary division was established between the ruler and the ruled where the former was superior, Eurocentric, hegemonic and nationalist, as opposed to the inferior latter. The members of this superior group had little interest in the cultural and traditional history of India—a civilisation thousands of years old lying thousands of miles away. Against this backdrop of imperial–colonial disparity and inequality first in Victorian and then in Edwardian Britain, Rabindranath Tagore, who was already established as a leading literary figure in India, came to England on 16 June 1912 to 'witness the manifestation of that great awakening of eternal humanity in the heart of Europe;'[3] and in no time was drawn into its literary vortex. Rabindranath was fifty-one years old and this was his third visit to England[4]—a major turning point in his literary career.

THE LITERARY LANDSCAPE OF EDWARDIAN BRITAIN: THE RISE OF RABINDRANATH TAGORE

A survey of English literary fashion in the late nineteenth century, the period immediately before the start of the Edwardian era (1901–10), revealed the predominance of Rudyard Kipling in English literature. Britain's wide readership was then absorbed in Kipling's ballads, narrative poems, satires, fantasy, and essays. However, his writings were chiefly remarkable for his celebration of Imperialism. Other representative literary figures of the time were Hilaire Belloc, Henry Newbolt, and G. K. Chesterton—all of them sought to revive a style distanced from Victorian romanticism and aesthetics.

Alongside this circle was a group of poets equally dominating the literary scene; they were classified as old traditionalists, parochial and anti-modern. They included such names as Robert Bridges, Thomas Sturge Moore, Walter de la Mare and Ernest Rhys, who were among the acclaimed representatives of the traditionalists. The common features of their work were Romanticism, sentimentality and hedonism. Although the traditionalists were greater in number than the imperialistic writers (Tagore would later find his cultural home within the traditionalists during the early years of his English career), both camps failed to contribute any new forms of style and ideas to rescue English literature from its stagnant state. There were some exceptions during the Edwardian period, notably George Bernard Shaw, H. G. Wells, Thomas Hardy and W. B. Yeats, who through their work debated and discussed the issues of the time: the amorality, insensitivity, repression and philistinism of the English middle class. With the exception of these writers, the overall literary expectation of British readers was at a low ebb.

While English literature was passing through the doldrums, several literary movements during 1912 were foaming beneath the surface of the stagnant literary pool—the modernist movement in English literature was awaiting expressionism mostly from non-British contributors like Ezra Pound, Hilda Doolittle, Robert Frost and Thomas Stearns Eliot. Pound was convinced that the English literary tradition consistently resisted modernisation and that he should cut out practically all London poetry save Yeats, Eliot and stuff of really unusual interest.[5] Eliot made the same point when he observed that the situation of poetry in 1909 or 1910 was stagnant to a degree difficult for any young poet of later years to imagine.[6] One of the new modernist movements, Imagism, initiated by Pound, Eliot (American by birth, he became a British subject at thirty-nine) and others, favoured clear, simple and sharp language with a precision for imagery in their literary idiom. Sentimentality, romanticism and wordiness, typical of Victorian poetry, were rejected outright by Imagists. This was in sharp contrast to their contemporaries, who were by and large content to work within their traditional frame.

A daily newspaper, in its year-ending survey of English books (3 January 1914), found the year 1913 uneventful. Clearly, within such currents and cross-currents, in a milieu of restlessness and doubt the poetry-lovers of Britain were even ready to accept any foreign work.[7] Then Rabindranath Tagore came to London with two notebooks full of his English translations of his Bengali poems. The day after his arrival he handed over one of his notebooks to William Rothenstein, the principal architect of the India Society.

THE LAUNCH OF TAGORE'S ENGLISH CAREER:
GITANJALI—A REVIEW OF REVIEWS

Rothenstein's reaction to the poems was exuberant; Yeats was also ecstatic; Andrew Bradley and Stopford Brooke were equally exhilarated. After two readings of Tagore's poems in the presence of poets, intellectuals and artists in Rothenstein's drawing room on 27 June and 7 July, and one public reception at a London restaurant arranged by the India Society on 10 July, Rabindranath Tagore was fêted by literary London.[8] He was launched into his new English career.

The India Society published translations of 103 of Tagore's verses in a limited edition titled *Gitanjali*, which came out on 1 November 1912, while Tagore was in America. Yeats helped select the poems from the two notebooks (eighty-three poems from the first and twenty from the second) and also edited the manuscripts. *Gitanjali* was the third publication of the India Society. The English *Gitanjali* should not be mistaken as a complete English translation of the original Bengali verses. Out of 157 verses in the Bengali *Gitanjali*, only fifty-three translated verses were included in the English version; the rest were from other books;[9] Yeats wrote the introduction. The book was dedicated to Rothenstein who also drew a sketch of Tagore for the frontispiece. A week after its publication, the first review of *Gitanjali* appeared in *The Times Literary Supplement* (*TLS*). According to the reviewer, the divorce of religion and philosophy, spreading widely within the poets of England, failed to attain the harmony of emotions and ideas in their poetry:

> But this Indian poet, without any obsolete timidity of thought, makes religion and philosophy one. He contemplates the universe as a primitive poet might contemplate a pair of lovers, and makes poetry out of it as naturally and simply. As we read his pieces we seem to be reading the Psalms of a David of our time who addresses a God realised by his own act of faith and conceived according to his own experience of life.[10]

The critic of the weekly magazine *The Athenaeum* found a trance-inducing beauty in Tagore's poems. The Oriental mysticism, evident in these poems, was applauded for its simplicity and negation of movement and colour rather than its warmth and serenity. However, despite the sustained beauty and spiritual accomplishment, according to this critic,

> ... his (Tagore's) work exercises, upon a Western mind at any rate, a somewhat numbing effect, and one must doubt whether it is really consonant with the deepest meanings of the life of which it offers a key.[11]

A lengthy review of *Gitanjali* emerged from the pen of Evelyn Underhill in the weekly journal *The Nation*. The reviewer herself was one of the authors of mysticism. According to her, the poetry of mysticism which inspired and expressed the soul's direct vision of reality was a rare occurrence. This was due to the fact that the creator of this kind of poetry must be a reveller in reality as well as an artist, a lover and a seer supreme. This supreme quality, essential in mystic poetry of the highest order, was evident alike in the writings of the East and the West; in the Sufi Jelalu d'Din Rumi (Jalal ad-Dīn Muhammad Rumi), in the Franciscan Jacopone da Todi, in the Carmelite St John of the Cross. To this illustrious list was added the name of Rabindranath Tagore. According to the reviewer, Tagore's God was far from the concept of a static and transcendent absolute which readers had been taught to regard as the centre of Hindu mysticism. The deity to whom these songs were offered was at once the surviving spirit of creation and the creation's eternal source and end; both infinite and intimate, 'dark with excess of light,' and yet the friend and lover of each soul—'His song offering is the sacrament of his ineffable communion with the Divine Nature; and it is from this personal and impassioned intercourse—so characteristic of the mystical consciousness—that his loveliest melodies are born.'[12] Underhill was not fully content with writing the lengthy and adulatory review. She later wrote to Rothenstein:

> Myself, I felt it (the review) to be horribly inadequate although I tried my best. It was deliberately made as detached as possible, partly because it seemed to me that the personal note was much overdone in the Introduction (by Yeats) and partly because he is too big to sentimentalize over. And I hoped by being objective to help those out of touch with these subjects to understand his poems.[13]

The critic of *The Manchester Guardian* suggested that Tagore was profoundly influenced by European thought, but not in the least disoriented by that influence. The European influence had rather completely Orientalised him.[14] *The Daily News and Leader* commented:

> This is, indeed, a book of the soul—not the soul of the ascetic, who rejects life, but the soul of the seer and the lover who finds life the visible expression of the eternal. 'Oh East is East and West is West and never the twain shall meet,' said Mr. Kipling. In these poems the twain do meet, for they touch that ultimate chord of humanity which is the same by the Thames as it is by the Ganges and they touch it with a mingling of the thought of the West with the rapture and reverie of the East that is unique.[15]

Yeats's introduction to *Gitanjali* helped to establish the poet's identity, necessary in presenting a new author to a new readership. The poems of *Gitanjali* genuinely stirred the soul of Yeats. However, in the absence of any first-hand information, the biographical elements and poetic background were hastily collected by Yeats from personal conversations with Tagore's friends. These friends were emotionally and sentimentally carried away in their statements and this was very much reflected in Yeats's introduction to *Gitanjali*. 'Mr Yeats' introduction was too hyperbolical a strain,' observed one reviewer.[16] Even Tagore himself was very much abashed on reading such an amplified introduction. A few months later one London evening paper even commented: 'Mr Yeats has the honour of having introduced the Bengali poet to Western readers, but he puts into a certain speech some months ago a strain of praise so lofty that it would be almost a miracle to deserve and to sustain it.'[17]

On the whole, reviews of *Gitanjali* in the British press were complimentary and the book gained very quickly a triumphant success on its first appearance. Through this book, an alien poet received a rapturous welcome within the community of Edwardian poets in England and, furthermore, was acknowledged as one of their own. The budget edition of *Gitanjali* was published in March 1913 by Macmillan. It was reprinted a further eleven times within the space of a year, which was unprecedented for any book of verse at that time. *Gitanjali* was also a chief contributor to Macmillan's fortune, being the best-seller of the day in the British literary scene. It was in no doubt that the discovery of the Indian poet, Rabindranath Tagore, by the British public was an outstanding literary event of the pre-War period.[18]

Why did *Gitanjali* suddenly become a best-seller? There were several factors—complex, sometimes ambivalent, and different strata of the British readership were affected or touched by the poems in different ways. So, each factor needs to be scrutinised on its own. For some time, *Gitanjali* generated tremendous enthusiasm within the literary elite in Britain. They were overwhelmed on finding simplicity, serenity and an abundance of Eastern mysticism within those poems—the kind of mysticism that also prevailed in medieval Europe in the works of St Francis of Assisi, Thomas à Kempis or, in modern times, William Blake. Stopford Brooke wrote in a letter to Rothenstein:

> Mysticism of this lofty and profound kind is at root similar all over the world and this accounts for the strange unity of the East and the West in these poems, and makes them ready to find a sympathetic home among that large, quiet and silent group of English people who do not talk against any form of materialism, but think and feel apart in stillness of the eternal matters.[19]

Rothenstein and his fellow intellectuals were jubilant on discovering an Eastern gem and the India Society was specially credited for being its first publisher. Immediately after the review of *Gitanjali* appeared in the the *TLS*, Rothenstein wrote to Tagore in America, 'It is a great delight to us to feel that what we felt at once is shared by others, and that you have once and for all gained the ear of the West for your literature.'[20]

With a few exceptions, British poets, traditional and modern, hailed their newfound poet and his works with delirious fervour. They found in *Gitanjali* a marked deviation from the works of their familiar Anglo-Indian writers like Kashiprasad Ghosh, Michael Madhusudan Dutt, Toru Dutt, Sarojini Naidu and others, whose works were not free from English literary influence both in style and form. They had to take notice of a new kind of poetry independent of Western influence. Ezra Pound (who had left the US for Europe in 1907 when he was about twenty-two) was overwhelmed on finding the mastery of cadence and simple imagery in those instances of *vers libre* which fitted nicely into the Imagists' concept. In a letter to Harriet Monroe, he wrote:

> The appearance of the poems of Rabindranath Tagore is an event in the history of English poetry and of world poetry. I do not use these terms with the looseness of contemporary journalism. Questions of poetic art are serious, not to be touched upon lightly or in a spirit of bravura ... I speak with all gravity when I say that world fellowship is nearer for the visit of Rabindranath Tagore in London.[21]

However, according to Edward Thompson, that 'silent mass of intellectuals' referred to earlier by Brooke did not approach Tagore from a purely literary point of view. Shaw was silent about *Gitanjali*. Seamus Perry wrote: 'Pound's fellow Imagist T. E. Hulme ... deplored the romantic habit of invoking "the word infinite in every other line" and it is hardly surprising that the modern taste which Pound and his friends were otherwise actively forging should have taken against lines such as "On the seashore of endless worlds children meet. The infinite sky is motionless overhead and the restless water is boisterous."'[22] When the clamour settled, especially after the award of the Nobel Prize for Literature to Tagore in 1913, the intellectuals of Britain became more and more critical about the hyperbolic literary publicity surrounding Tagore; they became more Eurocentric with their comments and this was evident in the British press.

Gitanjali's popularity made Tagore a mystic cult figure overnight and that mystic seal was something he had to carry with him throughout his Western journey. Thompson opposed this narrow label of mysticism attributed to his works: 'When Rabindranath Tagore's first English book appeared, and was seen to be mystical and religious, expectation was satisfied—"Oriental literature" was known to be like that; the West had made up its mind about 'the East' ... Tagore, however, was not in the least like what [he] was supposed to be', wrote Thompson.[23]

Strange as it may sound, the socio-economic condition of Edwardian Britain had an indirect but telling influence on the rise of *Gitanjali's* popularity. As mentioned earlier, the new industrial revolution that encompassed Britain between 1900 and 1914 contained a mass society that now lived in an industrial age of change. At the same time there was ample evidence of a breakdown in social homogeneity—a characteristic of industrialisation—into a more marked and disturbing social division. The uneven distribution of wealth divided the society into *masses* and *classes*. This was evident in the description in Rowntree and in the statistics of Charles Booth.[24] Even upper-class Britain with growing affluence seemed unhappy. 'This era of craving for unlimited wealth possessed by affluent English society for their luxury and pleasure with sufficient leisure in hand had developed a feeling of emptiness within. As enjoyment of any kind cannot be satisfied with more enjoyment, increased enjoyment acts as fat in the fire,' explained Nirad Chaudhuri.[25] As a result the spiritual aspiration of the people, both within *masses* and *classes*, was at an all-time low. The presence of delicate subtlety and finer sensuality was found in Tagore's poems; in addition, a direct and playful approach to the poet's divinity—written in the form of Psalms of David—satisfied the spiritual expectations of the general reading masses. They were the major shareholders of *Gitanjali's* popularity.

Jonathan Rose in his book *The Intellectual Life of the British Working Classes* surveyed in detail the reading habits of Edwardian Britain, collecting data from over a hundred diaries of working-class people, biographies, oral history and archival material from the libraries of Britain, and found that the golden age of reading came, in the years before World War I. It was not the age of television or the Internet; so a major pastime and pleasure was reading books on a wide variety of subjects. One would not be surprised to find the presence of Bunyan, Defoe, Carlyle, Dickens and Ruskin on people's reading lists. Equally the Bible was popular reading material amongst the working classes. In addition to buying their own books, these autodidacts could resort to inexpensive editions of the best-sellers from around the world. Everyman's Library established by J. M. Dent, Ernest Rhys and others, started around 1906 to bring in many coherently edited series of cheap classics. Everyman's Library, according to Rose, made at least some effort to include Eastern literature: The Ramabhata, The Mahabharata, *Shakuntala*, Hindu Scriptures introduced by Rabindranath Tagore, as well as [the] Koran.[26] In such a milieu of uninhibited reading, *Gitanjali's* popularity within working-class Britain seemed evident.

A large number of British Christians were drawn towards *Gitanjali* in seeking solace for their spiritual afflictions, not only finding parallels with the Psalms but also feeling an affinity with the monotheistic views of its author and his connections with the Brahmo Samaj. 'Some of the underlying Christian truths which these poems certainly suggest come to us with the more arresting beauty,' wrote one critic of *The Baptist Times and Freeman.*[27]

NOBEL PRIZE FOR LITERATURE, 1913

On 14 November 1913, the Western World woke with surprise and bemusement to find that the Nobel Prize for Literature had been awarded to an Indian poet—Rabindranath Tagore. The West was baffled by the decision of the Swedish Academy for three major reasons. First, the Award, for the first time ever, was given to a non-European, excluding twenty-seven other eligible contenders, particularly Britain's Thomas Hardy, France's Anatole France and Austria's Peter Rosegger. Secondly, the literary works of the recipient, in the absence of translation, were still not available to readers in any European country except Britain. And the third reason, insignificant as it may seem in this day and age: the recipient had a non-European name 'Rabindranath Tagore', which was difficult to pronounce with a 'European tongue'; so many were unsure about the poet's origin. In addition, the news was so sudden and unexpected that most reporters failed to obtain biographical details of the winner within such a short time. One reporter of *The New York Times* went to dig out the vast storehouse of the New York public library to find only two Tagores in its index—and none of those was actually Rabindranath Tagore.[28] Even four months after the award and a year after the publication of *Gitanjali,* a library in London often received a request for a copy of the 'Jewish' writer's book *Gitanjali*, or 'Russian' Tagore's latest, or the 'Arab' poet's new volume of songs.[29] The correspondent of *The Times* incorrectly printed the poet's date of birth, but did present a fair amount of information about Tagore in a succinct piece, justifying the award. The paper wrote: 'the Swedish poets Karfeldt and Heidenstam, and the writer Hallstrøm, who are all members of the academy, have expressed their satisfaction with the award and state that the Indian poet's works, although they have only recently become known in the Western world, show an original and poetic vein of great depth and undoubted literary merit.'[30] Another paper commented: 'The award of a Nobel Prize to Mr. Rabindranath Tagore, the famous poet, writer and teacher, is a remarkable event in the history of the World's literature. He has brought great literature, the mind of the East to us in our own tongue.'[31]

However, Tagore's reception in and out of the British press as the new Nobel Laureate was ambivalent. On a personal level many of Tagore's English friends, Rothenstein, Rhys, Sturge Moore and others rejoiced and sent congratulatory messages. Members of the India Society, especially Rothenstein for being the prime mover of Tagore's international career, also took credit for Tagore's achievement. Surprisingly, however, there was no immediate response from Yeats or Pound, arguably two of Tagore's admirers. In fact it was a year later that Yeats wrote to Tagore about receiving the Nobel Prize: 'I have not written to you all these months because somebody told me how burdened you are with letters and answering letters.'[32] This indeed sounded too feeble as an excuse. Why was there such indifference? Was it because both Yeats and Pound were disillusioned by or envious of his success? This was indeed the same Yeats who, so convinced in 1912 that no man in his time could equal the lyrics of Tagore, would write in 1935 to Rothenstein stating Tagore does not know English.[33] It took Robert Bridges seven months to break his silence when he wrote this wry comment: 'that mysterious committee of international judges crowned you with bank notes.'[34] Shaw was indifferent. Even those papers that reviewed *Gitanjali* with much exuberance had suddenly changed their tone. *The Daily News and Leader* wrote:

> In awarding this year's Nobel Prize for Literature to Mr. Tagore the Nobel Committee have established their reputation for catholicity, ... On no other hypothesis can be explained the persistence with which the claims of Anatole France, assuredly the living writer with the most universal reputation, [have] been passed over. Or, again, their blindness to Hardy's pre-eminence; for Hardy is no longer a purely insular classic; no Continental critic worth his salt or heedful of his reputation now dares ignore Hardy; the Nobel Committee is a conservative body and the scepticism of Anatole France and the pessimism of Hardy are too unorthodox to find favour. Within the limits of choice they allow themselves they have made a fine and bold selection.[35]

The weekly journal *The New Age* could not hide their malice. Their correspondent was more resentful of the British Academy than Tagore. Referring to the denial of the Prize to Thomas Hardy, the reporter wrote: 'the British Academy has a perfectly comprehensible spite against any living English (writer).'[36] However, he was wrong, as ninety-seven members of the British Academy forwarded their nominations to the Swedish Academy in favour of Thomas Hardy as a Nobel Prize contender, whereas Tagore's name was proposed once and by only one person, Thomas Sturge Moore, in two simple sentences. Four years later, in 1917, Pound quipped in a letter to Iris Barry, 'Tagore got the Nobel Prize because, after the cleverest boom of our day, after the fiat of the omnipotent literati of distinction, he lapsed into religion and optimism and was boomed by the pious non-conformists. Also because it got the Swedish academy out of the difficulty of deciding between European writers whose claims appeared to conflict. Hardy or Henry James? ... it was also a damn good smack for the British Academic Committee, who had turned down Tagore (on account of his biscuit complexion).'[37] The most interesting comment appeared in the weekly journal *Truth* quoting from a Swedish book about Prince William of Sweden. Quite simply, the author claimed Prince William's visit to Calcutta brought about the award of the Nobel Prize to Rabindranath Tagore.[38]

Judging from the Western perspective, the award of the Nobel Prize to Tagore was an event of very great surprise. When Tagore's name was proposed to the selection committee (on 31 January 1913, for the award in November 1913) there was only the India Society's *Gitanjali* the judges had in front of them. With this slim volume of lyrics Tagore had to compete with Hardy, France and other well-established writers in the West, including their impressive corpus of work. So the Nobel Committee had to turn towards his body of work in Bengali for their evaluation. Tegner was the only man on the Committee who knew a little Bengali but how much he was involved in the evaluation process there is no record. Karfeldt, Hallström and Heidenstam had to lobby hard within the eighteen-member committee to justify Tagore's eligibility. Most of the members were in favour of shelving Tagore for a future year. But there were two points that went in Tagore's favour. Firstly, his writings had optimism and universalism—the two main elements that satisfied the criterion under 'outstanding work in an ideal direction' as required by the Nobel statute in assessing the merit of the literary award. This constraint was rigidly followed, particularly in the earlier days of Nobel selection. Secondly, since the initiation of the Prize all recipients were European. By awarding Tagore the prize, the Nobel Committee had at last left its Eurocentric hub and extended its horizons. The uniqueness in Tagore's case was that he was recommended for the Prize once and by one person only, and that was enough to be awarded the laurel.

Two years after being awarded the Nobel Prize, on 3 June 1915, King George V knighted Rabindranath Tagore, the major British accolade he received for his literary achievements.

GITANJALI AND AFTER

Eleven months after the publication of *Gitanjali,* Macmillan published Tagore's two subsequent books of verse, *The Gardener* and *The Crescent Moon.*

Unlike *Gitanjali, The Gardener* and *The Crescent Moon* did not receive rave reviews in the papers, but they were satisfactory. 'He does not in his poetry set the themes of life to great music; he speaks them in a soft voice to the heart with all the simplicity and directness in his power. He takes the little intimate things which comprise life and fashions them into pearls which reflect the colour of the sky, mightiness of love and life,' wrote one of the reviewers on *The Gardener*.[39] Ernest Rhys wrote: '*The Gardener* is not a book of mystical poems, but a lover's garland from an Indian garden.'[40]

About *The Crescent Moon* one reviewer commended, 'It is sheer genius and joy. There is nothing quite like it in any literature I know of. For simplicity and loveliness it is unmatched.'[41] The critic of one of the evening papers found that the frank simplicity of feelings in the poems of *The Crescent Moon* was marred by a too frequent use of refrain, and the honeyed flavour of diction that grew monotonous.[42] With the euphoria of *Gitanjali* still in vogue, the critic was tired of what he thought was the monotony of Tagore's poems. Readers had by that time become so familiar with Tagore's style that parodies of his poems appeared in some papers. Abundant presence of flutes, tears, south winds, flowers, woods, separation, smiles, boats, and streams had a tiring effect on the readers, remarked Thompson.[43]

After *The Crescent Moon* seven more volumes of Tagore's poems appeared in Britain before his death in 1941. Of these seven volumes, *Fruit-Gathering* (1916), *Stray Birds* (1917), *Lovers Gift and Crossings* (1918) and *The Fugitive* (1921) published by Macmillan were all translated by the poet himself. In addition to the list a volume of Kabir's poems, *One Hundred Poems of Kabir*, translated by Tagore, was published by the India Society in 1915 (later on published by Macmillan). In 1925, a small sheaf of verses by Tagore, translated by Thompson in the *Augustan Books of Modern Poetry Series* (Sixpence Series) was published by Ernest Benn, a niche publishing house in London. Finally a long prose poem 'The Child' was published by Allen and Unwin in 1931. *The Child* was the only work of Tagore that was first written in English and was originally inspired by watching a passion play in Germany. It was later translated into Bengali, titled 'Shishuthirtha.' His last book of verse, also produced by Allen and Unwin, in 1932 was *The Golden Boat*, a collection of poems translated by Bhabani Bhattacharya. Besides those individual volumes a collection of his major works *Collected Poems and Plays* was issued by Macmillan in 1936 to celebrate the poet's seventy-fifth birthday. Reviews in the British press of those books were increasingly unsatisfactory as the translations, unlike *Gitanjali*, were becoming more and more inadequate, there was too much paraphrasing and much of the quality and sharpness of Tagore's style was lost. According to Chaudhuri, Tagore failed to develop his English throughout his 'English' career, and that made a substantial contribution to his eclipse: 'Somehow or the other, he developed for his own English a love which was as infatuated as Chesterfield's love for his natural son—both being children of love.'[44] Of his latter works, only *Stray Birds*, a collection of 326 aphorisms, received a good press, otherwise reviews of his last two books *Lovers Gift and Crossing* and *The Fugitive* were succinct and disparaging.

A TWIST IN TAGORE'S ENGLISH CAREER

Eighteen months after the publication of *Gitanjali*, the *TLS* forecast: 'the popularity (a popularity unfailingly registered by the Nobel Committee) that caught him up in a flame is likely to fade as rapidly as it was aroused.'[45] The prediction was well anticipated by Tagore's English publisher Macmillan. They realised that the 'Tagore boom' would be short-lived. So they rapidly cashed in on the Tagore phenomenon while the going was still good; books were randomly being published one after another; sometimes six of his titles were printed within a year. Even a draft copy of one of his plays, *The King of the Dark Chamber*, was printed as a book while Tagore was revising the manuscript back in Santiniketan. Such was the pressure from his publisher; it just went on and without any let-up. Tagore's main concern was to submit the manuscript within the deadline set by his publisher, rather than to control the quality of his writing by writing freely without a time frame. For the same reason he changed his translators frequently. Also a dire need for money for his Santiniketan school compelled him to accept all conditions imposed by his publishers. The reviews were gradually either very critical or just passable. William Radice, while reviewing the book *Imagining Tagore: Rabindranath and the British Press*, wrote,

> Turning the pages of the reviews, I find most of them, of course, ignorant and half-baked, in the light of Tagore's Bengali œvre; but as a response to the English works alone, they do not seem to me so wrong: indeed most British critics now would say that the reviewers— even when the first flush of enthusiasm wore off—[were] kinder than they should have been.[46]

Eight years after the publication of *Gitanjali*, Thompson was bold enough to write directly to Tagore who was in the USA at that time, accusing him:

> As I have told you before, you—with great assistance from your publishers—have been your own worst enemy. You thoroughly deserve to have Rhys' book written about you! [In fact Thompson did not like Rhys' shallow praise of Tagore in his biography.] You have

been taking the line of least resistance for years, translating from a certain stratum—and that not the least striking one—of your work, and unconsciously mixing the wine of *Gitanjali* with water, till folks have found the draught tasteless. Why, O why? One sin is, you have increasingly paraphrased, instead of translating. You have lost far more of your own force than you need have done.[47]

In a solemn confession, Tagore wrote in February 1921 from America:

In my translations I timidly avoid all difficulties, which has the effect of making them smooth and thin. I know I am misrepresenting myself as a poet to the western readers. But when I began this career of falsifying my own coins I did it in play. Now I am becoming frightened of its enormity and am willing to make a confession of my misdeeds and withdraw into my original vocation as a mere Bengali poet.[48]

Was Tagore influenced by Western Orientalists? Perhaps he was. At one stage he became used to identifying himself as a mystic poet. After *Gitanjali*, when Yeats was trying to look for poems of a different mood for the next collection, Tagore preferred to stick to his other mystical verses, assuming wrongly that British readers might not like his non-mystical image. Tagore's publishers also preferred that his image remained that way in fear that sales of his work would decrease.

Eighteen years after the publication of *Gitanjali*, in 1930, one reader wrote a letter to a provincial paper, which perhaps summed up the reasons for Tagore's decline in poetic reputation in Britain. This letter was very much a representative explanation of the new generation of British readers:

His poetry has been translated in nearly every European language. Yet how alien it is ... What is a new world to Yeats, is a strange world to most of us. Not that Tagore's verse is difficult or obscure. It is crystal clear; but it is written from another continent. In its abstraction, its constant use of earthly things as spiritual symbols, it is nearer to the poetry of Shelley than to that of any other Western writer. But Shelley is unpopular with our newer poets, and so is Tagore. For Tagore's first concern is with God, a God of whom the East has never for a moment lost sight. So there is a conviction in his approach, a spontaneity in his devotion. But for a long time now our own poets have been on a different road. We simply have not the nerve nowadays to write mystical verse, to start as a poem 'Thou art the sky, and thou art also the nest. O thou beautiful!' And so, although Tagore's poetry has been popular amongst some people for some time, and though the very essence of his English will always give his verse distinction, it would be safe to prophecy that his work will not be at all closely related to the English poetry of his day ... But if we cannot imitate, we can approve and admire. And then there is much to be admired in a poet, a musician, a teacher and a thinker.[49]

TAGORE'S OTHER WRITINGS: PLAYS, SHORT STORIES, NOVELS, MEMOIRS

Of all his other works, fifty-two plays, operas and dance-dramas that were written in Bengali, only eight of Tagore's plays were published in Britain. These were, in order of appearance: *Chitra* (1913), *The Post Office* and *The King of the Dark Chamber* (1914), *Maharani of Arakan* (1916), *The Cycle of Spring* and *Sacrifice and Other Plays* (1917), *The Curse at Farewell* (1924) and finally *Red Oleanders* (1925). Of these *Chitra, Sacrifice and other plays* (a collection of four plays entitled *Sacrifice, The Ascetic, Malini* and *The King and the Queen*) and *Red Oleanders* were Tagore's own translations; the rest were by different translators.

In his lifetime most of his plays except *Red Oleanders* were performed once in a while in Britain, but none received much attention other than *Chitra* and *The Post Office*. *The Maharani of Arakan*, a one-act play based on Tagore's short story *Dalia*, was the first production of a Tagore play in Britain at the Royal Albert Hall in 1912. But to Western readers *Chitra* was rather more like a lyrical poem than a play. According to Walter de la Mare,

> 'Chitra' is only one more revelation of Mr. Tagore's astonishing mastery of English. To win not only idiom, fluency, cadence, but also atmosphere in an alien tongue is neither the least nor, for us, the least fortunate, of this poet's achievements. How many English writers, one may speculate, could return so grave and real a compliment.[50]

The Indian Art and Dramatic Society first staged the play in London's Prince of Wales Theatre, six years after its publication, on 4 May 1920, with an all-English cast. The first ever professional performance of *The Post Office* was staged at the Abbey Theatre in Dublin on 17 May 1913. The play was translated into English by a young Oxford student Devabrata Mukerjea and revised by Tagore himself. Yeats, who was also closely associated with the Irish theatre movement, arranged this special production of *The Post Office* through the Abbey in aid of the building of St Enda's College founded by Padraic Pearse. The play was directed by Lennox Robinson. About the play, *The Irish Times* wrote:

> Mr W. B. Yeats and others associated with the Abbey Theatre have already expressed a high opinion of Tagore, and their judgement was confirmed by the appreciation and applause extended to the

specimen of the author's art by Dublin play-goers, as it was presented in its English dress ... It is not a very imposing play, but it has many attractive and, at the same time, pathetic features.[51]

Later on, the same group staged the drama at the Royal Court Theatre in London.

Regardless of opinions, *The Post Office* was, and still remains, the most sought after of Tagore's plays in the West. In fact it is an all-time favourite of theatre directors interested in exotic, innovative and challenging productions. The most poignant production of the play was performed by Jewish children in an orphanage at the Warsaw Ghetto while awaiting deportation to the Treblinka death camp in 1943. The play was directed by Janusz Korczak, a paediatrician who ran the orphanage. Among other Tagore plays, according to Sisir Kumar Das, *The King and the Queen* and *Sacrifice* closely followed the Shakespearean model.[52]

As a piece of text, most of the plays by Tagore were not very appealing to readers. The abundance of metaphors, allegories, symbolism and abstractions were the main obstacles to Western readers in approaching Tagore's plays. In this aspect Tagore was closer to Maeterlinck. But readers often found his dialogue verbose and the plays themselves not very well edited. Tagore did not follow the conventional style of introducing the characters and situations of the play at the beginning in detail, even though the readers were unfamiliar with alien minds and culture.

The critic of *The Athenaeum* wrote:

> Mr. Tagore endeavoured to make a developing action, an interplay of characters, the vehicle for presentment of spiritual truths; but in both the burden of the message was disproportionate to the machinery devised for delivering it; characters and situations alike groaned under the weight of the ill-concealed transcendentalism.[53]

Whatever the merits of Tagore's own translations or Tagore's translators, the latter group was at least loyal to the original text; whereas Tagore took excessive liberties in chopping and changing his own works, resulting in a serious distortion of his own plays. A real tragedy was his last play *Red Oleanders* which received harsh criticism in the press, so much so that the poet had to explain the inner meaning of the play to his readers at the end. [54]

Of the ninety-five short stories by Tagore in Bengali, thirty-four in translation were collected in three volumes, all published by Macmillan: *Hungry Stones and Other Stories* (1916, thirteen stories), *Mashi and Other Stories* (1918, fourteen stories) and *Broken Ties and Other Stories* (1924, seven stories). Most of those stories were not translated by Tagore and neither were his three novels in English: *The Home and the World* (1919), *The Wreck* (1921) and *Gora* (1923). Thompson firmly believed that the original short stories in Bengali were comparable and occasionally surpassed the merit of most short-story writers from the West. Rhys enthusiastically wrote: 'as we read them we feel at once the touch of the born storyteller.'[55] Rothenstein wrote, 'I find a book of short stories, [of] which to my delight *The Postmaster* ...will always have a particular value for me.'[56] The critics of the British press, on the contrary, did not always agree with Tagore's friends. The failure of appreciation by readers of those stories was due to their lack of comprehension and basic ignorance of the customs, traditions and cultural situations that surrounded the context of the stories. Hence, most of the reviews were superficial, shallow and negative: 'As studies of Bengali life most of these tales are weirdly engaging; as fictions they will not suit—and doubtless were not written to suit—all tastes,' wrote *The Daily Telegraph* while reviewing *Hungry Stones and other Stories.*[57] Another reviewer wrote: 'These stories ... may sometimes seem remote and, to a Western sense, lacking in sharpness of edge.'[58]

A detailed account of the editing process for these short stories and the frequent changing of translators to meet his publishers' deadlines before going to the press has been vividly described by Thompson in his *Alien Homage.*[59] Thompson feared that the original stories were chopped and parts lopped off in translation to satisfy Western expectations, and therefore the finer qualities and sensitivities were lost. Tagore's own explanation was that Indian life was so foreign to British readers that it was likely to tax their imagination too much for a perfectly comfortable reading.

The reception of Tagore's novels was almost the same as that of his short stories. However, a section of intellectual readers appreciated *Gora*. The debates and dialogues between the characters of *Gora*—educated young men and women, and their interactions in the whirlwind of religious movements such as Brahmoism, Hindu orthodoxy and Christianity amidst political, psychological and social tensions—were presented in a stimulating way in this novel. 'We ought not in fairness to apply English standards to a novel written in Bengali for Bengalis any more than to Russians ... but to the Hindu of today these things (regeneration of India and the social evils that hamper it) are very living questions,' wrote the critic of *TLS*.[60] Some readers also appreciated the underlying theme of women's liberation in *The Home and the World*. Rothenstein, profoundly moved by the beauty of this novel, wrote to Tagore: 'I don't know when you wrote it but it seems to me to contain your ripest wisdom.'[61]

Among other books of Tagore published in translation, his memoir *My Reminiscences* was highly praised by readers: 'Your Autobiography especially has been a great pleasure' was how it was commended by Yeats.[62] According to *The Nation*: 'if it is safe to prophecy immortality for anything Sir Rabindranath Tagore has written, it is safe to prophesy it for this (My Reminiscences).'[63] From other assorted reports and interviews in the British press, Tagore's first interview with a special correspondent from *Christian Commonwealth* appeared on 21 May 1913 and described his own poetical background. Also for the first time, mainstream readers of Britain saw a photograph of Rabindranath Tagore. From the same interview, readers were also made aware that the poet had founded a residential boarding school where he engaged in experimenting with new forms of education systems as opposed to the stereotypical English educational structure introduced by the British in India. At the beginning of 1914, Tagore's school was visited by J. Ramsay Macdonald, the future Labour Prime Minister of Britain, who wrote a detailed account of his day in Santiniketan in a long article that appeared in *The Daily Chronicle*.[64]

NATIONALISM AND ITS AFTERMATH

After his return from America, Tagore delivered a series of lectures between 18 May and 25 June 1913 in different venues across England. The subjects of these lectures were mostly based on the philosophical and spiritual experiences of human living—the sort of discourses that he addressed to his students in Santiniketan from time to time. At the request of the Quest Society of London, Tagore initially agreed to deliver five public lectures on Mondays starting from 19 May 1913 at Caxton Hall in Kensington. The series was titled 'The Search for God.' Some of these lectures were also delivered at the Unity Club in Urbana (in Illinois), and at Harvard University during his visit to America. Five months later, the Quest Society's lectures were published by Macmillan in a collection, *Sadhana: The Realisation of Life*. About *Sadhana* the critic of *The Nation* wrote: '"Sadhana" is not a philosophical treatise, it is a personal statement, which makes free, but not exclusive, use of the philosophic formulae of Indian religion, in the course of expounding its author's vision of life. Its temper is at once individual, national, yet also universal; accepting all the natural links of our closely woven humanity, not as fetters, but as supports to the soul.'[65] Other reviewers found the philosophical aspects in *Sadhana* to be closer to Emerson and Edward Caird (1835–1908), a Scottish philosopher, showing that there was not much difference in the thought process between the East and West.[66]

Other collections of Tagore's essays, *Nationalism* (1917), *Personality* (1917), *Creative Unity* (1922), and the collection of his Hibbert Lectures,

The Religion of Man (1930), certainly aroused interest among the intellectuals even though they may not have accepted the arguments. *Personality* also included six essays delivered in the USA. The *TLS* wrote in its review of *Creative Unity*

> ... if Rabindranath's great dream is an association between East and West, in which the elements derived from the West are taken up into a free and creative Indian personality, he himself already gives an example of such organic union. His writings alone show the absurdity of affirming that East and West can never meet; hundreds of Western men and women in reading him must feel that here they are in contact with someone with whom they could converse far more fully about the things for which they most care than with the majority of their fellow-countrymen.[67]

Tagore's clarity in thought and arguments were better expressed in those essays, which were written directly in English and not translated.[68]

Of the essays that raised serious debate and controversy in the West *Nationalism* stood out, comprising three individual essays: 'Nationalism in the West', 'Nationalism in Japan' and 'Nationalism in India,' and a long poem *Sunset of the Century* (this is in fact five poems written on the last day of the nineteenth century under a common title). It was published during World War I in August 1917. The War itself provided the whole argument around *Nationalism*. He wrote:

> A nation, in the sense of the political and economic union of a people, is that aspect which a whole population assumes when organised for a mechanical purpose... But when with the help of science and the perfecting of organisation this power begins to grow and brings in harvests of wealth, then it crosses its boundaries with amazing rapidity. For then it goads all its neighbouring societies with greed of material prosperity, and consequent mutual jealousy, and by the fear of each other's growth into powerfulness. The time comes when it can stop no longer, for the competition grows keener, organisation grows vaster, and selfishness attains supremacy. Trading upon the greed and fear of man, it occupies more and more space in society and at last becomes its ruling force.[69]

Tagore firmly believed that modern war was the consequence of aggressive Western materialism—of science divorced from spirituality—by which these Nations would drag the rest of the world 'down into the bottom of destruction. Whenever power removes all checks from its path to make its career easy, it triumphantly rides into its ultimate crash of death.'[70] *The Cult of*

Nationalism emphatically carried this message of Tagore, which he addressed nearly forty times during his lecture tours in the USA, immediately after his visit to Japan in 1916. He wrote:

> The war, to my mind, is the outcome of overgrown materialism, of an ideal based on self-interest and not based on harmony. There are differences between capital and labour because both are working in the interest of their own selves—peace is but temporary and other clashes are bound to come. The self-interest of nations is the same. A new readjustment of things is necessary, a new age, when the idea of Nationalism will be discarded, when colonies, the storm centres of the world, will be discarded. I think the war has proved this quite conclusively.'[71]

The TLS treated the argument in *Nationalism* sympathetically. In a lengthy piece the reviewer wrote:

> This is not to admit that the poet's view is just. It is not true that the public action of England as a state has been inspired simply by the desire for power and material gain. One hopes that increasingly a great moral ideal is becoming discernible as that which the federation of peoples included in the British Commonwealth are called to realize. On the other hand, it would be vain to deny that the love of power and the love of gain are motives which have had their share in the building up of the British empire. If we do not think the poet's view fair, we may allow that from his standpoint it is explicable.'[72]

However, the critic found that Tagore had not given any guidance for practical solutions such as how the poet would like to substitute the present regime of India or how the economic needs of mankind are now to be supplied without a complex industrial organisation. Critics of *Nationalism* actually failed to realise that the book was not a series of solutions for the problems of Nationalism, but was actually a grievous warning of the evil that would stem from it—evil that one can argue is still present in the world today.

Tagore's condemnation of Western nations as organised political bodies built to satisfy material greed, mechanical organisation and imperial aggression was certainly not what his British audiences expected to hear, especially when Europe was at war. As a result, his image of the 'Mystic poet of the East' received a serious knock for the first time. This was aggravated further when he renounced the knighthood in protest after the Jallianwala Bagh massacre of 1919. His British audience looked upon the renunciation as a deliberate insult to both King and Crown. 'The literary elite which had sat at Tagore's feet in 1912 had come for insight into the universal human heart, not into the affairs of the Punjab or of Bengal,' wrote Ratcliffe.[73]

In spite of the flurry of social engagements during his 1920–1 visit, Tagore's sensitive mind felt a lack of warmth and enthusiasm in his English friends. He came to Britain to seek support from them for his proposed university, which he idealised as 'the world meeting in one nest.' Regrettably, he did not receive any positive response; the whole concept was considered by his English friends as Utopian—the idea of a dreamer, too idealistic and unrealistic. Rothenstein wrote to Max Beerbohm: 'Alas, that the strong wine of praise and the weak wine of worship, should have gone to this good man's head.'[74] Tagore was further appalled at the result of the Dyer Debates in the Houses of Parliament and at the report of the Hunter Commission. He wrote to Andrews:

> The result of the Dyer debates in both Houses of Parliament makes painfully evident the attitude of mind of the ruling class of the country towards India ... The unashamed condition of brutality expressed in the speeches and echoed in their newspapers is ugly in its frightfulness.[75]

Frustrated, Tagore left England for continental Europe with a heavy heart, visiting country after country in war-torn Europe, promoting his message of East–West fellowship and seeking support for his university. He firmly believed that World Peace could only be achieved when East and West would meet together on common ground; where knowledge would flow in two streams—from the East and from the West—and in their unity there would be perceived the oneness of truth that pervaded and sustained the entire universe. He acted like a one-man peace envoy, received in Europe with 'the kind of welcome that might have been expected for any heavenly visitant in the hell to which man has reduced mankind,' described by a columnist of the weekly journal *The Nation and Athenaeum*.[76] Tagore, with his mission and charisma, with flowing grey beard and hair, long robe, and penetrating eyes, fitted nicely with the prophetic iconography of the West, a 'wise man of the East', rather than a poet. In mainland Europe he received sympathetic encouragement for his university. In 1921 when Tagore's university became a reality, his English friends were prompted to raise funds for it, which Tagore tried to stop as his vanity was hurt.

During 1926, his controversial tour in Fascist Italy at the invitation of Mussolini resulted in an international backlash, especially within Europe. The British press followed the event closely. During the months of July and August in 1926 *The Manchester Guardian* reported Tagore's Italian sojourn, and the arguments and counter arguments about Tagore accepting the Fascist dictator's invitation. However, in contrast to his cold reception in

1920–1, in 1926 he was warmly received in England again, reminiscent of the summers of 1912 and 1913. A large number of his images appeared in the papers during this visit.

GENESIS OF A POET-PAINTER

Tagore's creativity took a new turn in the last two decades of his life. Fascinated by the strange and fantastic shapes he constructed from corrections he made in his manuscripts, he began to develop his own drawing style, which was quite original and unique. Other than sporadic drawings when he was young Tagore did not practise art in a serious way during his first sixty years. However, he watched with interest as the new art movement unfolded in India and the West. He visited many museums and art galleries in Europe and the USA. This broadening of interest was sudden, and without any formal training or confidence in his inherent sense of pattern and balance, he painted over two thousand canvases before the end of his life. A prolific output from an amateur modernist painter indeed! His paintings were first exhibited in Paris in 1930. Britain hosted his paintings for the first time during an exhibition at Birmingham City Art Gallery on 2 June that year, and then subsequently in London on 4 June. An art critic of *The Birmingham Mail* wrote about the paintings:

> Some of these ... are of astounding power. Their very deep tones and wonderfully harmonious sequences produce exactly the same effect of rhythmical balance as that which is to be observed in the purely linear work, and indeed we might sum up the whole of this exhibition as being a marvellous example of the sense of balance and of harmony, even into the most fortuitous of its forms ... the rhythmic quality, whether of colour or of line, is the predominant factor, and it is a most instructive exercise to accompany the study of these drawings by a reading of the poems of the artist, for in both there is an outstanding quality of quietude.[77]

Eight years later, in 1938, his paintings were exhibited in the Calman Gallery in London; that was the last exhibition of his paintings in Britain during his lifetime.

TURN OF THE TIDE

After the Jallianwala Bagh massacre Tagore became more and more critical about British rule in India. Once he had had an unreserved faith in the English justice of *Boro Ingrej*, the Great English Heart in England, as opposed to the administrators and clerical English-men within the colonies.

This had now crumbled. While India was passing through political turmoil with such incidents as the police atrocities in Solapur for wearing the 'Gandhi cap,' Gandhi's Salt March, the arrest of Abdul Gaffer Khan at the border of Peshawar and riots in Dacca (now Dhaka, capital of Bangladesh), Tagore was in London as a helpless onlooker. During this period he wrote a series of articles in *The Spectator* showing his frustration with the British administration of India. In his article, 'An Appeal to Idealism,' he condemned Europe saying:

> Once Asia in her spring time of exuberant life offered the world her spiritual ideals, to-day Europe in the illumination of her intellect has brought her science and also her spirit of service. But unfortunately she has not come to Asia to reveal the generosity of her civilization, but to seek an unlimited field for her pride and power, trying to make these things eternal. She has come with her need and not with her wealth; and therefore she has belied her own mission and used the truth itself for a utilitarian purpose of self-aggrandizement.[78]

In the context of the riots in Dacca, he wrote in a letter to the editor: '... that this event at Dacca has alienated, more than anything else in Bengal, the sympathies of those who were still clinging to their faith in British justice. Other happenings had shaken public confidence, but this has struck at its very foundation.'[79] In his article on Gandhi's refusal to attend the Round Table Conference in 1930, Tagore initially did not approve of the decision, but later in the same article he did.[80] From letters, essays and interviews that appeared in the British press during 1930, one can gauge his anguish and conflict. His faith in British justice was at its lowest ebb. Once he had held in the highest esteem the greatness of British civilisation from its history and literature. He had established a close relationship with the finest English minds of his time. The articles and letters published in *The Spectator* were testimonies to the erosion of his own convictions. Now he became the severest critic of the administrators of his own country, and he became more isolated.

When another war loomed over Europe, Rabindranath's faith in Western civilisation totally deserted him. His last message to Europe came on his eightieth birthday, *Crisis in Civilization*, an abstract of which was published in *The Manchester Guardian*. It said in part:

> The failure of humanity in the West to preserve the worth of their civilization and the dignity of man which they had taken centuries to build up weighs like a nightmare on my mind. It seems clear to me that this failure is due to men's repudiation of moral values in the guidance of their affairs and to their belief that everything is determined by a

mere physical chain of events which could be manipulated by man's cunning or might. The consequences of this belief are proving terrible to man.[81]

It was his last warning to the West. A year before his death, Oxford University conferred on him a DLitt (honoris causa). In its four hundred-year-old tradition, this was the first time the conferrer went outside Oxford to give it, rather than the recipient coming in to receive it. This was not so significant for Tagore, but it was significant for Oxford to uphold its own institutional prestige.

From 10 July 1912 until his death on 8 August 1941, Tagore's twenty-nine-year relationship with Britain followed an uneven path. Although enthusiasm for Tagore from the British public was not always uniform—sometimes intense, sometimes low—and he was either praised or rejected, he was in the media spotlight throughout the course of his British association. The British media never lost sight of Rabindranath Tagore. He was widely reported upon in newspapers and journals. Reviews of his books, writings, interviews, lectures, news of his travels, meetings with like-minded figures and exchanges with them—whether they be political, philosophical or educational—his ideas, photographs, sketches and cartoons—all appeared in the press with equal importance.

The media even followed him when he was away from the British Isles. There were reports about him not only in the mainstream broadsheets and the tabloid press but also in countywide regional papers. Even in papers that did not fit the remit or ethos of Tagore—such as *The Bazaar Exchange and Mart* (an exclusive business paper), *Broad Arrow* (military journal), *Ladies Field* (women's fashion magazine), *Psychic News* (a magazine on parapsychology) and *Municipal Journal of Public Works*—he was intermittently featured. Rarely in history were there instances of a poet from one country being so exhaustively reported about in the media of another. In those twenty-nine years he was praised and revered by a section of intellectual Britain for the clarity of his thought, as a thinker with integrity and honesty and a great visionary of his time.

Decades of Oblivion

Soon after his death in 1941, Rabindranath Tagore faded rapidly from British memory. The new generation of academics found his literary works too wearisome and outdated for further cultivation: evidently he was ignored. Although in the sixties and in the early seventies some new translations by Aurobindo Bose appeared from a London publishing house, these translations too failed to impress modern poetry lovers. Other than a few radio programmes and some cultural events organised by Indian settlers in Britain, the poet's birthday centenary celebrations in 1961 passed unnoticed by the British public. There was no initiative of any kind, either at the government level or by any private enterprise, to keep his works alive for posterity. It is difficult to believe that up to 1970, Rabindranath was largely unread, and to the new generation of reading public the name Tagore was almost unheard of in Britain. A British newspaper columnist wrote in August 1986: 'For every hundred Indophiles who lap up the latest Rushdie or Narayan there is perhaps one intrepid adventurer who dips into a collection of Tagore's verse, his novels or his plays; and it is fairly probable that the dip won't last long, because Tagore in translation can be difficult to like.'[82]

RESTORING TAGORE: A NEW DAWN

In 1985, William Radice, then a young Oxford poet, published an anthology, *Rabindranath Tagore: Selected Poems* from Penguin Modern Classics. This was a collection of new translations, directly from the original Bengali, in clear and sharp modern English. Radice's translation, the first of its kind, drew the attention of modern poetry lovers in Britain and once again struck a chord in them. Since its first publication, the collection has gone through several editions, to favourable reception.

Following the publication of Radice's collection, André Deutsch published *Art of Rabindranath Tagore* by Andrew Robinson, unfolding for the first time the entire vista of Tagore's paintings to Britain's contemporary art lovers. Macmillan broke its silence after fifty-five years by publishing some new titles and also reprints of the old volumes with new forewords, namely *Rabindranath Tagore: Selected Short Stories* by Krishna Dutta and Mary Lago (1991); *Glimpses of Bengal* (1991) and *Rabindranath Tagore: An Anthology* (1997) by Dutta and Robinson; and new reprints of *My Reminiscences* and *Nationalism* came out in 1991.

Another collection of selected short stories by Tagore was published by Radice through Penguin in 1991. Ketaki Kushari Dyson's *I Won't Let You Go*, a collection of new translations of Tagore's poems and songs appeared from Bloodaxe (1993), and was received well in the *Poetry Review* (London, 1993). The reviewer John Bailey commended: 'Mrs Dyson has succeeded in these new translations in restoring a sense to the reader of Tagore's real and remarkable genius as a poet ... if any translation can put Tagore back on the map where he belongs.'[83] Heinemann brought out a translation by Kaiser Haq of the novella *Quartet* (*Chaturanga*); a biography of Tagore *Rabindranath Tagore: The Myriad-Minded Man* by Dutta and Robinson came out from Bloomsbury in 1991: 'Judicious, sympathetic and exceedingly well documented,' wrote the reviewer of *The Times*.[84] In 1997, Cambridge University Press published 346 letters and exchanges between Tagore and a range of personalities titled *Selected Letters of Rabindranath Tagore*, edited by Dutta and Robinson.

Thus, towards the end of the last century, there was a veritable flurry of publications about Tagore which appeared from high-street publishers, indicating a restoration of Tagore in Britain. Satyajit Ray's films based on Tagore's stories, such as *Tin Kanya* (Three Daughters), *Charulata* ('Broken Nest') and *Ghare Baire* (*The Home and the World*), made a huge impact on Western audiences. The real strength and sharpness of Tagore's short stories, previously lost in weak translations, became apparent in those films. About *Charulata*, Penelope Houston commented that 'the interplay of sophistication and simplicity is extraordinary in the film.'[85] The timing of the feature films along with an authentic documentary of Tagore's life, also produced by Ray as a tribute at the centenary of the poet's birth, contributed its share to the revival process.

A wide variety of Western composers both modern and old used Tagore's lyrics in their musical compositions. Tagore himself was aware of this growing new musical phenomenon during his lifetime. He is now well intertwined into the Western musical fabric. Professor Carlo Coppola of Oakland University in Rochester, USA, identified over one hundred composers worldwide to date that have set Tagore's words to music, including some well known British composers, namely Frank Bridge, Maurice Besly, Eric Fogg and more recently, Jonathan Harvey and Naresh Sohal.[86] In May 1992, one of Tagore's allegorical poems *Debatar Gras* (Snatched by the Gods) was used in an opera by Param Vir, its libretto having been written by William Radice. *The Sunday Independent* praised it as '[a] hugely accomplished achievement, crossing the cultural divide as the musically European work of an ideologically Indian Composer.'[87] There is now a growing trend amongst British singers and musicologists to study Tagore songs (Rabindra Sangeet) in their original form.

In 1986, the Rabindranath Tagore Festival Committee was formed to celebrate the 125th anniversary of the poet's birth in a UK–India collaboration. Under the auspices of the Festival Committee, together with a London-based cultural group, an international seminar was organised at the Commonwealth Institute in London for the first time since the poet's death, to discuss Tagore's creativity and talents. Papers presented in that seminar were later published by Macmillan in a collection titled *Rabindranath Tagore: A Perspective in Time* edited by Mary Lago and Ronald Warwick (1989). As a part of the celebration the Museum of Modern Art in Oxford, in collaboration with the Festival Committee, exhibited fifty paintings of

Tagore at the Barbican Art Gallery in London which subsequently toured Manchester, Glasgow, Bradford and Oxford.

During the early 1960s there was an influx of Bengali settlers into Britain. To keep their culture alive on foreign soil these settlers set up several cultural organisations all over Britain. Celebrating Tagore through his songs, operas and dance dramas was top of their agenda. Around the 1980s these cultural centres became vibrant, and through their cultural initiatives, the native people of Britain became more and more aware of Tagore's contribution towards the Indian performing arts, which they were unaware of during his lifetime. It is undeniable that these settlers contributed their share to the recent Tagore resurgence in Britain. It is through their relentless campaigning that the Bengali language, along with other languages, is now taught in British schools, predominantly where there are large Bengali communities.

In 1985, the Tagore Centre UK was established in London by a group of Tagore enthusiasts with the aim of promoting and archiving Tagore's work in Britain. Currently the Centre with its branch in Glasgow is the most thriving educational association outside India with a keen mission to disseminate and foster all areas of Tagore's continuing heritage. In 2000, the Centre succeeded, by negotiating with other education bodies, in including Tagore within the English Literature syllabus as part of the National Curriculum for schools in England and Wales. The Centre has also published several worthwhile titles including *This World is Beautiful* (1988) by Sakti Bhattacharya, Kalyan Kundu, Jill Parvin and Kalyan Sircar—an anthology aimed at young readers in schools, new translations of *Parrot's Training* (1993) by Debjani Chatterjee and *The Post Office* (1996) by William Radice, and a collection of fantasies and satirical poems titled *He* ('Sey', 2003) by Kalyan Kundu and Anthony Loyens. Among other publications were two volumes of essay collections: *Purabi: A Miscellany in Memory of Rabindranath Tagore, 1941–91*(1991) edited by Dutta and Robinson, and *Rabindranath Tagore: A Creative Unity* (2006) by Amalendu Biswas and Charles Gordon-Graham. In 2000, a Calcutta publisher brought out an important volume *Imagining Tagore: Rabindranath and the British Press (1912–41)* based on the research carried out at the Centre by Kalyan Kundu, Sakti Bhattacharya and Kalyan Sircar. In 2002, an award-winning head teacher and noted educationalist Michael Marland, in his book *Managing Arts in the Curriculum*, suggested: 'Rabindranath Tagore warrants a significant place in the secondary schools arts curriculum. Most famous for his poetry, he also wrote fifteen plays of which The Post-Office ... is eminently suitable for secondary schools.'[88]

Now Tagore is slowly appearing in British classrooms and his poems are being included in several curriculum-based anthologies specifically for schools, something that has not happened earlier. Nowadays the subject of Tagore can often be found within the dissertations of undergraduates in colleges and universities all over the UK.

In the new millennium more and more Tagore publications have appeared from publishing houses. Joe Winter's *Gitanjali*, which is the translation of the entire Bengali *Gitanjali* following the same rhyming as in the original verse, was published from Anvil Press (2000); Radice's *Particles, Jottings, Sparks* from Angel Books (2001); a valuable document of letters and exchange of two great visionaries, *The Geddes–Tagore Correspondence* edited by Bashabi Fraser from Edinburgh University (2002); Radice's recent translation of *Gitanjali* (a new retranslation of the poems from the original Macmillan volume) from Penguin (2011), and finally Michael Collins's *Empire, Nationalism and Post-colonial World* from Routledge (2011), a new interpretation of Tagore's English writings on history, politics and society—these works are further additions to the literature about Tagore.

In 2011, Britain celebrated the 150th anniversary of Tagore's birth where institutions and organisations, large and small, joined in commemorating the event. Dartington's Tagore Festival, The Tagore Centre UK's three-day international seminar at the University of London, a memorable cultural evening *Gitanjali* by a London group at the Royal Festival Hall, and many others were all part of this commemoration. Keeping this in view, The Tagore Centre UK's commemorative volume *Rabindranath Tagore: A Timeless Mind* edited by Amalendu Biswas, Christine Marsh and Kalyan Kundu is an important publication. Twenty-nine scholars on Tagore have contributed to this volume. There is a growing trend that non-Indian Tagore scholars are eagerly learning the Bengali language so that they can dip into the original writings and explore the canon of his works, apparently sealed away from the West for so long. This is indeed a new global phenomenon.

Recent Western interest has extended towards Tagore's other faculties that were not highlighted much during his lifetime. There is new appraisal of his educational ideas, including those on women's education, his thoughts on rural regeneration, and his deep concern for the preservation of nature and the environment and the saving of our fragile ecosystem. All of this was expressed in his writings. In his early years of managing his estates in rural Bengal, Tagore observed the progressive decaying of the village community. That insight motivated him in later life to establish an experimental institution of rural regeneration—Sriniketan, alongside his experimental educational institution Santiniketan. Sriniketan was one of the pioneering schemes of self-help in India actively supported and largely overviewed by Leonard Elmhirst, an agricultural economist and son of a Yorkshire clergyman who spent several years in Santiniketan. Cottage industry, handicrafts, dairy farming and agriculture using modern techniques were all part of the curriculum at Sriniketan. On his return to England, Elmhirst and his wife Dorothy took a leading role in revitalising the Devon countryside setting up Dartington Hall Trust in 1926 with similar radical schemes of regenerating rural England through arts, social justice and sustainability. Other than education and the arts, catered to by the Dartington International Summer School and Schumacher College, the Trust currently runs several charitable programmes,

Tagore's reception in Britain in 1912–13 was timorous, transitory and insecure. His works were not assessed holistically. After a century, Tagore has now passed the test of time. With the rise of India as an economic power, the advancement of Information Technology and social networking with Facebook, Twitter, Linked in, and You Tube, and the wide distribution and exchange of information and ideas, Britain is now becoming more aware and inquisitive about the cultural landscape in India and its heritage. Rabindranath Tagore is obviously one of their growing interest areas. He is now constantly in the process of rediscovery and, through the process of rediscovery, Tagore's place among the great artists and thinkers of the world is becoming secure as a growing number of British people are becoming fascinated by his life and work.

Apart from the Tagore Centre UK in London, two more centres of Tagore studies have been founded in Britain: the Scottish Centre of Tagore Studies in Edinburgh Napier University (2012) and The Tagore Centre for Global Thought at India Institute, King's College, London (2012).

Notes

1. Cited from the address delivered at the unveiling ceremony of the bronze bust of Rabindranath Tagore in London on 7 July 2011. For the full text of the address, see http://www.princeofwales.gov.uk/speechesandarticles/a_speech_by_the_prince_of_wal es_at_the_unveiling_of_a_bust_o_1054271606.html
2. Sengupta, *History of the Bengali-Speaking People,* 258.
3. Thakur, *Parassey, Rabindra Racanabali,* vol. 22, 443.
4. In 1878, Tagore was sent to England for higher study in pursuit of a career leading to admission to the Bar. He was admitted to University College London but returned home after 483 days without any academic qualifications. In 1890, he came to England again, accompanied by a friend. However, having no apparent objective, he returned home after twenty-nine days.
5. Page, ed., *The Letters of Ezra Pound, 1907–41,* 177. The letter was written to Harriet Monroe on 26 August 1917.
6. Stead, *The New Poetic,* 45.
7. Aronson, *Rabindranath Tagore Through Western Eyes,* 2.

8. The India Society was founded in London in June 1910 by William Rothenstein with the objective, as written in the Society's constitution, 'to promote the study and appreciation of Indian art, music and literature; ancient and modern, by means of publications by correspondence with kindred societies and with museums of literary records relating to branches of Indian culture or by such other means not being contrary to the rules, as the Society or the Executive Committee shall time to time determine.' Between 1912 and 1915, India Society published three works of Tagore, viz. *Gitanjali, Chitra* and *One Hundred Poems of Kabir.*

9. Out of the 103 poems included in *Gitanjali*, fifty-three are taken from the Bengali *Gitanjali*; the remaining are taken from his other books of verse— *Naivedya* (sixteen), *Gitimalya* (sixteen), *Kheya* (eleven), *Sishu* (three), *Chaitali* (one), *Kalpana* (one), *Utsarga* (one), *Smaran* (one) and one song from his play *Achalayatan.* The total actually comes to 104 as in one translation he had combined two poems into one.

10. *TLS*, 'Mr Tagore's Poems,' 7 November 1912, 492.

11. *The Athenaeum*, 'Gitanjali,' London, 16 November 1912, 583.

12. *The Nation*, 'An Indian Mystic,' London, 16 November 1912, 320–2.

13. Lago, ed., *The Imperfect Encounter*, 68.

14. Lascelles Abercrombie, 'The Indian Poet,' *The Manchester Guardian*, Manchester, 14 January 1913, 6.

15. *The Daily News and Leader*, 'An Indian Poet,' London: 21 January 1913, 4.

16. *The Spectator*, London, 'Recent Verse,' 15 February 1913, 278–9.

17. *Pall Mall Gazette*, London, 'Under the Banyan Tree,' 14 October 1913, 7.

18. *Daily Dispatch*, London, 'The Tagore Boom,' 19 February 1914, 4.

19. Lago, ed., *The Imperfect Encounter*, 20.

20. Ibid., 61.

21. Parekh, ed., *Tagore and Poetry, Chicago*, 92–4.

22. Seamus Perry, 'Rabindranath Tagore Revived,' *TLS*, 16 September 2011, 3–4.

23. Thompson, *Rabindranath,* viii [Preface].

24. Joseph Rowntree and Charles Booth were social reformers. Charles Booth's book *Life and Labour of People of London* (London, 1908) is relevant here.

25. Chaudhuri, *Atmaghati Rabindranath*, 143.

26. Rose, *The Intellectual Life of the British Working Classes,* 136.

27. *The Baptist Times and Freeman*, 'Rabindranath Tagore,' 13 February 1914, 122.

28. *The New York Times*, Section vi, 'The Hindu Poet Won the Nobel Literary Prize,' 20 November 1913, 4.

29. *The Daily Citizen*, 'London Chat,' London, 7 February 1914, 4.

30. *The Times*, London, 'The Nobel Literature Prize,' 14 November 1913, 8, and 'Swedish Tribute to Mr. Tagore,' 15 November 1913, 13.

31. *The Daily Chronicle*, 'Indian Poet Honoured,' 14 November 1914, 7.

32. Chakravarty, ed. *Poets to a Poet,* 151. Letter from Yeats to Tagore, 12 September, 1914.

33. Nirad C. Chaudhuri, 'Tagore: The true & the false,' *TLS*, 27 September 1974, 1029–31.

34. Chakravarty, *Poets to a Poet*, 59. Letter from Robert Bridges to Tagore written on 7 June 1914.
35. *The Daily News and Leader*, 'Nobel Prize for Indian Poet,' 14 November 1913, 1.
36. *The New Age*, 'Readers and Writers,' 20 November 1913, 80.
37. Page, ed., *The Letters of Ezra Pound*, 159–60. Letter written to Iris Barry on 25 January 1917.
38. *Truth*, 'Notes from Paris—The Prince and the Poet,' London, 24 December 1913, 1502–3.
39. *The Observer*, 'Life and the Poet,' London, 12 October 1913, 4.
40. Ernest Rhys, 'Rabindranath Tagore,' Everyman, London, 14 November 1913, 145.
41. E. W. Lewis, 'The Eastern Standpoint,' *The Christian Commonwealth*, London, 17 December 1913, 220.
42. *Pall Mall Gazette*, 'Under the Banyan,' 14 October 1913, 7.
43. Thompson, *Alien Homage*,.51.
44. Chaudhuri, *TLS*, 27 September 1974, 1029–31.
45. *TLS*, 'East and West,' 14 May 1914, 236.
46. William Radice, 'Books Reviews and Notes,' *Archiv Orientálni*, 68, No. 5, Czech Republic, 2000, 510–12.
47. Thompson, *Alien Homage*, 47.
48. Ibid., 48.
49. R. E. Warner, 'The Work of Rabindranath Tagore,' *Oxford Mail*, Oxford, 27 May 1930, 4.
50. Walter de la Mare, 'Poets from Afar,' *The Westminster Gazette*, London, 7 February 1914, 6.
51. *The Irish Times*, 'Abbey Theatre,' Ireland, 19 May 1913, 9.
52. Das, *The English Writings of Rabindranath Tagore*, vol. 2, 25.
53. *The Athenaeum*, 'Drama,' 7 November 1914, 486.
54. Rabindranath Tagore, '*Red Oleanders*: Author's Interpretation,' *The Manchester Guardian*, Manchester, 28 August 1925, 25.
55. Ernest Rhys, *Rabindranath Tagore: Biographical Study*: London: Macmillan, 1915, 47.
56. Lago, *Imperfect Encounter*, 246.
57. *The Daily Telegraph*, 'Hungry Stones,' 29 November 1916, 4.
58. *The Manchester Guardian*, 'Sir Rabindranath Tagore's Stories,' Special Supplement, 26 April 1918, 3.
59. Thompson, *Alien Homage,* 22.
60. *TLS*, 'New Novels: *Gora*,' 28 February 1924, 126.
61. Lago, *Imperfect Encounter,* 255.
62. Chakravarty, *Poets to a Poet*, 154.
63. *The Nation*, 'Memories of a Poet,' 25 August 1917, 536–7. This is the lengthiest review of the book.
64. J. Ramsey Macdonald, 'Mr Rabindranath Tagore's School,' *The Daily Chronicle*, 12 January 1914, 6.

65. *The Nation*, 'The Circle and the Centre,' 13 December 1913, 499.
66. *The Manchester Guardian*, 'Poet and Philosopher,' 6 January 1914, 4.
67. *TLS*, 'Man the Creator,' 31 May 1917, 259.
68. Das, ed., *The English Writings of Rabindranath Tagore*, vol. 2.
69. Tagore, *Nationalism*, London: Macmillan, 1917, 9–10.
70. Das, ed., *The English Writings of Rabindranath Tagore*, vol. 2, 426.
71. *The New York Times*, 'India Will be Free, Tagore, Poet, Says,' Section 1, New York, 19 November 1916, 6.
72. *TLS*, 'The Protest of a Seer,' 13 September 1917, 435.
73. Thompson, *Alien Homage*,31.
74. Lago, *Imperfect Encounter,* 269.
75. Andrews, *Rabindranath Tagore*, 85.
76. *The Nation and the Athenaeum*, 'A League of Spirit,' London, 9 April 1921, 49–50.
77. *The Birmingham Mail*, 'Poet as Artist,' Birmingham, 4 June 1930, 9.
78. Rabindranath Tagore, 'India: An Appeal to Idealism,' *The Spectator*, London, 7 June 1930, 932.
79. Ibid., 'Great Britain and India,' *The Spectator*, London, 30 August 1930, 280.
80. Ibid., 'The Round Table Conference,' *The Spectator*, London, 15 November 1930, 724.
81. *The Manchester Guardian*, 'Dr. Tagore and the War", 1 April 1941, p. 6.
82. Ian Jack, 'Master of Arts,' *The Observer*, Colour Supplement, London, 31 August 1986, 20–3.
83. John Bailey, *Poetry Review*, Vol. 83, No. 1, London, 1993, 22–4.
84. P. N. Furbank, 'The Wisest Fool in Calcutta,' *The Times*, 9 March 1995, 38
85. Andrew Robinson, *Satyajit Ray: The Inner Eye*, London: André Deutsch, 1989, 156.
86. Carlo Coppola, 'Tagore in Western Musical Garb,' in *Rabindranath Tagore—A Creative Unity,* edited by Amalendu Biswas and Charles Gordon-Graham, The Tagore Centre UK, London, 2006, 9–39.
87. Nicholas Williams, 'Opera Param Vir,' *The Sunday Independent*, 13 July 1996, 10.
88. Marland and Rogers, *Managing the Arts in the Curriculum.* 40–1.

Works Cited

Tagore's Works in Bengali

Thakur, Rabindranath: *Rabindra Racanabali*, vols. 1–28. Visva-Bharati: Kolkata, 1978.

Tagore's Works in English

Gitanjali. London: Macmillan and Co., 1913.
The Gardener, London: Macmillan and Co., 1913.
Crescent Moon. London: Macmillan and Co., 1913.

The Post Office. London: Macmillan and Co., 1914.

Nationalism. London: Macmillan and Co., 1917.

Collected Poems and Plays. London: Macmillan and Co., 1936.

Das, Sisir Kumar, ed. *The English Writings of Rabindranath Tagore*, vol. 1(1994), vols. 2 and 3 (1996). New Delhi: Sahitya Akademi.

Works on Tagore in English

Andrews, C. F. *Rabindranath Tagore: Letters to a Friend.* London: George Allen and Unwin Ltd., 1928.

Aronson, Alex. *Rabindranath Tagore Through Western Eyes.* Kolkata: Riddhi, 1943.

Chakravarty, Bikash. *Poets to a Poet.* Kolkata: Visva-Bharati, 1998.

Chaudhuri, Nirad C. *Atmaghati Rabindranath.* Kolkata: Mitra and Ghosh, 1992.

Lago, Mary, ed. *Imperfect Encounter: Letters of William Rothenstein and Rabindranath Tagore, 1911–41.* Cambridge, Mass.: Harvard University Press, 1972.

Marland, Michael, and Rick Rogers. *Managing the Arts in the Curriculum.*London: Heinemann, 2002.

Page, D. D., ed. *The Letters of Ezra Pound, 1907–41.* London: Faber and Faber, 1971.

Parekh, Shailesh, ed. *Tagore and Poetry, Chicago.* Kolkata: Rabindra Bharati University, 2010.

Rose, Jonathan. *The Intellectual Life of the British Working Classes.* New Haven and London: Yale University Press, 2001.

Sengupta, Nitish. *History of the Bengali-Speaking People.* Kent, England: Grantha Neer, 2001.

Stead, C. K. *The New Poetic: Yeats to Eliot.* London: Hutchinson, 1964.

Thompson, Edward. *Rabindranath Tagore: Poet and Dramatist.* Calcutta: Riddhi-India, 1948.

Thompson, E. P. *Alien Homage: Edward Thompson and Rabindranath Tagore*, Delhi: Oxford University Press, 1993.

PART FIVE

The Americas

Tagore in the Plaza Hotel, Buenos Aires, Argentina, 1924. Courtesy: Sonia Berjman's *La Victoria de los jardines: el paisaje en Victoria Ocampo*, Buenos Aires, Papers Editores, 2007. Photo credit: Archivo General de la Nación, Departamento Documentos Fotográficos (Argentinean National Archives, Department of Photographic Documents).

Part Five

The Americas

30

ARGENTINA

PAULA SAVON AND SONIA BERJMAN

If you walk through San Isidro, in the suburbs of the city of Buenos Aires, you surprisingly come across Tagore, not the great Indian poet, but a little street that bears his name: 'Today, 7 May 1961, marks the day that a hundred years ago a great poet was born in Calcutta, a great friend of this homeland and all the homelands (his homeland was the world), a teacher .... Today a side street will be named after him ...' wrote Victoria Ocampo in *La Nación*.[1] Ambassadors, politicians, writers, cultural personalities and the general public attended that event.[2] The person who had conceived and realised the idea was also present: Victoria Ocampo. Tagore became known in Argentina when he obtained the Nobel Prize and achieved fame through the friendship with Ocampo, the grande dame of Latin American literature.

The relationship Tagore had with our country went through four phases: 1913: Obtaining the Nobel Prize; 1924: Visit to Argentina; 1941: Tagore's death; and 1961: Celebration of Tagore's birth centenary.

COMMEMORATION OF TAGORE'S BIRTH CENTENARY (1961)

We start with this date because it was the poet's last great moment of remembrance. Argentine tributes included radio programmes, such as the presentation from the president of the Sociedad Argentina de Escritores (Argentine Writers' Society), Fermín Estrella Gutiérrez, and the broadcast of *Chitra*; exhibitions, as in the Museo Nacional de Arte Decorativo (National Museum of Decorative Art) containing manuscripts, books and paintings by Tagore; and lectures given in the same Museum, beginning with one by Victoria Ocampo entitled 'Historia de una amistad' (Story of a friendship), followed by those from Ángel Battistessa, Víctor Massuh, Frida S. de Mantovani, Marcos Victoria, Enrique Pezzoni and Osvaldo Svanascini. Finally, Tagore's books were edited afresh, newspaper articles were published in his honour and a commemorative stamp was issued. The number of edited books was impressive (see Works Cited).

The article from *La Nación* on 7 May 1961 entitled 'En el recuerdo de Rabindranath Tagore' (In memory of Rabindranath Tagore), outlining his life, devoted a few paragraphs to his visit to Buenos Aires and included a photo of the poet in his Plaza Hotel room, which was his first stopover in the city. Here we find: 'Buenos Aires opens its arms to him on 6 November, 1924 ... He gives lectures, writes on these same pages, speaks and tells us of a promising future, of a responsibility, of a transcendent and powerful life. Our intellectuals get to know him and, logically, immediately love him. From this deep relationship is born an affection which transposes the criticism of his work and spreads widely and generously to men. The patriarchal silhouette of the poet passes through our city and leaves an indelible memory.'[3]

On that Sunday, 7 May 1961, Victoria claimed in the same journal: 'Today, when some of Tagore's friends meet ... I only hope we can come together in brotherhood like he dreamt that all men would do, and that we achieve a few minutes out of the daily routine to enter a region that belongs to all times.' The President of India, Rajendra Prasad, and the Prime Minister, Jawaharlal Nehru, joined in the celebrations by sending a message to the Argentine people: 'Through his poetry, the poet Tagore was able to demonstrate universality of emotions and universality of human aspirations. ... His literary production has the positive quality of bringing people from all over the world together on a human level.'[4]

This fraternal relationship between India and Argentina had begun much earlier. Despite the fact that until 1900 the presence of Indians in this country was rare,[5] in 1920 an Argentine Consulate had already been set up in Calcutta. In 1943, a Commission of Commercial Exchange was created in Buenos Aires, which would then become an Embassy in February 1949, when diplomatic relations were established. Many years later, in April 2009, Argentina would open another Consulate in Mumbai.

Tagore's Visit to Argentina (1924)

What was happening in Argentine literature when Tagore arrived in our country? Argentine literature has always been characterised by a cleft between a position called 'exocentrism' or 'Europeanism' and another with a *Criollo* or 'national' base. In the second half of the nineteenth century, literary movements became consolidated, inspired by French Romanticism and by popular sources, and by popular habits and history, without ignoring the scenery of the Pampa (the pampas); foreign influences did not veil vernacular literary movements. In the 1870s appeared José Hernández's poem whose protagonist is the *gaucho Martín Fierro*, a representative of the men who inhabit and work in the Pampa. He is still considered the typical figure of Argentine literature.

Modernism emerged in Latin America at the end of the nineteenth century as a reaction to Romanticism and as an expression of an American and Argentine literary process influenced by the Parnassians, a group of French poets who set a new standard of formal precision in lyrical poetry from the 1860s to the 1890s. This was partly a reaction against the emotional extravagance of Romanticism, and French Symbolists and it was influenced by Greek, Germanic, Norse, pre-Columbian, and Far Eastern mythology. Buenos Aires was its main stage, and Nicaraguan Rubén Darío was its most important exponent. The 'postmodernismo o Generación del Centenario' (Postmodernism or the Centennial Generation) appeared around 1910, a hundred years after Argentina became independent from Spain. An important component in the ideological climate of the time was Hispanism: the spirit of reconciliation with Spain and Spanish heritage that became widely accepted particularly after the Spanish-American War. It gives way to a new vision of the past and feeds the myth of race. The other aspect of the movement is a cultural Nationalism in the context of modernisation, secularisation and increasing immigration that lead to finding a proper national literary tradition. Representatives of the nationalist reaction are Ricardo Rojas, Leopoldo Lugones and Manuel Gálvez.

Within this cultural horizon, many Argentine intellectuals were attracted by Eastern cultures.[6] There was a proliferation of Orientalist popular editions with the translation of several principal works, including the *Bhagavad-Gita*, parts of the Mahabharata, the *Arabian Nights* and the *Rubaiyat* quatrains by Omar Khayyam.[7] Almost simultaneously (1915–17) appeared the first translations of Rabindranath Tagore's texts by Joaquín V. González and Carlos Muzzio Sáenz Peña.

At the time of Tagore's visit in the 1920s, some intellectuals still clung to Europe and refused to accept the new North American cultural hegemony. Some of these learned nonconformists, such as the aforementioned Carlos Muzzio Saénz Peña, began to frequent the East with the expectation of discovering a new civilisation, inspired by a philosophy and a body of principles with roots contrary to the cultural foundations of the West. This spiritual and philosophical Orientalism was a return to a mysticism that, even with important Catholic vestiges, led to a kind of new spirituality, definitely opposed to monotheistic religiosity. In 1919, Julio Noé expressed it like this: 'Persian poetry, Hindu legends ... have for us men of this century an intimate and transcendent significance that to men of yesterday had remained undiscovered. In no other way can one explain the weird thirst of some modern westerners to drink from these ancient fountains...'[8]

Other intellectuals such as Ángel de Estrada, Joaquín V. González, Carlos Aldao, Ernesto Quesada, Arturo Capdevila, Álvaro Melián Lafinur,

Víctor Mercante, Emin Arslán, Jorge Max Rohde, Ricardo Güiraldes, Manuel Gálvez and Alberto Candioti also had a genuine interest in the intricate Eastern cultures, exceeding by far the reason of simple exoticism or a mere mystical search. Almost all of them travelled around Asia apart from their incursions around the Old World or the United States.

In 1931, Victoria Ocampo began publishing *Sur* magazine, one of whose basic premises was to establish a fruitful cultural dialogue between the two Americas (initiated by Waldo Frank) and between these regions and Europe (promoted by Ortega y Gasset); this magazine became one of the major instruments for the spread of Rabindranath Tagore's work in Argentina and in the whole of Latin America.

In the first week of November 1924, the Dean of the Facultad de Filosofía y Letras (School of Philosophy and Literature, Universidad de Buenos Aires), Coriolano Alberini, appointed a reception committee 'on occasion of the arrival of the thinker and poet Rabindranath Tagore' to accompany him, 'to greet him and participate in the tributes he will receive.'[9] The reception committee was chaired by Ricardo Rojas, the renowned writer, teacher, journalist, public speaker and researcher, who deeply influenced the culture of Argentina.[10] Some other members of the committee were Félix Outes, Clemente Ricci, Emilio Ravignani and Enrique Loudet. They also sent invitations[11] to a large number of renowned people, associations, leagues and centres, which contributed to the felicitation from different cultural spheres. Thus, a large committee was waiting for 'the arrival of the poet Rabindranath Tagore ... to welcome him ... The poet Tagore, who was already feeling somewhat unwell, retired sick to the Plaza Hotel, where he was accompanied by Mr. Ricardo Rojas ... In addition to suffering the effects of fatigue, he also had a fever.'[12]

The welcome was overwhelming. The press literally deified Tagore. Some journalists had moved to the city of Montevideo, the last stop before Buenos Aires, two days earlier and joined the ship on which the poet was traveling. The following extract is an example:

> The visit to the country of a representative man with the grandeur of Rabindranath Tagore is a source of deep satisfaction for Argentina. ... Rabindranath Tagore will find in Buenos Aires an atmosphere of cordiality and affection, trained for a long time in the reading and appraisal of his work. He arrives, then, as an old acquaintance, whom we have to thank for the incomparable pleasure that he has provided us with so many subtle pages of illusion and mystery, deep love and refined mysticism.[13]

The figure of Rabindranath Tagore was idealised: He was a representative from the distant and exotic East, a noble Bengali gentleman from Calcutta, somewhat dark-skinned with a venerable grey beard, dressed in the traditional style of his country, considered a 'thinker and poet,' a 'great Indian artist,' an 'eminent traveller' and an 'illustrious bard and great philosopher', 'illustrious guest' and 'eminent Indian poet, 'a Superior Being who visits us.'[14]

The newspaper *La Nación* in its extensive article on the occasion of his arrival, had already referred to him as the 'greatest contemporary poet of the East,' the 'glorious poet of immortal poems,' and a 'wonderful apostle and Indian poet,' describing his image with high-sounding words which were repeated in other Argentine periodicals. Here we get a more intimate insight:

> Wrapped up in a thick coat, lying on the bed, a blanket over his feet, his wonderful head, the same head that artists have not needed to idealize, rests on a cushion against a corner in the sleeping compartment. The white beard and white hair, in twisted loops, surround the noble dark face; his deep black eyes have an expression of sweetness that could never be forgotten. These sweet eyes look very deeply, and with an absolute serenity. Deeply serene is his countenance in which not a single wrinkle is noticed. There is no trace of frowning on his high, noble forehead, which seems to [rise] even under the white loops. There is a great light in his face.[15]

In an article in *La Nación* of 7 November 1924, the poet expressed an almost prophetic message:

> ... Europe has two wings: one, powerful; the other, failing ... If European civilisation succumbs, here it can be reborn. You are a new nation, and it is not unlikely that you will find yourselves with the inheritance of the European civilisation, having to do your part with your own intimate resources that have not been developed yet, thus, making a perfect match.
>
> I come to these new countries with the yearning to stimulate them, so that they aim at the true civilisation, without the European imbalance and with both wings equally spread.
>
> ... what interests me here is not the industrial progress, the modernized Argentina, which is something external, adopted; nor am I interested in seeing the state of its economic progress. What I ardently want to find is the typical, the genuine, that the country has. I want to know native customs, all those things in which, naturally, its national spirit has been expressed. I want to get in contact with the earth's environment, I want to know the farm, the ranch; I want

to see the typical dances, hear folk songs, their *vidalitas* [vidalita is a folksong], music that was born in their fields, in their villages, in the mountains.

When he came to know that in Buenos Aires there was 'intense curiosity about the new art', the poet said that perhaps it would be a 'favorable environment here to [hold] a Bengali art exhibition.'[16]

But, upon arrival, Tagore was ill and was placed in the care of the physicians Castex and Beretervide. The article 'Estada del poeta hindú Rabindranath Tagore' (Stay of the Hindu poet Rabindranath Tagore) in *La Prensa* mentions that the 'illustrious guest will need two or three days of absolute rest, due to the ailment that afflicts him.'[17]

Victoria Ocampo gave him a spiritual welcome with an article 'La alegría de leer a Rabindranath Tagore' (The joy of reading Rabindranath Tagore):

I have noticed ... that there are two kinds of books: those whose reading gives us pleasure and those which give us joy.... We are well away, incidentally, from the person of whom I speak. ... After having evoked *Recherche du temps perdu*, so extraordinary and so devoid of joy, is when the happiness of delving into the work of Rabindranath Tagore seems more sensitive. I think of it, then, as one does of a warm bath after an arid and dusty trip; I desire it as one desires the greenery of the trees, the blue of the sky, after a long stay in the city; I go to it as one would go towards a friend.[18]

On 9 November 1924, *La Nación* also announced: 'Rabindranath Tagore colaborará en La Nación' (Rabindranath Tagore will contribute articles to *La Nación*). The greatest personalities from all over the world have written for this highly respected Argentine newspaper, founded in 1879 by the former President of the nation, Bartolomé Mitre. The article mentioned:

Rabindranath Tagore's essays granted to La Nación will be published monthly ... Rabindranath Tagore does not ordinarily mix his literary task with journalistic work. This is an exception which must give us satisfaction. It is, no doubt, a compliment to those in South America who follow the development of his thought ....

Ketaki Kushari Dyson has gathered eighteen articles published during 1924 and 1925.[19] Tagore was a popular author who was widely read by the Argentine cultured class of the 1920s. His books could be found in public and home libraries. The most popular part of his work was his poetry and some plays with a clear spiritual content and a mysticism which integrated easily into Western sensitivity. 'If music can be defined as the embroidered outline of silence, Tagore's poetry could, in turn, be characterized as a wavy—and delightful—shore of the ineffable ... It allows us ... and leads us—starting from the real, to introduce ourselves on tiptoe, gradually, from reality into the Mystery.'[20]

Tagore was appreciated in Argentina's intellectual environment, but unfortunately, no access was available to his work in its translations from its original language. This led some renowned writers, such as Jorge Luis Borges, to make critical comments on his language and writing.[21] The admirable thing about Tagore's poems is that no preparation is needed to read them. This is, for example, what André Gide said after translating *Gitanjali* into French. But, as one commentator wrote: 'In my opinion, a similar thing can be said of the complete works of Tagore ... But if no scholarly preparation is required to read it, I think that a great spiritual preparation is essential to appreciate it.'[22] Victoria Ocampo organised a meeting between Gide and Tagore in Paris in 1930.[23]

ARGENTINE TRANSLATIONS

Today, versions of his books available in the Biblioteca Nacional Argentina (National Library of Argentina) are in Spanish, Italian, English, French, German, Catalan and Portuguese. But there are no direct translations from Bengali to Spanish: we only have access to *translated translations*, usually from English versions made by the author himself or by others. To pour the poetry of Tagore into our language, versified prose with biblical phraseology was used. Zenobia Camprubí recreated Tagore in exalted lyrical tones.

The first Argentine translations were done by Joaquín V. González and Carlos Muzzio Sáenz Peña (For the list of translations see under Works Cited).

The early translators of Tagore were well-known personalities in the Ibero-American culture; among them, Zenobia Camprubí´s versions had a wider appeal. These translators are worth mentioning:

> Carlos Muzio Saenz Peña (1885–1954), Argentine writer, translator and journalist (founder and director of the legendary newspaper *El Mundo*);
> Joaquín Víctor González (1863–1923), Argentine politician, historian, educator, philosopher, and writer. Founder of the Universidad Nacional de La Plata and the Instituto Superior del Profesorado in Buenos Aires, member of the Real Academia Española and jurist (International Permanent Court of Arbitration in The Hague). His complete works include twenty-five volumes;
> Alberto Girri (1919–91), Argentine poet of the so-called *Generación del 40* (1940s Generation). He published some thirty books in

an ascetic and extremely intellectual language. He wrote for the
magazine *Sur* and the newspaper *La Nación;*

Zenobia Camprubí Aymar (1887–1956), Spanish storyteller,
translated the English prose poems by Tagore into Spanish.[24] Zenobia's
versions were strongly influenced by her husband, the famous writer
Juan Ramón Jiménez. He helped with these compositions which were
more re-creations than literal translations.[25]

Juan Ramón Jiménez (1881–1959), Spanish Nobel Prize for Literature
laureate (in 1956), was influenced in his poetry by modernism, by
Rubén Darío and the French symbolists. *Platero y yo* (1917) stands out
from his vast body of prose. Jiménez employed his own orthography,
which distinguished his work and his texts even more. The search
for a closer congruity between the pronunciation and the spelling
of words, accentuating the 'plastic value' of the word on the written
page, can be seen in these translations of Tagore's works, published
by Editorial Losada:[26]

Alicia Molina y Vedia (1898–1983) translated *El naufragio* (*The
Wreck*), Buenos Aires: Futuro, 1946; *El alma y el mundo* (*The Home
and the World*), Buenos Aires: S. Rueda, 1950 (both reprinted in 1952
by S. Rueda); and *Recuerdos de mi vida* (*My Reminiscences*), Buenos
Aires: Futuro, 1947;

Heriberto Lionel Charles translated *Aves errantes* (*Stray Birds*),
Buenos Aires: Ulysses, 1946 (re-issued with an introduction by
Osvaldo Svanascini. Buenos Aires: Kraft, 1953); and

Anatole and Nina Saderman translated *Una juventud en la India—
Gora*, Buenos Aires: Futuro, 1945.[27]

From Tagore's Death Until the Present

Argentine cultured society reacted to Tagore's death with shock. Articles
were published in the principal newspapers. Some samples are given below.

La Prensa, on 8 August 1941, published 'Rabindranath Tagore:
Falleció ayer en Calcuta' (Rabindranath Tagore: He passed away yesterday
in Calcutta), giving a summary of his life and work. It highlighted his
educational work in Bolpur and Santiniketan, the political and philosophical
aspects of his thought, and emphasised his extraordinary originality as a poet
and composer. The article ended: 'Tagore visited our country in 1924, and
showed the universality of his culture and the superior quality of his spirit in
the conferences given in prestigious rostrums.'

La Nación of 8 August 1941 related in 'Ha fallecido en Calcuta el poeta
Tagore' (The poet Tagore has died in Calcutta):

The extraordinary coming together of people from the most diverse latitudes and, above all, the rapprochement of East and West is one of the most notable facts of contemporary times.... Thus, a figure like Rabindranath Tagore who, for our times, appears wrapped in an atmosphere of legend, and whose work was hardly known except in fragmentary versions and through dubious [pieces of] information [about his life] is not only perfectly known to us for his work, but we have even been able to see him and listen to him from close quarters. ... He was warmly welcomed and listened to with respect: the respect and warmth which he aroused was enhanced by his venerable priestly appearance and by the wisdom and the sweetness of his word. We remember the time he spent in our country, an event that was indeed a sign of our times, with deep admiration for his enduring work. This memory will stay with us.

After the poet's death a number of books were published about him in Argentina (see under Works Cited). The poet's work was also spread through the magazine *India eterna y actual* (Eternal and present India), published for twenty-five years, founded by María Renée Cura (1927–2007), who was Victoria Ocampo's secretary and a great admirer of India. She founded the Centre for Indian Studies called *Anand Bhavan* (inspired by the one in Allahabad) in 1977. She was awarded the Padmashri (a high civilian award) by the Indian government in 1984. In the Clásica y Moderna bookstore, Tagore's texts were read;[28] lectures have been delivered on him[29] and his work has been the subject of papers in university seminars, for example, 'Música y silencio. La Palabra creadora en la obra de Rabindranath Tagore' (Music and Silence: Creative Word in Rabindranath Tagore's works) and 'Concepción Dios-mundo en la obra de Rabindranath Tagore' (The God-world concept in the work of Rabindrananth Tagore) by Paula Savon.[30]

As to the acceptance of Tagore's plays, in July 1920, *Amal* (*The Post Office*) was staged at the Teatro Nacional Cervantes in Buenos Aires. 'It did not receive a favourable review, ... but it was offset by the accurate and magnificent scenery on stage which stood out, the composition of which was unhesitatingly classified as delightful scenes.'[31] Since the end of the 1990s until 2004, *Un cuento del Mahabharata* (A tale from the Mahabharata), based on *Chitra*, devised as a monologue and played by Laura Obligado was intermittently staged in small theatres.[32]

Tagore was also an inspiration to filmmakers. Pablo César directed an Indo–Argentine production entitled *Unicornio: el jardín de frutas* (Unicorn: the garden of fruits). Oscar Barney Finn included Tagore's character, played by Eduardo Pavlovsky, in *Cuatro caras para Victoria* (Four faces for Victoria,

1992). Contemporary musicians such as Daniel Santoro have revived Tagore's legacy.[33] The Buenos Aires Philharmonic Orchestra performed *Sinfonía Lírica* by Alexander Zemlinsky[34] at the Centro Cultural Borges.

The Bengali poet greatly influenced Western education. His innovative methods of doing away with classrooms and allowing students to be in contact with nature, and the principle of giving them greater freedom, introducing music, singing and painting were practised in Tagore's school in Santiniketan and then spread around the world. These ideas on education influenced Maria Montessori (1870–1952), who went to India in 1939 and, indirectly, Johan Heinrich Pestalozzi, the great Swiss educator, who had contact with Montessori. *La Escuela Serena* or *Escuela Activa* (a school belonging to the sisters Olga and Leticia Cossettini) put these principles into practice in the city of Rosario in Argentina, taking those educators as models. In Argentina there are several schools that bear Tagore's name, including one in the Department of Jáchal (San Juan Province) and another in Villa Claudina (Córdoba Province).

TAGORE AND OCAMPO (1890–1979)

Tagore's visit to Argentina is remembered in India as well as in Argentina because of his meeting with Victoria Ocampo. She dominated his stay in Argentina in every way, even in Tagore's reminiscences. Argentina was the ground where the encounter and relationship of these two personalities, one Bengali and the other Argentine, the Nobel Prize winner and the creator of *Sur*, were acted out. They apparently belonged to opposite worlds but had the same sense of existence. Both were universalists and cosmopolitans, but at the same time they had their roots in their homeland. Geographically speaking, this attachment derived in Tagore from the 'golden' Bengal countryside and in Ocampo from the Argentine Pampas.

Vijaya was the Bengali name that Tagore gave to Victoria. It means 'victorious', showing a double play on words and expressing his feelings for her. When she read poems from *Gitanjali*, even before knowing Tagore personally, Victoria felt 'that the future has just been revealed to me instantly, like an unknown landscape in the light of lightning, in the night. Just the time needed to recognize it, guide me in it: rocks in front and a solitary tree, a mountain, a single path to climb.'[35]

After the Buenos Aires meeting, Victoria had always described their relationship with concepts and ideas related to gardens and nature, comparing Tagore's love of nature to a mirror, where she saw reflected in it that which was herself.

Tagore was influenced in his paintings by Argentina: the poet began painting encouraged by Victoria after his visit to this country. He liked to draw flowers that seek the sun, landscapes, animals. His depiction of an exotic and exuberant fauna and flora may have had a double origin: the influence of American Indians' crafts and the reading of William H. Hudson's descriptions of South America. Tagore had met him personally in London in 1912 and imagined our country through his writing. Their common interest in Hudson was another point of deep attachment between Victoria and Tagore, as both appreciated and read his books. They also both appreciated the 'criollo' painter Pedro Figari, whose exhibition Tagore visited just soon after his arrival in Buenos Aires.

According to Ketaki Kushari Dyson, Tagore deeply influenced Victoria as a poet. *La laguna de los nenúfares* (The lagoon of the water lilies), her prose poem for children that narrates the life of Buddha, has great similarity with Tagore's *The Post Office*.[36] Victoria also took Tagore's autobiography *My Reminiscences* as a model for her own to which she gave the title *Testimonios y autobiografías* (Testimonies and Autobiographies).[37]

When Tagore arrived, the first gesture from Victoria was to send a bouquet of flowers to his hotel with the note: 'I feel relief to send you flowers, because you know very well that they are not "merely color and scent" for us, but "beauty and joy free from need,"'[38] referring to a quote from *Sadhana*. When after his illness he was allowed to take his first walk, Victoria took him to visit Palermo Park; and when choosing the country-house that would be his abode in Buenos Aires for his convalescence—Miralrío—it was important for her that it was surrounded by natural scenery.

The journey to Argentina and Rabindranath Tagore's and his secretary Leonard Elmhirst's stay in Buenos Aires from 6 November 1924 to 4 January 1925 (which is late spring and early summer in Argentina) are described in detail in the excellent book by Ketaki Kushari Dyson, *In your Blossoming Flower-Garden*, and in the *Diary* kept by Elmhirst, preserved in Dartington Hall, UK.

This is how Victoria remembers Tagore's stay in 'Miralrío':

It was a new house, a copy of the Basque ones. From the balconies on the first floor and the ground floor corridor one could see the river and a round tipa [Tipuana tipu] tree in the foreground to the right. It was the season of the most abundant and perfumed flowers ... The espinillos (*acacia caven*) were in flower and perfumed the air with their small gold coloured blossoms. It was the season of roses, paraiso (*melia azedarach*, *Ghora neem* in Bengali) and honeysuckles. I filled up the rooms with flowers. I even put up flowers on the stairs. ... Tagore and I looked at the sky, the river, the land in spring, from the balcony of what would be his room ... We arrived in San Isidro ... in the middle of a storm. ... 'No, it is not the sea. It is fresh water.' ... 'It's

so wide!' ... That balcony was to be 'his balcony.' ... It was the only
thing I could give him: the smell of rain on the slope grass, the tipa
tree shadow with yellow-flowers, the immensity of this unequalled
river and shreds of clouds pushed by the wind. ... In Miralrío, Tagore
wrote in the mornings, wandered in the garden, or came to walk in
my garden. From the balcony of his room, he carefully gazed with
binoculars at rufous hornero and benteveo [flycatcher] birds. He read
Hudson. In the afternoons the rows of admirers would arrive. He often
sat on the grass, under the tipa tree, near the ravine, and made his
visitors sit in a semicircle.[39]

And this is the way Tagore remembers it:

Last year it was about this time that I was in San Isidro and I still
vividly remember the early morning light on the massed groups of
strange flowers, blue and red, in your garden, and the constant play
of colours on the great river which I was never tired of watching from
my solitary window.[40]

    You express regret in your letter that I could not continue my stay at
that beautiful house near the river till the end of summer. You do not
know how often I wish I could do so. It was some lure of duty which
drove me from that sweet corner with its inspiration for seemingly
futile idling[41] ... my mind often wonders back to that balcony in
San Isidro seeking for your ministration of love ....[42] The picture of
that building near the great river where you housed us in strange
surroundings with its cactus beds that lent their grotesque gestures
to the atmosphere of an exotic remoteness, often comes to my vision
with an invitation from across an impossible barrier. There are some
experiences which are like a treasure island detached from the
continent of the immediate life, their charts ever remaining vaguely
deciphered—and my Argentine episode is one of them. Possibly you
know that the memory of those sunny days and tender care has been
encircled by some of my verses—the best of their kind—the fugitives
are made captive, and they will remain ... I am sure, thought unvisited
by you, separated by an alien language.[43]

    One of the desires of the poet upon arrival was to get to know the
'auténtica' (authentic) Argentina. After a walk around the countryside during
a stay in Chapadmalal, Tagore wrote in Bengali a poem influenced by the
vision of a dead cow, that inspired in him thoughts associated with time and
death: 'A Skeleton' (Konkal) of which Victoria asked the poet a translation
into English. This resulted in an incident that sheds light on the problems
associated with the translations of his work.

Victoria relates a vivid experience she had the week before Christmas 1924 when the two of them travelled to a huge ranch located in the Buenos Aires province:

So I asked my friend Martinez de Hoz to allow me to spend a few days with him in Chapadmalal. That would be an opportunity for him [Tagore] to see a ranch ... The place is exceptionally beautiful, some twenty kilometres from the Atlantic Ocean, with a magnificent park ... One afternoon ..., I entered his room when he was finishing a poem ... 'Translate that poem to me' [I requested]. Leaning on the pages lying before him, I could see, indecipherable, ... the delicate, mysterious strokes of the Bengali letters. Tagore took the page and began to translate literally, he told me. What he read, at times faltering, seemed extremely illuminating ... Then I asked Tagore to write down the English version. He gave it to me the following day, written in a precious manuscript. I read the poem in his presence, and I could not hide my disappointment. 'But such and such things that you read to me yesterday are not here,' I reproached him. 'Why did you delete them? They were the core, the heart of the poem.' He replied that he thought those things might not interest Westerners.[44]

Victoria Ocampo relates in her autobiography:

In these two months I got to know him, I learned how he could experience the most unexpected, the most opposite states of mind: capricious, indulgent, cheerful, harsh, tender, impersonal, distant, scrupulous. Variable as the weather. I learned, then, that there was no distinction between him and other men, other than his poetic genius and his spiritual and physical beauty. The difference was not little. At the age of sixty-three Tagore, with his white hair, extremely expressive eyes, high stature and slow, determined pace, his unchanged calmness and sweetness (in appearance), was impressive. It took a while for me to overcome the shyness that paralysed me in his presence.[45]

The poet, who carried in his soul the weight of a deep loneliness, found in Victoria someone able to value him in his most human aspects. They shared moments of deep interpersonal communion of thoughts and feelings, and after his departure, Tagore wrote from the boat to his host:

I am drifting further and further away from your shore and now it has become possible for me to set the vision of my everyday surroundings at San Isidro against a background of separation. ... For me the spirit of Latin America will ever dwell in my memory incarnated in your

person. ... When we were together we mostly played with words and tried to laugh away our best opportunities to see each other clearly. ... I tell you all this because I know you love me ... Therefore I believe that your love may, in some way, help me in my fulfilment ... But I accept my destiny and if you also have the courage fully to accept it we shall ever remain friends.[46]

During his convalescence in San Isidro the poet had become accustomed to a high and hard-backed chair, and at the end of the stay, Victoria insisted that Tagore should take the chair with him: it is exhibited today at Rabindra Bhavana in Santiniketan. When the last and fatal illness forced the poet to stay in bed, he asked for the chair to be near him. He became obsessed with its emptiness. He couldn't stop looking at it and then wrote one of his last poems: 'The empty chair' (written just a few months before his death, on 6 April 1941). Its beginning in English prose translation (by Ketaki Kushari Dyson) is:

One more time, if I can, I would like to find that seat on the lap of which the message of a caress from a foreign land is spread. ... It will keep for ever locked in my years the speech of that beloved woman who has spread this seat for me with her love from a foreign land. It will keep forever alive the sad—tender message of that woman whose language I did not know but whose eyes were eloquent.[47]

Purabi is a book of poems by the poet published in India in October 1925, with the dedication, 'To Vijaya', the name the author gave to Victoria. She called him 'Gurudev' (divine guru), in common with many of his admirers emphasising her admiration.[48] When he sent Victoria a copy from Calcutta, the poet wrote in a letter from 29 October 1925:

I am sending to you a Bengali book of poems which I wish I could place in your hand personally. I have dedicated it to you though you will never be able to know what it contains. A large number of poems in this book were written while I was in San Isidro. My readers, who will understand these poems, will never know who my Vijaya is with whom they are associated. I hope this book will have the chance of a longer time with you than its author had.[49]

This collection of poems points to a renewal in Tagore's poetry. *Purabi* and *Mahua*, in particular, marked the resurgence of an old feeling of love, together with a renewed intellectual vigour and philosophical meditation:[50] This is Krishna Kripalani's assessment:

... whatever was her memory in other places, in Bengali literature Vijaya will always be appreciated as a semi-mythical figure, Tagore's last platonic love, which inspired some of his most lyrical poems .... In his own land or wherever, the Indian poet has not had a greater admirer or more sincere devotee than this lady from a foreign land whose home was beyond the seas, who did not know the poet's language and whose language he knew neither. The only Bengali word that she learned and remembered was Bhalobasa: 'There is NO history BUT of the soul.'[51]

Purabi includes twenty poems written in 'Miralrío' and others dated later and written in other countries. Some were translated into English, but there is no published translation of all the poems. Although we read only translated versions and not the original Bengali, the heartfelt words of love for Victoria touch us. In his writings, the Argentine spring fragrance is evoked over and over again. 'Foreign flower' ('Bideshi phul') was written the day after his arrival in Miralrío, after having carefully observed the garden during the morning. All the verses begin with 'Flower, foreign flower...,' perhaps identifying Victoria with a flower in this 'foreign country.' The scenario is, without a doubt, a garden in which leaves let out a whisper.

The poem 'Guest' ('Atithi') goes like this:

Lady, you have filled these exile days of mine
With sweetness, made a foreign traveller your own
As easily as these unfamiliar stars, quietly,
Coolly smiling from heaven, have likewise given me
Welcome. When I stood at this window and stared
At the southern sky, a message seemed to slide
Into my soul from the harmony of the stars,
A solemn music that said, 'We know you are ours—
Guest of our light from the day you passed
From darkness into the world, always our guest.'
Lady, your kindness is a star, the same solemn tune
In your glance seems to say, 'I know you are mine.'
I do not know your language, but I hear your melody:
'Poet, guest of my love, my guest eternally.'[52]

On a visit to Villa Ocampo, they gazed at its rose garden and spoke of Hamlet and Shakespeare. At the end of the day Tagore wrote a poem which mentions—not roses—but jasmines which could also be found at Miralrío and at Villa Ocampo. Tagore refers to the silent love linking them in 'Apprehension' ('Ashanka'). After reading the English version which the poet sent her, Victoria wrote a deeply felt letter in which she compared Tagore with the sun and herself with a tree.

In spring when everything was in bloom in Miralrío, Tagore wrote 'The last spring' ('Shesh basanta'). This poem associated with Victoria refers to the gardens and balconies in Miralrío and Villa Ocampo.

> Before this day is done
> grant me a wish:
> Let us gather
> spring flowers
> for the last time.
> Out of many a spring
> that are yet to visit
> your bower,
> give me one
> —I implored.[53]

Another poem of *Purabi* is 'Bipasha' (the river Beas), alluding to one of the five rivers in the Punjab. The constant view of the Río de la Plata from the balcony of Miralrío had evidently evoked it. In this poem, Victoria is likened to a lotus in a fountain. Let us remember that the Argentine writer liked to watch the moon reflected in the water-lily fountain in the garden at Villa Ocampo, and that she also wrote *La Laguna de los Nenúfares* (*The water lilly lagoon*). *Vaitarani* is also a poem related to a river. It is a philosophical poem about a mythical river. It begins: 'Oh! Vaitarani, your flow is like a liquid sword, it has no sound, no gestures, no waves ...' Does the *Río de la Plata* not look like a liquid sword at certain times of the day, seen from a balcony in the ravines of San Isidro?

In 'The Key' ('Chabi'), 'Honey' ('Madhu') or 'The Lord of the Forest' ('Banaspati') we can find traces of the relationships between the poet and Victoria. This is especially true for 'The Unseen one' ('Adekha'), where the author begins by saying: 'She will come, I wait for that hope ...' and ends with '... and my heart knows that she has come.'

The poem 'The indifferent one' ('Udasin') is dated 1934, almost a decade after the South American sojourn, and goes like this:

> When I called you to the arbour,
> fragrance still lingered in the mango grove.
> Don't know why your thoughts were elsewhere,
> why your door was closed.[54]

According to Ketaki Kushari Dyson, one of the most eloquent evocations of the relationship between the two is the novel 'Farewell Song' (*Sesher kabita*, 1929). It presents a parallel to the Oriental–Occidental relationship and reminds us of the two real people with opposite characteristics:

'Tagore and Victoria. ... The work concludes with a farewell poem—"The last poem"—with a dialogue between the protagonists. It talks of flowers, tears, forgiveness, fragrances and moon-lit nights. All the stanzas end with: Goodbye, my friend, goodbye.'[55]

After his departure, and despite Tagore's insistent wish to meet Victoria again, it was only in 1930 that they met in Paris. After the 'first literary encounter' and the second 'personal' one, this was their 'third meeting.' With the help of her many contacts, Victoria organised an exhibition of the poet's paintings and drawings in the Gallerie Pigalle in Paris in 1930. These paintings had their origin as doodles and scribbles on the margins and in the text of the *Purabi* manuscript.

> The notebook in which he wrote at that time bore witness to it ....
> This notebook, I thought, was the beginning of Tagore the Artist, of his need to translate his dreams with a pencil or brush. I marveled so much at his doodles that I encouraged him to continue. When I met him, six years later in France, he was already painting, not doodling, and the exhibition I organized for him with the help of my French friends was a success.[56]

After the exhibition, Tagore wrote to Victoria Ocampo from London: 'I hope that some day we will meet in India.'[57] But they did not see each other again. And Victoria commented after Tagore's death: 'I would never see him at his home, as he wanted. I left him with a "farewell" on the train that took him to London, in summer 1930. Now, it's a goodbye.'[58]

In the second part of her autobiography (*Testimonios II*), Victoria included the following text written just after she had found out about the death of her friend:

> Rabindranath Tagore has died in his India. Midway between Buenos Aires and Mar del Plata the radio announced it to me. The car runs on the deserted road. The grey winter sky covers the plain that extends everywhere. ... It is a melancholic road when the sun and blue sky do not sing around it; sad for those not in love with space.
>
> Like me, Tagore was so much in love with space, and for the same reasons: his child's eyes would have spelled it out, they had become accustomed to it. He had spied its rumors, drunk its wind in the morning; he had populated it with his solitude: he wouldn't have fitted in anywhere else.
>
> That desert road in the middle of the plain was the best place to receive the news of his departure. What surrounded me was so according to what he preferred. ...

For him, for me, there is no place where we feel more at home than in that Pampa 'toujours recommencée'.[59]

Victoria Ocampo remained linked to Tagore's life and work. She was that woman with an oval face and penetrating eyes who appears in many of his drawings and paintings. Victoria Ocampo continued her relationship with India throughout her life. She was awarded the Desikottama, the honorary doctorate, by Visva-Bharati University, delivered by the then Prime Minister Indira Gandhi during her visit to Argentina in 1968. The Jawaharlal Nehru University (New Delhi) organised a seminar in memory of Victoria in 1991. It is interesting to note that Victoria Ocampo was invited several times to be the Argentine Ambassador to India, but she never accepted it. It may have been a challenge to restart her relationship with the Tagore legacy.

Present Situation

Currently, there is a vacuum in our country surrounding the Bengali poet due to a 'generational oblivion.' His memory is fostered almost exclusively by mature adults many of whom received his work as an inheritance from their parents.

The celebration of Tagore's 150th birth anniversary in 2011 could have been a signal for renewed efforts to make the poet known, as had been the years 1913, 1924, 1941 and 1961. UNESCO even had declared 2011 a 'Tagore's year.' However, few activities were carried out. We may mention the event conducted by the Centro Cultural Borges and Villa Ocampo on 10 December 2011.

In San Isidro at Villa Ocampo, there is an eloquent testimony of Rabindranath Tagore's relationship with Argentina. It is a bronze plaque written in beautiful Bengali script that says: 'Your home is in the loving heart that understands you and not anywhere else. Rabindranath Tagore, San Isidro, November 1924.'

Notes

1. The name was imposed by decree No. 2868, on 15 April 1961, Municipalidad de San Isidro. See: Victoria Ocampo: 'La Navidad de Tagore en Punta Chica' (Tagore's Christmas in Punta Chica), *La Nación* newspaper. 7 May 1961.
2. *La Nación*, 8 May 1961.
3. Ibid., 7 May 1961.
4. Ocampo, 'La Navidad de Tagore.'
5. In 1885, the National Census in Argentina reported the presence of six nationals from India, a figure that by 1913 had risen to sixty.

6. Axel Gasquet, 'El Orientalismo Argentino, 1900–40.' From *Nosotros* magazine to Grupo Sur, Working Paper 22 (University of Maryland: College Park, 2008).
7. *Rubáiyát de Omar-Al-Khayyam*. Trans. Carlos Muzzio Sáenz-Peña, foreword by Álvaro Melián Lafinur and drawings by Próspero López Buchardo: La Plata: *Nosotros* magazine, Joaquín Sesé & Cía, 1914; *Rubáiyát de Omar Khayyam*, trans. Joaquín V. González, Buenos Aires: s/n, 1926.
8. Julio Noé, 'refacio' Carlos Muzzio Sáenz-Peña in *Samsara* (short poems). (Buenos Aires: Mercatali Printer's: 1919) 5–7.
9. Note from Dr Alberini, *Álbum 9914*.
10. Ricardo Rojas (1882–1957). In 1909 he created the School of Humanities at the Universidad Nacional de La Plata; Dean of the School of Philosophy and Literature at the Universidad de Buenos Aires; Doctor 'Honoris Causa' and President of the latter university. 29 July, the day of his death, is designated in his honor as 'National Culture Day.'
11. Many of these invitations and their replies are in *Álbum 9914*, Museo Ricardo Rojas.
12. *Álbum 9914*.
13. *La Prensa*, 6 November 1924.
14. Note from the dean of the School of Arts, 2 November 1924 (*Álbum 9914*); note from the Circle of graduate teachers in the Academia Nacional de Bellas Artes, November 1924. (*Álbum 9914*); note by the Asociación Teosófica Argentina, 10 November 1924 (*Álbum 9914*); note by Asociación Wagneriana de Buenos Aires, November 1924 (*Álbum 9914*); and Note by A. Curutchet, November 1924 (*Álbum 9914*).
15. *La Nación*, 7 November 1924.
16. Ibid., 7 May 1961.
17. *La Prensa*, 8 November 1924.
18. *La Nación*, 9 November 1924.
19. El maestro de escuela' (The schoolmaster), 'Un mensaje de Tagore a Rusia' (A message from Tagore to Russia), 'El entrenamiento del loro' (The Parrot's Training, with illustrations by Abanindranath Tagore), 'Riqueza voraz' (Voracious wealth), 'Verdad' (Truth), 'Ciudad y poblado' (City and village), 'Mi escuela' (My school), 'Mi vida' (My life), 'Libertad' (Freedom), 'Los nuevos tiempos' (The new times), 'De noche' (At night), 'Oro fugitivo' (Fugitive gold), 'El editor' (The editor), 'Para los niños' (For the child), 'Giribala Manbhanjan,' 'La enseñanza de la religión' (The teaching of religion), 'Navidad' (Christmas,) 'Un mensaje del poeta' (A messsage from the poet: a farewell message to the Argentine people). See Kushari Dyson, *In Your Blossoming Flower-Garden*, 468–9.
20. Eduardo González Lanuza. 'La poesía de Tagore' (Tagore's poetry). Sur 270 (1961), 47.
21. Albino Gómez, 'Borges, a calzón quitado' (Online) Accessed 25 November 2011. URL: <http://www.enfocarte.com/7.32/ensayo.html>. Also see URL: <http://lacasadeasterionb.homestead.com/v3n11borges.html>

22. *La Nación,* 9 November 1924.

23. Ibid., 16 November 1969.

24. The works published by Losada in Argentina are: 'Offering lyric,' 'The gardener': *El jardinero,* '*The Postman of the King*': *El cartero del rey,* 'The new moon,' *La luna nueva, The king of the dark room, El rey del salón oscuro, The King and the Queen, El rey y la reina,* 'Malini, The ascetic,' *Malini. El asceta,* 'Mashi and other short stories,' *Mashi y otros cuentos,* 'The harvest,' *La cosecha,* 'Cycle of spring,' *Ciclo de la primavera, Chitra:* dramatic poem; 'Stray birds: feelings,' *Pájaros perdidos: sentimientos,* 'The older sister and other tales,' *La hermana mayor y otros cuentos,* Glimpses of Bengal, *Entrevisiones of Bengal.*

25. Enrique Díaz-Canedo. *Juan Ramón Jiménez en su obra.* México: 1944, 99; R. Johnson: 'Juan Ramón Jiménez, Rabindranath Tagore, and "La Poesía desnuda."' *The Modern Language Review,* 60, no. 4 (1965), 534–46.

26. Pairs of consonants are reduced as 'ns' to 's', 'pt' to 't,' silent implosive consonants are ignored and the duality 'j/g,' and 's/x' are simplified by adjusting it to the real sound of spoken Spanish: 'j' and 's'. See *La ortografía de Juan Ramón Jiménez* (On line) Acc. December 2nd, 2011 URL: <http://irati. pnte.cfnavarra.es/iesocintruenigo/joomla/images/stories/imagenesieso/R%20 A%20F%20A/actividadesytextos/laortografiadejrjdos.pdf>

27. The main publishing houses which published Tagore´s texts were Losada, Aguilar and Sur. Others: Cooperativa Editorial Limitada, Ulises, Librería Perlado, Américalee, Longseller, Santiago Rueda Editores, Editorial de Grandes Autores, Orbis, Glem, G. Kraft, Sociedad Americana, Tor; more recently: Futuro, Vergara, Nuevo Siglo, Hemisferio, Errepar, Kier. Recently, Editorial Lumen has published anthologies of the works of Tagore on various topics: wisdom, love, truth, wealth, childhood, etc.

28. *La Nación.* 7 December 2008. (Online) Accessed 27 September 2011. URL: <http://www.lanacion.com.ar/1077890-viajar-a-pesar-de-todo>. *La Nación.* 18 January 1999. (Online) Accessed 27 September 2011. URL: <http://www.lanacion.com.ar/125006-yanes-con-el-duende-del-tango-a-cuestas>.

29. For example: Susana Brandanen, 'Poesía mística y vidas de grandes almas: Rabindranath Tagore.' *La Nación,* 2003. (Online) URL: <http://www. lanacion.com.ar/458007-agenda-cultural>; 'Tagore, educador' by Paula Savón in the Borges Cultural Centre, 2005.

30. Workshops on 'Palabra y silencio' (The word and silence), Academia Nacional de Ciencias de Buenos Aires, 2010 and about 'Concepciones de Oriente y Occidente sobre Dios y el Mundo' (The eastern and western God and world conceptions), Universidad Kennedy, Buenos Aires, 2008.

31. *La Nación.* 20 July 1920, and Pellettieri Osvaldo, *Dos escenarios: intercambio teatral entre España y la Argentina* (Buenos Aires: Galerna, 2006), 69.

32. *La Nación,* 7 May 1999; 10 May 2003; 3 July 2003; 11 November 2004. (Online) Accessed 25 November 2011. URL: <http://www.lanacion.com. ar/194096-chitra>

(Online) Accessed 25 November 2011. URL: <http://www.lanacion.com. ar/508317-en-escena>

(Online) Accessed 25 November 2011. URL: <http://www.lanacion.com. ar/495013-en-escena>

(Online) Accessed 25 November 2011. URL: <http://www.lanacion.com. ar/652889-en-escena>.

33. *La Nación*, 8 November 2008. (Online) Accessed 19 September 2011. URL: < http://www.lanacion.com. ar/1066558-descamisado-gigante>.

34. *La Nación*. 6 April 2007. (Online) Acc. 19 September 2011. URL: <http:// www.lanacion.com.ar/897564-la-filarmonica-con-un-programa-osado>.
La Nación. 6 August 1997. (Online) Acc. 19 September 2011. URL: <http:// www.lanacion.com.ar/74345-la-sinfonica-de-estreno>;
La Nación.11 August 1997. (Online) Acc. 21 September 2011. URL: <http:// www.lanacion.com.ar/74635-los-apremios-del-tiempo >.

35. Victoria Ocampo, *Testimonios*, vol. 2, Buenos Aires: Sur, 1941.

36. Ibid., *La laguna de los nenúfares*. Madrid: Revista de Occidente, 1926, and Buenos Aires: Sur, 1982.

37. Ocampo's *Testimonios* was published in ten volumes, from 1935 to 1978 by the Editorial Sur and other foreign publishing houses. Six volumes of her autobiography were published posthumously.

38. Kushari Dyson, *In Your Blossoming Flower-Garden*, 373.

39. Ocampo, *Tagore en las barrancas San Isidro;* Ocampo, *Autobiografía IV, Viraje*. Buenos Aires: Sur, 1982. The River Plate is so wide that it is often confused with a sea since you can´t see the bank on the other side.

40. 30 December 1930, Kushari Dyson, *In Your Blossoming Flower-Garden,* 424.

41. 2 August 1925, ibid., 415.

42. 31 March 1925, ibid., 411.

43. 14 March 1939, ibid., 455.

44. Ocampo, *Autobiografía IV*, 77–8.

45. Ibid., *Testimonios II*, 436–7.

46. 13 January 1925, Kushari Dyson, *In Your Blossoming Flower-Garden,* 390–2.

47. Kushari Dyson, *In Your Blossoming Flower-Garden*, 327. Kripalani, 'Victoria Ocampo: Puente cultural entre continentes,' *Sur* 346, Buenos Aires (1980), 105.

48. What follows superscript 48 in the essay is taken from Berjman, *La Victoria de los jardines.*

49. Ocampo, *Autobiografía IV,* 56; Kushari Dyson. *In Your Blossoming Flower-Garden,* 416.

50. See Sukumar Sen, *History of Bengali Literature*, Delhi: Sahitya Akademi, 1960.

51. Kripalani, 'Victoria Ocampo: Cultural bridge,' 107. See Ocampo, 'Tagore on the banks of the River Plate' in *Rabindranath Tagore: A Centenary Volume* (New Delhi: Sahitya Akademi, 1961), 47.

52. William Radice (Transl), Rabindranath Tagore: *Selected Poems*. London: Penguin Classics, 2005.

53. *Poems from Purabi*, Transl. from Bengali by Kshitis Roy, New Delhi: Rupa & Co. (2003), 19–23.
54. Kushari Dyson, *In Your Blossoming Flower-Garden*, 304–5.
55. Berjman, *La Victoria de los jardines*, 158.
56. Ocampo, 'Tagore on the banks of the River Plate,' 40.
57. Ibid., *Testimonios I*, 453.
58. Ibid., 454.
59. Ibid.

Works Cited

Spanish translations of Tagore's works (See also Chapter 27, the essay on Spain and Latin America.)

Tagore, Rabindranath, trans. Joaquín V. González. *Cien poemas de Kabir* [*One Hundred Poems of Kabir*]. Buenos Aires: San Martín, 1915. (Republished later by other publishing houses: La Plata: Atenea, 1918; Buenos Aires: Juan Roldán y La Facultad, 1923).

——, trans. Carlos Muzzio Sáenz Peña. *Poemas.* [Poems.] Buenos Aires: Ediciones Mínimas No. 2 and 18, 1915–17.

——, trans. Carlos Muzzio Sáenz Peña. *La cosecha de fruta* [*Fruit-Gathering*]. Buenos Aires: Sociedad Cooperativa Editorial Limitada, 1917. [2nd ed. with Foreword by Joaquín V. González].

——, trans. and foreword by Carlos Muzzio Sáenz Peña. *El jardinero* [*The Gardener*] Buenos Aires: Colección Nobel, 1924. [Published in Santiago de Chile, 1933].

Edited Books on Tagore in 1961: Commemoration of the Centenary of His Birth

Ocampo, Victoria. *Tagore en las barrancas de San Isidro* [Tagore on the ravines of San Isidro]. Buenos Aires: Sur, 1961.

Rabindranath Tagore, Volumen conmemorativo del centenario, 1861–1961 [Memorial volume of the Centenary 1861–1961]. Buenos Aires: Embajada de la India en Buenos Aires.

'Rabindranath Tagore (1861–1961)', *Centenario* [Centenary] No. 270 Sur (special issue).

Seis de mayo: Nacimiento de Rabindranath Tagore, 1861–1961 [May 6th: Birth of Rabindranath Tagore, 1861–1961; NB Tagore was born on 7 May 1861]. Buenos Aires: Ministerio de Educación y Justicia.

Tagore, Rabindranath, Canto del sol poniente [Song of the setting sun]. Buenos Aires: Comisión Argentina de Homenaje a Tagore en el Centenario de su Nacimiento.

Tagore, Rabindranath, *Libro de los cumpleaños* [Birthday book]. Traducción y prefacio por Victoria Ocampo. Buenos Aires: Sur.

Books Written After the Poet's Death

Berjman, Sonia. *La Victoria de los Jardines. El paisaje en Victoria Ocampo.* Buenos Aires: Papers, 2007.
Delchi, Arturo Montesano. Delchi, ed. *Rabindranath Tagore y su obra.* Buenos Aires: Ferrari, 1941; Adrián A. Madril. *Tagore y la sociedad teosófica.* Buenos Aires, n.d.
Ferrari, Germán. *Tagore, soñador de esperanzas.* Buenos Aires: Longseller, 2001.
Lojo, María Rosa. *Las libres del Sur.* Buenos Aires: Sudamericana, 2004.
Monti, Lisandro. *Tributo a Tagore.* San Juan, [San Juan, 1994.]
Tummer, Lía. *La sabiduría de Rabindranath Tagore.* Buenos Aires: Deva's, 2004

Secondary Sources

Álbum 9914, archive from the Museo Ricardo Rojas in Buenos Aires.
Berjman, Sonia. *La Victoria de los Jardines: El paisaje en Victoria Ocampo.* Buenos Aires: Papers editores, 2007.
Kripalani, Krishna. *Tagore: A life.* New Delhi: Malancha, 1961.
Kushari Dyson, Ketaki. *I Won't Let You Go: Selected Poems of Rabindranath Tagore.* New Delhi: UBSPD, 1993.
———. *In Your Blossoming Flower-Garden: Rabindranath Tagore and Victoria Ocampo.* New Delhi: Sahitya Akademi, 1996.
'Rabindranath Tagore: centenario (1861–1961),' *Revista Sur* 270. Buenos Aires, Mayo-Junio 1961.
Rabindranath Tagore: volumen conmemorativo del centenario (1861–1961). Buenos Aires: Embajada de la India, 1961.

31

BRAZIL

JOSÉ PAZ RODRIGUEZ

B razil has a distinguished legacy of discovering and publishing Tagore's works over a long period of time. The reception given to Tagore was always extraordinary, starting with the publication of *Gitanjali*, with the title *A Offerta lyrica*, in 1914.[1] This was followed in 1915 by the edition of *The Crescent Moon*, translated as *A lua crescente*[2] by Plácido Barbosa which achieved four editions until 1926. In 1927, *The Gardener* was published, translated by Francisca de Basto Cordeiro under the title *O jardineiro*.[3] She originally intended to write a biography of Tagore, as she revealed in a letter from Rio de Janeiro, dated 23 July 1931 and sent to Tagore's secretary at Santiniketan. Her wish, however, was not fulfilled.

The greatest impact Tagore received was through the school-reader entitled *As mais belas histórias* (The most beautiful stories), published in 1954. Twelve editions had come out in 1959, and more than forty in 1962 and over a hundred editions in 1970. The coordinator of this anthology was the pedagogue Lúcia Monteiro Casasanta, a follower of the educational principles of the Escola Nova ('New School') Movement which had many adherents also in Brazil. He introduced Tagore's poem 'Sleep-Stealer' of *The Crescent Moon* in a translation by Abgar Renault in the section of 'intermediary reading.' Thus, as Marcus Vinícius de Freitas wrote: 'Tagore became a popular author among millions of children in Brazil, thanks to a small narrative taken from the book *A lua crescente* (*The Crescent Moon*).' Between 1939 and 1946, Tagore's work was further disseminated in Brazil by the edition of six works published by Livraria José Olympio (Rio de Janeiro) as part of the collection *Rubaiyat*. In very beautiful and careful editions, with covers designed by eminent artists, among them Tomás Santa Rosa, this collection included old and modern works of Oriental literature. Tagore was represented by *Gitanjali*, *The Gardener*, *The Crescent Moon*, *Fruit-Gathering*, *Stray Birds* and *Reminiscences*. The translations from English were done by the poets Guilherme de Almeida, Abgar Renault and Gulnara Lobato de Morais

Pereira. In the 1960s, owing to the Tagore birth centenary in 1961, Tagore was celebrated in several Brazilian cities and universities. A book exhibition was held at the Biblioteca Nacional (National Library) de Rio de Janeiro and some plays were performed. The promoter of most of these activities was the poet and educator, Cecília Meireles. In the 1970s, three Tagore volumes were translated by Raul Xavier and Gasparino Damata and published by Livros do Mundo Inteiro (Books from the Whole World) under the general title *Tagore: Obras seleccionadas* (Tagore: Selected Works). In the first volume are included *The Gardener, The Crescent Moon, Gitanjali* and the poem 'The Swan'(from *Balaka)*. The second volume contains the novel *The Wreck,* and the third *The Home and the World.* In the 1990s, Paulus Editora (São Paulo) published ten books by Tagore in translations by Ivo Storniolo and Jairo Veloso Vargas. Storniolo published in 2003 a comprehensive poetical anthology by Tagore under the title *Poesia mística: Lírica breve* (Mystical Poetry: Short Poems).

CECÍLIA MEIRELES (1901–64)

Cecília Benevides de Carvalho Meireles was born in Rio de Janeiro. She was an exceptional writer, both in poetry and in prose. She wrote articles on education in numerous journals and a great deal of children's literature on which she was considered an authority. In the 1930s, she became an educator, following the principles of the Escola Nova Movement. The principles of this Movement allowed no discrimination by gender, race or religion. In 1934, she organised the first children's library in the country, and in 1935 she started to teach Luso-Brazilian (Portuguese as spoken or written in Brazil) literature and literary techniques and literary criticism at the Universidade Federal de Rio de Janeiro, besides giving courses and delivering talks in Portugal (at the universities of Lisbon and Coimbra), Chile and the USA. She even gave classes on Brazilian literature and culture at the University of Texas.

As an adolescent, Meireles started to appreciate India and her culture, and she kept this sensibility towards the Orient all her life. That is why in her chronicle *Meus Orientes* [My Orients] she wrote: 'The East has been a constant passion in my life … because of its poetical profundity which is another way of being endowed by wisdom.' In 1920, at the beginning of her career, she participated in the literary movement called 'spiritualist,' within which stands out the group around the magazine *Festa*, with its representatives Tasso da Silveira (1895–1968) and Tristão de Ataíde, a pseudonym of Alceu Amoroso Lima (1893–1983), who were friends of Meireles and also admirers of Tagore. Nevertheless, she never wanted to be affiliated to any literary movement, although she had an affinity with Symbolism and later to Modernism. According to Cristina Gomes, Meireles's poetry is intimate and reflective, with a philosophical tone and a profound feminine sensibility. Life, love and time are the recurrent themes of her poems which were of a melodious quality. All her sadness and disenchantment, as arising out of the loss of her parents, then her grandmother and her first husband, marked her lyrical poetry.

Cecília Meireles was a great admirer of M. K. Gandhi, dedicating to him several beautiful poems and articles. In 1953, when she was fifty-two years old, she visited India. Invited by the Indian government, she participated in an international congress which was dedicated to Gandhi and presided over by Prime Minister Jawaharlal Nehru. She also received a Doctorate Honoris Causa from the University of New Delhi. A result of her trip is her book *Poemas escritos na Índia* (Poems written in India, 1961). It contains a poem dedicated to Tagore with the title 'Cançãozinha para Tagore' (Short Song by Tagore). She also wrote essays and reminiscences, some published later in Brazilian newspapers, on varied themes of India, her people, landscapes, cities, temples and important and admired personages like Gandhi and Tagore. These texts were published posthumously in the volumes *Crónicas de viagem* (Chronicles of a Journey) and *Obra em prosa* (Works in Prose), edited by Leodegário de Azevedo Filho (1998), further in the anthology *O que se diz e o que se entende* (What is said and what is meant, 1980).

Cecília Meireles dedicated herself to organising performances of Tagore's plays and of exhibitions. Cecília Meireles herself translated the play *The Post Office* which was performed at the Teatro Municipal of Rio de Janeiro in May 1949 thanks to the support of Krishna Kripalani and his wife Nandita (who were then members of the Indian diplomatic mission). Maria Fernanda, Meireles's daughter, played a role in the play. Tagore's birth centenary in May 1961 was celebrated with a special number of the *Jornal do Brasil*. Under the heading *Da Índia distante* (From distant India) it printed an essay by Meireles entitled *Homenagem a Rabindranath Tagore* (Homage to Rabindranath Tagore). In the *Cadernos Brasileiros* (*Brazilian Notebooks*), she wrote a beautiful piece with the title *Um retrato de Rabindranath Tagore* (A Portrait of Rabindranath Tagore).[4] Coordinated by Cecília Meireles, several commemorative publications came out which were translated by Guilherme de Almeida, Abgar Renault and Cecília Meireles. They were, among other works, the story 'A Fair Neighbour' from *Mashi and Other Stories*, seven poems from *Purabi*, which Tagore had dedicated to Victoria Ocampo, and *The Post Office* (all translated from English). In 1962, Cecília Meireles's translation of *Four Chapters*, from French, appeared in the collection of Nobel Prize winners, with an introduction by the translator and her essay on Tagore's relationship with Brazil.

In April 1962, the Biblioteca Nacional of Rio de Janeiro organised a major bibliographical and photographic exhibition with her help; a catalogue was published.[5] With the support of the Comissão Brasileira (Brazilian Commission) of Unesco, Cecília Meireles wrote a booklet in English, published in 1961, with the title *Rabindranath Tagore and the East–West Unity*. In the same year, the Sahitya Akademi, New Delhi, included a chapter under the title 'Tagore and Brazil' by Cecília Meireles in *Rabindranath Tagore: A Centenary Volume*.

The love and appreciation that Cecília Meireles had for Tagore led her not only to translate several of his works but also to dedicate to him six beautiful poems and numerous articles.

To bring out the spirit of Cecília Meireles and her love for Tagore, here are a few lines from the diary written during her visit to Kolkata (then Calcutta) in 1953 and published in 1959, entitled *Transparência de Calcutá* (The Transparency of Calcutta). Unable to visit Santiniketan, although she had come as far as Kolkata, she remarked:

Well, if one day I happened to return to this country, the first thing to which my wishes would lead me would be, naturally, to visit the University of Santiniketan. It was—and continues to be—like a symbol, in my heart. Founded by a poet—and a poet like Tagore!— early this century, dreaming of realising the 'place of peace' through an integral, intellectual, moral, artistic education, at the same time tied to the glorious past of India, to contemporary humility and to a future which could be dreamt as fraternal,—everything in that institution was attracting me: the origin, the methods, the objectives. Meanwhile, here, some ninety miles from that university, obeying a travel plan which it is necessary to carry out, I will not be able to see Santiniketan: I will continue to keep it in my imagination, with its trees, its teaching in the open air, its preoccupation to give the students a correct inner training, and means to express it. Santiniketan will continue to be a lyrical place, with music, dance, poetry, popular festivities, weaving, painting,—science, philosophy, in a bucolic environment, with the villages around, the fruit baskets, the milk jars,—the old life enriching the present, and the present life enriching the old.... I shall not see Santiniketan. Such is our destiny: we receive what we never expected; we don't achieve what we sometimes expect.[6]

Besides Bráulio Prego, Plácido Barbosa and Francisca de Basto Cordeiro, Brazilian translators already mentioned, three more translators deserve to be touched upon:

Guilherme de Almeida (1890–1969)

Guilherme de Almeida, born in Campinas, São Paulo, was a lawyer, journalist, poet, essayist and translator. At the age of forty he was elected to the Academia Brasileira de Letras (Brazilian Academy of Letters, Rio de Janeiro). In 1932, he supported the Constitutional Revolution of São Paulo. He was a member of several other academies and the author of numerous books of poetry published between 1917 and 1953. Besides Tagore, he translated Charles Baudelaire, Paul Verlaine and Jean-Paul Sartre.

In 1979, the Casa Guilherme de Almeida, a literary museum situated in the house where he lived from 1946 until his death, was founded in São Paulo In it a Centro de Estudos de Tradução Literária (Centre for Literary Translations) is maintained. Most recently, in 2011, a lecture and dance show was organised by Lúcia Fabrini de Almeida that was named 'Guilherme e Tagore: Afinidades eletivas' (Guilherme and Tagore: Elective Affinities).

Almeida translated two works by Tagore: *Gitanjali* (1932) and *The Gardener* (1939), both published by Companhia Editora in the *Rubaiyat* series. *Gitanjali* got a new edition in this same series in 1939. These books were repeatedly reprinted in the following years.

Abgar Renault (1901–95)

Abgar Renault, born in Barbacena, was a professor, educator, politician, poet, essayist and translator, his full name being Abgar de Castro Araújo Renault (Minas Gerais) (which indicates the name of the region from which his parents hailed). He did his primary, secondary and higher studies in the city of Belo Horizonte. He held numerous teaching posts in secondary and university centres, and even rose to Minister of Education and Culture during the government of Nereu Ramos. For many years he was a representative of Brazil at UNESCO. He was a translator of English, North American, French, Spanish and German poets and became a specialist in Shakespeare. He translated three works of Tagore from English: *The Crescent Moon, Fruit-Gathering* and *Stray Birds*. All three books were reprinted several times, as were the ones translated by Almeida. The quality of his translations can be fathomed by the praise he received in many reviews.

Ivo Storniolo (1944–2008)

Born in Ibitinga-São Paulo, Ivo Storniolo was master of Sacred Scripture of the Pontifical Biblical Institute of Rome. After studying Philosophy and Theology he became a specialist in C. G. Jung's psychology. He became a priest and a professor of biblical exegesis in São Paulo and Campinas. He was one of a team of translators of the Bible into the Portuguese language. He carried out important work at the Paulus Editora Brasileira, directing the collection of books 'Amor e Psique' [Love and Psyche]. From 1991 onwards, he translated not less than nine works of Tagore and an anthology of Tagore's poems for Paulus Editora.[7] In 2003, the above-mentioned anthology *Poesia mística: Lírica breve* (Mystical Poems: Short Poems) and in 2007 the beautiful book *Meditações* (Meditations), with essays by Tagore on art, women, education, the search for truth, meditation and the possibility of rebirth, came out. Many of the titles were translated from the Italian versions done from the Bengali by the Italian missionary Marino Rigon, who has lived in Bangladesh since 1953.

RECENT ACTIVITIES

There were other admirers of Tagore. The group around the magazine *Festa*, followers of the 'spiritualist' current, joined the literary movements of Symbolism and Modernism.[8] After Tagore's death, Otávio Tavares wrote a brief report entitled 'Tagore: filósofo, escritor, poeta e dramaturgo' [Tagore: philosopher, writer, poet and playwright] in the *Revista da Semana* [Weekly Review] (Rio de Janeiro).[9] In 1986, Neuza Moraes de Baptista published a book with the title *Tagore e o Evangelho* (Tagore and the Gospel) in Edições Paulinas. In 1961, the centenary year of Tagore, the Ministry of Education and Culture prepared an anthology of his works. Done with the assistance of the ministry, it had a beautiful introduction on Tagore as writer and educator. The Biblioteca Nacional in Rio de Janeiro organised a bibliographical exhibition, inaugurated on 2 April 1962. The catalogue printed for this exhibition was illustrated with photos, designs and manuscripts of Tagore. The introductory note was drawn up by the Director General Adonias Filho.

The government of Brazil issued a commemorative postal stamp with Tagore's picture. Several of his books were distributed free among libraries and cultural centres, which also received records of his songs. An exhibition called 'Tagore no Brasil' (Tagore in Brazil) took place in Rio de Janeiro and then was taken to other cities of the country. Also a special volume was published with the title 'In memoriam de Tagore.' This information on the events mentioned here is taken from the special number *O Correio da Unesco* (The Unesco Courier) of December 1961, dedicated in monographic form to 'Tagore, uma voz universal' [Tagore, a universal voice].

In May 1967, the play *The Post Office*, translated by Cecília Meireles and directed by the actress Alzira Miguel, was performed in the city of Porto Alegre. A booklet was published on that occasion. On 30 May 1967, the

Tribuna da Imprensa [Press Tribune] of Rio de Janeiro published an article devoted to Rabindranath Tagore where the performance was mentioned. On 7 May 1968, Tagore's 107th birth anniversary was celebrated at the Museu de Arte Moderna of Rio de Janeiro. A booklet was published on that occasion. On the same date, the deputy and second secretary of the Legislative Assembly in Rio de Janeiro, Mauro Werneck, made a proposal at the Assembly, asking for a vote of greetings to India for the events of Tagore's anniversary.

On 27 May 2011, a Colóquio Internacional [International Symposium] with the title 'Rabindranath Tagore e a Cultura da Índia' [Rabindranath Tagore and the Culture of India] took place at the Universidade Federal de Minas Gerais (UFMG), in the city of Belo Horizonte, to celebrate Tagore's 150th birth anniversary. It was organised by the Centro de Estudos sobre a Índia [Centre for Studies on India], which functions in this university, and in collaboration with the Indian Embassy and the Consulate in Belo Horizonte.[10]

NOTES

1. Editora O Pensamento of São Paulo, in a translation by Bráulio Prego reissued in 1929.
2. In Rio de Janeiro, by Tipográfica Besnard.
3. In Rio de Janeiro, by Editora Vida Doméstica.
4. No. 2, Rio de Janeiro in April–June also in 1961.
5. http://objdigital.bn.br/acervo_digital/div_iconografia/icon1285814.pdf.
6. In Crônicas de Viagem 3. Rio de Janeiro: Nova Fronteira 2000, 211–13 (slightly shortened).
7. In 1991, the translations of the following works were published: *Gitanjali, The Gardener, Fruit-Gathering, Stray Birds, The Fugitive* and *Lover's Gift, Crossing*. In 1994, *Sadhana* was published.
8. We may mention the poets Francisco Karam (1902–69), Alceu Amoroso Lima (1893–1983) who used the pseudonym Tristão de Ataíde under which he is better known, Ronald de Carvalho (1893–1935), Tasso da Silveira (1895–1968), Emílio G. Moura (1902–71), Murillo Araújo (1894–1980), Carlos Drummond de Andrade (1902–87), Murilo Mendes (1901–75), Graciliano Ramos (1892–1953), Augusto Frederico Schmidt (1906–65), and Gilberto Freyre (1911–87), a Brazilian of universal renown.
9. 16 August 1941, 42.
10. There is an Internet blog dedicated to Tagore with the name 'Casa Poética de Tagore.' It is coordinated from São Paulo by Marli Savelli de Campos, and the author of this study is a contributor.

Works Cited

Andrade, C. Drummond de. 'Tagore.' Rio de Janeiro: *Correio da Manhã*, 5 May 1961.

Calazans, João. 'O indu e o mineiro' [The Hindu and the miner]. Vitória: *A Tribuna*, 23 March 1943.

Gouvêa Leila V. B., ed. *Ensaios sobre Cecília Meireles* [Essays about Cecilia Meireles]. São Paulo: Humanitas-FAPESP, 2007.

Lamego, Valéria, ed. *A farpa na lira. Cecília Meireles na Revolução de 30* [The hook and the lyre: Cecilia Meireles in the revolution of 1930]. Rio de Janeiro/São Paulo: Record Editora, 1996.

Loundo, Dilip. 'Cecília Meireles e a Índia: viagem e meditação poética' [Cecilia Meireles and India: Tour and poetic meditation] in *Ensaios sobre Cecília Meireles*. São Paulo: Humanitas, 2007, 129–78.

Loundo, D., and Rita Ray. *Cecília Meireles: Travelling and Meditating—Poems Written in India and Other Poems*. New Delhi: Embassy of Brazil, 2003.

Meireles, Cecília. 'Abgar Renault e Rabindranath Tagore.' Belo Horizonte: Panorama, *Arte e Literatura* no. 5, 1948, 13.

———. *Abgar Renault e Rabindranath Tagore*. Belo Horizonte: Diário de Minas Gerais—Suplemento Literário, 20 July 1968.

———. *Apresentação*" no livro de Tagore *Çaturanga*. Rio de Janeiro: Delta Editora, 1962.

———. *Crônicas de viagem (2). (Obra em prosa)*. Rio de Janeiro: Nova Fronteira, 1999.

———. *Crônicas de viagem (3). (Obra em prosa)*. Rio de Janeiro: Nova Fronteira, 2000.

———. *Homenagem a Rabindranath Tagore*. Rio de Janeiro: Jornal do Brasil, 7 May 1961.

———. 'Necessidade de poesia' [Need for poetry]. Rio de Janeiro: *Leitura* no. 25, January 1945 (Tagore and A. Renault)

———. *Obra em prosa*, vol. I: *Crônicas em geral*. Tomo 1. Rio de Janeiro: Nova Fronteira, 1998.

———. *O que se diz e o que se entende (Crônicas)*[What is said and what is meant]. Rio de Janeiro: Nova Fronteira Editora, 2002 (5 chronicles on Tagore).

———. *Rabindranath Tagore and East–West Unity*. Rio de Janeiro: Brazilian National Commission for UNESCO, 1961.

———. 'Tagore and Brazil,' in *Rabindranath Tagore—A Centenary Volume*. New Delhi: Sahitya Akademi, 1961, 334–7.

———. *Tagore e o Brasil* no livro de Tagore *A noite de núpcias*. Brasília: Coordenada, 1968.

———. *Um retrato de Rabindranath Tagore* [A portrait of Rabindranath Tagore]. Rio de Janeiro: Cadernos Brasileiros, no. 2, April–June 1961.

———. ed. *Homenagem a Rabindranath Tagore. Poeta, dramaturgo, ator, musicista, novelista, pintor, educador* [Tribute to Rabindranath Tagore: Poet, dramatist, actor, musician, novelist, painter, educator]. Rio de Janeiro: Embaixada da Índia, 1961.

576   José Paz Rodriguez

Meireles, Cecília, et al. *Tagore*. Associação Brasileira do Congresso pela Liberdade da Cultura, 1961 [a twenty-three-page booklet].

Moraes de Baptista, Neuza. *Tagore e o Evangelho*. São Paulo: Edições Paulinas, 1968.

Rego, José Lins do. 'Coração da Índia.' *Jornal de Alagoas*, 2 October 1942.

Silveira, Tasso da. 'A Lua Crescente de Tagore.' João Pessoa: *A União*, 25 December 1942.

Tavares, Otávio. *Tagore: Filósofo, escritor, poeta e dramaturgo*. Rio de Janeiro: Revista da Semana, 16 August 1941, 42.

32

COSTA RICA

SOL ARGÜELLO SCRIBA

Costa Rica is a small Central American country with a population of 4.5 million. Spanish is the official language, although there are a few small groups which speak Mesoamerican and Caribbean languages. The population is a mixture of Amerindian, Spanish, African, Asian—especially Chinese—and mulatto people. The country has a democratic system and its population votes every four years to elect a President and the Parliament (Congress).

This essay presents research about Tagore's reception in Costa Rica. It establishes what the social situation was like when his work appeared in our country for the first time, and what it is like now, and especially which areas of culture he influenced. Costa Rican society began to hear about Tagore some time after he received the Nobel Prize in 1913. It is very unlikely that we would have heard anything of him in our country or throughout the American continent had he not received this award.

HISTORICAL, SOCIAL AND CULTURAL CONTEXT

Costa Rica's independence from Spain in 1821 did not result in significant economic or social change. Since it was a poor country, it depended on the General Captaincy of Guatemala, an administrative division of Spain, and México.[1] Rural life improved progressively. During the second half of the nineteenth century, the economy changed. England ruled the coffee trade, the most important product in Costa Rica's national economy. A coffee oligarchy, dependent on the English market, began to rise. By the end of the nineteenth century and during the first years of the twentieth century, a desire for Latin American solidarity gained an impetus, perceived in the search for an identity. Poetry became a highly valued means of literary expression.

José Enrique Rodó Piñeyro (1871–1917) published an essay titled *Ariel* in 1900, based on Shakespeare's *The Tempest*. This work became the paradigm of the Latin American man with ideals such as education for all, but with a Christian sense of charity and a Greco–Latin ideal of beauty. The aspect of Hispanic ancestry and the rejection of North American materialism and expansionism were emphasised. The idea was to achieve Latin American unity without considering the differences. A movement arose, called *El Arielismo* (The Arielism), that demonstrates how aristocracy had lost its social and political power, and that the class that would substitute it for governing Latin American countries had to be educated with spiritual and cultural values in order to avoid the influence of materialism on youth.

The rebirth of culture sought by the Latin American and Caribbean union (as one nation) was expressed through newspapers and journals, which had previously been used for the spreading the ideals of independence and now, once more, was seen to be of service for promoting union between the countries. Hence, intellectuals and writers thought it was important to publish the literary writings and essays of Latin American thinkers and writers. Costa Rica was no stranger to this new trend, and its intellectuals and writers embraced this movement by publishing and propagating a humanistic culture.

CULTURAL JOURNALS IN COSTA RICA AT THE BEGINNING OF THE TWENTIETH CENTURY

By the end of the nineteenth century, there was an effort to consolidate national literature, a common aspect of all first generations of writers. It was the dawn of urbanisation and modernisation of Costa Rican society, and the affirmation of modernism as a literary paradigm. It was also the affirmation of *Arielismo,* anarchism as a political vision, and mysticism, influenced by the Theosophists. The discovery of Sanskrit by Europeans produced a series of translations of literary works from Sanskrit into English, French, and German, which were also translated into Spanish in the nineteenth century, precisely as a consequence of the arrival of German philologists in Latin America, who made the earliest translations of Sanskrit literature into Latin American Spanish. This established the first contact with India, so that when Tagore appeared there was an obvious enthusiasm for getting to know the works of an author from a far away country, whose appearance represented, for some, the 'wisdom of the Orient' and for others 'poetic beauty.'

Although Costa Rica had a small population during the early twentieth century it is remarkable that many cultural journals and magazines— especially literary ones—flourished. The objective of these publications was not only to inform, but also to educate the Costa Rican population, in addition to being a means of exchange of ideas with other journals in Central and Latin America. To inform and to educate also constituted the reason why the poetic and educational works of Rabindranath Tagore were admired and seen as inspiring.

All journals used to publish poems by amateur as well as known writers, and very gradually, as isolated events, the poetry of Tagore or news about his work and life appeared, until it became a constant presence in the cultural magazine *Repertorio Americano*.

Pandemonium was the first magazine to publish a poem called 'Al niño' (To the boy) by Tagore.[2] This poem is actually composed of two poems from the book *La luna nueva* (*The Crescent Moon*). *La luna nueva* was published in Spanish in 1915 by the translator Zenobia Camprubí, the wife of the Spanish poet Juan Ramón Jiménez, in Madrid. Apart from this poem, there was a section about Tagore's life and work and, finally, some news reports about his circle and opinions, taken from other newspapers which Joaquín García Monge, a Costa Rican writer, educator and thinker, considered topical and relevant at the time. In 1914, *La luna nueva* had not yet been published, hence the above-mentioned poem published in an issue of *Pandemonium* is a mystery, since we do not know who translated it, or where it came from.

The poem, as mentioned, comprises two parts: the first one is called *Cuando y por qué* (When and Why), and immediately, without title, with a few handwritten lines which may have been added by the magazine owner, there was poem number 3 called *El manantial* (The source). What is remarkable is that no effort was made to highlight bibliographical data or sources.

Although these poems were not translated by a poet, as the text followed the English as closely as possible, still we can appreciate and feel the emotion of the poetic images created by the author. Sadly, there was no direct translation of these poems from the Bengali into Spanish, but only from their English version.

As late as 15 November 1914, an explanatory note was published in *Pandemonium* concerning Tagore receiving the Nobel Prize, called *Rabindranath Tagore, Hindu poet*,[3] followed by two poems of Tagore translated into Spanish. The perspective of the news seems to indicate that it was actually the summary of a longer piece of information on Tagore. Information travelled very slowly, by ship, so this text on Tagore should have taken many months before arriving from Europe or the United States.

The article began with an explanation of Alfred Nobel's testament, which indicates why the literature prize should be awarded specifically to the person who writes the most distinguished *idealistic* work. This was the rationale behind awarding the prize to Tagore for his book. As the article notes, '*Gitanjali* (*Ofrendas poéticas*) is no doubt the most idealistic work published in a long time.'[4] It goes on to say in the next paragraph: 'Its author, Rabindranath Tagore, is considered the prophet of Hindu Nationalism,' which draws our attention since it speaks about Tagore's nationalist aspect. However, the use of the term 'prophet' makes us think that he was considered a thinker, much in the Judeo-Christian tradition, a prophet in the sense that he announced the path for people to follow or communicated divine revelation.

The aforesaid article said that Tagore's father was 'famous among his fellow-countrymen, no matter what their caste was.'[5] In addition it mentioned that his family was a most important one in Bengal, that his grandfather Dwarkanath was received by Queen Victoria and that 'his father is the maharshi or lord of Tagore.'[6] There is an error of translation in the article of the word 'maharshi' (*maha*=great, *rishi*=seer). The translation turned out to be 'lord of Tagore', and seemed to become confused in the article with the term 'landowner.'

Later on, the text summarised Tagore's biography and explained that his literary outpourings began when he was very young. The text highlighted Tagore's educational works and teaching methods, with emphasis on his outdoor lessons: 'He came to London to study Law, but grew weary of the field and soon he went back to India, where he devoted himself entirely to his art. He founded a school in Nolepur [*sic*], near Calcutta, with 200 students; he himself created the teaching methods and, under his guidance, teachers he has summoned guide their own students in the open air.' ('Bolpur' was misspelled as 'Nolepur.')

As for Tagore's poetic work, the article stated that it was only known in Europe, and by his own English translations in rhymed prose, of such a simple, selected and precise expression that its meaning was never obscure; and he expressed admirably the agreement between idea and emotions caused by the meditative contemplation of the universe. 'When reading such poems slowly and aloud, they reveal all their beauty and allow us to see that they have been written by a musician who, indeed, is familiar with music more subtle than ours. In the Indian original, such poems are not read or recited, but sung; the breath and the words intertwine closely, to the point that certain modulations of the music have a particular meaning: some are used for nocturnal songs, some for morning songs, and other ones for seasons, in such a way that a Hindu recognizes, from the very first rhythms, the environment and the object of the poem.'[7]

Further on, the article adds: 'No poet has ever known more powerfully than Rabindranath Tagore how to express the intimacy of the human soul with nature and, at the same time, to profess a clear and broad philosophy. Such lyrical mysticism is incomparably elevated.'[8] The author compared

Tagore's poetry to the Song of Songs and the Psalms, both from the Christian Bible.

The desire of the author of the article to educate its readers about India by means of literature and poetry, but, above all, through a writer of Tagore's stature, is quite evident. Therefore, that author is considered an ambassador of India. There are small errors in the information due to lack of knowledge, despite the objectivity of the news.

As far as Tagore the educator is concerned, two aspects were highlighted: the first being that the author was an innovator of education by creating methods for such purpose, and secondly, that lessons were taught outdoors under the trees. Tagore's essays on education had still not arrived, but it is probable that these aspects would have caught the attention of Costa Rican thinkers and teachers and that Tagore would be read along with other European writers in the Escuela Normal (a Teachers' College), where Costa Rican teachers studied. The educational topic would be revisited later by Costa Rican educational theorists such as Roberto Brenes Mesén, Omar Dengo and, later on, Emma Gamboa. Tagore's educational ideas would influence our educators, especially in university classrooms, and in primary and high schools as well.

The writer values *Gitanjali* because its songs are purified or cleansed from pain or sorrow, sadness or fear, and this was the way in which Latin American readers would perceive Tagore's work: valuing more the beauty and harmony present in the poem.

The bi-monthly magazine *Athenea* published articles on varied topics in addition to literary ones from 1917 to 1920. The publishers were Alsina Bookstore, where *Pandemonium* was also brought out. The editors were Justo A. Facio and Rogelio Sotela, and for some years Joaquín García Monge, who published *Repertorio Americano*, one of the longest-running cultural magazines in the Americas.

In 1918, another poem by Tagore appeared in this magazine.[9] This time it had the name of the poet and it was called *Ejemplos XII* (Examples No.12), as if eleven poems from the author had been previously published, but it did not provide the bibliographical source nor the identity of the translator. The poem belongs to the book *La cosecha* (*Fruit-Gathering*).

The illustrated bi-monthly magazine *Minerva Revista Hispanoamericana* was first published on 15 February 1914. An essay on *Tagore and his Nobel Prize* was first published in *Pandemonium,* but in *Minerva*, on 1 September 1914, the same essay was called 'A Hindu poet,'[10] and was published, along with the poems *Las flores* (The Flowers), *Sencillez* (Simplicity) and *El silencio de la belleza* (The Silence of Beauty). The article begins thus: 'As can be remembered, the Hindu poet Rabindranath Tagore has been awarded the

Nobel Prize of Literature in 1913,'[11] which is remarkable since by then the news was already known in Costa Rica. Another interesting detail is that Tagore is said to have founded his school in *Bolepur*, not *Nolepur*, as mentioned later also in *Pandemonium* in November of the same year. It mentioned wrongly that Tagore 'has three sisters and three brothers who have become locally renowned: one of them is a famous philosopher.' This information seems to have an *oral*, not a *written* source.

The article and the poems 'Las flores' and 'El silencio de la belleza' were published two months later in *Pandemonium*[12]. The essay ended with three 'fragments from Tagore.' The style of the translation indicates that it was translated in Latin America, not in Spain, although the translator was in search of a more universal language, given that other countries in Latin America would read the magazine as well.

Joaquín García Monge published *Repertorio Americano* (1919 to 1958); its last extraordinary number was issued in 1959. With the presence of Tagore in *Repertorio Americano*, a second stage of his reception began when the Indian author came to be appreciated in Costa Rica. One of the first works of Tagore published in Costa Rica is *El jardinero de amor* (The Gardener of Love, based on *The Gardener*), printed in García Monge's publishing house *El Convivio*, founded in 1916 and advertised in *Repertorio Americano*.

In *Repertorio Americano,* Tagore's visits to different countries were reported and some of his stories and poems, essays and interviews published, especially those written during his stay in Argentina. García Monge culled the news from Argentinean newspapers. It was through *Repertorio Americano* that Tagore was also valued in other Latin American countries.

García Monge did not idealise Tagore, although some newspapers talked about Tagore as a 'Hindu holy man.' His poetic and educational work dominated the news. Tagore became important as an educational reformer. His vision of childhood and education were highly regarded, especially in a country like Costa Rica, which proposed that magazines and newspapers should not only inform but also educate. Even though *Repertorio Americano* evolved along with Costa Rican society, it kept alive the original ideals of Pan-Americanism: freedom and the spiritual development of the individual. Its articles covered several cultural topics, from scientific to literary. Writers from all of Latin America participated, among whom was the Chilean poet Gabriela Mistral (1889–1957). She and Tagore met in 1930 in New York, although they had no conversation.[13]

Repertorio Americano also reported the events surrounding Tagore's eighty-ninth birth anniversary in its issue of July 1950. After Tagore's intensive travelling and his return to India from Argentina in 1924, news about the author appeared intermittently. This magazine never reproduced any of Tagore's paintings, although it did know that one purpose of his travels was to raise funds for his school in Santiniketan through the sale of paintings. Instead, Tagore's reception was limited to poetry, spirituality and his educational vision.

Hilda Chen Apuy

Almost ten years after *Repertorio Americano* ceased to be published, the first study on Tagore appeared, written by Hilda Chen Apuy (b. 1923), in the *Revista de la Universidad de Costa Rica*[14] Hilda Chen Apuy tells us in her book *De la vida, del amor y la amistad. Un puente entre culturas* (2008) about the time when, in 1941, Joaquín García Monge gave Tagore's book *El jardinero de amor* (The Gardener of Love) to her and how Tagore became a teacher in her life. She had read one of his poems published in a newspaper along with the poet's photograph when she was a small girl, and she had cut out the poem and the image of Tagore, and had glued them next to her bed as if he were a saint.

Hilda Chen Apuy is now an emeritus professor of the University of Costa Rica, an educator and distinguished international lecturer. Awarded many international honours, she was the first Costa Rican and Latin American student to attend an Indian University, viz. the Banaras Hindu University (1957). She made further studies in Asian Civilisation and Sanskrit, thanks to UNESCO, founded the Sanskrit Department at the University of Costa Rica, and established courses on India, China and Japan in art, literature and history. To her belongs the credit for creating a course on Rabindranath Tagore and his works, which has been taught for thirty-two years at the School of Philology, Linguistics and Literature, University of Costa Rica. After Hilda Chen Apuy retired, Sol Argüello Scriba has continued to teach the Tagore course and courses on Sanskrit language and literature. Hilda Chen Apuy's interest lay in opening the doors of Costa Rica, a small country, to Asian culture as part of the human heritage. She always said to her successor, 'Never abandon Tagore,' and he never did. The students have considered Tagore inspiring, close to their minds and at the same time distant.

Tagore in Costa Rican Education

The Costa Rican educational thinker, educator and reformer of education, Omar Dengo, decided that future educators should read the great authors of world literature, and among them also Tagore. He himself was influenced by Tagore's educational philosophy. He quoted him in some of his works as an inspiration, and so did Roberto Brenes Mesén and later Emma Gamboa, to name a few.

Recently, María Eugenia Dengo, daughter of Omar Dengo and a former Minister of Education of Costa Rica, published a book called *Tierra de maestros*.[15] She presented a series of writings on different educators who left their imprint, and she talked about the admiration they all felt for Tagore's work, both in education and literature. She also mentioned how Tagore continued to be read at university.

University students of the Tagore course have frequently taken to research or to creative activity. For example, Irene Ulloa wrote on Tagore's novel *The Home and the World* which was only available in English; several years later the Spanish translation arrived. Irene Ulloa made a fine translation of Tagore's dialogue *Karna and Kunti* (*Karna y Kunti*) and of the story 'A Wife's Letter' ('Carta de una esposa'), translated from the Bengali into English by Ketaki Kushari Dyson and Prasenjit Gupta respectively for www.parabaas. com.

There are also several articles by Roberto Morales about different works of Tagore. The first were written when he was a student, and he continued writing on Tagore as a university professor. Recently, Silvia Quesada prepared adaptations of *The Gardener* (*El jardinero*) and the *The Post Office* (*Cartero del rey*), for presenting them at the University seminar, 'Rabindranath Tagore, a bridge between two worlds: India and Costa Rica,' on Tagore's 150th birth anniversary and celebrating her thirty-one years at the University of Costa Rica (on 21 and 22 September 2011). The Indian Hispanists Shyama Prasad Ganguly (Jawaharlal Nehru University, New Delhi) and Indranil Chakravarty (Mumbai) participated.

The seminar was made possible through the efforts of the Indian Council for Cultural Relations of the Indian government and the Business Attaché of the Embassy of Costa Rica in India, Ana Lucía Nassar. The programme was magnificent, and many students, professors and people who wished to know more about Tagore were able to participate. The research of Jackeline García and Sol Argüello Scriba on Tagore's influence on the educational thinking of Roberto Brenes Mesén and Emma Gamboa, important Costa Rican educators and thinkers, was presented. A few months afterwards, the public could enjoy samples of Tagore's paintings at the Museum of Costa Rican Art through the efforts of Ana Lucía Nassar.

From 2011, the new Spanish Literature programme was made official for the entire country. Among the readings proposed was *El cartero del rey* (*The Post Office*). During July 2012, Sol Argüello Scriba trained teachers from different regions of the country on how to study and understand this play. It was impressive to hear from thirteen and fourteen-year-old high school students how they identified with the sick boy Amal, how they interpreted him and, in some cases, how they represented him in a performance.

Conclusion

Rabindranath Tagore's poetry left such a deep impression on readers in the early twentieth century that he was not forgotten over the years. One reason was that Tagore's poetic creation became the ideal for Costa Rican writers, because Tagore gave an impetus to the birth of a Costa Rican national literature that started to gradually move away from European models to look for its own path, as had happened also with the Bengali language and literature (the Bengal Renaissance) in the nineteenth century. The birth and affirmation of the Costa Rican and Latin American identity occurred through Latin American Spanish and not through the Spanish spoken in Spain. Related to this were the struggles to prevent the imposition of models with a European vision of beauty and aesthetics, and also the struggles for independence and social awareness through education and cultural development. Some intellectuals considered Tagore's poetry as mysterious echoes from the distant Orient, full of wisdom, but Costa Ricans could relate to Tagore's literary and educational work which is full of emotion and inspiration. It is still left to be explored how many of Costa Rica's poets were inspired by the images created by Tagore.

Ever since he was awarded the Nobel Prize, he has been read and continues to be read in Costa Rica. Young readers also enjoy his stories and poems, and they want to read more about Tagore because it is not only the lyrical emotion that appeals to their spirit, but they feel that the author deals with various relevant topics of justice, Nationalism, knowledge, and art. That is why they want to read more of Tagore and Indian literature.

Notes

1. The Captaincy General of Guatemala, also known as the kingdom of Guatemala, was a subdivision of the Spanish Empire colonial administration and belonged to the viceroyalty of New Spain (Mexico). Its governors were the Captains General who ruled Control America, except Panama.
2. *Pandemonium*, 9, no. 120 (15 October 1914), 732.
3. Ibid., no. 122 (15 November 1914), 790.
4. Ibid.
5. Ibid.
6. Ibid.
7. Ibid.
8. Ibid.
9. *Athenea*, 1, no. 15 (15 July 1918), 314.
10. *Minerva*, 2, no. 5 (1 September 1914), 35–6.
11. Ibid., p.15.
12. *Pandemonium*, 9, no. 122 (15 November 1914), 790–1.

13. I have dealt with these topics in two articles: the first one was published in Spanish in the book *Redescubriendo a Tagore* (see Ganguly and Chakavarty, *Redescubriendo a Tagore*, 288–308), and the second one in its expanded English version in the *Hispanic Horizon* magazine of the Jawaharlal Nehru University, in 2012.

14. Chen Apuy, *Rabindranath Tagore*, 89–105.

15. Dengo, *Tierra de maestros.*

WORKS CITED

Argüello Scriba, Sol. 'Tagore and Latin America: Some considerations from the Repertorio Americano.' *Hispanic Horizons Review*, New Delhi: Jawarhalal University, 2012.

Chen Apuy, Hilda. *De la vida, del amor y la amistad. Un puente entre culturas.* Editorial Universidad de Costa Rica, 2008.

———. *Rabindranath Tagore.* Revista de la Universidad de Costa Rica. No. 26, Julio 1969 San José, Costa Rica, 89–105.

Dengo, María Eugenia. *Tierra de maestros.* Editorial de la Universidad de Costa Rica, 2010.

Facio, Justo, and Rogelio Sotela, eds. *Athenea.* San José, Costa Rica, 1917–20.

Ganguly, Shyama Prasad, and Indranil Chakravarty. *Redescubriendo a Tagore. 150 aniversario del nacimiento del poeta indio.* Amaranta Ediciones, Mumbai: Manjul Graphics, 2011.

García Monge, José Joaquín. *Repertorio Americano.* San José, 1919–58.

Ovares, Flora. *Crónicas de lo efímero. Revistas literarias de Costa Rica.* Editorial EUNED, San José, 2011.

Ovares, Flora, and Hazel Vargas. *Trinchera de ideas: el ensayo en Costa Rica, 1900–30.* San José Editorial Costa Rica, 1986.

Quesada, Álvaro. *La formación de la narrativa nacional costarricense (1890–1910).* San José: Editorial Universidad de Costa Rica, 1986.

Quesada, Ovares, and Santander Rojas. *Antología del teatro costarricense, 1890–1950.* Editorial Universidad de Costa Rica, San José, 1993.

Rojas, Margarita, and Flora Ovares. *Cien años de literatura costarricense. Generación del Repertorio Americano.* San José: Farben Norma, 1995.

33

Mexico

Xicoténcatl Martínez Ruiz

Commercial contacts between Mexico and India, at least via a sustained trade route, date from the colonial era. In the seventeenth century, a particular route used the Philippines as a point of exchange of goods. Catarina of San Juan—an iconic woman (d. 1688) of supposedly Indian origin—contributed to the cultural exchange and commerce between 'New Spain' (the formal name of Spanish colonial Mexico until independence in 1821) and India with various culinary items, as can be seen in the similarity between curry and *mole*, a spicy sauce of Mexican cuisine[1]. In 1914, José Vasconcelos (1882–1959), Mexican philosopher, writer, and politician, began another kind of rapprochement and comparative study between Mexico and India. It was initiated in the midst of the Mexican Revolution when he read the works of Rabindranath Tagore, who had just been honoured with the Nobel Prize. Here we present some responses from the Mexican community to Tagore's Nobel Prize, especially by Vasconcelos and Octavio Paz (1914–98). By surveying Tagore's reception in Mexico we can see how it is still valid and what made Tagore's work relevant for our time.

José Vasconcelos Brought Tagore to Mexico

For Vasconcelos, Tagore's Nobel Prize was an incentive for many writers and social ideologists to escape from dogmatism. Argentina was the first country in Latin America to welcome Tagore which provided an impetus for rethinking the cultural and intellectual relationship between Asia and Latin America. The echoes of Tagore's work are not only present in Vasconcelos's essays of appreciation, but he also put Tagore's social and cultural ideas into practice. When he was Secretary of Education from 1921 to 1924, Vasconcelos began—in the midst of an ongoing nationwide revolution—a struggle against educational backwardness and illiteracy, focusing on the diffusion of culture, appreciation of indigenous art, promotion of libraries, and creation of rural schools. Above all, he created a veritable army of literacy teachers whose central concept was to teach and disseminate the books which Vasconcelos considered classics. This collection included books from Plato to Dante, from Tolstoy to Tagore. It was an emblem of the reconstruction of a country through education. Vasconcelos distributed books free of charge; the number of copies is uncertain, but it was probably more than 10,000 and included Tagore's *The Crescent Moon* and *Nationalism*. After Tagore's visit to Argentina, Vasconcelos always believed that Mexico should invite Tagore. Although Tagore never visited Mexico, this does not belittle the impact of his thought and literature. His educational ideas are more relevant than ever.

Tagore's aesthetics represented an inspiration for the literary profession in Mexico. This was expressed in Vasconcelos's essay *Indology*, written in 1926. This is an example of how Tagore's voice became a guide for the literary profession at that time. Tagore offered inspiration and literary guidance to Mexican writers, poets and philosophers. Moreover, Mexican scholars of the humanities in the first two decades of the twentieth century considered the Bengali poet's literature as part of a global tradition where the voices of Asia and the Mesoamerican cultures spoke out in harmony.

Tagore's Aesthetics and its Mexican Reception

The Atheneum of Youth founded in 1909 was a Mexican cultural, literary, philosophical and humanistic movement of the first quarter of the twentieth century. Its intellectual activity drew the attention of the country's literary circles as well as of various similar Latin American groups. At the heart of this movement was a discussion not only of European literature and philosophy but also of the Eastern traditions, particularly of Tagore's literature. The central problem was the access to his works provided by translations circulating in Mexico. This remains a problem even today. This movement began with writers and philosophers such as Antonio Caso, Pedro Henríquez Ureña, Alfonso Reyes, Rafael López, José Vasconcelos, and others[2]. The aesthetics and literature of Tagore were echoed when the positivist vision and the dehumanisation of society were criticised.

In this movement José Vasconcelos's vision stands out in its search for literary sources that were not necessarily Greco-Roman. He found this kind of inspiration in the aesthetics and thought of South Asia and Japan. The reception of Tagore's literary work and Vasconcelos's drive to move towards a dialogue with Asia caused Alfonso Reyes to call him 'Zapotec–Asian.' It means that Vasconcelos was influenced by pre-Hispanic civilisations of Mexico with special reference to Zapotec culture, located in the southern Mexican state of Oaxaca, when dealing with his studies on Asian traditions. By the linguistic construction, 'Zapotec–Asian', Alfonso Reyes acknowledged that Vasconcelos himself was a bridge of encounters between Mexico and Asia, something new at that moment of intellectual discussions. Vasconcelos built a unique bridge between ancient Mexican thought and Indian tradition. In 1929, amid post-revolutionary imbalances agitating the country, his inclination towards India's aesthetics made Vasconcelos go beyond the dissemination of Tagore's work in literary circles. He strove to implement Tagore's and Mahatma Gandhi's ideas through social strategies and actions.

In 1916, Mexico was immersed in an extremely complex and difficult situation. In the international context of World War I combined with a worldwide moral crisis, the essays of writers and intellectuals like Vasconcelos brought about respect and recognition for India's literary and philosophical traditions. It was at that moment that the admiration for the Indian poet grew, along with Vascocelos's re-reading of Indian texts that he shared with various Latin American writers. All this allowed Tagore's works to become a port of entry for South Asian culture. The dissemination, impact and responses to Tagore's work increased in national importance when José Vasconcelos returned from exile to Mexico to occupy two strategic posts from 1920 to 1924, as the Rector of the National University of Mexico and the head of the Ministry of Public Education. It was then that he distributed editions of *Nationalism*, *The Crescent Moon*, *Personality* and *Sadhana* in Mexico along with works by authors like Tolstoy and Plato.

The Emergence of Scholarly Interest: Octavio Paz

After Vasconcelos, the impact and response to Tagore's works broadened and, in the 1960s, they occupied a literary and poetic position that acted as a bridge between Mexico and India. The main protagonist in constructing this bridge was Octavio Paz.

Octavio Paz, the Nobel Laureate of Literature in 1990, recognised Tagore's work as a bridge between India's literary, philosophical, humanistic, and religious traditions and the world. Paz wrote:

[Rabindranath Tagore]'s work, as well as himself, was a bridge between India and the world. Admired by the greatest in Europe, such as W. B. Yeats and André Gide, in the Hispanic countries he also had numerous and fervent readers. He visited Buenos Aires and was a friend of Victoria Ocampo, to whom he dedicated a book of poems. A great poet, Juan Ramón Jiménez, in collaboration with his wife, Zenobia Camprubí, translated a large part of Tagore's work. Those translations influenced many young poets of the time, including Pablo Neruda. In one of his first books, *Twenty poems of love and a song of despair*, at certain times the echo of Tagore's voice is audible.[3]

These echoes were already manifest when, in 1967, Octavio Paz attended a conference at the University of Delhi, which was dedicated to Tagore's manuscripts. Paz said at the conference:

> Tagore's interest in the relationship between painting and poetry appeared early on in his work. When he first read the Japanese poets, he commented: 'They don't write poem-songs, but poem-paintings.' ... Indeed, Tagore did not fall into the temptation of the ideogram or the poem-painting. This differentiates his attempt from Apollinaire's .... Tagore wanted to sing with lines and colors. That is why he does not begin with words and letters, but with lines and stains, which are always rhythmical.[4]

Octavio Paz, along with Gabriela Mistral and Pablo Neruda, recognised Tagore's influence on Latin American literature. Recently, Jaime Sabines, another Mexican poet, expressed his appreciation for Tagore, whom he considered not only a literary influence but also a spiritual guide.

RELEVANCE OF TAGORE'S EDUCATIONAL PHILOSOPHY TO CONTEMPORARY MEXICO

Tagore's philosophy of education stresses the place of poetry and music as opposed to present-day education. Today, the humanities are allowed to be pushed into the background by various educational reforms. Martha Nussbaum's book *Not for Profit: Why Democracy Needs the Humanities* refers to Tagore as a defender of the humanities and the arts to promote a critical, humanistic and creative education.

In 1917, Tagore asked: Which innovation do we want in our school curriculum today? The answer is condensed in these lines, as quoted by Nussbaum:

> History has reached a point at which the moral man, the man with integrity, is ever ceding more space, almost without realising it ... to the commercial man, the man limited to a single end. This process, helped by the marvels of scientific progress, is reaching massive proportions, with an immense power, which causes the moral imbalance of man and darkens his most human side under the shadows of a soulless organisation.[5]

We must reconsider what Nussbaum calls the 'humanistic side' of education and its impact on the future of democracy. This reconsideration proposes studying other educational models, such as that designed by Tagore.

Present Situation

In 1964, the Centro de Estudios de Asia y África (CEAA) was founded as a specialised Centre of Studies at El Colegio de México, in Mexico City, a prestigious research centre focused on the social sciences, where the study and research of Asian languages is part of the postgraduate programmes in Asian Studies. Over the 1960s various projects of UNESCO focused on East–West relationship; one of these was the creation of this Centre in Mexico. Since its foundation it nurtured a high interest in philosophy, literature, history, religions, and even more in the study of classic and modern Asian languages. The study of Sanskrit, Hindi and Bengali by PhD students is the basis of a major project of translation from Asian languages into Spanish. This is the scenario from which some translations of Tagore's works from Hindi versions into Spanish have been published. A recent example of this is the translation into Spanish of *Kabuliwala* in 2009.

In 2011, the response to Tagore reached a peak in Mexico with the Ministry of Public Education reprinting timeless classics of world literature, including the works of Tagore, which were first published in the 1920s in Spanish translation.

Notes

1. Paz, *Vislumbres de la India,* 412–13.
2. Quintanilla, *Nosotros, la juventud del Ateneo en México,* passim.
3. Paz, *Vislumbres de la India,* 438.
4. Paz, 'Los manuscritos de Tagore,' in *Obras Completas de Octavio Paz,* 2.
5. Nussbaum, *Sin fines de lucro,* 7.

Works Cited

Bovet, Pierre. *L 'Educateur.* June 11, Ponencia de Tagore el 5 de mayo (1921).

Chen-Apuy Espinoza, Hilda. 'Nacionalismo y Arte en la India.' *Estudios de Asia y África,* [Studies of Asia and Africa] 19, no. 2, 1984, 268–77.

Duque–Saberi, Isabel A. 'La India en México' in *Simbiosis de culturas: los inmigrantes y su cultura en México* [Symbiosis of cultures: the immigrants and their culture in Mexico], edited by Guillermo Bonfil Batalla, *México: Fondo de Cultura Económica y Consejo Nacional para la Cultura y las Artes* [Mexico: Collection of economic culture and National Advisor for culture and the arts], 2003, 217–43.

Fell, Claude. *José Vasconcelos. Los años del Águila (1920–25)* [The years of the eagle]. México: Universidad Nacional Autónoma de México, 1989.

Hernández Luna, Juan, ed. *Conferencias del Ateneo de la Juventud* [Conferences of the Atheneum of youth]. México: Universidad Nacional Autónoma de México, 1962.

Noeli, Morejón, Acevedo Guiomar and Jesús Chaix. 'Kabuliwala.' *Estudios de Asia y África*, 44, no. 1, 2009, 95–103.

Nussbaum, Martha. 'Education and Democratic Citizenship: Capabilities and Quality Education.' *Journal of Human Development and Capabilities*, 7, Issue 3, 2006, 235–395.

———. *Sin fines de lucro. Por qué la democracia necesita de las humanidades* [*Not for Profit: Why Democracy Needs the Humanities*]. Buenos Aires: Katz Editores, 2010.

Paz, Octavio. *Obras Completas de Octavio Paz* [Complete Works of Octavio Paz], vol. 2, México: Fondo de Cultura Económica, México, 1994.

———. *Vislumbres de la India* [*In Light of India*]. México: Fondo de Cultura Económica, México, 1996.

Paz Rodriguez, José. 'Tagore, un precursor de la nueva educación en la India'[Tagore, a precursor of the New Education in India]. *Revista Recre@rte* 3 Junio (2005): accessed 28 March 2012. http://www.iacat.com/revista/recrearte/recrearte03/Tagore/tagore.htm

Quintanilla, Susana. *Nosotros, la juventud del Ateneo en México* [We, the youth of the Atheneum in Mexico]. México: Tusquets Editores, 2008.

Taboada, Hernán G. H. 'Oriente y mundo clásico en José Vasconcelos.' *Cuyo. Anuario de Filosofía Argentina y Americana* [The Orient and the classical world in José Vasconcelos], vol. 24, 2007, 103–19.

Tagore, Rabindranath. 'The problems of education.' *Bangadarsham Journal*, Calcutta. June 1906.

Vasconcelos, José. *Estudios indostánicos* [Hindustan studies]. Michigan: University of Michigan Library, 1920.

———. *La raza cósmica: misión de la raza iberoamericana* [The cosmic race: the mission of the Ibero–American race]. Madrid: Aguilar, 1967.

———. *Memorias II. El desastre, el proconsulado* [Memories II. The disaster, the proconsulate]. México: Fondo de Cultura Económica, 1993.

34

United States of America

Anna Feuer

Introduction

This essay examines the reception by Americans of Rabindranath Tagore's writing in English translation. Tagore's international career was launched from London, where he gained the esteem of the poets Ezra Pound and W. B. Yeats, and American critics first encountered Tagore through the writings of his British admirers. Accordingly, we see some fluidity between the British and American experiences of Tagore: British and American critics responded to the same translations of Tagore's Bengali work, translated by Tagore himself, and American newspapers and literary journals often ran or responded to reviews of Tagore's works by British authors.

However, the evolving political and cultural scene of the United States during World War I and through the interwar years distinguishes the American encounter with Tagore from the British and tells us much about the American perception of the Asian 'Other' during that time—roughly the period during which Tagore published and made appearances in the United States. Sujit Mukherjee has characterised the American intellectual climate during this period as decidedly anti-idealist; as such, American readers received Tagore's work as the obscure and mystical writings of an Eastern religious philosopher.[1] Likewise, Stephen Hay has suggested that American hawkishness, particularly on the Eastern Seaboard, and post-War disillusionment with Wilsonian idealism ran counter to Tagore's critiques of Nationalism and militarism.[2]

Americans' political sentiments and literary tastes, often at odds with the internationalist message of Tagore's lectures and the unfamiliar style of his verse, only underscored Tagore's otherness for most of his American readership. Certainly America's experience of Tagore was characterised by the readers' perception of the poet as something of a cultural and religious ambassador from the East, a strange mystic with a message for the Western world. Tagore's perceived 'Easternness' elicited respect from those who admired his efforts to impart Oriental insights to the Occident and adverse criticism from those who regarded the 'Tagore craze' as a short-lived fad. Whether Tagore's identity contributed or detracted from his popularity, it certainly eclipsed his role as a writer and artist and coloured American critical engagement with his work. Indeed, in 1961, on the occasion of the 100th anniversary of his birth, participants at the All-India Bengali Literary Conference in Bombay paid tribute to Tagore as 'Ambassador Extraordinary to America.'[3]

As I shall discuss in this essay, only a handful of scholars have closely examined the American impression of Tagore's work or Tagore's time spent in the United States. Mukherjee's *Passage to America* (1964) provides the deepest and most detailed analysis, while Hay's 1962 essay on Tagore in America offers useful details about the poet's impressions of the United States and his American interlocutors. I am indebted primarily to Mukherjee and Hay for their detailed accounts of the American reaction to Tagore and their inclusion of a range of primary sources.

INDIA AND THE UNITED STATES

While Tagore cut an unusual figure in the United States, he was not the first Indian 'spiritual ambassador' to address American audiences. Swami Vivekananda, follower of the mystic Ramakrishna Paramahamsa, arrived in the United States in 1893 as a delegate to the Parliament of World Religions in Chicago. In a speech that elicited a three-minute standing ovation, Vivekananda praised Hinduism as a 'religion which has taught the world both tolerance and universal acceptance. We believe in not only universal toleration, but we accept all religions as true.' In response, the *New York Herald* proclaimed Vivekananda 'undoubtedly the greatest figure in the Parliament of Religions. After hearing him we feel how foolish it is to send missionaries to this learned nation.'[4] Vivekananda established chapters of his Vedanta Society in New York, Boston, and San Francisco, and he is widely credited with introducing the practice of yoga to Americans. By the time of his death in 1902, Vivekananda had spread awareness of Hinduism to a population that previously had minimal engagement with Indian thought or religion.

Vivekananda introduced to the American intellectual mainstream a body of knowledge that Transcendentalist thinkers had explored and embraced in the early nineteenth century. Ralph Waldo Emerson, Henry David Thoreau, and Bronson Alcott drew from Hindu scriptures, including the Vedas and the Bhagavad Gita. However, the Transcendentalists did not visit India, nor did they encounter Indians, and hence their engagement with

Indian thought was refracted through the scholarship of English Indologists, especially William Jones.

The Theosophical Society, founded in New York in 1875 by the American lawyer Colonel Henry Steel Olcott and the Russian noblewoman Helena Petrovna Blavatsky, attempted to apply lessons from Indian religious texts to a Western context.[5] However, the movement remained something of a fringe interest and did not make its way into American literary circles to the extent that it influenced thinkers and writers in England and Ireland. While Vivekananda's ground-breaking 1893 lecture bolstered the enthusiasm of Theosophists and other avant-garde thinkers for Hindu systems of thought, most Americans had almost no exposure to Indian philosophy or, more specifically, to Bengali literature, until the awarding of the Nobel Prize to Tagore in 1913.

THE FIRST REACTIONS

The American expatriate poet Ezra Pound, one of Tagore's most enthusiastic advocates, is largely responsible for introducing Tagore to American audiences. After attending a reading of Tagore's work at the London home of the painter William Rothenstein in 1912, an excited Pound sent six of Tagore's poems to Harriet Monroe, editor of the new *Poetry* magazine based in Chicago. They appeared in the December issue. As *Poetry*'s Foreign Correspondent, Pound provided an introduction to the poems that proclaimed the publication of Tagore's work in English 'an event in the history of English poetry and of world poetry.'[6]

Initially, American critics paid little attention to the English publication of Tagore's poems. Editors were content with quoting Pound's review of the poems in the English publication *Fortnightly Review*, first published in March 1913. Although Pound's review praised Tagore for 'bring[ing] us a quiet proclamation of the fellowship between man and the gods, between man and nature,' his enthusiasm hardly reached readers beyond *Poetry*.[7] *Literary Digest* mentioned that *Poetry* and the *Atlantic Monthly* were the only publications to take note of Tagore's early translations by August 1913.[8]

While Pound was the most prominent of Tagore enthusiasts, he was not alone in his efforts to engage an American readership. In his analysis of first reactions to Tagore, Mukherjee emphasises the role of the forgotten freelance journalist Basanta Koomar Roy. Roy met Tagore in January 1913 during Tagore's first trip to America at Urbana, Illinois. In his biography of Tagore, Roy claims that he encouraged Tagore to have his Bengali work translated into English in order to be considered for the Nobel Prize. Following their first encounter, Roy wrote an article for *Open Court* titled 'India's Greatest Living

Poet,' in which he stated that Tagore's verses 'are read by the thousands... they are known by heart, sung, and recited by the millions. No Western poet has ever had such a constituency of contemporaries.'[9]

Roy would become a factor in Tagore's literary successes in the American market, given that he translated Tagore's Bengali prose, poetry, and fiction following the awarding of the Nobel Prize. However, prior to November 1913, when the Prize was awarded, Tagore remained unknown to most readers outside of *Poetry*'s small circulation.

On 14 November 1913, the *New York Times* reported the awarding of the Nobel Prize for Literature to 'Babindranath [*sic*] Tagore.' Mukherjee notes the *Times*'s highly racialised handling of the news: the second sentence of the article read, 'It is the first time that this prize has been given to anybody but a white person.' In a subsequent article, the *Times* suggested, 'Babindranath Tagore, if not exactly one of us, [he] is, as an Aryan, a distant relation of all white folk.'[10] The *Los Angeles Times* scorned Stockholm's decision to grant the Prize 'to a Hindu poet whose name few people can pronounce, with whose work fewer in America are familiar, and whose claim for that high distinction still fewer will recognise.'[11]

The New York *Evening Post* reacted more favourably toward the news while still focusing on Tagore's Indian identity: in the award is 'a sharp rejoinder in the recognition of Europe of the fact that the East can contribute something more to the West than a burden for the white man to bear.'[12] The Philadelphia *Public Ledger* understood the award as an indication that 'the races of the earth are drawing ever closer together, growing ever more ready to recognise and acclaim service, wherever the servitor and brother.'[13]

The Nobel Prize served as Tagore's official and most effective introduction to the American literary readership and book trade. The initial reactions of American media outlets to the award demonstrate the lens through which American readers and critics viewed Tagore and his work, forever conscious of the fundamental difference of his literary tradition and philosophical and religious grounding. Mukherjee offers a useful summary of American expectations of Tagore as a figure representative of Eastern culture. As a result, deep consideration of Tagore's literary merit was overshadowed by his role as an 'international symbol,' a personification of the American understanding of India, of Eastern spiritualism as a contrast to the West.[14]

TRANSLATIONS

Tagore's career in English is unusual in that he translated his work from the original Bengali himself. Basanta Koomar Roy translated a few of Tagore's previously untranslated poems into English and included them in his biography of the poet, *Rabindranath Tagore: The Man and his Poetry* (1915). A 1914 issue of the American journal *Poet Lore* includes a translation of 'The Bayadère' by Roy Temple House; House's translation is a poetic interpretation of a French prose version.[15] However, as Tagore provided the translations for most all of the volumes of his poetry sold in the United States, this essay will discuss Americans' reactions to Tagore's own work.

The simplicity of *Gitanjali's* song-poems, both in form and content, made them easily translatable. Tagore describes how the English poems poured out of him in 'an urge to recapture, through the medium of another language, the feeling and sentiments which had created such a feast of joy within me.'[16] *Gitanjali* ran into twelve reprints even before Tagore received the Nobel Prize, indicating the sensational response to the quality of his translation in that volume.[17] However, Mukherjee characterises Tagore's success with *Gitanjali* as 'uniformly injurious' to his later work, as it 'seems to have persuaded him that the devotional aspect of his poetry was the aspect most suitable for translation and most accessible to foreign appreciation.'[18] J. C. Ghosh has also described Tagore's English work as 'one-sided,' so focused on applying a mystical tint as to eliminate words and phrases that strayed from the motif and replace them with words that he thought would be more American-friendly.[19]

To demonstrate the qualitative deficiencies of Tagore's translations, Mukherjee offers an analysis of the first poem in *Lover's Gift and Crossing* (1918). In a typical *Balaka* poem titled 'Shah-jahan,' Tagore points to the Taj Mahal as a concrete symbol through which to meditate upon the immortality of artistic achievement. Mukherjee finds the poem, in comparison with the Bengali original, 'truncated and simplified in translation, the English version offers only a solitary picture, with none of the burden of history and brooding time that hovers over the original poem.'[20]

Other critics have suggested that Tagore's emphasis on the mystical or devotional element of his work often resulted in translations that were flimsy, drawn out, and ultimately out of synch with American literary tastes. In his essay 'Tagore's Poetry in English,' collected in *Rabindranath Tagore: American Interpretations* (1981), Melvin D. Palmer compares an English translation of a poem from *Gitanjali* to Carl Sandburg's 'The Harbor,' a poem that contrasts the claustrophobia of the city with the openness of the sea, published in 1914. Both poems were included in Monroe's 1917 anthology titled *The New Poetry*. Palmer concludes from his comparison that Tagore's work lacks 'economy, concreteness, freshness,' visible in Sandburg's poem and expected of modern poets by American critics. Juxtaposed with Sandburg's vivid images and concise language, Tagore's translation is overly abstract, his images too ephemeral, and his phrases strung with clunky articles and prepositions. Palmer offers as example the line: 'The speech of my heart will be carried on in the murmurings of a song.'[21]

Despite the limitations of his translated work, Tagore's reputation in America was primarily that of a poet rather than a playwright or novelist. His short stories were deemed inaccessible by the few American critics to take interest in them. The *New York Times* expressed the challenge of Tagore's fiction for American readers: 'To the Occidental, caste is ludicrous; but it is at the root of the tragedies of Tagore's stories of Indian life... Is the Western reader able to acknowledge their reality?'[22] A similar misunderstanding motivated the lukewarm reception of Tagore's novels. A critic wrote in the *Boston Evening Transcript* of Tagore's prose, 'We are as much occupied with constructing for ourselves a clear conception of home life in Bengal as we are with grasping the psychological study [Tagore] gives us of the Eastern woman emerging from the seclusion of the zenana.'[23]

Tagore's writing for the theatre was even less suited for English translation or production upon the American stage: the most successful of his dramatic works, *The Post Office* (1914) and *The King of the Dark Chamber* (1914) were both examples of symbolic drama and further perpetuated the American understanding of Tagore as an obscure mystic. The Union of East and West staged a very limited run of *Sacrifice* and *The Post Office* at the Garrick Theatre in New York in December 1920.[24] The production received mixed reviews: writing in *Billboard*, Patterson James praised Tagore as 'a real poet, whose genius survives the mob adulation he received a few years ago when the Nobel Prize was awarded him,' but warned that 'both *The Post Office* and *Sacrifice* bear the marks of poetry, not a drama.'[25]

THE EMERGENCE OF SCHOLARLY INTEREST

The 'Tagore craze' was never stronger in America than in the few years immediately following the awarding of the Nobel Prize, and no piece of Tagore's work elicited a greater response than *Gitanjali*. The *New York Times* included *Gitanjali* as one of the hundred best books of the year.[26] Roy and the English writer Ernest Rhys published, almost simultaneously, the first English-language biographies of Tagore, in 1915. Rhys's book commanded attention from American reviewers but elicited mixed responses: the *Nation*, in its review of Rhys' book, identified Tagore as evidence of the decline of European taste into 'emotional obscurantism.'[27] The *Dial*, in contrast, opined that Tagore's 'Hindu poetry' revealed to Western thinkers 'the charlatanism of our culture, the restlessness and materialism of our life.'[28]

The less-than-enthusiastic reception of a biography by the English historian and translator Edward Thompson, titled *Rabindranath Tagore:*

His Life and Work, published some six years later, indicates the waning of American interest in Tagore as the memory of the Nobel Prize faded from people's minds. Thompson's critical work received almost no attention in the United States save for a review by the Indologist and Sanskritist W. Norman Brown. As a scholar well versed in Indian history and Bengali literary culture, Brown bemoaned American indifference to Tagore's literary merits and insisted that America's reading of Tagore's English-language work was based on 'inadequate appraisal;'[29] that is, for Brown, the only adequate gauge by which to judge Tagore is his Bengali writings.

Tagore's translations may not have best represented his literary talent. However, that his work was so frequently overlooked and dismissed by prominent American writers and critics is explained somewhat by poor timing. A Romantic in the vein of Emerson, Thoreau, or Walt Whitman, Tagore arrived in America at a time when Romanticism was falling out of fashion. Palmer explains that by the second decade of the twentieth century 'the Romantic temperament and mood and the concepts that had for a time in the nineteenth century linked East and West were rapidly falling away.'[30] Mukherjee adds to Palmer's claim by suggesting that Tagore's limited success in America was due to the anti-idealist character of post-World War I American intellectual life, best seen in the ideas of George Santayana or John Dewey. Nor did Tagore's work correspond to either of the trends that dominated American literary discourse between 1910 and 1925, represented by the 'neo-classicists' Irving Babbitt and Paul Elmer More and the 'radicals' Van Wyck Brooks and H. L. Mencken.[31]

Stephen Hay points out that the American post-War political climate also made for an unfavourable reception of Tagore's anti-nationalist and anti-war sentiments. Tagore's lectures, in which he decried the dangers of twentieth-century Nationalism, were taken poorly on the hawkish East Coast. Hay suggests that by the time Tagore arrived in the United States for the second time in 1920, the Wilsonian idealism that had characterised the early years of the second decade of that century had given way to the affluent and decidedly more cynical Harding years. Indeed, the Providence *Bulletin* mocked Tagore's exoticism: 'Rabindranath Tagore expresses the opinion that we Americans get our souls from steam boilers...an East Indian like Tagore has to be satisfied with a second-hand soul that formerly occupied a rabbit or a cabbage.'[32]

TAGORE'S VISITS TO THE UNITED STATES AND AMERICAN RESPONSES[33]

Tagore's arrival in Urbana in October 1912 was beset with annoyances. He faced difficulty passing through customs and was hassled by a reporter. Indeed, Tagore wrote to Rothenstein about his first impressions of the States:

'Though it is too early for me to pronounce any opinion on this country, I must say I do not like it. America, like an unripe fruit, has not got its proper flavour yet. It has a sharp and acid taste.'[34]

Tagore had travelled to Urbana to visit his son, Rathindranath, who was studying agriculture at the University of Illinois, and to acquire rest and treatment for piles. He found the plains of Illinois more favourable: 'The country round is flat and open, which has a great attraction for me, reminding me of our own scenery.'[35]

Tagore's in-person appearances in America are especially important to his reception by American critics. The white-robed and long-bearded Tagore seemed to many American audiences the walking embodiment of the East and only further distracted American critics from the content of his writing. Moreover, the differing reactions to Tagore's appearances and work across the country and over a time span of eighteen years (Tagore made his final trip to America in 1930) tells us something about the changing American political climate and understanding of Asia in the first half of the twentieth century.

In Urbana, Tagore was embraced by the local Unitarian community—unsurprisingly, given Unitarians' affinity with the Hindu reformist Brahmo Samaj movement, with which Tagore was affiliated. (See Chapter 35, the 'Canada' essay in this volume.) Tagore remained in Urbana until December, when he accepted an invitation from *Poetry* editor Harriet Monroe and was received at her home in Chicago and the two began a life-long friendship and correspondence. He also accepted invitations to speak at the Congress of the National Federation of Religious Liberals and at Harvard Divinity School, further cementing the American image of Tagore as something of a religious emissary or preacher from the East.

In September 1916, motivated by the need to raise funds for Santiniketan, Tagore began a formal speaking tour of the United States, sponsored by the J. B. Pond Lyceum of New York (which hosted speaking sessions with prominent literary figures such as Matthew Arnold.) He began the lecture circuit in Los Angeles and worked his way east, facing mixed responses from the different regions. Tagore loved what he perceived as the integration of civilisation and nature present in California, and was received generally very favourably as he made his way east to Salt Lake City, Des Moines, Chicago, Indianapolis, Detroit, Cleveland, New York, and Boston. Upon awarding him the Yale Bicentennial Medal, the president of Yale University welcomed Tagore 'as one of the great brotherhood of seekers for light and truth, we honour you as one to whom it has been given to help thousands—yea, millions—in that search.'[36]

In New Haven and at New York's Carnegie Hall, Tagore's audiences were standing-room only. However, critics writing for East Coast publications—those whom Hay identifies as hawkish—responded less favourably to Tagore's espousals of internationalism and anti-militarism. 'If one may judge by the expressions of the Eastern newspapers,' wrote the Columbus, Ohio, *Dispatch* in 1916, 'Sir Rabindranath Tagore, the Hindu poet, is not wholly pleasing his audiences in that section of the country.'[37] Tagore decided to cancel the remainder of his lecture tour on the East Coast, which was scheduled to end in April 1917. He cited exhaustion, 'I have not felt like a human being... I have felt like a bale of cotton being transported from town to town'—but privately he expressed the feeling that he was hopelessly out of place. He hated Manhattan's skyscrapers—'there is no grace, no beauty, just bulk'—and grew frustrated with Americans' gawking: 'Here in America, on Fifth Avenue, I am a laughing stock!... The very women turn to look at me and laugh!'[38]

Tagore returned to America for a third time in October 1920. Upon his arrival, the lack of publicity indicated that American enthusiasm for Tagore had largely run its course; however, he maintained a loyal following amongst women's groups and religious organisations and delivered a resounding speech on 'Race Conflict' before the National Federation of Religious Liberals at Rochester. In 1929, Tagore attempted to travel to the United States from Canada, where he had been invited to lecture at a conference at the Canadian National Council of Education, but he lost his passport in Vancouver and was treated disrespectfully by the U.S. Consul there. The unpleasant incident heightened Tagore's awareness of American prejudice and xenophobia, but the damage was largely corrected in 1930, when Tagore travelled to the United States following a trip to the Soviet Union, where he had received an official welcome. Perhaps wary of the political implications of Tagore's travels, Tagore was granted a special visit with President Herbert Hoover and welcomed by a banquet in New York, organised by the Tagore Welcome Committee headed by Henry Morgenthau. The ceremony that marked Tagore's last visit to the United States provided the opportunity to meet several prominent Americans, including Sinclair Lewis, Helen Keller, and Will Durant. Following his lecture on the prophet Zoroaster at the Hotel Ritz-Carlton, Keller deemed Tagore 'the supreme prophet in a movement that would result in a world-wide awakening of the brotherhood of all nations.'[39] The next year, in celebration of Tagore's seventieth birthday, his American admirers formed an American Tagore Association to safeguard the legacy of his American career.

TAGORE IN AMERICAN MEMORY

On the occasion of Tagore's centennial in 1961, a committee of American academics and writers that included W. Norman Brown and the authors

Norman Cousins and Pearl Buck organised a programme featuring productions of Tagore's plays and choreography and a discussion panel comprising Indian and American scholars. In connection with the centenary celebrations, Joseph Dees published a pamphlet titled *Tagore and America* for the United States Information Service. Recounting Tagore's efforts to bridge the cultural divide between Eastern and Western nations, Dees admires 'the phenomenon of the Man himself... Universal Man come out of the Orient.'[40] While Dees wrote enthusiastically of Tagore's Eastern wisdom, his impassioned account is tempered by its Cold War context: he points out the 'innate contradiction in [Tagore's] uncritical praise of the Soviet education system' and suggests that Soviet values threaten 'the very bases of the cultural and religious traditions' that Tagore sought to impart to his Western audience.'[41]

Following Dees's publication, Sujit Mukherjee (1964) published what is still the most detailed account and classic monograph of Tagore's reception in the United States. Alex Aronson previously had published a volume titled *Rabindranath Through Western Eyes* in 1943, but his analysis devotes little space to the American experience of Tagore and instead focuses primarily on British, French, and German experiences.

Mary Lago of the University of Missouri published a critique of Tagore's traditions, lyric poems, short fiction, dramas, novels, and personal writings. In her conclusion, titled 'The Inescapable Man,' she marvelled at his literary output: 'Critics who have kept him on a pedestal designed for a god have done him a disservice. When he is reduced to a human scale his achievements are enhanced: it does not seem possible that one man, even by living for eighty years, could have done so much.'[42] Later, in 1989, Lago, with Ronald Warwick, edited *Rabindranath Tagore: Perspectives in Time*. American contributors to the volume included David Kopf, Professor of History at the University of Minnesota and author of *British Orientalism and the Bengal Renaissance* (1969), and Kristine M. Rogers, who had received a grant from the National Endowment for the Humanities to translate the 252 letters that Tagore wrote to his niece during 1886–96.

Tagore's drama fared best among American audiences decades after his final visit. Krishna Shah's staging of *The King of the Dark Chamber* was entered in the Midwest Colleges Drama Conference, where it took honours, after a successful run at the University of Iowa in 1960. It was produced at the Jan Hus House off Broadway in February 1961; a minor sensation, it attracted full or near-capacity houses at each production. Howard Taubman of the *New York Times* praised it as a 'striking amalgamation of mime, song, dance, and poetry. Its appeal is to the mind as well as the senses.' Robert Brustein, writing in the *New Republic*, affirmed, 'In [Tagore's] hands, the conventions of Eastern theatre are liberating devices rather than restrictions, freeing his imagination to an extent almost unequalled in modern Western tradition.'[43] Howard Taubman also published a follow-up piece comparing the themes of Tagore's play and Dylan Thomas's *Under Milk Wood*.[44]

In 1981, to observe the 120th anniversary of Tagore's birth, a group of American scholars, including Hay and Palmer, remembered Tagore in a collection of critical essays titled *Rabindranath Tagore: American Interpretations*. Ira G. Zepp of Western Maryland College, who had chaired the first Tagore panel at the American Academy of Religion in 1977, edited the collection.

More recently, Panchanan Saha published *Tagore and USA* in 2009. While Saha's account is more concerned with Tagore's impressions of Americans than with American responses to Tagore's writing and personality, it includes a useful appendix of letters and essays by American writers about Tagore and his work. Saha highlights Tagore's simultaneous admiration for and disappointment with American society. On the one hand, Tagore encountered in America a 'forward marching idealism' that he found promising and rejuvenating;[45] on the other, he condemned 'the spirit of the machine' that so pervaded American life.[46] A 2009 article by Assistant Professor Amardeep Singh of Lehigh University, published in the travel journal *Journeys*, reflects upon Tagore's varied impressions of the United States as examples of 'reverse Orientalist' travel writing, whereby Tagore's moral critique of modern liberal governance implicates the United States in the European imperialist project.[47]

In *Provincializing Europe* (2000), his influential examination of the European assumptions underlying the categories utilised by modern social science practices, Dipesh Chakrabarty examines Tagore's advancement of a particular function of the poetic in the world of the modern: the poetic, for Tagore, was 'a powerful means of transfiguring the real and historical Calcutta'[48] and served to 'reconstitute (not deny) a reality that contained material and other forms of deprivation.'[49] Gayatri Spivak has also examined Tagore extensively, notably in a 2002 article in which she places a 1932 poem in an intertextual relationship with J. M. Coetzee's 1999 novel *Disgrace*.[50]

In a 2003 article on 'Rabindranath Tagore and the Aesthetics of Postmodernism,' Kenneth R. Stunkel of Monmouth University contrasts Tagore's cosmopolitan humanism with contemporary postmodern thought furthered by, among others, the Subaltern Studies collective, with which Chakrabarty and Spivak are associated. Pointing to work presented at a conference titled 'Home and the World: Rabindranath Tagore at the End of the Millennium,' convened at the University of Connecticut in 1998, Stunkel suggests that the result of the postmodern approach is to 'overshoot

and diminish Tagore as an artist and humanist' and presents Tagore's life and
work as 'instructive non-Western contrasts to extravagant skepticism that has
washed over the humanities in American and European higher education.'[51]
Many of the papers presented at the 1998 Connecticut conference are
collected in *Rabindranath Tagore: Universality and Tradition* (2003), edited
by Patrick Colm Hogan of the University of Connecticut and Lalita Pandit
of the University of Wisconsin La Crosse. Despite Stunkel's criticism,
Hogan assumes a humanist perspective in his introduction, on 'Tagore
and the Ambivalence of Commitment.' 'Explaining the inconsistencies in
Tagore's political positions—Tagore was an advocate of India's anticolonial
national movement and yet a staunch critic of the nationalist project—
Hogan suggests that he was in 'consistent pursuit of an anti-dogmatic,
empathetic universalism in a world that is itself constantly changing and full
of contradictions.'[52]

While Tagore remains underappreciated by the intellectual mainstream
in the United States, he is a central figure for American scholars of Bengali
literature and religion, such as Clinton B. Seely, professor emeritus at the
University of Chicago, and Tony K. Stewart of Vanderbilt University.
Celebrating Tagore (2009), edited by Seely with Rama D. Datta, includes
papers presented at a conference on Tagore at Fayetteville State University in
North Carolina in 2004;[53] Stewart has translated Tagore's Vaishnava poetry.[54]

Increasingly, a field in which Tagore's work appears particularly
influential is education. The first American to examine Tagore's approach
to education was W. W. Pearson, whose 1916 volume *Shantiniketan: The
Bolpur School of Rabindranath Tagore* included Pearson's first impressions
of Santiniketan, an account of the schoolboys' daily routine, and a
comparison of Bengali boys and English boys.[55] The contemporary interest
in Santiniketan is in part due to University of Chicago philosopher Martha
Nussbaum's ardent championing of Tagore as a model internationalist and
educator. In *Not For Profit: Why Democracy Needs the Humanities* (2010),
she points to Tagore's 'All-the-World University' at Santiniketan and his
interdisciplinary educational philosophy to support her claim that education
in the humanities plays a crucial role in the democratic process. Similarly,
David T. Hansen of Teachers College at Columbia University and Robert
Sylvester of Bridgewater State College, Massachusetts, have written about
Tagore's ethical and internationalist vision of education.

Present Research Position and Prospects

In 2011, to commemorate the 150th anniversary of Tagore's birth, Visva-
Bharati University at Santiniketan and Harvard University Press published

The Essential Tagore, edited by South Asian scholars Fakrul Alam and Radha Chakravarty and with a foreword by Amit Chaudhuri. The anthology received favourable and extensive attention by the *New York Times*, the *New Yorker*, *Bookforum*, and other American and foreign publications and was named 'book of the year' by Nussbaum. On its publication, Kumkum Bhattacharya, former director of publishing at Visva-Bharati, told the *New York Times* that the book aimed to expand appreciation for Tagore beyond 'the restricted circle of aficionados' of Bengali literature.[56]

There is a small but active community of Americans who demonstrate their love of Tagore's literary and artistic works and internationalist vision. Among other notable seminars and exhibits, the Philadelphia Museum displayed a rare collection of Tagore's drawing and paintings alongside the works of other twentieth-century Indian artists as part of a 2008 exhibition titled 'Multiple Modernities: India, 1905–2005.' Harvard University's Mahindra Humanities Center celebrated the centennial of Tagore's Nobel Prize with a performance of Tagore's poems and musical compositions. Recent events on Tagore's work include an April 2014 seminar titled 'The Kaleidoscopic Mind of Rabindranath Tagore,' convened by the Pennsylvania Humanities Council.

Most notably, the Smithsonian hosted a symposium titled, 'Santiniketan to Smithsonian: A Tribute to Tagore,' in 2011. The event featured remarks by Tagore scholars from Santiniketan and elsewhere. The Smithsonian also screened Satyajit Ray's documentary film on Tagore and presented music and dance acts that drew from his compositions. The Asia Society in New York displayed Tagore's drawings and paintings, most of which had never been shown in the United States, in a 2011 exhibition curated in conjunction with the National Gallery of Modern Art in New Delhi. There are a number of appreciation societies devoted to Tagore in the United States, the most prominent of which is located in Houston, Texas. The Tagore Society of Houston, together with the University of Houston, co-sponsor the Tagore Passport Operating Scholarship, which funds doctoral students' travel to India to conduct research on Tagore's life and work.[57] It should also be mentioned that the United States has produced more doctoral dissertations on Tagore than any other nation except India and Bangladesh.

Tagore's legacy is most vivid in Urbana, where the Channing Murray Foundation Tagore Center hosts the Annual Tagore Festival, a celebration of Tagore's intellectual and cultural contributions. Keynote speakers have included the Indian Ambassador to the United States, the Bangladeshi High Commissioner, and the mayor of Champaign, Illinois.[58] The November 2012 Festival featured an address on Tagore's meeting with the Urbana Unitarians by Rebecca Manring of Indiana University. There is also a

Rabindranath Tagore Chair in Indian Cultures and Civilizations at Indiana University, Bloomington. The chair is currently held by political scientist Sumit Ganguly.

The Harvard economist Amartya Sen, in a 1997 essay for the *New York Review of Books*, noted that 'especially in Europe and America, the excitement that Tagore's writings created in the early years of this century has largely vanished.'[59] However, as the centenary of the 1913 Nobel Prize for Literature has produced new interest in Tagore's life and work among American writers and publishers, the small community of Tagore appreciators in the United States may seize upon this momentum to raise his profile as a writer and thinker of ongoing aesthetic and intellectual value.

NOTES

1. Mukherjee, *Passage to America*, 113–14.
2. Hay, 'Rabindranath Tagore in America,' 439–63.
3. Martin C. Carroll, in his address to the All-India Bengali Literary Conference in Bombay, 1–3 January 1961 quoted in Mukherjee, *Passage to America*, 112.
4. 'God in America: Swami Vivekananda.' <http://www.pbs.org/godinamerica/people/swami-vivekananda.html>
5. 'Brief History of the Theosophical Society.' <http//www.theosophical.org/the-society/history-of-the-society>
6. Pound, *Poetry*, vol. 1 (December 1912), 92–4, quoted in Mukherjee, *Passage to America*, 9.
7. 'Tagore's Poems,' *Poetry: A Magazine of Verse*, 1 (1912), 93, quoted in Palmer, 'Tagore's Poetry in English,' 82.
8. Mukherjee, *Passage to America*, p. 10.
9. 'India's Greatest Living Poet,' *Open Court*, vol. 27 (1913), 385 quoted in Mukherjee, *Passage to America*, 26.
10. 'Our Case Isn't Desparate,' *New York Times*, 15 November 1913, 10 quoted in Mukherjee, *Passage to America*, 29–30.
11. *Los Angeles Times*, 15 November 1913 quoted in Aronson, *Rabindranath Through Western Eyes*, 9.
12. Quoted in Mukherjee, *Passage to America*, 30.
13. Philadelphia *Public Ledger*, 16 November 1913 quoted in Hay, 'Rabindranath Tagore in America,' 445.
14. Mukherjee, *Passage to America*, 113–14.
15. *American Poet Lore* 25 (January–December 1914), 61.
16. Letter dated 6 May 1913, *A Tagore Reader*, 20–1 quoted in Mukherjee, *Passage to America*, 120.
17. Mukherjee, *Passage to America*, 124.
18. Ibid.
19. *Bengali Literature* (London, 1948), 169 quoted in Mukherjee, *Passage to America*, 124.

20. Mukherjee, *Passage to America*, 133.
21. Palmer, 'Tagore's Poetry in English,' 87–9.
22. *New York Times*, 10 October 1926, 11, quoted in Mukherjee, *Passage to America*, 160.
23. Boston *Evening Transcript*, 9 July 1919, quoted in Mukherjee, *Passage to America*, 174–5.
24. Tagore, *Three Plays*, 79.
25. James, 'The Union of East and West.'
26. Mukherjee, *Passage to America*, p. 36.
27. Mukherjee, *Passage to America*, 42.
28. 'Tagore, Poet and Mystic,' LVIII (10 June 1915), 459–61, quoted in Mukherjee, *Passage to America*, 42.
29. 'Tagore as Bengali Poet,' *Books*, 1 May 1927, 14, quoted in Mukherjee, *Passage to America*, 58.
30. Palmer, 'Tagore's Poetry in English,' 83.
31. Mukherjee, *Passage to America*, pp. 112–13.
32. Providence *Bulletin*, 8 December 1916, quoted in Hay, 'Rabindranath Tagore in America,' 448–9.
33. Detailed accounts of Tagore's travels in the United States are provided by Hay, "Rabindranath Tagore in America," pp. 441–60, and Mukherjee, *Passage to America*, pp. 65–107.
34. Letter from Rabindranath Tagore to William Rothenstein, 31 October 1912, quoted in Hay, 'Rabindranath Tagore in America,' 441.
35. Ibid.
36. *Yale Daily News*, 7 December 1916, quoted in Hay, 'Rabindranath Tagore in America,' 447.
37. Columbus *Dispatch*, 29 November 1916, quoted in Hay, 'Rabindranath Tagore in America,' 448–9.
38. Quoted in Hay, 'Rabindranath Tagore in America,' 449.
39. New York *American*, 3 December 1930, quoted in Hay, 'Rabindranath Tagore in America,' 460.
40. Dees, *Tagore and America*, 38.
41. Ibid., 30.
42. Lago, *Rabindranath Tagore*, 146–7.
43. Robert Brustein, 'Off Broadway's Trials and Triumph,' *New Republic*, 6, March 1961, 21–2, quoted in Tagore, *Three Plays*, 83–4.
44. Tagore, *Three Plays*, 83–4.
45. Saha, *Tagore and USA*, 145.
46. Ibid., 15.
47. Singh, 'Veiled Strangers.'
48. Chakrabarty, *Provincializing Europe*, 171.
49. Ibid., 172.
50. Spivak, 'Ethics and Politics in Tagore, Coetzee, and Certain Scenes of Teaching.'
51. Stunkel, 'Rabindranath Tagore and the Aesthetics of Postmodernism,' 238–9.
52. Hogan and Pandit, eds., *Rabindranath Tagore*, 11.

608   Anna Feuer

53. Datta and Seely, *Celebrating Tagore.*
54. For example, with Stewart and Twichell, *The Lover of God.* Bhanusimha Poems
    9, 10, 11, 12, 13, 14 and 15 in their translation also came out in *The Drunken
    Boat* 3, no. 4 (Winter 2003), http://www.thedrunkenboat.com/tagore.html.
55. Pearson, *Shantiniketan.*
56. Sharma, 'The Essential Tagore Joins East and West.'
57. 'Tagore Scholar Passport Operating Scholarship.'
58. 'History of the Tagore Festival.'
59. Sen, 'Tagore and his India.'

WORKS CITED

Aronson, A. *Rabindranath Through Western Eyes.* Allahabad: Kitabistan, 1943.
'Brief History of the Theosophical Society.' Theosophical Society in America, https://
    www.theosophical.org/the-society/history-of-the-society.
Chakrabarty, Dipesh. *Provincializing Europe: Postcolonial Thought and Historical
    Difference.* Princeton: Princeton University Press, 2000.
Datta, Rama D., and Clinton B. Seely, eds. *Celebrating Tagore.* New Delhi: Allied
    Publishers, 2009.
Dees, Joseph. *Tagore and America.* United States Information Service, 1961.
'God in America: Swami Vivekananda.' American Public Broadcasting Service,
    2010. http://www.pbs.org/godinamerica/people/swami-vivekananda.html
Hay, Stephen N. 'Rabindranath Tagore in America.' *American Quarterly,* 14, no. 3
    (1962), 439–63.
'History of the Tagore Festival.' University of Illinois at Urbana-Champaign, http://
    tagore.business.uiuc.edu/history.html
Hogan, Patrick Colm, and Lalita Pandit, eds. *Rabindranath Tagore: Universality and
    Tradition.* Cranbury, NJ: Rosemont Publishing, 2003.
House, Roy Temple, trans. 'The Bayadère.' *American Poet Lore* 25 (January–
    December 1914), 61.
James, Patterson. 'The Union of East and West presents "The Post Office" and
    "Sacrifice".' *The Billboard,* 25 December 1920, 59.
Kirsch, Adam. 'Modern Magus.' *The New Yorker,* 30 May 2011, 75.
Lago, Mary M. *Rabindranath Tagore.* Boston: G. K. Hall and Co., 1976.
Mukherjee, Sujit. *Passage to America: The Reception of Rabindranath Tagore in the
    United States, 1912–41.* Calcutta: Book Land Private Ltd., 1964.
Palmer, Melvin D. 'Tagore's Poetry in English: A Candid View.' In *Rabindranath
    Tagore: American Interpretations.* Edited by Ira G. Zepp, 78–98. Kolkata:
    Writers Workshop, 1981.
Pearson, W. W. *Shantiniketan: The Bolpur School of Rabindranath Tagore.* New York:
    Macmillan, 1916.
Saha, Panchanan. *Tagore and USA.* Kolkata: Biswabiksha, 2009.
Sen, Amartya. 'Tagore and his India.' *New York Review of Books,* 26 June 1997.
Sharma, Anuradha. 'The Essential Tagore joins East and West.' *New York
    Times,* 21 February 2012. http://india.blogs.nytimes.com/2012/02/21/
    the-essential-tagore-joins-east-and-west/

Singh, Amardeep. 'Veiled Strangers: Rabindranath Tagore's America, in Letters and Lectures.' *Journeys* 10, no. 1 (2009), 51–68.

Spivak, Gayatri. 'Ethics and Politics in Tagore, Coetzee, and Certain Scenes of Teaching.' *Diacritics,* 32, nos. 3–4 (2002), 17–31.

Stewart, Tony K., and Chase Twichell, transl. *The Lover of God: Rabindranath Tagore's Songs of the Poet Sun-Lion.* Introduction and Postscript by Tony K. Stewart. Port Townsend, WA: Copper Canyon Press, 2003.

Stunkel, Kenneth R. 'Rabindranath Tagore and the Aesthetics of Postmodernism.' *International Journal of Politics, Culture and Society,* 17, no. 2 (2003), 237–59.

Tagore, Rabindranath. *Three Plays.* Trans. Ananda Lal. New Delhi: Oxford University Press, 2001.

'Tagore Scholar Passport Operating Scholarship.' University of Houston Department of English, http://www.uh.edu/class/english/tagore-scholarships/index.php

Zepp, Ira G., ed. *Rabindranath Tagore: American Interpretations.* Kolkata: Writers Workshop, 1981.

35

Canada

Kathleen M. O'Connell and M. A. Serhat Unsal

Although there has been considerable coverage of Rabindranath Tagore's visits to the United States, relatively little has been written about the impact Tagore has had in Canada and the manner in which his presence, writings and concept of art have been disseminated. This essay represents a partial foray into that world, with the hope that it will stimulate further research in areas that have not been covered. The first two sections of this essay discuss aspects of the socio-political, religious and cultural climate in North America generally—and Canada specifically—which would have affected and preconditioned the response to Rabindranath's Nobel award and his later influence upon Canadian art and culture. Sections three to five discuss Tagore's 1912 visit to North America, the reception of his Nobel award, his influence on the Canadian artists known as the Group of Seven and his 1929 visit to Canada. The final two sections discuss the way in which Tagore's legacy has been celebrated in Canada following his 1929 visit and his growing legacy within the network of global human consciousness through the Internet, which affects not only Canada, but the world as a whole.

THE SOCIO-POLITICAL BACKGROUND

Over the period of Tagore's life, several developments in North America worked in unison to build the groundwork for the reception of his philosophy and literary works on the continent. As colonies, Canada and India were not permitted to establish direct diplomatic or trade relations. Despite the early lack of official ties, the two regions were linked by two major historical trends: first, patterns of human migration and second, cultural exchange.

The history of Indian migration and settlement in North America began around the time of Queen Victoria's Diamond Jubilee in 1897 when Sikh veterans of the British Army in India crossed Canada on their way home.[1] Upon arriving in the Punjab and finding conditions inhospitable, some of these men decided to return to Canada to seek employment. In 1906, there was a sudden spike in immigration from India as a result of a decrease in Chinese immigrant labour due to a $500 head tax imposed on each new Chinese migrant worker by the Canadian government.[2] The reduction in the number of Chinese workers created a labour shortage that was subsequently filled by East Indian workers.

Eventually, the labour shortage turned into a job shortage and Indian migrants began to face considerable racism from the local unemployed white settlers. In 1907, a serious anti-Asian riot erupted in Vancouver, and the anger of the local population was directed against Asian businesses as well as Sikhs living in the downtown area. When the violence abated, the rioters forced the Canadian government to take action on their behalf. In order to restrict immigration, the Canadian government passed the 'continuous journey' rule requiring immigrants to travel directly to Canada from the country of their birth, or citizenship, without stopping along the way, which was an impossibility for any passenger arriving from India. Throughout the period, the British government in India watched nervously as fears mounted that the ill-treatment of Indians in Canada would cause a backlash in India. And that is exactly what happened after the infamous *Komagata Maru* incident of 1914.

That year, a Sikh businessman based in Singapore, Gurdit Singh, chartered the Japanese ship *Komagata Maru* to carry Sikh, Muslim and Hindu passengers from India to Canada to challenge the continuous journey rule. After arriving in Vancouver, the ship was denied docking facilities by the Canadian authorities, and passengers were kept waiting for several months and refused medical assistance; the deteriorating conditions led to a number of deaths. Then, at the end of a months-long stalemate, the boat was forced to return to India, stirring resentment in India and among the Indian diaspora worldwide. Rabindranath had in fact rejected several previous invitations to speak in Canada to protest the treatment of the passengers of the *Komagata Maru* and during his subsequent journey to Canada in April 1929, one of the places he made a point to visit in Vancouver was the gurdwara on 2nd Avenue.[3] Nevertheless, despite the protests and calls for reform of racist anti-immigration laws, these heavy-handed measures resulted in success for the Canadian government's racist benefactors, and between 1914–18 only one East Indian man was permitted to enter Canada. Thereafter, throughout the interwar years, the number of East Indian immigrants remained very low.[4] In fact, the numbers did not pick up again until well after World War II.

A Transforming Cultural and Religious Climate in North America

While the political and immigration policies generated a generally negative climate for intercultural exchange within North America, there were countervailing, interpersonal connections being created throughout the world among religious and literary circles that would work towards a favourable reception of Tagore's works. This section of the essay explores some of the religious, cultural and psychological influences in North America in the late eighteenth and early nineteenth centuries that would have affected the manner in which Tagore was received.

Unitarian–Brahmo Samaj links between India (Calcutta), USA (Boston) and Canada (Toronto)

One factor that would influence Tagore's reception in America and Canada involved a synergetic change that began in the 1830s when British and North American religiously liberal Unitarians encountered similarly-minded individuals among the Bengali Brahmo Samaj in Calcutta. This would have included such individuals as Rammohun Roy, Keshub Chandra Sen, Protap Mazumdar and members of the Tagore family, including Rabindranath's grandfather Dwarkanath, who had supported Unitarian–Brahmo Samaj connections in Calcutta, as well as his father Debendranath, a leader in Brahmo activities. The history of the manner in which these two groups interacted and impacted one another is a fascinating study,[5] and it should be noted that both groups, as well as influencing one another, had an impact on their respective societies and cultures that was out of all proportion to their numerical strength. It is particularly significant that when Rabindranath first came to North America, it was largely through Unitarian and academic circles that he became known, and that such circles would already have had some familiarity with the Bengali Brahmo Samaj and the Tagore family. Significantly, it was the extended Unitarian–academic–artistic circles in Boston and Toronto that initially found Tagore's work so attractive.

Historically, many of the social reforms of the period known as the 'Bengal Renaissance' had Unitarian links. The majority of such reforms had their origin in the city of Calcutta, which represented the first site of extended East–West interface within India. Dwarkanath Tagore came in contact with Reverend William Adam—who would later serve as first minister of the new Unitarian Church in Toronto, Canada, in 1846—and other Unitarians through Rammohun Roy, who had converted Adam from a Scottish Baptist position to one of Unitarianism, while helping him translate the Bible. Rammohun Roy, Dwarkanath Tagore and William Adam had found common ground in their socio-religious concerns, and in September 1821 the Calcutta Atmiya Sabha was replaced by the Calcutta Unitarian Committee. By 1828, Rammohun, Dwarkanath and other close associates decided that a more indigenous form of ceremony would better serve the group, and the Brahmo Sabha was formed in August with meetings regularly conducted in Bengali. Rammohun Roy continued his close association with British Unitarians after he left for England, and when he died in Bristol in 1833, it was Lant Carpenter, a Unitarian, who delivered his eulogy in a Unitarian church.

Following his years in India (1818–38), William Adam, the Scottish Presbyterian, who had been converted to a Unitarianian position by Rammohun Roy, went to Boston, where among other endeavours, he became a lecturer of Oriental literature at Harvard University.[6] It seems likely he would have had contact during this time with the Transcendental Club, which had been founded in 1836 and included such members as Ralph Waldo Emerson (a Unitarian who was teaching at Harvard), Henry David Thoreau and later Walt Whitman. Adam's influence extended to Canada, when in 1846 he moved to Toronto to serve as the first minister of the new Unitarian Church. Though there were a number of Canadian clergy having come out of Harvard Divinity School, Adam represented the first of a trio of Unitarian clergymen that had Calcutta-Boston-Toronto associations. Toronto was at the time beginning a period of rapid growth, and Adam attracted an increasing number of members from the academic and artistic community who were seeking a more cosmopolitan type of religious and cultural synthesis that was less authoritarian, as well as being open to emerging scientific analysis and the exploration of non-Christian thought. Adam was followed in Toronto by Charles Dall, who headed the Toronto congregation from 1850–4. Dall provided another link between Calcutta, Toronto and Boston, having spent thirty years in India—largely in Calcutta—with the Unitarian mission, where he had close contact with the Brahmo Samaj and the Tagore family. He had received his education in Boston, graduating from Harvard in 1840, where he would have been under the influence of such figures as Emerson.[7]

A third Calcutta–Toronto–Massachusetts link was provided through Jabez T. Sunderland,[8] who had spent his first four years as a Unitarian pastor in Northfield, Massachusetts, where he had been in close touch with Boston Unitarians and other cultural figures. Sunderland provides us with the most direct connection to Rabindranath in that during his Calcutta stay he went to Jorasanko, the locality of the Tagore family home, where he heard Rabindranath's music and poetry.[9] Sunderland was as much a cultural–political emissary as a religious figure when he came to Canada to head the Toronto Unitarian church from 1901 to 1905. Sunderland shared his knowledge of India, Calcutta and also of the Tagore family with his Toronto congregation. What is especially significant about this is that it would become the congregation of Arthur Lismer, a prominent artist and member of the Group of Seven, when he arrived in Toronto. Lismer had emigrated to Canada from Sheffield, England, where he had been a member of the Unitarian Church, and of the Theosophical Society. In later years, Lismer would recall hearing about Tagore from speakers at the Sheffield Unitarian church.[10]

After leaving Canada, Sunderland returned to America, where he lectured widely on Indian religions and social conditions. Sunderland established contact with Rabindranath during his 1912 visit to the United States and published articles about him as early as 30 January 1913. In appreciation of Sunderland's book *India in Bondage,* Rabindranath wrote in 1928: 'The facts, which the Reverend Dr. Sunderland has set down in his book, are impressive. They corroborate the great saying of Abraham Lincoln which he quotes on the title page, "No nation is good enough to rule over another nation."'[11]

The American Civil War, Transcendentalism and Theosophy

Concurrent with the cross-cultural personal relationships and ideological transformations being created by the Unitarian–Brahmo connection were various historical events, along with new religious and literary currents, that would all challenge provincial perceptions and create the need for a broader understanding of humanity. Historically, the United States had just emerged from the first modern, industrial war in human history, the US Civil War. In the aftermath of this bloody conflict Americans began to search for a message of tolerance, unity, and peace.

Among those intellectuals and artists seeking a new humane vision were a group called the New England Transcendentalists, who became an influential voice of change. It began with the establishment of the Transcendental Club in Boston in 1836. The transcendentalists began seeking other sources of inspiration such as India and Eastern philosophies and scriptures to help them create an alternative vision to an emerging industrial society stricken with warfare and religious dogmatism they saw surrounding them. Such a vision privileged the artist, seeking a more personal relationship to spirituality, nature and morality. Many of the writings and ideas were disseminated through the Chautauqua camps, a progressive adult education movement that travelled through various parts of the United States and Canada. Sylvia Du Vernet in her study of the Canadian Chautauqua Association writes:

'Canadian educators and intellectuals were very much cognizant of Tagore's creative educational philosophy as it was practiced at this school of the arts at Shantiniketan. They were also familiar with his writings in prose and poetry.'[12] These same artists and intellectuals were also drawn to theosophy, which provided another important route of transmission for ideas from India to the West.[13]

The first Canadian theosophical lodge was established in Toronto 1891, expanding to three by 1922. It was attended by prominent artists and academics including Group of Seven Painters Arthur Lismer, Lawren Harris, Fred Varley and Jock Macdonald. Another link here would be the New Education Fellowship, an international organisation which had theosophical roots, and to which both Lismer and Tagore belonged. In fact, Tagore was president of the Indian Branch of the New Education Fellowship.[14]

The North American visits of Swami Vivekananda and Protap Mazumdar—both Bengalis from Calcutta, who were acquainted with the Tagore family—and their appearance at the Parliament of Religions, an adjunct of the Chicago World Fair that ran from 11 to 27 September in 1893, acted as a prelude to Tagore's own visit.

NORTH AMERICAN RECEPTION OF TAGORE'S NOBEL PRIZE

Rabindranath Tagore arrived in America in October 1912, following a four-month stay in England, during which he had impressed the leading writers and thinkers of London with his manuscript of *Gitanjali*. During Rabindranath's six-month stay in the United States, *Gitanjali* was published in England and was receiving widespread recognition, so that by the time of his return to London in April 1913, Macmillan had reprinted his book of poems ten times.

After arriving in North America, Rabindranath, with his son Rathindranath and daughter-in-law, Pratima Devi made their base in Urbana, Illinois, where Rathindranath had obtained a degree in agriculture in 1909, and where he hoped to continue his studies. One of the important initial contacts that Rabindranath made was with the local Unitarian church and its pastor Rev. Albert Vail. Rev. Vail had organised a comparative religions group, and Tagore's first public lecture in North America took place on 10 November at the Urbana Unitarian Church. This would become part of a lecture series and the basis for Rabindranath's book *Sadhana*, published in New York by Macmillan in 1913.

Knowledge of Tagore's *Gitanjali* was also travelling across the Atlantic. Ezra Pound, an American, who had met Tagore in England, recommended his poetry to Harriet Monroe, the editor of *Poetry* in Chicago. This resulted in the publication of six poems in the journal *Poetry* in December 1912, with a short introduction by Pound, and became the first representative selection from *Gitanjali* to be published in North America. Harriet Monroe invited Tagore to Chicago in January 1913, and introduced him to her circle of friends, including Harriet Moody, who would become a patron of the family.

One of Tagore's interests in the West was examining the educational systems. Besides his lectures at the Chicago Unitarian Church and the University of Chicago, he writes about visiting a school, which is most probably Dewey's Laboratory school, which was connected to the University. Although there is no evidence that Tagore and Dewey ever met personally, it is likely that Tagore would have become familiar with his theories during this visit, if not earlier,[15] as well as through his later association with Leonard Elmhirst.[16] His biographer Prabhat Kumar Mukhopadhyay writes about Tagore's lecture at the University of Chicago and that America had given him new ideas about his school at Bolpur. Among the books on the methods and problems of education which Tagore sent back to his teachers in Santiniketan were a large number of books on science and scientific subjects.[17]

In February 1913, Tagore also received an invitation to give three lectures at Harvard by James Houghton Woods, Professor of Indian Philosophy. Tagore's lectures were from the *Sadhana* series, but his educational work was also becoming known. Ellery Sedgwick, editor of the *Atlantic Monthly* from 1908–38, met Tagore during his Harvard lectures and requested him to write an article on Santiniketan, which was published in July 1913. During the same trip, he spoke on 'Race Relations' at the annual Congress of Religious Liberals at Rochester (see the 'United States of America' essay in this volume).

George Mackenzie: The First Canadian to Publish Tagore's Poetry

The earliest collection of Tagore's verses from *Gitanjali* to emerge in Canada was arranged by George A. Mackenzie of Toronto and published in Toronto under the title *Song Offerings from India* in August 1913, almost three months before the Nobel Prize was announced. The book consisted of eight poems that Mackenzie had rendered into rhyming verse. The verses differ from those published by Harriet Monroe in January 1913. Not much is known about how Mackenzie, a Toronto poet and lawyer, became interested in Rabindranath's work, though a likely connection would have been the Toronto Arts and Letters Club. The Club, founded in 1908, provided a significant cultural centre for Canada, which brought together a remarkable group of writers, musicians, painters and patrons. It represented the avant-garde cultural activities of Canada by producing plays and sponsoring exhibitions and concerts. As well as playing an important role in furthering the Group of Seven style of painting, the Arts and Letters Club provided an introduction of Tagore's writings and dramatic works to Canadians. Those who first brought Tagore to the attention of the Arts and Letters Club were Group of Seven members Arthur Lismer, Fred Varley, Lawren Harris and Jock MacDonald.

Mackenzie had in fact sent a fan letter to Tagore sometime in 1913 to which Tagore responded on 2 December 1913, thanking Mackenzie for sending him one of his poems. From Tagore's response, it is obvious that Mackenzie had expressed how deeply his own work had been inspired by Tagore's verses. Tagore responded from Bolpur writing to Mackenzie: 'I much appreciated the fact that you had found my translations an inspiration of your own verse.'[18]

The Nobel Prize: 14 November 1913

Rabindranath left for England in April 1913, where he stayed until 4 September, when he sailed from Liverpool on the *SS City of Lahore*. He received the news of the Nobel award from India. Although there were some negative responses in the media to Tagore's Nobel award, such as an editorial on 15 November 1913, in the *New York Times* expressing resentment that the Nobel Prize for Literature passed over all Occidental writers for 'a Hindu bard with a name hard to pronounce and harder to remember,' it was generally received in a favourable light. The *Outlook* of 29 November 1913 carried a detailed and lengthy article on Tagore, concluding:

> The award will interpret the East to the West as the East has never before been interpreted. It thus becomes a historic event, a turning point in the understanding of one hemisphere by the other.[19]

In Canada, news of the award was reported widely, albeit briefly, in both the English and French language press. *The Globe* wrote on 14 November 1913: 'The Nobel prize for literature was awarded today to the British Indian Poet, Rabindranath Tagore, the first time on record that this prize has been given to anybody but a white person. The works of Tagore were scarcely known outside of British India until recently, when some of them were translated into English.'

Tagore and The Group of Seven

The group of painters known as 'The Group of Seven' and their interpretations of the Canadian landscape would seem to be one of Canada's best kept secrets, in that this distinctive group remains relatively unknown outside

Canadian borders. The group, who were influenced by Tagore's writings, originally consisted of Franklin Carmichael (1890–1945), Lawren Harris (1885–1970), A. Y. Jackson (1882–1972), Frank Johnston (1888–1949), Arthur Lismer (1885–1969), J. E. H. MacDonald (1873–1932), and Frederick Varley (1881–1969). Two artists who have been linked with the group are Tom Thomson (1877–1917) and Emily Carr (1871–1945).

In general, the painters shared a frustration with the conservative, imitative quality of Canadian art and the provincial nature of their society, and they held a common interest in Eastern art and religions that included theosophy. They rebelled against the tenets of nineteenth century naturalism by viewing the relationship between art and nature in a manner that shifted the focus from verisimilitude towards subjective expression. They argued that the unique Canadian landscape required a distinctive painting style and following their first exhibition at the Art Gallery of Toronto in 1920, began to identify themselves as a landscape school. They laid new emphasis on the 'Artist as Seer,' a concept which Tagore's writings helped reinforce.

Arthur Lismer, who, as mentioned previously, came from a Unitarian background, arrived in Toronto in 1911 from Sheffield, England, where he and Fred Varley had been friends before coming to Canada. Fred Varley was another Group of Seven member who was influenced by Tagore; Ann Davis, in her study of the Group of Seven, notes that he had read Tagore's work as early as 1918 and was strongly influenced by Tagore's concept of art, the role of the artist and the 'oneness of nature.' Davis indicates that Varley's work can be analysed 'in terms of the specifics of Tagore's philosophy.'[20] Varley's role in bringing Tagore to Canada in 1929 will be discussed in greater detail elsewhere in this essay.

The Arts and Letters Club, under the direction of Roy Mitchell, produced Tagore's *Post Office* in 1914, with Lismer in the role of the Fakir, and Lawren Harris and J. E. H. MacDonald as stage designers.[21] The play was staged three times between December 1914 and January 1915. By popular demand, a fourth performance was added in March. The group also produced Tagore's *Chitra* in 1916. M. O. Hammond reflected in his journal about *Chitra*, jotting down the following: 'A lovely, weird poetic chant from India. Big crowd.'[22] Augustus Bridle, chairman of the Program Committee at the Arts and Letters Club, wrote that the Club's staging of *Chitra* was 'scenically and historically the finest in the history of the Club.'[23] Both plays were North American debut performances. Roy Mitchell's interest in Tagore was related to his pioneering efforts in the 'Little Theater Movement,' which sought to only produce plays that had never before been staged in North America. Nevertheless, Lismer's Group of Seven friends were likely the key catalysts who introduced Tagore's dramatic works to Mitchell. In fact,

Lismer, like Rabindranath, was connected to a progressive, international educational circle called The New Education Fellowship,[24] and it is possible they would have attended some of the same European conferences. Lismer headed various art education programmes at the Art Gallery of Ontario and was known to have an interest in Tagore's educational work. Lawren Harris shared a similar interest in Tagore's theories of art.[25]

TAGORE'S VISIT TO CANADA IN 1929

Rabindranath came to Canada in the spring of 1929 to participate in the Triennial International Conference sponsored by the National Council of Education of Canada.[26] Significantly, by this time, Fred Varley and Jock MacDonald were both in Vancouver teaching at the Vancouver School of Decorative and Applied Arts, where they met artist Emily Carr[27] and became part of the group that used to gather in the studio of photographer, John Vanderpant, where Tagore had his portrait taken in 1929. This was the group that pushed for Rabindranath's invitation to the Triennial Conference.[28]

This would mark Tagore's tenth foreign tour, his only visit to Canada, and his penultimate trip to North America.[29] There had been a previous invitation to Canada during his 1916 visit to North America, but he had declined because of Canada's 'Continuous Journey' regulation that blocked immigration from India. In particular, he was aware of the *Komagata Maru* incident in 1914, when Indians had been barred from landing in Vancouver. *The Toronto Daily Star* of 27 September 1916, in an article entitled 'Hindu Shuns Canada', reports that although receiving invitations to visit Toronto and Montreal, Tagore had indicated that he would never visit Canada on account of the manner in which his countrymen had been treated, and that he would not set foot on Canadian or Australian soil while his countrymen were treated as they were.

The overall theme for discussion at the Triennial was 'Education and Leisure,' and it included delegates from England, France, Italy, Germany, Australia, New Zealand, India and Japan.[30] One of the themes Tagore highlighted during his trip was educational freedom, which he discussed in an interview on the way to Canada, stating: 'I do not see any factor which will lighten India's load except the free and intensive dissemination of learning among the lower classes. In this programme I look to America and Canada for aid, since it is in these countries that education has attained its highest form and the student class has the greatest freedom.'[31]

Tagore arrived in Victoria on the *R M S Empress of Asia* via Japan on the morning of 6 April 1929, accompanied by B. W. Tucker of the American Mission, a teacher at Santiniketan at the time, as well as A. K. Chanda, from Santiniketan. Following his arrival, Tagore was joined in Vancouver by C. F. Andrews, one of his close associates at Santiniketan. And, though Tagore spoke relatively little about the practical workings of his school at Santiniketan during his Canadian visit, Andrews had published an article on Tagore's school and its needs that was featured in the April issue of the *Canadian Forum*.[32] The Victoria *Daily Colonist* reported wide interest in Tagore's arrival, and hundreds had to be turned away at the theatre on the evening that he delivered his first address. His lecture, entitled 'The Philosophy of Leisure', set out his central thematic concerns for the conference. These included the necessity of freedom in education, the importance of the role of the artist in society, and the need to preserve a sense of leisure in our everyday life to allow for the unfolding of the creative imagination and the potential for human cooperation.

This was the period of the 'Roaring Twenties,' with great technological and social changes in evidence. William Lyon Mackenzie King was then Canadian Prime Minister and Herbert Hoover had become President of the United States. It was a period of new horizons in mass communications and rapid transportation: Charles Lindbergh had made the first solo flight across the Atlantic a few years earlier, and Canada was now linked by radio from coast to coast. Automobiles were being produced on assembly lines, and Canadian women had just that year been legally declared to be 'persons' under the law, and thereby eligible to hold office. Other dimensions of life were also being challenged as religious and psychological systems faced re-evaluation in the light of Freudian analysis and Darwinian theory. Globally, the League of Nations had been created in 1919–20, with Canada being among the first countries to join.

Tagore's first address noted these changes and argued for the essential need of leisure to counterbalance a world increasingly dominated by rapidity, pragmatic organisation and global consolidation. Though acknowledging the almost irreversible momentum of material progress, Tagore expressed concern that such rapid exterior growth was not being accompanied by a comparable expansion of the deeper creative forces of the personality.

A second lecture was delivered at the Vancouver Theatre on 8 April 1929. *The Vancouver Sun* reported: 'Thousands sought to see and hear Tagore Monday night, but could not gain admission ... They saw in him a leader of thought who had the secret gift of the born artist.'[33] Clifford Dowling of the *Daily Province* reported that it was common criticism on the street that Tagore had talked over nine-tenths of his audience, but he went on to say: 'To those who take art and its wherefore casually it was, perhaps, unintelligible, but to those who have pondered art seriously, it was an illumination and a sensible explanation to hitherto inexplicable conundrums.'[34] From summaries reported in the papers, we can gather that the lecture was a variation of his essay, 'The Artist,' again with a theme that emphasised the vital role of the creative artist in illuminating and furthering civilisation.

In an interview with Noel Robinson of the *Vancouver Star* following his talk, Tagore elaborated further on the vital role of creative individuals in educating and changing society and the need for organising a body of public opinion. 'You can never rescue humanity from this condition by organisations and institutions,' he observed, 'It is individuals who have always helped humanity ... Our efforts must be directed towards organising such a body of public opinion among all the nations of the world that it will be overwhelming in its strength.'[35]

Tagore avoided the usual public luncheons and other functions preferring to keep to his room for reasons of health, though he continued to meet people in his room. As mentioned above, one public appearance that he did make was a visit to the Vancouver Sikh Temple on 2nd Avenue, where he spoke to a large gathering. He also met with the Governor General of Canada and his wife, Lord and Lady Willingdon. His final address was delivered on 14 April to the delegates of the conference, and in it he noted that the needs of East and West are not of such a different nature when it comes to freedom and leisure, adding:

> Canada is too young to fall a victim to the malady of disillusionment and skepticism, and she must believe in great ideals in the face of contradictions–for she has the great gift of youth ... She will have to solve, for the salvation of man, the most difficult of all problems, the race problem, which has become insistent with the close contact of communities that had their isolation for centuries in their geographical and cultural exclusiveness.[36]

Tagore had received invitations from various American universities and it was proposed that he stay in Los Angeles for a time before visiting other cities in the USA and proceeding on to England and Europe. However, for various reasons, including an unpleasant incident that arose with American immigration authorities in Vancouver when he mislaid his passport, he abandoned his further travels. After a brief stop in Los Angeles, he returned to India via Honolulu, Tokyo and Saigon.

Following Tagore's departure, Noel Robinson wrote in *The Vancouver Star* that: 'one thing is certain—he has made us think.... He has set an ideal before us—-practical or impractical, as we choose to regard it—the ideal of beauty and truth, individual, national, international, as a counter-balance to the materialistic philosophy, which is, admittedly, the danger of this age of discovery and commercialism.'[37]

TAGORE IN CANADA AFTER 1929

Research for this essay revealed a hitherto unknown Canadian exhibition
of Tagore paintings that took place in Toronto at the Art Gallery (now
AGO or Art Gallery of Ontario) in December 1930. There in *The Globe*,
10 December 1930, was a small advertisement:

THE ART GALLERY
(Dundas St. between Beverley & McCaul Sts.)
ANNUAL EXHIBITION OF LITTLE PICTURES
By Members of the Ontario Society of Artists
Also
Exhibition of Indian Paintings
By Rabindranath Tagore
Open Daily—10 a.m. to 5 p.m.
General Admission 25 cents—Members Free

Research in the AGO archives led to the discovery of a file that contained
letters pertaining to the exhibition, and also further evidence linking Tagore
with the Group of Seven. By 1930, MacDonald had become principal of the
Ontario College of Art, and Arthur Lismer headed the Teachers' Summer
Course in Art. Credit for bringing the exhibits to Toronto goes to Lawren
Harris. Harris's sponsorship was indicated by a letter from the New York
Rabindranath Tagore Exhibition Committee addressed to him, dated 24
November 1930, indicating that:

The Poet has accepted your very kind offer to exhibit his paintings at
the Art Gallery of Toronto from the first of December until the 20th ....
I understand from Mr. Williams that you have agreed to pay for the
expense of shipping the pictures from New York to Toronto and back
to New York, and that you will take care of the insuring and framing
of the pictures and their sales.[38]

Tagore was planning to come to Canada for the exhibition, and he wrote
to his daughter-in-law Pratima Devi that he would visit Canada before 27
December, when he would be sailing for Europe.[39] Apparently he felt the
paintings would sell better in Europe.

TRANSLATIONS AND ACADEMIC CENTRES OF TAGORE ACTIVITIES

Published translations of Tagore's works from the Bengali to English by
translators in North America have been relatively few.[40] This is perhaps
due to the accessibility of Tagore's own translations, of new translations by

W. Radice, K. Kushari Dyson and others that have come out in Europe, as well as others from India

Over the past three decades there have been numerous North American academic conferences on Tagore, which have resulted in bringing together Tagore scholars. Some of the American Universities that have hosted Tagore conferences include: the University of Chicago (where Bengali studies have been centered); The University of Illinois, Urbana—where Tagore's son Rathindranath studied in 1912, and which Tagore visited—is the site of an annual Tagore lecture; the University of Connecticut; the University of North Carolina; and the University of Texas. A major two-day Tagore symposium was also hosted by The Smithsonian Institute in Washington DC in 2011.

Throughout Canada, there have been scattered academic programmes on Tagore, but two academic centres that have provided a consistent focus on Tagore are the University of British Columbia and the University of Toronto which has offered a course on Tagore since 1993. With assistance from the Government of India, bronze busts by Bengali sculptor Gautam Pal have been installed on each of these campuses. The University of British Columbia hosted Tagore conferences in 2002 and 2011, and the University of Toronto hosted conferences in 1986 and 2005 (each featuring a Tagore exhibition by Niladri and Ranu Chaki, from their private collection).

Academic publications include *Presenting Tagore's Heritage in Canada*, (edited by Joseph T. O'Connell, et al., Toronto: Rabindranath Tagore Lectureship Foundation, 1989); this represented the proceedings from the 1986 Tagore symposium, held at St. Michael's College in the University of Toronto; *Rabindranath Tagore: Facets of a Cultural Icon*, Commemorative issue, *University of Toronto Quarterly* (edited by Kathleen and Joseph O'Connell, 77, Number 4, Fall 2008); this was a selection of conference proceedings from the 2005 symposium 'Claiming a Cultural Icon: Interpretations and Misrepresentations of Rabindranath,' held at New College in the University of Toronto; and Kathleen M. O'Connell, *Rabindranath Tagore: The Poet as Educator*.

COMMUNITY INSTITUTIONS AND EVENTS, AND INDEPENDENT INITIATIVES

Tagore's legacy has been widely celebrated within Canada by the Bengali Indian and Bangladeshi communities, which the limits of this essay prevent exploring in depth. Such groups regularly hold *Rabindra-jayanti* functions to celebrate the poet's birth anniversary. Visiting and local vocal artistes of Rabindra Sangeet are apt to be featured performers throughout the year, as are dramatic groups performing Tagore's plays and dancers his dance-dramas.

The written programmes for Bengali community events often include translation of portions of Tagore's work. Several Bengali newspapers are published from Toronto, which contain some Tagore material and notices of Tagore-related events. The *Bangla Journal* edited by Iqbal Hasnu published a special issue on Tagore in 2012. The TSS (Toronto Sanskriti Sangstha) funded the production of a two-CD set on Tagore's literary work containing *Chhelebela* and *Jibansmriti*. Within Canada there are also 'multi-cultural' TV programmes and even channels that provide outlets for good quality Tagore-related programmes or portions thereof.

The broader arts community has also demonstrated an interest in Tagore. In 1989, the National Ballet of Canada staged *Tagore*, choreographed by Glen Tetley with the score *Lyric Symphony* by Viennese composer Alexander Zemlinsky (1871–1942). The Menaka Thakkar Dance Company has presented and toured with numerous Tagore pieces: *Karna-kunti* (1986); *Farewell to Heaven* (1996); *Land of Cards* (2000); *In the Further Soil* (2001, revived 2011); and *Chitra* (2006). The Art Gallery of Ontario (AGO) featured an installation 'Tagore and Mrs. E' by Rachel Kalpana James in 2000.

The Canadian Broadcasting Corporation (CBC)/Radio Canada has produced at least two radio programmes on Tagore: the CBC 'Ideas and Tapestry' featured a Tagore programme in 1997 created by Piali Roy, and Eleanor Wachtel of CBC 'Writers and Company' featured a programme on Tagore in 2011 that included interviews of Uma Das Gupta and Martha Nussbaum.

Tagore's 150th birth anniversary celebrations created considerable interest in the poet. Again, the activities were most widely celebrated in British Columbia and Ontario, particularly within academic and community groups. In Vancouver, a Tagore 150th Committee was set up, which sponsored a seminar and a one-woman performance of *Chandalika* by the Bharatanatyam dancer Maithili Prakash. The University of British Columbia held a special Tagore evening, organised by Mandakrantha and Tirthankar Bose with lectures by Amartya Sen and Sugata Bose, and an evening of dance and music by students and faculty. The Tagore Society of Vancouver held a two-day seminar on Tagore in November 2013.

In Toronto, the Tagore Anniversary Celebrations Committee Toronto (TACCT) in conjunction with the Indian Consulate was set up to help coordinate activities. These included a *mela* and production of *Chandalika*, organised by Manashi Adhikari, the setting up of a special TACCT website on Tagore by Ananya Mukherjee and a two-day Tagore film Festival at New College, University of Toronto. Other activities included a production of *The Post Office* (*Dakghar*) by Pleiades Theatre, directed by John Van Burek and translated (though not published) by Julie Mehta, and a special 'Tribute to Tagore' held at the Royal Ontario Museum.

In the fall of 2013, TACCT (http://www.tagore150toronto.ca) sponsored a large Tagore event 'Inspirations' at the G. Weston Recital Hall in Toronto, celebrating Tagore's Nobel Centenary.

Again, it was the link with the Group of Seven that produced one of the most significant and far-reaching events connected with Tagore's Sesquicentennial: *The Last Harvest*, an exhibition of Tagore's paintings, which was mounted at the McMichael Gallery, home of the Group of Seven paintings. The exhibition—which was greatly facilitated by the energetic efforts of Joseph O'Connell and McMichael Director Victoria Dickenson— was curated by Professor R. Siva Kumar and organised by the Ministry of Culture, Government of India, and the National Gallery of Modern Art. It was done in collaboration with TACCT and Panorama India. The National Gallery of Modern Art in New Delhi has in turn expressed interest in holding a Group of Seven exhibition at the NGMA.

Tagore and the Web: A New Medium for Tagore's Message within Canada and Beyond

In early June 1930, Rabindranath Tagore met H. G. Wells in Geneva. During their conversation, Wells drew attention to how the radio had brought the world together. Wells went on to suggest that in the future, a new medium might arise, allowing human beings to communicate in entirely different ways. To this Rabindranath replied, 'We have to create the new psychology needed for this age. We have to adjust ourselves to the new necessities and conditions of civilisation.'[41] This dialogue took place more than fifty years before the Internet and the World Wide Web as we now know it became a popular medium, yet it seems that both Tagore and Wells could envision a future technology that would connect people around the world and transform the way they communicate with one another.

The Internet, which forms the structural backbone of the World Wide Web, has indeed become a medium that connects people from disparate regions of the globe, facilitating transfer and sharing of content that transcends race, creed, national boundaries, and language altogether. However, it wasn't always so. While the pioneers of the web envisioned a technology that would facilitate two-way communication, during the early years of the web's development, information flow was decidedly one-way— data providers 'dictated' content, which was read passively by an audience of consumers. Then, just before the dawn of the new millennium, the web was radically transformed. In today's Web 2.0, there are millions of web users across the globe, constantly creating, modifying, and uploading new material to the web.

It is not surprising to find that Rabindranath's legacies continue to thrive in this new, digital environment of modern, technologically-enabled media and it is apparent that the collaborative nature of the web has not only led to an increase in the popularity of Tagore, which had shown steady decline especially in North America in the decades following the 1930s, but the web has also become a major conduit to introduce Tagore's literary and artistic achievements to an entirely new generation worldwide. This is an indication of how well Tagore's thought continues to resonate with people today within the new 'psychology' being conjured by the Internet age.

For example, a Google search of 'Rabindranath Tagore' yields close to nine million 'hits.' When results are narrowed by region, we find that there are close to 25,600 websites in Canada and 5,300,000 in the United States that mention Rabindranath Tagore. A search in YouTube reveals over 10,000 videos related to Rabindranath Tagore, and each one has anywhere from hundreds to tens of thousands of views. A Google image search reveals over 1.2 million images related to Tagore on the web. Turning to web analysis tools, a search on Google Trends, which charts the number of times a search term was used on Google reveals a steady increase in Tagore-related searches between the years 2004 and 2012.[42] When narrowed by region to reveal results from the United States, we see the same result—a steady increase in search volume, with notable peaks starting in 2010 and continuing to the present.

A search of 'Rabindranath Tagore' on Twitter, the popular online social networking and microblogging utility, reveals hundreds of quotes by Tagore being posted and re-posted by users at any given time. Since Twitter posts are restricted to 140 characters, short quotes are very popular. In all, a quick survey of the 'Twitterverse' or 'Twittersphere' reveals that Tagore is very much in the hearts and minds of web users around the world. And given that Twitter's main demographic consists of young adults between the ages of eighteen and twenty-nine, it seems that Tagore's words are reaching a younger generation.[43]

If we turn our attention to the immensely popular social networking utility Facebook, we find that numerous Rabindranath Tagore 'fan pages' have been generated by different users.[44] The most popular fan page has over 300,000 'likes' by other Facebook users. Moreover, many of Tagore's works now have similar user-generated fan pages, which act as vehicles to discuss the significance of each work and share related material.

Turning our attention to Amazon.com, a rudimentary search reveals that several works of Tagore's works that are available for sale on the global bookseller's website have received online ratings and reviews by readers. User-generated reviews like these possess great value due to the sheer number of readers they can potentially reach.

A search on Tumblr, a popular photo blogging site, again reveals thousands of references to Tagore, including quotations, translations of his poems in various languages, articles about Tagore, photographs of Tagore posing with notable and famous figures of his day, photos or scans of his artwork, tributes to Tagore by individual Tumblr users, and numerous links to videos and multimedia posts of Tagore's songs and writings. As of April 2012, Tumblr had fifty million users worldwide and over twenty billion posts. Running a search for Tagore on Pinterest, a similar web tool allowing users to share photos and commentary via captions, also reveals several Tagore-related 'pins' created by users worldwide. Finally, a search on Pearltrees, the online information curation site, also brings up several Tagore-related collections; to cite one example, the Pearltrees user 'alaineng' has created and curated a collection of Tagore's works in French on the web with numerous links to books and articles.[45]

What this brief survey reveals is the expanding presence of Tagore within the network of global human consciousness enabled by the web. Commemoration of important days in Tagore's life, such as the awarding of the Nobel Prize, his birthday, and the anniversary of his death, are now broadcast widely by way of Twitter and Facebook posts by individual users; his photographs are shared over a wide array of social networks; his books are reviewed and recommended by a new generation of readers and his voice continues to resonate across the globe due to the dedicated efforts of a new generation of fans. Keeping all of this in mind, and given the nature of social networking on the web, one may only presume that Tagore's popularity will spread in the years to come within Canada and beyond as the web grows to accommodate an ever-expanding number of new users.

NOTES

1. Nayar, *The Sikh Diaspora in Vancouver,* 16.
2. Singh, 'The Political Economy of Immigrant Farm Labour,' 94.
3. Ashok Bhargava, 'My Journey with Tagore,' *Asian Journal,* 16 September 2011, accessed 17 November 2013, http://asianjournal.ca/sep%2016_11/ot_head7.html.
4. Nayar, *The Sikh Diaspora in Vancouver,* 17.
5. Lavan, *Unitarians and India.*
6. Hewett, *Unitarians in Canada,* 45.
7. Lavan, *Unitarians and India,* 81.
8. Ibid., 144.

9. Ibid., 154.

10. McLeish, *September Gale*, 9.

11. Lavan, *Unitarians and India,* 179.

12. DuVernet, *Canadian Chautauqua Association,* 97.

13. Theosophy was formulated in New York City in 1875 by Colonel Henry Olcott, who had served in the Union army during the Civil War, and Madame Helene Petrovna Blavatsky, a Russian, who had travelled widely, studying spiritualism.

14. Mukherjee, *Education for Fullness,* 428.

15. See Das, *Santiniketaner Bidyalayer Siksadarsa,* 70–1.

16. Dorothy and Leonard Elmhirst were personal friends of Dewey, and would probably have shared his educational ideas with Tagore.

17. Mukherji, *Life of Tagore,* 146–7.

18. National Archives of Canada, George Allan Mackenzie fonds, CAIN No. 261021: George Whitaker Correspondence, 1875–1920, Robindranath [*sic*] Tagore [between 1975 and 1920]; Archival reference no. R7699-0-4-E. I am indebted to Linda and Roy Harris for their assistance in obtaining the letter.

19. 'A Bengali Poet,' *New York Times,* 15 November 1913, 10; *Outlook* (1893–1924), *American Periodicals.*

20. Davis, *The Logic of Ecstasy,* 129.

21. McCann, 244.

22. *M. O. Hammond Diaries: Excerpts* (Toronto: Arts and Letters Club Archives).

23. *Papers of the Arts and Letters Club of Toronto* (Toronto: Arts and Letters Club Archives).

24. Grigor, *Arthur Lismer,* 103–4.

25. See Davis, *The Logic of Ecstasy,* note 129, 190.

26. This section draws from a much longer article 'Freedom, Creativity and Leisure in Education,' which also draws from my study of Tagore's educational work: *Rabindranath Tagore: The Poet as Educator.*

27. Emily Carr's correspondence with Lawren Harris and others indicates a shared interest in Tagore. One of the three books bequeathed in her will was Tagore's *Gitanjali.* See Morra, *Corresponding Influence,* 301.

28. See Reid, *A Concise History of Canadian Painting,* 189.

29. For further discussion of Tagore's 1916 invitation, see Mukhopadhyay, *Rabindra Jibani,* vol. 2, 567–8.

30. For the conference proceedings, see Lang, *Education and Leisure.*

31. Mahalanobis, *Rabindranath Tagore's Visit to Canada,* 3.

32. See C. F. Andrews, 'Rabindranath Tagore,' *Canadian Forum* (April 1929), vol. 9, 236–8.

33. *The Vancouver Sun,* 9 April 1929; *Rabindranath Tagore's Visit to Canada,* 16–17.

34. *The Daily Province,* 11 April 1929, *Rabindranath Tagore's Visit to Canada,* 24.

35. *Vancouver Star,* 12 April 1929, *Rabindranath Tagore's Visit to Canada,* 28–9.

36. Mahalanobis, *Rabindranath Tagore's Visit to Canada,* 67.

37. Quoted in Mahalanobis, *Rabindranath Tagore's Visit to Canada,* 34–6.

38. Art Gallery of Ontario Archives.
39. Dutta and Robinson, *Selected Letters of Tagore*, 395.
40. For further North American publications, see the 'United States of America' essay in this volume.
41. 'Tagore and H. G. Wells,' excerpted from: *A Tagore Reader*, edited by Amiya Chakravarty. Accessed 5 September 2012, http://www.schoolofwisdom.com/history/teachers/rabindranath-tagore/tagore-and-hg-wells.
42. Accessed 12 September 2012, http://www.google.com/trends/?q=rabindranath+tagore&ctab=0&geo=all&date=all&sort=0.
43. Accessed 16 September 2012, http://www.ragan.com/Main/Articles/Pew_Report_The_demographics_of_Twitter_users_44999.aspx.
44. Accessed 16 September 2012, http://www.facebook.com/search.php?q=rabindranath+tagore.
45. Accessed 17 September 2012, http://www.pearltrees.com/#/N-s=1_4490950&N-u=1_283282&N-p=36620721&N-fa=2799246&N-f=1_4490950.

Works Cited

'A Bengali Poet,' *Outlook*, 23 November 1913 (New Outlook, 1–165, no. 6; Jan. 1870–June 1935, [microfilm], American Periodicals, v104–6. UMI, 1979, reel 407).

Das, Anathnath. *Santiniketaner Bidyalayer Siksadarsa.* Calcutta: Visva-Bharati, 1989.

Davis, Ann. *The Logic of Ecstasy: Canadian Mystical Painting, 1920–40.* Toronto: University of Toronto Press.

Dutta, Krishna, and Andrew Robinson, eds. *Selected Letters of Tagore.* London: Cambridge University Press, 1997.

DuVernet, Sylvia. *Canadian Chautauqua Association.* Muskoka, Canada: Muskoka Graphics, 1985.

Grigor, Angela. *Arthur Lismer: Visionary Art Educator.* Montreal: McGill-Queen's University Press, 2002.

Hewett, Phillip. *Unitarians in Canada.* Toronto: Fitzhenry & Whiteside, 1978.

Lang, S. E., ed. *Education and Leisure: Addresses Delivered at the Fourth Triennial Conference on Education, held at Victoria and Vancouver, Canada, April 1929.* Toronto: Dent, 1930.

Lavan, Spencer. *Unitarians and India.* Boston: Beacon Press, 1977.

Mahalanobis, P. C. *Rabindranath Tagore's Visit to Canada.* New York: Haskell House Publishers Ltd., 1977

McCann, Gillian. 'A New Dharma for the Nation: The Toronto Theosophical Society and Albert Smythe, 1891–1945.' PhD Thesis., University of Toronto, 2002.

McLeish, John B. *September Gale.* Toronto: J. M. Dent & Sons Ltd, 1973.

Morra, Linda M., ed. *Corresponding Influence: Selected Letters of Emily Carr and Ira Dilworth.* Toronto: University of Toronto Press, 2006

Mukherjee, Himangshu Bhushan. *Education for Fullness.* Bombay: Asia Publishing House, 1962.

Mukherji, Probhat Kumar. *Life of Tagore.* Calcutta: Indian Book Co., 1975.

Mukhopadhyay, Prabhat Kumar. *Rabindra Jibani*, vols. 1–4. Calcutta: Visva-Bharati, 1988. [Probhat Kumar Mukherji and Prabhat Kumar Mukhopadhyay are the same person, and the Bengali book is Tagore's biography too.]

National Archives of Canada, George Allan Mackenzie fonds, CAIN No. 261021.

Nayar, Kamala E. *The Sikh Diaspora in Vancouver*. Toronto: University of Toronto Press, 2004.

O'Connell, Kathleen M. *Rabindranath Tagore: The Poet as Educator*. Calcutta: Visva-Bharati, 2002.

———. 'Freedom, Creativity and Leisure in Education: Tagore in Canada, 1929.' In *Rabindranth Tagore: Claiming a Cultural Icon*. Ed. Kathleen and Joseph O'Connell, 219–33. Kolkata: Visva-Bharati, 2009.

O'Connell, Joseph, and Kathleen M. O'Connell, eds. *Rabindranth Tagore: Claiming a Cultural Icon*. Kolkata: Visva-Bharati, 2009.

Reid, Dennis. *A Concise History of Canadian Painting*. Toronto: Oxford University Press, 1973.

Singh, Hira. 'The Political Economy of Immigrant Farm Labour: A Study of East Indian Farm Workers in British Columbia,' in *The South Asian Diaspora in Canada: Six Essays,* edited by Milton Israel, 87–112. Toronto: Multicultural History Society of Ontario, 1987.

The Art Gallery of Ontario, Exhibition Curatorial 1930 series, Box 13, File 21.

SELECT BIBLIOGRAPHY

Detailed lists have been given under 'Works Cited' at the end of every chapter. This is a brief selection of books in Bengali and English which are basic to many of the contributions in this volume.

TAGORE'S WORKS

Chaudhuri, Sukanta, ed. *Rabindranath Tagore: Selected Poems*. New Delhi: Oxford University Press, 2004.

——. *Rabindranath Tagore: Selected Short Stories*. New Delhi: Oxford University Press, 2000.

Das, Sisir Kumar, ed. *The English Writings of Rabindranath Tagore*, vol. 1 (1994), vols. 2 and 3 (1996). New Delhi: Sahitya Akademi.

Das, Sisir Kumar, and Sukanta Chaudhuri, eds. *Rabindranath Tagore: Selected Writings on Literature and Language*. New Delhi: Oxford University Press, 2001.

Das Gupta, Uma, ed. *Rabindranath Tagore: My Life in My Words*. New Delhi: Penguin Books, 2010.

Ghosh, Nityapriya, ed. *The English Writings of Rabindranath Tagore*, vol. 4. New Delhi: Sahitya Akademi, 2007.

Kushari Dyson, Ketaki. *I Won't Let You Go: Selected Poems of Rabindranath Tagore*. New Delhi: UBSPD, 1993.

Radice, William. *Rabindranth Tagore: Selected Poems*. New Delhi: Penguin, 1985, 1995.

——. *Rabindranth Tagore: Selected Short Stories*. New Delhi: Penguin, 1991.

——. *Rabindranth Tagore: Gitanjali*. New Delhi: Penguin India, 2011.

Siva Kumar, R. *Rabindra Chitravali*: *Paintings of Rabindranath Tagore*. Kolkata: Pratikshan, 2011.

Tagore, Rabindranath. *Gitanjali*. London: Macmillan and Co., 1913; New Delhi: UBS Publishers and Distributors, 2010 (15th reprint).

——. *Letters from Russia*, trans. Sasadhar Sinha. Calcutta: Visva-Bharati, 1960.

Thakur, Rabindranath. *Rabindra Racanabali* [Tagore's Complete Works], 15 vols., Kalikata, Paschim Banga Sarkar, 1368 (B.S.) [1962].
——. *Rabindra Racanabali*, vols. 1–28. Visva-Bharati: Kolkata, 1978.

TAGORE'S LETTERS

Andrews, C. F., ed. *Rabindranath Tagore: Letters to a Friend.* London: George Allen and Unwin Ltd., 1928.
Bhattacharya, Sabyasachi, ed. *The Mahatma and the Poet: Letters and Debates between Gandhi and Tagore.* New Delhi: National Book Trust, 1997.
Das Gupta, Uma, ed. *A Difficult Friendship: Letters of Edward Thompson and Rabindranath Tagore, 1913–40.* New Delhi: Oxford University Press, 2003.
Dutta, Krishna, and Andrew Robinson, eds. *Selected Letters of Rabindranath Tagore.* Cambridge: Cambridge University Press, 1997, 2005.
Lago, Mary, ed. *Imperfect Encounter: Letters of William Rothenstein and Rabindranath Tagore, 1911–41.* Cambridge, MA: Harvard University Press, 1972.

ABOUT TAGORE

Chatterjee, Ramananda, ed. *The Golden Book of Tagore.* Calcutta, 1931.
Das Gupta, Uma. *Rabindranath Tagore: A Biography.* New Delhi: Oxford University Press, 2004.
Dutta, Krishna, and Andrew Robinson. *Rabindranath Tagore—The Myriad-minded Man.* London: Bloomsbury, 1995.
Hogan, Patrick Colm, and Lalita Pandit, eds. *Rabindranath Tagore: Universality and Tradition.* Cranbury, NJ: Rosemont Publishing, 2003.
Kripalani, Krishna. *Rabindranath Tagore: A Biography.* London: Oxford University Press, 1962, Calcutta: Visva-Bharati, 1980 (2nd ed.).
Lesný, Vincenc. *Rabindranath Tagore: His Personality and Work.* Translated by Guy McKeever Phillips. London: George Allen and Unwin, 1939.
Mukherjee, Himangshu Bhushan. *Education for Fullness: A Study of the Educational Thought and Experiment of Rabindranath Tagore.* Bombay: Asia Publishing House, 1962.
Mukherji, Prabhat Kumar. *Life of Tagore.* Translated by Sisir Kumar Ghosh. Calcutta: Indian Book Co., 1975.
Pal, Prasanta Kumar. *Rabijibani*, vols. 1–9. Calcutta: Bhurjapatra, 1982–2003.
Pearson, W. W. *Shantiniketan: The Bolpur School of Rabindranath Tagore.* New York: MacMillan, 1916.
Thompson, Edward J. *Rabindranath Tagore: Poet and Dramatist.* London, New York, Bombay: Oxford University Press, 1926.

Winternitz, Moriz. *Rabindranath Tagore: The Poet's Religion and World Vision.* Translated by Debabrata Chakrabarti. Kolkata: Winternitz Society for Literature and Culture, 2011.

ABOUT TAGORE'S INTERNATIONAL RECEPTION

Aronson, Alex. *Rabindranath through Western Eyes.* Allahabad: Kitabistan, 1943 (2nd rev. ed.: Calcutta: Riddhi, 1978).

Bangha, Imre. *Hungry Tiger: Encounters between Hungarian and Bengali Literary Cultures.* New Delhi: Sahitya Akademi, 2008.

Biswas, Amalendu, et al., ed. *Rabindranath Tagore: A Timeless Mind.* London: The Tagore Centre UK, 2011.

Frenz, Horst, ed. *Nobel Lectures: Literature, 1901–67.* Amsterdam: Elsevier Publishing Company, 1969.

Ganguly, Shyama Prasad, ed. *The Kindred Voice: Reflections of Tagore in Spain and Latin America.* New Delhi: CSPILAS, Jawaharlal Nehru University, 2011.

Gnatyuk-Danil'Chuk, Aleksandr P. *Tagore, India and [the] Soviet Union: A Dream Fulfilled.* Calcutta: Firma KLM, 1986.

Hay, Stephen. *Asian Ideas of East and West: Tagore and His Critics in Japan, China and India.* Cambridge, MA: Harvard University Press, 1970.

Ivbulis, Viktors. *Tagore: East and West Cultural Unity.* Kolkata: Rabindra Bharati University, 1999.

Kämpchen, Martin. *Rabindranath Tagore in Germany.* Shimla: Indian Institute of Advanced Study, 1999.

Kushari Dyson, Ketaki. *In Your Blossoming Flower-Garden: Rabindranath Tagore and Victoria Ocampo.* New Delhi: Sahitya Akademi, 1996.

Mukherjee, Sujit. *Passage to America: The Reception of Rabindranath Tagore in the United States, 1912–41.* Calcutta: Book Land Private Ltd., 1964.

Nikolaev, Anna, and Nikolay Nikolaev. *Rabindranath Tagore and the Bulgarian Connection.* Kolkata: Visva-Bharati, 2009.

Tan Chung, Amiya Dev, Wang Bangwei and Wei Liming, eds. *Tagore and China.* New Delhi: SAGE India and Central Translation & Compilation Press, 2011.

Wojtilla, Gyula. *Rabindranath Tagore in Hungary.* New Delhi: Hungarian Information and Culture Centre, 1983.

Zepp, Ira G., ed. *Rabindranath Tagore: American Interpretations.* Kolkata: Writers Workshop, 1981.

CONTRIBUTORS AND EDITORS

SOL ARGÜELLO SCRIBA graduated in Classical Philology and studied Sanskrit and Literatures of India. She is director and professor of the Classical Philology Department of the Philology, Linguistics and Literature School of the University of Costa Rica. She has written several articles on Tagore and Sanskrit and is now translating the *Panchatantra* into Spanish.

AHMAD RAFIQ AWAD is one of the founders of Palestinian radio and TV, and a member of the Council of Palestinian Culture. He has been a professor in the Media and Television Department of the Al Quds University in Jerusalem since 2001. He is the author of several books on media and politics as well as of seven novels and three plays, some of which have been translated. He was named Arab Journalist of the Year in 1996 (in Cairo) and Best Writer in Arabic in 2003 (in Amman).

IMRE BANGHA is associate professor of Hindi at the University of Oxford. He studied Indology in Budapest and holds a PhD in Hindi from Visva-Bharati, Santiniketan. His publications include Hungarian translations from Bengali and other South Asian languages, as well as *Hungry Tiger: Encounter between India and Central Europe* (2007) and *Tagore: Beyond his Language* (2017). At present he is working on critical editions of various old Hindi works and on the European reception of Tagore.

FRANCE BHATTACHARYA is emeritus professor of Bengali Language and Literature, Institut national des langues et civilisations orientales, Paris. She holds a PhD and a DLitt in Indian Studies, Paris University. She is Doctor honoris causa, Rabindra Bharati University, Kolkata. She is the author of *Les intellectuels bengalis et l'impérialisme britannique* (Collège de France, Institut de Civilisation indienne, 2010) and translator of works by Rabindranath Tagore and Bankim Chandra Chattopadhyay, among others.

SONIA BERJMAN is an urban and landscape historian. She has a PhD in History of Art (Universidad de Buenos Aires), is a Docteur en Histoire de l' Art (Université de la Sorbonne), and she did post-doctoral research at

Dumbarton Oaks Research Library and Collection, Washington DC (an institute of Harvard University). Her publications include *La Victoria de los jardines* (Buenos Aires, Papers Editores, 2007) devoted to the Argentinean writer Victoria Ocampo, a friend of Tagore. Berjman is a Member of Honour at the ICOMOS (International Council of Monuments and Sites) Cultural Landscape International Committee.

Victor A. van Bijlert is associate professor of Indian religions, Dept. of Philosophy of Religion and Comparative Study of Religions, Faculty of Theology, VU University Amsterdam. He is the author of *Toen Jij de Snaren spande: De Gitali van Rabindranath Tagore, uit het Bengaals vertaald en ingeleid door Victor A. van Bijlert* (When you tuned the strings: The *Gitali* of Rabindranath Tagore translated with introduction by Victor A. van Bijlert), Leiden: Kern Institute, 1996.

Liviu Bordaş holds a PhD in Philosophy from the University of Bucharest. He is a scientific researcher and programme director at the 'New Europe College' Institute for Advanced Study in Bucharest. Besides writing many articles and contributing chapters to books, he published a volume on Romanian cultural contacts with India during the period 1780–1860 (*Iter in Indiam*, 2006), and he has forthcoming books on Mircea Eliade (*Eliade secret*) and on the reception of Tagore in Romanian culture.

Sawitree Charoenpong is an assistant professor at the Department of History, Faculty of Arts, Chulalongkorn University, Bangkok, Thailand. She is studying India–Thai Relations (1927–45) with a focus on the roles of Rabindranath Tagore, Swami Satyananda Puri, and Subhas Chandra Bose. Her India-related publications in Thai include 'Struggle for Indian Freedom: The Movement in Thailand.'

Alexander Cherniak was born in Leningrad (St Petersburg) and graduated from St Petersburg State University (Department of Oriental Studies) in 1995. During1995–8, he studied and taught in India, and since 1999 he has lived and worked in Israel. He is a lecturer in Hindi language and literature, University of Haifa, and lecturer in Sanskrit language and literature, Tel Aviv University. He is the translator of Mahabharata, Book VI: *Bhishma (Bhishma-parva)*, 2 vols., (New York: Clay Sanskrit Library, 2008–9).

Sandagomi Coperahewa, PhD (Cambridge), is a senior lecturer in Sinhala and the Founder Director of the Centre for Contemporary Indian Studies (CCIS), University of Colombo. His main research interests are sociology of modern Sinhala, language policy and planning as well as the social history of language. Apart from his major publications related to the Sinhala language, he edited a commemorative volume titled *Remembering Rabindranath Tagore* (University of Colombo, 2011).

UMA DAS GUPTA, historian and Tagore biographer, did her DPhil from the University of Oxford. She retired as professor, Social Sciences Division, Indian Statistical Institute, Kolkata, in 2004. Her publications include *A Difficult Friendship: Letters of Edward Thompson and Rabindranath Tagore, 1913–40* (2002), *Rabindranath Tagore: A Biography* (2004), *The Oxford India Tagore: Selected Writings on Education and Nationalism* (2010), *Rabindranath Tagore: My Life in My Words* (2006), and *Rabindranath Tagore: An Illustrated Life* (2013).

ANNA FEUER studied imperial history and international relations at the University of Oxford and the School of Oriental and African Studies (SOAS), University of London, as a Marshall Scholar. Her areas of research interest include history and literature of the British Empire, particularly in South Asia and Ireland, and contemporary South Asian politics. Her work on the historiography of empire has been published in the University of Virginia's *Essays in History*. She lives in Washington DC.

SHYAMA PRASAD GANGULY is former professor and chairperson of the Centre of Spanish, Portuguese, Italian and Latin American Studies of the Jawaharlal Nehru University (JNU), New Delhi. He has taught and researched on Spanish and Latin American cultures and societies for nearly four decades. He has made a pioneering contribution to the subjects of Tagore reception in the Spanish-speaking world and Cervantes's *Don Quixote* in India. He has also edited or authored bilingual poetry anthologies. His honours include Doctor honoris causa from the Los Andes University of Colombia, Gabriela Mistral Medal from the Government of Chile and the Order of Merit for Distinguished Services from Peru. Recently he gifted memorabilia relating to Victoria Ocampo and Tagore to the Visva-Bharati University.

DO THU HA is Head of Department of Indology (Philology and History) and Dean, Faculty of Oriental Studies, University of Social Sciences and Humanities, Vietnam National University, Hanoi. She was visiting professor at the Maureen and Mike Mansfield Center for Asian Studies, Montana University, USA, and held the Dr Ananda Coomaraswamy Fellowship of the Sahitya Akademi (2009) and an ICCR Fellowship at Calcutta University (2010). Apart from articles and research reports, she has authored or co-authored fifteen books about India.

MARTIN HŘÍBEK's doctoral research was on the poetics and politics of the Durga Puja festival in Calcutta (2009). He is a lecturer in Bengali and Indian Studies at the Charles University in Prague. Besides Bengali literature, he teaches courses on Hinduism and Indian nationalism. He has conducted seminars on Indian films and Indian culture and society. His recent publications are on nature symbolism in Bengali literature, and Rabindranath Tagore and Czechoslovakia.

Viktors Ivbulis holds a DPhil from the Institute of Oriental Sciences, Moscow (1983), with a dissertation on Tagore. His areas of research include Rabindranath Tagore, history of India and Hinduism, and literary theory (subjects he taught at the University of Latvia between 1972 and 2012). He is professor emeritus of the University of Latvia and full member of the Latvian Academy of Sciences. He is the author of *Rabindranats Tagore* (in Latvian, Rīga, 1978), *Literaturno-hudozhtvennoe tvorchestvo Rabindranata Tagora* (Literary Creation of Rabindranath Tagore, in Russian, Rīga, 1981), *Tagore: East and West Cultural Unity*, Calcutta, 1999; *Rabindranats Tagore: Romāns „Mājās un pasaulē un citi darbi* (The novel *The Home and the World* and other works, in Latvian, Rīga, 1999). His Tagore books in Russian and English were awarded prizes by the USSR Ministry of Higher education and by the West Bengal Government.

Ana Jelnikar holds a PhD from SOAS, London. She has been an ICCR (Indian Council for Cultural Relations) foreign research fellow at the Presidency University in Calcutta and a visiting scholar at the Research Centre of the Slovenian Academy of Sciences and Arts in Ljubljana. She is the translator of the first Slovenian edition of C. G. Jung's *Man and His Symbols*, as well as eight books of Slovenian poetry.

Mirja Juntunen was born in Finland but has lived in Sweden since the age of eight. She holds a PhD from Stockholm University for her thesis 'The Town Plan in Jaipur: Its Sources and Narrations,' 2004. She was a lecturer in Hindi at Stockholm University until 2012 and the head of The Nordic Centre in India between 2006 and 2012. She has also worked at Uppsala University (Sweden) and Aarhus University (Denmark).

Martin Kämpchen studied German Literature in Vienna, and Comparative Religions at Santiniketan, leading to a PhD in both places. He has translated Tagore's poems from Bengali to German, wrote his German biography and published several books on Tagore's relationship with Germany including *Rabindranath Tagore in Germany* (1999) and *My dear Master: Correspondence between Rabindranath Tagore and Helene Meyer-Franck / Heinrich Meyer Benfey* (2010). *Anubhave, anudhyane Rabindranath* (2016). He lives in Santiniketan.

KALYAN KUNDU obtained his PhD in Botany from both Calcutta and London Universities. While pursuing biomedical research on muscular dystrophy at the Institute of Neurology, London, he became interested in the work, philosophy and life of Rabindranath Tagore. This passion led him to form an archive of Tagore's work in Britain, out of which eventually, in 1985, The Tagore Centre UK was born. He is now the Chairperson of the Centre. He has authored and edited several publications in English and Bengali including *This World is Beautiful* (an anthology for young Tagore readers), *HE* (translation of Tagore's fantasy writing *Sé*), *Imagining Tagore: Rabindranath and the British Press (1912–41)*, *Rabindranath Tagore—a Timeless Mind*, and two Bengali books, *British Patra-patrikay Rabindra Prasanga* and *Itali Safare Rabindranath and Mussolini Prasanga*.

XICOTÉNCATL MARTÍNEZ RUIZ is the Coordinator of Academic Systems in the National Polytechnic Institute, México, and Editor-in-Chief of the *Journal Innovación Educativa*. He conducted a project on Tagore and Gandhi in this Institute. He is director of the project Cultural House of India in Mexico, founded by Octavio Paz. He has a PhD in philosophy, Lancaster University, and a Master's degree in Asian Studies with specialisation in Sanskrit from El Colegio de México (CEAA). He has given talks on Tagore and Indian Philosophy in México, India, Italy, the Czech Republic and England and is the author of academic papers, books, and translations from Sanskrit to Spanish.

LAURENT MIGNON is university lecturer in Turkish at the University of Oxford. His research interests include modern Turkish literature and intellectual history, minority literature, socialist literature, biblical themes in Turkish literature and modern Jewish intellectual history. He taught modern Turkish literature and comparative Arabic and Turkish literature at Bilkent University in Ankara from 2002 to 2011.

NIKOLAY NIKOLAEV was born in Bulgaria, studied Bengali Language and Literature at Visva-Bharati between 1988 and 1991 and worked for the United Nations in various countries. He is an official at the Department of Immigration and Citizenship in Australia. He co-authored the book *Rabindranath Tagore and the Bulgarian Connection*, Kolkata: Visva-Bharati, 2009, with Anna Nikolaev.

KYOKO NIWA holds a PhD in Comparative Literature from Jadavpur University. She is a reader of Bengali Language and Literature at Tokyo University of Foreign Studies. She has published essays on modern Bengali literature in journals and translated a selection of modern Bengali poetry into Japanese. Her recent book is a volume on Tagore in Japanese.

KATHLEEN M. O'CONNELL is a scholar of comparative literature and modern Bengali culture. She offers courses at the University of Toronto on Rabindranath Tagore and Satyajit Ray. Her writings on Tagore include *Rabindranath Tagore: The Poet as Educator* (2002, 2012) and *Bravo Professor Shonku* (English translation of three stories by Satyajit Ray, 1985). Together with Joseph O'Connell she was the editor of the 'Rabindranath Tagore: Facets of a Cultural Icon' issue of the *University of Toronto Quarterly* (2008) and of *Rabindranath Tagore: Claiming a Cultural Icon* (2009).

JOSÉ PAZ RODRIGUEZ is retired tenured professor at the University of Vigo (Spain) and Academic member of the Galician Academy of the Portuguese Language (AGLP). His research interests extend to Tagore as an Educator, Cinema and Education, and The New School Movement in the world. He divides his time between Ourense-Galiza (Spain) and Santiniketan. He is the author of several articles on Tagore in English, Spanish, Portuguese and Bengali.

HANNELE POHJANMIES is a Finnish writer, translator and independent scholar. She studied biology and geography at the University of Helsinki and published on a wide range of subjects including environmental issues, developing countries, literature and psychology. She has translated into Finnish nine collections of poetry, seven of which are from the English poems of Rabindranath Tagore.

MARIO PRAYER is associate professor at Sapienza University, Rome, specialising in the history of society, politics and culture in 20th century Bengal, Mahatma Gandhi, and Indo–Italian relations in the 20th century. He is the author of *In search of an Entente: India and Italy from the XIX to XX Century—A Survey* (1994), *Internazionalismo e nazionalismo culturale. Gli intellettuali bengalesi e l'Italia negli anni Venti e Trenta* (1996), and *The 'Gandhians' of Bengal: Nationalism, Social Reconstruction and Cultural Orientations, 1920–42* (2001).

MD. BADIUR RAHMAN is professor at the Department of Arabic and Persian, University of Calcutta. His research area is Arabic literature. His articles include 'Tagore in Arabic Translation,' 'Tagore in Arabic Books and Translation' and 'Tagore in the Land of Arabian Nights.'

FRANÇOISE ROBIN is professor of Tibetan Language and Literature at Institut national des langues et civilisations orientales, Paris. Her research focuses on the contents, dynamics and social implications of contemporary Tibetan culture in China, including poetry and fiction, women's writings and the young Tibetan cinema. She has also published translations of proverbs, folktales and contemporary Tibetan literature (*Neige* by Pema Tseden, 2013), as well as analyses of the situation in Tibet (*Clichés tibétains*, 2011).

SUPRIYA ROY has worked in Rabindra-Bhavana, the Tagore Research Centre of Visva-Bharati, Santiniketan as a librarian and archivist for three decades. She has been series editor for the *Tagore Travelogues* for Visva-Bharati and has edited among other books, *Letters from Java: Rabindranath Tagore's Tour of Southeast Asia, Talks in Japan, Journey to Persia and Iraq, The Diaries of Rathindranath Tagore*, and *Letters from a Sojourner in Europe*. In 2011, she curated an exhibition on Rabindranath in Kuala Lumpur. Other (ICCR) exhibitions curated by her which have travelled all over the world are: *Rabindranath Tagore and the Romance of Travel, Pilgrimages to the East* and *An Encounter with Japan*. The gallery on the life of Rabindranath at the Rabindranath Tagore Institute in Mauritius was also prepared by her.

PAULA SAVON, born in 1964, is licentiate in Oriental Studies, specialised in the area of Indian Studies, and associate professor in History of Oriental Art and Culture (Universidad del Salvador, Buenos Aires). She is researching on Rabindranath Tagore's poetry and has published several articles on the subject.

SERGEI SEREBRIANY was born in Moscow and has lived there since. He graduated in 1968 from the Institute of Oriental Languages, Moscow State (Lomonosov) University, and his research interests include South Asian languages and literatures and Indian culture in general, as well as comparative study of cultures (civilisations). He is the director of E. M. Meletinsky Institute for Advanced Study in the Humanities, Russian State University for the Humanities, Moscow. He is the author of *Vidyapati* (1980, in Russian), Vidyapati's 'Purusha-pariksha' (translation from Sanskrit into Russian, 1999), and *Rūs aur Bhārat: sāhitya, cintan, itihās* (in Hindi, 2009).

TAN CHUNG, now based in Chicago as Honorary Academician of Yunnan Academy of Social Sciences, was given the name 'Asoka' by Tagore at Santiniketan in 1929 (the year he was born). He retired in 1994 from Jawaharlal Nehru University as professor of Chinese Language. From 1971 to 2004, he served at various times as Head of the Department of Chinese and Japanese Studies of Delhi University, as Chairman of the Centre for Afro-Asian Languages and the Centre for East Asian Languages of JNU, as Professor-consultant and Head of East Asia Research in the Indira Gandhi National Centre for the Arts, New Delhi, and as Co-Chairperson of the Institute of Chinese Studies, Delhi. He has written and edited twenty books in English and Chinese. He received the high Indian civilian award of Padma

Bhushan and the China–India Friendship Award from the Chinese Premier, both in 2010.

M. A. SERHAT UNSAL is an independent researcher from Toronto with degrees in Political Science (York University) and Adult Education (Ontario Institute for Studies in Education/University of Toronto). His main interest has been the interdisciplinary study of the junctions between biology and society. He contributed a paper entitled 'Implicit Racism and the Brain: How Neurobiology can Inform Anti-Colonial, Anti-Racist Pedagogy' to the edited volume *Anti-Colonialism and Education: The Politics of Resistance*. His recent interests include the neurobiology of spirituality and artistic creativity.

ELŻBIETA WALTER works at the Chair of South Asian Studies, Oriental Faculty, University of Warsaw. She is the author of the first Bengali grammar in Polish (*Gramatyka języka bengalskiego*, Warszawa: Wydawnictwo Akademickie Dialog, 2008). She is an author of several translations from Bengali into Polish such as *Folk Tales of Bengal, Pather Panchali, Na hanyate,* and *Dakghar,* and written articles on Bengali literature and culture. She was a co-author and an editor of the Tagore anthology *Poeta swiata*, Antologia (Warszawa: Wydawnictwa Uniwersytetu Warszawskiego, 2011).

WEI LIMING is professor and Head of the Department of Afro-Asian Languages, Peking University, and Fellow of the University's Centre for Eastern Literature Studies. She is Editor-in-Chief of the *Journal of Eastern Literature Studies*, and Deputy Secretary of the Association of Eastern Literatures within the Chinese Association of Foreign Literatures. She has written widely on modern Indian literature and Tagore. She received an award for educational technique innovation from Beijing Municipality, and for her teaching achievement from Peking University.

KIM WOO JO is professor at the Department of Indian Studies, Hankuk University of Foreign Studies (HUFS), Seoul, since 1994. She did her PhD in Santiniketan. She has published many papers on medieval Indian literature and modern Indian literature including Rabindranath Tagore, and co-authored several books on Asian literature, Indian woman, Indian communalism, etc. She was chief editor of the *Korean–Hindi Dictionary* and translator of *Papad Mein Phool* (Korean Poetry Anthology in Hindi). She is working on Indian and Korean Romantic Poetry. She was president of the Korean Association of Indian Studies and Director of the Institute of South Asian Studies, HUFS.

INDEX